OUR STRUGGLE FOR THE FOURTEENTH COLONY

Volume II

A Da Capo Press Reprint Series

THE ERA OF THE AMERICAN REVOLUTION

GENERAL EDITOR: LEONARD W. LEVY

Claremont Graduate School

OUR STRUGGLE FOR THE FOURTEENTH COLONY

CANADA AND THE AMERICAN REVOLUTION

by Justin H. Smith

Volume II

DA CAPO PRESS · NEW YORK · 1974

Library of Congress Cataloging in Publication Data

Smith, Justin Harvey, 1857-1930.
  Our struggle for the fourteenth colony.

  (The Era of the American Revolution)
  Reprint of the 1st ed. published in 1907 by Putnam,
New York.
  Bibliography: p.
  1. Canadian Invasion, 1775-1776. 2. Canada—History
—1775-1783. I. Title.
E231.S654 1974   971.02′4   74-12272
ISBN 0-306-70633-4

This Da Capo Press edition of *Our Struggle for the Fourteenth Colony* is an
unabridged republication of the first edition published in New York and London in 1907. It is reprinted from a copy in the collections of the University
of Delaware Library.

Published by Da Capo Press, Inc.
A Subsidiary of Plenum Publishing Corporation
227 West 17th Street, New York, N.Y. 10011

Manufactured in the United States of America

SIR GUY CARLETON, 1783

OUR STRUGGLE FOR THE FOURTEENTH COLONY

CANADA AND THE AMERICAN REVOLUTION

BY

JUSTIN H. SMITH

Professor of Modern History in Dartmouth College ; author of
" The Troubadours at Home," "Arnold's March
from Cambridge to Quebec," " The
Historie Booke," etc.

315 Illustrations and 23 Maps

VOLUME II

G. P. PUTNAM'S SONS
NEW YORK & LONDON
The Knickerbocker Press
1907

The Knickerbocker Press, New York

CONTENTS AND ILLUSTRATIONS

The Illustrations are included in the Index also

SOURCES OF THE ILLUSTRATIONS: 1, attached to the title of an illustration, signifies that the original is in the Continental Congress Papers, Library of Congress; 2, Washington Papers, Library of Congress; 3, Emmet Coll., N. Y. Pub. Lib. (Lenox Branch); 4, S. Adams Papers, N. Y. Pub. Lib. (Lenox Branch); 5, Wheelock MSS., Dartmouth College; 6, Dreer Coll., Hist. Soc. of Penna.; 7, American Antiquarian Soc., Worcester, Mass.; 8, Winsor, Narr. and Crit. Hist. of America; 9, photographed by the author; in other cases the source is stated below. Full-page illustrations are starred.

Frontispiece. Sir Guy Carleton (water-color by W. Welling, 1783, owned by the Baroness Dorchester).

CHAPTER XXI. THE CRISIS OF ARNOLD'S EXPEDITION

The aspect of Quebec, November, 1775. Cramahé, the Lieutenant-Governor. Measures to prepare Quebec for defence. These of little value, particularly because many of the people are not loyal. Sentiment when Arnold approaches. Why British reinforcements have not been sent. Some do arrive at this juncture, but they count for little. Meanwhile the Americans prepare to cross and attack. A review. Information. Difficulties about crossing the river. Maclean arrives at Quebec. Effects of his coming. The Americans cross. It is possible to take Quebec by a *coup de main*, but it does not seem prudent to attempt that. Arnold endeavors to draw Maclean out or excite an uprising in the town; but he is unsuccessful and blockades the city. Dixon's death. News comes that a formidable sally is to be made, and, as the American powder and muskets are found to be in a bad condition, Arnold retires to Pointe aux Trembles. The sojourn there

PAGE

CHAPTER XXII.   BEHIND THE SCENES

Interest in Arnold's expedition and a desire to secure (what
Congress has repeatedly urged) the adhesion of Canada
prompt Montgomery to go to Quebec. His efforts to persuade the troops to re-enlist. Difficulties: dread of a
Canadian winter; the small pay; arrears of wages; colonial
jealousy; dislike of Schuyler; the already protracted stay;
the independent spirit of the New Englanders; apparent
lack of anything to fight for. About 800 remain. Why is
not another army ready? There is no general plan to wage
war against England, for it has been thought that peaceful
opposition can secure redress, especially if she sees the
Colonies dare to fight. Opposition of Dickinson's party
to the Canada operations. Minor difficulties,—particularly the attitude of New York, due to Tory sentiment and
the machinations of Great Britain. New York has to be
handled carefully. Action of Congress. What might
have been done in Canada. Montgomery's work at Mon-
treal, his preparations and his hopes...................   **36**

CHAPTER XXIII.   THE GREAT DUEL BEGINS AGAIN

Montgomery is governed by a sense of duty, not ambition,

CHAPTER XXIV.   THE ASSAULT

CHAPTER XXVII.   GRAVE OMENS

The pleasure-loving, easy-going character of the Canadians. They do not value liberty or understand the controversy between the Colonies and England, and are not a heroic race. They lack leaders favorable to the Americans. The nobles retain a little of their influence. The clergy, ailed by the women and the ignorance of the men, have a a great power, Carleton is still at work upon the people. The Americans discredit themselves through the weakness and poor appearance of their army, its disorderliness, and the quarrels of its chiefs (particularly that between Schuyler and Wooster), by oppressing the people, by exercising military rule, by banishing men on suspicion, by Wooster's general unfitness for his place, and by Arnold's decree forcing paper money upon the Canadians. By the end of March, it is evident that the Americans have made a great mistake. There are signs that the Canadians desire to recover a good standing with Great Britain, and a revolt led by Beaujeu seems especially ominous   208

Illustrations. P. 296, Lord George Germain[8] (Murray,
Impartial History, i., p. 190); 299, John Thomas (portrait
owned by Miss Sarah Williams); 302, *Woedtke to Schuyler, Apr. 18, 1776[3]; 305, *Château de Ramezay, Montreal
(photograph by H. T. Perrault); 315, Deschambault[9];
320, St. Louis Gate, Inside, 1776 (from a model by Mr.
Th. O'Leary); 322, John Thomas, signature.

CHAPTER XXXI.   THE APOSTLES OF LIBERTY

Illustrations. P. 327, Charles Carroll of Carrollton (after
a portrait by Gilbert Stuart, Med. Hist. Soc.); 330, Charles
Carroll, signature[8]; 333, John Carroll (portrait by Gilbert

CHAPTER XXXII. THE CEDARS

The flight from Quebec, on second thought, seems less disgraceful than at first, and it is believed that a successful stroke may re-establish American credit. A chance soon offers itself. The British posts west of Montreal are centres of hostile activity, and signs multiply that Montreal is threatened from that quarter. Bedel is posted at the Cedars to guard the approach, but goes to Montreal, leaving Butterfield in charge. Butterfield is attacked by Forster with Canadians, Indians, and a few regulars, and shamefully surrenders. Sherburne, sent to relieve him, does the same. Young, near St. Anne, imitates their example. This leaves the road to Montreal open. But Arnold posts himself at Lachine with some troops and Forster retreats. Forster's prisoners, threatened with massacre, sign an agreement for an exchange. Arnold confirms this in substance, and during the truce Forster slips away. Wretched condition of the American army. The Commissioners leave and Thomas dies.................................. 357

CHAPTER XXXIII. THREE RIVERS

Congress orders six more regiments, commanded by Sullivan, to Canada. After many embarrassments they arrive. Sullivan, though he realizes the confusion, is hopeful. It is decided to attack the British advance post at Three Rivers. Thompson is detached for that purpose, but the

MAPS IN VOLUME II.

OUR STRUGGLE FOR THE FOURTEENTH COLONY

XXI

THE CRISIS OF ARNOLD'S EXPEDITION

'SUPERB, tremendous!' Large words are these, and rather suspicious; but, when one faces the mighty front of Quebec, they have to be spoken. Rising grandly from a majestic river, the vast rock towers high and broad, with a splendor of sunshine on its brow and an abyss of shadow at its feet. Gibraltar is no doubt more lofty, but hardly seems more solid. Belgrade, while resembling it, looks far less bold and threatening. George Sand was reminded of Angoulême; but Angoulême has no such river to double its height. Montjuich might suggest it; yet merely as a strong hand suggests a mailed fist. Chapultepec is justly famous; but that is only a piece of shapely bric-à-brac beside Quebec. Ehrenbreitstein may be compared with it; but so may the Rhine be compared—if one please—with the St. Lawrence. The Morro of Havana sits haughtily enough on the waves; but the Walled City of the North would make light of its pride. In beauty and in power it stands eternal; and it recalls not only the saying of old Froissart,

I

that once 'every fayre town had high, strong walls,' but those far grander and far more ancient words: 'In the beginning God created the heavens and the earth.'

Looking across from Point Levi, the Americans could make out the principal features of the city. At the water's edge, on a fringe of earth filched from the river, extended the Lower Town, where the tall Hurons, gorgeous with sunflower-oil, paint, and beaver mantles, had beached their canoes by the hundred; and where Father LeJeune, the Jesuit Superior, in his close cassock and wide black hat, had called the Indian children to his door with a bell, taught them a *Pater* and an *Ave*, and clinched the good effect with a porringer of pease. Now, a solid cluster of warehouses and residences crowded the scanty sands, and an upper and a lower battery at the river-front defended them.[1]

Behind, rose the gray precipice, inclining downward toward the right, but still high where it turned a sharp angle and followed back along a little river, the St. Charles. In the midst of the cliff, a winding road and a zigzag footpath could be seen struggling upward, leading past the roomy palace of the bishop at the brow of the rock, and—on the left, a little higher—past a long, yellowish building of two stories overhanging the abyss on props, which was Castle St. Louis, built by Frontenac as a residence for the governors. Farther back stood the fine tower of the cathedral, attended by the spires of the Jesuits, the Récollets, the Ursulines and the Hôtel Dieu, so striking a group on so massive a foundation that artists

---

1 § For the meaning of 'Point Levi' (French *Pointe de Lévy*) in 1775 see Smith, Arnold's March, pp. 450-452. Old Quebec: Parkman, Jesuits, pp. 2, 20, 46, 47; Royal Mag., Nov., 1759; [Jefferys], Nat. and Civil Hist., p. 8; Kalm, Travels, III., pp. 97-109; Anburey, Travels, I., p. 51; Silliman, Tour, p. 232; Parkman, Old Régime, pp. 288, 477; Id., Montcalm, II., p. 208: Gaspé, Canadians, pp. 6, 7; Murray, Report, 1762 (Can. Arch., B, 7, pp. 34-40); Hawkins, Picture, pp. 155-169: Marr, Remarks (Can. Arch., M, 384); Mackellar, in Doughty, Siege, II., p. 272. Blockhouse: Caldwell, Letter; Doughty and Dionne, Quebec, p. 131. The Lower Town has grown at the expense of the river since 1775.

thought a forest of steeples on a mountain of rock almost sufficient for a likeness of Quebec ; while among the spires, leafless but still suggestive of beauty, stood the grove of the Seminary, the orchard of the Récollets, and the tall shade-trees of the hospital garden, watered by a now freezing brook. A 'Holy Hill of Zion' the early theocracy of Quebec had tried to make it, and its architecture still suggested that name.

Zion had walls ; and here a line of old batteries and fresh-looking palisades crested the precipice. To the left of the Castle, the rising cliff mounted to its climax in a rounded pinnacle of dark slate, studded with sparkling quartz crystals, known as Cape Diamond, from which the rigging of the ships looked like spider's web ; and here stood a small square fort, called the citadel, joined by a sloping curtain to a very high cavalier. A fortified windmill surmounted the cavalier ; while on the summit of the cape hung a sort of iron cage, in which the bodies of strangled felons had formerly been left for the winds, the rains, and the birds. Below, on a shelf some fifty or sixty feet from the top, stood a blockhouse ; and beyond— almost wholly ought of sight—were hints of walls, towers, and bastions on the farther side of the town.

Over against this eagle's nest on its cliff stood a handful of ragged, half-starved Americans, shivering in the November gale. Thus far they had certainly accomplished wonders. 'Arnold has made a march that may be compared to Hannibal's or Xenophon's,' boasted Joseph Warren to Samuel Adams. 'This march of Arnold's is equal to Xenophon's retreat,' thought Jefferson. 'Some future historian will make it the subject of admiration,' predicted Schuyler. 'The march of Col. Arnold and his troops,' thus a British author was already preparing to fulfill the prophecy, 'is one of the greatest exploits recorded in the annals of nations.' 'It is not in the power of any man to command success,' wrote Washington to his officer, 'but you have done more—you have deserved it.'[2]

Yet this was not enough. Running his eye over the towers, walls, and forts of Quebec, each of them edged with old gold by the pale sun of November ninth, Arnold himself realized that. Could he obtain possession of this town, and so draw the thorn from the foot of America? The Commander-in-chief believed that he could, and many others held the same opinion. 'We expect, every hour, to be informed that Quebec has opened its arms to Colonel Arnold,' wrote Jefferson to Randolph ; 'In a short time, we have reason to hope, the delegates of Canada will join us in Congress, and complete the American union, as far as we wish to have it completed.' Carleton had little hope. 'The prospect at Quebec is not much better,' he said, when writing (November 5) of the foregone conclusion at Montreal ; and even stiff Maclean, in spite of his narrow zeal, feared they were to be 'Undone.' Arnold, for his part, was ready to try ; his brave men, fresh from their victory over the wilderness, might shiver but did not flinch ; and even for Quebec it was not well to be over-confident.[3]

Indeed, the Provincials appeared to have a good fighting

---

[2] § Warren, Dec. 5, 1775: S. Adams Papers. Jefferson to Page, about Dec. 10, 1775: Am. Antiq. Soc. Sch. to Hancock, Nov. 22, 1775: 4 Force, III., 1633. Murray, Present War, I., p. 569. Wash. to Arnold, Dec. 5: 4 Force, IV., 102.

[3] § Jefferson, Nov. 29, 1775: Writings (Ford), I., p. 491. Carleton to [Dartmouth], Nov. 5, 1775: Pub. Rec. Off., Colon. Corres., Quebec, 11, p. 445. Maclean to Barrington, Nov. 20, 1775: War Off., Orig. Corres., Vol. 12.

chance and more too ; for a fortress, however impressive, must have a garrison, and Quebec had Cramahé, the trembling Lieutenant-Governor.

Carleton regarded this functionary as useful, and that appears a very strong point in his favor ; but, after all, the lion would no doubt say a good word for the jackal. The Lieutenant-Governor should have worn—probably he did—a dry semi-smile forever on his face ; a smile that could warm into eager cordiality or fade into ironical patronage ; a smile that scraped an incessant apology for the thinness of soil behind it ; a smile like a prickly pear in the desert,—a touch of dusty green, a hint of gummy moisture, even the miracle of a small yellow blossom once in a while, but all well guarded from general consumption by fifty thorns for every flower. He never treated anybody roughly, at least nobody who could strike back, but some of those he dealt with must have wished that he would ; and he was happy to perform a kind act when invited thereto by some who could do him a favor, but his resources of kindliness were exhausted – or nearly so—by this prudent expenditure.

Carleton's long absence at the front left the responsibility for Quebec with Cramahé, and there was need enough of providing for defence. Until September, 1774, the tenth and fifty-second regiments had been stationed there ; but Gage drew them away, and, when affairs began to look threatening in the lake region, Carleton sent all but a scrap of the remaining garrison to the frontier. Alarmed at their defenceless condition, some of the British citizens twice requested to be organized as militia, but evidently the Governor did not care to place weapons in suspected hands ; and when, on the nineteenth of July, an attempt was actually made to form a British corps, the number that came together did not exceed seventy. Canada, and especially Quebec, had seemed so detached from the rest of the continent, that many did not believe it would become involved in the dispute with England ; and others, friendly to the Colonials, did not wish to take up arms. Carleton viewed the Canadians of the city with some confidence, however, and acknowledged the need of defence by taking steps to organize them.[4]

Schuyler's entry into Canada changed the situation. 'The confusion this has thrown everything into is inexpressible,' wrote a gentleman from Quebec. 'At one time,' reported another, 'St. John's was said to be invested by five thousand Provincials ; then it was said they were retired ; then the River Chambly (that is, Richelieu or Sorel) was said to be full of them, and that they were sending circular letters about the country ; [and] then Montreal was said to be surrounded by them.' 'Soon after, unexpectedly and all on a sudden,' Mrs. Carleton's passage for England was taken ; and, only five days after Montgomery planted his foot before St. Johns, the ship *Lydia*, Captain Deane, set sail with her and her family.[5]

Saturday evening, September the ninth, precisely while Arnold was straining every nerve to march from Cambridge, the active organization of a militia began at Quebec, and twenty-five gentlemen volunteered to do sentry duty. On the seventeenth, 'at the request of the Lieutenant-Governor, the British and Canadian inhabitants assembled on the parade ; the latter were formed into eleven companies, the former into six '; and seventy-two men were ordered to mount guard at six o'clock every evening. Two days later, Mr. Thompson was directed to

---

4 § Two regts.: Gage to Carleton, Sept. 4, 1774 (Pub. Rec. Off., Colon. Corres., Quebec, 10, p. 159. Quebec letter, Oct. 1, 1775: 4 Force, III., 925. Ursul. de T. Riv., I., p. 362. Requests: 4 Force, II., 1125 ; III., 1723 (Account); Almon, Remembrancer, 1776, Part I., p. 131. July 19: Quebec letter, July 20, 1775 (Can. Arch., B, 20, p. 8). Detached: Quebec letter, Sept. 30, 1775 (4 Force, III., 845). Canadians: Carleton's letter, July 3, 1775 (Centenaire, p. 42, note); Quebec Gazette, July 6, 7, 1775.

5 § Quebec letter, Sept. 17, 1775: 4 Force, III., 726. Id., Oct. 1, 1775: ib., 924. Id., Sept. 18, 1775: ib., 728.

A VIEW OF QUEBEC FROM THE SOUTH SHORE, 1759

'get the greatest number of Canadian Carpenters' he could : some to be employed in 'cutting & preparing Picketts,' some in 'setting the Picketts with all the Expedition possible,' and some in laying platforms for cannon ; while 'Fraser the Carpenter with his Men' attended to repairing the blockhouses and sallyports. Ten days more, and the gates were ordered to be 'lock'd at 9 O'Clock, and the Keys to be carried to the Main guard.' Daily lessons in cannon-practice began to be given by a bombardier, and infantry target-shooting followed. Five transports from Boston, sent up to bring forage, were held, and several private vessels were taken for government service. Then an embargo was laid upon the shipping in order to man them ; and, on October third, one of the vessels, the snow *Fell*, 'compleatly equipped with sixteen 9-pounders besides swivels, etc., and 100 true tars, on board of which Commodore Napier hoisted his flag, haul'd out into the stream.' [6]

'On Saturday, the 28th of October, Mr. John Dyer Mercier, [ex-Coroner of Quebec], as he was going into the Upper-Town, was laid hold of by the Town Sergeant, and conducted to the main guard, and there confined' : thus wrote a British merchant from Quebec. Arnold's Indian messenger had placed his letters from the Great Carrying-Place to Mercier and Schuyler in the hands of the British authorities, and they knew that a force was on the move against them. Probably Cramahé did not believe the Provincials could pass the mountains, but the guards were reinforced. On the third of November, it became certain that the impossible had been accomplished, and a flood of steel was pouring down the Chaudière.

---

[6] § Quebec Gazette, Sept. 14, 21 ; Oct. 5, 1775. Quebec letter, Sept. 18, 1775 : 4 Force, III., 728. Vialar, Ord. Book. Lindsay : Can. Rev., No. 5, Sept., 1826, p. 8c. Cramahé to Dartmouth, Sept. 30, 1775 : Pub. Rec. Off., Colon. Corres., Quebec, 11, p. 413. Id. to Gage. Sept. 20, 1775 : Pub. Rec. Off., Am. and W. I., Vol. 130, p. 677. Transports : Howe to Secy. State, Dec. 3, 1775 (ib., Vol. 305, p. 198).

Upon that, some one in authority announced signals for 'turning out the whole Militia of the Town,' ordered the gates firmly 'Shut at 6 O'Clock every Evening from this day,' had all the boats on the south shore of the St. Lawrence destroyed or confiscated, and sent spies across to meet the Americans. On the eighth Cramahé learned that Arnold's advance guard had been 'within two Leagues & a half of the St. Lawrence' the evening before; and the next day the guards were doubled, the officer at each gate was directed to 'Examin carefully the Environs' every morning before opening the doors, and warnings against 'a Surprise' went forth. All this looked vigilant and effective.[7]

But it meant little. For all Cramahé's complacency over the 'better posture of defence' and the reassuring tales of ordnance made ready, the British government found that 'about the 6th of November there were only nine Pieces of Cannon, provided with Carriages, mounted on the Ramparts.' No canoe could enter or leave the harbor without a pass, wrote a citizen; and 'the means made use of to get Canadians from the neighboring country to do duty in town had so intimidated the inhabitants,' that few ventured into Quebec, and there was 'hardly a supply of provisions from hand to mouth, much less to stand out a siege.' 'A very poor stock of provisions and a far less stock of firewood,' said another epitome of the situation.[8]

The citizens, even though under arms, could not be depended on. Baby, a staunch loyalist, reckoned only about

[7] § Quebec letter, Nov. 9, 1775: Maseres, Add. Papers, p. 107; Verreau, Invasion, p. 374. Cramahé to [Dartmouth], Nov. 9, 1775: Pub. Rec. Off., Colon. Corres., Quebec, 11, p. 459. Ogden, Journal, Nov. 5, 7, 8. Vialar, Ord. Book. Ainslie, Journal, Nov. 3. Cramahé to Howe, Oct. [Nov.] 8, 1775: Pub. Rec. Off., Am. and W. I., Vol. 130, p. 729. Mercier, Memorial: Cont. Cong. Papers, No. 41, II., p. 134. REMARK XLII.

[8] § Cramahé to [Dartmouth], Sept. 30, 1775: Note 6. Cannon: cf. Quebec Gazette, Oct. 5, 1775, with Précis of Oper., and see Pell's Diary (Mag. Am. Hist., 1878, p. 43). Quebec letters: Maseres, Add. Papers, pp. 94, 110.

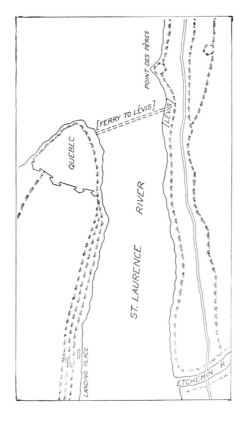

FROM A MAP DRAWN BY A BRITISH CAPTAIN, 1759

one-half of them as reliable.   Many neglected the service, others thought it hard, and the greater part had felt dissatisfied from the very first.   They received no ammunition except—when doing sentry duty—four rounds in the evening, and this caution was understood as a mark of distrust.   The captain of a brig from Quebec, taken prisoner off Cape Ann at the end of September, believed that city would yield without firing a shot, if attacked before Carleton could throw himself into it.   Even Cramahé admitted (November 9) that the militia were ' with Difficulty brought to mount Guard, and consequently [were] not much to be depended on.'   ' The lower sort,' wrote the Governor from Montreal, 'are not more loyal than here.'   Soon after the companies formed, what Mr. Ainslie, Collector of Customs, termed ' the anarchical method of calling town meetings ' had begun to flourish.   ' In these noisy assemblies the masks of many dropt . . . Reports of Mr. Montgomery's successes were most industriously spread — the enemies of Government . . . address'd the fears of the timid, & spoke to this effect : '' Our force is small indeed, theirs is now great & it increases daily— let us be prudent—let us remain neuter—let us secure with our effects good treatment from the friends of Liberty, for they will sooner or later take the town. . . .   Why suffer our property to be destroyed ?'' ' [9]

As Arnold approached, the house grew more and more divided.   Fear increased his pitiful six hundred and seventy-five to twelve or fifteen hundred, and superstition magnified their power.   ' Assuredly a miracle must have been wrought in their favor,' whispered the Canadians ; ' it is more than a human undertaking in this degenerate

---

[9] § Baby : Verreau, Invasion, p. 314.   Quebec letter, Sept. 18, 1775 : 4 Force, III., 728 (cf. Vialar, Ord. Book, Nov. 3).   Lindsay : Can. Rev., No. 5, Sept., 1826, p. 89.   Brig : Wash. to Sch., Oct. 4, 1775 (Writings, III., p. 156).   Cramahé to [Dartmouth], Nov. 9, 1775 : Note 7.   Carleton to Dartmouth, Nov. 5, 1775 : Note 3. Ainslie, Journal (Introd.).

age.' The linen frocks of the riflemen had astonished the warmly clad peasants, and the rumor spread that cold had no power over these warriors. Then a curious accident, changing *toile*—the French word for this linen—into *tôle*, sheet iron, completed the picture : a superhuman phalanx, marching on to battle in gleaming suits of plate-armor. Carleton had vanished. Perhaps the Americans had got him, thought many. While some talked of making a good defence, others talked of making a good capitulation. If report said truly, noted Ainslie in his Journal, 'some of ye over prudent had drawn out articles of surrender to be laid before the people.' In fact, a considerable number of British and Canadian citizens met secretly, and undertook to contrive means of compelling a surrender.[10]

'Just now,' wrote a citizen while Arnold stood surveying the town from Point Levi ; 'Just now an order is come down for eight men from each of the six companies of the British Militia to appear on the parade *without Arms*, to receive One Shilling and a pint of Porter for the business they were to do. Orders are also given for a party of Marines, to be on the parade *armed*. So we are inclined to judge the intentions of our Government to be to force us to a defence of the town, and sacrifice our lives and properties. The Shilling and a pint of Porter are supposed to be considered as King's money to enlist us, and subject us to military discipline. The Lord protect us from our enemies within and without!'[11] What such people would prefer to do, when offered their choice between the open

---

[10] § 675: Arn. to Wash., Dec. 5, 1775 (Me. Hist. Soc. Coll., I., p. 386). 1500: Legge to Dartmouth, Dec. 29, 1775 (Pub. Rec. Off., Colon. Corres., N. Sco., Vol. X., p. 84, inclos.; Carleton to Dartmouth, Nov. 5, 1775 (Note 3); Quebec letter, Nov. 9, 1775 (Maseres, Add. Papers, p. 110). Miracle: Quebec letter, Nov. 9, 1775 (Verreau, Invasion, p. 376). Tôle, etc.: Ainslie, Journal, Dec. 2. Cramahé to [Germain], Nov. 19, 1775: Bancroft Coll., Eng. and Am., Aug., 1775–Dec., 1776, p. 169. Ainslie, Journal. Meeting (possibly the same as that mentioned below, at which Williams spoke): Lindsay in Can. Rev., No. 5, Sept., 1826, p. 89.

[11] Quebec letter, Nov. 9, 1775 (P.S.). Maseres, Add. Papers, p. 111.

hand and the clenched fist of the Provincials, could easily be imagined.

But how did Quebec, that pivot of empire, happen to be left so long without a garrison? Carleton was compelled, of course, to use every available man against Schuyler, but why did not Great Britain send him reinforcements?

In September, four regiments were assigned to Quebec, and on the twenty-seventh a letter for the commanding officer, giving careful instructions about navigating the St. Lawrence, left Whitehall by a special messenger. This was added : ' It being of very great importance that the Regiments ordered to Quebec should get to that Place before the Winter, every possible effort must be made to secure that Object.' Yet for some reason—a storm, perhaps—these troops landed at Staten Island. Nor was this England's only effort. On December sixth, Lord Germain wrote General Clinton that, in consequence of a gale, two regiments destined for Quebec had ' put into Milford Haven,' and would now be added to the southern expedition. [12]

But why did not the army and navy already in America do something for this vital point?

On October the tenth, ' a Vessel arrived [at Boston] express from Quebec,' reported General Howe, with letters to Gage from Carleton and Cramahé. Howe ordered a battalion of marines into the transports at once ; but, when he applied to Admiral Graves for a convoy, the Admiral consulted his captains ' and others well acquainted with the River Saint Lawrence, ' as he stated, ' upon the probability of their getting up. ' Cramahé found by the records of the

---

1 2 § Four Regts. (17th, 28th, 46th, 55th): Can. Arch., B, 37, p. 111 ; Pownall to Com'g ff., Sept. 27, 1775 (Pub. Rec. Off., Am. and W. I., Vol. 431, p. 82) ; Mem. kindly furnished by Brit. War Off., June 23, 1902. (They actually embarked in Sept.) Germain: Pub. Rec. Off., Am. and W. I., Vol. 130, p. 759. See also Pownall to Carleton, Sept. 25, 1775: Can. Arch., Q, 11, p. 244.

Custom House that two ships had arrived as late as the twenty-fourth of November ; but all the gentlemen consulted by Graves were of the opinion, 'that hard Gales of Wind and Snow Storms, would not only prevent their getting up, but perhaps endanger the loss of the whole Convoy.' Howe then decided to procure 'smaller vessels better adapted to working their way up the River St. Law-

rence, but not being able to have them fitted for sea in reasonable time to undertake the voyage with the least prospect of succeeding,' he 'judged it most prudent to decline sending the Reinforcement.' One day before the certainty of Arnold's coming was known in Quebec, news arrived that no relief could be expected from Boston. 'It is impossible,' wrote Lord Germain bitterly to Howe; 'It is impossible to turn one's thoughts to Canada, without . . . lamenting the obstacles which prevented the execution of the Measure you had with so proper a Zeal proposed for the safety of it, and which, I will venture to say, could not have failed.' The color of the tears poured by the loyalists at Quebec itself could be imagined. And so, as it seemed, Andromeda stood chained to the rock once more. Was there to be a Perseus? [13]

On the twelfth of October, the *Hunter* sloop-of-war, Captain McKenzie, slid into the Basin and cast anchor ;

---

[13] § Howe to Secy. State, Nov. 27, 1775: Pub. Rec. Off., Am. and W. I., Vol. 305, p. 193. Id. to Carleton, Oct. 13, 1775: Can. Arch., Q, 11, p. 288. Graves to Stephens, Nov. 2, 1775 : Pub. Rec. Off., Admirals' Disp., N. Am., Vol. 6, Bundle 485. Cramahé to [Dartmouth], Nov. 9, 1775: Note 7. Germain to Howe, Jan. 5, 1776: Pub. Rec. Off., Am. and W. I., Vol. 431, p. 110.

but her men were needed aboard.   When the little American army crossed the threshold of civilization (November 3), only the wavering militia stood behind the walls of Quebec.   This was a Friday.   Saturday evening brought a schooner from famishing but loyal Newfoundland and a sloop from St. John's (now Prince Edward's) Island with two of Maclean's captains and some men ; and, on Sunday, a London ship delivered a few more from Newfoundland,—about one hundred and twenty in all ; but Cramahé described the greater number as 'Irish Fishermen unacquainted with the Use of Arms,' and others were traders or artisans not intending to enlist.[14]

Sunday evening, the white sails of His Majesty's frigate *Lizard*, Captain Hamilton, lighted up the harbor. Even below hatches there was brightness, for she carried thousands of muskets and twenty thousand pounds in gold; and after her followed two or three brigs, full of arms, ammunition, uniforms, and bribes for the Indians, which the Continental Congress had vainly tried to catch.   But the *Lizard* could send ashore only some thirty-five marines. It was not considered safe to land her shining cargo.   The merchant ships went on bolting their freight day and night.   Briand talked of leaving the country.   Cramahé reached his boiling point, profanity: ' It is your damn'd Committees that have thrown the province into its present State,' he told MacAulay ; and then, sitting down, he moaned to Howe: ' There is too much Reason to apprehend, the Affair will be soon over.'[15]

---

[14] § Hunter: Cramahé to Dartmouth, Oct. 25, 1775 (Can. Arch., Q, 11, p. 264); Graves to Stephens, Sept. 26, 1775 (Pub. Rec. Off., Admirals' Disp., N. Am., Vol. 6, Bundle 485).   Nov 3: Quebec letter, Nov. 7, 1775 (4 Force, III., 1396); Caldwell, Letter ; Carleton to Dartmouth, Nov. 5, 1775 (Note 3).   Recruits: Quebec Gazette, Nov. 9, 1775 ; Callbeck to Shuldham, Jan. 10, 1776 (Pub. Rec. Off., Admirals' Disp., N. Am., Vol. 5); Finlay, Journal, Nov. 14 ; Caldwell, Letter ; Cramahé to [Dartmouth], Nov. 9, 1775 (Note 7); Account (4 Force, III., 1723).   Newf.: J. Parsons, Jr., to N. Y. Com., May 30, 1775 (4 Force, II., 851); Newf. letter in N. Eng. Chron., June 22, 1775 ; Prowse, Newfoundland, p. 338.

[15] § Lizard, etc.: Hamilton to Graves, Nov. 9, 1775 (Pub. Rec. Off., Admirals Disp., N. Am., Vol. 6, Bundle 485); Montg. to Sch., Nov. 13, 1775 (4 Force, III.,

Was Arnold, then, to be Wolfe's compeer? The goal stood in full view; the prize could almost be touched ; not a minute was lost. With all possible speed the troops hurried on to Point Levi. Canoes were gathered in every quarter,—the worn-out men carrying twenty of them some eight leagues on their shoulders. Dugouts brought the number of boats up to thirty-five or forty ; and all were kept out of harm's way at the mouth of the Chaudière, several miles up the St. Lawrence. Provisions, also, had to be collected, and the bare feet, weary of plodding about in snow and ice, covered with ' savage shoes ' of fresh hide. Details worked at scaling ladders. One party marched fourteen miles to a forge, hammered out spear points all night, and marched back the next day. And, when enough men had come up, the lofty red pines witnessed a grand review.[16]

What a review that was ! Hollow eyes and pinched faces recorded the battle with the wilderness. Morgan's figure, an athlete's at Cambridge, seemed now a monk's. Bigelow's good six feet of patriotism stood for seven, so thin was he. Less flame burned in Greene's cheeks, though still more, perhaps, in his look. Dearborn did not appear at all, for he was down with fever in a peasant's cottage not far from St. Mary, and his keen blue eyes were near closing forever. Habiliments had fared no better. Some of the men had boasted uniforms, when

---

1602); Précis of Oper.; Dartmouth to Carleton, Aug. 2, 1775 (Can. Arch., Q, 11, p. 198) ; Cramahé to Howe, Oct. [Nov.] 8, 1775 (Note 7). To catch brigs: Hancock to Wash., Oct. 5, 1775 (4 Force, III., 950); Wash. to Broughton, Oct. 16, 1775 (ib., 1975); Reed to Broughton, Oct. 19, 1775 (ib., 1109) ; Wash. to Hancock, Dec. 7, 1775 (4 Force, IV., 214). Gold left aboard: Hamilton to Graves, Nov. 9, 1775 (*supra*). Loading: Arnold to Montg., Nov. 13, 1775 (4 Force, III., 1635). Nov. 16, the Adamant, with Guy Johnson, Brook Watson, and Ethan Allen aboard, sailed from Quebec (Quebec Gazette, Nov. 16; Cramahé to [Dartmouth], Nov. 9, 1775: Note 7 ; Allen, Narrative, p. 38). Briand : Maseres, Add. Papers, p. 118. Cramahé: ib., p. 101. Cramahé to Howe, Oct. [Nov.] 8, 1775 : Note 7.

16 On the authorities for Arnold's operations covered by this Chapter see REMARK XXXI. Up to his reaching the Plains of Abraham, they have been studied in Smith, Arnold's March, Chap. II. See also Capt. Ward's letter in Gammell, S. Ward, p. 339: 'marched through snow and ice barefoot' to Quebec.

they left Cambridge, and some had not; but now all dressed alike,—in rags dyed by the forest and the soil. Heads were as bare as feet; while the gaunt faces hid beneath ragged beards that young cave-dwellers might have envied. The sight was pathetic, laughable, glorious; but perhaps the ludicrousness of it came uppermost, and one at least of the soldiers thought that they all resembled 'the animals which inhabit New Spain, called the Ourang Outang.' [17]

On the left of the American line at Point Levi, and about four miles above the present ferry to Quebec, stood a big stone mill, worked for Major Caldwell's benefit by the co-operation of a tiny stream and a water-wheel huge enough to make amends. One day a boat rowed over toward it from the *Hunter*, and a man stepped ashore in the bushes. His object was to obtain something from the mill, but the object of the Americans was to obtain him. When the boat drew off, perhaps to find a better landing, some of Arnold's riflemen and Indians made a dash for the fellow that had landed. Discovering the danger, he swam for it and swam well. Bullets made the water boil round his head in vain; but finally one of the savages overhauled him and took him prisoner. He was a midshipman, brother of the *Hunter's* captain; but the only items of information sifted from his ingenious loquacity were things his captors knew or did not wish to know: among the latter that five regiments were on their way from Boston and twenty thousand Hanoverians from Europe. [18]

Very different another visitor. John Halsted of New Jersey, superintendent at the mill, had labored actively on the liberal side, and some days since had been exiled or had exiled himself to the Island of Orleans, just below

---

17 § Stocking, Journal. Bigelow: Essex Inst. Hist. Coll., XXXIII., p. 249.
18 § See particularly the Journals of Henry and Ogden.

the town. He took the first opportunity to join Arnold ; and, besides turning over to the Americans a quantity of wheat and flour stored in the mill, reported, among other things, that all the militia except a hundred 'Tories' were ready to lay down their arms. The Americans felt rather pleased than otherwise to hear that some ultras would fight. All they wanted now was to get at them.[19]

That, however, did not prove absolutely easy. The strait of the river at Quebec was under the *Lizard's* guns ; the *Hunter* moved up to the next narrow place, a little

CALDWELL'S MILL (REBUILT), 1902

above the mill ; several smaller armed vessels hovered about ; and guard-boats did patrol duty from sloop to frigate all night. Still, the Americans had no thought of despairing. 'Our situation now seem'd somewhat tick-

[19] § Halsted: Can. Arch., Q, 10, p. 28 (he signed petition for Assembly); the Amer. Journals, particularly Ogden's ; Caldwell, Letter ; Halsted, Memorials (Cont. Cong. Papers, No. 41, II., p. 142 ; III., pp. 401,463); LeMoine, Album du Touriste, p. 165.

lish,' remarked Ogden ; 'We determined however [to] make a bold push for Quebec at all events.' But here their old enemy, Nature, stepped in. The same gale that held Carleton spellbound at Montreal, blew here. Friday night, the tenth, found the St. Lawrence foaming like a whipped courser. Very well ; to-morrow, then, said the Americans. Saturday night, however, did no better : a canoe could not live in the waves. It was a nightmare for the army,—straining every muscle, yet rooted to the spot. But, happily, the city could not get away. Sunday morning found her still on the cliff. She seemed only waiting for something to happen.[20]

And that day something did happen. One of the 'town-meetings' was in session at the chapel of the bishop's palace, and a Mr. Williams held the pulpit, preaching the doctrine of a good capitulation. Suddenly a noise was heard at the door. A grim old man entered with other grim men behind him, listened an instant, and then strode fiercely forward. Even in his skin he would have been taken anywhere for a soldier and a royalist.

'Out of that pulpit !' he shouted.

The command alone would have been sufficient, for this intruder was Allan Maclean, arrived that moment from the west ; but in an instant the furious Highlander pulled Williams down by the arm, and began exhorting the people to loyalty with a slogan-and-broadsword eloquence.[21]

Driven from Sorel by Major Brown's cannon, Maclean had sent a part of his force to Carleton, and with the rest

---

[20] § Ogden, Journal, Nov. 7. Wind: Arnold to Montg. and to Wash., Nov. 13, 1775 (4 Force, III., 1635, 1636); Cramahé to Germain, Nov. 19, 1775 (Bancroft Coll., Eng. and Am., Aug., 1775–Dec., 1776, p. 169.

[21] § Verreau (Berthelot), Invasion, p. 235 ; MS. in Can. Arch., M, 99. (Jenkin Williams of Quebec signed a petition for an Assembly.) The description of Maclean and minor details of the scene are inferential.

moved down the St. Lawrence. At Three Rivers he stripped the barracks and magazines, took all the gunpowder from the merchants, and then decided to set out for the capital. Half-way there, he met a couple of Indians in a canoe ; and, by a stupid mistake, one of them handed over a letter from Arnold that he was carrying to Montgomery. It announced the arrival of the Kennebec detachment near Point Levi, and so revealed to Maclean the danger of Quebec. The hostile winds checked his ships, but he strode on by land ; and now here he stood, the King's senior officer on the ground, with some two hundred stout and true men at his back, ready for anything—except surrender.[22]

This was not a large force, but it counted for more than it numbered. Five hundred men of Marseilles, chanting the song which took a new name from them, electrified France and tipped the scale toward red Revolution at Paris in 1792, because they were united and resolute. Maclean's corps had a similar influence. Many of his followers had belonged to Fraser's Highlanders, a corps of picked men who marched under Wolfe's banner in kilt, bonnet, and black feather, and swung their broadswords high at the victory of the Plains. Every officer was a veteran, and none of the captains had served fewer than twenty years. ' No danger or difficulty could startle, or make them deviate from their duty,' boasted their leader ; and Carleton himself described them officially as ' officers of merit.' Gorgeous in scarlet jackets with blue facings and white lace, dark tartan kilts, tartan hose, and blue bonnets edged with a checker-work of white, red, and green, the brawny Highlanders marched about the town as if

---

22 § See Vol. I., p. 469. Verreau (Badeaux), Invasion, p. 174. Cramahé to [Germain], Nov. 19, 1775: Bancroft Coll., Eng. and Am., Aug., 1775–Dec., 1776, p. 169. Ogden, Journal, Nov. 13. Arnold to Wash., Nov. 14, 1775: Me. Hist. Soc. Coll., I., p. 373. REMARK XLIII.

already victors, and their presence was not only a shield, but a sword and a banner also.[23]

With red-hot energy and zeal, Maclean set about organizing and inspiring the defence of Quebec. He was no believer in the French of Canada, and could honestly satisfy the British merchants that he would show no preference to the noblesse. This no doubt aided him to ' Reconcile' them, as he said he did ; but apparently he applied a still more potent argument. From the first, every effort had been made by the loyalists of Canada to represent their visitors from the south as highwaymen. The Colonials had ' attempted to invade, and consequently to plunder' the province, wrote a gentleman in Quebec to his father. ' Those vagabonds, who come with no other view but that of plunder and pillage,' said a writer in the *Quebec Gazette*. Allen's raiders, especially his Canadians, were reported as merely in quest of loot. ' Rebel banditti,' snarled a letter from Quebec, pointing at Schuyler's troops, just as Arnold drew near.[24]

The Americans realized the power of such an idea, and cried out against Carleton for misrepresenting them. ' This Villain,' wrote Lieutenant Copp, ' has worked up the People against Us, by representing us as the worst of Banditti; . . . This has caused the People to resist.' But no doubt all on the British side took so convenient a ground more or less honestly, and such an argument fitted Maclean's intense and narrow zeal peculiarly well. Besides, in the rough-and-tumble about St. Johns, cases

----

[23] § Mars.; Rose, Century, p. 35.   Fraser's: Hawkins, Picture, p. 390.   Maclean to ———, May 25, 1776: Can. Arch., Q, 12, p. 69.   Carleton to Germain, July 13, 1776: ib., p. 104.   Uniform: Gage to Maclean, June 12, 1775 (Can. Arch., B, 173, p. 1); Maclean to Barrington, May 11, 1776 (ib., p. 334) ; Groves, 42d, pp. 2, 9.

[24] § Maclean to Barrington, Nov. 20, 1775: Can. Arch., M, 317, p. 259.   Id. to ———, May 25, 1776: ib., Q, 12, p. 69.   ' Banditti,' etc.: Quebec letter, Sept. 30, 1775 (4 Force, III., 845); Quebec Gazette, Oct. 5, 1775 ; Ainslie, Journal (Introd.); Quebec letter, Nov. 7, 1775 (4 Force, III., 1396): Verreau (Badeaux), Invasion, p. 167.

I have not been able to cross the River, but is now moderated and intend crossing this Evening with about 40 Canoes; to prevent which the Hunter Sloop & Lizard Frigate lie opposite — however expect to be able to evade them. I have received the agreeable Intelligence that St. Johns is in our hands and Montreal invested. The Merchant ships in the Harbour (about fifteen) are loading Day & Night, & some already Sailed —

FROM ARNOLD'S LETTER TO WASHINGTON, NOV. 13, 1775

of pillage must have occurred, and he—fresh from the scene—could give the full details. Obviously, then, he made it look very dangerous indeed to admit 'fifteen hundred' or even half that number of naked, famishing strangers into the town, particularly as they showed extraordinary spirit, bore arms in good earnest, and had a following of irresponsible Canadians. However fine their pretensions, better sup with them at the end of a long spoon, said timidity and even common prudence. Some, however, knowing the truth about the Provincials, worked the other way, and nobody could tell yet—in spite of Maclean—which view would finally prevail.[25]

Sunday night the wind still raged, and this gave the Scotchman twenty-four hours more ; but Monday evening the river seemed calm enough to attempt. Clouds covered the sky ; and darkness, punctuated sharply by the lights of Quebec and the vessels, hid the bluffs on both sides. Behind this curtain, on the south shore, many figures crept noiselessly about. The fleet of dugouts and canoes floated down to Caldwell's mill ; and, at eight or nine o'clock, Arnold and a part of the troops paddled off into the unseen.

As they neared the other side they found a British boat rowing along between them and the land. It looked like ruin.

'Lie on your paddles and let her pass !' ordered Arnold under his breath.

All obeyed ; and the patrol went by without seeing them. The *Hunter*, swinging at her anchor above, prevented their landing at the point selected; but they finally beached their craft, and then felt their way down, looking for a place to ascend the bluff, until they

---

25 § Copp, before Quebec, Dec. 7, 1775: Pub. Rec. Off., Am. and W. I., Vol. 186, p. 237. See Macpherson to Read, Dec. 16, 1775. Read, G. Read, p. 115 ; Marshall, Wash., II., p. 296.

reached the spot where Wolfe had landed,—a happy augury.[26]

Time and again the flotilla crossed in safety, except that one canoe broke apart midstream, and her passengers had to be towed the rest of the way; but, about four o'clock, the moon broke through the clouds; the wind freshened; the tide ebbed swiftly, exposing many rocks off the mill; and the journeys had to cease. About five hundred men, brought together from their scattered points of disembarkation, now stood shivering under the huge wall of the river on the north shore. Something must be done. But what?[27]

On and attack! was the impulse of Arnold, Morgan, and all the bolder spirits; and in fact the hour for a supreme audacity had struck. No sentries had been encountered. Parties despatched promptly both up-stream and down to guard against discovery had found no enemy stirring. A reconnoissance observed only signs of repose. Just beyond the bluff, less than two miles away, lay Quebec, still waiting to be taken. Confident that Arnold's men could not pass the warships, the citizens were asleep; and as yet they dreamed only of securing their property in the suburbs and laying up supplies. St. John's Gate stood open. The fastenings were out of order. Nobody appeared to know where the keys hung. There were no matches to fire the cannon with, it was said. One quick rush, and the news would soon have been flying far and wide through town and country and overseas, ' Quebec taken!'[28]

---

[26] § Besides the Journals, Arnold's letters to Montg. and Wash., Nov. 13, 14, 20: 4 Force, III., 1635, 1636, 1684, 1695.

[27] § See Note 26. There is a difficulty about the moon: Smith, Arnold's March, p. 460.

[28] § Besides the Journals, see Account (4 Force, III., 1723); Marshall, Wash., II., pp. 319–321 (based largely on the now lost Journal of Lieut. Heath, or Heth, of Morgan's Company); and Morgan's autobiog. (interesting but inaccurate) in Hist. Mag., June, 1871, p. 379.

But every finger of good sense pointed the other way. One could not easily imagine that a gate had been left open ; sentries were heard singing out their calls on the ramparts ; report had exaggerated Maclean's force ; the Americans had been able to transport only three-quarters of their feeble number ; and the scaling ladders were still on the other shore.   Even more alarming seemed another fact.   A fire had been lighted in a vacant house to warm the men, especially those chilled in the river ; and a patrol-barge, catching sight of the blaze or else wishing merely to avoid the current, had drawn into the Cove while the flotilla was paddling north for the third time. When discovery seemed inevitable, the barge was hailed and ordered ashore.

' Yes,' came the answer ; but it headed away.

' Fire ! ' cried Arnold ; but even the argument of lead failed to persuade the crew, and, with many doleful cries and lamentations, the patrol hurried off.

Who could suppose that for hours no echo of this event would reach the executive ear ?   Even Arnold would not urge an assault ; and after a little, clambering up the bluff, his troops crossed the Plains of Abraham and threw themselves down in their blankets on

LOOKING UPSTREAM FROM WOLFE'S COVE, 1902

the floors of Major Caldwell's roomy mansion, about a mile and a half from Quebec.[29]

All the heroism of the wilderness, then, had been merely a libation spilled on the sands of the St. Lawrence ?

[29] § In particular, Ogden's Journal and Arnold to ——, Nov. 27, 1775 : Sparks MSS., No. 66, I., p. 23.   Conn. Gazette, Dec. 22, 1775 (Providence letter). Caldwell, Letter.   REMARK XLIV.

The stubborn leader would not admit it, and his fertile brain was busy. Montcalm had left the fortifications to meet Wolfe, and in that way lost Quebec : perhaps a taunting challenge would bring Maclean out. The Americans, roused ere long by a timid sally from the town, paraded near the walls in such a manner as to conceal their fewness, gave three bold huzzas, and waited. Within the city rose a tremendous commotion. Citizens and soldiers armed and hurried to the ramparts. Cries of alarm burst out : ' The gate is open ! ' ' St. John's Gate is open ! ' ' There are no matches for the cannon ! ' The keys of the gate could not be found : ' Quick, handspikes here, and ropes ! ' At last the gate was fastened, and matches came from the *Lizard.* But the Americans waited in vain for a battle. Though in tatters they were deeply respected. Arnold, whose trading in horses at Quebec was remembered, might be called a horse-jockey; but only from the wall. Cheer answered cheer, and a few charges of cannon-balls, grape, and canister followed; but no Montcalm was in town, and the people stayed on the ramparts.[30]

Arnold then undertook to frighten Quebec with a haughty and threatening summons, hoping to make the authorities yield or the people revolt. ' On surrendering the Town,' he wrote to Cramahé, ' the property of every Individual shall be secured to him ; but if I am obliged to carry the Town by storm, you may expect every severity practised on such occasions'; and toward evening Ogden, with a white flag and a drum, marched boldly ' within 4 Rod of St. Johns Gate ' to deliver the letter.

---

[30] § Besides the American Journals (particularly Humphrey's) see Ainslie's; also Thompson in LeMoine, Quebec Past and Present, p. 197. The description of the doings in town is based upon the Account (4 Force, III., 1723) which, though inaccurate in some details, appears substantially reliable. Arnold's horse business: Sparks MSS., No. 57, XI., p. 336 (his voyages); Carleton to [Dartmouth], June 7, 1775 (Pub. Rec. Off., Colon. Corres., Quebec, 11, p. 283). REMARK XLV.

The parley was still beating and the flag still waving, when an answer came in the shape of an 18-pound shot, spattering the American envoy with dirt and stunning his drummer with fright. Thinking this might have been a mistake, Ogden was despatched again with the same missive the next morning, but only to hear a cannon-ball pass just over his head ' in a verry streight direction '; and a third attempt produced no better fruit. Yet one arrow still remained in Arnold's quiver. Quebec, in want of provisions and fuel, ' if blocked up by a superior force, must, as soon as the frost sets in, surrender,' he thought ; and he stopped every road effectually. In a few days Cramahé was complaining : ' they actually prevent fuel or refreshments of any kind being brought in.' ' We can get nothing into the Town,' admitted Maclean.[31]

Facing life instead of death now, the Americans themselves needed provisions ; and their poverty, backed by their respect for the law, stood somewhat in the way. Just inside of a mile from the city was the General Hospital, in reality a convent. The next day after Arnold's final rebuff, his troops appeared at the door. ' The tattered clothes that covered them, and their pitiful, haggard faces excited compassion,' recorded the nuns ; ' They asked a little something to eat of our servants, who notified us. All we could give these troops, famished and exhausted with fatigue, was a few loaves ' ; yet the Americans made no trouble, and soon withdrew. Indeed, though sundry provisions intended for the city were captured and a few ' tories ' lost some livestock, the rations had to be limited

[31] § Ainslie, Journal.   Arnold to Cramahé, Nov. 14, 15, 1775: 4 Force, III., 1685.   Arnold's letter, Dec. 16, 1775: Conn. Gazette, Jan. 26, 1776.   Ogden's and Haskell's Journals.   Cramahé, Nov. 19, denied the firing on a flag of truce (Bancroft Coll., Eng. and Am., Aug., 1775–Dec., 1776, p. 169); but Arnold's letter of Nov. 15 to him and the American Journals seem decisive.   Arnold to Montg., Nov. 14, 1775: Me. Hist. Soc. Coll., I., p. 374.   The quotation from Cramahé is from his letter of Nov. 19.   Maclean to Barrington, Nov. 20, 1775: Can. Arch., M, 317, p. 259.

still so closely that Morgan, Hendricks, and Smith complained hotly, and one day Arnold ordered Lieutenant Simpson and his men to seize a herd of cattle feeding beyond the St. Charles River.[32]

' Come on, lads ! ' cried the ready lieutenant ; and the party, running down to the ferry, near the mouth of the river and almost under the city walls, threw themselves boldly into the crowded boat, thinking the gunners would not fire upon their own people. The boat—already aground, as it proved—was fixed solidly on the bottom by this added weight ; and most of the Americans, jumping into the water, pushed, pulled at the rope, and plied the handspikes with might and main. Above them rose the lofty battlements,—the heavy guns darkly silhouetted against a clear, sunset sky. Men could be seen preparing to fire the cannon, while the motionless boat, like a rock in a pond, made a perfect mark.

' A shot ! ' cried Henry suddenly, noticing a flash ; and at the word a 36-pound ball took off brave Sergeant Dixon's leg below the knee. ' Oh, Simpson,' he cried, ' I am gone !' and fell. Amid a shout of triumph and a roar of artillery from the ramparts, he was tenderly borne away. The limb was amputated, but the patient sank. ' The doctor advised him to drink a bowl of tea,' noted Thayer in his Journal. ' Said the noble spirited sergeant, " I would not if it would save my life." ' So died the first American martyr before Quebec, and the Plains of Abraham gave him a fitting grave.

Meanwhile anxiety reigned in the city. No one could feel secure with such enterprising foes in the vicinity. ' The Enemy without,' however, were ' not so much to be dreaded, as their numerous friends within the Town,' ob-

---

[32] § Hospital: Mgr. de St. Vallier, Part II., Chap. IV., p. 400. **Complaints, Dixon, etc.:** Henry, Journal, pp. 86, 87, 98, 185. Dixon: Thayer, Journal, Nov 18.

served Cramahé.   Captain Hamilton, after giving orders
for sending ashore the equipment of the *Lizard* and *Hunter*, was adding to himself, ' If the Place is not betray'd

into the hands of the
Rebels before we can ac-
complish it.'   Maclean
felt equally •troubled :
' our provisions are by
no means adequate to
maintain the Number
of inhabitants,' he re-

ST. LOUIS GATE (OUTSIDE), 1775

flected, ' and now if we turn out some thousands,
We run very great risk of having the Canadian Militia
Mutiny.'   The Americans appeared to have Quebec fairly
in a corner, for Montgomery to bag.[33]

But suddenly, in a moment and between two days, the
scene shifted.   On the eighteenth of November, a friend
or pretended friend of the invaders left the city, and informed Arnold that Maclean's troops were to make a
sally the next day ' with seven field pieces and all their
force,' as Captain Topham heard ; for the weakness of the
Americans had been discovered.   Previous alarms had
been received with joy.   Though in want of everything
but stout hearts, the Provincials were always 'prepared and
anxious to see him,' as their leader declared.   But now
the threat seemed unusually serious.   A servant of Arnold's, who had been captured, escaped at this time and
said that eight hundred were under arms in Quebec ; Captain Napier in the *Fell*, ' with two hundred men,' was reported close at hand ; and the *Lizard* stole up the river as
if to cut off the Americans' retreat.   A strict examination
of arms and ammunition was ordered ; and so many of the

³³ § Cramahé, Nov. 19: Note 31.   Hamilton to Dartmouth, Nov. 20, 1775:
Can. Arch., Q, 11, p. 339.   Maclean to Barrington, Nov. 20, 1775: Can. Arch., M,
317, p. 259.

cartridges, 'which to appearance were very good,' proved worthless, that not over five rounds per man could be depended upon. Nearly one hundred muskets also were unserviceable. 'Right about face,' was the only rule of war that fitted the situation. A council was held; the men were ordered to lie on their arms, ready to march at a moment's notice ; what guards and invalids had remained on the other shore were looked out for ; and, about three o'clock the next morning, the Americans buried themselves in the forest. The heroic expedition—planned with care but not with knowledge, sadly belated, and cruelly unlucky—had entirely failed.[34]

All one could hope for now was safety ; and even that seemed precarious enough. Over frozen ground the troops limped almost barefoot some twenty miles up the St. Lawrence. 'We might have been tracked all the way,' declared Stocking, a serious man, 'by the blood from our shattered hoofs,'—*feet* they could hardly be called after going so long shoeless ; and the men could not possibly march farther in that condition. Fortunately, they found themselves in a safe and pleasant spot, to which the silvery shimmer and silken rustle of many poplars gave the name Aspen Point (*Pointe aux Trembles*).[35]

Here the great bluff of the river politely stepped back a little, giving place to a church of St. François de Sales, a nunnery and a straggling village of farmhouses, mostly stone, which sunned themselves comfortably at the foot of cultivated slopes. Pimply Bigot with his beautiful Madame Péan, the Canadian Pompadour, and a choice following of transiently paired couples, had found this an agree-

[34] § Topham, Journal, Nov. 19. Humphrey's, Stocking's, and other Journals. Arnold to Wash., Nov. 20, 1775: Me. Hist Soc. Coll., I., p. 379. Id. to Montg., Nov. 14: ib., p. 374. Id. to Id., Nov. 20, 1775: Sparks MSS., No. 52, II., p. 31. Id. to ———, Nov. 27, 1775: ib., No. 66, I., p. 23. Id. to ———, Nov. 25, 1775: Me. Hist. Soc. Coll., I., p. 382. REMARK XLVI.

[35] § Stocking, Journal. Letter in Henry's Journal, p. 185.

able place to make a halt on their lively way to Montreal. When Wolfe attacked Quebec, it became a place of refuge for women and children. What counted for more, the Chevalier de Lévis had considered it a strategic point of value, and the French had taken post there against Murray. So the troops broke ranks with confidence, and took up their quarters gladly in the houses.[36]

Gloomy days followed. Happily, nobody knew the truth about Maclean's reported plan of a sally : that his field-pieces were not in order, and, since the morning the Americans crossed the river, he had not thought of attacking them ; and so the chagrin of a needless retreat had not to be borne. But none the less there were bitter 'heart burnings' over the failure to capture Quebec ; and the assurance that keen disappointment would be felt at home, added pitch to the flame. Provisions and fuel were known to be hurrying into the city, and every wagon-load meant a cargo of toil and suffering for the Americans. The preparations for defence were going on undisturbed. Every one could foresee—what proved to be the case— that many enemies of liberty in the Colonies would term the withdrawal a defeat and pluck up new courage. Some began to realize that after 'having their constitutions Racked' by such fearful hardships, they would never be themselves again. 'Indeed,' said Lieutenant Humphrey to his Journal, 'was one of the officers from Cambrig here Now to review our men he would Really think one half of them was fiter for the Genll hospital than the field.' Every one found himself, like Ward, 'as poor as a church mouse.' Clothing for such a number could not be obtained, and the more than usually cold weather bit hard. 'Some severe Peripneumonias, Anginas, etc.,' noted the

---

36 § Bouchette, Descr. Topog., p. 409. Bigot: Parkman, Montcalm, II., pp. 18, 19. Refuge: ib., II., 224. Strategic: ib., II., 361 ; Lévis, Journal, p. 284. Henry, Journal, p. 91. Morison, Journal.

surgeon. 'Poor Arnold, I wonder where he is,' groaned Washington in the midst of his own troubles. He was here.[37]

AT ASPEN POINT, 1902

Yet, in many ways, the sharp contrast with what had gone before made even the present situation look bright. At last, food enough could be had, and a chance to recruit 'worn out natures,' as Captain Ward phrased it. Some

[37] § Sallying : Caldwell, Letter. Heartburnings: Henry, Journal, p. 83. Disappointment: Sch. to Hancock, Nov. 22, 1775 (4 Force, III., 1633). Q. reported taken: Eddis, Letters, Nov. 17. At Quebec: Arnold to Montg., Nov. 20, 1775 (Sparks MSS., No. 52, II., p. 31); Nov. 25, 1775 (Me. Hist. Soc. Coll., I., p. 381); Letter (Henry, Journal, p. 185). Defeat: Mayor of Albany, Dec. 25, 1775 (Pub. Rec. Off., Am. and W. I., Vol. 186, p. 231); Cuyler, Dec. 24, 1775 (ib., p. 233); Hutcheson to Haldimand, Jan. 16, 1776 (Can. Arch., B, 20, p. 79). Racked: Thayer, Journal, Nov. 22. Humphrey, Journal, Nov. [22]. Ward to [sisters], Nov. 26, 1775: Sparks MSS., No. 25, p. 52. Senter, Journal, Nov. 21. Wash. to J. Reed, Nov. 28, 1775: W. B. Reed, Letters, p. 18.

poor leather was obtained, and all the shoemakers among
the troops worked at moccasins. Ogden was sent off to
Montreal for clothing.   Good news, which had always
managed somehow to arrive at the gloomiest points ever
since they left Cambridge, cheered the spirits of the men :
Montreal had fallen.   Several comrades, mourned as lost
in the wilderness, crawled into camp with pinched faces
but joyful hearts. Signs could be discovered that Quebec,
though well aware how the Americans were straitened,
was perhaps wavering, after all ; and Arnold still hoped
to 'knock up a dust with the garrison.'   On November
twenty-eighth, Morgan went back to watch the city ; and
the 'Worthy Inhabitants of Point Levi' were requested
the same day to furnish the British forces no supplies, as
they were 'endeavouring to subvert the Rights and Liberties of Mankind and this Colony in particular.'   Thereafter the work of getting provisions into Quebec went on
rather less merrily.[38]

In a different way also the time counted : Canadians
and Americans had another chance to get acquainted.

The little one-story cottages of flint cobbles—and those
of wood no less—were certainly plain enough.   The
sitting-room kitchen (where the huge fireplace had now
been stoned up for the winter) with a big, square, cast-
iron stove in the middle of the floor, a pine bureau, a pine
cupboard, a few red-bottomed pine chairs, and at least
one canopied bed covered with homespun sheets and
coarse blankets,—eked out perhaps with a room off, to

---

[38] § Ward to [sisters]: Gammell, S. Ward, p. 339. Moccasins, etc.: Thayer
Journal, Nov. 21 ; Haskell, Journal, Nov. 21 ; Arnold to Montg., Nov. 20, 1775
(Sparks MSS., No. 52, II., p. 31). Ogden: Arnold to Merchants, Nov. 20, 1775
(Me. Hist. Soc. Coll., I., p. 380).   News: letter in Henry, Journal, p. 185. Comrades: Humphrey, Journal, Nov. [22].   Quebec: Hamilton to Dartmouth, Nov.
20, 1775 (Can. Arch., Q, 11, p. 339); Arnold to Montg., Nov. 25, 1775 (Me. Hist.
Soc. Coll., I., p. 381).   Dust: Arnold to ———, Nov. 25, 1775 (ib., p. 382). Morgan: Topham, Journal, Nov. 28 ; Morgan, Autobiog. (Hist. Mag., June, 1871, p.
379). According to Morgan, the riflemen's powder was found to be in a better
condition than the rest.   Arn. to Pt. Levi, Nov. 28: at Château de Ramezay,
Montreal. Ainslie's and Finlay's Journals, Dec. 2.

supplement the sleeping accommodations,—this could not be termed luxurious; but it seemed so to exiles just from the woods. The ever-simmering pot appeared the very emblem of hospitality; and the lively group chattering gossip and pulling at long pipes round the hot stove whole evenings through, looked kindly, as indeed they were, and artless, as perhaps they were not. On the other side, to deal with the Americans, whose gold and silver —though running very low—could be had at a good rate for whatever they bought; to hobnob with bold, stalwart soldiers talking nothing but liberty, fraternity, and away-with-taxes; to see one of them eat beef enough at a single meal to last a whole family of the peasants a week, gave prosy life a new quality. Both parties were in truth highly pleased. The behavior of the Provincials created a fund of pleasing traditions and even fraternal songs. The visitors found many a thing—indeed, the 'zeal and fervency' of Catholic worship—to 'give a severe and additional stroke at early prejudices,' as Henry phrased it; and the fraternization of the two elements, begun in the Chaudière valley and continued before Quebec, seemed to be progressing here at a wonderful speed.[39]

Yet after all, in spite of sympathy and good-will, it still remained a hard question of power. Arnold's brave volunteers were admirable, but they had not captured Quebec. Reinforcements were talked of; but day followed on after day, the paling November sun dropped lower and lower, there began to be ice on the St. Lawrence every morning,[40] and Montgomery did not come.

---

[39] § Stone (ed.), Letters, pp. 16–20. Kalm, Travels, III., p. 150. Anburey. Travels, *passim*. Henry, Journal, pp. 91–93. Morison, Journal. Gold: Arnold to Montg., Nov. 20, 1775, P.S. (Sparks MSS., No. 52, II., p. 31). Morison (Journal, Nov. 20) speaks very emphatically of the good relations between the Americans and the Canadians. REMARK XLVII.

[40] Topham, Journal, Nov. 21.

BEHIND THE SCENES

WEEK after week Montgomery had listened for news of Arnold's reaching Canada, but listened in vain. Unfounded rumors floated about the camp, to be sure. As early as October the second, a report of his arrival 'seemed to gain ground'; and, on the day St. Johns fell, an officer at Laprairie wrote home that word to that effect had arrived from Cambridge; but the General summed up the case at this very time in the tone of hope deferred: 'Not a word of Arnold yet.'[1]

Before he closed his eyes for his first night's rest in Montreal, however, intercepted letters informed him that his distant ally had 'certainly arrived in the neighborhood of Quebeck'; and four days later, 'with great pleasure,' he was able to forward Schuyler a letter from the seemingly buried expedition. It had been his intention to winter at Montreal, unless he returned home; but the appearance of this little band of daring comrades before the capital appealed mightily to his heart. Bedel, sent forward in pursuit of Carleton, had orders to follow on—in case the British got past Sorel—until he 'joined Colonel Arnold, if that could be done'; but Montgomery had still more in mind. 'If the season remain favorable and the troops will follow me, I shall lend a hand to Arnold,' he assured his brother-in-law.[2]

---

[1] § Montg. to Bedel, Oct. 2, 1775: Emmet Coll. Letter, Nov. 3, 1775: 4 Force, III., 1342. Montg. to Sch., Nov. 3, 1775: ib., 1392.

[2] § Montg. to Sch., Nov. 13, 1775: 4 Force, III., 1602. Id. to Id., Nov.17: ib., 1633. To Winter at M.: Mrs. Montg. (L. L. H[unt], Biog. Notes, p. 8). Montg.

And the General had even a stronger motive than sympathy for making a campaign in the dead of a northern winter. The plan of Samuel Adams to merge Canada in the Union of Colonies, though obscured by the smoke of war, had not been abandoned. Apparently Adams had been following his classic method of spreading ideas through personal influence and good-will; for, according to his biographer, 'a mutual friendship had sprung up within a year' between the political and the military leaders of the campaign. Only a week after planting himself before St. Johns, the soldier showed himself also a statesman of the Bay Colony sort. 'I shall endeavour, if successful, to have Deputies sent from Canada to the Congress,' he wrote, 'giving them assurances that, before an accommodation takes place, Canada must have a free Government; that the Congress will as soon give up the Massachusetts Government to the resentment of the Ministry, as relinquish this point.' It was his political ambition to help the northern province 'make a part of that union now so formidable to tyrants'; and in Brown's instructions, at the time of La Corne's overtures, Montgomery stated this proposition in detail, describing himself as 'at the head of an auxiliary Army to effect these purposes': union and free government.[3]

The Adams party in Congress followed this line with unflagging energy, and succeeded in drawing the majority after them. 'What they expect from your Endeavours,' wrote their spokesman to Schuyler in October, 'is, that the Canadians be induced to accede to a Union with these Colonies—and that they form, from their several Parishes, a Provincial Convention & send Delegates to

to [Bedel], Nov. 16, 1775: Saffell, Records, p. 27. Id. to R. R. Liv., Nov. 13, 1775: Liv. Papers, 1775-1777, p. 63.

[3] § Wells, S. Adams, II., p. 339. Montg. to Sch., Sept. 24, 1775: 4 Force, III. 840. Id. to R. R. Liv., Oct. 5 [1775]: Liv. Papers, 1775-1777, p. 51. Id. to J. Brown, Oct. 6, 1775: 4 Force, III., 1098.

this Congress.' Their rights would be held as dear as any, in religious no less than in civil matters; and they would be ensured the blessings of a free government, the security of life and the security of possessions. When the Congress, early in November, appointed a committee of its members to visit Schuyler and confer with him about the northern interests of the United Colonies, these gentlemen received formal instructions to exert their 'utmost endeavours' in the same direction; and they in turn, addressing Montgomery, expressed the 'ardent wishes' of the Congress that he should 'cherish the first dawnings of liberty' among the Canadians, and pursue the policy embodied in their instructions.[4]

On finding himself in Montreal, the American general 'made the inhabitants acquainted with the views of Congress' relative to the province, and symptoms of a cheering response were not entirely wanting. The people of the suburbs, in their address to him, said: 'We now OPENLY ENTER into the union and association, as we did in our hearts the moment the address of the 26th of October, 1774, was handed to us'; and, when Montreal drew up the plan of capitulation, its 'haughty terms' cast a shadow in the form of an anonymous argument in French against them, favoring a union with the Colonies.[5]

These things, however, while they showed how the wind of logic was beginning to set, could be reckoned only as encouraging straws. Confidence is a plant of slow growth, said Burke; and only a few days had passed since Montgomery had found himself compelled to admit, that perhaps the Americans would have to give up the Canadian enterprise. Chambly, with its light screen of masonry; St. Johns, ill provisioned for a siege; and Mon-

---

4 § Hancock to Sch., Oct. 12, 1775: Am. Antiq. Soc., Worcester, Mass. Journ. Cong., Nov. 2, 8. Com. to Montg., Nov. 30, 1775: 4 Force, IV., 445.

5 § Montg. to Sch., Nov. 19, 1775: 4 Force, III., 1682. Suburbs: Can. Rev., Vol. II., No. 4, Feb., 1826. For union: Can. Arch., B, 185, 1, p. 129.

treal, fortified only against a raid, had fallen; but the
stronghold of British power, the rock of Quebec, lifted its
brow of stone as proudly as ever, and its wharves were a
spacious threshold, over which British legions, arriving
safely by sea, could still march to victory. To that prospect every royalist now pointed. The fringe of British
power has been torn, they said, but warp and woof are
intact. Beware! The Capital stands; and the fleets of
the King will soon find it. 'Till Quebec is taken, Canada
is unconquered,'—in these words the American chief sum-
marized the crisis.[6]

Montgomery, quick to understand the tactful line of
policy, conversed with leading people frankly. In particular, he discussed this most vital question with Pelissier,
the proprietor of certain famous iron-works near Three
Rivers called the *Forges St. Maurice*, who—being French
but not Canadian—could understand the people without
sharing their prejudices. It was his judgment that so long
as the British flag shone above the western Gibraltar, an
Assembly or Convention could not prudently be summoned; and Montgomery concurred in that opinion. To
Quebec, then, he must go; and he would go in earnest.
'The King's friends [there] are exceedingly alarmed, and
expect to be besieged,' he wrote to Schuyler, 'which, with
the blessing of God, they shall be.'[7]

As their term of service would shortly expire, Montgomery began to urge re-enlistment upon the troops the
day he entered Montreal; but he soon found himself in a
very strait place. The upper end of Lake Champlain had
a way of freezing in December, while the deeper water toward the north did not close effectually until nearly two

---

[6] § Pelissier to Hancock, Jan. 8, 1776: 4 Force, IV., 595. Montg. to R. R.
Liv., Dec. 16, 1775: Liv. Papers, 1775-1777, p. 81. Id. to R. R. Liv., Nov. —, 1775:
4 Force, III., 1638.

[7] § Pelissier: Note 6. Forges: Burton to Commrs. of Trade, May 31, 1763
(Can. Arch., B. 7, p. 61). Montg. to Sch., Nov. 13, 1775: 4 Force, III., 1602.

I think it exceedingly necessary, that General Webster should be accommodated with a house. You will therefore be so good as to have one got ready for him. I am told that which Major L'Estrange occupies is the most suitable. Should any repairs be found necessary do let them be made immediately, as the General will be there today.

I am Sir your most Ob

Arch'd Montgomery

Colonel Bedel

months later; consequently, should the men remain in Canada until New Year's, they could not get away for something like six weeks more, and the pass might perhaps be sealed even before the middle of December. This prospect had made them very nervous about continuing the campaign after St. Johns fell; and, in order to lull their fears, the General had promised an immediate release, on the surrender of Montreal, to all who would follow him across the St. Lawrence.[8]

Addressing the men now in a proclamation, he thanked and praised them for their services, which 'merited,' as he said, the 'applause of their grateful countrymen,' and gave notice that passes, rations, and a passage across the river would be furnished all who desired to return home; but, at the same time, he begged them 'not to lay him under the necessity of abandoning Canada, of undoing in one day what had been the work of months,' and promised all who would stay until the fifteenth of April a complete outfit of winter clothing at Continental expense, besides a dollar of bounty. How many will remain? he then anxiously asked himself. Anticipating some trouble, he had written his chief a fortnight before, 'Send everybody you possibly can immediately down.' 'Should they refuse to re-enlist, how dreadful the consequences!' General Schuyler had already exclaimed, thinking remotely of this very crisis.[9]

'I have had great difficulty about the troops,' reported Montgomery when his proclamation was two days old; 'I am afraid many of them will go home.' Unfortunately, his warm exhortation had fallen on very cold ground. It made its appearance in a squall of snow, and the soldiers

---

[8] § Trumbull, Journal, Nov. 14. Montg. to Sch., Nov. 13, 1775: 4 Force, III., 1602. Sch. to Hancock, Nov. 27, 1775: ib., 1681. REMARK XLVIII.

[9] § Proclamation, Nov. 15, 1775: 4 Force, III., 1683. Montg. to Sch., Nov. 3, 1775: ib., 1392. Sch. to Hancock, Oct. 20, 1775: ib., 1124.

discussed it with their feet soaked and chilled in the miry slush of the streets, breakfastless and fireless. The northeast wind had come back, and with it a raw, heavy, unremitting storm. The sixteenth continued very bad; the following day found the earth well covered with snow; and, though the sky was clear the next morning, it wore the settled frown of winter.[10]

In those days the cold season of Canada possessed the terrors of Arctic night for people to the south; and the dread of it had almost produced a mutiny in Wooster's regiment, when ordered to St. Johns. What the men had actually suffered, hardened their fears into convictions. Easton's were not the only half-naked troops. Even about the middle of September, the men had seemed 'thinly and poorly' clad. Near the end of October, Congress recommended sending them blankets and shirts from the King's stores at New York; but that meant a far and slow journey. 'I feel so much for them in their unhappy situation,' wrote Schuyler in November, 'destitute of every necessary to guard against the inclemency of the season.' The committee sent north used the same word as Montgomery to describe their condition,—'half-naked'; and Chaplain Trumbull now found the men, huddled together in the northeaster at Montreal, 'very impatient.'[11]

The offer of a suit of clothes was a tangible though slight inducement; but little else encouraged the men to stay. A captain received twenty dollars per month in paper money, and a private six and two-thirds. 'Amazingly low,' said Schuyler of the officers' pay, and no doubt the men said quite as much of their own. 'Scanty

---

10 § Montg. to Sch., Nov. 17, 1775: 4 Force, III., 1633. Trumbull, Journal, Nov. 15-18.
11 § Wooster's: Sch. to Hancock, Oct. 21, 1775: 4 Force, III., 1130. Half-naked: Montg. to Sch., Dec. 5, 1775 (4 Force, IV., 188). Sch. to Hancock, Sept. 19, 1775: 4 Force, III., 738. Secret Journ. Cong., Oct. 26, 1775. Sch. to Hancock, Nov. 11, 1775: 4 Force, III., 1520. Report: 4 Force, IV., 442. Trumbull, Journal.

pittance,' echoed Montgomery, pointing out that articles which travelled all the way from New York to the army in Canada brought a price accordingly. Captain Lamb, ardent patriot though he was, came near resigning, for his pay amounted to only 'such a trifle' that he found himself drawing on his personal funds, and saw that 'by and by his family must starve at home.' And yet here was not the hardest feature of the case. In this improvised army, accounts were not regularly kept ; and often men had to do without their wages, because General Schuyler could not be sure what was due. Many, he informed Congress, went 'naked and penniless,' who might have money owing them ; and some, when discharged, offered their claim for two-thirds of it. As late as August, Schuyler had not been able to settle the accounts of the Green Mountain Boys for capturing Ticonderoga, though he recognized that many of them were 'most truly necessitous.' If men ' are not paid off when asked to re-enlist,' he very sensibly remarked, 'they will seldom re-enlist in the service.'[12]

Among the New England men, the Colonial jealousy which cursed all sections alike and had shown itself in the northern army from the beginning, tended to deaden interest in an enterprise led by two New Yorkers ; and Schuyler's nerves, harrowed by pain, disappointment, and anxiety, shed abroad no soothing influences. ' If Job had been a General in my situation, his memory had not been so famous for patience,' he fumed ; and, however that might have been, the General in Job's place would certainly not have shone in Holy Writ. ' Scandalous want of subordination '; ' vast variety of disagreeable

---

[12] § Journ. Cong., July 29, 1775. Nov. 4, Congress made the pay of a captain in a ' marching ' regiment $26 2/3 ; see Journ. Cong., Nov. 4 ; Sch.'s Ord. Book, Nov. 19, 1775. Sch. to Hancock, Sept. 20, 1775 : 4 Force, III., 839. Montg. to Sch., Oct. 9, 1775 : ib., 1096. Lamb: Id. to Id., Nov. 20, 1775 (ib., 1684). Sch. to Hancock, Aug. 6 ; Oct. 21, 1775: ib., 48, 1130.

and vexatious incidents,' arising 'almost every hour';
'tormented . . . by a parcel of scoundrel artificers';
'most scandalous inattention to the publick stores,'—
this was his language, in official reports to the President
of Congress, with reference to occurrences that might
have been expected; and no doubt in the freedom of off-
hand speech—especially when he addressed subordinates—

JOHN JAY

greater reserve could hardly be expected. How different the ring of Washington's letters to Hancock! and,
writing Schuyler, he quietly observed, 'I have met with
difficulties of the same sort, and such as I never expected;
but they must be borne with. The cause we are engaged
in is so just and righteous, that we must try to rise

superior to every obstacle in its support.' Schuyler did try ; but he tried too often in vain.[13]

Two phases in particular of his irritability bore unhappy fruit at this time in Montreal.

David Wooster, a Connecticut major-general and commander-in-chief of the Colony's troops, did not relish finding himself placed by Congress below his junior, Montgomery, lately a mere captain in the British service ; and he did not hesitate about saying so. ' My appointment in the Continental army, you are sensible, could not be very agreeable to me,' he informed Schuyler. Yet Montgomery got on with him at St. Johns as Damon with Pythias. ' I think it exceedingly necessary, that General Wooster should be accommodated with a house. You will therefore be so good as to have one got ready for him. I am told that which Maj[r] Elmore occupies is the most suitable,' he wrote to Bedel, when his offended colleague approached. A few days later, he invited Wooster to live with him ; and he honored him with all the attentions in his power. As a matter of fact, his orbit showed no sign of being affected in the least by contact with his Connecticut compeer ; yet he managed so well that Rev. Mr. Trumbull believed nothing of importance was done without Wooster's advice, and he found himself able to report : ' Mr. Wooster has hitherto behaved much to my satisfaction.'[14]

Not so Schuyler. Hearing that Wooster had stumbled against the prerogatives of the commander-in-chief of the department, he notified Congress that he felt ' these insults from a General Officer with all that keen sensibility that

---

[13] § Sch. to Hancock, Sept. 25, 29 ; Nov. 20: 4 Force, III., 796, 839, 1617. Wash. to Sch., Dec. 5, 1775: Writings (Ford), III., p. 267.

[14] § Wooster: Johnston, Record, p. 37. Wooster to Sch., Oct. 19, 1775: 4 Force, III., 1107. Montg. to Bedel, Oct. 27, 1775: Emmet Coll. B. Trumbull to ———, Nov. 3, 1775: Conn. Hist. Soc. Coll., VII., p. 169. Montg. to Sch., Oct. 31, 1775: Sparks MSS., No. 60, p. 17. See p. 40.

a man of honour ought,' and would have sent Wooster's
regiment on without its commander, had he not been told
bluntly that it would not go.   No shrewder scheme to
embitter colonial jealousy than such a quarrel could well
have been invented.[15]

At the same time, Schuyler angered large numbers of
the privates.   In every army men have tried to escape
duty by shamming illness, and very likely he did not slander some of the troops in asserting that they swallowed
tobacco juice or burnt their tongues with chocolate in order to seem feverish and get a discharge.   But the unhealthy conditions at Nut Island and St. Johns must have
produced a great deal of sickness that was very real, even
if not often fatal ; and the General's treatment of the invalids did not lean toward over-indulgence.   ' They pretend
sickness and skulk about,' he assured President Hancock ;
' nor can I get the better of them, although I do not suffer
a ration of provision to be issued unless I countersign the
order, and the sick, or pretended sick, do not get half
allowance.'[16]

On the other side of this matter, a sergeant and nineteen
soldiers directed a joint letter to the Honorable Governor
and Council of Connecticut, and said: ' When our Doctors
of the Connecticut Troops thought us unfit for duty [at St.
Johns] and not like to be any more this campaign we was
sent of to Ticonderoga.   And when we came their we was
veuid [viewed] by the Head Docter of the Continent, we
was veuid by the General Schuyler also and such men as
the docter returned sick, the General damd all in heaps
and swore, dam them for their sickness and said he would
pay them for it, and said they should have but 4 ounces
of fresh meat a day, and a gill of rice which is now fullfild

---

15 § Sch. to Hancock, Oct. 14, 1775 : 4 Force, III., 1065.
16 § Sch. to Trumbull, Oct. 12, 1775 : 4 Force, III., 1033.   Id. to Hancock,
Oct. 18, 1775 : ib., 1093.

on us your poor suffering subjects and soldiers.'   At Fort
George, so Lieutenant Gibbs informed Governor Trumbull, no provisions, fresh or salt, were allowed his convoy of invalids, and only the 'good fortune' of borrow-
ing a little money saved them from distress.   At Albany,
Phelps, the Connecticut commissary, advanced some funds
to keep the poor fellows from actual suffering, but Gibbs
heard afterwards that Schuyler 'would not allow him a
farthing of it' ; and when Phelps, in default of a hospital,
put some of them into taverns and private houses, he was
blamed for doing so.   'Many oblige[d] to sell their blankets and shirts to git home and others begging on the
road,' observed the Lieutenant, adding, 'I beg there may
be some provition . . . if not we must expect never to
raise any more men.'   Certainly Schuyler had many ex-
cuses ; he was often blamed unjustly ; no doubt his mistakes were exaggerated ; and he stayed in office only at the
urgent request of
Congress ; b u t
the fact remained
that he made
himself intensely
hated.   Echoes
of it all reached the front, of course; and good Chaplain
Trumbull declared, 'Our men have had such a Taste
of the Officers in the New York department, that . . .
I believe it will be impossible ever to enlist them to Serve
this Way again under any Officers but their own.'[17]

But there were deeper reasons for not re-engaging.   In
the first place, ordinary men could see little sense in it.
They had been told that redcoats, papists, and savages
proposed to come and ravage their homes; and now the red-

17 § Letters from sergeant et al., Gibbs, and Young (Oct. 13, 10, 16, 1775)
Trumbull Papers, IV.   Injustice to Sch.: Sch. to Albany Com., Nov. 2, 1775 (4
Force, III., 1524).   Resignation : Hancock to Sch., Nov. 30, 1775 (ib., 1717).
Trumbull : Note 14.

coats were prisoners, the savages friends, the papists brethren, St. Johns overpowered, Montreal captured, and not a stick of British timber floating on the lakes. Their pledge had been kept, though it meant far more time and hardship than any one had expected. What more needed to be done? There was no war. They had no country but Great Britain, no flag but the crosses of St. George and St. Andrew, no cause but self-defence. On the other hand, their time of service had come to an end ; they were now free ; the homes they had sallied forth to defend, their wives, children, friends, and interests, entreated them loudly and often pitifully to go back. If work did remain to be done, it was the turn of others. Would not the others come? Then why should brave men be sacrificed for cowards?

The New York troops earliest in the field had not left the streets from which they were gathered until August, and perhaps had little to invite them south. Many of the rest from that Colony had not yet worn off the novelty of campaigning. At the worst, their homes did not seem far away: two lakes and a river almost measured the distance. But the Connecticut men, with mountains behind them, had been in the field much longer. Hinman's regiment set out for the north before the first of June ; Waterbury's *Orderly Book* was opened on the third of that month, and Wooster had instructions on the nineteenth to march for New York. In fact, the recruiting for these regiments had begun about the first of May, and now the men longed for their firesides. ' An unhappy homesickness prevails,' complained Schuyler. ' Indeed they are homesick,' remarked Montgomery of the New Englanders.[18]

And what could have been more proper? Home was

18 § Hinman: N. Y. Cong. to Albany Com., June 1, 1775 (4 Force, II., 1269). Waterbury, Ord. Book. Johnston, Record, pp. 35, 37, 39. Sch. to Hancock. Nov. 20, 1775: 4 Force, III., 1617. Montg. to R. R. Liv., Oct. 5, [1775]: Liv. Papers, 1775-1777, p. 51.

the right place for every man who possessed such a blessing, when victory had crowned the hills with sunset.   ' I
must go home, if I walk by the side of the lake, this winter,'
exclaimed Montgomery himself.   The commander, indeed, standing in full view of the world, might well have
personal inducements to smother his longings for the
hearth ; but humble Jonathan and Eleazer had not.   A
certain small cottage, with rusty hollyhocks in the front
yard, and a plain, tired-faced woman in the kitchen hush-
ing a little boy with stories about ' father,' was their
world ; and no sooner did they get a discharge at Ticonderoga than, without waiting for boats to Fort George,
they slung their heavy packs across their shoulders, even
though still invalids, got across the lake as they could,
and struck off through the woods.   Schuyler looked upon this as proof positive they had been shamming, and
they would have retorted, perhaps, that anything was better than a longer stay with him; but in reality it mainly
showed how powerful was the lodestone that could draw
them—little in the pocket, little in the mouth, little on the
back, but much in the heart—some two hundred miles by
wintry roads over hills and rivers, through frost and
through snow, to their modest haven.[19]

Still another thing rendered the New Englanders particularly eager to be off.   The very qualities that prompted
the eastern provinces to lead in the movement against
Great Britain, made their people peculiarly independent
in temper.   Anxious, more than anxious, though he was
to keep an army in the field, Governor Trumbull felt
pride instead of impatience when he saw his troops homeward bound at the end of their term.   ' The pulse of a
New England man,' said he grandly, ' beats high for
liberty ; his engagement in the service he thinks purely

---

[19] § Montg. to Sch., Nov. 13, 1775 : 4 Force, III., 1602.   Sch. to Hancock:
Note 18.

voluntary ; therefore when the time of enlistment is out he thinks himself not holden without further engagement.' The New Yorkers had less of this temper ; besides, Colonial feeling offered them a strong reason for sticking by their leader ; and the consequence was that most of them, resolving 'to see an End to the Campaign' provided they could return in season to plant their corn, agreed to serve until the middle of April ; but the New Englanders at Montreal, with the exception of perhaps two hundred from Connecticut who remained with General Wooster, crossed the St. Lawrence and hurried south.   In all, only some eight hundred effectives were left on the island ; and out of these Montgomery had first of all to provide a garrison.[20]

But had not the Continental Congress, foreseeing the possibility of all this, made ready a new army, to step into the places of the old ? Garnier, the French representative at London, informed his chief that most people in England considered such a course the axiomatic policy for the Americans [21] ; and, on purely military principles, very likely they reasoned well.

The case was by no means so simple, however. The Colonials in general had not agreed upon rebellion, were not conspiring for independence, did not look for serious war.   More than four years before the passage of the Stamp Act (1765), a gifted young law-student named John Adams took notes of Otis's fiery argument before the Superior Court of Massachusetts against the Writs of Assistance, and fifty-six years later he said, 'Then and there the child Independence was born ' ; but no angels and no Wise Men from the East came to inform plain shepherds of the great event.   Governor Ward of Rhode Island

---

[20] § Trumbull: Wash., Writings (Sparks), I., p. 164. Ritzema, Journal, Nov. 14, 28.   Montg. to Sch., Dec. 5, 1775: 4 Force, IV., 188.   Sch. to Hancock, Nov. 27, 1775: 4 Force, III., 1681.   Montg. to Sch., Nov. 24, 1775: ib., 1694.

[21] Stevens, Facsimiles, No. 872.

prophesied as early as 1766 : ' These colonies are destined
to an early independence ' ; but such a man, though he
ate no wild honey, was a veritable John the Baptist, a
voice crying in the wilderness.[22]

In August, 1774, Benjamin Franklin assured the Earl
of Chatham that, ' having
more than once travelled
from one End of the con-
tinent to the other, and kept
a great variety of company,
eating, drinking, and con-
versing with them freely,'
he had ' never heard, in any
Conversation, from a n y

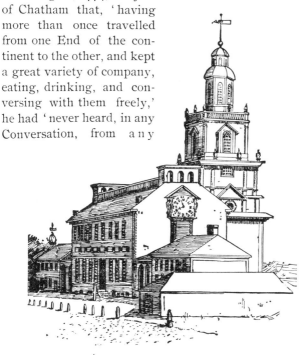

'INDEPENDENCE HALL ' IN 1778

Person, drunk or sober, the least Expression of a wish
for a Separation.' Franklin, to be sure, had then been
out of the country for some years ; but, had a widespread conspiracy to rebel against England existed, signs

---

[22] § Adams: Winsor, Narr. and Crit. Hist., VI., p. 11. Ward: Knapp, Burr,
p. 33.

of it would almost certainly have appeared before he went abroad.   If not, they must surely have made themselves visible in his correspondence during the interval ; and in that case a statement like his would have been highly disingenuous, if not absolutely false.[23]

Dr. Warren, even after standing forth as the champion of liberty, proclaimed, ' Our wish is that Britain and the colonies may, like the oak and ivy, grow and increase in strength together ' ; and he wrote Joseph Reed, ' I verily believe, that the night preceding the barbarous outrages committed by the soldiery at Lexington, Concord, etc., there were not fifty people in the whole colony that ever expected any blood would be shed in the contest between us and Great Britain.'   ' I wish,' explained the Father of the Revolution to Arthur Lee only a fortnight before Pitcairn rode out of Boston, ' I wish for a permanent union with the mother country, but only on the principles of liberty and truth ' : which amounted to saying that he desired though he did not expect it.   Flanders has stated that Jay allowed the thought of independence ' no tolera-tion, until all hope of conciliation and harmony was cut off.'   Washington wrote Captain Mackenzie in October, 1774 : ' I am well satisfied that no such thing is desired by any thinking man in all North America '; and, even when he took command of the army at Cambridge, he ' abhorr'd ' the idea.   John Adams recorded that, after he became suspected of leanings in this direction, in July, 1775, he was ' avoided, like a man infected with the leprosy.'   The same month, Timothy Dwight argued with some of his Whig intimates in favor of independ-ence, but he admitted that his views met with ' a hostile, and contemptuous' reception.   In October, Governor Tryon sent the British government word, as the con-fidential opinion of an eastern member of Congress, in-

---

23 § Franklin : Works (Bigelow), V., pp. 445, 446.

directly obtained, 'They don't wish for independency.'
John Jay declared that, 'until after the second Petition
of Congress,' the fate of which became known in Philadelphia on the ninth of November, 1775, he 'never did
hear any American, of any class, or of any Description,
express a wish for the Independence of the colonies.'
After Montgomery had been in Montreal two weeks, the
author of the Declaration of Independence assured John
Randolph, 'There is not in the British empire a man who
more cordially loves a union with Great Britain than I
do. . . . We want neither inducement nor power, to declare and assert a separation. It is will, alone, which is
wanting.' As late as the first great Fourth of July, it
has been estimated that no less than two-fifths of the
people were Tories.[24]

Official action told the same story. A week after the
clearing smoke revealed fellow citizens gasping in their
blood on Lexington Green, the Massachusetts Congress
declared : 'We profess to be his loyal and dutiful subjects,
and so hardly dealt with as we have been, are still
ready, with our lives and fortunes, to defend his person,
family, crown and dignity.' When Benedict Arnold and
his company set out for Cambridge, they formally dis-
avowed 'every thought of rebellion.' On the second of
June, 1775, the Continental Congress listened to an ardent
wish from the New Hampshire Convention for the preservation of a connection with England ; 'to our view,' said
the Convention, 'the thought [of war] is shaded deep in
horrours.' A month after the capture of Ticonderoga, the

---

[24] § Frothingham, Warren, pp. 435, 486. S. Adams to A. Lee, Apr. 4, 1775:
4 Force, I., 238. Flanders, C. Justices, I., p. 82. Wash.: Writings (Sparks),
II., p. 399 ; [Palfrey] to S. Adams, May 24, 1776 (S. Adams Papers). J. Adams,
Works, II. p. 513, note (the feeling was doubtless personal in part). Dwight,
Travels, I., p. 159. Tryon to Dartmouth, Oct. 10, 1775: Pub. Rec. Off., Am. and
W. I., Vol. 185, p. 569. Jay: Colburn, Am. Indep., p. 3. Journ. Cong., Nov. 9,
1775. Jefferson to Randolph, Nov. 29, 1775: Jeff., Writings (Ford), I., p. 491.
Narr. and Crit. Hist., VI., p. 2, note. For further testimony, including Madi-
son's and Gov. Penn's, see Wash., Writings (Sparks), II., pp. 406-501 ; Froth-
ingham, Rise, p. 453, note ; Colburn, Am. Indep. REMARK XLIX.

Congress of New York assured the Canadians that it reckoned allegiance to the King and attachment to the illustrious house of Hanover among the 'most singular blessings' of the Colony. When Virginia gave Daniel Morgan the commission under which he marched his riflemen to Cambridge, the authority to which it pointed was 'the spirit of the British constitution.' [25]

To sit in the Pennsylvania Assembly during the session of 1775–1776, one had to swear 'true allegiance to King George,' and promise under oath to be faithful 'against all traitorous conspiracies and attempts whatsoever.' The instructions of the Pennsylvania Delegates to the second Congress had in view only the redress of grievances and a restoration of harmony between England and the Colonies; and, while Montgomery was preparing to cross the St. Lawrence, they were ordered to 'dissent from, and utterly reject, any propositions, should such be made,' that might lead to a separation from Great Britain. On the twenty-eighth day of November, the Assembly of New Jersey directed its Delegates in Congress 'utterly to reject any propositions, if such should be made, that might separate this Colony from the Mother Country.' Porter's Commission, given by Massachusetts in January, 1776, was dated, 'in the Sixteenth Year of the Reign of his Majesty King George the Third.' To sum it up, the Congress affirmed solemnly in July, 1775, that it did not mean 'to dissolve that Union' which had 'so long and so happily subsisted' between the two shores of the Atlantic; and, in the following October, instructed Schuyler to offer the Canadians merely 'that Security to their Persons and Property,' which was 'derived from the British Constitution.' [26]

---

[25] § Journ. Mass. Cong., Apr. 26, 1775. Arnold: 4 Force, II., 383. N. H., May 23 : Journ. Cong., June 2, 1775. N. Y. Cong., June 12, 1775 : 4 Force II., 1294. Morgan: Graham, Morgan, p. 53.

[26] § Pa. Assembly: 4 Force, IV., 1536. Pa. Deleg. 4 Force, II., 456 ; III.,

An easy reply to all this became fashionable in England. Rising in the Parliament, while Montgomery was drawing near Montreal, Lord Lyttleton denounced the 'insidious, traitorous, false expressions of loyalty' uttered by the Colonists.[27]   In short, the dutiful language of Americans was commonly said and often believed to come from elaborate and concerted hypocrisy.

But who would have undertaken to indict the whole Continent on such a charge?   And, if the leaders went about to deceive one another as well as their followers, how could so great and hollow a conspiracy have lasted? The President of Congress made an ample and conclusive answer to Lyttleton's accusation, when, pointing to 'the unprepared state of the Colonies' at the beginning of the war and the nearly total want of 'everything necessary to carry it on,' he pronounced these facts 'a most striking proof of the weakness or wickedness of those who charge them with an original intention of withdrawing from the Government of Great Britain.'   In a word, either these men were substantially honest, or they were substantially mad ; and the Continental Congress had little resemblance to Bedlam.   Not rebellion, but constitutional resistance, was the purpose of America :—a resistance authorized by Blackstone, when he wrote that, 'In cases of national oppression, the nation hath very justifiably risen as one man, to vindicate the original contract, subsisting between the king and [the] people.' [28]

The strong political opposition in England, the shock to her commerce and revenue, her merchants alarmed, her manufacturers starving, taxes augmented, France and Spain preparing to strike,—these were elements from

---

1408. N. J.: 4 Force, III., 1857. Porter, Colon. Mag., I., p. 3. Journ. Cong., July 6, 1775.   Hancock to Sch., Oct. 12, 1775: Am. Antiq. Soc.

[27] Lyttleton : 4 Force, VI., 135.

[28] § Hancock to Mass. Council, Apr. 30, 1776 : 4 Force, V., 1139.   Blackstone : W. Smith, Works, I., p. 26.

which the Colonists were taught, by friends across the water as well as by their own reasonings, to expect success. 'There is nothing upon earth more sure,' wrote a gentleman from London, 'than that one year's determined resistance must reduce this country to any terms.' [29]

A single issue of the *Boston Evening Post* contained statements enough, hailing from the same quarter, to jus-

JOHN DICKINSON

tify that expectation. 'The resolution of the Americans relative to their exporting nothing from thence to England,' said one letter, 'will affect government more than may be generally imagined. Even in the article of tobacco they will sustain vast loss; for the duty on that commodity only for the present year, it seems, amounts

[29] London letter, Feb. 10, 1775: 4 Force, I., 1223.

to upwards of 220,000 l.' 'It has been calculated,' added another, 'that Great Britain sustains a loss of upwards of 1000 l. per day, exclusive of government duties, while this nation continues at variance with her American Colonies.'   'The matter grows serious—People begin to *feel* and *fear*,' observed a third.   'People in general here are in favour of America,' noted another ; 'the manufacturing towns will, in general, petition.'   In view of such statements, it was not surprising to learn from the same paper of its having been ' intimated to some considble Merchants, that the Ministry would be ready to meet any conciliatory measures that might be proposed with reference to America.' [30]

On the hither side of the Atlantic, to choose a single illustration, Joseph Warren argued that merely stopping the exportation of flaxseed to Ireland would set a million hungry mouths clamoring against the policy of the Ministers, and he reckoned that cutting off the trade of Great Britain with her American colonies and her West Indies would not only rouse the merchants against their government, but reduce the revenue of the country an eighth part. From the effects of non-importation ' on two former occasions,' to use the words of a prominent Colonial, ' and an apprehension that the trade of America was necessary to the inhabitants of Great Britain, it was generally hoped the obnoxious acts would soon be repealed. An appeal to arms, independence, and an alliance with France, were events at that time neither intended nor expected.'   In fact, the Congress itself admitted that it had counted upon the severance of commercial intercourse as 'the ultimate step of the controversy,' the finishing stroke against oppression. [31]

---

[30] Boston Evening Post, Mar. 20, 1775.

[31] § Warren to S. Adams, Aug. 21, 1774: Frothingham, Warren, p. 343. Ramsay, So. Car., I., p. 232. Journ. Cong., July 6, 1775.

Why, then, an army? Why, then, battles? Dickinson, addressing the Assembly of New Jersey in the most formal manner, as a special representative of the Continental Congress, answered the question: 'It was necessary to convince Britain that we would fight, and were not a rope of sand.' 'We must drub him [Howe] soundly, before the sceptred tyrant will know we are not mere brutes, to crouch under his hand, and kiss the rod with which he designs to scourge us': in these words Jefferson explained the presence of an army at Cambridge. A week after Arnold set out for Quebec, John Day, a Tory from Nova Scotia, wrote Mifflin, with whom he said he 'could once boast of being on a footing of the strictest friendship,' 'I hear you are in Arms to convince the World that Americans dare fight.' 'Britain at the expense of three millions has killed a hundred and fifty Yankees,' remarked Franklin to Dr. Priestley ; and many believed that thrifty John Bull would tire of oppressing the Colonies, if he found they had the pluck to make it costly.[32]

The Canada expedition, aside from its purely protective merit, seemed to most of its friends a part of this general plan, and so Dickinson characterized it before the New Jersey Assembly. 'We have as yet resolved only on defensive measures,' asserted Franklin more than three months after Schuyler received instructions to cross the boundary. 'If we once had that Province secured, we should convince the people of England of the weakness of the ministers' plan,' said Leffingwell to Silas Deane ; and the latter assured his wife that 'the reduction of Montreal and Quebec would . . . give the ministry a blow indeed.' It was the opinion of the 'Friends in England,' reported Thomas Lynch, that the complete reduction of

---

[32] § Dickinson, Dec., 1775: 4 Force, III., 1874. Jefferson to Randolph, Nov. 29, 1775: Jeff., Writings (Ford), I., p. 491. Day to Mifflin, Aug. 22, 1775: Hand Papers. Franklin to Priestley, Oct. 3, 1775: 4 Force, III., 940.

Canada during the winter 'must certainly produce Peace
in the Spring.' Montgomery himself looked forward to
the capture of Quebec, not as a telling move in a war,
but, as the 'final blow to Ministerial politicks in this Province' ; instead of counting himself a rebel, he bewailed to
Carleton 'the melancholy & fatal necessity which obliged
the firmest friends of the Constitution to oppose an officer
of the Crown' ; and, in urging the accession of Canada to
the Continental Union, he merely represented the league as
destined, with the blessing of God, to 'establish the rights
of all the Colonies on a firm basis.' 'May Heaven still
prove propitious,' exclaimed Schuyler in announcing the
triumph at Montreal to Trumbull, 'and Britons and Americans once more regard each other with the fond tenderness
of a parent and child!' Washington himself, Commander-
in-chief of the embattled forces, hoped for the capture of
Quebec as a measure that would 'much embarrass' the
Administration ; and the President of Congress, writing
to Montgomery on the last day of November, urged him to
continue gathering laurels till he should find ' our oppres-
sors reduced to reason, and America restored to her constitutional liberties.' [33]

Unfortunately the whole Colonial plan of campaign was
wrecked. George the Third, not merely the Father but
the Surgeon of his people, seemed to feel that all the
opposition of his transatlantic subjects, if brought quickly
to a head, could be lanced off with but a few drops of
blood, and the patient restored to tranquil health. Confident of his chirurgical talents, he courted rather than
dreaded resistance, treating with contempt not only the

[33] § Dickinson: Note 32. Franklin to Hartley, Oct. 3, 1775: 4 Force, III.,
940. Leffingwell, June 4, 1775: Conn. Hist. Soc. Coll., II., p. 258. Deane, Oct.
2, 1775: ib., 308. Lynch, Nov. 14, 1775: Pub. Rec. Off., Am. and W. I., Vol. 186,
p. 39. Montg. to Sch., Nov. 17, 1775: 4 Force, III., 1623. Id. to Carleton, Oct. 22,
1775: Sparks MSS., No. 52, II., p. 58. Id. to Brown, Oct. 6, 1775: 4 Force, III.,
1098. Sch. to Trumbull, Nov. 18, 1775: 4 Force, III., 1603. (See also Id. to Alb.
Com.: ib., 1595). Wash. to Sch., Dec. 18, 1775: Wash., Writings (Ford), III., p.
288. Hancock to Montg., Nov. 30, 1775: 4 Force, III., 1718.

opinions of America but those of his own capital. 'The Colonies must either triumph or submit,' he announced in the fall of 1774 ; and, a few months later, his majority in the House of Commons, on the motion of his chief minister, declared almost eagerly that rebellion existed. As time passed, the prospect only darkened. The opposition in England proved impotent, the King resolute and supreme. America then found an unwelcome issue forced

John Dickinson
June 20ᵗʰ–1774

upon her. Congress had to choose either the right hand or the left, decide either to be firm or to bend ; and all could see that measureless consequences hung upon the choice.[34]

John Dickinson of Pennsylvania, possessor of a fine seat at Fair Hill overlooking Philadelphia, the Schuylkill, and the country round, owner and also user of what John Adams called a 'very grand library,' was peculiarly fitted to enjoy the social pinnacle, yet ready enough to descend into the forum ; was a modest, refined, agreeable person, yet capable of no little activity and zeal ; was a gentleman and a scholar, yet not unwilling to lead the masses ; and such a man could not fail to wield a great influence. On the question of American rights he stood with the patriots, and the news of Lexington struck a Boanerges note from his sensitive heart. 'The rescript to our petition is written in blood,' he cried ; 'The impious war of tyranny against innocence has begun.' But a contest in

---

[34] § George III. to North, Sept. 11, 1774: Wash., Writings (Sparks), VI., p. 532. Commons (Feb., 1775): 4 Force, I., 1542, 1547.

arms had no attraction for one so delicate, studious, conservative by temperament, cautious because wealthy, and —as some thought—physically timid ; the Quakers brought their non-resistant influence to bear ; and his mother dinned into his ears, ' Johnny, you will be hanged; your estate will be forfeited and confiscated ; you will leave your excellent wife a widow, and your charming children orphans, beggars, and infamous.' [35]

Dickinson, besides all his other claims to consideration, ' was so honest a man,' said Jefferson, ' and so able a one, that he was greatly indulged even by those who could not feel his scruples '; and when he rose to speak,—tall, slender as a reed, pale as ashes, hardly more than a shadow, yet powerfully in earnest ; and when, with eyes aflame and a voice quivering with emotion, he poured forth weighty arguments and solemn appeals, wakening all the fears and knitting together all the doubts of the many Delegates who feared and doubted, his words fell not in vain. Around him gathered a large body of the members, especially of those from the middle Colonies. ' Accommodation ' was his battle-cry ; and once, following John Adams from the hall of Congress, he exclaimed, ' Look ye ! If you don't concur with us in our pacific system, I and a number of us will break off from you in New England, and we will carry on the opposition by ourselves in our own way.' With such a leader and so strong a party drawing in one direction, and the Adamses with their associates tugging as hard in the other, Congress found it difficult enough to settle the essential issue, which—meaning life or death not only for the country but for the Delegates—came near doing the miracle of Aaron's rod, and swallowing bodily all other questions. [36]

---

[35] § J. Adams, Works, I., p. 228 ; II., pp. 379, 401, 408. **Dickinson to A. Lee,** Apr. 29. 1775: 4 Force II., 443.

[36] § Jefferson, Works (Wash.), I., p. 11. J. Adams, Works, I., p. 178 ; II., pp. 360, 410, 419. (Adams's remarks about Dickinson were likely to be colored somewhat by personal feeling.) Flanders, C. Justices, I., p. 139.

For the same reason, what was attempted could not be done efficiently. 'It is amazing to me,' exclaimed Samuel Mott, 'that the Colonies should have so little sense of the importance of this expedition [to Canada], as not to give us a good large army, well furnished, in due season'; and so felt many another. But hints from within Congress have explained this mystery. 'Our councils have been hitherto too fluctuating,' remarked Governor Ward at the beginning of November; 'one day measures for carrying on the war were adopted; the next, nothing must be done that would widen the unhappy breach.' 'Many gentlemen in high stations and of great influence,' John Adams told his wife, 'have been duped by the ministerial bubble of commissioners to treat. And in real, sincere expectation of this event, which they so fondly wished, they have been slow and languid in promoting measures for the reduction of that province. Others there are in the colonies who really wished that our enterprise in Canada would be defeated, that the colonies might be brought into danger and distress between two fires, and be thus induced to submit. Others really wished to defeat the expedition to Canada, lest the conquest of it should elevate the minds of the people too much to hearken to those terms of reconciliation, which, they believed, would be offered us. These jarring views, wishes, and designs occasioned an opposition to many salutary measures which were proposed for the support of that expedition, and caused obstructions, embarrassments and studied delays.'[37]

In fact, many of the reasons for hindering the Canada campaign draw their sap from the very heart of the situation. As every thoughtful man could perceive, it was a bridge into a thick cloud, and no one could see the farther

---

[37] § S. Mott to Trumbull, Oct. 6, 1775: 4 Force, III., 972. Ward to his brother, Nov. 2, 1775: J. Ward, S. Ward, p. 10. J. Adams, Works, IX., p. 419.

A letter from London 6th of December says the present intention of the Ministry is to declare all meetings and associations in America illegal and treasonable — To guard the coast against all traffic and communication with Holland, France, and Spain. To corrupt Mr. York, and to employ a military force, chiefly from Canada, if necessary, having the

FROM RICHARD HENRY LEE'S LETTER TO SAMUEL ADAMS, FEBRUARY 4, 1775.

end of it. Washington's position before Boston could easily be explained: he stood evidently for self-defence, for resistance to aggression; but the northern operations had shown from the first an uncontrollable trend of their own, and this pointed—no matter what some men alleged or intended—toward separation and independence. There had always been the same dilemma about it : perilous to follow its logic but absurd to stop. The argument that invading Canada and shooting the King's redcoats did not attack the Crown, might perhaps be theoretically sound, but in the eyes of common-sense plans like that amounted to 'doing the work of the Lord deceitfully '; therefore could not prosper; therefore ought to be dropped. ' Make the tree good and the fruit will be good,' taught John Adams : in other words, lay aside pretences if you wish to succeed. Moreover, the notion of softening the King by fighting his troops, however shrewd it might be, was much too subtle to fire the popular heart, and for this reason also a more strenuous and explicit programme seemed necessary. As the soldiers trooping home from Montreal showed, the Canada enterprise required a flag and a foe : a flag meant a nation, and a foe meant a war. This Dickinson was fully able to see or to sense. He felt that an advance northward led toward independence ; and for this deep reason, as John Adams plainly intimated, ' every measure for the service in Canada, from the first projection of it,' was ' opposed and obstinately disputed ' by his party, so that no proposal could be carried except ' by a bare majority ' and after the delays of slow, hard fighting.[38]

Minor obstacles, also, yet very substantial ones, hampered the friends of the expedition. The Congress, a political debating society, had no executive. There was not even a Board of War as yet. Every proposition came be-

---

[38] § J. Adams, Works, IX., p. 412 (to Chase, June 24,1776); II., pp. 503, 419.

fore the whole body. The army at Cambridge alone would have been enough to occupy all the time it had for military affairs. Virginia made claims for defence against 'negroes and ragamuffins' that could not be ignored. Other sections required attention. A thousand petty details gorged the Journal. Personal jarrings, the inveterate differences between the Colonies, and—as Ward put it confidentially—the 'jealousies' entertained by the south toward the north, helped throw sand on the axle. No less harmful was the lack of information. 'They have never yet known the difficulties you have had to contend with,' wrote Livingston to Schuyler, 'or the state of the army of Canada.' Communications were very slow, and it always seemed natural to wait a bit and learn what had occurred meanwhile. Were St. Johns to fall as early as many expected, it looked as if the campaign might be concluded before the existing army would expire by limitation. Most likely nobody in Congress understood why a general re-enlistment could not be counted upon. Probably too much was expected of the Canadians. And apparently, whenever forcible action was proposed, the state of sentiment in New York must have been found strongly and peculiarly embarrassing.[39]

Loyalism, at least in the early stages of the conflict with Great Britain, had a real air of virtue, 'Dear Sons,' exhorted Colonel Thomas Gilbert, 'If those wicked sinners, the Rebels, entice you believe them not, but die by the sword rather than be hanged as Rebels.' The worship of anointed royalty, the worship of legality, the worship of church establishment, the worship of office, the worship of the old-home idea, the worship of tradition, the worship of a text: ' Fear God, honor the King,'—all these were added to numberless influences of habit, friendship,

---

[39] § Ward: Note 37. R. R. Liv. to Sch., Jan. 12, 1776: Emmet Coll. Can. regt.: Hancock to Sch., Oct. 12, 1775: Am. Antiq. Soc.

association, timidity, and interest ; and several of the ties and motives had more strength on the Hudson than within the restless towns of New England.[40]

Certain special arguments reinforced them. In May, 1775, a gentleman in London expressed the opinion that ' the mercantile connections ' of the middle province were ' as little friendly to American liberty ' as any he knew. ' I fear there is a chain of toryism extending from Canada through New York,' said John Adams. ' There is a Combination in that Colony,' wrote Samuel Adams, ' of high Church Clergymen & great Land holders,' the former favoring the absolute authority of Parliament as the only hope for an ' American Episcopate,' and the latter dreading to find a spirit of liberty among their ' bondsmen.' Cadwallader Colden knew of ' peculiar Indulgences and Favours intended by Parliament ' for that section ; and Lord North bestowed one of them by omitting New York from the bills restraining Colonial trade.[41]

Indeed, it was firmly believed that His Majesty's government intended to corrupt that Colony. Sayre wrote over to Samuel Adams that four members of the New York Assembly had ' touched £1000 each from ye Treasury ' ; and William Lee, besides naming three men said to have received a thousand guineas, declared that Ministers openly boasted of sending large sums for such purposes. ' We have the strongest persuasion,' declared the Congress of Massachusetts to the Continental Congress, ' that the settled plan of the British Administration is to break the chain of union of the Colonies at New York ; and we are sure that the evidence of such design, and

---

[40] § Gilbert : 4 Force, II., 508. See Flick, Loyalism, pp. 32–36, etc. ; Van Tyne, Loyalists, p. 25, etc.; Tyler, Am. Hist. Rev., I., p. 25 ; Id., Lit. Hist., I., pp. 298–300, etc.; Quarterly Rev., Vol. 188, pp. 430, 436, 438, etc.

[41] § London, May 5, 1775 : 4 Force, II., 508. J. Adams to J. Sullivan, June 23, 1776: Works, IX., p. 407. S. Adams to A. Lee, Mar. 4, 1775: S. Adams Papers. Colden to Dartmouth, June 7, 1775: Pub. Rec. Off., Am. and W. I., Vol. 185, p. 360. Bills: London letters (4 Force, II., 508, 122); Pownall, (ib., 276).

their machinations for that purpose, cannot escape your attention.' Besides, fear joined hands with hope to keep the province from declaring for Liberty. In April, 1775, Dartmouth informed Gage that certain regiments, intended for Boston, would go to New York and take post on the Hudson ; and, as this purpose had been known in a general way to Samuel Adams months before, no doubt the leading citizens of New York felt the lion's paw, by anticipation, long before London letters of July thirty-first explained the plan.[42]

Naturally enough, then, John and Samuel Adams were not the only ones who felt suspicious. Samuel Mott believed the Colony of New York 'unsound at heart.' Joseph Warren confided strong doubts to Samuel Adams. Colden testified that his fellow-citizens were looked upon by their neighbors on the east 'as highly inimical to their Designs,' and he believed that Ticonderoga had been captured in order to 'produce an explicit union with them' or expose the Colony to 'Destruction.' Ethan Allen alluded very frankly to the number of Tories in the province. John Brown hinted that Schuyler's delay was due to influences of that color, and probably they did suggest some of his doubts about the 'propriety' of advancing. General Wooster said to Governor Trumbull : 'Your Honour well knows the suspicious light in which the New York Congress are viewed by the rest of the Continent,' and protested against being placed under their orders. Even Washington seems to have shared the feeling : 'In this instance the Congress at New York have judged properly,' he observed in September, adding,

---

[42] § Bribes: R. H. Lee to S. Adams, Feb. 4, 1775 (S. Adams Papers); Sayre to S. Adams, Apr. 4, 1775 (ib.); W. Lee to S. Adams, Apr. 10, 1775 (ib.). Mass. Cong. to Cont. Cong., May 27, 1775; 4 Force, II., 721. Dartmouth to Gage, Apr. 15, 1775 : Bancroft Coll., Eng. and Am., 1775, p. 109. S. Adams to Bowdoin, Nov. 16, 1775: Mass. Hist. Soc. Proc., Ser. 1, XII., p. 227. London letters: 4 Force, II., 1755.

' I wish I could extend my approbation equally to the whole line of their conduct.' [43]

In February, the Assembly had voted to send no delegates to the second Continental Congress. Only three out of thirteen members appointed in April on the Committee of Correspondence and Inquiry favored doing so. As late as the twenty-eighth of June, the Provincial Congress declared itself ' deeply impressed with the importance, the utility, and [the] necessity of an accommodation with our Parent State.' Poughkeepsie officials cut down a liberty-pole. Allan Maclean found no less than four hundred men on the Mohawk ready to shoulder British muskets. After the capture of Montreal, Richmond County refused to send Delegates to the Provincial Congress, on the ground that all prospects of reconciliation with England had vanished. Westchester County got up an insurrection ' against liberty ' ; and four men were believed to be at work in that section recruiting for the British army. As time passed, some of the loyalists—to borrow Allen's phrase—were ' savingly converted '; but, near the close of 1775, Robert R. Livingston remarked : ' As for the politicks of our province it still moves in the same rascally channel in which it has hitherto run,' and Governor Tryon believed on the last day of January, 1776 : ' The Majority of this Province are Loyal.' [44]

If, then, Dickinson—though determined in his own fashion to resist Great Britain—dreaded a vigorous campaign at the north, all this force of loyalist sentiment in

---

[43] § S. Mott to Trumbull, Aug. 3, 1775: 4 Force, III., 18.   Warren to S. Adams, June 15, 1774: S. Adams Papers.   Colden : Note 41.   Allen to N. Y. Cong., June 2, 1775: 4 Force, II., 891.   J. Brown : Vol. I., p. 315.   Wooster to Trumbull, Aug. 24, 1775: 4 Force, III., 262.   Wash. to Wooster, Sept. 2 : ib., 632.

[44] § N. Y. Ass., Feb. 23, 1775: 4 Force, I., 1290.   Com. C. and I.: ib., 1324 (cf. ib., 1290).   N. Y. Cong., June 28, 1775: 4 Force, II., 1329.   Pough.: 4 Force, II., 176.   Maclean : Gage to Secy. State, Sept. 20, 1775 (Pub. Rec. Off., A. and W. I., Vol. 420, p. 257).   Richmond Co., Dec. 15, 1775: 4 Force, IV., 428.   Westchester Co., etc.: N. Y. Cong. (ib., 402, 403).   Allen: Note 43.   R. R. Liv. to Montg., Nov. 29, 1775: Liv. Papers, 1775-1777, p. 73.   Tryon to Carleton : Pub. Rec. Off., Am. and W. I., Vol. 186, p. 329.   See also 4 Force, III., 457.

New York must have been fiercely hostile to it. Moreover, it was able to present itself in the Continental Congress, not only with no brand of treason upon it as yet,
but supported by a body-guard of weighty considerations.
The social and commercial intercourse of New York with
Canada, easier and therefore closer than any other Colony
enjoyed, gave her a special voice in what concerned that
province. Ticonderoga was the natural and almost inevitable base of military operations at the north, and New
York did not wish alien troops to press her soil without
full authorization. Even when she desired men from another Colony to garrison the lake forts, her invitation wore
the coyest air : ' There is no doubt but that our brethren
of Connecticut will feel great reluctance at the idea of
ordering any of their troops to march within the bounds
of this Colony,' she said ; ' But we pray you to cast away
all fears of offending us upon this occasion.' Even under
the stress of British invasion and in dire need of cannon to
repel the foe, Massachusetts had shown the utmost caution
about encroaching on the reserve of another Colony ; the
General Congress felt, as Jefferson said, a ' great desire
not to go too fast for any respectable part ' of the body ;
and the reasons for not estranging New York had extraordinary force. Every Colony and the assembled representatives understood as well as Lord North, how serious
its defection from the Union of Colonies would be, and
could estimate as fairly the strategic value of the Hudson.
No matter how exasperating or suspicious to ardent
patriots, the sentiment of that quarter had to be very
tenderly studied.[45]

Samuel Adams, however, was not the man to sleep

---

[45] § The election of delegates to the second Cont. Cong. can be seen now to
have drawn the line between ' patriots ' and loyalists (Becker, Am. Hist. Rev.,
IX., p. 85); but such lines are always more or less obscure and fluctuating at
the time. It was only the Declaration of Independence that changed an obscure line into a yawning chasm (see Flick, Loyalism, p. 54). N. Y. Cong. to
Conn., May 25, 1775: 4 Force, II., 705. Jefferson, Works (Wash.), I., p. 11.

I is proper that you sh. know the Mans)

try now openly boast of their having last year sent large sums to
New York, to bribe the members of that Assembly & the Names of

FROM WM. LEE'S LETTER TO SAMUEL ADAMS, APRIL 10, 1775

X There is prohibition in this Colony of keepg
Chocol. to buy maize & feed land holders ~ of the

FROM SAMUEL ADAMS'S LETTER TO A. LEE, MARCH 4, 1775

upon his great plan for adding a northern empire to the league of Colonies. Hancock, the President, and John Adams, the orator, aided him. Lynch, 'a solid, firm, judicious man,' 'as constantly attended Congress' with motions for supplies 'as ever nurse did her patient with a bolus.' 'It appears to me,' wrote Richard Henry Lee to Washington, 'It appears to me that we must have that country [Canada] with us this winter, cost what it will.' Other determined members took the same view ; and the Congress, embarrassed and almost paralyzed as it was, did all that could reasonably have been expected. During the summer, four regiments from New York, three from Connecticut, and one from Massachusetts were assigned to Schuyler, besides the battalion of Green Mountain Boys and some other troops,—a nominal strength of nearly eight thousand ; and this, about ten times the British force in Canada, seemed ample. Much sickness was reported from the army, but not of a fatal sort ; and the Congress, after allowing so wide a margin of safety, might easily suppose nothing further necessary, beyond urging—as it did—the completion of the New York regiments. As yet, the march of events was so slow that even a dilatory body had no great difficulty in keeping abreast of them.[46]

By the first week of October, however, the situation had changed. Montgomery had committed himself to a forward movement, and Arnold had taken aim at the heart of Canada. Both advances were likely to require support ; both might be delayed ; the troops had enlisted only for the year ; the losses from sickness were proving serious ; and the process of raising new forces would cer-

---

[46] § J. Adams on Lynch: Works, II., p. 360. Lynch to Montg., Nov. 14, 1775: Pub. Rec. Off., Am. and W. I., Vol. 186, p. 39 ; to Sch., Jan. 20, 1776 : Sparks MSS., No. 60, p. 61. Lee to Wash., Oct., 22, 1775 : 4 Force, III., 1137. Sch.'s circ. letter, July 21, 1775: Lossing, Sch., I., p. 366. Sickness: Sch. to Hancock, Sept. 25, 1775 (4 Force, III., 796).

tainly be slow. Congress knew all this. Not a day could safely be wasted, and no doubt the friends of the Canada enterprise pointed that out. But all they could accomplish, after debate, was to authorize the enrollment of a Canadian regiment, and bid Schuyler (October 12) consult with his principal officers about the number of troops required from the north and ' the best Method of procuring Men.' [47]

On the last day of October, Congress listened to a series of letters from Schuyler. Troops would be needed,—were needed already, he said ; and there was ' too, too much reason ' to believe that very few of the present army would re-engage. This meant a crisis ; and Schuyler made it look the worse by adding, that already the lateness of the season would prevent raising troops in the Colonies. That depended, perhaps ; but the icy breath of winter could be felt at the door, and certainly the swiftest and most positive action was called for. Again, however, the Opposition stepped in. Two days later, Congress merely voted to despatch a committee northward. Then another struggle followed, no doubt, over their instructions ; but, after about a week of delay, they received orders ' to make use of every argument' that could induce the troops to re-enlist or at least remain until they could be relieved ; and they were empowered, in concert with General Schuyler, ' to raise any number ' of men that could be procured in Canada, New York, or New England. Two months' pay and the settlement of all arrears were to be offered as a bounty for re-enlistment ; arrangements were made for certain increases of salary; clothing was promised ; and authority was given to buy six months' provisions for three thousand men. Three days later, after receiving further instructions, the committee set out for the north ; and, on the twenty-second,

---

[47] § Hancock to Sch., Oct. 12: Am. Antiq. Soc.   Journ. Cong., Oct. 3, 5, 11.

Schuyler expected it 'momently' at headquarters, Ticonderoga. Once more the party of Samuel Adams had won the battle, but at how pathetic a loss of dead and buried time![48]

Fairly on the ground and well posted about the campaign, the committee made, perhaps, a few sad reflections. Had Schuyler planted two thousand men at St. Johns in earnest about the middle of August, he would have found the works quite incomplete and the supplies quite inadequate. The British could not have stood a siege; and to sally into that wooded country would have given the Provincials just the sort of fighting they liked. Two weeks might have finished the business; and then a strong column, hastening to Quebec and from Quebec to Montreal, should have ended the campaign within the next month. Or, had Montgomery been given three thousand men on the first of October, he could easily, with such a backing, have enrolled a thousand Canadians, and then have sent at least that number of his best troops to secure the two cities. Or, at the very worst, a sufficient force to dominate the rural districts below and reinforce Arnold could certainly, in either case, have been spared; and, by the first of December, while snugly housed garrisons were smoking their pipes in all the chief points of the province, Canadian Delegates, fully satisfied the Colonies could hold their own, might have been toasting their good brethren of the Congress in old Madeira at the City Tavern, Philadelphia. As it was, the committee arrived in season to witness the exodus of disbanded soldiers, realize the hopelessness of urging political union—which the Congress had earnestly enjoined upon them to do—while the military issue remained in doubt, and learn that now it would be practically impossible for

---

[48] § Journ. Cong., Oct. 16, 31; Nov. 2, 8, 11. Instructions: Sparks MSS., No. 52, II., p. 123. Sch. to Wash., Nov. 22, 1775: 4 Force, III., 1635. REMARK L.

troops to pass Lake Champlain, even could they be raised, before 'about the beginning of February.' The grand opportunity had evidently been lost.[49]

A less brilliant opportunity remained, however, and Montgomery proposed to make the best of it. As rapidly as possible, the business at Montreal was disposed of. Some of the prisoners begged permission to remain there ; and when the General, pursuing his conciliatory policy, granted their petition, a number of officers protested so vigorously that he declared he would hold the command no longer. But their action had grown out of honest zeal for the cause, and, seeing their mistake, they apologized in a way that perhaps drew leader and followers more closely than ever together. Conferences were held with laymen and the clergy. James Livingston was commissioned to enlist a regiment of Canadians, and received the well-earned sword of a colonel. Three Rivers, the only town of importance in Canada besides Quebec and Montreal, decided to submit, and sent a deputation to crave kind treatment. 'Gentlemen,' replied Montgomery, 'I feel greatly mortified that you should entertain any fears about your property. I am sure that the Continental troops will never be stained with any imputation of injustice. We are here to conserve, not to destroy. If Providence continues to favor our efforts, this Province will soon possess a free government.' But the General's greatest care was to procure clothing. Some time before, Schuyler had proposed to buy woollens at Montreal, and now that plan was perforce adopted. James Price loaned five thousand pounds (York currency), and out of this and the stores captured with the fleet Montgomery was able to provide for Arnold's detachment and to equip

---

[49] § Works not completed in August : Claus, No. Am. Notes and Queries, I., No. 1, p. 24. Tavern : Scharf and Westcott, Phila., I., p. 289, etc. Hopelessness : Com. to Montg., Nov. 30, 1775 (4 Force, IV., 445). Impossible : Report of Com. (Sparks MSS., No. 52, II., p. 63).

about three hundred men of his own for a campaign at Quebec.[50]

Many dangers threatened the voyage toward the capital. Contrary winds might stop him. The cold weather might throw a boom of ice across the river. The British vessels of war might sink his fleet. But without hesitation Montgomery determined to spread his canvas and accept the chances. On his return—his victorious return—he announced, a Convention should be called, and Canada take her place among the self-governing United Colonies ; so on to Quebec and away with the last barrier ! 'I have courted fortune and found her kind,' he wrote ; 'I have one more favor to Solicit.' Little doubt about her answer could be felt. Mrs. Montgomery, waiting by the Hudson, received one day a thrice-welcome message. 'I live in hopes to see you in six weeks,' it said.[51]

[50] § Montg. to Sch., Nov. 24, 1775: Dunlap, New Netherlands, II., p. 23. Clinton et al. to Montg., Nov. 23, 1775: 4 Force, III., 1695. D. Campbell to——, Mar. 28, 1776: Liv. Papers, 1775-1777, p. 145. Conf.: Montg. to Sch., Nov. 19, 1775 (4 Force, III., 1682). T. Riv.: Verreau (Badeaux), Invasion, p. 179 ; Ursul. de T. Riv., I., p. 365. Sch. to Hancock, Sept. 25, 1775 : 4 Force, III., 796. Montg. to R. R. Liv., Dec. 17, 1775: Liv. Papers, 1775-1777, p. 89. Montg. to Sch., Dec. 5, 1775: 4 Force, IV., 188. Price: Id. to Id., Nov. 24 (4 Force, III., 1694).

[51] § Montg. to Sch., Nov. 19, 1775: 4 Force, III., 1682. Id. to R. R. Liv., Nov. 13, 1775: Liv. Papers, 1775-1777, p. 63. Id. to Mrs. M., Nov. 24, 1775: L. L. H., Biog Notes, p. 15.

XXIII

THE GREAT DUEL BEGINS AGAIN

IF ever a soldier deserved well of fortune, it was Montgomery when setting out in winter to conquer the citadel of the north. No greedy ambition clamored within him; no professional enthusiasm spurred him on. The career of arms, once a gallant vocation, had lost its glamour in his view. No glint of self-interest sharpened his eye. 'Disinterested and generous motives will forever, I hope, prevent me from serving myself or my family at the expense of the public,' he wrote his wife with reference to promoting a near relative. As the leader of freemen should, he longed only for peace with honor. 'My family and farm,' were the glories that illumined his dreams. 'O fortunate husbandmen ! *Would I were at my plough again!*' was his inmost feeling. 'I . . . sigh for home like a New Englander,' he confessed.[1]

And he more than sighed. No hint of shirking could be found in his conduct. '*I shall always be ready to contribute my mite to the public safety*,' was his voluntary pledge. But, when it began to seem as if his task had nearly been accomplished, he wrote to his official superior, 'I most earnestly request to be suffered to retire, should matters stand on such a footing this winter as to permit me to go off with honour'; and he went so far as to propose Charles

---

[1] § Montg. to Mrs. M., Oct. 9 ; Dec. 5, 1775: L. L. H [unt], Biog. Notes, pp. 13, 16 (see pp. 6, 17). Id. to R. R. Liv., Sr. and Jr., Oct. 5 ; Nov. 13 ; Dec. 16, 17, 1775 : Liv. Papers, 1775–1777, pp. 51, 63, 81, 89.

Lee for the Canada command.   But duty ruled him as
effectually as pride or ambition has ruled others.   He saw
'a prize of such value at stake' before the United Colonies that he would not halt for his own ease.   It was
'of the utmost importance,' he understood, 'to finish this
business at once,' that the Ministry might 'have no hopes
left of carrying on their infernal plan in this important
quarter.' [2]

And his cheerful anticipations appeared to have reasonable grounds.   Quebec stood at the tip of a high ridge of
rock extending for some three leagues down the St. Lawrence, and sloped inevitably toward the St. Charles.   One
consequence was that, from the opposite side of this little
stream, an eye could survey the interior of the fortifications, and, if it happened to be the eye of a cannon, could
reconnoitre it in force.   Later a splendid citadel, a crown
of beauty and of strength, was placed upon the brow of
Cape Diamond; but in 1775 the works at that point, while
important, had neither extent nor massiveness, and the
principal defence on the land side consisted of a wall
reaching from the Cape, nearly three hundred and fifty
feet higher than the St. Lawrence, to the bluff above St.
Charles River, there fifty or sixty feet in height.   A small
polygon at each end, six bastions between them, a shallow
ditch, a low and imperfect counterscarp, and an unfinished
glacis strengthened the wall somewhat; and a valley
beyond, sixty-nine feet deep from the summit of the Cape,
served to a certain extent as another and far larger moat. [3]

But, unfortunately for Quebec, the Heights of Abraham,
running along the farther side of this valley at a distance
of about eight hundred yards from the town, rose ten feet

[2] § Montg. to Sch., Oct. 31; Nov. 13, 1775: Sparks MSS., No. 60, p. 17; 4
Force, III., 1602.   Id. to R. R. Liv., Sr. and Jr., Dec. 16, 17: Note 1.

[3] § For the fortifs., see Murray's report, June 5, 1762: Can. Arch., B, 7, p. 1;
Marr, Remarks: ib., M, 384, p. 111; Précis relative to Fortifs. in Am.: Pub.
Rec. Off., Am. and W. I., Vol. 289, p. 35; Doughty, Fortress, *passim*; Hawkins,
Picture, pp. 155–169.

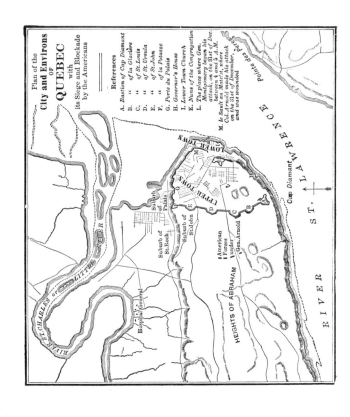

Plan of the
City and Environs
OF
QUEBEC
with
its Siege and Blockade
by the Americans

References

A. Bastion of Cap Diamant
B.   "   of la Glacière
C.   "   of St. Louis
D.   "   of St. Ursula
E.   "   of St. John
F.   "   of la Potasse
G. Porte du Palais
H. Governor's House
I. Lower Town Church
K. Nuns of the Congregation
L. The place where Gen.
   Montgomery began his
   attack, on the 31st of Dec.
   between 4 and 5 A.M.
M. le Sault au Matelot, where
   Col. Arnold made his attack
   on the 31st of December,
   and was wounded

78

higher than Cape Diamond, and not only commanded
the wall to its very foundations in many places, but could
enfilade the flanks of the bastions inside and a considerable extent of the ramparts.   Neither a covered way nor
outworks had been provided.   The two exits toward
the Plains—St. Louis Gate, near the Cape, and St. John's
Gate below—were pronounced by General Murray 'ill-
placed and not defended'; and Palace Gate, which looked
down the St. Charles River bluff toward the Intendant's
Palace hard by, fell under the same condemnation.   The
'irregular, unwrought stone' of the walls lacked solidity.
The cheeks of the embrasures had in many cases broken
out under the pressure of the earth, and the roots of
shrubs growing in the joints of the revetment had for
years been threatening to burst it.   A breach might be
made by artillery 'in two Days Time,' reported Marr, the
British engineer.[4]

Several attempts had been made since the Conquest of
1760 to have the defences improved.   Both Gage and
Carleton had repeatedly pointed out their weakness.   In
fact, the government had thought very seriously of building new fortifications.   At least four plans for a citadel
went over to London.   Some slight repairs appear to have
been made.   But, when the Americans entered Canada,
however formidable the bluff toward the St. Charles,
however tremendous the St. Lawrence front, Quebec's
third side left much to be desired.[5]

Under the menace of invasion, something was now
accomplished.   It had been the French plan to carry the
wall along the verge of the bluff all the way round.   Some

---

[4] § See Note 3; also Carleton to Shelburne, Nov. 25, 1767 (Can. Arch., Q, 5,
1, p. 260); Gage to Hillsborough, Jan. 7, 1769 (Pub. Rec. Off., Am. and W. I., Vol.
125, p. 91); Carleton's Instructions, Jan., 1775, § 50 (Can. Arch., M, 230, p. 134);
Frederick to Townshend, Jan. 25, 1773 (Dartmouth Papers, II., Pt. 1, p. 42);
Hawkins, Picture, pp. 164, 168; Doughty, Fortress, p. 71.

[5] § See Note 4.   Maclean's letter to Barrington (Note 7) shows that no
substantial improvement had been made since Gage, Murray, and Marr wrote.

blocks of masonry were erected, and the foundations for others laid ; but the approach of Wolfe obliged the occupants to complete their defences with palisades in lieu of stone work. Many—perhaps nearly all—of the posts had since fallen, but they were now renewed. The merlons, embrasures, and sally-ports were repaired ; barriers were constructed between the Upper and Lower Towns and at the ends of the latter ; platforms for cannon hastily laid ; barracks provided. A blockhouse outside St. Louis Gate supplied the place, to some extent, of outworks ; and two other such constructions, either new or freshly repaired, occupied positions in the circuit.[6]

Yet the city remained, from a strictly military point of view, decidedly weak. Maclean groaned over ' the difficulty of defending it Even with a good garrison ' ; and that, according to Murray, meant at least three thousand men. ' The walls in a ruinous situation,' wrote Arnold ; and Montgomery himself summed up the case in clear though purposely exaggerated terms : ' a great extent of works, in their nature incapable of defence, manned with a motley crew ' of sailors, militia, and recruits, honeycombed with disloyalty. The supplies were inadequate, and all hope of succor lay far below the horizon.[7]

Very promising, too, seemed the political outlook. Good-will, or at least a strong desire to do the Colonials no harm, was not confined to the Chaudière *habitants*, the disaffected militia, nor the farmers at Aspen Point. Though the red woollen caps of the peasants, which had grown so familiar about Montreal, changed to grey in the district

---

    6 § Marr, Remarks : Can. Arch., M, 384, p. 111. Id., Report, July 1, 1778 : ib., B, 154, p. 6. Letter from Quebec, Oct. 1, 1775 : 4 Force, III., 924. Alsopp, Petition, Sept. 3, 1790 : Can. Arch. (separate). Thompson, in LeMoine, Quebec Past and Present, p. 195. Carleton : Note 4. Lindsay : Can. Rev., No. 5, Sept., 1826, p. 89. Caldwell, Letter.
    7 § Maclean to Barrington, Nov. 20, 1775 : Can. Arch., M, 317, p. 259. Murray : Note 3. Arnold to Wash., Dec. 5, 1775 : 4 Force, IV., 190. Montg. to Carleton, Dec. 6, 1775 : Warren, Am. Rev., I., p. 432 (corrected from Lindsay : Can. Rev., No. 5, Sept., 1826, p. 89).

of Quebec, the ideas under them remained about the same. 'Was a vigorous effort to be made on your side,' a citizen of the capital had affirmed in September, 'this Country would be your own'; and nothing had occurred in the two following months to weaken that opinion. About the same time, three of Maclean's captains and a French officer had undertaken to rouse the people about and below Quebec; 'but to no purpose.' In October, 'Civis Canadiensis' published a fiery address to the Canadians in the *Quebec Gazette*. 'The Apostle commanded, "Fear God, honor the king,"' he reminded them; 'hence to refuse obedience on any pretext is to resist the express orders of God'; but, as an address a week later called them 'abominable in the eyes of God and men' for their 'perfidy,' it seemed evident that little was expected. Indeed, the people declared flatly that they would not defend 'a parcel of pension-drawers nor their miserable French laws.' All the *habitants* near Quebec on the south shore—so Roy, the historian of that district, has found—were 'strongly sympathetic,' and the Journal of Monsieur Baby, a prominent citizen of the capital, extended this description to the whole region.[8]

As the troops of Congress drew near, the sympathy did not fail to warm. 'All the Canadians in the country join them,' said a gentleman in Quebec with reference to Arnold's troops. 'The inhabitants are our friends on both sides of the river to Quebeck,' wrote Montgomery from Montreal ten days later; and the Quebec region, the Montreal region, and the St. Lawrence region between, contained substantially the whole population of Canada. Within twenty-four hours after, Carleton penned a despatch to

---

[8] § Quebec letters, Sept. 17; Oct. 1, 1775: 4 Force, III., 726, 925. Maclean, Return, Nov. 18, 1775: Can. Arch., M, 317, p. 248. Quebec Gazette, Oct. 5, 12, 1775 (in French). Letter of Oct. 24, 1775, quoted by Maseres, Add. Papers, p. 97 (un tas de b—— pensionnaires ni leurs f——loix françoises). Roy, Lauzon, III., p. 65. Baby, Journal (the author has not seen this MS.; but Mons. Roy writes him: 'Ce manuscrit me donne la preuve que presque tous les habitants des paroisses de la région de Québec sympathisaient en 1775 avec l'armée du Congrès.').

the government, informing it that not only the 'base Desertion of the Canadian Peasantry' still continued, but the
noblesse were deeply offended at finding themselves and
their followers classed as militia instead of regulars. 'The
french seem for the most part in our favour,' noted Lieutenant Humphrey just after crossing the St. Lawrence;
and three weeks later, when Montreal and the fleet were
known to have been taken, an officer put it still more
strongly : 'The inhabitants are all in our favour and are
excessive kind.' 'The inhabitants are very friendly and
give all the assistance they dare to do at present,' said
Arnold on retiring to Aspen Point; and, near the end of
the month, a Quebecker testified, 'The Canadians, are in
general, favourable to the Americans.' Some of them, in
fact, went beyond sentiments and even beyond friendly
assistance.   While the Kennebec detachment was approaching the capital, a party of the most forward actually
took up arms against the government, and there was 'an
engagement near the Town,' a citizen reported ; and, some
time later in November, the people at Pointe à la Caille
rose en masse, and prevented a vessel laden with provisions
from sailing to Quebec.[9]

The Americans were few, no doubt, but they were
exceedingly choice.   Almost all, if not quite all, had volunteered twice over, and every man wore the laurel of
triumph.   Victors over the enemy composed one wing ;
victors over nature the other.   'Surely God is with this
people, or they could never have done what they have
done,' exclaimed the pious Canadians ; and so it looked.
Montgomery had shown himself just the man to win and
hold the people, and even the loyal nuns could not help

---

[9] § Quebec letter, Nov. 9, 1775: Maseres, Add. Papers, p. 94.   Montg. to
Sch., Nov. 19, 1775: 4 Force, III., 1682.   Carleton to Dartmouth, Nov. 20, 1775:
Pub. Rec. Off., Colon. Corres., Quebec, 11, p. 519.   Humphrey, Journal, Nov. 15.
Letter before Quebec, Dec. 5, 1775: 4 Force, IV., 190.   Arnold to Montg., Nov.
20, 1775: Sparks MSS., No. 52, II., p. 31.   Account, end of Nov.: 4 Force, III.,
1723.   Quebec letter, Nov. 7, 1775: ib., 1396.   Ainslie, Journal, Dec. 2.

THE INTENDANT'S PALACE

admiring this rebel and heretic. 'Montgomery and Arnold deserve statues of Gold,' exclaimed Charles Lee ; and the men who had won such plaudits could still win them. Samuel Adams and his allies appeared to have got the ball rolling in Congress, and the more or less tardy support of that body could be reckoned upon. Obstacles lay ahead ; but 'I have been so used to struggle with difficulties,' observed the General, 'that I expect them of course' ; and forewarned was in a sense forearmed. Arnold felt there were not enough troops, as every one did ; but he still believed that Quebec would not hold out long. 'I do think there is a fair prospect of success,' Montgomery assured his superior ; and, almost at the same time, Washington wrote Hancock, 'Upon the whole, I think affairs carry a pleasing aspect in that quarter.' [10]

Following the Commander-in-chief's directions, Arnold had tried, from the Great Carrying-Place on, to get into touch with the western army ; and, in spite of some bad luck, he lodged in Montgomery's hands at least one despatch written from the southern bank of the St. Lawrence. After passing the river, he could send letters with almost the certainty of a post; but, in order to safeguard the most precious information, he more than once commissioned trusty subordinates to explain the situation by word of mouth at the upper city. The General, on his side, was careful to communicate with the junior officer; and in these ways a close understanding came to be established. [11]

[10] § God: Letter, Dec. 6, 1775 (4 Force, IV., 204). Nuns: Mgr. de St. Vallier, Part II., Chap. IV. Lee to R. Morris, Dec. 9, 1775: Bancroft MSS., I., 21. Montg. to Sch., Dec. 18, 1775: 4 Force, IV., 309. Arnold to Wash., Nov. 20 ; Dec. 5, 1775: 4 Force, III., 1695 ; IV., 190. Montg. to Sch., Dec. 5, 1775: 4 Force, IV., 188. Wash. to Hancock, Dec. 4, 1775: ib., 180.

[11] § Wash.'s instr. to Arnold, Sept. 14, 1775: Writings (Ford), III., p. 121. Despatches: Arnold to Sch., Oct. 13 ; Nov. 7 (4 Force, III., 1062, 1633) ; Id. to Montg., Nov. 8, 13, 14, 16 (ib., 1634, 1635, 1684, 1685). Id. to Id., Nov. 20 (Sparks MSS., No. 50, II., p. 31); Id. to Id., Nov. 25, 30 (2) (Me. Hist. Soc. Coll., I., pp. 381, 386); Id. to Wash., Nov. 8, 13, 20 (4 Force, III., 1635, 1636, 1695); Id. to Easton (at Sorel), Nov. 14 (Me. Hist. Soc. Coll., I., p. 373.) (Most if not all of these letters appear in more than one collection, and Arnold wrote others.) See also Montg.

Montgomery, though eager to join Arnold had to struggle ' day after day ' with his difficulties at Montreal ; but
at last, on the twenty-eighth of November, he was able
to hoist anchor and set sail.   Several of the vessels that
' Mr. Prescott made us a present of,' as he pleasantly
phrased it, carried his men, stores, and light artillery.
Heavier cannon in bateaux joined the expedition at Sorel.
There James Livingston also embarked, with what Canadians—less than two hundred—he had been able to enlist
for his regiment in eight days ; and Major Brown, with
about a hundred and sixty men recruited from Easton's
and Bedel's disbanded corps, made ready to follow from
the same point.[12]

By this time, as an officer said, the troops began to
doubt whether they would be able to get down the river.
A crust of ice would have sawn the vessels through, and
the frost had been darting long crystals over the water
for nearly three weeks, the winter set in ' very cold &
stormy ' at Montreal while they were preparing to sail,
and the course was to take them each day nearer Labrador ;
but happily the weather moderated in season.   Adverse
winds or no winds at all would have ruined the expedition;
but a fresh southwest breeze sprang up.   The *Hunter*, the
Fell, and an armed schooner or two—no contemptible
squadron—had sailed up the St. Lawrence and might
have demolished the American fleet; but the breaking ice
cut their cables, the rising wind forced them back to Quebec, and the same auspicious gale ' wafted ' the Provincials

---

to Sch., Nov. 13, 17, 19: 4 Force, III., 1602, 1633, 1682 ; Odgen, Journal ; Humphrey, Journal ; Ritzema, Journal ; etc.   Montg. to Arnold: see Arnold's
replies ; Humphrey, Journal, Nov. 17, 22 ; Dec. 1. REMARK LI.

 1 2 § Departure: Montg. to Sch., Nov. 24 ; Dec. 5, 1775 (4 Force, III., 1694 ;
IV., 188) ; Ritzema, Journal, Nov. 28. Lt. Artill, etc.: Haskell, Diary, Nov. 27.
Bateaux: Thayer, Journal, Dec. 2. J. Liv. to ——, [Feb., 1776]: Am. Hist.
Rec., III., p. 181.   J. Liv., Certif.: Board of War Papers, II , p. 261. (See Montg.
to Sch., Nov. 19, 1775: Sparks MSS., No. 60, p. 26.) Canads.: Sch. to Hancock,
Jan. 13, 1776 (4 Force, IV., 666). Brown: Campbell to ——, Mar. 28, 1776 (Liv.
Papers, 1775-1777, p. 145); Arnold to Hancock, Feb. 1, 1776 (Sparks MSS., No.
52, II., p. 38) ; Field, Pittsfield, p. 57.

rapidly on toward Aspen Point. 'Providence smiles on us,' observed an officer with a smile of his own.[13]

Happy signs of their approach preceded them. On the twenty-eighth of November, Captain Goodrich and a strong party set off hastily up the river : it was to meet ammunition and cannon some distance above. 'This day received intelligence from Generall Montgomery of his Being In the River,' noted Lieutenant Humphrey on December the first, with no more capitals than his feelings required; and now the soldiers began to wonder a little what their new commander would be like. He was no amateur in war like all their other officers, they realized, but a regular. How would he rule them? How would he lead them? And was he actually coming, at last? Ogden, arriving the next day with stores of various kinds, cleared away all doubt on the last head ; and, at nine o'clock in the evening, a topsail-schooner with several other vessels from above turned in at the Point. A boat soon scraped on the beach. It brought the General; and, in a foot of snow, amid the flare of torches and lanterns, Colonel Arnold, at the head of a detachment, saluted him at the water's edge.[14]

All other doubts vanished then. ' He is a gentle polite Man tall and Slender In his make bald on the top of His Head Resolute mild and of a fine Temper and an Excellent General,' burst forth Humphrey. Noticeably pock-marked, but 'well limbed, tall and handsome,' observed Henry ; with an air and manner that ' designated the real soldier.' General Montgomery, cried Morison, ' was born

[13] § Ice, etc.: Letter of N. Y. Off., Dec. 7, 1775 (Pub. Rec. Off., Am. and W. I., Vol. 186, p. 261); Legge to Dartmouth (Pub. Rec. Off., Col. Corr., Vol., X., p. 84). Brit. vessels: Arnold to officers, Nov. 24, 25, 30, 1775 (Me. Hist. Soc. Coll., I., pp. 381, 386); Id. to Montg., Nov. 25 (ib., p. 381); Humphrey, Journal, Nov. 24-26, 30. Officer, Dec. 6, 1775: 4 Force, IV., 204.

[14] § Escort, etc.: Arnold to Dugan, Nov. 27, 1775 (Me. Hist. Soc. Coll., I., p. 385) ; Humphrey, Journal, Nov. 28 ; Haskell, Diary, Nov. 27. Humphrey, Journal, Dec. 1, 2. Snow: Ainslie, Journal, Dec. 1. Arrival: Senter's, Humphrey's, and other Journals ; see REMARK LII.

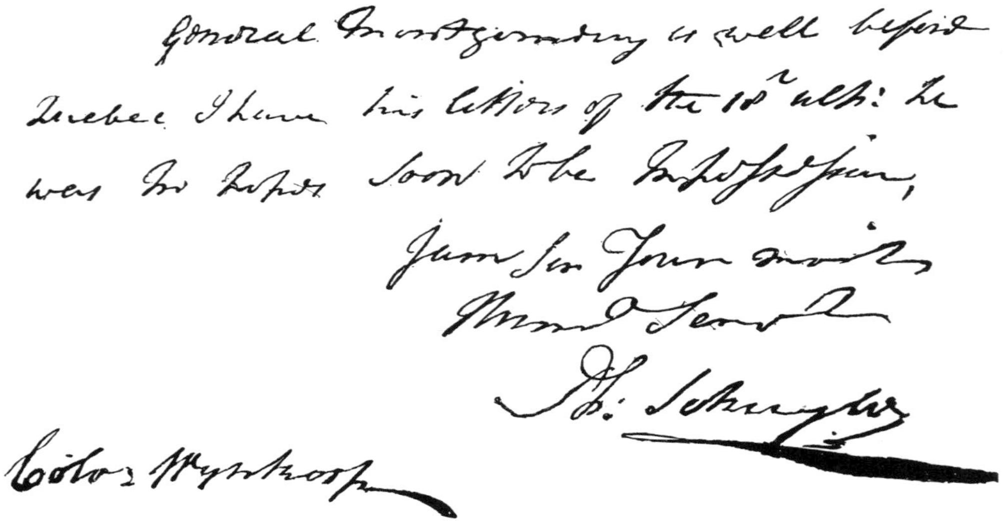

General Montgomery is well before

Quebec. I have his letters of the 10th ult.: he

was to report soon to the [illegible],

I am Sir Your most

Obedient Servant

Ph. Schuyler

Doctor Wynkoop

FROM A LETTER DATED JANUARY 7, 1776

to command. His easy and affable condescension to both
officers and men, while it forbids an improper familiarity,
creates love and esteem ; and exhibits him the gentleman
and the soldier.' Better still, the admiration was mutual.
Rags could not blind the eyes of a veteran. ' An exceed-
ing fine one,' he pronounced Arnold's corps ; ' There is a
style of discipline among them, much superior to what I
have been used to see this campaign.' At the proper moment he made a short but ' energetic and elegant ' speech,
as a soldier described it. There was praise for the wonderful march ; there was confidence that such courage would
persevere to the glorious end ; and—not least—there was
a promise of something to shield their bodies from the
northeast gales. Huzzas answered him. Feet might be
deep in snow, but heads were above the clouds. Montgomery's arrival ' gave us warmth and animation,' said
Henry. [15]

The next day found the old stone church of St. François
de Sales dripping with half-frozen sleet ; but the order
to distribute new clothing cheered the soldiers not a
little, especially as their backs were to be dressed in
captured British uniforms ; and very promptly the movement on Quebec began. What heavy cannon had been
landed above, out of harm's reach, went back into the
bateaux, for the enemy's vessels had now gone down
to be laid up for the winter ; and, toward evening, after
cutting through a wide fringe of ice, Captain Thayer
and his men set out for a trip of eighteen miles in the
dark. It grew so cold, he said later, ' that we strove
with the utmost Eagerness to Row, in order to keep
ourselves from being frozen. . . . Besides, such a
prodigious snow storm rais'd that we separated, and
could not come up with each other until I order'd some

---

[15] § See the Journals. Montg. to Sch., Dec. 5, 1775 : 4 Force, IV., 188.
Speech : Henry, Journal, p. 94, and other Journals.

guns to be fir'd, by the flashing of which with the utmost difficulty we rejoin'd.' To cap these difficulties, 'The Batteaux being heavy and quite frozen, got on the Ground amongst Rocks, and the men . . . jump'd into the river, being up to their armpits in the water, and with the utmost difficulty reach'd the shore, from whence they brought some horses.' [16]

Two days later, with equal enthusiasm though less hardships, the rest of the troops—'bloody backs' themselves, now—went swinging down toward Quebec, drawing a long red mark across the snow. Sealskin moccasins, thickly lined with hay or leaves, kept their feet warm ; the ammunition and light artillery formerly lacking went with them ; and their numbers, though feeble, were greater than before. Heads were high, hearts beat fast, and inevitably a little bragging was done, though in no trifling mood.

'In this part of the world,' commented a soldier, ''t is time for men to think of winter quarters rather than attacking fortified towns ; however, we are *Americans and American soldiers.*'

Carleton's 'runaway Frolicks' will not answer here, observed another, adding: 'They look upon [us] in the Light of Freebooters, but we are in hopes a few Shot & Shells will soon remove their prejudices.'

The town 'cannot hold out long,' said an officer; 'they are much divided amongst themselves, and a prodigious panick has seized them all.'

'Success must attend our General,' exclaimed a New Yorker, 'for a braver man does not tread on American nor on English leather.'

In this temper, canopied with a titanic whirl of break-

---

[16] § Ainslie, Journal. Roy, St. François, *passim*. Humphrey, Journal. Montg. to Sch., Dec. 5, 1775: 4 Force, IV., 188. Brit. vessels: Arnold to offs., Nov. 30, 1775 (Me. Hist. Soc. Coll., I., p. 386). Thayer, Journal.

ing storm-clouds, the troops pushed on till they could see the weather-vanes of Quebec. Before them lay now the glorious Plains of Abraham. Below, rolled the majestic outlet of the Great Lakes, filling all beholders—as one of them said—with 'astonishment and rapture'; while, on the left, the dark St. Charles wound on through white meadows to join the St. Lawrence. The scene looked worthy of heroic deeds; and this little army seemed to be marching along the vast rim of a crystal world, sharp with zest and radiant with promise, to achieve them. Small indeed were its numbers; but that fact could not belittle the issue. Figures are not the measure of importance; and the fall of Julius Cæsar, though but one man lost his life, was a tremendous event.[17]

Carleton had been expected in Quebec November the tenth, but did not appear. Day after day, more than a week dragged past without bringing so much as a word from him. Widespread rumors announced his capture by the enemy. The friends of the Americans in the garrison grew bolder as each sun failed to bring him. But again the intrepid Governor escaped from all his perils. Approaching Aspen Point, on their retreat from Quebec, Arnold's men saw an armed schooner and what the surgeon called a brig sailing at full speed down the river, and expected to be fired upon. But not a gun spoke; and they wondered. A few hours later the faint roar of cannon floated up from below; and again they marvelled. It was Carleton. After passing the American batteries at Sorel, he kept on till he reached Maclean's wind-bound vessels. Captain Napier took him aboard the *Fell;* a favoring breeze carried him down the river; he went ashore at Aspen Point, but, with his usual good fortune,

---

[7] § Letter, Dec. 6, 1775: 4 Force, IV., 204. Carleton to Howe, Jan. 12, 1776: Pub. Rec. Off., Am. and W. I., Vol. 130, p. 673. Humphrey, Journal, Dec. 5. Henry, Journal, pp. 91, 94, 185. Letters: Pub. Rec. Off., Am. and W. I., Vol. 186, pp. 237, 261; 4 Force, IV., 204. The clouds are inferred.

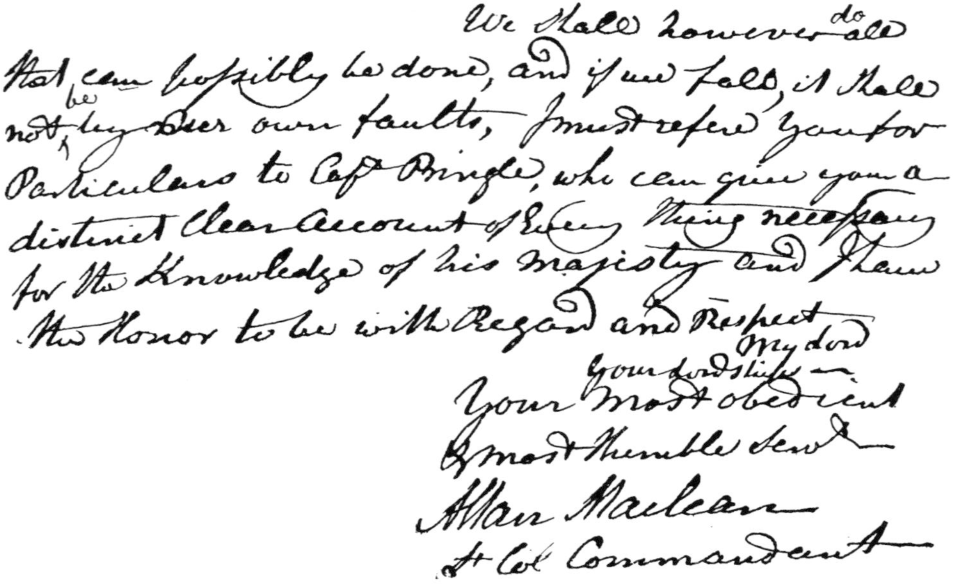

We shall however do all that can possibly be done, and if we fall, it shall not be by our own faults, I must refer You for Particulars to Capt Pringle, who can give you a distinct Clear Account of Every thing necessary for the Knowledge of his Majesty and I have the Honor to be with Regard and Respect

My Lord

Your Lordships

Your most obedient

& most Humble Servt

Allan Maclean

Lt Col Commandant

FROM A LETTER TO BARRINGTON WRITTEN JUST BEFORE CARLETON ARRIVED

set off again just before the Americans appeared; and the
cannon-fire at Quebec announced his arrival. Again the
champions were face to face.[18]

'On the nineteenth (a happy day for Quebec), to the
unspeakable joy of the friends of Government, & to the
utter dismay of the abettors of sedition & rebellion, Gen.
Carleton arrived . . . we saw our salvation in his
presence': in these words Ainslie recorded the loyalist
feeling. Already the town had good officers, but it
lacked a chief. Cramahé, at such a time, did not count.
Surrendering his military position, he sealed himself up
indoors. 'I believe he was thoroughly frightened,' said
Major Caldwell a few months later. Carleton gave the
spear a head,—in fact a triple head; for he combined
authority, ability, and unswerving determination. Even
those not fully in sympathy with all his ideas, recognized
him as the fit and appointed leader, and stepped at once
into their proper places of subordination. Maclean, a
soldier, but not a statesman, and only partially aware of
the delicate political situation, had regarded the Governor's
military policy as rather unenterprising; but he now saw
that he was to have all the fighting he wished. Caldwell,
offended at the favor shown the Canadian noblesse, had
ignored the Governor for six months; but he soon presented himself with sincere dutifulness. Even the
Americans understood the meaning of the General's
presence. 'Carleton,' said a home letter, 'Carleton, we
are told, is determined to hold out to the very last.'[19]

---

[18] § 10th : Hutcheson to Haldimand, Dec. 4, 1775 (Can. Arch., B, 20, p. 55).
No word: Cramahé to Germain, Nov. 19, 1775 (Bancroft Coll., Eng. and Am.,
Aug., 1775-Dec., 1776, p. 169). Rumors: Pa. Ledger, Dec. 16, 1775; Howe to
Secy. State, Dec. 9, 1775 (Pub. Rec. Off., Am. and W. I., Vol. 305, p. 210). At
Aspen Pt.: Henry, Journal, p. 185; Arnold to Montg., Nov. 20, 1775 (Sparks
MSS., No. 52, II., p. 31); Lindsay, Can. Rev., No. 5, Sept., 1826, p. 89; Senter,
Journal, Nov. 19. Ainslie, Journal, Nov. 19. Précis of Oper. Carleton to
Dartmouth, Nov. 20, 1775: Pub. Rec. Off., Colon. Corres., Quebec, 11, p. 519.

[19] § Ainslie, Journal. Cramahé: Caldwell, Letter. Maclean to Germain,
May 10, 1776: Can. Arch., Q, 12, p. 59. Caldwell: Letter. Letter, Dec. 6, 1775:
4 Force, IV., 204.

What measures of defence had been taken met with his approval. The embargo on the shipping—with the exception of the loaded fur-vessels—had been twice extended, and now covered also the 'British Inhabitants and Seafaring People.' Captain Hamilton of the *Lizard*, though his commission to Quebec had been fulfilled, had decided to remain there, 'stepping out of his own line'— as Germain said approvingly—because it was believed that otherwise the city would not be defended. Under his orders, McKenzie of the *Hunter* had done the same ; the vessels had been laid up, and the seamen, the £20,000 brought by the frigate, and the ammunition brought by both vessels been ordered ashore. Two councils had been held and the means of defence investigated. The truth about the provisions in town was not divulged : men were merely given to understand that a supply for eight months could be reckoned on ; but 'firewood, hay, [and] oats' were known to be 'scarce.' The militia had been assembled and squarely asked whether they would fight. 'Yes,' the Canadians had answered equivocally, 'if the British will' ; and the British—moved by loyalty, prudence, instinctive combativeness, fear of Maclean, and a natural reluctance to step forth into open rebellion—had concluded to lead off under the colors. The captains of the merchant vessels had promised their assistance. Numbers had been footed up ; and it appeared that, besides what might come from above, the garrison could muster officers included, six artillerymen, two hundred Royal Highland Emigrants, thirty-seven marines from the *Lizard*, two hundred and seventy-one seamen from the armed vessels, who must have known something of military service, seventy-four men from the other shipping, eighty artisans, two hundred British militia, and three hundred French militia : a total of eleven hundred and sixty-eight.[20]

---

20 § Carleton to Dartmouth, Nov. 20, 1775: Can. Arch., Q, 11, p. 318.   Em-

Without delay, the Governor reinforced the stiffening process begun by Maclean. He felt keenly that many 'Enemies within, and foolish People, Dupes to those Traytors,' had to be counted upon, and understood well 'the natural fears of Men unused to War.' Cramahé, though often urged to order the suspected away, had not wished or had not dared to act; but Carleton, while he recognized the fate of the town as 'extremely doubtful to say nothing worse,' intended to sink, if sink he must, with pennant at masthead, and in three days clearly announced his policy. 'Whereas information has been given me,' he proclaimed, 'that some persons resident here have contumaciously refused to enroll their names in the Militia Lists, . . . and that others, who have enrolled their names, and had for some time carried arms . . . , have lately laid them down; and also that some persons are busy in endeavouring to draw away and alienate the affections of His Majesty's good and faithful subjects . . . : for these reasons and in order to rid the Town of all useless, disloyal, and treacherous persons,' those who will not serve in arms must 'quit the Town in four days' and the District of Quebec before December first with their families, 'under pain of being treated as rebels or spies,' if thereafter found within these limits; and all their provisions must be appraised and sold to the government. Upon this, a long and wrathful procession filed out. John McCord, Bondfield, and several others prominent in the old political agitations could be seen in the line, and four or five militia officers appointed by the Lieutenant-Governor.

---

bargo, etc.: Quebec Gazette, Oct. 5, 26; Nov. 16, 1775; Cramahé to Dartmouth, Oct. 25, 1775 (Can. Arch., Q, 11, p. 264); Hamilton to Dartmouth, Nov. 20, 1775 (ib., p. 339). (Hamilton's duty was to transport the money and arms and convoy the storeships to Quebec.) Germain to Carleton, June 21, 1776: Can. Arch., Q, 12, p. 44. Provisions, etc.: cf. Ainslie, Journal, Nov. 30, with Cramahé and Hamilton (Can. Arch., Q, 11, 324, 329). To Hamilton, Nov. 16: ib., p. 345. Militia: Caldwell, Letter. Account: 4 Force, III., 1723. Council and Returns, Nov. 16, 1775: War Office, Orig. Corres., N. Am., Vol. 12. Maclean's Return, Nov. 18, 1775 (Can. Arch., M, 317, p. 248) was 240, counting drummers and all others. More were enrolled in the militia later.

Some of the exiles were capable of helping the Americans more or less, and one of them—a New Jersey lawyer named Edward Antill—received the appointment of Chief Engineer; but their presence doubtless counted less for Montgomery than did their absence for Carleton.[21]

'Cabals then ceased,' recorded Major Caldwell. That did not mean, however, that everybody now in the city was a fighting Tory. For various reasons many hearts dwelt outside, not attended by the corresponding bodies. A multitude of citizens detested the very thought of war. The stern realities of muskets and cannon, battle-smoke, fire and blood were shocking to these good people. Truth to tell, life had gayer traditions at Quebec than even at Hochelaga. In the last days of French

THE GENERAL HOSPITAL VIEWED FROM THE NORTH SIDE OF ST. CHARLES RIVER

rule, old Bigot—pimply but able and gracious—had lived there like a prince with his Canadian *amie*, little Péan's handsome, proud wife. Through the late war, twenty persons had feasted every

21 § Carleton to Dartmouth, Nov. 20, 1775: Note 18. Cramahé, etc. Caldwell, Letter. Proclamation, Nov. 22, 1775: 4 Force, III., 1639; Letter, Dec. 6, 1775 (4 Force, IV., 204). Montg. to Sch., Dec. 5, 1775: ib., 188. Antill, Memorial, Mar. 4, 1782: Cont. Cong. Papers, No. 41, I., p. 81. Lindsay: Can. Rev., No. 5, Sept., 1826, p. 89.

day at his table; and every evening citizens had crowded the gallery of his great ball-room, to watch the fine people and copy their manners. Even the humble folk had been gay and careless. Young women passed their days at the window, taking a stitch now and then in some fancy needlework, but ready, should a good-looking young fellow—even a stranger—enter the room, to drop everything on the instant, sit down by him, and burst into a sparkling torrent of chat, laughter, jokes, and those make-believes of wit, puns. The well-to-do British fell naturally into easy ways, especially as the long winters taught them idleness.

> ' When loudly-blustring winds arise
> And hoarsely-hurling, sweep the skies, . . .
> Then from abroad, my friend[s], retire
> And jovial croud the high-pil'd fire ':

so the Poets' Corner of the *Quebec Gazette* had pointed, only a few weeks before, to the approaching cold season. Particularly hard it was for the belles and beaux to give up their jolly drives on the Sainte Foy Road, now occupied by the Americans; and some, perhaps many, of the people were still disposed to escape hardship, secure their property, and welcome Liberty by surrendering the town. But now those influential enough to lead in such plans had mostly gone; and fines, plus ' the black hole on bread and water,' were counted upon to steady the lower class.[22]

To give his few regular troops a little ' Consistence,' Carleton combined the Royal Fusiliers, the marines from the *Lizard*, and the Emigrants into one corps under Maclean, who stood second in authority over the garrison. Major Caldwell took charge of the British militia; Colonel

---

[22] § Cabals, fines, etc.: Caldwell, Letter. Old Quebec: Parkman, Montcalm, II., pp. 18, 21, 28, 33; Kalm, Travels, III., p. 282. Gazette, Sept. 28, 1775. LeMoine, Pict. Quebec, *passim*. To surrender: Account, 4 Force, III., 1723; Wash. to Hancock, Dec. 31, 1775 (Writings (Ford), III., p. 305).

Voyer led the Canadians; and Captain Hamilton commanded the seamen. Thanks to the arrival of the Fusiliers and heavy pressure on the people, the garrison rose to eighteen hundred at the close of November. How a certain element would act, should it get a chance, nobody felt sure. With a total population of five thousand, the edifice of military despotism had a narrow base, and something untoward was liable to happen; but Carleton intended to guard all the vital points with his few trustworthy men. Work on the fortifications continued; and ease and high-piled fires were soon forgotten. What to expect from the enemy, could hardly be guessed for a while. Country people declared that Aspen Point overflowed with forty-five hundred of them, and one fellow got a drumming out of town for circulating such tales over-industriously. But a number of dark figures creeping toward Cape Diamond bastion in the night of December fifth announced that something definite would soon be known; and, when the long red line filed across the Plains the next day, Quebec stood watching it, silent and determined. Indeed, it was the time for silence. The time for pandemonium was coming.[23]

Montgomery's first operation was to select favorable positions and bar the roads. The fringe of beach along the St. Lawrence, rather wide at Wolfe's Cove and wider still at the Lower Town, rounded the point of Quebec, and, following the St. Charles, broadened into ample meadows above the city. On this low ground stood the General Hospital; and toward it, beginning at the old Palace of the Intendant, straggled the suburb of St. Roch.

[23] § Carleton to Barrington, May 14, 1776: War Off., Orig. Corres., N. Am., Vol. 12. Id. to Germain, May 14, 1776: 4 Force, VI., 456. Caldwell, Letter. Maclean to Germain, May 10, 1776: Can. Arch., Q, 12, p. 39. Numbers, etc.; Ainslie, Journal, Nov. 30 (70 Fusil.; 320 Emig.; 22 Artill., etc.; 330 Brit. Mil.; 543 French Mil.; 400 Seamen; 50 Masters and Mates of trading vessels; 35 Marines; 120 Artificers; 5000 total popul.). 4500, etc.: ib., Dec. 2, 3. 'Chalmers' Journal, Dec. 5. For Caldwell: LeMoine, Quebec Past and Present, p. 202. REMARK LIII.

The occupation of this region was committed to Arnold, with Morgan on his exposed left; and a couple of field-pieces were given him to help repulse a sortie, should one be made. As for the Hospital, 'Like the city of Montreal,' wrote the sisters of big Salaberry with gentle sarcasm, 'we have surrendered without firing a single shot'; and there a large detachment was placed. The York troops occupied the Plains of Abraham; the headquarters were fixed among them at the Holland House, a long, high-peaked French mansion on a low but sightly eminence; and squads took post at Beauport and elsewhere to aid in sealing up the town. Once more Quebec retired from the world. Hardly a bag of wheat or a whisper of trustworthy news could steal into it. About a thousand able-bodied men penned up eighteen hundred.[24]

Next, Montgomery proceeded to summon the town; but, desiring to address Carleton privately or to gain some other end, he did this in a peculiar way. Craving admittance at Palace Gate, a woman announced that she had an important communication for the Governor, and was immediately conducted to him. She then produced a letter, and explained that it came from the American general.

'Call a drummer,' said Carleton to an aide; and presently the drummer appeared.

'Take that letter with a pair of tongs,' bade the General, 'and throw it into the fire.' This done, he ordered the woman out of town, and told her to report at the

---

[24] § Arnold, etc.: Caldwell, Letter; Graham, Morgan, p. 92. Hospital: Mgr. de St. Vallier, Part II., Chap. IV., partic. pp. 400, 416 (the nuns were treated with the greatest possible courtesy); Senter, Journal, Dec. 5. Humphrey, Journal, Dec. 7, 8. Haskell, Diary, Dec. 8. Holl. Hse.: LeMoine, Pict. Queb., p. 413. Humphrey, Journal, Dec. 7. Outposts: Ainslie, Journal, Dec. 7. Carleton to Howe, Jan. 12, 1776: Pub. Rec. Off., Colon. Corres., Quebec, 12, p. 23. Montg. to Sch., Dec. 18, 1775: 4 Force, IV., 309 ('upwards of 800'). Id. to R. R. Liv., Dec. 16, 1775: Liv. Papers, 1775-1777, p. 81 ('little more than 800 men fit for duty'). (These figures do not seem to include the Canadians under Livingston, whom he considered of little value; see his letter to R. R. Liv., Dec. 16, 1775: Liv. Papers, 1775-1777, p. 81.) The part of St. Roch near the Intendant's Palace was often called the Suburb of the Palace; see the map on p. 78. REMARK LIV.

American headquarters how she and the message had been received.

'Such,' he added, 'shall be the fate of all other embassies, unless they come to entreat the King's mercy.'[25]

Montgomery then resorted to another ruse. He addressed the Governor in a fierce and haughty tone, painting in strong colors the weakness of the garrison. With equal intensity be pictured the ardor of the Americans, —'accustomed to success, confident of the righteousness of the cause . . . , inured to danger and fatigue, and so highly incensed' by the firing upon Arnold's flag of truce and by the misrepresentations of their character, that it would not be easy to restrain them until the proper moment. 'Should you persist,' he added, 'in an unwarrantable defence, the consequence be upon your head'; and he wound up with an awful warning to destroy no stores. Fraternal epistles to the merchants, both English and French, were then drafted.

SAMUEL WARD

In these, Montgomery bewailed 'the unhappy necessity,' which forced him to 'carry on Hostilities' against their town because British troops held it; depicted the dreadful prospect now before its inhabitants,—'The City in flames at this severe season'; repelled the slanders against his troops 'progapated . . . by Ministerial Hirelings'; and entreated them to help secure his peaceable admission. A copy of the lurid note to Carleton—probably not really intended for him, but de-

---

[25] § Lindsay: Can. Rev., No. 5, Sept., 1826, p. 89. (Indirect discourse restored to the direct form.)

signed to stimulate the Americans and affright the garrison—was enclosed with each of these, and an old woman smuggled them into Quebec. As the messenger, however, went to prison for a few days before being drummed out of town, Montgomery did not learn what became of his letters, and so he adopted a still more ingenious plan. A flight of Indian arrows fell presently in the streets. Are the Americans mad or are they mocking us? queried some. They were neither. Each arrow had these letters in its head.[26]

Disarming the people of St. Roch at night—by invitation, the royalists believed—the besiegers, under the shelter of the bluff, gradually advanced their outpost within a hundred and fifty yards of the city wall. Behind this shield, Captain Wool of the artillery was ordered to plant five mortars in the suburb, and 'heave bums into the city' as marginal notes to the letters. That he did; and every night the delighted Provincials watched the long flight of some forty or fifty such burning comments across the sky. 'Agreeable to prescription, fifty-five more of the fire pills were given to the Charletonians last evening,' noted the surgeon gleefully in his Journal, adapting the metaphor to his vocation.[27]

To increase the alarm, Arnold's riflemen advanced. 'These men,' said Thacher, 'are remarkable for the accuracy of their aim; striking a mark with great certainty at two hundred yards distance. At a review, a company of them, while on a quick advance, fired their balls into objects of seven inches diameter at the distance of two hundred and fifty yards'; and, as better nerves and muscles

---

[26] § Carleton to Howe, Jan. 12, 1776: Note 24. Id. to Germain, May 14, 1776: Can. Arch., Q, 12, p. 14. Montg. to Carleton, Dec. 6, 1775: Lindsay (Can. Rev., No. 5, Sept., 1826, p. 89); Can. Arch., Q, 12, p. 16; Jos. Smith, Journal; Warren, Am. Revol., I., p. 432. (See p. 80.) Id. to Merchants, Dec. 6, 1775: Can. Arch., Q, 12, p. 18. Caldwell, Letter.

[27] § Ainslie, Journal, Dec. 5, 7. 'Chalmers' Journal, Dec. 9, 11. Senter, Journal, Dec. 9, 11. Arnold letter, Dec. 16, 1775: Conn. Gazette, Jan. 26, 1776. Carleton to Howe, Jan. 12, 1776: Note 24. Caldwell, Letter.

never clothed the human frame, no doubt they did all
their imperfect weapon permitted. Not less daring than
skillful, a number of them climbed into the cupola of the
Intendant's Palace, and fired from that point of vantage
until a British 9-pounder made the place uninhabitable.
Within reach of the 'twisted guns,' no one cared to show
so much as an ear.[28]

Yet none of these was the grand stroke. On the tenth,
men guarding the walls discovered something new in the
blackthorn bushes near the windmill on the Heights, and
fired at it; but the next day it seemed larger instead of
smaller.[29]

It was an American battery planted at the most advantageous point, about seven hundred yards from the town.
No earth for a parapet could be obtained from the frozen
soil. But a party of Canadians cut a great quantity of
fascines; these were made into gabions; the gabions, when
filled with snow and placed in position, were drenched with
water; and in this way a redoubt that fitted well into the
crystalline scenery grew quite rapidly. It was hard work,
piling it up on the shelterless Heights in the bitter night
air. Some of the men, owing to difficulties of transportation, had not received their new clothing yet. A blistering
northeast wind full of lancets cut them to the marrow, and
scarified their faces to a raw, bloody red. One soldier got
lost in a snow-storm, and presently found himself under
the walls with a hole in his thigh. Once, after a rain,
a 'perfect hurricane' set in from the northwest, and in half
an hour the country was glacé with ice. Both of Major
Meigs's feet were frozen at the battery. One night the
working party had to give up, fairly 'beat off' by a snow-

---

[28] § Thacher, Mil. Journal, p. 33 (one suspects a misprint. Rifle experts
assure the author that such a feat, with the arm of that day, was impossible).
Ainslie, Journal, *passim*. 'Chalmers' Journal, Dec. 16.

[29] § Marr, Remarks: Can. Arch., M, 384. Finlay, Journal, Dec. 10. Haskell,
Diary, Dec. 11.

storm ; but, when the fifteenth of December dawned, five
6- and 12-pounders and a howitzer stood in a trim row behind the grey breastwork.[30]

This major menace ready and in full view, Montgomery
wrote Carleton a letter really intended for him, demanding
surrender and 'offering him a safe conduct to embark for
England.' The cannon fired a few rounds, and then Arnold and Aide-de-camp Mac-
pherson put on their blanket
coats, tied a handkerchief or
something like one on a stick,
and set out for the town, preceded by a drummer beating
for a parley.

'We desire to speak with
General Carleton,' announced
Arnold boldly, when under
the wall; and a messenger
carried his words to the Governor.

JOHN LAMB

But Carleton had settled
his line of policy two months before : 'I shall return
no answer, nor enter into any Correspondance with
Rebels,' he had stated, 'not thinking myself at liberty to treat otherwise those who are Traytors to the
King, without His Majesty's express Commands.' Besides, he feared the ideas of the Americans more than he
feared their guns.

'I will not see them,' he replied sternly.

'Will he send some one to receive a letter?' persisted
the envoys.

'Make the best of your way off and take your letter with

[30] § Carleton to Howe, Jan. 12, 1776 : Note 24. Brit. and Am. Journals, Dec.
10-15. Arnold : Note 27. Letter, Dec. 16, 1775 : 4 Force, IV., 290. Caldwell,
Letter. Montg. to Wooster, Dec. 16, 1775 : Sparks MSS., No 52, II., p. 60.
Montg. to R. R. Liv., Dec. 17, 1775 : Liv. Papers, 1775-1777, p. 89. Clothing :
Henry, Journal, p. 94. 'Arnold's' Ord. Book.

you,' answered the officer; 'He will receive nothing from Mr. Montgomery.'

'Mr. Carleton will remember this by and by,' retorted Macpherson, but Arnold and he could only withdraw. Most of the people on the wall 'seemed disposed to listen to terms,' the Aide-de-camp thought; yet some of the 'raw sailors' could hardly be kept from firing.[31]

Then Montgomery began a cannonade in earnest, and the enemy replied with 13-inch shells and 32-pound balls. Before long 'a great pillar of smoke' flew up from the ice-battery, and its fire ceased. A gun had burst, the men on the wall concluded, and probably they were not far from the truth; but after some time the bombardment began again. Torrid enough were the Heights now; and the next day Montgomery admitted that battery and guns had been 'very near destroyed already.' The men suffered not a little; but, as the enemy conceded, they kept at work even 'brisker than before.' In the midst of it, just as a shot had knocked over a gun and wounded a number of soldiers, the General himself appeared.

'This is warm work, sir,' he quietly observed to Lamb.

'It is, indeed, and certainly no place for you, sir,' was the Hotspur answer.

'Why so, Captain?'

'Because there are enough of us here to be killed without the loss of you, which would be irreparable,' replied Lamb.

'Dec. 19 . . . The Enemys Works totally demolished,' recorded an officer on the ramparts; but the Americans

---

31 § 'Chalmers' Journal, Dec. 15. Ainslie and Meigs, Journals, Dec. 15. Haskell, Diary, Dec. 14, 15. Montg. to R. R. Liv., Dec. 16, 1775: Liv. Papers, 1775–1777, p. 81 (REMARK LV.). Id. to Wooster, Dec. 16, 1775: Sparks MSS., No. 52, II., p. 60. Carleton to Howe, Jan. 12, 1776: Pub. Rec. Off., Colon. Corres., Quebec, 12, p. 23. Policy: Id. to [Dartmouth], Oct. 25, 1775 (Pub. Rec. Off., Colon. Corres., Quebec, 11, p. 433). Arnold: Note 27. Macpherson to Read, Dec. 16, 1775: Read, G. Read, p. 115. Lindsay: Can. Rev., No. 5, Sept., 1826, p. 89. Letters, Dec. 16, 1775: 4 Force, IV., 290. To some extent the dialogue is constructive.

clung to the ruins five days longer. Then they gave up.[32]

Where did Montgomery find himself now? The letters to Carleton and the merchants were skillfully designed to warn the citizens against resistance, and to show that in case of surrender no injury need be feared ; but they had accomplished nothing. The mortar battery was intended to make the people rise and open the gates in preference to enduring the horrors of a siege; but the shells were only five and a half inches in diameter, and the townsfolk —who had reckoned on seeing each of them scatter a house or two—soon went about the streets much as usual, laughing at the ' bombettes,' as they called them. The battery on the Heights was expected by many to open a breach; but that also accomplished nothing. The shot had no more effect on the wall, noted a citizen, ' than peas wou'd have against a plank.' Military science might pronounce Quebec weak ; but that was on the supposition of an adequate offence. Thirty-two-pounders could still hold their own against 6- or 12-pounders ; and, to creatures without wings, an unbreached wall thirty feet high was an obstacle, even though it could be seen to the very foot. Everything tried had totally failed. The problem of Quebec remained unsolved, and every bastion seemed to have crooked itself into a stony interrogation-mark.[33]

As Montgomery had understood before he left Montreal, a regular siege was impracticable. Trenches could not be dug in the frozen earth, nor lived in if made ; the subsoil of rock forbade mining ; no one in the American forces had the skill to direct such works ; and the artillery was inadequate. Why not settle down to a blockade, then ?

[32] § 32s, etc.: Montg. to R. R. Liv., Dec. 16, 17, 1775 (Liv. Papers, pp. 81, 89), Finlay's, ' Chalmers ' and Ainslie's Journals, Dec. 15-24. Lamb: Irving; Wash., II., p. 154. Senter, Journal, Dec. 24.

[33] § Ainslie, Journal, Dec. 11, 14 (error for 15). 30 feet, etc.: Id., Feb. 12 ; Verreau (Sanguinet), Invasion, pp. 112, 117.

The troops numbered too few at best, and there was danger that such fatigues and hardships would quite wear them out. Besides, the British cannon-fire had to be considered. Shells and balls had already seasoned the camp of Arnold's men with an excess of pepper. The Colonel was driven from his quarters by them. One night, while Captains Topham and Thayer were sleeping together, a ball passed very neatly through the bed between them. One day, just as Montgomery stepped from his sleigh at the Hospital, a shot carried off the horse's head and smashed the vehicle into ' a thousand pieces.' Under such a cannonade, it was no easy task to keep the cordon close and shut Quebec off from supplies ; and, as more and more heavy guns were mounted on the ramparts, this was bound to grow increasingly difficult.[34]

Above all, a blockade would be very slow, and time was priceless. 'Possession of the town, and that speedily, I hold of the highest consequence,' declared the General as his works flew to pieces. Washington hungered for the powder, arms, blankets, and clothing of the Quebec magazines : ' I do not know where else I can apply,' he wrote Montgomery. The party in Congress that supported the Canada campaign was urgent for the immediate political adhesion of the province. About the middle of November Lynch had exclaimed, ' We wait in a state of the most anxious Suspence for Accounts of the total Reduction of Canada and their accession to our League.' The committee from Philadelphia had just now bidden Montgomery to employ his ' utmost endeavours ' to that end. And further, so long as Quebec remained in British hands, the Canadians could not be expected to recognize Continental money.[35]

---

[34] § Siege, etc.: Montg. to R. R. Liv., Nov. —, 1775 (4 Force, III., 1638). Fire: e. g , Topham and Dearborn, Journals, Dec. 16 ; Thayer, Journal, Dec. 8; Fobes, Narrative, *passim;* Ainslie, Journal, Dec. 8, 24. Vs. blockade : Montg. to Sch., Dec. 18, 1775 (4 Force, IV., 309).

[35] § Vs. blockade : Montg. to Liv., Nov. — (Note 34) Montg. to Sch., Dec. 18,

FROM A LETTER TO GENERAL SCHUYLER NOV. 11, 1775.

Indeed, it seemed very doubtful whether a blockade would be possible. The time of Arnold's men—at least the majority—would expire with the year; they had done their full duty and more; their mission to Canada had ended; they had not been paid even the meagre wages promised; many of their families were suffering; like the rest, they had no country except England; Montgomery himself was thinking still of 'accommodation' with Great Britain; and, if proving that America was in earnest could down Lord North, had they not done enough? Some of the men would no doubt remain, but some would go. Even venturesome Arnold considered two thousand necessary; and the loss of but a few, aside from its moral effect on the rest, on the Canadians, and on the enemy, might easily prove fatal. As for new troops—assuming that in some way they could reach Canada—Schuyler's recruiting officers reported little success. [36]

Resources were likely to be no more plentiful than men. Already Montgomery found himself in want. The demands for specie had not been met. For months past, Congress had been offering soldiers a bounty for bringing their own blankets to camp. What powder Schuyler possessed had been sent down to New York by orders from Philadelphia, and of lead only a trifle was left him. Montgomery received instructions to look about secretly for saltpetre in Canada,—sure sign of a lack farther south; and he was driven to ask whether the catapult and ballista

---

1775: 4 Force, IV., 309. Wash. to Montg., Jan. 12, 1776: ib., 657. (It seems reasonable to suppose that the idea had been conveyed earlier. Indeed, Montg. did not need to be told anything so obvious.) Lynch to Sch., Nov. 11, 1775: Emmet Coll. Com. to Montg., Nov. 30, 1775: Sparks MSS., No. 52. II., p. 68. Canads.: Montg. to Sch., Dec. 18, 1775 (4 Force, IV., 309). Money: Ainslie, Journal, Dec. 30.

[36] § Time out: Campbell, Dec. 31, 1775 (4 Force, IV., 480); Haskell, Diary, Jan. 30, 1776; Montg. to Sch., Dec. 26, 1775 (4 Force, IV., 464). Letter, Feb. 9, 1776 (ib., 706). Pay: Hawley to Gerry, Sept. 11, 1776 (S Adams Papers); Arnold to Wash., Dec. 5, 1775 (4 Force, IV., 190). Accommodation: Montg. to R. R. Liv., Dec. 17, 1775 (Liv. Papers, 1775-1777, p. 89). 2000: Arnold to Montg., Nov. 20, 1775 (Sparks MSS., No. 52, II., p. 31). Recruits: Sch. to Hancock, Dec. 14, 1775 (4 Force, IV., 260).

might not be revived.   Sending any supplies past Lake
Champlain would be extremely difficult for two months.
Schuyler proposed to retire ; the Committee of Congress,
which Montgomery longed to see in Canada, returned
south from Ticonderoga ; and a British armed vessel,
passing up the Hudson, jarred the line of communication.[37]

Successes had made a victory at Quebec look easy and
certain to the public.   Montgomery's presence before the
town seemed a guaranty of its fall.   His promotion to the
grade of major-general had the appearance not only of a
reward given to him but of a pledge given by him.   He
was expected to win.   'In all probability,' announced
Schuyler.   'I have very little doubt,' wrote Knox to
Washington.   'We have reason to expect it,' felt Edmund
Pendleton.   'I flatter myself, that it will be effected,' said
the Commander-in-chief.   Indeed, a report flew with
the wind that already the Americans held the rock,
and Almon published this in his *Remembrancer* at
London.   When Arnold failed, it had been understood
that support was at hand, and the attack would be resumed at once ;   but a failure on Montgomery's part,
especially as British reinforcements must surely arrive in
the spring, would seem very different.   A tremendous
revulsion might come.   The resounding encomiums of
Congress for ' exploits so glorious in their execution, and
so extensive in their consequences ' would perhaps turn to
irony in the public mind, and blast the unlucky general
forever.   This, to be sure, he could ignore, though honor
was the very breath of his heart ;   but the ruin of the

[37] § Montg. to Wooster, Dec. 16, 1775: Sparks MSS., No. 52, II., p. 60.
Specie: Sch. to Hancock, Nov. 18, 1775 (4 Force, III., 1595); Montg. to Sch., Dec.
26, 1775 (4 Force, IV., 464).   Blankets: Sch., Ord. Book, Nov. 19, 1775 (see
Journ. Cong., Nov. 4).   Powder, etc.: Sch. to Hancock, Nov. 27, 1775 (4 Force,
III., 1681).   Saltpetre: Id. to Montg., Nov. 30, 1775 (Am. Antiq. Soc.).   Catapult:
Montg. to R. R. Liv., Dec. 17, 1775 (Liv. Papers, 1775-1777, p. 89).   Retirement:
Wash. to Sch., Dec. 24, 1775 (Wash., Writings (Ford), III., p. 292).   Com., etc.:
Montg. to Sch., Nov. 24, 1775 (4 Force, III., 1694); Id. to R. R. Liv., Dec. 17,
1775 (Liv. Papers, 1775-1777, p. 89); Holmes to Bedel, Dec. 16, 1775 (Saffell,
Records, p. 28).   Vessel: N. Y. Com., Dec. 5, 1775 (4 Force, IV., 186).

Canadians who had espoused his side, the loss of the four-teenth Colony, and the deadening blow at the patriot cause,—here were things that could not be forgotten.[38]

From all sides, these urgencies bore in savagely upon Montgomery. The weight of Canada, the weight of America pressed upon his bosom. January first—the end of his army—stood at the gate ; and every measure to win Quebec had failed.

---

[38] § Promotion: Journ. Cong., Dec. 9, 1775. Sch. to Alb. Com., Nov. 18, 1775: 4 Force, III., 1595. Knox, Dec. 17, 1775: Knox Papers, II., p. 4. Pendleton to Woodford, Dec. 7, 1775: Dreer Coll. Wash. to Sch., Dec. 5, 1775: Writings (Ford), III., p. 267. Almon, Remembrancer, 1776, Part I., p. 134. Hancock to Montg., Nov. 30, 1775: 4 Force, III., 1718. Canads: Montg. to R. R. Liv., Oct. 5, 1775 (Liv. Papers, 1775-1777, p. 51).

XXIV

THE ASSAULT

MORE or less clearly, all the Provincials could see the dead wall now before them, yet they were not ready to give up ; and a certain terrible thought, which had been lurking this long while at the back of the army's mind, began to come forward and assume a definite shape.

Montgomery himself, though disappointed, was not overwhelmed. It was a hope, rather than an expectation, that had failed. No professional military man could suppose that 12-pounders would beat 32-pounders, merely because the charges were rammed home by Sons of Liberty. Shrewd calculation, and not blind confidence, had suggested his measures. There had seemed to be a chance of working upon the Governor by alarming the timid, stimulating the disaffected, or fatiguing the garrison into discontent, and so leading him to surrender in despair or to sally in desperation. Besides, the battery was sure to cost the enemy a great amount of ammunition. Its failure would perhaps give them a sense of security, 'and security dwells next door to destruction,' said the American leader. And, furthermore, it would mask his preparations for what he really intended to do, though reluctantly, should Quebec prove obstinate.[1]

Even before he took leave of Montreal, the General had

---

[1] § Montg. to R. R. Liv., Nov. —, 1775 : 4 Force, III., 1638. Id. to R. R. Liv., Dec. 16, 1775 : Liv. Papers, 1775–1777, p. 81. Id. to R. R. Liv., Dec. 17, 1775 : ib., p. 89. Id. to Wooster, Dec. 16, 1775 : Sparks MSS., No. 52, II., p. 60. Id. to Sch., Dec. 5, 18, 1775 : 4 Force, IV., 188, 309. Campbell to Wooster, Dec. 31, 1775 : 4 Force, IV., 480.

studied that prospect and read its logic. An escalade, an assault over unbroken walls, was what it suggested. ' To this we must come at last,' he wrote a near relative ; ' If my force be small, Carleton's is not great. The extensiveness of his work, which, in case of investment, would favour him, will in the other case favour us. Masters of our secret, we may select a particular time and place for attack ; and to repel this, the garrison must be prepared at all times and places.' The motley and undisciplined forces within the walls, most of them living amid the soft influences of home life, seemed to lack the iron hardness for deadly cut and thrust ; and some of them, well-wishers to the patriot cause, might fraternize—or at least might falter—when eye to eye with friendly Americans. Fortune, too, marched on the Provincial side. ' "Audaces Fortuna juvat " is almost an axiom,' said Montgomery ; and the career of every noted soldier seemed a demonstration of the principle. ' Wolfe's success was a lucky hit, or rather a series of such hits,' he reflected ; and what leader could have better ground to count upon the fickle goddess than himself? Nor was this a mere unreasoning appeal to luck, a gambler's recklessness. Great captains have taken exceptional risks because they have felt in themselves the power to seize upon unexpected chances. Men of that kind have had a right to scorn perils that should appall

JOHN MACPHERSON

weaker minds, and have often won a victory where a defeat seemed probable. Above all, there was a mightier argument than probabilities of success : it simply must be tried. To assault might be a dreadful risk, but not to assault was a dreadful certainty.[2]

Without loss of time, the General began to plant his ideas in the minds of the officers, one by one ; and they promptly took root there. ' If the insulting foe does not surrender shortly,' one of Arnold's detachment wrote home within twenty-four hours after returning to Quebec, ' I believe it is the general's intention to carry the town by storm.' If shot and shell cannot remove the ' prejudices ' of the Quebeckers, announced Lieutenant Copp the next day, 'we are determined to storm. . . . The more Danger, the more Glory.' ' Getting in readiness to storm the city,' noted Haskell on the twelfth. Montgomery's calm and attested courage made the peril seem contemptible. ' To die with such a man is to die with a hero indeed!' exclaimed an officer.[3]

' But the approbation of the whole army was necessary,' as private Stocking well said ; and the General took care—especially as enthusiasm had been checked a little by the strictness of his discipline—to ensure the cordial support of rank and file. When the second summons was insultingly rejected, on December fifteenth, a proclamation rang like a trumpet through the camp, as if in reply. ' The General having in vain offered the most favorable Terms of accommodation to the Governor and having taken every possible step to prevail on the Inhabitants to desist from seconding him in his wild Scheme of Defence,' nothing remained ' but to pursue vigorous Measures for the speedy Reduction ' of the last Ministerial stronghold. ' The Troops flushed with continual Success confident of the Justice of their Cause and relying on that Providence which has

---

[2] § Montg. to R. R. Liv., Nov. —, 1775 : 4 Force, III., 1638. Id. to R. R. Liv. Dec. 17, 1775 : Liv. Papers, 1775–1777, p. 89. Ramsay, Am. Rev., I., p. 241.

[3] § Stocking, Journal, Dec. 5 (most of this was evidently written later). Letter, Dec. 6, 1775 : Henry, Journal, p. 189. Copp, Dec. 7, 1775 : In Tryon's of Jan. 5, 1776 (Pub. Rec. Off., Am. and W. I , Vol. 186, p. 237). Humphrey, Journal. Officer, Dec. 7, 1775 : Pub. Rec. Off., Am. and W. I., Vol. 186, p. 261.

uniformly protected them,' proclaimed their leader, 'will advance with alacrity to the Attack of works incapable of being defended by the wretched Garrison posted behind them. . . . A vigorous and spirited Attack must be attended with Success ' ; and, by the rule of war, the victors shall have the effects of those active in fighting against them, 'misleading the inhabitants and distressing the Friends of Liberty': a one-hundredth part of the whole to be reserved, however, for the soldiers particularly distinguished in the contest. Does Carleton throw down the mailed glove? Then let it be war.[4]

Yet the die had not really been cast. Montgomery was only feeling the edge of his blade ; and, though a council of field-officers met that evening, no decision to storm was reached. The General said that he was not 'certain whether or no the troops [would] relish this mode of proceeding '; and, should they not, he would by no means 'press it upon them, well knowing the impossibility of making troops act with the necessary vigour on such an occasion, if their minds are possessed with imaginary terrors.' But each officer commanding a regiment received orders, the next day, to hand in a list of all who engaged 'to distinguish themselves by activity and bravery in the attack '; and, after this experiment, he felt able to describe the troops as ' well inclined to an escalade.' [5]

Another council met that night. Montgomery underestimated the strength of the city. The sixty or seventy Fusiliers were the only men he would call troops. In all, he reckoned on but few more than twelve hundred ; and

[4] § Stocking, Journal, Dec. 5. Proclamation : Can. Arch., Q, 12, p. 20, confirmed by 'Arnold's ' Ord. Book, Dec. 15. Some Canadians feel quite bitter still about the intention to confiscate certain private property ; but, as Risley (Law of War, p. 141) says, ' Private property has always been, and always must be, liable to seizure as "booty" on the field of battle, or when a town which refuses to capitulate is carried by assault.'

[5] § Council, etc., Dec. 15: Orders (Can. Arch., Q, 12, p. 20); ' Arnold's ' Ord. Book, Dec. 15, 16 ; Van Wagenen, Dec. 16, 1775 (4 Force, IV., 290). Montg. to Wooster, Dec. 16, 1775: Sparks MSS., No. 52, II., p. 60. Montg. to R. R. Liv., Dec. 17, 1775: Note 1.

he looked upon the Governor as resisting only in desperation, wishing perhaps 'to be covered by death from
the disgrace and shame' of his political and military non-
success. Regarding his own strength,
or rather his own weakness, the General had no illusion. 'Little more than
800 men fit for duty' could be mustered for the assault, he knew, though
some declared that they numbered
fifteen hundred.[6]

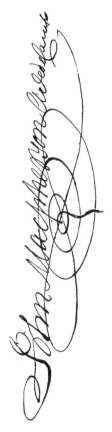

Nor were those in command of the
Yorkers wholly satisfactory, for it had
been necessary to 'encourage all officers to stay who had influence enough
to engage men,' or could be of service
in any other direction. Next the General in importance among them flour-
ished a pictorial fraud, the Deputy
Quartermaster-General. An o v e r-
grown spaniel that had wriggled into
the company and more or less into the
fur of mastiffs, Donald Campbell had
a very military air, no doubt. Most
of such brains as fell to him—and
they were ample in quantity—nature had planted in his back, and
nothing had been able to entice them
very far into his cranium : but he
possessed the heartiness of good round
oaths and the culture of messroom
stories. His characterless mind, corky
enough to serve as a life-preserver, had floated him along

[6] § Council, Dec. 16: Dearborn and Humphrey, Journals ; Armstrong,
Montg., p. 212 ; Arnold, letter, Dec. 16, 1775 (Conn. Gazette, Jan. 26, 1776),
Montg. to R. R. Liv., Dec. 16, 17: Note 1. Id. to Wooster, Dec. 16, 1775: Sparks
MSS., No. 52, II., p. 60. Arnold (letter, Dec. 16) reckoned the garrison at 1500.

on the easy waves of rudderless good-fellowship, and lu had so far helped by saving him from a fatal rock. A fawner to the very turn of his fat shanks, he doubtless knew how to make rebukes more terrible to subordinates and compliments more palatable to superiors by a certain barracks bluntness, cultivated for the purpose; while his large body filled out a uniform so plumply, and his handsome head brandished a gold-laced hat so convincingly, that few could doubt he was a man. Undeniably, he possessed the energy and readiness of a hearty digestion, and, as a graduate from the regular British service, he had proved of great assistance in licking the untutored Colonial army into military shape; but the qualities of a real soldier he lacked.[7]

Lieutenant-Colonel Zedtwitz, who figured next, was destined for a bad end, but did not intend it should be a bullet. Captain Cheeseman, on the other hand, deserved to march shoulder to shoulder with Montgomery; Aide-de-camp Macpherson had every quality of head and heart that a young hero need possess; and little Burr, transferred from Arnold's vicinity to Montgomery's as a second aide, showed no lack of intelligence and spirit. There was fine as well as coarse material—indeed, the very finest sort—among the Yorkers, as well as in Arnold's division; and Montgomery and his officers, weighing, as best they could, both resources and hazards, now made the momentous choice: they decided to storm Quebec.[8]

' Which if resolved upon,' Dearborn had confided to his Journal, ' I hope will be undertaken with a proper

---

nearly 1000 of them disaffected. 1500 (' our army then present '): J. Liv. to ———, [Feb., 1776] (Am. Hist. Rec., III., 1874, p. 181).

[7] § Montg. to R. R. Liv., Dec. 17, 1775: Note 1. The sketch of Campbell is based upon his conduct, his letters and statement (Note 22), letter of Commrs. of Cong., May 10, 1776 (Sparks, Corr. I., p. 512), his Memorial (Cont. Cong. Papers, No. 41, II., p. 363), Caldwell's Letter, and Henry's Journal, p. 128. REMARK LXVII.

[8] § Zedtwitz: see Chap. XIV., Note 26. Burr: ' Arnold's ' Ord. Book, Dec. 12, 1775; Arnold to Wooster, Dec. 31, 1775: Sparks MSS., No. 52, II., p. 33. For Cheeseman and Macpherson see the text below.

sense of the Nature & Importance of such an attack, & vigorously Executed'; and this wise hope was now in the way of fulfillment. 'I propose the first strong north-wester,' wrote the General, 'to make two attacks by night—one with about a third of the troops on the lower Town having first set fire to some houses which will in all probability communicate their flames to the stockade lately erected on the rock near St. Roque [Roch], the other upon Cape Diamond bastion by escalade'; and the preparations for these attacks were soon 'ripening fast.' Arms and ammunition underwent a careful scrutiny; spears, hatchets, and ladders were provided. Mont-gomery met Arnold's officers 'to compose some matters, which were happily settled,' as Meigs believed; and at sunset, on the twenty-fifth, at a review of the Kennebec detachment, he addressed the men in a brief but 'very sensible, Spirit'd manner,' as his auditors agreed. The necessity and good prospects of the attack were pointed out. 'Nothing is wanting to ensure victory,' he added, 'but the valor already so triumphantly displayed under the most unparalleled sufferings; and, if we succeed, we shall rescue a province from the British yoke, win it for our country, and obtain for ourselves immortal honor.' 'Our heroic general seemed resolved on victory or death,' recorded one soldier. We were 'enraptured,' said an-other. Some of the reflective felt that the plan might be 'rash'; but all misgivings were swept away, and with a cheer the soldiers cried, 'Whatever your Excellency is pleased to command, we are ready to obey.'[9]

It was hard to believe that anything so terrible as the storming of a fortress lay in prospect. The hush of snow had fallen. The stillness of dead winter had come. The

---

[9] § Dearborn, Journal, Dec. 15, 16, 22, 25. Montg. to Wooster, Dec. 16, 1775: Sparks MSS., No. 52, II., p. 60. Letter, Dec. 16, 1775: 4 Force, IV., 290. 'Arnold's' Ord. Book, Dec. 16–25. Meigs, Journal, Dec. 23. Morison, Journal: Penna. Mag., 1890, p. 435. Stocking, Journal (under Dec. 5). Doubtless Montg. ad-dressed the Yorkers in a similar strain. REMARK LVI.

thousand smokes of the thousand hearths in Quebec rose each morning into the keen air, sometimes—like a forest of stalagmites—appearing to prop the dense blue sky, and sometimes dropping and melting into a flood of grey that rolled torpidly over the housetops, and—like an aërial glacier—dripped slowly and heavily down the precipice. Little by little each morning, a disk of brass pushed up from somewhere toward the east, slid imperceptibly along the leaden horizon, and sank amid pale glories in the upper St. Lawrence. On clear nights the quiet stars appeared to come close, blinking their lovely eyes as if to watch the better over the sleeping camp ; and now and then a broad illumination, splendid yet restful, played across the northern heavens. Linked together by a close comradeship which supplied the place of every luxury and almost every comfort, the men passed many contented and even jovial hours. For variety, they visited in the homes of the sociable Canadians ; and on Sunday they listened to Chaplain Spring at the Hospital church, staring in amazement the while at its rich decorations of 'Carved & guilt work,' as Dearborn's Journal—with no thought of punning—described it. Strife, rage, and battle often began to seem remote, impossible, absurd ; but soon the boom of a cannon or the spiteful crack of a rifle announced that blood was dyeing the white drifts, and gave notice that before long a great flood of crimson was to flow.

Affairs in town had settled down, meanwhile, into a routine of subdued excitement. The garrison felt annoyed by the occasional rifle-balls and 'bombettes,' and answered by knocking off the chimneys of the American guard-house under the bluff in St. Roch, and pelting every spot where an enemy appeared to lurk. The ditch was kept clear of snow. Lanterns were swung out from the wall on poles, when the moon did not shine. Everything like a signal was watched and studied. The bells hung in silence yet expectantly, ready to sound an alarm. An attack seemed likely, but no certainty could be felt ; for, if anybody made his way into town, he ran the chance of being taken for a spy and of finding the news he brought discredited. One night, however, the sentry at Palace Gate saw the enemy actually coming—thousands of them, he swore it — seven deep. The drums beat to arms. The cathedral bell clanged a tocsin. 'Every man ran arm'd to his post, & there the Garrison remain'd waiting the attack but no enemy appear'd.' [10]

At length Caldwell's clerk, whom the Americans had captured, got away and brought the definite information that an assault was to be made. Five hundred scaling ladders were ready; and every 'rebel,' thus it went about the city, had been promised £200 in plunder. It had lately been reported in town that Montgomery's troops were beginning to scatter, and the clerk's news gave the citizens a shock. [11]

For many good reasons it was hard to believe him. The piles of snow and ice had made even the weakest of the defences 'exceedingly strong,' said a Quebecker. 'Can these men pretend,' exclaimed Ainslie ; 'Can these men pretend that there is a possibility of approaching our walls loaden with ladders, sinking to the middle every step in snow !' 'No man after having been exposed to the air but ten minutes,' he wrote one day, 'cou'd handle his arms to do execution.' 'This is no wall-scaling weather,' said his diary at another time ; 'the night was clear &

10 § The British Journals ; Thompson in LeMoine, Quebec P. and P., pp. 197–199 ; Verreau (Sanguinet), Invasion, p. 116 ; Senter's, Topham's, Dearborn's and other American Journals ; Ursul. de Québec, III., p. 132.

11 § Ainslie, Journal, Dec. 20, 22, 23. 'Chalmers' Journal, Dec. 21.

inconceivably cold—it is employment enough to preserve ones nose. The wind is at N W peircingly keen.' Yet the people hardly felt satisfied. The conquest of the wilderness and the passing of the St. Lawrence could not be forgotten. A man who called himself a deserter came in, and reported that Montgomery's troops numbered some two thousand. Three more 9-pounders from the *Lizard* were planted on the flank of each bastion, and opened their mouths for grape and canister. Carleton began to pass his nights usually at the Récollet

BREBOEUF

monastery, the general rendezvous of the garrison; while a part of the troops lay there in their clothes with their arms beside them, and the rest stood on guard. If thoughts of Wolfe inspired the besiegers, Frontenac, buried in the Récollet church, Montcalm, sleeping under the chapel of the Ursuline Convent in a grave dug by an exploding shell, and Brebœuf, a silver bust of whom, enshrining his skull, stood in the Hôtel Dieu :—these exhorted the garrison. What was more tangible, all steadied their courage by the calm lines

of the Governor's face, and when he declared that he would
never grace a rebel triumph, braced themselves for solid
blows. Evidently Greek was to meet Greek, whenever the
struggle should come.[12]

But would it come? A new foe, more terrible than
Fusiliers or Highlanders now attacked the besiegers,
pierced their lines, penetrated the camps, and struck them
down in their very beds. It was the small-pox, always
lurking about Quebec. On the morning of December
twentieth, Haskell awoke to find himself and his bed-fellow
' broke out ' ; and, by the next day, the dreadful epidemic
was rapidly spreading in the army. But the Americans
met even this enemy with a bold front. The sick, as fast
as discovered, were taken several miles away ; everything
possible was done to prevent contagion, and the ravages of
the pestilence — as well as the pleurisy, pneumonia, and
other ' very prevalent ' diseases—were partially checked.[13]

Soon, however, another enemy threatened ruin. There
had been serious friction in Arnold's detachment. Captain
Hanchet, apparently much offended somewhere on the
wilderness march, had twice refused to obey orders after
reaching the St. Lawrence, ' and thereby,' said Montgomery, ' given room for harsh language ' from Arnold, which
aggravated the trouble. Two of the other captains appeared to side with him. Major Brown, full of the old
Ticonderoga hostility, co-operated. All of these proposed
that a separate corps should be formed of the three companies, with Brown for its commander ; and on that basis
the captains promised to remain after the expiration of
their time. Montgomery, however, could not countenance
any such insubordination, and the malcontents then showed

---

[12] § The British Journals, *passim*. Carleton: Ainslie, Journal, May 1,
1776. Frontenac, etc.: LeMoine, Maple Leaves, 1894 ; Parkman, Montcalm,
II., p. 309 ; Id., Jesuits, p. 391.

[13] § Small-pox, etc.: Ainslie, Journal, Dec. 9 ; Haskell, Diary, Dec. 20–22 ;
Senter, Journal, Dec. 23 ; Henry, Journal, p. 107.

themselves 'very averse' to the assault. 'I shall not compel you,' said the General; 'I want no persons with me who go reluctantly'; and for a time this new difficulty seemed to bar his way. Dr. Senter offered to lead one of the companies; but he would be needed, unfortunately, at the Hospital. Finally, however, Montgomery's address rode the wave, and harmony returned.'[14]

The Americans were now 'under orders at a moment's warning for an attack,' and Wednesday evening, the twenty-seventh, which was stormy, seemed the fitting time. About midnight, the expected signal passed through the camps. The men turned out. A sprig of hemlock was placed in the front of every cap, to distinguish friend from foe. Smith, Hendricks, Topham, and Thayer moved off toward the Plains to help Montgomery assault at Cape Diamond, while the rest of Arnold's force began their march against the Lower Town. But suddenly the sky cleared, and the attempt had to be given up. With the 'most sensible pleasure' Montgomery saw the good disposition of the troops, he told them; and 'it was with the greatest reluctance he found himself called upon by his duty to repress their ardor'; but he felt that he would be 'answerable for the loss of those brave men whose lives might be saved by waiting for a more favorable opportunity.' No doubt he felt also that his chance of succeeding would be better in a storm, though by a delay he risked even the chance of trying.[15]

Then another stroke fell. Sergeant Singleton, and perhaps other deserters, carried into Quebec the plan of attack, and soon the movements of the garrison showed that steps

---

[14] § Smith, Arnold's March, p. 416. Thayer, Journal, Dec. 2, 7. Montg. to Sch., Dec. 26, 1775: 4 Force, IV., 464. Id. to ———, Dec. 26, 1775: Dunlap, New Neth., II., p. 24. Senter, Journal, Dec. 27. Campbell to ———, Mar. 28, 1776: Liv. Papers, 1775-1777, p. 145.

[15] § Campbell: Note 14. 'Arnold's' Ord. Book, Dec. 21, 28. Journals of Thayer, Humphrey, Dearborn, et al., Dec. 27, 28.

to frustrate it had been taken. ' Masters of our secret,'
Montgomery had said. That was the condition of success ;
and the Americans were masters of their secret no longer.
Well had the General prophesied, ' Fortune often baffles
the sanguine expectations of poor mortals.' His task now
was not to make bricks without straw, but bricks without
clay. The hand of the New Year was on his latch, and it
came to break up his army and scatter the hopes of the
Colonies. Anticipating their near release, men had already
begun to steal away. ' His situation,' wrote a gentleman
of the army afterward, ' not only justified [an attack], but
made it a matter of indispensable duty ' ; yet here he stood
with not even a plan left him. What barest possibility of
success remained ? [16]

Well, the enemy had learned that while a feint would be
made upon the Lower Town, the real attack would strike
the bastion at Cape Diamond ; and the weight of the assault
might be shifted from the second to the first. Montgomery well understood that the Lower Town, instead of
being Carleton's weak point, had been specially guarded.
Houses bad been torn down, windows planked up, barricades erected, cannon planted. The road to the Upper
Town had been blocked and armed with cannon at every
turn ; and, with the paving-stones alone, the garrison could
slaughter an army there. At least one life had been lost
in brave attempts to reconnoitre these defences, and something could certainly be made out from the opposite shore.
Thayer, in particular, studied them. Doubtless Montgomery saw, then, as Wolfe had seen, that the Upper Town
could not be conquered from the Lower. But it seemed
very likely that, as most of the wealth of Quebec lay be-

---

[16] § Henry, Journal, p. 105. Arnold to Wooster, Dec. 31, 1775: Sparks
MSS., No. 52, II., p. 33. Letter, Feb. 9, 1776 : 4 Force, IV., p. 706. Movements:
Journ. Cong., Jan. 24, 1776. Fortune: Montg. to Sch., Dec. 5, 1775 (4 Force, IV.,
188). To break up army: see Chap. XXIII., Note 36 ; also Wash. to Hancock,
Feb. 9, 1776: Writings (Ford), III., p. 406. Desertion: Macpherson, Order to
Langlois, Dec. 30, 1775 (Can. Arch., B, 184, 1, p. 19).

low the bluff, if the Americans could get possession there, Carleton would be forced by the people to surrender in order to prevent the destruction of their property. At all events, a stroke like that would reassure the Canadians, and probably hold the American army together. So Brown's handful of men were ordered to make a lively feint at Cape Diamond bastion, and Colonel Livingston, with his Canadians, to do the same near St. John's Gate. Possibly one or two of the gates could be set on fire. Meanwhile Arnold, with most of his own men and a part of Lamb's artillery, would pass down the St. Charles, round the turn, and assault one end of the Lower Town ; and Montgomery, with his Yorkers, would march into the lion's mouth below Cape Diamond, and attack the other end. It was a hard chance, but the only one; and even that hung upon the favor of the weathercock.[17]

Thursday, the twenty-eighth, was ' clear & mild '; Friday, ' Clear, fine weather ' ; Saturday, the last day of the year but one, '.Fine Weather & clear.' But the wind blew up the river now. By afternoon it brought clouds, and soon a cold, blustering snow-storm began. At a quarter past four o'clock, when the sun was supposed to be setting, one could hardly see. Favored at last, thought Montgomery. It was the night of all nights to assault Quebec,—a night when Fortune could keep a tryst without fear of detection. Dark ? No ; black,—black as the bore of a loaded rifle. The tempest actually raged. The ' thick small Snow ' whirled furiously and drifted high. The hail seemed to hiss, as it cut the air. With

---

[17] § Guarded: Montg. to Wooster, Dec. 16, 1775 (Sparks MSS., No. 52, II., p. 60). Defences (more will be shown later): Caldwell, Letter ; Thompson in LeMoine, Quebec P. and P., p. 196; Alsopp, Petition and Témoignage (Can. Arch., separate) ; Maclean, Certificate (Can. Arch., M, 116, p. 23); Marr, Report, July 1, 1778 (Can. Arch., B, 154, p. 6); Lindsay, Can. Rev., No. 5, Sept., 1826, p. 89 ; Henry, Journal, pp. 171, 172. Life: 'Chalmers' Journal, Dec. 24. Thayer, Journal, Dec. 31. Wolfe to Pitt, Sept. 2, 1759: Can. Arch., Report, 1898, p. 4. Reasons: Henry, Journal, p. 174 ; Stocking, Journal, Dec. 5; Antill (Davis, Burr, p. 70) ; Price to Sch., Jan. 5, 1776 (4 Force, IV., 668). For the plan see Note 22. REMARK LVII.

a strange tug at the heart, the Americans realized that their hour had come [18]

Though heroes, they were men. The beaver blanket on Montgomery's couch told him of the wife whose loving thoughtfulness had sent it; and, while he waited, his mind paid a little visit at the home for which he sighed. Major Meigs no doubt wrote a short letter to Mrs. Meigs, for that had been rather a constant employment of his lately. Rough Morgan agonized inwardly with his awful fear of death,—an inheritance, perhaps, from a renounced but unescapable ancestry. Macpherson, now only in his twenty-first year, thought of his father's home—'the most elegant seat in Pennsylvania,' John Adams called it—his grey-haired mother, and his pretty sisters. Ward could not forget the 'dear Girls,' to whom he had written not long before, and doubtless read once again the letter from 'Debby' that had made the wilderness campaign with him. And Arnold, however tumultuous, must have had a thought or two of motherless little Benedict at New Haven, teasing Aunt Hannah for something more about papa.[19]

But, though men, they were heroes also. The General perhaps recalled his father-in-law's parting words, 'Take care of your life!' and his own reply, 'Of my honor, you would say, Sir.' Morgan gathered his tremendous powers for the first of his many famous battles. Arnold lived over again the bold and triumphant rush at old Ticonderoga. Thayer meditated on 'Liberty, that Dearest of names, and property, the best of Charters,[which] gave an additional desire to extirpate the malignant root of Arbitrary power.' 'A man that enlists into this service

---

[18] Weather: the Journals, particularly Ainslie's and ' Chalmer's.'

[19] § Montg. to Mrs. M., Dec. 5, 1775: L. L. H., Biog. Notes, p. 16. Meigs, Journal, *passim*. Morgan: So. Lit. Messenger, Sept., 1854, p. 563. Macpherson: LeMoine, Quebec P. and P., p. 208. J. Adams, Works, II., p. 428. Ward to [sisters]: Sparks MSS., No. 25, p. 52. I. N. Arnold, B. Arnold, p. 47.

should not be afraid of dying,' reflected Topham. Ward thought of the letter from his noble father : ' You will give me the highest satisfaction by devoting your life, while Heaven graciously continues it, to the public service ' ; and of what he himself had written the dear girls : ' The wise men say that life is a journey, and seeing we must go through with it, and seeing 't is the *end* we ought to look at, why should we be troubled at any perverse accidents on the way.' Macpherson, who had wished ' the roughs as well as the smooths of a soldiers life,' calmly sealed a letter to his father—' the last this hand will ever write you'—saying, ' I experience no reluctance in this cause, to venture a life which I consider is only lent to be used when my country demands it.' And Cheeseman, dressing with more than his usual care, quietly put five pieces of gold into his pocket : ' That,' he said, ' will be enough to bury me with decency.'[20]

Soon after midnight, however, it looked like another disappointment ; for the storm showed signs of breaking,

FAÇADE OF CASTLE ST. LOUIS, ERECTED IN 1698

as it had broken on Wednesday night. To and fro across his room at Holland House paced the anxious leader, halting now and then to look from the window ; and finally, despairing of the sword, he caught at the only straw he could see : to make a last demand for surrender, while he still had an army before the walls. ' Let me once more entreat you,' so he worded a letter to the Gover-

20 § Montg.: L. L. H., Biog. Notes, p. 5. Thayer, Journal, Dec. 30. Topham, Journal, Dec. 28. Gammell, Ward, p. 338 ; Ward to [sisters]: Note 19. Macpherson to Read, Dec. 16, 1775: W. T. Read, G. Read, p. 115 ; Id. to his father, Dec. 30, 1775: Hist. Mag., Jan., 1861, p. 19, and LeMoine, Quebec, P. and P., p. 208. Cheeseman: Letter, Feb. 9, 1776 (4 Force, IV., 706).

nor; 'Let me once more entreat you to have compassion on the unfortunate Inhabitants of Quebec. . . . Embrace the opportunity I offer you of retiring in a manner suitable to your rank—you shall not be a Prisoner—You shall have a safe Conduct to New York or wheresoever else you may chuse—the Lieutenant Governor shall have the same Indulgence. I engage in the most solemn manner for the security of the Lives and Properties of the Citizens, our dispute is not with them—we bear them no malice. . . .' But the storm grew furious again, and the letter was never sent.[21]

About half-past four or five o'clock in the morning, Malcolm Fraser, Captain of the Main Guard in Quebec, rushed down St. Louis Street, crying like a tocsin: 'Turn out! turn out! turn out!' and the city awoke with a start and a cry. Two rockets had gone up from the foot of Cape Diamond bastion; firing had begun there; men were seen creeping toward the walls. Out rang the great bell of the cathedral. One by one, but all quickly, the other bells took up the tale. The bells of the Jesuit college and the Récollet monastery pealed and clamored. The gentle prayer-bell of the Ursulines joined in the turmoil, while the sisters fell on their knees in the dark chambers. The nuns of the Hôtel Dieu, praying in the vaults, felt the jar and heard the dull clang of their own bell swinging furiously; and far away, in the Lower Town, Our Lady of Victory re-echoed the cry for help.[22]

---

[21] § Senter, Journal, Dec. 31. Montg. to Carleton: see REMARK LVIII.

[22] § Principal sources of the account of the assault (when the place where the source may be found is not indicated below, see the name in the List of Sources at the end of Vol. I.): The American Journals of Dearborn, Haskell, Henry, Humphrey, Meigs, Melvin, Morison (Penna. Mag., 1890, p. 435), Nichols, Porterfield, 'Provincials,' Senter, Stocking, Thayer, Tolman, and Topham (see REMARK XXXI.); the recollections of Fobes and Nichols ; Heath's Journal, reflected in Marshall's Life of Washington ; Morgan's autobiog. (Hist. Mag., June, 1871, p. 379); Arnold's letters of Dec. 31, 1775 (Sparks MSS., No. 52, II., p. 33), Jan. 2 (4 Force, IV., 670), Jan. 6 (ib., 589), and Jan. 14, 1776 (ib., 674); Campbell's letters of Dec. 31, 1775 (ib., 480), and Mar. 28, 1776 (Liv. Papers, 1775–1777, p. 145), and statement (Lib. Cong., U. S. Rev. MSS., VII.); J. Liv. to cousin, Jan. 25, 1819 (Bancroft Coll., separate); Ritzema's Journal and letter of Jan. 3, 1776 (4 Force, IV., 1113); anonymous letters, 4 Force, IV., 582, 705, 706, 707 ; letter from Montreal, Jan. 8, 1776, in Tryon's of Feb. 8, 1776 (Pub. Rec. Off., Am. and W. I., Vol. 186, p. 309); Wooster to Warner, Jan. 6, 1776 (ib., p. 313); Account

The dogs barked madly. Cannon began to thunder. A storm of shells came in from the American mortars in St. Roch, and the city walls quivered with the retort. Fireballs flared and sputtered at the angles of the bastions. Drums beat wildly up and down the streets in the dim glow of lanterns and the smoky flare of torches. Officers roared their orders. Citizens rushed hither and thither to their posts. Boys and old men of seventy shouldered guns. Squads of sailors, artisans, and Emigrants, in green coats faced with scarlet; squads of the Fusiliers, in red with facings of blue ; squads of militia, in green coats, buff breeches, and buff waistcoats, met, stared threateningly at one another in the dim light, and then hurried on.[23] Children woke up and held their breath, too frightened to cry. Even at the General Hospital, the nuns were sure that a 'fatal' hour had come, for the town blazed,

---

pub. by Cont. Cong. (Journal, Jan. 24, 1776 ; 4 Force, IV., 1651); the British, Canadian Journals (see REMARK XLV.); Carleton to Howe, Jan. 12, 1776 (Pub-Rec. Off., Colon. Corres., Quebec, 12, p. 23); Caldwell, Letter ; Maclean's letters. May 21 (Can. Arch., M, 317, p. 330), and 25 (Can. Arch., Q, 12, p. 69), 1776 ; Sanguinet and Badeaux in Verreau, Invasion pp. 118, 182 ; Lindsay's account (Can. Rev., No. 5, Sept., 1826, p. 89); Barnfair's letter (Middlesex Journal, June 22, 1776, reprinted in Hist. Mag., Oct., 1869); British return of prisoners (Can. Arch., Q, 12, p. 37); American lists of prisoners in Journals of ' Ware ' (i. e. Tolman) and Nichols ; Mgr. de St. Vallier, Part II., Chap. IV.; Ursul. de-Québec, III.; pp. 131, 132, 133 ; MS. Records of Hôtel Dieu ; Anburey, Travels, I., pp. 58–62 ; Silliman, Tour, pp. 308–317 ; Mass. Hist. Soc. Coll., I. (1792), p. 111 ; Thompson in Anderson, Siege and Blockade, p. 63. The narratives to be found in the newspapers of the day seem to have been based upon one or more of the sources mentioned above (e. g., N. Y. Packet, Feb. 1, 1776 ; Conn. Gazette, Feb. 2 and Mar. 15, 1776 ; Essex Journal, Feb. 9, 1776 ; N. H. Packet, Feb. 9, 1776). Graham had special information to use in writing his Life of Morgan. A few other items might be mentioned, but they add nothing significant. Several more or less careful accounts have been compiled (e. g., Cullum, Sketch ; Dawson, Battles; Arnold, Arnold ; LeMoine, Quebec P. and P.; Garneau, Canada ; Anderson, Siege and Blockade) ; but none of them has been based upon a complete study of the sources. The author has carefully and repeatedly inspected the ground, gleaned information from local antiquarians, and made use of all the available maps and views of that period (e. g., Marr, MS. Plan of Quebec ; Bartlett and Welford, Atlas of Battles ; Faden, Quebec, 1776 ; Habermann, Lower Quebec ; Holland, Plan ; Leizelt, Upper Quebec, 1765; Sayer and Bennett's maps ; Smyth, Quebec [1759]; Duberger, Model, about 1800). All the accessible works relating to Quebec archæology have been studied, particularly Doughty's and LeMoine's; and both these gentle men have kindly given additional information. For the author's method of using the sources, see REMARK LIX.

23 Lindsay, Can. Rev., No. 5, Sept., 1826, p. 89 ; London letter in Conn. Gazette, Oct. 27, 1775 ; Ainslie, Ord. Book, Nov. 24, 1775. Apparently Carleton changed the uniform of Maclean's corps to secure ' Consistence ' (p. 97). The evidence about the uniforms at this time is not entirely satisfactory.

and the thunder of its cannon shook their stone walls;
and in fear and trembling they knelt for the Communion.
So fiercely blew the gale, that only three miles to one
side nothing could be heard, though much was seen; but
a frightful din, whirling and writhing in the tempest,
swept far up the St. Lawrence. The city was one ring of
fire, one crater of tumult; yet intelligence controlled the
uproar, and, in the midst of it all, Governor Carleton, calm,

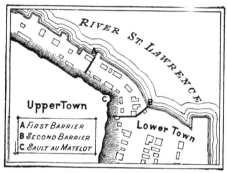

A SKETCH PLAN (APPROXIMATELY CORRECT) OF
THE LOWER BARRICADES

alert, fearless, passed down the steps of the Castle, and
walked across to the Récollet monastery, the place of
assembling.

For a time the firing raged all along the bastions and
beyond the polygon above Charles River; but in a little
while the attack seemed to be dying out. An attempt to
burn Palace Gate came to nothing, and the similar attempt
at St. John's Gate flashed in the pan. Livingston's Canadians were soon scampering for shelter. Brown's men
kept up a rattling fire below Cape Diamond bastion, but
made no serious move toward assault. What did it mean?
The answer came from some frightened school-boys, rushing up from the Lower Town, and shouting at the top of

their voices that Americans had got in there. What ? Yes, had got in, they insisted. Carleton sent Maclean to investigate. He was soon back. 'By God, sir, it 's true ! They 're there,' he burst out.[24]

Two-o'clock-in-the-morning courage is rare, says a high authority ; but at two o'clock the Americans had paraded. Arnold's men gathered in St. Roch, and, when the signal-rockets went up, they set out on a run along the fringe of shore below the bluff to reach their point of attack. In all, there were probably about six hundred, including a few Canadians and Indians.[25] No 'cannon fever' raged among them. Every man had freely volunteered for the assault, and every heart beat full and high.

First came Arnold with Captain Oswald and the forlorn hope of twenty-five or thirty. Lamb, with a brass 6-pounder on a sled, went next ; and Morgan, leading the van of the main body, followed. For a space, the bluff sheltered them. Holding their heads low against the storm, and covering the locks of their guns with handkerchiefs or the edges of their coats, the men dashed forward in Indian file ; and the forlorn hope, a hundred yards or so in advance, pushed swiftly on—silent and unperceived, like a rapier-thrust in the dark—to their striking-point.

Not so fared the main body. Palace Gate once passed, they found that the sailors posted along the top of the bluff knew what was going on. Down spurted a thousand red messages of flame, 'a dreadful fire,' as a Quebecker testified. Many of the shots flew wild ; but the marksmen knew the ground, the way was narrow, and the life-or-death race was a good third of a mile long. ' Met the wounded men very thick,' said Dearborn.

Brave Hubbard was one of these. Leading his com-

---

[24] REMARK LX.
[25] REMARK LXI.

pany on, he stopped suddenly, death-struck, and leaned against a building.

'Are you wounded, Captain?' asked one of his men.

'Yes; march on, march on!' he gasped.

An orderly sergeant was shot down at Fobes's side. 'I'm a dead man,' he groaned; 'I wish you would turn me over,' for he lay face-up. Fobes did so much for him, and then hurried on.

Let the dead bury the dead, had been the strict order: other work for the living; and not a few gallant fellows, dropping under the shock of a severe but not mortal wound, struggled in the snow till exhausted, then grew numb, and at last froze.

Before long the cannon had to be abandoned: it could not be dragged fast enough through the drifts; but Lamb and Morgan pressed their men on after Arnold without delay. At last these advanced parties entered a very narrow street, and quite soon—just before reaching the point of the bluff—came to something squarely across the way: it was the close barricade, with two 12-pounders full of grape-shot behind it, that had been observed—and, so far as possible, studied—from a distance.

The plan had been to open here right and left, let the cannon on the sled fire once or twice, then charge, and shoot through the portholes; and Morgan was to make a circuit on the ice, meanwhile, and attack in the rear. But nothing could be done as proposed, and hard fighting was the only choice. As well as possible the few troops were formed. 'Now, lads, all together! Rush!' cried Arnold, or something like it: nobody could remember afterward just what it was; and in a moment the men were up to the barricade, and shooting into the portholes. One cannon had been fired, but the charge did little harm; the priming of the other flashed.

So far Arnold had marched in the front; but his time

had come, and a stray bullet, splintered on a rock, a gun or a stone house, cut its way through his left leg. For a while he stood leaning on his musket, heartening the troops; but pain and the loss of blood finally drove him back. For some distance, aided by two men, he hobbled along, crying: 'Rush on, brave boys, rush on!' But, before

SAULT AU MATELOT PRECIPICE IN 1902
The Americans passed through this street (*La Canoterie* or Dog Lane)

Palace Gate was reached, he could only drag the wounded limb after him, and the rest of the distance to the Hospital he was carried.

The voice of the soldiers then called on Morgan to lead

them, and Greene—since Morgan knew something of war —cordially assented. The cannon were silent now, yet the barrier had still to be taken. High and forbidding it stood, with muskets and bayonets behind; but a ladder was set up, and Morgan mounted it.

'Now, boys, follow me!' he cried; 'Follow me!'

His head rose above the barrier. That was the signal, and at once a great blaze poured over from beyond. Bluff, barricade, houses,—all were visible at last. For a moment, the American leader was wrapped in flame. The next instant he dropped sheer to the snow, and there, like a scorched rag,—there he lay.

But soon the rag stirred. Another second, and Morgan was on the ladder again, going up. One bullet had cut his whiskers; one had gone through his cap; the burning grains of powder had shot deep into his face; the shock had stunned him; but he was alive and unwounded.

Stooping low as he climbed up, he straightened quickly at the top of the ladder, and gave a bound. How his men cheered! Over he went, fell on the muzzle of a cannon—bruising his knee—and rolled beneath it. For an instant the bayonets could not reach him; and now the rest were over, Porterfield ahead, and the guard were flying. Into a house they rushed; and while the riflemen, after sending plenty of bullets to keep them company, charged with pikes, Morgan himself dashed round the corner, and found them escaping the back way.

'Down with your arms, if you want quarter!' he shouted; and they all surrendered. The outer door of the Lower Town was now open.

Farther up the street, a guard of citizens and school-boys met the invasion, and astonished enough they were. These men, dressed like British soldiers, offering hands instead of bayonets, joyously shouting 'Liberty forever!' or '*Vive la liberté!*' instead of battle-field curses,—these men acted like brothers, not enemies ; yet no doubt they were Americans, for every cap had on the front of it a piece of white paper inscribed, 'Liberty or Death !' the Yankee war-cry. Some of the Quebeckers got away, and some tried to resist ; but the captain at least, while he pretended to be drunk, seemed far from hostile. Had the fraternization, from which Montgomery hoped so much, begun ? It looked that way ; and people came from beyond in squads to give themselves up.

Just ahead, rose the precipice of Sailor's Leap (*Sault au Matelot*), the very point of the Upper Town ; and, on the farther side of it, some two or three hundred yards from the first barrier, stood a second. Beyond that were cannon—the flashes of the muskets dimly revealed them—cannon on a high platform, that could fire over the barrier, and fire down. What should be done ?

DANIEL MORGAN

Long after it was all over, one could say. The barrier gate was open. Morgan passed through it with an interpreter, and scrambled up to the defences on the edge of the bluff, near where Carleton had posted himself. The garrison were doing nothing : they seemed paralyzed. Indeed, that they were. A panic had struck the people, when they heard that the enemy had taken the barrier ; and the dipping balance of destiny paused. So Major Caldwell wrote General Murray ; and he added that, had the Americans pushed on, they might have won the whole of the Lower Town and let Montgomery in at the other side. The prize for which they had suffered everything and risked everything lay once more at their feet!

To push on was precisely what Morgan urged; but the 'hard reasoning' of his officers, as he said afterward, beat him out of it. Only a small part of the troops had yet come up, and the prisoners outnumbered them; would it be safe to go on, leaving these a chance to recapture the battery and cut the line of retreat? It was pitch-dark and storming furiously still; the guides had been killed or disabled; nobody understood the alleys or the defences; the troops might easily get lost. Besides, this was the place, they said, where they had been ordered to wait for Montgomery; and in a few minutes he would no doubt arrive. The best plan—was it not?—was to obey orders, wait for more men, and not hazard everything by rashness.

More men, however, did not come at once. Indeed, the rest of the division seemed very slow; and very slow they were, in fact.

Snow five or six feet deep much of the way; drifts piled higher still; a path filled as soon as made; a gale that swept their breath away; cold that stiffened them; no light but musket flashes; no street at all until they neared the barricade; storehouses, docks, and boats blocking the way; hawsers, that moored vessels to the shore, catching men under the chin, and snapping them down fifteen feet into some hole; all the loose odds and ends of such a place—lumber, broken anchors, rotting spars, discarded chains—tripping them up; cakes of ice wedged into the open spaces; the abandoned sled and cannon plugging the narrow way; a maze without a clue; no guides; a plunging fire that could not be answered,—these were not things to render marching easy. A few had been lucky enough to slip through them, but the greater number had not.

Still, reinforcements arrived. Hendricks, placed in the rear, found an opening by chance, and hurried to the front. Greene, Meigs, and Bigelow came up with troops, cheering, and got a cheer back. Here and there a single officer or man worked his way forward. Little by little a considerable force gathered; and finally, as day began to appear, the men called loudly on Morgan to head an attack. They were hastily and roughly formed, and then, seizing the ladders, they dashed round the point.

But things were very different there now. The panic had yielded to authority. Maclean's concise report had been made. Troops had gathered. Caldwell had come down with reinforcements, and able officers had come with him. Lieutenant Anderson was already sallying from the barrier to attack the Americans. 'Surrender!' he cried to Morgan. Morgan snatched a rifle and replied. Anderson fell with a bullet in his brain, but his party managed to drag him within and shut the gate. For a moment fraternizing was tried again, and the men behind the barrier heard the Americans call a number of citizens by name. 'Are you there, my friend?' a pleasant voice would ask. They quaked in fear of treachery, and the Canadians in particular shrank from the barricade; but their only reply was bullets and grape-shot.

Then the fighting began in earnest, and soon every American, however fraternal before, was battle-mad. Weariness disappeared. The passion of slaughter set in. Throats got sandy, and eyes blood-red. Some prayed, some cursed, some laughed, some cheered; all fought. No; not all. Most of the guns proved useless, for snow had got into the priming, and the heat of hand or body melted it there. Hardly one in ten would fire. Some of the troops took the captured muskets, but there were not enough of them.

Yet something could be done. A mound was built

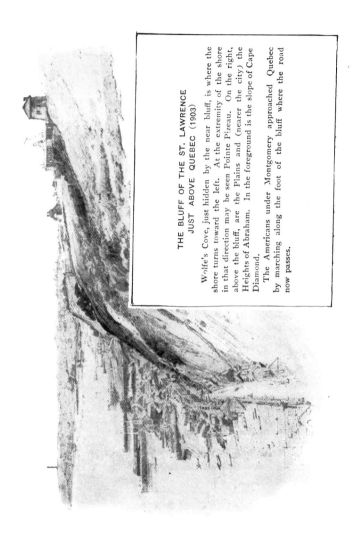

THE BLUFF OF THE ST. LAWRENCE
JUST ABOVE QUEBEC (1903)

Wolfe's Cove, just hidden by the near bluff, is where the shore turns toward the left. At the extremity of the shore in that direction may be seen Pointe Pizeau. On the right, above the bluff, are the Plains and (nearer the city) the Heights of Abraham. In the foreground is the slope of Cape Diamond.

The Americans under Montgomery approached Quebec by marching along the foot of the bluff where the road now passes.

against the barricade. Ladders were set up, and one of them was fixed on the inside to go down by. A rush was made. Spear in hand, Morgan climbed one ladder and Porterfield another. Humphreys, Lamb, Greene, Meigs, Nichols, Heath, and many more faced the bullets and grape-shot as they did the snow-flakes. But it was all too late. The houses beyond the barrier had been filled with soldiers and sailors, and their muskets blazed incessantly from the upper windows. Across the street waited a double line of the Fusiliers with fixed bayonets. To try going down the ladder inside or making the drop of twelve feet, in the face of so many bullets and bayonets, was mere suicide.

Here died most of the Americans killed that morning. The space was narrow ; the enemy's fire converged ; even the random shot found a target. Intrepid Humphreys fell, with one bullet in the body and another in the head ; Cooper and Thomas fell ; Tisdale got a ball in the shoulder ; Topham was wounded ; Steele had two fingers shot off while taking aim ; Taylor was hit ; the left side of Lamb's face was torn away. Not long after, the be-loved Hendricks, whose courage and animation made him seem to his men 'all Soul,' received a ball near the heart, staggered back a few paces, fell, and was dead. Every officer's clothing was cut more than once. Of the sheltered enemy, few could be reached.

Yet the Americans would not give up. They dared their foes to sally and fight in the open. 'Our rifles are for sale cheap, come out and try them!' they cried. They emptied their guns—those who could—at the win-dows. They tried to outflank the barricade, though only to find that it reached from bluff to river. Time and again the ladders were mounted. This thing and that were attempted, but always in vain. They listened, then, for the merry music of the Yorkers' muskets. All at once a brisk firing broke out in a new quarter. Cheers greeted it. 'Montgomery!' they shouted; 'Quebec is ours!'

Thicker and thicker grew the enemy, however; and fighting in the open against men protected seemed a losing game. Better take shelter from tempest and bullets in the houses, it was thought, and let the riflemen try conclusions from the windows. Friends might come; and anyhow, lives would be saved. Morgan was not of that opinion. His grand figure towered, his wonderful eyes blazed, he gnawed his lip, his terrible voice cut through the uproar.[26] But the weary men panted for a breathing space; so the houses were occupied, and many went back as far as the other barrier. Then Morgan ordered those around him to take shelter, and the battle was continued by firing from the windows. But in every heart rose a question like the cry of a drowning man: The General, where is he?

Montgomery had decided to stimulate his men by leading them in person; and, with a corps of nearly three hundred, he set out betimes for his long circuit. From his quarters, it was about a mile to Wolfe's Cove, and then some two miles to the defences of the Lower Town at *Près de Ville* or the Potash.

The first part of the journey was hard, the second frightful. Here the men had to march into the very teeth of the storm, and it was impossible to face the horizontal sweep of snow and hail with an open eye. Stumbling along in single file, with a precipice above and a steep bank below, they fought a battle every furlong of the way. The deeper the path grew, as the line moved along, the worse it became, for the slumping of the men filled it with holes, and nobody could tell where his foot was going when he set it down. Blocks of ice piled up by the tide

---

26 So. Lit. Messenger, Sept., 1854, p. 563; Henry, Journal, p. 111.

often barred the way. Not once, but repeatedly, the men could pass round some obstacle only by scaling the slope on their left for fifteen or twenty feet; and then, to get back safely to the route, they had to sit down, with the skirts of their coats under them, and slide,—thankful enough if they did not slide too far. One officer got a fall that it was feared he would never recover from [27]; and no doubt others fared the same. Those who carried the ladders had to move so slowly that all behind them were checked, and there came to be long gaps here and there. Every one felt chilled and tired.

Just about the time when night has been said to be darkest, the head of the line reached a strong, close palisade fifteen or twenty feet high. This the carpenters attacked with saws ; but, before their work was completed, Montgomery impatiently crowded the posts away from the rock and entered. There was a blockhouse on the Cape above, but not a shot came down. [28] Fortune again. About a hundred yards farther, but not yet quite at the point of the Cape, stood another palisade. This also was cut through, and still there was no alarm. Montgomery stepped within. Macpherson, his aide, and Cheeseman, captain of the first company, with a group of others—Burr among them—attended him. The rest were slow to come up, and Montgomery sent back to hurry them on. Soon, but not soon enough, a party of fifty or sixty—possibly more—were at hand ; and the leaders, quietly advancing round the point of Cape Diamond, entered a sort of road some twenty-four feet wide. [29]

Just ahead, in the middle of the narrow pass, the form of a building seemed to shape itself dimly in the darkness and whirling snow. A blockhouse ? No ; only a

---

[27] Wooster to Cong.. Mar. 6, 1776: 4 Force, V., 511.
[28] REMARK LXII.
[29] Anburey, Travels. I., p. 58.

dwelling, Simon Fraser's house [30]; but four small cannon had been mounted in it; the walls had been loopholed for muskets; a small detachment of Canadians was on guard there; and a squad of sailors under Adam Barnfair—a small Jack Falstaff afloat, the master of the *Fell* before she was taken by the government—had charge of the guns. Or rather, should have had. Entombed under the Cape and buried by the storm, what could there be for them to dread? Only melancholy; and so all had been drinking. Before they dreamed of an enemy, he was upon them; and, overwhelmed with panic, they fled. But the Americans were a little slow, and Barnfair had not wits enough to be wholly a coward. At the bottom of his muddy intelligence lurked a grain of the mastiff. With a curse, he vowed he would not go without firing a gun first, and turned back. Possibly others turned back with him.

Montgomery was peering keenly through the storm at that instant. There seemed to be portholes in the house, and a faint glimmer of light. Was it the slow match of a gun? He could not be sure. Indeed, it made no difference. What worried him was the tardiness of his men. Many or few, however, he could wait no longer. Drawing his sword and tossing the scabbard away, he cried to those at his back: 'Come on, my good soldiers! Your general calls. Come on!' And, with a spring, the head of the column rushed forward at the double quick. Only a few paces ahead lay victory, Quebec, Canada.

But at that moment came a blaze, a roar, a fierce rush of air; and, the next instant, dark forms were toppling over into the snow. One lay motionless: it was knightly Macpherson. Another rose, staggered on, plunged, and fell: that was Cheeseman, with the gold for burial ready

---

30 § Témoignage in support of Alsopp's petition of Sept. 3, 1790: Can. Arch (separate). Fraser rented the house from Alsopp.

in his purse. Another lay quietly on his back, then painfully drew up his knees, raised a forearm and hand, as if calling Heaven to witness, and then, like the others, lay quite still : that was Montgomery. A few more could be seen near them. Some limped back or crawled back with cries and groans. The column halted.

Oh, for another Montgomery or another Morgan now ! No doubt the loss of the three leaders is disheartening ; but soldiers expect to die. No doubt the muskets are too damp to shoot ; but spears and bayonets can still prick, and perhaps the way is clear. If the attack was worth making, it is worth following up ; and there is vengeance to take, besides. But Campbell, who assumes command, is fonder of swearing at the enemy than fighting him. An unsafe place, this : better get out of it. He confabulates instead of charging, and presently he orders a retreat. The column hurries away. The British cannon speak again, at their leisure, and then hold their peace. There is no pursuit, and soon there are none to be pursued; and the dead rest alone in their failure and their glory.

WHERE MONTGOMERY FELL

This was why Morgan's men did not hear Montgomery coming. Gradually it dawned upon them that something was not right, else how could so many of Carleton's troops be spared to fight their division? Every moment their case grew harder. A barricade, cannon, windows full of muskets, a street full of bayonets, a bluff edged with fire, and the whole force of the garrison were now focused upon them. Fatigue, the loss of their leader, the heaps of dead and wounded, the peril, darkness, cold, and uncertainty had exhausted the strength of many and chilled the ardor of some; but those who could fight still fought stubbornly on from the windows.

And now Fortune made another of her dark proffers. A stone house formed a part of the barrier. But it was more than a house; it was a castle, and the castle a keystone. The door, which stood under the eaves, opened into the narrow street held by the Americans; but the end had a gable window looking down on the British side of the barrier, and two or three of the unerring riflemen, posted there, while others loaded for them, could do blithe execution among the enemy. Perhaps, after all, the barrier might be won. The Americans could not see the chance, but at least they could feel their way to it; and already they occupied the first floor.[31]

But Caldwell's men had a full view of the window, and perceived the danger. A sailor tore away the ladder fixed by the Americans on the inside of the barrier, and it was planted against the gable. Brave Dambourgès and valiant Nairne rushed up and threw themselves into the darkness; a party followed; their bayonets were quickly plying the astonished Provincials; and, after a dreadful conflict, they cleared the place. Then Caldwell got another cannon—a 9-pounder—turned upon the Americans, and the houses could no longer protect them. Victory was out of the question now; yet some, believing still that Montgomery might come and need them, favored holding on at any cost until night. Retreat, however, seemed the wisest course, and to this a council of the officers finally brought themselves.

But Carleton's eye had been watching; and, when the

---

[31] REMARK LXIII.

time arrived, he sent Laws out of Palace Gate, with a choice party and some cannon, to attack in the rear. Laws was supported by Macdougal, Macdougal by Fraser, and Fraser by Hamilton,—five hundred men in all. This was something Arnold's men had not counted upon, for they believed that a sortie during an assault was almost unheard of. Montgomery must have seen the danger; but he planned to keep the enemy busy in the Lower Town, and the Potash, had it been won, could not have been outflanked; besides, no reserves, to prevent a sortie from Palace Gate, could possibly be spared.

Rushing on, all zeal and courage, Laws burst into the midst of the American rear.

'You are all my prisoners!' he cried, with drawn sword.

'How your prisoners? You are ours,' they answered.

'No, no, my dear creatures; I vow to God you are all mine; don't mistake yourselves.'

'But where are your men?' And then Laws noticed that he was alone: nobody had been able to keep pace with him. But he knew they were coming.

'Oh ho,' he replied, 'make yourselves easy about that matter; they're all about here; they'll be with you in a twinkling.'

A good many twinklings passed, however; and, as they did not appear, some of the Americans were for sacrificing this enemy who refused to surrender. But Meigs[32] prevented that, and before long the British troops, aided by the prisoners they released, were masters of the post.

Morgan proposed to cut a way out, and many would have joined him; but some preferred to wait for Mont-

---

[32] That this was done by Meigs is apparently proved: see Meigs, Journal. Dec. 31; Haskell, Diary, Jan. 25; Wash. to French, Aug. 8, 1776 (5 Force, I., 853).

gomery, and others realized there was positively no hope. Nearly one in five of the Americans—perhaps more than one in five—had been killed or wounded,[33] and almost all the rest were utterly exhausted. With cannon before and behind them, and musketry fire from the rear, the front, and the flank, they found themselves, as Carleton said, 'compleatly ruined; . . . caught as it were in a Trap'; and at last, about nine or ten o'clock, on the promise of 'good quarters & Tender usage,' they began to give up their arms.[34]

Morgan, however, choked at the thought of surrender, and burst into tears of rage. His back to a wall, he defied the host of enemies. Upon that, they furiously demanded his sword.

'Come and take it, if you dare!' he thundered. Then they threatened to shoot him.

'Shoot, if you will!'

But his men begged him not to throw his life away; and at length, catching sight of a person in clerical dress, he asked:

'Are you a priest?'

'I am.'

'Then I give my sword to you. No scoundrel of those cowards shall take it out of my hands.'[35]

And so the battle ended. 'A complete failure,' says Trevelyan.[36] No doubt; but that is not the wonder.

---

[33] REMARK LXIV.

[34] For a discussion of the chief hard questions, see REMARK LXV. The author has considered many others with equal care, but does not regard them as entitled to a place here.

[35] From Graham, Morgan, p. 103 (derived from Dr. Hill), thrown into a somewhat more direct form by the present author.

[36] American Revolution, Part I., p. 381.

The wonder is that creatures of flesh and blood dared venture into such death-traps ; and but for the narrowest of chances—not once but repeatedly—the ' failure ' would have been a splendid and famous victory.

But the facts were facts ; and the last sun of fateful 1775, the avant-courier of glorious '76, bade good-night at Quebec to a doleful scene : Montgomery dead ; Arnold a cripple nailed to his bed ; Morgan and Lamb, with almost the whole artillery company and Kennebec division, fast in prison. The army, already small, was now a shred ; and there it lay, buried in the drifting snows of a Canadian winter, beaten and broken-backed, its friends far away and the enemy close at hand, mutely asking in a half-conscious way what the fate of it was to be.

XXV

TO THE RESCUE!

SOME thought the war in Canada neared its end like the year, that last day of December ; but in reality it was only beginning. The close of 1775 was the opening of 1776. The breadth of the struggle was soon to be extended, its energy deepened. Philadelphia on the one side and London on the other were to throw their full power into the contest, and Canada was to feel the weight of armies instead of battalions.

A look at the American lines before Quebec just then was almost enough, however, to break the heart of a patriot. All day the gloomy storm continued, and it answered well to the feelings of the troops. The defeat and death of Montgomery were soon reported. Almost equally depressing was the uncertainty about Arnold's division, for the line of communication with it had been broken. 'They will either carry the lower town, be made prisoners, or [be] cut to pieces,' was all their leader himself could say. At the General Hospital, stretched on piles of straw reddened with their blood, the wounded men were raising their hands to heaven and moaning piteously, ' Montgomery is dead ! Montgomery is dead ! ' Touched with compassion the Mother Superior sent them coverlets and linen for bandages ; and the nuns, though relieved that an enemy had failed, went about repeating sympathetically, ' Poor Montgomery is dead ! ' but the hurt of the soldiers lay too deep for bandages or even for sympathy. The split bullet that disabled Arnold had struck his leg midway between ankle and knee, passed down between the bones and lodged above the heel. It was a most painful wound ; and he lay on his bed pallid from weakness and acute suffering, with the gout coming on, and an amputation—if nothing worse—threatening. 'Oh Liberty!' 'Oh Virtue!' 'Oh my country!' the dejected troops were groaning ; and it was cursing Campbell, whose theory of war was to avoid risks, that had command. Should the enemy come, unconditional surrender, of course.[1]

And he came. Round a corner in St. Roch appeared a column shouting, ' D—— the dogs, we 'll take them all.' But Captain Wool had gathered some stragglers, invalids, and seven or eight of Lamb's artillery company, and awaited them with a brass 6-pounder.

'You lie ; take that !' he cried, returning their epithet with a charge of grape.

By good fortune, Major Duboys with Clinton's regiment and Livingston with his Canadians were just marching down to take the place of Arnold's detachment at the General Hospital, and the British imagined they were coming to charge ; so the column retreated round the corner and went back to Quebec, merely capturing the advanced post in St. Roch, the five little mortars, and a pair of 3-pounders.[2]

The Americans, knowing that—as Livingston admitted —the garrison had it in their power to ' cut off ' their annoying visitors altogether, expected a return in greater

[1] § Haskell, Diary, Dec. 31 ; Ainslie, Journal, Jan. 1: Senter, Journal, Dec. 31 ; etc. Arnold to Wooster, Dec. 31, 1775: Sparks MSS., No. 52, II., p. 33. Mgr. de St Vallier, Part II., Chap. IV., p. 413. Gaspé, Mém., p. 38. Arnold's letters, Jan. 2, 4, 6, 1776 : 4 Force, IV., 670, 854, 589. Arnold to Cong., Jan. 11, 1776: Sparks MSS., No. 52, II., p. 34. ' Arnold's ' Ord. Book, Jan. 1.

[2] § Senter, Journal, Dec. 31. Campbell to ——, Mar., 1776 : Liv. Papers, 1775-1777, p. 145. Carleton to Howe, Jan. 12, 1776: Pub. Rec. Off., Colon. Corres., Quebec, 12, p. 23. Caldwell, Letter. Ainslie, Journal, Dec. 31. ' Chalmers' Journal, Dec. 31.

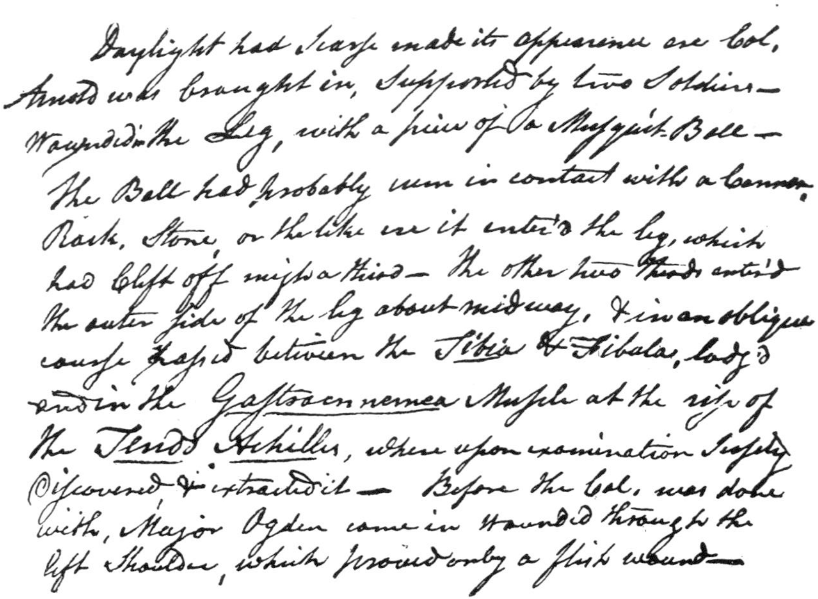
Daylight had scarse made its appearence ere Col.
Arnold was brought in, supported by two Soldiers—
Wounded in the Leg, with a piece of a Musquet Ball—
The Ball had probably come in contact with a Cannon,
Rock, Stone, or the like ere it enter'd the leg, which
had Cleft off nigh a third— The other two thirds enter'd
the outer side of the leg about midway, & in an oblique
course passed between the Tibia & Fibula, lodg'd
in the Gastrocnemea Muscle at the rise of
the Tendo Achilles, where upon examination I safely
discovered & extracted it— Before the Col. was done
with, Major Ogden came in wounded through the
left shoulder, which proved only a flesh wound—

ARNOLD'S WOUND (EXTRACT FROM DR. SENTER'S JOURNAL)

force, and the surgeons 'entreated' Arnold to be carried out of reach. To no purpose, however, recorded Doctor Senter; for 'he would neither be removed, nor suffer a man from the Hospital to retreat.'

'Bring my sword!' he cried; 'Load my pistols, and lay them on my bed! I will kill as many as I can of them, if they come into the room.'

Everybody turned soldier; beside each pallet of straw was laid a musket; the Hospital was to be stubbornly defended. But the red column did not come back. People were singing in Quebec about the 'blacksmiths, tanners, shoemakers, skillful tailors and clever wig-makers' outside, and boasting that Arnold knew how to play the horse-jockey better than to frighten them,—quite as the Russians might have shouted at Zürich that Masséna's father sold wine, and before Friedland that Ney's made barrels; but apparently they preferred to do their singing and boasting out of reach. Eighteen hundred men in arms, led by a British major-general and officered by veterans trained in British victories, seemed willing to be imprisoned by a mere handful of Colonial volunteers. Perhaps they would change their minds, but at all events there was time to breathe.[3]

New Year's Day poor Montgomery entered Quebec at last; but it was on a sled. A bloody fur cap with his initials in the top had suggested that the American leader was no more, and one of the prisoners identified his body. Pierced in the head, groin, and thigh, the harassed chieftain now gained the victory of repose; but he found it only in frozen ground, attended by the smoky glare of a few torches and lanterns. Those about his coffin rejoiced, however soberly, instead of weeping; and of all who

---

[3] § J. Liv. to ———, [Feb., 1776]: Am. Hist. Rec., III., p. 181. Senter, Journal, Dec. 31. Arnold to ———, Jan. 6, 1776: 4 Force, IV., 589. Song (in French): Canadiana, I., p. 189.

loved him only one poor creature—a beautiful spaniel—discovered his grave and mourned there.[4]

Less fortunate than he, as it almost seemed, those of his followers who lived and were free, now thought anxiously of the future. The uncertainty regarding Arnold's men grew less and less hopeful. Duncan, one of the 'volunteers' that had marched through the wilderness, offered to go and find out what had become of them; he went but did not return. Overwhelmed by the disaster, more than a hundred soldiers insisted that their time was out and hurried off up the river, to enlist for the easier service at Montreal or perhaps to make their way home; while others followed their diminishing figures with longing and irresolute eyes, and were soon to follow them with legs as well. The whole American force, including invalids and men detached 'on command,' amounted to about six hundred, besides the timorous Canadians. The magazine contained no lead and but few bullets or buckshot, the storehouse not pork enough to last a week, and the treasury hardly four or five hundred pounds. Medicine as well as food was lacking. Arnold and his troops felt a deep grievance against the Yorkers, for they believed that, if Montgomery's men had pressed on, there would have been a triumph instead of an overthrow.

THE HOUSE TO WHICH MONT-
GOMERY'S BODY WAS
CARRIED

---

4 For Montg.'s Burial, etc., see REMARK LXVI.

Naturally this imputation was resented, with bitter gibes at the airs of superiority put on by the 'Yankeys'; and the fact that Campbell, who had ordered the retreat, was the one person to profit by the disaster, threatened to drive this wedge very hard and fast through the woe-begone army.[5]

But the partial eclipse of courage and resolution soon ended. Meigs, who came out on parole the next day to get the prisoners' effects, cleared up all uncertainty about Arnold's division, but at the same time—so it went about the camp—declared that Carleton himself did not believe he could hold out much longer. Indeed, on hearing that he treated the 'rebel' prisoners well, their comrades promptly argued that so bold an attack must have 'struck terror' into him. Campbell found himself compelled to summon a council; and fighting Arnold was chosen leader in his room 'by the Unanimous Voyce of the field officers and Captains.' The main body drew back about a mile from Holland House; but the troops were planted on the roads in such a way as to bar them still yet give mutual support in case of a sortie, while the advance posts remained close to the city. Instead of withdrawing the magazine to a safer place and so exciting the distrust of the Canadians, it was decided to bring cannon from the old battery on the Heights and plant them round it. Ramparts of 'frozen snow,' valuable against musket-fire, rose about the camp; and most of the men fit for duty stood guard or lay on their arms both day and night. In short, what seemed the wise policy was bravely followed: to 'put the best face on matters

---

[5] § Duncan: Senter, Journal, Jan. 1. Nos., etc.: Arnold to Wooster, Jan 2, 5, 1776 (4 Force, IV., 670, 854); Id. to Wash., Jan. 14, 1776 (ib., 674); Campbell to Wooster, Jan. 2, 1776 (Sparks MSS., No. 60, p. 51). Against the Yorkers: Arnold to ———, Jan. 6, 1776 (4 Force, IV., 589); Topham, Journal, Dec. 31; Nichols, Diary, Dec. 31. J. Liv. (to ———, Jan. 25, 1819: Bancroft Coll.) said that Campbell might 'unquestionably' have taken the post. For gibes of Yorkers: Ainslie, Journal, April 9, 10 (Spies).

and betray no marks of fear.' A new flag had just been thrown to the free winds at Cambridge (January 2), and the shivering, unpaid soldiers before Quebec acted as if they knew it.[6]

'The burden lies very heavy on me, considering my present circumstances,' wrote Arnold; 'I find myself unequal to the task'; but —he added—'I have no thoughts of leaving this proud town, until I first enter it in triumph.' Indeed, though able only to lie on his back and 'scrawl,' he still believed that, were 'proper methods' adopted, the capital 'must inevitably fall.' The enemy he reckoned at fifteen hundred, but he was 'well assured more than one half of the Inhabitants of Quebec would gladly open the gates,' if not prevented by the 'strict discipline and watch kept over them, the command of the Guards being constantly given to Officers of the Crown, known to be firm.' It was 'generally agreed,' he reported, that the provisions could hardly last through March, though Carleton would permit no one to investigate the stores. Fuel was lacking, without a doubt. To capture the town seemed 'an object of vast importance.' Its overflowing magazines; its great stocks of cannon, arms, and uniforms; the vessels laid up in its docks; the captives in its prisons, and its dominating influence on Canadian politics,—all forbade retreat. Some force needed to be rallied, then, and quickly rallied, to strengthen the American grip.[7]

First the Canadians, for they were nearest. Nothing was left untried that could possibly feed their courage. When Montgomery did not reappear, somebody explained

[6] § Haskell, Diary, Jan. 2, 4. Senter, Journal, Jan. 2. Letter, Jan. 5, 1776: 4 Force, IV., 582. Council: Campbell to Wooster, Jan. 2, 1776 (Sparks MSS., No. 60, p. 51); 'Arnold's' Ord. Book, Jan. 3. Fobes, Narrative, [Dec. 31]. 'Chalmers' Journal, Jan. 13. Arnold to Wash., Jan. 14, 1776: 4 Force, IV., 674. Id. to Cong., Jan. 11, 1776: Sparks MSS., No. 52, II., p. 34. Flag (Union Jack with 13 stripes): Preble, Flag, p. 217. REMARK LXVII.

[7] § Arnold, letters of Jan. 4, 5, 6, 1776: 4 Force, IV., 854, 589. Arnold to Cong., Jan. 11, 12, 24, 1776: Sparks MSS., No. 52, II., pp. 34, 37.

that he had gone to Boston through the woods to lead
new forces northward. So long as the fate of Arnold's
division could be doubted, people were given to believe
that it had taken the Lower Town, besides disposing
of six hundred enemies; and, when they saw Major Meigs
coming out, they crowded round him to hear the good
news confirmed. To offset the defeat, after it could not
be denied, another assault—this time with four thousand
men—was announced; while a story shivered through
the parishes that Carleton had strung up sixty Canadian
prisoners over the ramparts without giving them time to
say, 'Lord, have mercy on me!' and then had thrown
their bodies to the dogs in the ditch;—at least, so a spy
reported in Quebec. Some of the people had compromised themselves deeply, while others were ardent and
honest believers in the cause; and many of both sorts—
their nervous backs almost writhing in the thick blanket-
overcoats bound round them with worsted sashes, and
their frightened eyes blinking hard under the fur caps
that nearly buried them—rallied in alarm to the American
headquarters. Arnold believed that a new Canadian
regiment could be raised, and commissioned officers to recruit it; while, to equip these men, an order was issued
to search houses and take, in exchange for a receipt,
what arms could be found. [8]

In this way he reckoned on getting three or four hundred men; but in a few days his hopes fell to 'two or
three hundred,' and very soon they dropped still lower.
'The peasants,' noted Dr. Senter, 'however friendly disposed, thought it too precarious a juncture to show

---

[8] § Ainslie, Journal, Jan. 1; Feb. 28. 'Remark. Occurr.' Journal, Jan. 7, 17,
Senter, Journal, Jan. 3. Roy, Lauzon, III., p. 65. Dress: Anburey, Travels
I., p. 71. Canads. joined: Arnold to Wooster, Jan. 4, 1776 (4 Force, IV., 854)
Regt.: Id. to Cong., Jan. 12, 1776 (Sparks MSS., No. 52, II., p. 34); Id. to
Wooster, Jan. 5, 1776 (4 Force, IV., 854); Id. to Wash., Jan. 14, 1776 (ib., 674).
Vouchers, Jan. 1, 1776: Cont. Cong. Papers, No. 35, p. 219. Arms: Order to
Langlois, Jan. 3, 1776 (Can. Arch., B, 184, 1, p. 20).

Ticonderoga Novr: 30th 1775.

Dear General

You send me such agreeable Accounts, and serving frequently, that I am under the necessity of sending an hour before Day, to announce the Glad Tidings to my Superiors, President and us in my Bosom myself in hour before I received Your Letter, I believe he could easily perceive, that I knew his Character,

FROM SCHUYLER'S LETTER TO MONTGOMERY

themselves in that capacity, and those nigh rather retreated back into the country, than gave any assistance.'
Doubtless, too, there was another reason for their diffidence.
'Of Canadians,' Montgomery had reported, 'I might be
able to get a considerable number, provided I had hard
money, with which to clothe, feed, and pay their wages;
but this is wanting.' Colonel Livingston himself had
never received 'a shilling of pay.' Canadian volunteer-
ing, therefore, had not met with encouragement; and
now, when cash was more lacking than ever, the people
alleged, so Livingston said, that, 'as they had been refused before the storming, they did not think proper to
come after the Retreat,'—certainly a very delicate morsel
of their traditional politeness.[9]

But, after all, their backwardness did not matter very
much. Something more than Canadian volunteers was
required. 'What cannot Soldiers do, who are fighting for
Liberty and their Country?' exclaimed Arnold; but his
inmost thoughts were on cannon, howitzers, powder, lead,
shells, and specie. 'An experienced general,' with
at least three thousand men, better five thousand, better
still 'eight or ten thousand,' was the need, he felt; and
from the bottom of his heart, like every other man behind
the snow ramparts, he prayed for 'reinforcements.'[10]

Reinforcements! Pacing to and fro among the drifts
on the top of the great ridge, an American sentry—
shrivelled up with cold, and buffeted by a gale from
the northeast that drew a deep veil of grey over the
splendid sky—beheld, when the drifting snow permitted,
a vast, enshrouded body of dead white, stabbed here and

---

[9] § Cf. Arnold's letters of Jan. 12, 14: Note 8. Senter, Journal, Dec. 31,
Montg. to R. R. Liv., Nov. —, 1775: 4 Force, III., 1638. J. Liv. to ——, [Feb.,
1776]: Am. Hist. Rec., III., p. 181. Not encour.: Hazen to Sch., Apr. 1, 1776 (4
Force, V., 751).

[10] § Arnold to ——, Jan. 14, 1776: Conn. Gazette, Feb. 23, 1776. Id. to
Cong., Jan. 11, 1776: Sparks MSS., No. 52, II., p. 34. Id. to Wooster, Jan. 2,
1776: 4 Force, IV., 670.

there with a cluster of brown cottages, and bleeding ragged streaks of dark stone walls ; while—single or in groups, outposts of the gloomy forest—leafless trees whistled in the blast, or funereal evergreens bowed low before it. To escape this prospect, he could survey the grey cliffs and the bluffs of rusty sand that scarred the white, or watch the hoary tide of the St. Lawrence, where the heaving blocks of thick ice froze and broke, rose and fell, ebbed and flowed, crushed, ground, and groaned in the aimless melancholy of an Arctic winter ; while, if he turned his eyes to the south for cheer, his vision had to travel across the drifts—if it could—one hundred and eighty miles to Montreal, one hundred and fifty more to Ticonderoga, then one hundred to Albany, one hundred and fifty more to New York, and finally one hundred to Philadelphia, where sate the Conscript Fathers under the waiting bell of Independence Hall in a maze of perplexities. All these miles of snow must be tediously paced off before the needs of the struggling soldiers could even be told, and again paced off to bring back word they were not forgotten.

Yet an atom had been set in motion across that sea of frost. Even while the battle continued, Edward Antill, who had been near Montgomery when he fell, wrapped himself in a heavy furred mantle such as every man of position wore, sprang into one of the light, hooded sleighs used by people of means, and set out for Montreal.[11]

Changing horses at the posting stations, he sped on across the narrow plains and through the long, straggling villages. Aspen Point soon lay behind. Down one steep

11 § This paragraph and the next two: Campbell to ——-, Mar. 28, 1776 (Liv. Papers, 1775–1777, p. 145); Stone (ed.), Letters, pp. 13, 34, 35, etc.; Anburey, Travels, I., pp. 100–103, etc.; Marr, Remarks (Can. Arch., M, 384, p. 85); Henry, Journal, p. 93. T. Riv.: Bouchette, Descr. Topog., p. 309 ; Letter, Dec. 17, 1775 (4 Force, IV., 296). For Château see Chap. XXX., Note 11. (These facts are given for the purpose of acquainting the reader further with the Canada of 1776. The conduct of Antill's man is inferred from the rapidity of the journey.) Ritzema, Journal, Jan. 2, 1776.

bank of the Jacques Cartier River slid the tough but creaking vehicle—all of pine—and up the other bank it crawled. Although the *corvées* would not begin breaking roads until the storm ended, the way could not be missed, for young evergreens had been set all along, forty or fifty yards apart, to mark it ; but the piety or superstition of the driver was a real danger. Between every two villages, more than one great wooden cross reared themselves beside the highway, adorned with a wax figure of the Virgin and Child or of Christ on the Tree set into the upright behind a square of glass, and hung about with hammer, tongs, nails, and flask of vinegar ; and at every such emblem the travelling peasants felt bound to alight, kneel in the snow, and say a long prayer. Antill's man, however, satisfied his conscience by repeatedly crossing himself ; and with few pauses the pair of big, round bells at the horses' necks jingled on past Cape Santé, and their hoofs—no longer shoeless, as in summer —crunched firmly up *Charles Lee* the slope at the Falls of Richelieu, now muffled by the frost ; while the driver, instead of plying a whip, encouraged them with unflagging talk.

Now and then, in default of a tavern, Antill ate some bread and eggs at a private house and drank some milk, for no time could be spared to buy provisions of his own and have them cooked, as was customary ; and so, after many hours that seemed many days, he caught sight of the stone monastery of the Récollets at Three Rivers, and presently was telling his dismal story to Captains Lyon and Goforth, who commanded the guard at that post. Then forward he crunched again, leaving the great Lake St. Peter—here and there quite wind-swept—on the left, catching a glimpse of Sorel, far in the distance across the St. Lawrence, and passing below the tall, slender spire of Lavaltrie, where Carleton had found himself becalmed in November; until, before the close of January the second, he sadly shook hands with General Wooster at the Château de Ramezay, Montreal.

Wooster had become now the ranking officer in Canada. On him lay the direct responsibility for the province, with all that implied. Montgomery's death, Arnold's wound, and the critical situation stood clearly forth in Antill's despatches, and he found himself called upon to set out for Quebec 'as instantly' as he could. Already Arnold confessed himself 'exceedingly apprehensive' about the fate of his men, and two days later came another express with tidings of their loss. 'For God's sake,' said Arnold, 'order as many men down as you can possibly spare, consistent with the safety of Montreal.'[12]

But Wooster himself was in straits. There was 'but little confidence to be placed in the Canadians' round him, he felt sure; and the Americans had many 'enemies in the country.' They were also 'in the greatest need of cash.' Price had enabled them to 'subsist as an army,' having already advanced about £20,000; but now he was 'almost out of that article' himself, and could find no one in the city willing to lend. There were 'but five or six hundred men for the garrisons' of Montreal, Chambly, and St. Johns, 'and many of those few not to be depended on.' 'The soldiers mutinous, and with little discipline,' explained an officer: 'not a sous to pay them with, which makes them so.' In fact, I've not 'rec'd a Farthing since I left you,' a man was just writing home. To all of which Lieutenant-Colonel Ritzema, whom Montgomery had considered an able officer, added a little more: 'no one capable to command them.'[13]

---

[12] § Arnold to Wooster, Dec. 31, 1775: Sparks MSS., No. 52, II., p. 33. Campbell to Wooster, Dec. 31, 1775: 4 Force, IV., 480. Arnold to Wooster, Jan. 2, 1776: ib., 670.
[13] § Wooster to Sch., Jan. 5, 1776: 4 Force, IV., 668. Price to Sch., Jan. 5: ib.,

The logic of this 'very critical and dangerous situation,' as Wooster called it,—and especially of the last item,—was inexorable. Some generals in his place would have figured to themselves that a retreat from Quebec was impossible. The Americans had no means of transporting food—to say nothing of the sick, the ammunition, and the cannon—save by the favor of the Canadians, and that would turn to bitter and active hostility at the first sign of flight. To attempt a march of one hundred and eighty miles through deep snows in the piercing cold of January, poorly fed, unprepared for battle, bushwhacked by the natives, and pursued by a well ·equipped, well provided enemy three times as numerous, would mean destruction. Some generals might also have felt that a total overthrow of the remnant still before Quebec would not improve the

SCHUYLER'S ALBANY HOUSE

situation above, and might possibly have fancied that, should a part of the Montreal garrison be despatched to Arnold, the hostile but quite unorganized Tories—with his strengthened army on one side, the Colonies on the other, and the guns of the citadel aiming point-blank at their chimney-pots —would not be likely to rise. Wooster, however, did not permit imagination to riot in this manner. What impressed his guarded intelligence was that he and the rest might, 'perhaps, be all sacrificed,' and equally plain lay the path of his duty : Montreal 'must be secured for a retreat.' [14]

668.   Ritzema to ———, (N. Y. Com. Safety), Jan. 3, 1776: ib , 1114. Letter, Montreal, Jan. 8, 1776, in Tryon's of Feb. 8, 1776: Pub. Rec. Off., Am. and W. I , Vol. 186, p. 309.   Montg. to R. R. Liv., Oct. 5, 1775: Liv. Papers, 1775-1777, p. 51.

14 § That the Canadians would probably have acted as is here suggested

' I little expect,' he said, ' with the troops who remain, to be able to continue the siege. . . . I shall not be able to spare any men to reinforce Colonel Arnold.' ' What they will do at Quebeck,' he added, ' for want of money, God only knows,' but none could be spared from Montreal. Above all, he decided that he could not go down, himself, though Arnold assured him that his presence was ' absolutely necessary ' ; and a council of officers, Ritzema included, 'agreed to a man' in this decision, —not so much probably, because they believed he would do great things at Montreal, as because they knew he would not at Quebec. The burden was conveyed by despatch to Schuyler. Warner, of the Green Mountain Boys, was urgently entreated to recruit and forward men ; Colonel Clinton was sent down the river to take command, and Price to raise funds outside of Quebec that he could not find inside of Montreal ; but nothing more was done. ' God only knows what the event will be,' remarked Wooster ; but this was just his modesty. He really felt no doubt.[15]

After Arnold's letter of January the second arrived, outlining the full dimensions of the misfortune, Antill bundled himself again in his furs, crossed the ice-bound river through the avenue of small pines that marked the road, startled the drowsy garrison at St. Johns, and struck for the south. Eight days of Arctic adventure, hardship, and peril, this link of the journey represented. It was John Brown's wild feat of ten months before done backward, only with ice forming instead of breaking, and the mercury shrinking a little closer into the bulb each day ; but the envoy had, to keep him warm, these words

---

will appear later from the narrative. Wooster to Sch., Jan. 5, 1776: 4 Force, IV., 668.

[15] § Wooster to Sch., Jan. 5, 19, 1776: 4 Force, IV., 668, 1004. Id. to Warner, Jan. 6, 1776 : ib., 588 (for what is evidently a more correct copy, see Pub. Rec. Off., Am. and W. I., Vol. 186, p. 313). Arnold to Wooster, Jan. 2, 1776: 4 Force, IV., 670. Id. to Wash., Jan. 14, 1776: ib., 674.

Within this half Hour Mr Antill arrived
with the unfortunate Accounts contained in the
Inclosed. My Amiable & Gallant Friend General
Montgomery is no more, he fell in our service
full Attack on Quebec on the 30 Ulto: My Feelings
on this unhappy Occasion are too Poignant to
admit of Expression; May Heaven avert any
further Evils.—

FROM SCHUYLER'S LETTER TO WASHINGTON, JAN. 13, 1776.

just penned by Ritzema to a member of the New York Committee of Safety : ' For God's sake, sir, exert yourself . . . . Let us have men and money ; otherwise, by Heavens, Canada is lost.'[16]

At length, in the dusk of January thirteenth, the wearied traveller caught sight of a throng of wooden houses one story or—here and there—a story and a half in height, with Dutch gable-ends of brick toward the street and iron horses in the place of weathercocks, crowded into a narrow intervale between the Hudson and a sharp hill crested with the edge of a boundless pine forest. It was Albany, and very attractively twinkled the lights through the clean, bright window-panes ; but the sleigh kept right on through the town, and, about a mile beyond it, drew up at a stately brick mansion in a grove,—the city residence of Philip Schuyler. The hour-hand of the tall clock on the stairs was then reaching toward the figure six, and the dining-room shone with candles and silver.[17]

A terrible gloom fell upon the General's vivacious countenance as he read the despatches. ' You send me such agreeable Accounts, and so very frequently ; That I am under the Necessity of scribling an Hour before Day, to announce the Glad Tidings to my Superiors,' he had written Montgomery no long while before. ' The gallant Montgomery is no more ; the brave Arnold is wounded ; and we have met with a severe check,' was his agitated epitome of the tidings he now read ; and to that he added, already picturing Carleton at the gates of Montreal, ' May heaven avert any further evils ! ' ' Nothing but the

---

[16] § Stone (ed.), Letters, pp. 34, 73 (pines set in the ice). Wooster to Sch.. Jan. 5, 1776: 4 Force, IV., 668. Brown: Vol. I., Chap. III. Ritzema to ——— (N. Y. Com. Safety), Jan. 3, 1776: 4 Force, IV., 1114.

[17] § Sch. to Hancock, Jan. 13, 1776 (6 P.M.): 4 Force, IV., 666. Sch., Colon. N. Y., II., p. 277. Munsell, Collections, II., pp. 336, 419; III , p. 404. Carroll, Journal, p. 53. The clock, candles, and silver are inferential.

immediate march of a body of troops into Canada can secure that Province,' he felt instantly.[18]

But what could he do? The few soldiers at Ticonderoga would be free in three days, and—thoroughly disgusted at having to lug pork-barrels instead of shaking King George's throne—were determined to quit the service. All the recruiting parties together had so far sent in only twenty men. Interest in Canada had waned. A nearer peril now filled the public eye. The Highlanders along the Mohawk, roused by the zealous loyalty of Sir John and Colonel Guy Johnson and by the missionary fervor of Allan Maclean, seemed in earnest—since they found themselves debarred from joining the regiment of Emigrants—to do something on their own account. About seven hundred Tories were in arms in Tryon County, and they had cannon. Albany was in confusion and alarm, and the melancholy news from the north only added to its danger and its panic. ' Every countenance is changed,' said an excited letter ; ' Whigs depressed and melancholy, and immediately animated and revengeful, or rather spirited for a noble and vigorous effort in the cause of liberty; whilst the Tories prick up their ears.' Minute-men from the country round and from Berkshire were flocking in, to defend the settlements against Johnson's fierce partisans ; but they had no artillery and very little powder. At so critical a moment few could spare even a thought for distant perils.[19]

The General himself was in poor health and a thoroughly disgusted frame of mind. 'Let me ask you, Sir, when is the time for brave men to exert themselves in the cause of liberty and their country, if this is not?' had been

---

[18] § Sch. to Montg., Nov. 30, 1775: Am. Antiq. Soc. Id. to Hancock, Jan. 13, 1776: 4 Force, IV., 666.   Id. to Wash., Jan. 13, 1776: ib., 666.   At Montreal: Id. to Wooster, Jan. 14, 1776 (in Id. to Hancock, Jan. 29: 4 Force, IV., 880).

[19] § Sch. to Hancock, Jan. 13, 1776: 4 Force, IV., 666.   Recruiting: Report of Com. (Sparks MSS., No. 52, II., p. 63). Tryon Co. Com. to Sch., Jan. 11, 1776: 4 Force, IV., 667. Letter, Albany, Jan. 15, 1776: ib., 682.

Washington's response to his proposed resignation ; but, though Schuyler then decided to remain at his post, he did not fail to ' frankly avow ' that he still felt ' a resentment ' against the Connecticut men. The danger in Tryon County was close at hand and its dimensions lay easily within the compass of his abilities. He was preparing to march there in person, and within a few days he actually did set out for a sharp and successful campaign. What, then, could he do for Canada ? He could send no men ; and, in spite of a very pointed hint from the Commander-in-chief, he could not go himself. [20]

What he felt came within his duty and powers he did

JOHNSON HALL

—as usual—with activity and zeal. Like Wooster, he begged the immediate assistance of the Green Mountain Boys, offering ' forty shillings, lawful, as a bounty to the men, and a month's pay to the officers, ' besides an allowance for rations from the hour of leaving home ; and he furnished Colonel Warner with funds for recruiting. On the same terms, Colonel Fellows was authorized to raise a regiment in Berkshire. The enlisting already set on foot in the Colony of New York for four companies to garrison the lake posts received, no doubt, a fresh impetus. But the crisis called for 'an immediate reinforcement, that is nowhere to be had, but from you,' he wrote the Com-

20 § Sch. to Hancock, Jan. 13, 22 ; Feb. 10, 1776: 4 Force, IV., 666, 802, 990. Id. to Wash., Jan. 5, 13, 1776 : ib., 580, 666. Wash. to Sch., Dec 24, 1775 : Wash., Writings (Ford), III., p. 292. Id. to Id., Jan. 27, 1776: ib., 375. Id. to Hancock, Jan. 30, 1776: ib. 383. Tryon Co. Exped.: Sch., 4 Force, IV., 818.

mander-in-chief; and, in reply, Washington had to report that recruiting for the army at Cambridge had proved so slow, that five thousand militia had been called in to man the lines. A great part of these had gone home, and 'the rest [were] induced to stay with the utmost difficulty and persuasion,' although their withdrawal would have exposed the patriot cause to complete ruin in case of an attack. ' In short I have not a man to spare,' he confessed.[21]

But no one called upon Washington in the name of his country vainly. A council of general officers—which John Adams also attended—met promptly; and, at the suggestion of the commander, it was decided to ask Massachusetts, New Hampshire, and Connecticut for one regiment each. These would form a part of the quota already called for, except that the term of service would be extended to January 1, 1777, 'if that should be necessary'; and Washington favored granting two months advance pay, as a special inducement.[22]

Antill, however, did not pause at Albany for results. Springing into his sleigh again, he set out for Philadelphia so hurriedly that a despatch from Schuyler to the Congress was overlooked. Sleepy Kingston, in the shadow of the Catskills, had the tale soon; and, by the way of Poughkeepsie and Samuel Smith, it travelled down the other side of the river to New York and to Governor Tryon's delighted ear. Turning eastward, it spread across the mountains, beating hard on the parsonage door at Pittsfield as it hurried past; and at length, on the seventeenth

21 § Sch. to Hancock, Dec. 8, 1775; Jan. 14, 22, 29, 1776: 4 Force, IV., 219, 671, 802, 880. Id. to Wash., Jan. 13, 1776: ib., 666. Wash. to Sch., Jan. 18, 1776: Writings (Ford), III., p. 355.

22 § Council, Jan. 18, 1776: Sparks MSS., No. 52, II., p. 252. Wash. to Sch., Jan. 18, 1776: Wash., Writings (Ford), III., p. 355. Id. to N. Eng. Govts., Jan. 19, 1776: ib., 362. Weare to Wash., Jan. 21, 1776: 4 Force, IV., 810. Wash. to Trumbull, Jan. 21, 1776: Writings (Ford), III., p. 363.

of January, the envoy from Quebec himself, sad and worn, laid it wearily on the table of Congress.[23]

Everywhere the tragic news fell upon the patriots like the shadow of a thunder-cloud on a garden. 'It has . . . Stunned the Advocates for Rebellion,' said Tryon. The 'bad Heads . . . begin to totter,' exulted Major Skene. 'Great confusion' in the American army at Cambridge, a deserter announced at Boston. 'The Country are greatly alarmed,' wrote Barnabas Deane to his brother, Silas. Governor Trumbull himself, though his were the eyes of St. John and the chin of Herod the Great, felt both vision and courage troubled. 'Let our eyes be upon the Lord!' he prayed; 'May we humbly and patiently bear his chastisement!' Even the Commander-in-chief, who had been counting upon the 'vast pleasure' of a letter from within the walls of Quebec, and fully believed that 'To whomsoever Canada belonged, in their favour, probably, would the balance turn,' felt with awful keenness the 'sad reverse of our affairs.'[24]

THOMAS ALLEN'S PARSONAGE

This, however, did not last. With the spring of steel, Washington recovered himself. 'But for the loss of the gallant chief, and his brave followers,' he declared, 'I should think the rebuke rather favorable than otherwise;

---

[23] § Sch. to Hancock, Jan. 14, 1776: 4 Force IV., 671. Tryon's No. 30, Feb. 8, 1776: Pub. Rec. Off., Am. and W. I., Vol. 186, p. 339. Antill: Journ. Cong., Jan. 17, 1776. Hancock to Wash., Jan. 20, 1776: 4 Force, IV., 781.

[24] § Tryon to Carleton, Jan. 31, 1776: Pub. Rec. Off., Am. and W. I., Vol. 186, p. 329. Skene, Jan. 28, 1776: ib., p. 333. Hutcheson to Haldimand, Feb. 2, 1776: Can. Arch., B, 20, p. 91. B. Deane, Jan. 22, 1776: Conn. Hist. Soc. Coll., II., p. 351. Trumbull: Stuart, Life, frontispiece; letter, Jan. 21, 1776 (ib., p. 245, note). Wash. to Arnold, Jan. 12, 1776: Wash., Writings (Ford), III., p. 334. Id. to Id., Jan. 27, 1776: ib., 379. Id. to Sch., Jan. 27, 1776: ib., 375.

for, had the country been subdued by such a handful of men, it is more than probable, that it would have been left to the defence of a few, and rescued from us in the spring. Our eyes will now be open not only to the importance of holding it, but to the numbers which are requisite to that end.' In the same spirit Richard Henry Lee expressed a hope, that the ill fortune in Canada might yet turn out well by teaching moral discipline, and urged pouring in troops enough to reduce Quebec before the enemy could relieve it. Trumbull, without waiting to hear from either Cambridge or Philadelphia, set on foot a regiment for the northern service, exhorting his people ' freely and cheerfully to engage in, and undertake the same for the sake of the love of their country, and all the dear-bought rights and privileges thereof, the happiness of themselves and all posterity ! ' Some, among them Jedediah Huntington, tried to believe that after such good news the Ministry would be less eager to hurry troops into America in the spring ; but others, like Josiah Bartlett, caring more for action than for consolation, preached that ' no cost or pains must be spared' to gain Canada, and that it would be 'of almost infinite advantage' to secure it before British reinforcements could arrive.[25]

As for Montgomery, John Adams—not fully understanding the circumstances that had forced him to attack —mingled the word 'inexperience' in his praise ; but it was soon clear that the laurels nipped by the frosts of Canada had merely been pruned for a still higher and still more generous growth. Not only were the encomiums of Burke, Fox, and Barré in the House of Commons

---

[25] § Wash. to Reed, Jan. 31, 1776: Writings (Ford), III., p. 398. Lee, Feb. 7, 1776: S. Adams Papers. Trumbull: 4 Force, IV., 931, 934. Trumbull to Griswold, Jan. 18, 1776: Trumbull Papers, Conn. Hist. Soc. Huntington to Trumbull, Feb. 15, 1776: Mass. Hist. Soc. Coll., 5th Ser., IX., p. 510. Bartlett to N. H Com. Safety, Jan. 20, 1776: 4 Force, IV., 784.

anticipated, but it could already be seen that his glorious death was to broadcast seeds of heroism, the noble harvest of his blood. From every lady's eye at Philadelphia spake the eloquence of tears. 'Revenge!' cried even the blasé Charles Lee.[26]

In the hall of Congress, where Antill ended his mission by answering questions for two hours, all these feelings wrought with special intensity, for there was the focus of the country. Some men shared more or less fully, perhaps, the sentiments of Tryon and Skene, but even these were saddened by the loss of brave citizens. The hall became so still that between question and answer, the crackling of the two great fireplaces at the right and the left of President Hancock's low platform seemed noisy.[27]

Samuel Huntington's keen legal face looked a little more grey than usual, a sure sign of a struggle behind it. General Floyd's military figure stiffened as he followed Antill's account of the battle. On Governor Ward's fine countenance could be read what he wrote his son, the Captain, at Quebec: 'The poet justly said, "Dulce et decorum est pro patria mori."' Sturdy Sherman, closing tight his vice-like jaws, gazed with unwinking steadiness at the envoy, four-square to every wind that blew. Wilson, the canny Scotch barrister, forgot briefs and longed to grasp a sword. Yonder, a face that was knuckles all over, with a nose like the beak of a galley, told every one who glanced that way that McKean stood for war to the knife. George Wythe, who looked the bald-headed eagle that he was, once the teacher but now the colleague of Jefferson, glared this way and that as if searching for some British enemy to tear in pieces. Samuel Adams, struck to

---

[26] § J. Adams to Knox, June 2, 1776: Works, IX., p. 384. Burke, etc.: 4 Force, VI., 314. Phila.: Lynch to Sch., Jan 20, 1776 (Sparks MSS., No. 60, p. 61). Lee to Wash., Jan. 24, 1776: Sparks, Corres., I., p. 135.

[27] § Antill before Cong.: Smith, Private Journal, Jan. 18; Hancock to Wash., Jan. 20, 1776: 4 Force, IV., 781. The scene is constructive.

ROBERT MORRIS

the marrow, took the blow with a shaking head but an un-
shaken heart, as he had taken many a rebuff in the earlier
stages of the controversy. The kingly brow of Robert
Morris neither rose or bowed; and he sat grandly still
and musing, with eyes that carried far beyond the present
like the eyes of Pope Julius the Second. Franklin, removing his big spectacles and slowly laying down his thick
handful of papers, put on the look of one able to tear
the thunderbolt from Jove and the sceptre from a tyrant.
'Poor gallant fellow,' murmured Lynch to himself; 'if a
martyr's sufferings merit a martyr's reward, his claim
is indisputable.' And then he pondered,—deeply, intensely. Lord Drummond had assured him that America
could have accommodation with Great Britain on the
terms Lynch himself would have dictated had England
lain at his feet, and it had been his intention just now to
' move for a mode of application for peace.' Should he
offer the motion? 'No,' he finally decided; 'it must
wait a little till we cool and set ourselves on a footing in
Canada.'[28]

'A footing in Canada!' With a start, some of the consciences in that room awoke. The energy of a few had
saved the record from a total blush, but it looked red
enough now. Priceless time had been lost. Divided
counsels had paralyzed good purposes all the way along.
Difficulties ought to have been foreseen, shortages provided
for in advance, developments anticipated instead of
awaited. Wages and supplies might have been looked
after more carefully. Action should have followed closer
upon knowledge.

---

[28] § Mainly from portraits hanging in Independence Hall, and the text
and portraits of Sanderson's Signers and the Nat. Portrait Gallery. Ward:
John Ward's Biog., *passim;* letter to his son, Gammell, Ward, p. 338. S.
Adams: Wells's Life, II., pp. 340, 341. Lynch to Sch., Jan. 20, 1776: Sparks
MSS., No. 60, p. 61. Franklin: Turgot's famous *mot.* Those named appear
from the Journal to have been in attendance. Drummond: Lynch to Sch.,
Jan. 20, 1776 (*supra*).

The report of the committee sent north had been read two days before Christmas, and again three days later; yet, although it recommended, since men were not re-enlisting freely, ' the immediate raising three Regiments,' nothing had been done except refer it by resolution to a special committee—apparently a compromise committee—with Dickinson at its head. Some of the Delegates must have been eager to act, for Harry Livingston, sent down from the army with letters, was detained day after day for three weeks to carry despatches back. But Dickinson made no report, and Livingston had to return empty-handed. On January the sixth, a letter from Schuyler, repeating his wish that a large force be sent immediately into Canada, was read. ' I do most sincerely believe,' he added, ' that, unless such a measure be adopted, we shall severely repent of it.' Still nothing was done; but, recorded a member, ' Monday Morning [January 8] was assigned to consider this Business & Nothing else to interfere, the Delegates to be upon Honor to meet punctually at 10 O'Cloc.' Evidently some of them felt very much in earnest.[29]

Monday brought this party reinforcements. A letter from Montgomery announced that his feeble army stood before the walls of Quebec, and declared it ' absolutely necessary to make the most formidable preparations ' for holding Canada in the spring. Enclosing this, came a note from Schuyler, urging that no time be lost in setting about the preparations. Possibly the rumor that Montgoymer had been killed, Arnold taken prisoner, and the army totally defeated had reached Philadelphia, as Schuyler presumed, and opened some eyes; but at all events the old fear that England might be able ' to turn the force

---

[29] § Journ. Cong., Dec. 23, 26. Report: Sparks MSS., No. 52, II., p. 63. R. R. Liv. to Sch., Jan. 12, 1776: Emmet Coll. (see Montg. to R. R. Liv., Dec. 10, 1775: Liv. Papers, 1775-1777, p. 81'. Sch. to Hancock, Dec. 31, 1775: 4 Force, IV., 480. Smith, Private Journal, Jan. 6.

of that Province, as well as the Savages, against our defenceless frontiers ' awoke again, and, without waiting longer for Dickinson, Congress broke its leash. [30]

It was assumed that two battalions or regiments could be made up from the men in Canada. James Livingston's corps would be a third. The First Pennsylvania and Second New Jersey battalions—already organized under Bull and Maxwell—were ordered to march north ' immediately.' Another, lately authorized in Pennsylvania, was assigned to the same field ; and New Hampshire, Connecticut, and New York were to raise one each. These would make nine in all, nominally over six thousand men. Their pay was to equal that given at Cambridge ; and various measures were voted to facilitate their march as well as prepare for the new campaign. [31]

It was this Congress, already in motion at last and haunted by remorse for its delays, that received the five-fold shock from Arnold, Campbell, Wooster, Schuyler, and Antill, a multiplied tale of disaster, helplessness and peril. Not so startling but no less alarming, a letter of Montgomery's written five days before his death declared —in what sounded now like a voice from the other world— that, in the judgment ' of several sensible men acquainted with this Province ' as well as in his own, the Colonies could not expect a union with Canada until they had ' a force in the country sufficient to ensure it against any attempts ' that might be made for its recovery. [32]

Yet the session passed without a proposal. ' Providence has, hitherto, been pleased to crown our attempts

---

[30] § Montg. to Sch., Dec. 5, 1775: 4 Force, IV., 188. Sch. to Hancock, Dec. 26, 1775: ib., 463 [Sch.'s letter of Dec. 31 appeared before Congress two days earlier than that of Dec. 26]. Journ. Cong., Jan. 8, 1776. Hancock to N. Y. Conv., Jan. 12, 1776: 4 Force, IV., 1073.

[31] § Journ. Cong., Jan. 8-10. Hancock to N. H. Com. Safety, Jan. 12, 1776: 4 Force, IV., 654. New Pa. battals.: 4 Force, IV., 507. REMARK LXVIII.

[32] Montg. to Sch., Dec. 26, 1775: 4 Force, IV., 464. Antill was examined Jan. 18 ; but it seems fair to assume that he made a statement on the seventeenth, when he delivered his despatches.

with success,' has been the President's complacent language until now, and men required a little time to adjust themselves to the change. Their task was to grapple with destiny, and first of all they wished to look their foe in the eye. The next day (January 18), it was proposed to put on mourning ; but, with Roman spirit, Governor Ward and others combatted the idea. 'Such Proceedings may cause too much Alarm at such a critical Juncture,' they protested, and the motion failed. Self-control like that vetoed hurry; and nothing was done now save to consider the tidings again and refer the letters to five members. But Dickinson had no place on this committee. It was a fighting corps : Lynch, Wythe, Sherman, and Ward, with Samuel Adams in the position of helm ; and, beginning on the nineteenth, resolutions in a flood came before Congress and passed it.[33]

First, it was voted 'that the American army in Canada be reinforced with all possible despatch, as well for the security and relief of our friends there as for better securing the rights and liberties not only of that colony, but the other United Colonies.' Washington should send one battalion to Canada 'with the greatest expedition possible,' if it could be spared, and, on the same condition, a general officer to command there. Steps were taken to set Bull's and Maxwell's regiments in motion, or at least what companies were ready. It was decided to address the authorities of New Hampshire, Connecticut, New York, and Pennsylvania, and urge on the raising of troops for the north. Bounties were voted ; money to stimulate recruiting provided ; inducements offered for arms and blankets; advances of pay recommended ; artillerymen called for ; blank commissions issued, 'from the necessity of the case,' to save time ; a second Canadian

---

[33] § Hancock to N. Y. Conv., Jan. 12, 1776: 4 Force, IV., 1073. Journ. Cong., Jan. 17-19. Smith, Private Journal, Jan 18.

regiment of one thousand—under Moses Hazen, Colonel, and Edward Antill, Lieutenant-Colonel—authorized ; De Haas put in place of Bull ; the collection of all the obtainable specie in the Colonies requested ; flints, powder, lead, given out ; a reassuring address to the Canadians prepared ; measures adopted to place needed supplies within reach of the Indians, in order to preserve

Robt Morris,

their ' confidence and friendship' ; and expresses hurried off in all directions on these and other matters. Learning soon of Washington's plan to obtain troops, Congress promptly endorsed it. 'The very first companies' that could be organized for the new Canada regiments were to be sent on without waiting for more. ' Immediate,' ' forthwith,' ' all possible expedition,' ' the utmost despatch,' were the labels on all this business ; and warm approval or hearty praise was dealt out liberally to reward activity or excite emulation. One question, however, remained unanswered. Had Congress the rod of Moses ? Could muskets, powder and ball, equipments, blankets, gold and silver, discipline be made by vote ? [34]

As Arnold's express crossed an ocean of drifts with tidings, an express from Carleton traversed an ocean of waves. Laden with despatches and verbal messages, Lieutenant Pringle of the *Lizard* embarked November the twenty-second aboard the *Nancy*, and, on the third day after Christmas at two o'clock in the afternoon, stepped into the office of Lord George Germain, that small Nemesis of despotism, bred by despotism itself. [35]

----

[34] § Journ. Cong., Jan. 19-29. Hancock to Wash., Jan. 20, 1776: 4 Force, IV., 781.
[35] § Hamilton to Dartmouth, Nov. 20, 1776: Can. Arch., Q, 11, p. 339. Précis

As His Lordship read the despatches, his cold and haughty face grew black ; and all the more—now that he could no longer despise the Provincials—he longed, like his Master, to crush them. ' It will require a very large and powerful Land and Naval Armament to reconquer the Country, and seize a proper hold of it,' Cramahé had written ; and a powerful expedition was resolved upon. ' I fear the Delays commonly attending a large Armament,' the experienced Governor had added on reaching Quebec ; and a small but efficient advance force was ordered equipped. No need here of a miraculous rod. ' Whereas Lord George Germain, one of his Majesty's Principal Secretaries of State, has acquainted Us, that it is the King's intention that every effort be made to send relief to Quebec ' : in that wise the Admiralty issued its commands. Here it was a magazine, not a rock, to be smitten.[36]

All this created a situation boiling with chances. Perhaps the victory at Quebec had led to a feeling of security in the town, and therefore weakened the influence of the fighters. Perhaps the friends of America and those in favor of neutrality would now declare that they had done enough to prove their loyalty. Perhaps the citizens who loved comfort would refuse to endure the hardships of the blockade longer. Everything showed that firewood was beginning to fail[37] ; and perhaps the women and children might not care to freeze, even if the men did not mind it. Perhaps Carleton might find it necessary to make a sortie ; and, leaving behind all whom he could not thoroughly rely upon, might give Arnold the advantage of numbers as well

---

of Oper. Germain to Carleton, Feb. 17, 1776: Can. Arch., Q, 12, p. 1. Intelligence from Quebec: Can. Arch., Q, 11, p. 338. London letter: Conn. Gazette, Mar. 22, 1776.

[36] § Dict. Nat. Biog., XXI., p. 235. Cram. to Dart., Nov. 19, 1775: Can. Arch., Q, 11, p. 324. Carl. to Dart., Nov. 20, 1775: Pub. Rec. Off., Colon. Corres., Quebec, 11, p. 519. Germain to Carleton, Feb. 17, 1776: Can. Arch., Q, 12, p. 1. Admiralty Sec. (to Lutridge): Out Letters, Vol. 100, p. 429 (Pub. Rec. Off.). Précis of Oper.

[37] Haskell, Diary, Jan. 19, 26, 1776 ; Arnold to Cong., Jan. 24, 1776: Sparks MSS., No. 52, II., p. 37.

as position.   On the other hand, the people might resolve
to make an end of it, gather heartily round their chief,
come out in serried ranks, and sweep every American from
the roads.

In short, the issue at Quebec might be settled there any
morning in an hour ; but, if the two sides could master
their internal difficulties and then hold each other in check,
it would become a question of reinforcements.   England
had far to send, but an English pound sterling could travel
post, while a mere promise to pay was halted at every pike ;
America stood near, but she journeyed afoot, her shoulders
were burdened with every sort of encumbrance, and her
path at best was only a buckboard road.

XXVI

THE PLANS WORK OUT

EVEN Washington felt that there was 'little hope of Arnold's continuing the blockade,' and the case was hard he knew. 'Inconceivably more severe, than the rest of the Continental Army have experienced,'—so the committee of Congress regarded the service in Canada ; yet even they could not realize what it meant. 'A season the severest that has been known here this ten years,' was Campbell's description of the winter. The Canadians themselves could find no adjective sufficiently cold to satisfy them. 'It is freezing hard enough to split stones,' they would say. 'There has been little cannonading of late,' wrote James Livingston, 'owing to the severity of the weather,'—a veritable Truce of God. The British patrols could mount guard for only half an hour at a time. Some of the American sentries were 'froze dead,' said Melvin. A soldier at one of the blockhouses had a foot frost-bitten with a warm stove in the room, noted Finlay in his Journal. 'God bless Your Honour, I am glad you are come for I am blind,' murmured a Quebec sentry to an officer of the guard : his eyelids had frozen together while he paced his beat.[1]

Sometimes it snowed until the low sky seemed falling

---

[1] § (This paragraph and the next.) Wash. to Sch., Jan. 27, 1776 : Wash., Writings (Ford), III., p. 375. Com., [Dec. 23, 1775]: Sparks MSS., No. 52, II., p. 63. Campbell to ——, Mar. 28, 1776: Liv. Papers, 1775-1777, p. 145. J. Liv. to ——, [Feb., 1776] : Am. Hist. Rec., III., p. 181. Melvin, Journal, Feb. 10. Ainslie, Journal, Jan. 10, 28 ; Feb. 9, 10, 12 ; Mar. 6 ; etc. Finlay, Journal, Feb. 9, 17, 18. 'Chalmers' Journal, Jan. 29 ; Feb. 9 ; etc. Haskell, Diary, Feb. 10. Tolman (Ware), Journal, Feb. 9-12.

bodily, and sometimes a tempest came straight across the fields like a charge of the Light Brigade. 'Such a storm, I believe, never was known in New England,' remarked a Massachusetts man in his diary. 'A perfect hurricane,' said a Quebecker; 'impossible to face the weather but for a minute.' Once the British patrols could not reach their posts, —it blew so hard; and some got lost in the attempt. At least three men were stifled to death on duty. Sometimes the citizens had to dig their way out of their houses, or use a window of the second story for a door. 'Many of the guns are deeply buried in this drift,' recorded Ainslie, 'altho their muzzles are at least 30 foot from the bottom of the ditch.' While, if a thaw came, one had to choose between ridges 'cover'd with clear ice' and the 'Ponds knee deep,' that lay between them.

Yet, so far as concerned the Americans, all these hardships were merely incidental. The people of Quebec, who complained so bitterly of the frost, had ramparts; but the besiegers were constantly exposed to an attack from more than double their number. 'We are in expectation every night that the enemy will come out upon us,' wrote one of them. More than once a large party sallied forth as if intending to give battle; and, though always retiring when boldly faced, it appeared like a threat of something formidable. A predicament like theirs, confessed Major Caldwell, would have prevented him 'from sleeping very sound.' When the enemy did not come in person, they sent messages,—unless the cold stopped everything: 'A plenty of 36-pound balls come to our door without hands,' wrote Major Brown to his father. The small-pox, in spite of all that orders could do, ravaged the cantonment; and, from one cause and another, the number of soldiers fit for

duty—including some two hundred Canadians—frequently shrank to five hundred. 'The men,' reported Arnold,
'are obliged to lay on their arms constantly, and to mount
Guard every other night.' 'No officer, no Soldier is
to go from his Quarters, upon Pain of Being Punished
instantly,' said the orders. Many necessaries—to say nothing of comforts—were lacking. 'Quarters awful!' exclaimed an officer, 'such as no page in History can equal.'[2]

Schuyler had expected that cold alone would force
Montgomery to raise the siege, even while the soldiers
were comparatively fresh ; after the disastrous assault it
was 'generally believed,' so Governor Tryon reported, that
Canada had been 'entirely evacuated' by the Provincials;
but now, in spite of cold, peril, and exhaustion, the wee
specks were still crawling in and out of the drifts, and the
circling shadows of their muskets marked off the slow
hours. Communication with Quebec, admitted Caldwell, was 'effectually' blocked,—save for an occasional spy
or deserter. Should quicker means fail, Arnold had said
at Aspen Point, 'time and perseverance' could not ; and
he evidently held the same opinion still. Wooster, needless to observe, found it 'most surprising.' 'This is true
bravery,' commented fearless Trumbull ; 'It must convince Lord North that Americans are not all poltroons.'[3]

Some gleams of cheer visited the camp, however. The
keen northwesters, when not over-keen, braced the nerves
and keyed the spirits to concert pitch. After the storm came
skies of the purest and most radiant blue, bending flaw-
less overhead ; and below them lay an ocean of diamond

---

[2] § Haskell, Diary, Jan. 5, 25. Arnold to Hancock, Feb. 1, 1776: Sparks
MSS., No. 52, II., p. 38. Caldwell, Letter. Brown: Smith, Pittsfield, I., p. 259.
500, etc.: Arnold to Deane, Mar. 30, 1776 (4 Force, V., 549); Campbell to ———,
Mar. 28, 1776 (Liv. Papers, 1775-1777, p. 145). Arnold to Cong., Jan. 11, 1776 :
Sparks MSS., No. 52, II., p. 34. 'Arnold's' Ord. Book, Jan. 25 ; Feb. 3, 11, 21.

[3] § Sch. to Hancock, Jan. 10, 1776: 4 Force, IV., 622. Tryon to Dartmouth,
Feb. 8, 1776 : Pub. Rec. Off., Am. and W. I., Vol. 186, p. 305. Caldwell, Letter.
Arnold to Montg., Nov. 20, 1775: Sparks MSS., No. 52, II., p. 31. Wooster to
Cong., Feb. 11, 1776: 4 Force, IV., 1001. Trumbull to Sch., Feb. 14, 1776: ib., 1147.

A VIEW OF QUEBEC IN 1759

light, garnished with the sapphires of deep shadows lustrous even at their darkest. At night—most of all on Washington's birthday—splendid auroras filled the heavens with castles and crowns, flaunting banners, fires of victory, and such chariots as perhaps the servant of Elisha beheld, when the prophet had opened his eyes.[4]

Nor was the illumination confined to the sky. Aware that the Quebeckers needed heat, the Americans did all they could to kindle fires. A little party would crawl past the walls in the dark, clamber into a vessel, set a slow match, and then make off: so much good lumber would never help warm the garrison. By the same logic, the houses in St. Roch and the suburb near St. John's Gate were touched off, and all the cannon on the ramparts could not prevent it. 'Nobody was seen altho the distance from our sentries was not fifty paces,' confessed a citizen once. Another time, fourteen houses were burned at a single haul. 'The night was still & gloomy,' wrote Ainslie; 'the snow loaded clouds hung low, from them an orange tinge was reflected, & the snow as far as the flames gave light, was of a reddish yellow—The adjacent country seem'd cover'd with a pitchy fire, & the villages were just perceptible in a dismal gloom . . nothing was heard but the crackling of burning beams, & a hollow roaring of feirce flames.'[5]

The constant fear of attack helped season the ennui, and the military operations, though few, had their interest. Now and then the crack of an American rifle aroused the camp for a moment; and occasionally one of the cannon, distant though it now was from the town, would aim high and drop a ball among the houses by way of reminder. As for the 36-pound shot that came

---

[4] § Marr, Remarks: Can. Arch., M, 384, p 85. Ainslie, Journal, Feb. 22.

[5] § (This paragraph and the next.) Ainslie, Journal, Jan. 21, 23; Feb. 16, 20, 21; etc. Haskell, Diary, *passim*. Melvin, Journal, Jan. 22. Brown: Smith, Pittsfield, I., p. 259.

out, Brown found that a pair of them did very well for andirons.

Day by day, moreover, the shadows of the muskets grew shorter, and this meant that reinforcements were nearer. The pressure became too strong for Wooster; and, three weeks and a half after the disaster—quite delay enough to ruin everything—about a hundred and twenty comrades from Montreal entered the cheering camp. Sixty or seventy more followed soon; and, on the fourth of February, twenty-five men from Berkshire, welcomed with huzza upon huzza, headed the line of reinforcements from home.[6]

All the way down, these last had cheered the Sons of Liberty and confounded the Tories by proving that the lakes were now passable, and announcing that Yankees were pressing on behind 'as thick as the trees in the woods.' And they had some foundation for the boast. A traveller going south from Montreal assured Tryon that he 'met many Parties upon the Lakes hanging upon the Sleighs like Bees about a Hive.' When the wind blew strong from behind, they laid boards across the sleds and stood upon them, to act as living sails. Here and there grim piles broke the smooth white,—comrades frozen to death, six or seven together sometimes; but on they hurried, crossed the ice-waves of the St. Lawrence from Laprairie, tarried for a breath at Montreal, and then on again down the river. 'Can Europe any longer doubt of the virtue, perseverance, and spirit of Americans,' cried Schuyler, 'when they see citizens become soldiers, regardless of the comforts they might enjoy in their own habitations, and quitting them with alacrity, to undertake a march of many hundred miles, through

6 § Wooster to Sch., Jan. 19, 1776: 4 Force, IV., 1004. Arnold to Cong., Jan. 24, 1776 . Sparks MSS., No. 52, II., p. 37. Haskell, Diary, Jan. 24 ; Feb. 4. Berkshire: Sch. to Wooster, Jan. 26, 1776 (4 Force, IV., 1003). Account of arrivals at T. Rivers: Letter, March 24, 1776 (4 Force, V., 481).

RUINS OF THE ST. MAURICE IRON-WORKS (PELISSIER'S)

snow and over frozen seas, without tents, without any shelter from the inclemency of the weather, but the azure canopy of Heaven?'[7]

Other aids arrived. Deserters from Quebec entered the lines, reporting that a short allowance of provisions had been ordered, and that Carleton's mainstay, the seamen, were getting uneasy. Pelissier furnished two petards and promised a supply of shells by the first of April. On the last day but one of December, five horsemen trotted out of Philadelphia, escorting northward all the specie that had adorned the Continental treasury that morning. At Albany, this pale sunbeam crossed Antill; and, ten days afterwards, it threw a spot of brightness on Wooster's table at Montreal. Six weeks later about $5,300—raised by Schuyler on his personal credit—were dropped with a clink in the same place · a total of some 28,000 hard dollars for the months of January and February. Arnold had been made a brigadier-general, which seemed to show that Congress had a grateful eye upon the doings in Canada ; and, more than everything else, the splendid thought of a triumph, all the dearer for the blood and suffering it required, touched every sacrifice with the magical iridescence of glory. 'I already view the approaching day,' wrote Washington, with reference to the reinforcements ordered to Canada ; 'I already view the approaching day, when you and your brave followers will enter this important fortress, with every honor and triumph attendant on victory and conquest. Then will you have added the only link wanting in the great chain of Continental union, and rendered the freedom of your country secure.'[8]

---

[7] § Letter, Montreal, Jan 27, 1776: 4 Force, IV., 868. Tryon to Dartmouth, Apr. 15, 1776: Pub. Rec Off., Am and W. I., Vol. 428, p. 340. Boards: Bloodgood, Sexagenary, p. 47. Letter from Skene: Pub. Rec. Off., Am. and W. I., Vol. 186, p. 333. Sch. to Trumbull, Feb 5, 1776: 4 Force, IV , 944.

[8] § Arnold to Hancock, Feb. 12, 1776: 4 Force, IV., 1017. Haskell, Diary, Feb. 13 J. Liv. to ———, [Feb.,] 1776]: Am. Hist. Rec., III., p. 181. Arnold to

But, while the shadows of the muskets grew shorter, other shadows lengthened. For one thing, it became clear that Congress had not the rod of Moses. A committee, appointed to inquire what articles the army needed, reported at the end of December, that goods to the value of £116,467 were 'absolutely necessary, and ought to be imported as soon as possible'; while, considering also 'the best ways and means for supplying the Continental Treasury with silver and gold,' it could light upon nothing more talismanic than to send American produce 'to proper ports in Europe and the West Indies' for sale,— a process rather too slow for the crisis in Canada. A great part of the needed goods were nothing more extraordinary than woollens. 'All the wool in America cou'd not furnish its inhabitants with stockings,' it was said at Quebec, and apparently with some truth. Washington had suggested at Christmas that a house-to-house canvass be made in the towns of New Hampshire for blankets to keep his army from suffering; and the next month precisely that had to be done in Philadelphia.[9]

Another item called for 20,000 stand of arms. Tryon and other emissaries had urged all the gunsmiths in America to leave the country, Holt told Samuel Adams. 'Of a thousand stand the New York Convention contracted for,' said Schuyler in March, 'six only have been delivered.' Apparently Robert Boyd, Jr., was the contractor; and, while he boasted that no equally well appointed shop could be found in that or the neighboring governments, he confessed that his works had been frozen

---

Hancock, Jan 11, 1776: Sparks MSS., No. 52, II., p. 34. Pelissier to Cong., July 20, 1776: Cont. Cong. Papers, Letters, 78, P, XVIII., p. 73. Specie: Journ. Cong., Dec. 30, 1775; Sch. to Hancock, Jan. 13, 31, 1776 (4 Force, IV., 666, 898); Id. to Id., Mar. 6, 1776 (4 Force, V., 91), Wooster to Sch., Mar. 5, 1776 (ib., 516); Sch., Ledger. Arnold: Journ. Cong., Jan. 10, 1776 Wash. to Arnold, Jan. 27, 1776: Writings (Ford), III., p. 379. REMARK LXIX.

9 § Report : 4 Force, IV., 446. Wool : Ainslie, Journal, Mar. 8. Wash. to N. H., Dec 23, 1775 : N. H. Hist. Soc. Coll., II., p. 150. Journ. Cong., Jan. 19, 1776.

up all winter, and that, for lack of competent hands, the superintendent had to 'employ his own fingers at every piece of business.' Benjamin Rittenhouse was entreated by express to come to Philadelphia and manufacture gun-locks on his own terms. Many people had begun to make saltpetre, and powder-mills were grinding in a feeble way ; but, at the middle of February, 1776, John Adams wrote anxiously to James Warren : ' Don't fail, my dear friend, to inform me of every step in the progress of the manufacture of saltpetre and gunpowder.' Even barracks were lacking, and some Pennsylvania troops had to be quartered in a pest-house and an old gaol.[10]

The Second New Jersey regiment, it was announced by Hancock on January the twentieth, would ' set forward [at] the beginning of next week.' That was a Saturday. The following Tuesday, Colonel Maxwell wrote from Trenton that he hoped he should always obey Congress cheerfully, but his regiment lacked ' a great part of everything' except men. Some two hundred and eighty stand of arms were totally wanting, and so many of those on hand were scattered about in repair-shops that he could make no exact return. Much warmer clothing would be necessary; and so would various other articles, a part of which, he supposed, were making. On Thursday, Congress appropriated money to arm the men. Six days later, notified that nearly half the muskets and a large variety of other articles were still wanting, it ordered the company that

---

[10] § Holt, Jan. 29, 1776: S. Adams Papers. Sch. to Wash., Mar. 9, 1776 : 4 Force, V., 147. Boyd to N. Y. Cong., Feb. 23, 1776: 4 Force, IV., 1480. Pa. Com. Safety to Rittenhouse, Feb. 26, 1776 : 4 Force, IV., 1576. J. Adams, Feb. 14, 1776: 4 Force, IV., 1140. Journ. Cong., Nov. 7, 1775; Jan. 25, 31 ; Feb. 13, 1776.

was 'nearest furnished' to be equipped out of whatever
the regiment possessed, and sent on. Fifty blankets,
fortunately, had been picked up among the farmers.
February the second, the New Jersey Congress, besides
directing the county committees to supply Maxwell with
all the weapons they possessed, recommended, 'in the
most strong and explicit manner,' that every private citizen
who owned arms fit for immediate use let them go in the
same direction. Two days more, and one company moved
at last ; but three weeks later the hindmost of the regiment
had not set out. None of the First Pennsylvania battalion,
which Hancock bracketed with this of New Jersey as
expected to move about the twenty-second of January,
arrived at Three Rivers before March, and its rear had
not reached Albany on the twelfth of April.[11]

'We will not conceal that the circulating cash in this
Province is very small,' the New Hampshire Convention
had said to Congress ; but there was no lack of good-will.
On receiving Washington's call for a battalion to serve in
Canada, the Assembly deferred over Sunday the adjourn-
ment which it was just ready to vote, held a special session,
'very readily and cheerfully' ordered the regiment, appointed Timothy Bedel its colonel, allowed two months'
pay in advance, directed the Committee of Safety to equip
and send off the men, and put two more members upon it in
order to expedite the work. 'You may depend, sir, we shall
not fail to do our utmost to forward this reinforcement,'
the Committee of Safety assured the Commander-in-chief ;
and apparently the business was to move briskly, for Bedel
had informed Schuyler a month before that a number of
minute-men, already under his command, would be ready

---

11 § Hancock to Wash., 4 Force, IV., 781. Maxwell to Hancock, Jan. 23,
1776: ib., 813. Maxwell, Mem. and letter, Jan. 31: ib., 897. N. J. Cong., Feb.
2, 1776: ib., 1580. Maxwell to Hancock, Feb. 3, 1776: ib., 923. Shreve to Sch., Feb.
24, 1776 : Emmet Coll. Letter, T. Riv., Mar. 24, 1776 : 4 Force, V., 481. Sch. to
Wash., Apr. 12, 1776: ib., 871. Jones, Conquest, p. 21.

to march as soon as he received orders. Indeed, the regiment was expected at Montreal before the end of January; and Wooster's secretary, with a piquant phraseology happily suggestive of the Colonel's rustic vigor, believed that when it came they could 'give those fellows a sweat in Quebec.' Actually, a few of the men reached Three Rivers on the tenth of March, but on the twentieth, in spite of promising announcements, it had to be reported : ' The regiment is not near full nor gone.' No doubt there were good reasons,—chiefly a dearth of funds that Israel Morey lacked ' words sufficient to describe ' ; but this fact helped little beyond the border.[12]

' Colonel Porter, said to be an exceedingly active man, is appointed to the command ' of the Massachusetts regiment, stated Washington with satisfaction, and the Colonel could be seen writing letters on this business at two and three o'clock in the morning ; yet it was already the third of March, when the first company, after parading in front of the meeting-house and listening to a prayer from Mr. Hooker, set out from Northampton. Some people had been active in urging men not to enlist : and they no Tories, either, very likely. The failure to pay soldiers their due was now bearing fruit. ' Numbers that have gone home,' said Schuyler, ' have swore most bitterly that they will never re-engage in the service ' ; and it followed, of course, that all their friends were advised never to enter it. The special bounty offered in Berkshire just after Montgomery fell, discouraged men from enlisting without such an inducement. Further, the volunteers were required to bring ' a good effective fire-arm ' as well as a blanket, ' also, a

---

[12] § N. H. Conv. to Cont. Cong., May 23, 1775: 4 Force, II., 696. N. H. Com. Safety to Wash., Jan. 21, 1776 : 4 Force, IV., 810. N. H. Hse. Repres., Jan. 25, 1776: 4 Force, V., 18. Bedel to Sch., Dec. 19, 1775: Sparks MSS., No. 60. p. 39. Cole to ———, Jan. 24, 1776: Emmet Coll. Cole: Wooster to Sch , Feb. 21, 1776 (4 Force, IV., 1499). N. H. Com. Safety to Hancock, Feb. 8, 1776: 4 Force, IV., 964. Morey to Weare, Mar. 7, 1776 : 4 Force, V., 117. N. H. Hse. Repres. to Gerrish, Mar. 12, 1776: ib., 26. Letter, T. Riv., Mar. 24, 1776: ib., 481 (cf. Morey, *supra*). Johnson to Folsom, Mar. 20, 1776: ib., 440.

Here you are my instructions. & you
and from the Character you bear. Doubt not
you will pay due attention to them. I must
again recommend your making all possible
Dispatch, & that you may share in the glory
of excluding the Instruments of Ministerial
Tyranny from that fair Province, is the
Sincere wish of Sir Your most Obt.
G: Washington

Colonel Elisha Porter

good bayonet, a cartridge-pouch, and a hatchet, or tomahawk, or cutting-sword, if possible ' ; and Porter found it
hard to obtain such an equipment. Most of the men willing to enlist had served in the previous campaign and been
obliged to leave their guns behind, for which, said the
Colonel, they had not yet received pay. Nearly all
the muskets of any value had already been bought up by
the authorities of the Colony ; prices had risen ; and the
men discovered that all the pay they were to have would
scarcely arm them.[13]

' I hear men inlist cheerfully,' said Governor Trumbull
a fortnight after issuing his call. Everything in his power
was done ; and Colonel Burrell, a man of spirit and influence, took hold vigorously to raise the regiment, no doubt.
But — ' Our treasury is entirely exhausted of money,'
Trumbull confessed at the same time ; ' without which it
will be impossible to persuade the men to set forward to
Canada, nor can it be reasonable to expect it.' No blankets and very few arms could be found in the Colony, and
Connecticut men as well as others had arrears owing them.
Nor was this all. The resentment against Schuyler's
methods counted even more, perhaps. ' I shall be carefull
another year and that is the universal say of al the officers,'
Lieutenant Gibbs had written in October. Only one company of Burrell's passed Albany by the sixth of March.[14]

---

[13] § Mass. action : 4 Force, IV., 1272, 1403. Wash. to Sch., Jan. 27, 1776:
Writings (Ford), III., p. 375. For Porter : Mag. Am. Hist., Sept., 1893, p. 186.
Colon. Mag., I., p. 3. Porter to Warren, Mar. 15, 1776: 4 Force, V., 240. Porter,
Diary : Mag. Am. Hist., Sept., 1893, p. 187. N. Cook, Diary, p. 381. Sch. to
Hancock, Dec. 8, 1775 : 4 Force, IV., 219. Equipment: Mass. Council, Feb. 9,
1776. The company that set out on Mar. 3 reached Quebec in exactly a month
(Cook, Diary).

[14] § Trumbull to Hancock, Feb. 3, 1776 : 4 Force, IV., 930. Id. to Wash.,
Jan. 24, 1776: ib., 839. Id. to Griswold, Jan. 18, 1776: Trumbull Papers, Conn.
Hist. Soc. Burrell: Wash. to Sch., Jan. 27, 1776 (Writings (Ford), III., p. 375).
Trumbull to Wash., Feb. 2, 1776 : 4 Force, IV., 917. Blankets, etc. : Sch. to
Hancock, Feb. 10, 1776 (ib., 990). Arrears : Id. to Id., Feb. 20, 1776 (ib., 1214).
J. Trumbull, Jr., stated on Feb. 17 that £30,000.14.4 were due Conn. men for
pay (Cont. Cong. Papers, 153, I., p. 562). Gibbs to Trumbull, Oct. 10, 1775:
Trumbull Papers, Mass. Hist. Soc., IV. One Co.: Sch. to Hancock, Mar. 6,
1776 (4 Force, V., 91).

Congress itself undertook to find arms for the Second Pennsylvania regiment (St. Clair's); but Schuyler reported only one company of it at Albany on the twenty-first of March. Van Schaick's New York battalion had a good start, for it inherited three companies already in process when Antill brought the sad news from Quebec; but the Congress of New York confessed its inability to furnish it with any arms, blankets, or clothing, and Schuyler found himself ' distressed in the highest degree ' for these and every other necessary. As for Warner, from whom General Wooster had expected the most effective aid, he proved the greatest disappointment of all, perhaps ; for, instead of 736 men reported to Schuyler as enrolled, only 417 had arrived at Montreal on the fifth of March, and few more seemed likely to appear. Schuyler had actually advanced pay for the larger number; but, as the Ticonderoga accounts had not yet been adjusted, the ' truly necessitous ' men of the Grants could hardly be blamed for accepting their due as they could get it.[15]

Most of the troops went by way of Albany ; and there all the final touches had to be given their equipment, provisions be furnished, and transportation be provided for. Possibly Schuyler's ' nerves ' felt the difficulties of the case a little more keenly than others might have, and cried a little more loudly; possibly, here and there, another minute of prevision might have saved an hour of bustle ; but his troubles were many and grievous,—occasionally even ludicrous. Troops came up to him unarmed, half-armed, or with arms ' hardly worth carrying.' As the soldiers returning from Canada had been expected to leave their muskets for their successors, Albany was looked

15 § St. Clair : Journ. Cong., Jan. 3 : Feb. 16, 1776. Sch. to Hancock, Mar. 21, 1776: 4 Force, V., 452. 3 Cos.: Id. to Id., Feb. 15, 1776 (4 Force. IV., 1156). N. Y. Cong. to Sch., Feb. 22, 1776: 4 Force, V., 301. Sch. to N. Y. Cong., Feb. 21, 1776: ib., 318. Warner: Id. to Hancock, Mar. 19, 1776 (ib., 415); Wooster to Sch., Mar. 5, 1776 (ib., 416). (See Sch. to Wooster, Jan. 26, 1776: 4 Force, IV., 1003.) Ti.: Sch. to Hancock, Mar. 7, 1776 (4 Force, V., 103).

upon as a sort of arsenal ; but men whose wages had not
been paid seldom cared to surrender valuable firelocks on
trust.   The bad ones were taken and repaired ; but, in the
midst of it all, the supply of steel gave out.   The Tories
of Tryon County reluctantly helped ; but the list of their
confiscated pieces had no elasticity.   Men went about,
picking up what they could; but this resource was poor,
dear, and inadequate.[16]

Now the General found himself 'hard put to it' for
nails or felling-axes, and now for the mittens, woollen caps,
and Indian stockings required in Canada.   Last week no
hay could be had for the horses, and yesterday no horses
for the hay.   At one time, seventy-six sleds came when
a hundred and twenty had been expected, and at another
it was cargo that fell short.   'This moment,' the captains
of two Pennsylvania companies announced that no
moccasins—absolutely required for winter marching in
Canada—had been furnished their men ; the next, Major
Ogden gave notice that shoes—equally necessary after
the snow departed—could not be had at the north.   Even
men who had left home well clothed and well armed often
found their equipment in a bad condition after the long
march to Albany.   Now the recruits turned up sick and
there was no medicine, and Schuyler could only suggest
that Congress 'despatch a small vessel or two to Portugal
or the Islands for a supply' ; now they turned up grum-
bling and mutinous for want of their pay, and Schuyler
had nothing at all to propose.   The scarcity of salt was
'incredible' ; the Commissary-General could not 'possibly' furnish the troops with all the articles allowed
them by law ; to ease the military chest, people were
'recommended' to transport the troops gratis, with all

---

[16] § For Sch.'s troubles, see his letters : 4 Force, IV., 219, 622, 802, 829, 880,
938, 955, 990, 1146, 1156, 1214, 1481 ; V., 91, 147, 318, etc.   Journ. Cong., Feb. 5, 1776.
Jones, Conquest, p. 22.   Men who, contrary to orders, brought their muskets
home probably did not wish to reveal that fact.

the expense of time and patience that implied ; the lack of proper equipment caused longer or shorter detentions ; and every difficulty was the greater because the small frontier settlement at Albany could supply ' hardly anything.'

The diabolical embarrassments of the route, also, tripped up every calculation. The ice on the lower Hudson began to break up quite early. The upper course gradually followed suit ; and, wherever the river burst its bonds, the waters overflowed the roads. ' By the time it will be navigable,' remarked Schuyler, ' and the waters which are out subsided, the ice in the lakes will be too weak to venture troops on.' About the middle of March, the St. Lawrence had its turn of spring fever, overflowing in the same way and cutting the roads for three or four weeks. The General had believed that he could lead troops around Lake Champlain before the deepest portion of it froze, but there were no troops to go then ; and, after the deep snows began to melt, even if such a route—' hitherto not attempted '—actually did exist, it could not be used. While, then, Hancock was not exactly correct in pronouncing February, as he did, ' the only time before Summer, of crossing the Lakes,' he made no mistake in calling it the best ; and in that month the movement of troops only got under way.[17]

Nor was it enough merely to land the men in Canada : they must be kept alive still, and that meant a tremendous expense. No pork and very little beef could be obtained there before autumn ; and Schuyler found it necessary to send down about four hundred barrels of the former, at the appalling freight of seven dollars and a half per barrel, and a hundred and fifty head of the latter on the hoof.

---

[17] § Sch. to Wash., Mar. 9, 1776: 4 Force, V., 147. St. L.: Wooster to Wash., Jan. 21, 1776 (4 Force, IV., 796); Id. to Sch., Feb. 19, 1776 (ib., 1483). Route: Sch. to Hancock, Dec. 8, 1775: ib., 219. Hancock to N. Y., Jan. 12, 1776: ib., 1073.

Staggered by such bills, the military chest groaned over so small and so proud an item as the expense of a few British prisoners, who remained in Albany. 'It is even a great burden,' mourned Schuyler, 'that we are to furnish these with provisions.' Before January came to an end, all but $66,000 of the $240,000 in Continental paper

GENERAL CHARLES LEE

actually received by the northern department, had been expended ; debts had mounted up ; and now the Congress was ordering new expenses with a speed that no hand-press of 1776 could hope to equal.[18]

[18] § Sch. to Hancock, Feb. 15, 23, 1776: 4 Force, IV., 1156, 1481. Id. to Wash,. Mar. 9, 1776: 4 Force, V., 147. Id. to Lee, Feb. 29, 1776: ib., 356. Prisoners: Id. to Hancock, Jan. 29, 1776 (4 Force, IV., 880). Mil. Chest, Jan. 28, 1776: ib., 907.

As the plans were figured out, some nine thousand men—including Warner's regiment as promised—were designed for the Canada service ; but the crisis at the north forbade anything like deliberation and thoroughness, and incomplete rosters, much sickness, and a percentage of desertion brought the eight new battalions from the Colonies far below their nominal strength. Weaker yet proved the regiments to be formed in Canada. Two were to consist of Colonials already in the field. ' I shall be agreeably disappointed,' remarked Schuyler, ' if one can be raised there.' Everything stood in the way. The men were coming home as fast as they could get off. At the end of February, Lieutenant-Colonel Ritzema estimated that about nine hundred, 'the remnants of all [the] corps which had been there,' remained in Canada. Schuyler drew up a scheme for arranging the officers under the new plan, intended to reconcile claims and prejudices ; but, though it looked as ingenious and complicated as a game of solitaire, Wooster declared it would not satisfy Colonial jealousies and personal pretensions. Watching the privates disappear, the officers concluded they would have none to command ; deemed themselves unprovided for ; felt neglected, and therefore were sour. Wooster undertook to carry out the plan and failed ; and Ritzema advised Congress bluntly that the men from different sections had ' too opposite Characters ever to form a useful Corps.'[19]

Hazen, the appointed colonel of the Second Canadian regiment, seemed able to carry his banner far and high. After a boyhood passed at Haverhill in Massachusetts,

---

[19] § One regt. each from N. H., Mass., Conn., N. Y., N. J., N. H. Grants ; two each from Penn., the army in Canada, and the Canadians ; also the Berkshire men and Nelson's Co. of riflemen (Journ. Cong., Jan. 30). Shortages: Sch. to Hancock, Feb. 10, 1776 (4 Force, IV., 990); Id. to Wash., Feb. 14, 1776 (ib., 1146); Id. to Lee, Feb. 29, 1776 (4 Force, V., 356); Id. to Hancock, Mar. 19, 1776 (ib., 415). Id. to Id., Feb. 4, 1776: 4 Force, IV., 938. Ritzema, Feb. 27, 1776 : 4 Force, V., 313 ; Journal, Feb. 16. Plan for offs.: 4 Force, IV., 1216 ; Wooster to Sch., Feb. 13, 1776 (ib., 1218); Sch. to Hancock, Feb. 20, 1776 (ib., 1214).

he served in the Louisburg expedition, rose to be a captain of Rangers at the taking of Quebec in 1759, and, as
even Canadian Tories admitted, won the reputation of 'a
fam'd partizan, remark'd by Gen: Wolfe for a good soldier.'
Later, he obtained a lieutenant's commission in the 44th
Foot, and, soon after the Conquest, retired on half-pay.
Settling then near St. Johns, he not only carried on large
farming operations but owned saw-mills, a potash-house,
and a forge. When the Americans appeared there in
arms, he doubtless foresaw the losses that were sure to
befall him in case of war, and wished them elsewhere.
For a while, his trimming policy inspired confidence in
both camps. Then it inspired suspicion in both, and each
held him in turn as a prisoner. But Schuyler believed
him a ' friend '; and certainly principles, interests, necessity
or all combined brought him and his sword eventually to
the American army. On the tenth of February he unfurled
his flag in due form, directing his agents to enroll fit men
' at beat of drum or otherwise,' and give them one month's
pay as a bounty. But the Canadians, 'tho' prompt at a
short, desultory war,' said the committee of Congress, had
'some reluctance to more permanent engagements.' Besides, money for the promised bounties failed. ' For God's
sake send some Cash for that purpose !' cried Antill, the
lieutenant-colonel. But cash there was none ; and by
April the first, with some two hundred and fifty on his
roll, Hazen found himself compelled to stop. Livingston's
corps remained at about two hundred : a total of four hundred and fifty Canadians instead of two thousand.[20]

[20] § Hazen : Bull. Rech. Hist., 1901, p. 159 ; Hazen to Hancock, Feb. 18, 1776
(4 Force, IV., 1186) ; Quebec Gazette, Sept. 28, 1776 ; Foucher, Journal, Sept. 23,
1775 (Can. Arch.); Ainslie, Journal, Mar. 8 ; Verreau, Invasion, p. 71 (Sanguinet), p. 251 (Lorimier); Journ. Cong., jan. 22, 24 ; Sept. 24 ; Oct. 23, 1776 ;
Penna. Arch., Sec. Ser., XI., p. 99 ; Memor. (Cont. Cong. Papers, No. 42, III.,
p. 451). (Hazen was captain of a Co. of Rangers, and so commonly bore that
title.) Sch. to Hancock, Jan. 13, 1776 : 4 Force, IV., 666. Recruiting papers :
Can. Arch., B, 27, pp. 385, 397. Com.: Sparks MSS., No. 52, II., p. 63. Hazen
to Antill, Mar. 10, 1776: Can. Arch., B, 27, p. 387. [Antill] to [Hazen], Mar. 28,
1776: ib., p. 380. Hazen to Sch., Apr. 1, 1776: 4 Force, V., 751.

' Daily aids are going,' observed a member of Congress cheerfully ; but the real question was : What arrives ?[21]

A month and a day after Congress heard of Montgomery's death, Arnold had six hundred and seventeen of the rank and file, besides Livingston's Canadians, fit for duty. March eighth, a squad of men in uniform coats, knapsack on back, tomahawk at side, broad white belts crossing ' diamond-fashion' on breast and back—a cartouch-box hanging from one, and a canteen swinging from the other—trudged bravely but wearily, with drum, fife, and flag at their head, into Arnold's camp : they were the advance guard of the First Pennsylvania. Seventeen days more went by before the earliest from New Jersey appeared. By the twenty-second of March, less than fourteen hundred new soldiers from the Colonies had reached Three Rivers on their way to Quebec ; by the eighth of April only seventeen hundred and seventy-two ; and not another new face appeared until the twenty-seventh of that month.[22]

The small-pox was more prompt. At the close of February, ' near one hundred men in the Hospital ' were reported by Arnold ; and in three weeks they numbered about four hundred. Hazen believed that 'our strength in camp before Quebeck did not, on the 18th of March much exceed that of the day after General Montgomery's fall '; within two weeks more, Arnold admitted to his friend Silas Deane that ' the greatest part' of the New England men were down with the plague ; and, a little after the first of April, a captain serving there reported 'six hundred and odd present and fit for duty.' At the

---

[21] Chase to ———, Feb. 10, 1776: Arch. of Md., XI., p. 150.

[22] § Return, Feb. 18, 1776: 4 Force, V., 104. Arrivals: Cf. letter, Mar. 24, 1776 (4 Force, V., 481), with Haskell, Diary, Mar. 8, 25 ; Arnold to ———, Mar. 26, 1776 (4 Force, V., 512) ; Goforth to Jay, Apr. 8, 1776 (Bancroft Coll., Rev. Papers, I., p. 37). Uniform: Journ. Cong., Dec. 21, 1775 (see also Deane to Mrs. D., June 3, 1775: Conn. Hist. Soc. Coll., II., p. 252). Wooster to Cong., Apr. 27, 1776: Cont. Cong. Papers, No. 161, II., p. 309.

very time when the force was supposed to be swelling like the Solway at full of the tide it was noted, 'seventy odd men less this day fit for duty than there was two days ago.' Warner's recruits engaged only to the fifteenth of April, and by that time they would not, 'on an average, have done ten days' service.' To make it worse, 'Our surgeons are without medicine ; our Hospitals crowded, and in want of almost every necessary,' added Arnold. With a circuit of twenty-six miles, including three ferries, to guard, the troops needed for aggressive operations could be found only—in the Northern Lights.[23]

The cannon of Ticonderoga had been captured to salute the British in Boston with, and, as Knox had taken the best of them across the mountains, they could not be had for Quebec. Pelissier gave notice that a lack of coal would prevent him from supplying shot and shells before May, and by about that time a British fleet might be rounding Point Levi. The quantity of powder ordered up for Canada Schuyler pronounced ' vastly short ' ; and, even after another appropriation, the amount fell much below his demand. All kinds of military stores were lacking. ' We shall want everything,' wailed Montreal ; ' I have it not in my power to send anything, for I have nothing,' moaned Albany in response. ' Our flour is nearly expended,' reported Wooster ; ' we have not more than enough for the army one week. We can purchase no provisions or wood, or pay for transporting of anything without hard cash. We are now not able to pay half the debts we owe the country people. Our credit sinks daily ; all the provisions and wood that we want for the army, for two or three months to come, must be purchased and transported to camp by the middle of March ; after that time there

---

[23] § Arnold to Wash., Feb. 27, 1776 : 4 Force, IV., 1513. Hazen to Sch., Apr. 1, 1776 : 4 Force, V., 751. Arnold to Deane, Mar. 30, 1776 : ib., 549. Goforth to Jay, Apr. 8, 1776 : Bancroft Coll., Rev. Papers, I., p. 37.

New York Febry 28th 1776

Sir

I am to inform ... that I am appointed by the Continental Congress to the Command of the Troops in Canada — I hope and trust Mr I shall agree well together. I must request you immediately to contract and grind into flour twenty thousand (Bushels) Bushels of Wheat I must also desire that you will suffer the Parishes of Montreal to send ...

204

of their another Cloaths out of the Barn, the poor.

it first going out I must therefore conclude, Sir

Your Charles Lee
Major General

I have ordered that these two persons
to longer are it to your
from Brown Point;
disposition whether it would not be understood for it
is ready enough
is too late in the season to the folks of Richelieu
where it appears to me you ought to effectuate a Post

205

will probably be no passing for a month or six weeks ;
these things, therefore, must be provided immediately, or
the consequences will be dreadful.' For answer, this
drowning-cry had the $5,300 that Schuyler borrowed ;
and to suppose that much of so trifling a sum would reach
Quebec, would be to expect a rill from the Oasis of
Bahrieh to cross the Great Desert.[24]

When that mournful February handed the distaff on to
March, Arnold could barely ' hobble ' about his room ;
Clinton was proving only a makeshift ; Campbell sulked
in total eclipse ; Wooster was still securing the retreat. [25]

A few days before, Charles Lee had been ordered to go
north immediately and take command in Canada. What
sort of a rod he was likely to wield there, probably General Wooster at least could have guessed, for about the
hour his drowning-cry for money shuddered past New
York on its way to Philadelphia, Lee airily tossed him off
his first orders : ' I am to inform you that I am appointed
by the Continental Congress to the Command of the
Troops in Canada—I hope and dare say We shall agree well
together. I must request you immediately to contract
[for] and grind into flour twenty thousand Bushels of
Wheat.' But Montgomery had believed that Lee could
win success in the north ; ' General Lee, in my opinion,
is the man,' cried Ritzema ; Lee is the man, echoed Mc-
Dougall. Washington felt that there would be an advantage in sending a general who knew France and the
French, and could address the Canadians in their own

---

[24] § Ti. : Knox to Wash., Dec. 5, 1775 (4 Force, IV., 188) ; Sch. to Hancock,
Dec. 8, 1775 (ib., 219) ; Wash. to Sch., Jan. 27, 1776 (Writings (Ford), III., p. 375) ;
Sch. to Wash., Feb. 14, 1776 (4 Force, IV., 1146). Shells: Arnold to Cong., Jan.
24, 1776 (Sparks MSS., No. 52, II., p. 37). Powder : Sch. to Hancock, Feb. 4,
1776 (4 Force, IV., 938) ; Id. to Wash., Feb. 14, 1776 (ib., 1146) ; Id. to Lee, Feb.
29, 1776 (4 Force, V., 356) ; Wooster to Sch., Mar. 16, 1776 (Sparks MSS., Vol. 60,
p. 77). Wooster to Hancock, Jan. 27, 1776 : 4 Force, IV., 869. Sch. to Hancock,
Feb. 7, 1776: ib., 955. Wooster to Sch., Feb. 21, 1776: 4 Force, IV., 1499.
[25] § Arnold to Wash., Feb. 27, 1776: 4 Force, IV., 1513. Only glimpses of
Clinton appear in the docs. Campbell to ——, Mar. 28, 1776: Liv. Papers,
1775-1777, p. 145.

cherished idiom. Lee himself argued in that way ; and when, on the morrow of his first order, this gentleman was ' given up to the Southern Colonies, as the most exposed,' keen disappointment reigned. No single element of strength seemed to be left the army in Canada.[26]

' It is commonly said,' reported the French representative in England, ' that the Americans have made a capital and inexcusable mistake in neglecting to send, as soon as winter began, sufficient forces to ensure, with the capture of Quebec, the complete acquisition of Canada.'[27] Capital ? Yes, in the narrower and possibly in the broader view. Inexcusable? Yes again, in the eyes of the Revolution, were the charge made against a certain group in Congress. But whoever examined the hours that made up the winter, from its beginning to its end, would probably have added one other epithet : ' Unavoidable.'

The scraps of an army before Quebec, however, could not philosophize on the case. They were at the circumference, not the centre. All they could do was to drag along in their fever-and-ague of hopes and fears. All they could see was that some fine morning, in one way or another, the strange situation was likely to end.

---

[26] § Journ. Cong., Feb. 17, 28 ; Mar. 1, 1776. To Phila.: Sch. to Hancock, Feb. 26, 1776 (4 Force, IV., 1499). Lee to Wooster, Feb. 28, 1776: Am. Antiq. Soc. Montg. to R. R. Liv., Dec. 16, 1775: Liv. Papers, 1775-1777, p. 81. Ritzema to [N. Y. Com. Safety], Jan. 3, 1776: 4 Force, IV., 1114. McDougall to Jay, Mar. 17, 1776: Johnston, Jay Papers, I., p. 46. Wash. to Lee, Mar. 14, 1776 : Sparks, Wash., III., p. 315. Lee to Sch., Feb. 8, 1776: Sparks MSS., No. 60, p. 66. Duane to Stirling, Mar. 1, 1776: 4 Force, V., 37.

[27] Garnier to Vergennes (in French), June 4, 1776: Stevens Facsim., No. 872.

XXVII

GRAVE OMENS

DAY by day, a change was now creeping over the face of Canada—so a number of careful observers felt—like that which makes one say, Autumn is coming. The great-great-grandfathers of the *habitants* in old France had felt no strenuous cravings for 'Liberty.' Their ambition was to be happy in this world and feel easy about the next,—the second item really a part of the first. They could fight and they loved victory ; but, whether conquering or conquered, they desired most of all to get back to their farms. Home, wife, and children ; the cheery village, as the necessary non-ego, the complementary delight, of the home ; the Church, to fend off the prowling wolves of conscience and imagination ; and the priest, as the embodiment of the Church : these were the realities of life. If tyranny pinched them, it was hated and if possible overthrown,—not because it was tyranny, but because it made itself disagreeable. Certain lofty ideas and certain beautiful sentiments gave them pleasure, like the ribbons on a jacket ; but, if it came to a choice between the jacket and the ribbons, they knew very well which to surrender. Moreover, since the ribbons were unessential, they could be treated airily, capriciously. Constancy in trifles was no duty. Indeed, it argued heaviness of wit.[1]

---

[1] The author has had many opportunities for observing the country people in several quarters of France, and has, of course, learned from other

The peasant of Canada inherited this disposition and certain habits besides. For example, Captain Marr, who studied him rather closely, thought his vivacity due in part to an inborn preference for bread instead of meat. And, too, his natural traits were somewhat deepened by his environment. Each generation, after the race came to New France, had smaller learning than its predecessor, and for that reason a narrower horizon. 'The Discouragements they formerly met with in their Husbandry,' said Marr, 'made them careless and indolent; and the Length of their Winter when they have little or nothing to do enures them to Laziness.' To be sure, some went into the woods, but they were the few; and almost all had to get up the fuel for their ravening stoves, but that did not take long. The keenness and the changeability of the climate heightened their liveliness; and, in the total absence of any other attractions, their cosy homes and congenial spouses, their pipes and chat, their skating parties and social sleigh-rides became more and more their vital interests. More and more, they seemed 'incapable of long application to Labour' or anything else, 'unless where a certain Prospect of Gain' encouraged them to persevere.[2]

As all the Americans agreed, few, if any, understood the issue between Great Britain and the Colonies. 'Down with taxes!' they could feel, for they felt the taxes; 'Down with the nobles!' they could enjoy, for they hated the nobles; but all the broad phases of politics lay quite beyond their sky-line. The universal impulse to be free, the hints of boundless forests and unfettered

---

observers. This and the following paragraphs may be compared with those at the beginning of Chap. XIV. The latter have primary reference to the military quality of the people and the effect of a particular situation upon them; the former to their essential character. The two views of them are intended to be complementary.

[2] § Marr, Remarks: Can. Arch., M, 384, p. 85. See Casgrain, Perrault, *passim*.

winds, and the vaguely sensed principles of English liberty, had an influence, but as yet only one faint one,
upon the general mass. 'Too ignorant to put a just
estimate on the value of freedom,' observed Stocking on
the Chaudière. 'Many of the ignorant Canadians don't
know what they are themselves,' testified the Rev. Syl-
vanus Ripley ; 'their ideas of Liberty are very ill-digested.'
'Some few may be attached to us from principle ; sure I
am the majority are not,' concluded Ritzema after months
of experience in the field. Even at Quebec, where intelligence was naturally keener than among the farmers,
Pelton did not feel at all sure that people understood the
controversy. 'Having been so long habituated to slav-
ery,' thought Arnold, 'and having (as yet) but a faint
sense of the value of Liberty,' they needed 'every possible encouragement'; and this encouragement, as well as
the needful education in liberal politics, the Colonial
campaign among them had done little enough to supply.[3]

'Generous souls,' wrote Congress to the people of
Canada after the repulse at Quebec, 'Generous souls,
enlightened and warmed with the sacred fire of liberty,
become more resolute, as difficulties increase' ; but Marr
used a juster measure of their character when he said :
'If one stops & lodges at one of their Houses, they will
furnish him with a tolerable Bed, coarse but clean Sheets,
they will offer him what Provisions the Home affords,
with a very good grace ; but when a Bill is demanded, the
answer is, " What you please, we never tax Gentlemen " ;
by this means they often get three times the value of
what they furnish.' 'Very kind, neat and accommo-
dating, but a little deceitful withall,' was the judgment

[3] § Stocking, Journal, Nov. 3. Ripley to J. Wheelock, Mar. 7, 1776 : J.
Wheelock Papers. Ritzema to N. Y. Com. Safety, Jan. 3, 1776 : 4 Force, IV.,
1114. Pelton : N. Y. Calendar, I., p. 285. Arnold to Cong., Jan. 11, 1776 : Sparks
MSS., No. 52, II., p. 34. See also Rep. Com. Secret Corres., Cont. Cong. Papers,
No. 22, p. 211 ; Liv. Journal, Oct. 19.

HOUSE AT THE CORNER OF NOTRE DAME AND ST. PETER STREETS, MONTREAL
Occupied by the American Officers during the Winter of 1775-76

of Frye Bayley after an intimate acquaintance. The little graces and little arts of life engrossed their minds. People less fitted to play a heroic rôle, except in stark self-defence, could not easily have been contrived. Their virtues and their faults joined hands on that ; and Carleton, after seeing clearly what they were, gave this verdict : ' There is nothing to fear from them, while we are in a state of prosperity, & nothing to hope for when in distress.' [4]

To emphasize this unreliability, those in sympathy with the Americans had no leaders of their own blood. Not only the noblesse, lawyers, and priests, but the few solid Canadians outside those classes adhered still to the British, for the poverty and inefficiency of the Colonials had tended little to change, as a different policy might have done, their natural conservatism and their loyalty. In May, 1777, Carleton prepared a ' List of the principal persons settled in the Province who very zealously served the rebels in the winter 1775 and 1776,' and the only French name worth putting into it, Pelissier, belonged to a man from the old country. ' With respect to the better sort of people, both French and English,' admitted Hazen in April, 1776, ' seven-eighths are Tories.' The bracing influence of clear minds, powerful wills, and high social position was therefore lacking among the Canadian Sons of Liberty. They were grain cargoed in bulk ; and now it began to look as if the ship might roll. [5]

What steady pressure there was upon them counted as before against the Americans. The nobles had lost their ascendancy forever, though in some cases they retained more or less influence ; but the clergy still kept a power-

---

[4] § Secret Journ. Cong., Jan. 24, 1776. Marr, Remarks: Can. Arch., M, 384, p. 85.   Bayley, Narrative.   Carleton to [Germain], Sept. 28, 1776 : Pub. Rec. Off., Colon. Corres., Quebec, 12, p. 345.

[5] § List : Can. Arch., Report for 1888, p. XIV. Hazen to Sch., Apr. 1, 1776: 4 Force, V., 751.

ful grip on affairs. Good old Prince might kick up his heels when a bridle entered the pasture, but Jacques understood quite well that after a little play the bit would certainly be grinding in his teeth ; and the Church knew the same about Jacques. The pale shoot of free-thinking found absolutely no trellis of knowledge to support it and no beam of philosophy to harden it. To the Canadians Voltaire was not only unknown, as Parkman has said, but inconceivable ; and Briand, the son of a poor vinedresser, who had managed, though without extraordinary intellect or education, to reach a bishop's throne, was not the man to give up easily or exhaust his resources early. He knew, still better than General Murray, that his people were after all ' extremely tenacious of their religion.' Though now shut up in Quebec, he had found time enough in the previous months to lay down the line for his priests, and no doubt had occasional opportunities to assure them during the winter that it did not swerve. ' The clergy [are] our bitter Enemies,' remarked Arnold. They are ' unanimous . . . against our cause,' admitted Hazen, forgetting Lotbinière and Hoquette for the moment.[6]

Such a factor was bound to tell. Owing to their superior education, the women of Canada—particularly since they put on no airs of superiority—had a special influence over their husbands,[7] and through them the priests could work powerfully. Moreover, there were arguments for the men themselves.

The letter addressed by Congress to the Canadians in the autumn of 1774 had pleased and flattered them. When

---

[6] § Report, Com. Secret Corres,, Feb. 14, 1776: Cont. Cong. Papers, No. 22, p. 211. Parkman: Montcalm, I., p. 22. Briand: Lotbinière, Mém. (Can. Arch., M, 384, p. 1). Murray, Report, 1762: Can. Arch., B, 7, p. 55. Arnold to Cong., Jan. 24, 1776 : Sparks MSS., No. 52, II., p. 37. Hazen to Sch., Apr. 1, 1776: 4 Force, V., 751. Lotbinière: Ainslie, Journal, Apr. 6, 1776 ; Caldwell, Letter ; Lotb. to Cong. (Cont. Cong. Papers, Letters, 78, L, Vol. XIV., p. 267). Hoquette: Hazen to Antill, Apr. 20, 1776 (Can. Arch., B, 27, p. 398).

[7] Laterrière, Mém., p. 52.

the appeal to the people of Great Britain appeared, a gentleman was invited to translate it, and in due time he read his version to a large audience. All went finely for a while, and Jacques nodded approval to Pierre often enough; but by and by this thunderbolt fell: 'Nor can we suppress our astonishment, that a British parliament should ever consent to establish in that country a religion that has deluged your island in blood, and dispersed impiety, bigotry, persecution, murder and rebellion through every part of the world.' 'Oh, the perfidious, double-faced Congress!' cried the auditory. The impression passed after a little, for, like other impressions in that quarter, it did not strike deep. But fire still hid in the ashes, only waiting to be fanned; and the priests did not forget the paper.[8]

Most unfortunate it proved now for the American side that so few of the Canadians could read. Whenever a document fell at their feet, they had to ask some notary, priest, or noble to let them know what it said, and these British partisans did not neglect their opportunity to color and interpret its words. Papers printed by the Tories of New York, stating that Congress intended to deprive the *habitants* of their property and their Church, were read aloud by the clergy. Congress thought seriously of sending persons 'to explain vivâ voce to the People' the meaning of the dispute with England and the aims of the United Colonies; but evidently, for the present case, this excellent idea had arrived too late.[9]

In the letter that Antill carried south from Wooster, the situation of the Americans was painted in doleful colors and full details. This, in so far as he gave the facts, was not to be censured; but certainly, if the letter fell into British hands, it could not fail to prove unfortunate, and

[8] § Journ. Cong., Oct. 21, 1774. The incident. 4 Force, II., 231.
[9] Report: Note 6.

that very thing occurred. Duane's valet picked his master's pockets at night and copied for Governor Tryon what interesting papers they contained. In some such way, Tryon obtained Wooster's despatch, and then he thoughtfully forwarded it north to Montgolfier, Director of the Seminary of St. Sulpice at Montreal, one of the most active and influential churchmen in Canada. Now the General had not only revealed the weakness of the Americans, but had

SEMINARY ST. SULPICE

added to his other plaints this profound remark : 'There is but little confidence to be placed in the Canadians ; they are but a small remove from the savages.' Nothing more apropos than such a letter to fan their old suspicion of the Americans to life, as well as to kindle fresh fire, could possibly have been devised; the priests were exactly fitted to make the most of it ; and Montgolfier had it.[10]

Besides the prestige of intelligence and some education, besides the reputation for sagacity and fairness which had made them unofficial judges after the Conquest, besides their control of the women and their possession of useful documents, the clergy held a downright power, and that not merely redoubtable but awful. A young Canadian at the point of death was brought into the General Hospital near Quebec, and implored the ghostly offices of Father Rigaudville; but Rigaudville refused to minister, unless the man would publicly confess his great guilt in siding with the Americans, and even then, although he absolved the penitent, he would not allow his body an ecclesiastical in-

---

10 § Wooster to Sch., Jan. 5, 1776 : 4 Force, IV., 668 (Tryon speaks of it, in a general way, as addressed to Congress ; but his description fits this letter unmistakably. Perhaps a duplicate was sent to Philadelphia). Duane : London letter, 4 Force, V., 44. Tryon to Montgolfier, Jan. 31, 1776: Pub. Rec. Off., Am. and W. I., Vol. 186, p. 325.

terment. 'The Clergy refuse absolution to all who have shown themselves our Friends,' testified Wooster at Montreal, 'and Preach Damnation to all those that will not take up Arms against us.' Caldwell heard of but one priest, Lotbinière, who would absolve a 'rebel.' Substantially every pious Canadian—and they were all 'pious'—had to ask the question, What are taxes, even at the worst, beside an eternity of hell-fire? To be sure, Jacques might argue that Rigaudville had no business to meddle in politics; but which was to give the priests their orders, Bonhomme Jacques or the Bishop? Some persisted timidly; some persisted defiantly. At St. Michel de Bellechasse—and no doubt elsewhere—graves were dug for such by the roadside. But not many cared to face the Beyond without squaring accounts with the Church, and the priests made the most of it. Their total pressure, aided by what the gentry could do, amounted to something terrific.[11]

Carleton also was at work. Mysterious individuals, male and female, entered and left Quebec now and then. At least one of them received a pension afterwards for some unknown reason. Tryon's letter to Montgolfier passed on to the Governor by this method, and 'large pacquets' for the priests below Quebec were seen going out. Scarcely had the smoke of the assault cleared, when one of the prisoners, an Acadian, was taken in hand by the authorities, led to the scaffold in imagination, then promised his fortune for dutiful obedience, and finally sent up the river to labor in the King's interest. Quite a number of Canadian captives lay in Quebec under the shadow of the gibbet, and there was reason to believe—as Arnold anticipated—that some of them agreed to carry word for the

---

[11] § Rigaudville : Mgr. de St. Vallier, Part II., Chap. IV., p. 400. Wooster to Warner, Jan. 6, 1776: Pub. Rec. Off., Am. and W. I., Vol. 186, p 313. Caldwell, Letter. Roadside : Roy, Lauzon, III., p. 65. Verreau (Sanguinet), Invasion, p. 95. Report: Note 6.

Governor. 'There were . . . five or six taken prisoners with two or three savages, all of whom the General set at liberty,' recorded Finlay, on the outside of this business. In short, Hazen probably did not miss it greatly in believing that many priests, 'with other people of some consequence,' had carried on a correspondence with General Carleton 'the whole winter.' Something was likely to come of this.[12]

But nobody labored for the King so hard or so persistently as the Americans.

Strength was the gospel they needed to preach ; but their apostles were a meagre force, badly dressed, badly armed, badly drilled, badly paid, and badly fed. They called themselves the Liberators and Protectors of the Canadians ; but, as Bondfield, one of their principal friends, told Robert Morris, they never could have reached Quebec 'had not the Canadians opened the Road and led them by the hand to the very gates of the Capitol,' and Maclean bore witness, that '2000 of those fellows never could have done . . . any mischief had they not been joined by the Canadians.' The soldiers at Three Rivers lived in great part on alms, begging at every house in town, Whig or Tory ; and when Badeaux, the agent of the hospital, told the American commander that the nuns could not care for his sick indefinitely without payment, the officer was only able to reply,

'Tell them to have patience.'

'Very well, I will tell them to feed your soldiers on patience ; we shall see how fat they will get,' retorted Badeaux ; and the slap could only be answered by a blush.

'The best of causes are subject to vicissitudes, and disappointments have ever been inevitable,' proclaimed Con-

12 § 'Chalmers' Journal, Mar. 8. 'Shortt' Journal, Jan. 17 ; Mar. 18. Ainslie, Journal, Jan. 17 ; Feb. 28 ; Mar. 8, etc. Carleton to Barrington, May 14, 1776: War Off., Orig. Corres., N. Amer., Vol. 12. Acadian : Arnold to Wooster, Jan. 5, 1776 (4 Force, IV., 854). Finlay, Journal, Jan. 2. Hazen: Note 6.

gress very grandly to the Canadians after the disaster of December thirty-first; but even the *habitants* could see that, instead of some inscrutable decree of Providence, a simple lack of men and means had brought down the avalanche, and they beheld an army of the enthusiasts for Liberty melt away homeward, even when it had no enemy to fear. 'I am sure our Army are at the greatest remove from any kind of merit to found our hopes upon,' confessed Ripley.[13]

Besides failing to accomplish the good they should have done, the troops caused mischief that should have been avoided. Not only had the American principle of Freedom made the soldiers unruly, not only did Provincial jealousies and bickerings prevent harmony among them, but the treatment they met with rendered them actually mutinous, however brave and loyal at heart. 'Money is the sinews of War,' said James Livingston ; 'and without it it is impossible to keep up an Army already too ripe for Revolt.' 'I must beg leave,' wrote Wooster a week before Christmas, ' to enforce Gen. Montgomery's request, for the Paymaster or money to be sent forward, or we shall be overwhelmed with mutiny and disorder.' At the beginning of February, Schuyler hoped this could be brought about in 'a very few days.' By and by it actually was accomplished; yet on the twenty-first Wooster's hands went up again in despair : 'The Paymaster has arrived, but has brought nothing but paper money.' At Quebec, the same good fairy had been looked for since the latter part of January, and Livingston believed the consequences of delay were 'greatly to be feared.' But whether men would feel mightily pleased, after this long waiting, to

---

[13] § Bondfield to Morris, Feb. 4, 1776 : N. Y. Hist. Soc. Coll., 1878, p. 399. Maclean to Barrington, Nov. 20, 1775: War Off., Orig. Corres., N. Am., Vol. 12. Three Rivers : Verreau (Badeaux), Invasion, pp. 191, 196 ; Ursul. de T. R., I., pp. 367, 368. Secret Journ. Cong., Jan. 24, 1776. Ripley to J. Wheelock, Mar. 7, 1776: J. Wheelock Papers.

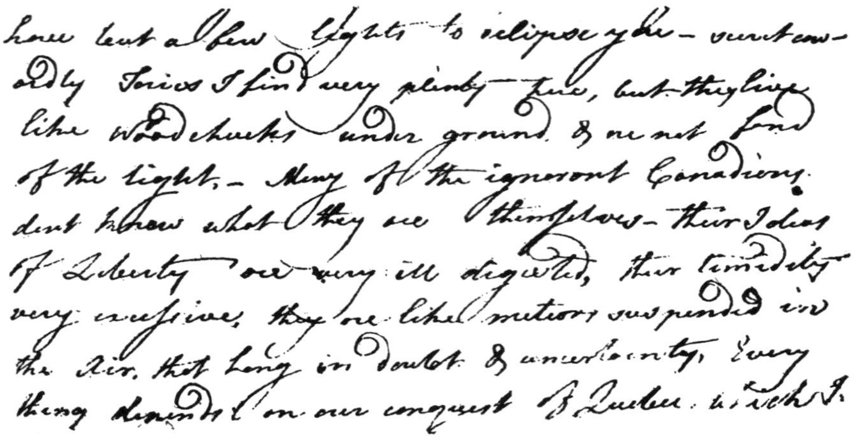

TWO EXTRACTS FROM RIPLEY'S LETTER TO WHEELOCK, MARCH 7, 1776.

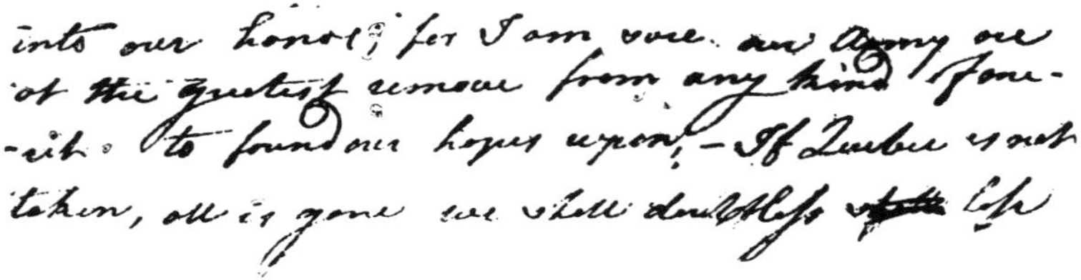

get a fraction of their six and two-thirds dollars a month and then have to offer it—perhaps in vain—at a discount of one-third, could easily be foretold.[14]

A worse thing, however, was possible, and it came to pass. Both at Quebec and at Montreal men were forced to serve after they were legally free. 'I hope you will think it necessary to send back every soldier who has deserted from us under pretence of his time being out,' hinted Arnold to his superior officer. But Wooster did not require the suggestion. Before this letter arrived, orders had been given ' to suffer no man to go out of the country, whether they would inlist or not '; and Schuyler approved of this action. Probably, as the generals believed, necessity justified their policy ; but it certainly made a queer footnote in the new Primer of Liberty for Canadian Beginners, and did little indeed to improve the morale of the troops. [15]

Quarrels among the chiefs undermined what vestiges of discipline remained. Hazen, though he had given Carleton his first notice of the invasion of Canada and perhaps offered suggestions about repelling it, had committed himself irrevocably to the opposite side ; but many of the Americans were unable to view his doings as a whole. At Montreal, he was 'Esteemed . . ., universally, an enemy in Grain,' as Gershom Mott—no doubt with some exaggeration—informed Samuel Adams ; and Antill was always mentioned there as 'a Very suspected Character.' Dugan, though a barber, had great influence among the Canadians: 'more than Livingston, Antill or Hazen,' Ritzema believed ; and both Arnold and Wooster com-

---

14 § See Vol. I., Chap. XIV. Goforth to Jay, Apr. 8, 1776: Bancroft Coll., Rev. Papers, I., p. 37. J. Liv., [Feb.], 1776: Am. Hist. Rec., III., p. 181. Commrs. to Cong., May 6, 1776 : Cont. Cong. Papers, No. 166, p. 29. Van Rensselaer to Sch., Feb. 22, 1776: Sch. Papers. Wooster to Sch., Dec. 18, 1775: 4 Force, IV., 310. Sch. to Trumbull, Feb. 5, 1776: ib., 944. Wooster to Sch., Feb. 21, 1776: ib., 1490. Sch. to Hancock, Feb. 23, 1776: ib., 1481.

15 § Arnold to Wooster, Jan. 4, 1776 : 4 Force, IV., 854. Wooster to Sch., Jan. 5, 1776: ib., 668. Sch. to Hancock, Jan. 29, 1776: ib., 880.

missioned him to raise troops as a colonel. Hazen and Antill, however, working together at Philadelphia, secured control of the new Canadian regiment, and made a sort of bargain to prevent the employment of Dugan. Dugan then hurried south, obtained some money from Congress, and got a commission to raise three companies of Rangers, with power to select their officers. So far as concerned himself, this proved of no great value, but the affair involved plenty of annoyance for Wooster, Hazen, and Antill, and plenty of damage for the cause.[16]

Brown, besides antagonizing Arnold at the lakes, had intrigued against him before Quebec, and now—looking for an assault of the city under his enemy's direction—informed his wife that he ' must be a Uriah.' That was merely suspicion ; but without a doubt Arnold refused him a promotion that Montgomery had given him reason to expect, charged him publicly at the camp with plundering the baggage of British officers at Sorel, and wrote Congress vigorously to the same effect. In fact, he stated that Montgomery himself, to the knowledge of several officers, took the ground that ' he could not in conscience or honour promote him (Maj^r. Brown) until those matters were cleared up.' Such a charge might have some basis or at least color without really signifying much. Brown denied it stoutly ; and the hatred between the two officers became as hot as the climate would permit.[17]

But another quarrel far outshone this one. As Wooster did not conceal the irritation caused by his Continental

---

16 § G. Mott to Adams, Feb. 21, 1776 : S. Adams Papers. Arnold to Dudevan, Jan. 13, 1776 : Can. Arch., B, 184, 1, p. 23. Ritzema, Journal, Feb. 16, 1776. Smith, Private Journal, Jan. 18, 25. Hazen to Antill, Mar. 10, 1776 : Can. Arch., B, 27, p. 387. Sch. to Hancock, Mar. 21, 1776 : 4 Force, V., 103. Journ. Cong., Mar. 28, 1776.

17 § Brown to his wife, Mar. 15, 1776 : Smith, Pittsfield, I., p. 259. (Here will be found a full account, from the Brown point of view, of the long running fight with Arnold that ensued. See Journ. Cong., June 27 ; July 30 ; Aug. 1, 1776.) Dugan, Deposition, Aug. 1, 1776 : Emmet Coll. Arnold to Hancock, Feb. 1, 1776 : Sparks MSS., No. 52, II., p. 38.

rank, Schuyler probably began to look for something unpleasant when the Connecticut general entered his department. At all events, he found it. On his march to Ticonderoga in the summer, Wooster ordered a court-martial at Fort George, and he was reported as giving men discharges. Probably this did not mean a deliberate intention to override his superior officer. Ignorance or, at the worst, a stubborn tenacity in asserting old-time prerogatives might explain it. But Schuyler sharply denounced this 'extraordinary conduct,' and felt it an 'indispensable duty' to write the offender a letter. The letter struck its recipient as 'founded in falsehood' and written with no motive except to 'insult' him. Wooster made a dignified and patriotic reply, however, disclaiming any intention to contradict authority or cause trouble; and, as he soon passed into the direct jurisdiction of Montgomery, the difficulty appeared to end.[18]

Montgomery's death, unfortunately, removed the buffer. About the middle of January, Wooster wrote his superior at Albany: 'Some of the persons [i. e. prisoners] you have sent back [i. e. set at liberty] have really behaved very illy.' 'Resolved Sir,' came the reply from Albany, 'Resolved Sir to be treated with the respect due to me as a Gentleman and as an Officer Intrusted with a Command by the Honourable the Representatives of Thirteen Colonies, it is my Positive Order that you cause all such Persons as have had my Permit to return into Canada, to be called before you, and there Confronted with their Accusers.' At the same time Schuyler informed Wooster that he had complained at Philadelphia of the 'unbecoming subacity' of his subordinate, and had explained to Congress this order about the ex-prisoners by saying : 'If they have abused

---

[18] § Journ. Cong., June 22, 1775. Wooster to Sch., Oct. 19, 1775: 4 Force, III., 1107. Sch. to Hancock, Oct. 14, 1775: ib., 1065. Wooster to Sch., Feb. 11, 1776: 4 Force, IV., 1217. See Sch. to Wooster, Oct. 23, 1775 (Cont. Cong. Papers, 161, II., p. 293) for another cause of trouble.

my Confidence, they are Scoundrels, and I will treat them Accordingly, without repenting that I gave them the Indulgence, for that was an Act of Humanity. If they are not Culpable, they are Injured and I too. I shall sift the Matter to the bottom and my Resentment *without any kind of exception*, shall be experienced by those that deserve it.' [19]

On this, Wooster also discharged both barrels. To Schuyler he retorted, 'I, also, claim a right to be treated' *et cetera*, asserting with equal force his intention to work for the good of the Colonies and his purpose to decide for himself, as the commanding officer in Canada, what the 'internal regulation of the Army' and 'the immediate

DAVID WOOSTER AS A YOUNG MAN

safety of the country' demanded. To Congress—with whom, unlike Montgomery, he felt perfectly free to correspond over the head of his superior officer—he forwarded the file of correspondence, and added : 'I know of no reason under Heaven why he should treat me thus cavalierly, but merely to indulge his capricious humour, which, in the course of the last year, he has dealt out very liberally' ; with more in the same tone. 'Either he or I must immediately quit this department,' was Schuyler's prompt ultimatum to Hancock. Neither left his post ; but naturally the bitter quarrel could not be concealed, and, as most of Wooster's men were from New York, the

---

[19] § Wooster to Sch., Jan. 14, 1776 : 4 Force, IV., 852. Sch. to Wooster, Jan. 26, 1776 (copy sent by Sch. to Congress) : Cont. Cong. Pap., 161, II., p. 273. Id. to Hancock, Jan. 25, 1776 : Cont. Cong. Pap., 153, I., p. 450.

situation of the Connecticut officer probably did not improve. Discipline must have been staggered by such dissensions ; and all this went on before quick-witted and fickle spectators, accustomed to the strict regularity of the British and French armies.[20]

More unfortunate still, the Canadians not only saw but felt the disorder.

At the beginning, extreme care had been taken to make the American troops regard their Canadian hosts as long-lost brothers, and circumstances had reinforced the lesson. Arnold's men entered Canada as actual suppliants ; and Montgomery's, finding themselves at the threshold face to face with British soldiers, realized the value of friendly aid. To a great degree, this remained the spirit of the military authorities. According to the records of the General Hospital, an officer who threatened Father Rigaudville for not furnishing beds enough to accommodate the American wounded, was cashiered. A nun at Three Rivers heard that a soldier stole some baby-clothes, and that, when the mother complained, the Provincial commander said, ' You shall have them back, and if you care to see the thief punished you need only go to the pine grove at 9 o'clock.' ' Please to advertise a silver spoon left with me by Captain Stout of Jersey, supposed to have been stolen at Montreal,' wrote Goforth. Traditions at Aspen Point attested the considerateness of American rule. At Quebec officers were directed ' Strictly to observe the Conduct of their Men,' that all disorder might be suppressed ' in the Verry Bud.'[21]

But soldiers have always had certain faults, especially in an enemy's country ; and it became increasingly

---

[20] § Wooster to Sch., Feb. 11, 1776 : 4 Force, IV., 1217. Id. to Cong., Feb. 11, 1776 : ib., 1001. Sch. to Hancock, Feb. 20, 1776 : ib., 1214. For an opinion on the quarrel see J. Adams to J. Thomas : Coffin, Thomas, p. 22.

[21] § Mgr. de St. Vallier, Part II., Chap. IV., p. 400. Ursul. de T. Riv., I., p. 370. Goforth (undated) : 4 Force, V., 753. Aspen Point : see REMARK XLVII. ' Arnold's ' Ord. Book, Jan. 23.

evident that some at least of the Canadians were not friends. Moreover, the distinction between a loyalist and a man who was merely disobliging could not in all cases be easily discerned. Expecting rough-and-ready fellows to pay more deference to a stranger than they did to their own officers ; to go hungry that sleek Tories might pile on superfluous flesh ; to trudge bare-footed that cantering enemies might splash them with mud ; to bear a harder discipline, while battling for Liberty, than despots ventured to impose ; to bear it at the order of a government that neither paid, fed, nor clothed them ; and to bear it that conspirators against them might be free and prosperous :—this, as the *Annual Register* itself admitted,[22] was expecting much ; and it seemed still more when the American troops began to enter the land as masters instead of suppliants, to succor Provincials rather than to liberate Canadians.

Goforth himself testified that privates on their way to Quebec were guilty of ' flagrant abuses.' A priest's house was broken into, and a watch taken from him. A man had a bayonet run through his neck in his own dwelling for insisting upon being paid. Women and children found themselves constrained by a similar logic to supply private soldiers with horses. ' The peasantry in general,' confessed Hazen, ' have been ill-used ; they have in some instances been dragooned, with the point of the bayonet, to furnish wood for the garrison, at a lower rate than the current price ; carriages, and many other articles furnished, for which certificates were given, not legible and without signature—the one half of consequence rejected by the Quartermaster-General. It is true, they have been promised payment, from time to time ; yet they look upon such promises as vague, their labour and property lost, and the

---

[22] Annual Register, 1776, p. 11.

Congress and the United Colonies as bankrupt.' Yet, after all, probably only a small fraction of the people really suffered abuse, and such acts could be charged against individuals, not the system.[23]

Another trouble, however, was broad and official. A state of war reigned in Canada and all the higher officers were Americans. This meant that foreigners, who had entered the province almost on their knees, now ruled it by the steel. ' The whole country left without any other kind of law than that of the arbitrary and despotick power of the sword,' was Hazen's description of the régime. ' Too frequently abused in all cases of this nature,' he justly added ; but, even when not abused, when enforced only as necessity appeared to require, the military law of strangers and aliens could not be agreeable. No way presented itself to get arms for Dugan's proposed regiment save to take what could be found and give certificates ' payable at the end of the campaign '; but that seemed extremely harsh. Wooster ordered many captains of the militia to resign,—very likely in consequence of hearing from Arnold that Carleton was endeavoring to rouse them ; but, however necessary the precaution, it provoked opposition. Lee's one order bade Wooster ' suffer the Merch[an]ts of Montreal to send none of their woolen Cloths out of the Town,' and no doubt this resulted in more or less vexation of trade.[24]

One instance of arbitrary rule overtopped all the rest. Montgomery had thought of disarming the Tories at Montreal,—' not so much from any apprehensions I have of them,' he explained, ' as to quiet the jealous apprehen-

---

[23] § Goforth: Note 21. Hazen to Sch., Apr. 1, 1776: 4 Force, V., 751. Commrs.: Note 14.

[24] § Garneau, Canada, III., p. 4. Hazen to Sch., Apr. 1, 1776: 4 Force, V., 751. Verreau (Sanguinet), Invasion, p. 96. Arms : Arnold to Dudevan, Jan. 13, 1776 (Can. Arch., B, 184, i., p. 22). (Cf. Chap. XXV., Note 8.) Militia: Letter, 4 Force, V., 481 ; Wooster to Wash.. Jan. 21, 1776 (4 Force, IV., 796) ; Souv. de Maisonneuve, p. 40 ; Verreau (Sanguinet), Invasion, p. 96 ; Ainslie, Journal, Feb. 24. Lee to Wooster, Feb. 28, 1776: Am. Antiq. Soc.

sions of the troops'; but, with victory perching on his banner, he felt it safe as well as politic to disturb them little. At Christmas, an anonymous letter informed him that the 'placemen' captured on the fleet were 'holding conversations big with the most inhuman sentiments, and the most disadvantageous to the cause of liberty,' and urged that he send them into the Colonies as soon as conveniently he could. After his fall they grew 'more bold,' as Wooster soon discovered. Just before the frost threw its crystal chains across the St. Lawrence, the schooner *Magdalen* had brought word from the government that 'as early as possible in the spring a very considerable Body' of Russians would be sent over; and, as Quebec seemed to be holding out, the royalists felt quite cheerful. 'In the Spring, the Wheel will turn,' observed Major Skene, with a look that could almost awaken yellow violets in January. 'Boldly my friend,' Governor Tryon exhorted Montgolfier, with fresh assurances of early and formidable reinforcements. The advice was followed; and stories of many hues, but all dark towards the Provincials, went flying among the people. The men sent back by Schuyler had seen the state of things above, and represented that St. Johns and the lake posts could easily be seized. 'Tories I find very plenty,' wrote Silvanus Ripley from Montreal. 'Very saucy,' was Mr. Secretary Cole's description of the Ministerial party. 'Already they cry, Victory,' added Pelissier.[25]

'It is my opinion,' said Arnold, 'that every soul who were in office at the reduction of the country, and others who are looked upon as inimical, should be immediately

25 § Montg. to Sch., Nov. 24, 1775: 4 Force, III., 1694. Anon. letter, Dec. 22, 1775: 4 Force, IV., 381. Wooster to Sch., Jan. 14, 1776: 4 Force, IV., 852. Magdalen: Lindsay (Canad. Rev., II., No. 4, p. 352). Pownall to Carleton, Sept. 8, 14, 1775: Can. Arch., B, 37, pp. 104, 106; see ib., O, 11, p. 338. Skene, Jan. 28, 1776: Pub. Rec. Off., Am. and W. I., Vol. 186, p. 333. Tryon to Montgolfier (in French), Jan. 31. 1776: ib., p. 325. Wooster to Sch., Jan. 14, 1776: 4 Force, IV., 852. Ripley to J. Wheelock, Mar. 7, 1776: Wheelock Papers. Cole to ——, Jan. 24, 1776. Emmet Coll. Pelissier to Hancock, Jan. 8, 1776: 4 Force, IV., 596.

sent over the lake, without respect of persons,' and Pelissier agreed that the royalists ought to be weeded out. With such support, Wooster felt satisfied of 'the great necessity of sending many of their leaders out of the Province,' and no less than forty sled-loads of wrathful Tories made the hard journey to Albany, leaving ten times as many indignant friends behind. One could easily prove the punishment high-handed, for the General himself charged some of the exiles with nothing more than 'base, ungenerous conduct.' Who then is safe? it was natural to ask. Like most benefactors, the Canadians probably had an adequate idea of the aid they had given their liberators, and felt the sting of ingratitude as well as the heel of tyranny. These Americans were usurpers in addition to being despots; and had not Jerry Dugan, the most popular Canadian officer, been almost crowded out? Liberators, indeed![26]

Beyond a doubt, the task of ruling at Montreal called for the wisdom of the serpent; but it fell — to David Wooster. 'I am informed,' confided Silas Deane to his wife, 'that Wooster talks high of his *Thirty years' Services.* . . . [I] am determined to do my duty, and will on no Occasion sacrifice the good of my Country to the whim of any old man, or old woman rather, or their sticklers— when Wooster was appointed, I washed my hands of the consequences, by declaring him, in my Opinion, totally unequal to the Service. This I did openly in the face of the Assembly, and if I tho't him unfit for a Major General of Connecticut Forces only '—the conclusion was unmistakable. 'General Wooster, I am informed,' said the reserved Washington, 'is not of such activity as to press through difficulties '; and, indeed, that could hardly be expected of a man whose eye was already turned back-

---

[26] § Arnold to Wooster, Jan. 4, 1776: 4 Force, IV., 854. Pelissier : Note 25. Wooster to Sch., Jan. 14, 1776 : 4 Force, IV., 852. Sch. to Hancock, Jan. 31, 1776: ib., 898. Wooster to Sch., Jan. 19, 1776: ib., 1004.

ward over a generation of work. As for sagacity and judgment, his defence against the complaint of discharging soldiers without authority to do so, told the story. 'I did not Discharge any men,' he protested, 'but only gave them a Furlough, . . . as the Term of their Inlistments were not expired.' In other words—and so the Commander-in-chief pointed out—he not only let needed men quit the service, but continued their pay ; and he looked upon an avowal of this as a triumphant vindication.[27]

Not that Wooster could fairly be called a cipher, however ; nor a knave ; nor a coward. In some ways he compelled respect. No doubt he was a bluff, hearty man of the people. He must have been a very effective general in the opinion of a hay-field. All the farmers within reach of his voice would have nodded approval—possibly as they did at church—of his honest zeal, his patriotism, and his plan of campaign ; and probably almost any hay-field problem could have been routed by his agricultural strategy. But his view of a really difficult situation took shape in the handy formula : 'God only knows,'—less an ascription to the wisdom of God than to the ignorance of Wooster ; and his notions of meeting it did themselves up in the parallel phrase : 'What we wish, we easily believe.' Congress, doubtless to make him grumble less about his rank, had thanked him 'for the very important assistance' contributed to the reduction of St. Johns ; and, as he had contributed nothing but bodily presence, any kind of cerebration at Montreal was clearly superfluous.[28]

From turret to foundation stone, from his dusty old cocked hat down to his coarse boots, every feature of his person—his uninspiring figure, his lethargic face, his dila-

---

[27] § S. Deane, [about July 15, 1775]: Conn. Hist. Soc. Wash. to Sch., Oct. 5, 1775 : Writings (Ford), III., p. 168. Wooster to Sch., Dec. 18. 1775: Sch. Papers. Wash. to Sch., Jan. 16, 1776: Writings (Ford), III., p. 348.

[28] § See Wooster's letters to Sch., Jan. 5, 19, 27, 1776: 4 Force, IV., 668, 1004 ; Sparks MSS., No. 60, p. 65. Cong. to Wooster, Nov. 30, 1775 : 4 Force, III., 1718.

tory eyes glowing covertly now
and then with a streak of plebeian
shrewdness—everything spoke the
sad word 'provincial': provincial
courage, provincial knowledge,
provincial pride, provincial obsti-
nacy, provincial dulness. His proper place was in a historical museum of the French and Indian War;
and, with due care to prevent the
sawdust from leaking, he might
long have made an impressive figure there in the eyes of his honest
country-folk. But, of all conceivable posts, Montreal just then was
about the least suitable for him.
'Cast about for a General to command us,' begged Ritzema grimly;
' He must be a military man, of
sound intellects, and an affable
deportment'; and this measure
of the need measured also the vac-
ancy. As a soldier, Wooster
was *vieux jeu,* or, to translate
French slang into English slang
just as good, a 'back number.' For
statesmanship, the triple-crowned
prejudices that helped give him a
provincial popularity disqualified
him. In a way, too, his sturdy
virtues were worse than vices, for
vices would have tried to hide or
even grace themselves among
people of opposite ideas, but convinced virtues, never ; while his

want of activity, at first sight a blemish, probably counted at Montreal as the very chiefest of his merits.[29]

Intellectually, at least, the disaster at Quebec had struck him with panic. He proved unable to hold his men in hand under immensely easier conditions than Arnold had at Quebec. He confessed that during his administration there had been 'many abuses' and, he feared, 'not a few embezzlements' in the commissary department. A report crept into Quebec that one of his orders provoked the people of Montreal to flat disobedience; and certainly Hazen protested that he 'could not Possibly be an Instrument' of carrying out some scheme that Wooster undertook. His basal idea of governing the city could be inferred from his own remark that he had 'permitted' certain of the merchants to choose a committee with a view of petitioning Congress. His general treatment of the Canadians doubtless followed logically from considering them as next door to the savages; and, as regarded the British Tories, probably Schuyler did not err in thinking him too much influenced by the implacable Walker, just freed from the dirty hold of an armed schooner.[30]

Among a people that loved politeness and deftness, he showed himself dull and blunt, if not brutal. When things began to look dubious, he ordered the public, under pain of exile, not to talk of the affairs of the Americans,—a masterpiece of stupidity. His proclamation after the disaster at Quebec declared in the same breath and with no sense of the incongruity, first, that Congress had sent an

---

[29] § Ritzema to N. Y. Com. Safety, Jan. 3, 1776: 4 Force, IV., 1114. The author's judgment is based upon the whole range of incidents and correspondence touching Wooster from his entry into the field of operations to the time of his summary dismissal from it. (See R. Morris to S. Deane, June 5, 1776: N. Y. Hist. Soc. Coll., 1886, p. 136.) His personal appearance is inferred from his mental and moral qualities, the well-known portrait of him at an earlier age, and other facts patent to the thoughtful reader.

[30] § Wooster to Sch., Mar. 5, 1776: 4 Force, V., 416. (See Sch. to Hancock, Feb. 23, 1776: 4 Force, IV., 1481.) Ainslie, Journal, Jan. 15. Hazen to Wooster, Feb. 15, 1776: Emmet. Coll. Wooster to Cong., Feb. 11, 1776: 4 Force, IV., 1001. Sch. to Hancock, Feb. 10, 1776: ib., 990.

army to deliver Canada from general servitude, and secondly, that men even suspected of co-operating or corresponding with Quebec should suffer close imprisonment or exile. When a number of citizens called to expostulate against the banishment of people, he cut this difficult knot at once in grand style : ' I regard the whole of you as enemies and rascals,'—at least, so Monsieur Sanguinet noted in his Journal. He denied that Major Campbell had any ground for calling him ' a damned old scoundrel ' and a breaker of his word ; but he certainly replied to a courteous note from Judge Fraser in this manner : ' Your breach of promise & insolent letter to me yesterday, justly merritt a sett of Iron orniments, which you & your associates have very lately been so fond of bestrowing on the friends of constitutional liberty, but as I disdain to follow your inhuman & Infamous example, I shall only order, & I do hereby order and direct you on receipt hereof to repare to the Fort at chambly, under such an escort as I shall direct, & there to remain in close abode till further orders.' This meant five weeks of confinement ; guards were set upon Mrs. Fraser, although Wooster knew that she was in a delicate state ; and finally the Judge was deported, — only to find, on reaching Albany, that ' no particular charge ' had been laid against him.[31]

Montgomery, though he knew the clergy worked against his cause, had ' winked at this behaviour,' and said highly agreeable things to them ; but Wooster, praise to God, was no such a trimmer. Chaplain Robbins, of the same staunch Puritan province, on seeing a Catholic boy enter a church and kneel for some time ' With the greatest devotion,' exclaimed, ' Oh when shall Satan be bound and Antichrist meet a final overthrow ? ' Under an admin-

---

[31] § Order, etc. : Verreau (Sanguinet), Invasion, p. 95. Proc., Jan. 6, 1776 : Can. Arch., B, 184, 1, p. 21. Wooster to ^ch., Jan. 19, 1776 : 4 Force, IV., 1004. Fraser, Memorial : Cont. Cong. Paper ^, No. 41, III., p. 151.

istration of that shade—as was natural, and as Hazen asserted—the clergy were 'neglected, perhaps in some instances ill-used'; and, according to Major Skene, who apparently kept in touch with Montreal, a military order shut up all the Mass houses on Christmas Eve. Many other such things were probably done, though not recorded. Antill, going north, met a friend of the cause at Iron Point, and 'could not help being greatly alarmed and much shocked, to hear of the great confusion and irregularity' prevailing at Montreal; and Schuyler, apparently after listening to the same informant, concluded that all was 'in confusion' in Canada.'[32]

At Quebec, meanwhile, a tremendously hazardous move was made. As early as the middle of December, Montgomery announced that he must 'soon be exceedingly distressed,' if specie did not arrive. Even before leaving Montreal, he had found that but few would accept Continental currency, and at Quebec he confessed that it 'would not be received by the inhabitants.' Several schemes to give the bills a standing were suggested; but the popular distrust could not be overcome. To make the situation peculiarly delicate, royalists had warned the Canadians in advance that the Provincials were going to rob them by the trick of paper money. 'You see men,' cried 'Civis Canadiensis' in the *Quebec Gazette*, 'You see men, against whom you have done nothing, come into the province with arms in their hands, and seize your property under the pretext of being your benefactors. Think you that these destitute people will let you quietly enjoy the fruit of your labors? They will take all they wish and pay with bills of credit. What will you do with such money? Alas, nothing.' Wash-

[32] § Montg. to Sch., Nov. 19, 1775 : 4 Force, III., 1682. Robbins, Journal, Apr. 30. Hazen to Sch., Apr. 1, 1776: 4 Force, V., 751. Skene: Pub. Rec. Off., Am. and W. I., Vol. 186, p. 333. Antill to Sch., Feb. 7, 1776 : 4 Force, IV., 1132. Sch. to Wash., Feb. 14, 1776: ib., 1146. REMARK LXX.

ington's orders to Arnold had been most emphatic : ' You will be particularly careful to pay the full value for all provisions, or other accommodations, which the Canadians may provide for you on your march ' ; and the wisdom of this rule had only grown since it was issued.[33]

As the legatee of Montgomery's necessities, Arnold hoped to ' rub along,' and he endeavored to comfort himself with the thought that, should the capital fall, ' paper money would soon have a currency ' ; yet, in spite of every device to ' beg, borrow and squeeze,' he often found nothing in his military chest but a few Portuguese coins. Price could aid him little, for Wooster admitted, about the middle of January, that every friend had been ' drained already ' ; and, after no very long stay at Quebec, he set out for Philadelphia with Thomas Walker. It finally became a question of stark necessity, if the blockade of Quebec was to continue. Possibly, indeed, no ' if ' could be added. Not only was it evident that any attempt to retire would be hazardous, but a man from Chambly, vouched for by Maclean, reported positively in Quebec, that Arnold's troops dared not go off, since their Canadian allies had sworn to ' cut them to pieces in their retreat,' unless another attempt were made to capture Quebec.[34]

Something, in short, really had to be done ; and, on the fourth of March—' drove to the last extremity [and] in want of almost every necessary,' as Antill said—Arnold issued this decree : ' To the Inhabitants of the District of

---

[33] § Montg. to Wooster, Dec. 16, 1775: Sparks MSS., No. 52, II., p. 60. Id. to Sch., Dec. 26, 1775: 4 Force, IV., 464. Schemes : Montg. to Sch., Dec. 26, 1775 (4 Force. IV., 464); Ritzema, Journal, Feb. 16 ; Wooster to Sch., Jan. 14, 1776 (4 Force, IV., 852) ; Sch. to Hancock, Jan. 29, 1776 (ib., 880) ; Id. to Id., Feb. 7, 1776 (ib., 955); Wooster to Sch., Mar. 5, 1776 (4 Force, V., 416) ; Journ. Cong., Feb 6, 17, 1776. Distrust : Garneau, Canada, III., p. 3 ; Quebec Gazette, Oct. 5, 1775 ; see also Chap. XIV. Wash. to Arnold, Sept. 14, 1775: Writings (Ford), III., p. 121. REMARK LXXI.

[34] § Arnold to Wash., Jan. 14, 1776 : 4 Force, IV., 674. Id. to Hancock, Feb. 1, 1776: Sparks MSS., No. 52, II., p. 38. Id. to Cong., Jan. 24, 1776 : ib., p. 37. Id. to Id., Jan. 11. 1776: ib., p. 34. Wooster to Sch., Jan. 19, 1776: 4 Force, IV., 1004. Id to Cong., Feb. 11, 1776: ib., 1001. Ainslie, Journal, Feb. 28. 'Chalmers' Journal, Feb. 28.

toutes Personnes qui refusent de la recevoir au Cours
& sans aucun Décompte, seront Considéré comme un
Ennemi des Colonies unies, et traitté Comme tel.
Donne sous notre Signature & le Sceau
de nos Armes au Quartier général au Camp Mars 1776.

Benedict Arnold

Brig.r General and
Commander in Chief
of the Army before Quebec

236

Quebec, . . . We have seen fit to give Circulation among the Public to a necessary Amount of the Paper money issued by Order of the honorable Congress, upon the general Credit of the united Colonies of the Continent. . . . Whoever shall accept the said Money of the Congress, shall receive the Amount of it in Gold and Silver within the space of three or four Months from the date of this Present; while on the contrary Every Person who shall refuse to accept it at Par and without Discount, shall be considered an Enemy of the united Colonies and treated As Such.' 'This Step could not be avoided, [but] I tremble for the consequences,' wrote Antill. ' If the rebels should come into the country,' a gentleman at Quebec had prophesied in August, 'they will want everything from the Canadians for their paper money, . . . and the Rebels will be obliged to have recourse to force to give it a circulation, or in other words to take what they want, which will make the Canadians fly to arms in defence of their property.' But this gentleman was evidently a Tory; and so far nearly all the soothsaying of that party had gone wrong. It was a most perilous move; one had reason to tremble; and yet nobody could certainly foretell off-hand the consequences of the decree.[35]

By the last days of March, however, some things had grown clear. The right method to win the Canadians had certainly not been followed. When Montgomery first entered the country, testified Hazen, ' the ready assistance which they gave on all occasions by men, carriages, or provisions, was most remarkable.' In November, Schuyler could perceive that they were beginning to believe in 'the strength of the Colonies,'—the main thing needful. But the proper steps to confirm this feel-

---

[35] § [Antill] to [Hazen], Mar. 28, 1776: Can. Arch., B, 27, p. 380. Decree (in French): Am. Antiq. Soc. Arnold to Deane, Mar. 30, 1776: 4 Force, V., 549 Letter, Aug. 20, 1775: 4 Force, III., 211.

ing had not been taken. Wrote an American officer : ' I must say I think this department has been neglected,' and many others felt the same. Troops enough to ensure the security of Canada or even to drive out the feeble British force at Quebec had not been sent. ' Liberty had meant chaos. ' The civil state of this Province is very bad,' testified Ripley. As Arnold admitted, the people in most of the parishes had found it necessary to mount guard for their own security. The Indian trade had been closed. All the large business was paralyzed; and, as Joseph Hawley pointed out, Canada did not enjoy even the business opportunities which open rebellion and a declaration of independence could have given. In fact, she had no commercial status at all, internal or external. ' Will they ever join with us heartily,' demanded Hawley, ' who, in order to do it, must sacrifice their trade ? ' [36]

' Should things not go well,' confessed Montgomery, ' I tremble for the fate of the poor Canadians.' Evidently they were not going well ; and soon, it was reported, they would not be going at all. Sears, one of the Montreal prisoners permitted to return home, reported that ' the Colonies had given over the thoughts of keeping this Province.' Others affirmed the same thing. Still others held that the Colonies would leave Canada to her punishment, after using her as a club against the Ministry and thus carrying their own point. ' We will never abandon you,' promised the Congress in January ; but by March various facts had appeared to prove either its impotence or its hypocrisy. Some recalled now how the Americans had been pictured to them in September : ' a set of miscreants, who while they were promoting their own

[36] § Hazen to Sch., Apr. 1, 1776: 4 Force, V., 751. Sch. to Hancock, Nov. 11, 1775: 4 Force, III., 1520. Letter, Mar. 24, 1776 : 4 Force, V., 481. Ripley to J. Wheelock, Mar. 7, 1776: Wheelock Papers. Arnold to Hancock, Feb. 12, 1776: 4 Force, IV., 1017. Wooster to Cong., Feb. 11, 1776: ib., 1001. Goforth to Jay, Apr. 8, 1776: Bancroft Coll., Rev. Papers, I., p. 37. Hawley to Gerry, Feb. 20, 1776: Austin, Gerry, I., p. 164.

Malignant ends, knew they were setting the Reputation, Safety and Welfare of a generous (but deluded) People at Stake, and involving them in certain Ruin.' Many realized that they had done much to excite the wrath of England ; and now, if America did not take care of them, where were they? Where were they, in fact ? ' Between Hawk and Buzzard,' Antill informed Congress. They did not hear the remark, but some of them could think it.[37]

However much the Canadians loved the Lord, they feared the Devil still more. Tales of prisoners hung on the ramparts of Quebec and then thrown to the dogs, declared Ainslie, served the King most effectively. ' The peasants are, in general, at present, for us, but I believe from no other motive than that we are the strongest side,' said Ritzema. Terror was the final argument still ; and therefore in exact proportion as respect for the Americans diminished, dread of the British and the wish to ' make their peace with their former masters'—as Wooster phrased it—increased ; so that the mischief grew with double speed. On the one hand, more was demanded of the United Colonies. The mere capture of Quebec would no longer ensure their joining the Union. On setting out for the capital, Montgomery had expected, after reducing that place, to call a convention and see Canada welded to the other Colonies ; but, after his batteries failed, he sent word to Schuyler that a full and palpable insurance against every possible attack from Great Britain would be necessary. The simple prolongation of this line of ascent carried it, by the middle of March, rather high. On the other hand, the Tories urged that it was not too late even

---

[37] § Montg. to Sch., Sept. 28: Force III., 954. Wooster to Sch., Jan. 14, 1776: 4 Force, IV., 852. Id. to Warner, Jan. 6, 1776: Pub. Record Off., Am. and W. I., Vol. 186, p. 313. Letter, Mar. 24, 1776 : 4 Force, V., 481. Secret Journ. Cong., Jan. 24, 1776. Quebec Gazette, Sept. 21, 1775. Antill: Smith, Private Journal, Jan. 18.

now to give a redeeming proof of loyalty. 'They are but a handful of Men,' hinted the priests.[38]

Others did more than hint. A plot was laid in January to overpower the garrison of Montreal. Beaubassin advised the massacre of the American troops loudly enough to be overheard. Woolsey headed an attempt to capture some of Arnold's men. An anonymous paper, 'very artfully written,' was found one morning at the church door in Three Rivers, 'calculated to stimulate the inhabitants to rise' and cut the Americans off. Under Wooster's very ear, Sanguinet cried to the Canadians of Montreal : 'Will you be more senseless than the beasts, which, looking at their hurts, rouse themselves against the men that have wounded them?' And it was found that soldiers were being quietly enlisted for the King even between Chambly and Sorel. Were such affairs accidents or were they symptoms? It mattered vitally which. Should Carleton succeed in winning over the Canadians and Indians, Washington assured the Massachusetts legislature, 'words are unnecessary to describe the melancholy effects that will, inevitably, follow.' Happily, nobody had really dared make head against the Provincials as yet. Sporadic malcontents were, perhaps, of no particular significance.[39]

But, as the days and nights were growing equal, the Americans at Quebec began to catch glimpses of something more serious. A number of priests from below had been arrested a few weeks before ' on account of their diabolical conduct' ; and, though Arnold dismissed them on parole, such treatment could hardly be expected to charm away

---

[38] § Ainslie, Journal, Feb. 28. Ritzema to N. Y. Com. Safety, Jan. 3, 1776 : Force, IV., 1114. Wooster to Hancock, Feb. 13, 1776: 4 Force, IV., 1132. Montg. to Sch., Dec. 26, 1775 : ib., 464. Wooster to Warner, Jan. 6, 1776: Note 37.

[39] § Cf. 'Chalmers' Journal, Feb. 28, with letter from Montreal, Jan. 8, 1776, in Pub. Rec. Off., Am. and W. I., Vol. 186, p. 309. Wooster to Sch., Mar. 13, 1776: 4 Force, V., 417. Letter, Jan. 27, 1776: 4 Force, IV., 868. Verreau (Sanguinet), Invasion, p. 103. Goforth to Jay, Apr. 8, 1776 : Bancroft Coll., Rev. Papers, I., p. 37. Wash. to Mass., Jan. 19, 1776: 4 Force, IV., 775.

their spirit of contradiction. Later, something was heard
of the mysterious packets that had left Quebec for the
same quarter. On the sixteenth of March, Captain Ayot
of Point Levi wrote to Arnold, in bad French but a good
spirit, that certain persons were telling all through the
parishes on that side how few the Americans before Quebec
really were, and actually prompting the people to 'Revolt.'

Carleton had in fact sent word to Beaujeu, the seig-
neur of Crane Island (*Ile aux Grues*) to cut off Arnold's
guard at Point Levi and thus break the blockade. About
thirty miles down the St. Lawrence the standard of the
King was set up. A convoy of provisions intended for
the Americans was seized. The movement grew 'more
formidable every day.' Peasants gathered fast. The ball
got started. Beaujeu, on the march with three hundred
and fifty men, boasted that as many more were coming
behind. The little force at Point Levi counted nothing
like that. As news of all this arrived, about the twenty-
second of March, many of the Americans before Quebec
fairly trembled. And well they might : it was an hour of
real, of mortal danger. 'God (and he only) can determine our fate,' exclaimed Brogden. [40]

But Arnold acted quickly. The posts at Point Levi and
Orleans Island were strengthened. Some boats that had
been armed with cannon got into motion. Brave Major
Duboys marched down the river with eighty men ; Colonel
Nicholson followed with seventy more ; and a large number of friendly Canadians joined these forces. An *habitant*
betrayed the advance party of the enemy ; and Du-

[40] § For the Beaujeu affair: Arnold to ——, Mar. 28, 1776 (4 Force, V., 512).
Id. to McNeill, Mar. 29, 1776 (Ford Coll.); Id. to Deane, Mar. 30, 1776 (4 Force,
V., 549); Ayot to Arnold (Can. Arch., B, 27, p. 389); Carleton to Germain, May
14, 1776 (4 Force, VI., 456) ; Caldwell, Letter ; Bull. de Rech. Hist., 1900, pp.
130, 132, etc.; Centenaire, p. 54 ; Haskell, Diary, Mar. 23 ; Senter, Journal ;
'Shortt' Journal, Mar. 18 ; Têtu, Evêques, p. 334 ; Pelton (N. Y. Calendar, I.,
p. 285) ; Mott to Goforth, Mar. 26, 1776 (4 Force, V., 753); Anon., Apr. 6, 1776 (ib.,
804); Finlay's and other British Journals, Apr. 6 ; Berthelot (Can. Arch., separate); Brogden to Goforth, Mar. 26, 1776 (4 Force, V., 753); Arnold to Clinton,
Mar. 22, 1776 (Dreer Coll.); Verreau (Sanguinet), Invasion, p. 105.

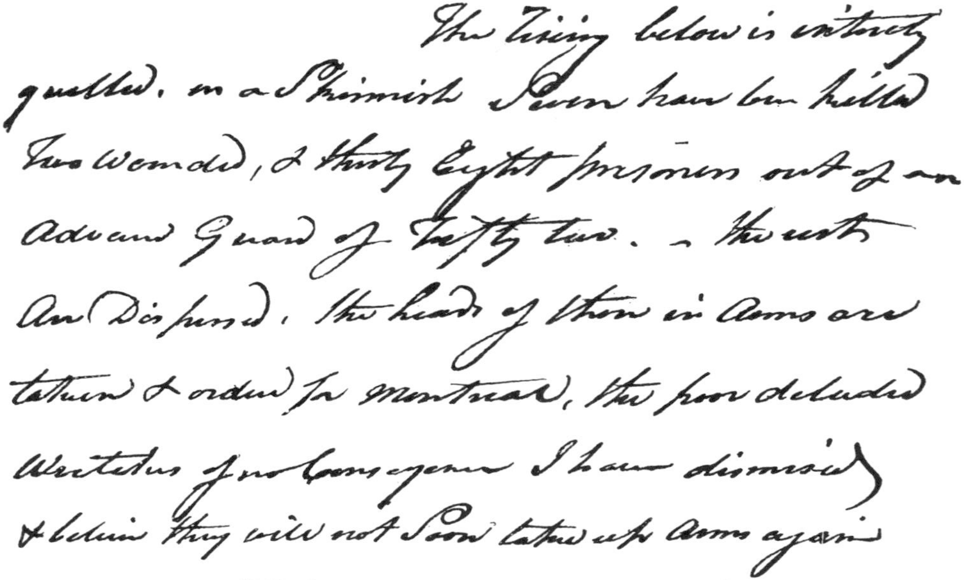

The Rising below is entirely quelled. in a Skirmish Seven have been killed Two Wounded, & thirty Eight prisoners out of an Advance Guard of Fifty two. — the rest are Dispersed. the heads of those in Arms are taken & order'd for Montreal, the poor deluded Wretches of no Consequence I have dismiss'd & believe they will not Soon take up Arms again

FROM ARNOLD'S LETTER TO MC NEILL, MARCH 29, 1776

boys—taking it by surprise at a priest's house—killed six or eight, wounded an abbé from the Seminary besides one or two laymen, and sent nearly forty prisoners to head-quarters. Upon that, Beaujeu's main body scattered. 'Thanks be to God!' cried Brogden.

Yet the real question remained. Noblesse, clergy, and peasantry had now combined under the royal flag, and had actually fought the Americans. Two months before, Pelissier had said that troops ought to be placed in the country districts, and Ritzema thought it necessary to 'awe' the people. It really began to look that way. I 'consider,' Washington had concluded at the end of January, 'that the important period is now arrived, when the Canadians and consequently their Indians must take their side': were they doing it? 'The Canadians taking up arms so early against us is of the most important consequence,' thought Hazen; 'Much depends on it,' Gershom Mott could see; and, like an earthquake, this tragic incident jarred harshly southward all the long way to Philadelphia. 'Alarming,' commented Schuyler as it shook Fort George; 'really alarming,' thought the Commander-in-chief at New York; 'of the utmost importance,' felt Congress.[41]

Yet Arnold, in reporting the affair, added: 'The inhabitants are generally in our favour.' All but the leaders of the rising were set free, and he believed 'they would not soon take up Arms again.' Certainly, complete quiet returned in that quarter. The commander at Three Rivers found many Canadians eager to get American appointments as captains of militia. More Provincial forces moved toward the seat of war. New plans to reduce Quebec ripened. England was far away. The St. Lawrence re-

41 §See Note 40. Pelissier to Hancock, Jan. 8, 1776 : 4 Force IV., 596. Ritzema to N. Y. Cong., Jan. 5, 1776: ib., 1115. Wash. to Sch., Jan. 27, 1776 : Writings (Ford), III., p. 375. Hazen to Sch., Apr. 1, 1776 : 4 Force, V., 751. Sch. to Wash., Apr. 12, 1776: 4 Force, V., 871. Wash. to Sch., Apr. 19, 1776 : Writings (Ford), IV., p. 28. Hancock to Sch., Apr. 26, 1776: 4 Force, V., 1086.

mained fast locked. And nobody on earth could sum up the words that passed in the dark confessionals under the tin roofs of the churches, the sharp remarks covered with banter that circled round the simmering stew-pots between puffs of the long pipes, and still less the half-conscious feelings that crept voiceless from heart to heart through this agitated sea of unlettered, inscrutable peasants. The clergy believed they knew, perhaps; but, six months before, their shrewdest calculations had been wofully, even ludicrously, disappointed. [42]

---

[42] § Arnold to ———, Mar. 28, 1776: 4 Force, V., 512. Id. to McNeill, Mar. 29, 1775: Ford Coll. Anon. letter (in French), Mar. 28, 1776: Can. Arch., B, 27, p. 394. Letter, Three Rivers, Mar. 24, 1776: 4 Force, V., 481.

XXVIII

NEW PLANS, NEW HOPES, NEW ATTACKS

A LL these weeks, the people going their narrowed ways
in Quebec knew nothing of the fresh thunderbolts
forging against them. Ignorance brought little bliss, however. The city appeared to be marching in a cul-de-sac,
and nobody pretended to make out what was lurking at
the farther end. Another assault was constantly looked
for. 'Thus we remained the remainder of the winter, always on the *qui vive*,' said Caldwell. 'If they make a
second attack,' muttered Ainslie, 'they will repent their
rashness'; but every one understood that repentance was
easy enough to be little dreaded by the Americans. Deserters and spies, who crept into the city shrouded in new
white blankets or were hoisted bodily over a gate, declared
that an assault was coming and gave the date. From a
look-out box thirty feet in air above Cape Diamond, the
snow beyond the Heights could be seen strewed with ladders. When a night proved 'dark and sleety,' timid
folks could almost hear the 'rebel' battle-cry. People
studied the Governor's face whenever he appeared, and
drew courage from his calm looks ; but they read there no
contempt for the danger.[1]

Consequently, while the amount of fighting may not
have been great, the amount of getting ready to fight was

---

[1] This and several following paragraphs are based on the British Journals ;
Vialar's, Lester's, and Ainslie's Ord. Books ; Caldwell, Letter ; Carleton to
Germain, May 14, 1776 (4 Force, VI., 456) ; Id. to Tryon, May 17, 1776 (Pub. **Rec.**
Off., Am. and W. I., Vol. 186, p. 739) ; Précis of Oper.; Dearborn, Journal.

immense. ' More guns mounted ' ; ' More guns mounted ';
' More guns mounted '; wrote a citizen day after day in
his Journal. By the ninth of March, a hundred and fourteen cannon—' none under 12-pounders,' noted Finlay—
squatted on the ramparts, besides a numberless brood of
mortars, howitzers, cohorns, and other minor sorts ; nor
did the work stop there. Soon after the assault, Carleton
visited the Lower Town and had new fortifications erected
in that quarter. Another blockhouse went up toward the
Heights. Will the ice in the river get solid enough now
to bear the Americans ? asked every one when the cold
grew intense at sunset and the gale died down ; and, after
the river did freeze hard, a trench was cut through the ice,
while barriers of heavy cakes closed the ends of the streets
in the Lower Town. Now and then all the cannon were
freshly scaled, or the ditch and ramparts cleared of snow.
On moonless nights, fireballs hung at the angles of the
bastions; and a composition was invented, which, after
giving a bright, steady light until nearly consumed, ex-
ploded and scattered hand-grenades, bullets, and scraps
of metal in all directions. As a rule, nobody took his
clothes off, day or night ; and, a great part of the time,
every man not on duty slept at a place of rendezvous with
a musket by his arm, under orders ' to be ready on a minute's warning.' The invalids and pseudo-invalids were
tried out on the parade, and over one hundred men fit for
battle or for guarding the prisoners were discovered. Nobody could escape Maclean. Every one had to do his part
of the sentry duty ; and, with few long intermissions,
the roar of heavy guns kept the windows jarring.

The stories of scanty firewood that comforted Arnold
had a very solid foundation. Fuel 'was much wanted,'
said Carleton, and some of the people found themselves
' in great Distress.' Even in January, one fire had to answer for six or seven families ; and March twentieth saw

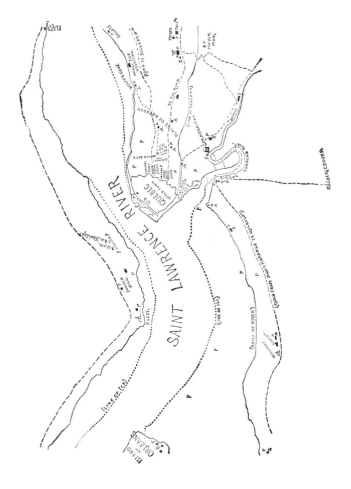

EDWARD ANTILL'S MAP (NORTH AND SOUTH REVERSED)

247

the last armful of 'the King's wood' served out. Party after party ventured under escort into St. Roch, to get fuel from what houses the Americans did not burn; and the picket fences there were trimmed to the snow. 'When that melts two or three feet,' they said, 'we'll find a second crop'; and they could hardly wait for the time to come. Provisions also grew short. Seven pence and a half for a pound of beef seemed 'very dear' the middle of January; but the price rose to nine pence in three weeks, and kept on climbing. Only about half of the wheat in town had been made into flour when the blockade began; and the one mill, driven by horses, ground but three bushels an hour. Much of the grain had to be boiled, and eaten whole. Cold weather, scant rations, fatiguing duty, and continual alarms made the time heavy if not exactly dull. 'A hard winter,' grumbled Barnfair. 'A close Blockade,' admitted the Governor.[2]

Many wondered why Carleton did not end it all by a sortie, and some blamed him. Maclean was doubtless one of the latter, and Caldwell certainly another.[3] But they did not balance all the chances, as the responsibility of command required him to do. The misfortune of losing Quebec would have been ten, perhaps a hundred, possibly a thousand fold greater than any advantage to be gained by driving the Americans from the suburbs and highways. The Governor's one duty at present was to save the capital, that is to say the flag, Canada, perhaps North America; and this he intended to do, regardless of glory or minor strategic advantages. 'Montcalm,' said Montgomery, 'permitting his courage to get the better of his discretion, gave up the advantages of his fortress, and came out to try

[2] § Council, Quebec, Nov. 16, 1775; War Off., Orig. Corres., N. Amer., Vol. 12. Barnfair, May 5, 1776: Middlesex Journal, June 22, 1776. Carleton to Tryon, etc.: Note 1. Report, Com. of Secret Corres., Feb. 14, 1776: Cont. Cong. Papers, No. 22, p. 211.
[3] Maclean to Germain, May 10, 1776: Can. Arch., Q, 12, p. 39. Caldwell, Letter.

his strength on the plain. Carleton, who was Wolfe's Quartermaster-General, understands this well, and, it is to be feared, will not follow the Frenchman's example.'[4]

Had it been possible to know the situation of the enemy,—but that he could not. There were telescopes enough in town, even after Maclean lost the spy-glass covered with green baize, that had become so familiar a sight on the ramparts; but none of them, even from the sentry-box on stilts, could explore the secrets of the American lines. The numbers in the besieging camp were naturally exaggerated by report. Even when only five hundred Provincials could pace the rounds, Caldwell barely ventured to believe that they did not exceed fourteen hundred. Tryon assured the Governor that he 'would not probably have one-fourth part of the ten thousand [proposed for Canada] to cope with'; but even that would be twenty-five hundred, and many more could lurk in the folds of the 'probably.' Spies could not easily ransack Arnold's camp, especially as it included several posts; and, if they announced the reinforcements that Sanguinet heard of at Montreal, the tale was twenty thousand. Deserters were the principal sources of information, as Caldwell stated; and nobody could be sure whether they were converts or emissaries. Early in April, Lee was said to be on the way with four thousand troops. One man reported that quarters for seven thousand had actually been ordered by the American commander. 'A Yankyade,' sniffed Ainslie; but who could be positive? Another fellow, who seemed very simple and open, called the enemy eleven thousand: it seemed unreasonable, but perhaps a trap had been set, and baited with the self-styled 'deserters' who gave smaller figures. Had there been enough such visitors, the algebraic pro-

---

[4] Montg. to R. R. Liv., Nov. —, 1775: 4 Force, III., 1638.

cess of elimination might have netted a mathematical certainty; but the line of guards only six hundred feet apart on the Plains, the patrols crossing every fifteen minutes between the Island of Orleans and the north shore, and the close watch maintained everywhere, reduced them to a minimum. We were 'very destitute' of intelligence all winter, confessed Finlay.[5]

Moreover, the interrogation mark above the American encampment was answered by a still blacker interrogation mark over the town. Confidential letters from loyalists outside assured Carleton that some of his Canadian officers corresponded with the enemy. General discontent was not only reported to Arnold, but recognized by at least one important officer of the garrison. Even in December, the sergeants proved remiss in duty, and had to be menaced publicly with a court-martial. A month after, it was given out in orders that, 'for the future,' if any man of the British militia should be found 'declaring he would lay down his Arms & refusing to do his duty,' he should be confined immediately in the Black Hole. Later, Maclean announced that the officers of both French and British militia had 'relaxed very much in their Duty,' and threatened to shut up those who left their posts, as had become the practice, to go to supper.[6]

Evidently this military frankness raised an outcry, for Carleton himself appeared presently in orders, complimented the garrison, and assured the troops that the purpose had only been 'to stimulate and awaken some few.'

---

[5] § Ainslie, Ord. Book, Feb. 6. Caldwell, Letter. Tryon to Carleton, Jan. 31, 1776: Pub. Rec. Off., Am. and W. I., Vol. 186, p. 329. Verreau (Sanguinet), Invasion, p. 98. Caldwell, Letter. 'Chalmers' Journal, Apr. 19. Finlay, Journal, Feb. 26, 28; Apr. 6. Ainslie, Journal, Feb. 28; Mar. 19; May 1. 'Shortt' Journal, Feb. 23. 'Remark. Occurr.' Journal, Mar. 8.

[6] § Lindsay: Can. Rev., No. 5, Sept., 1826, p. 89. Arnold to Wash., Feb. 27, 1776: 4 Force, IV., 1513. 'Chalmers' Journal, Feb. 14. Ainslie's and Lester's Ord. Books, Dec. 25; Jan. 26; Feb. 7, 12; Mar. 1, 2, 3, 9, 14, 26. Finlay, Journal, Feb. 13. Ainslie, Journal, Feb. 6; Apr. 13. Prisoners: next Chapter. 'Shortt' Journal, Mar. 2.

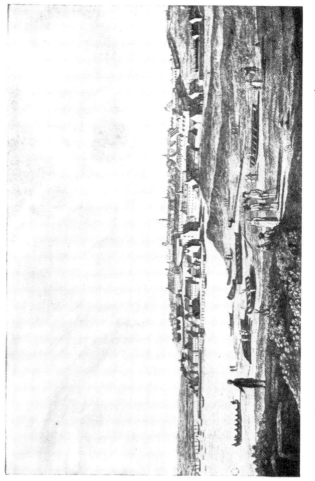

QUEBEC AS SEEN FROM NEAR THE MOUTH OF ST. CHARLES RIVER (1759)

Yet in March a captain was reprimanded, men had to be fined for not doing duty, a sergeant was reduced to the ranks, and, on the twenty-sixth, Maclean confessed publicly that he found himself 'obliged to make use of hard methods' to enforce discipline. Some of the troops would not wear their uniform. The number of deserters that got safely out of town produced alarm : three escaped at one time, with a sentry not over thirty yards away. The prisoners appeared to have good friends in the city. A 9-pounder near Palace Gate was found stuffed with rubbish. Maclean came near being shot from the walls one day while placing sentries outside. A mistake, this was said to be, and probably so it was; but all such incidents, taken together, proved that a tight rein and a convenient propinquity to the Black Hole were needed to ensure the defence.[7]

Carleton's Fabian policy had various other arguments in its favor. Frosts and storms waged a sort of warfare against the Americans that cost no British blood ; danger, hardships, poverty, weakness, hope deferred, and internal friction seemed likely to wear out the besiegers ; while the mere effort of keeping an army afoot at so great a distance and in spite of such difficulties was sure to weaken and might possibly discourage the Colonies. Let them alone, then, said common-sense.

But perhaps another point weighed even more in the statesmanlike mind at the Castle. To attack the Americans while allied with the Canadians might weld the two parties together ; whereas to attack them after the Canadians had become unfriendly and wished them out of the country, should that day arrive, would force a wedge of steel between them. The woollen caps, both red and grey, would then hail the British bayonet as a savior,

_____

[7] See Note 6.

friend, and brother; and Canada, healed of its dog-star madness, would rejoice to be loyal forever. Enough intelligence filtered into the city to show that the American and the Canadian did not love each other better day by day; and enough orders went forth to help on the mischief. Be still, and let the inexorable logic of the situation crystallize, bade statecraft.

Quebec, then, could only watch and wait; and above all it watched. As an old Greek sailor off Malea studied the sky, Maclean and his officers observed and analyzed the signs of the blockade. Flashes of fire, distant musketry, signals, a procession of sleighs, a group of soldiers, a rocket at Point Levi answered by a cannon at Sainte Foy, a roll of drums, a deserter in green on the Heights pointing at a bastion, a line of men carrying boards,—all these were noted and interrogated. A company was seen marching on snow-shoes in Indian file, and it had to be counted: 'ninety-six.' Huzzas were heard: 'we conjecture that they have had a reinforcement.' The dogs on the Plains barked more than usual: 'there is certainly some movement.' Voices were heard singing out, as sailors did when they heaved at a great weight; two men stole up to the walls on Cape Diamond and called out, 'Good morrow, gentlemen!' a party crept down from St. Roch, 'shouldering the wall' near Palace Gate; two hundred Americans marched up a 'hollow pass' in the bluff above the town : what new scheme did these operations betoken? On the fifth of March, a pole set in a fence near the General Hospital bore a strange flag,—red bordered with black. Some pronounced it a squaw's blanket edged with mourning, raised in memory of the Boston Massacre; but many wrung their hands and went about shivering to one another: '*Mon Dieu*, it's the bloody flag! we shall all be slaughtered!' Now and then an alarm sounded; the bells rang; the drums beat; the garrison hurried to their posts.

But there it ended. No enemy came. Quebec sank back to waiting and watching; and fear deferred made the heart weary, if not sick.[8]

On the second day in April, something new appeared on the Heights, and the glasses were soon levelled that way. It was an enormous grey periwig. On one side of it stood Edward Antill; a figure in scarlet on the other was pronounced Arnold; and the periwig—was General David Wooster. The retreat at Montreal had at last been secured, or at least enough troops had come down the river so that he felt safe against a sortie at Quebec. Indeed, not knowing the exact facts, he had feared there were now too many besiegers, thinking the city might surrender before he could win the glory of reducing it. ' I 'll scale those walls if there 's enough space between them and the heavens!' he had exclaimed with all the conviction of Tartarin; and April the First smiled a little more broadly than usual on seeing him arrive at Quebec to do it. Indeed, the fence-posts began working their heads through the snow just then, as if to look on.[9]

The first consequence of his arrival seemed rather negative. Wooster and Arnold had been well acquainted in Connecticut. In fact, it was on Wooster's advice that Arnold had been refused ammunition by the Selectmen of New Haven, when he proposed to march for Cambridge. At that stage, the first had been a major-general and the second a captain in the service of the Colony; but now both were brigadier-generals in the Continental army. Within a year, Wooster had lost one grade and Arnold had gained four grades. Wooster, however, held the advantage of seniority; and his age, his general quality, and

---

[8] § From the British Journals, mainly Ainslie's and Finlay's.

[9] § Ainslie, Journal, Apr. 2. Letter, Apr. 6, 1776: 4 Force, V., 804. Wooster to Wash., Feb. 25, 1776: 4 Force, IV., 1493. Goforth to Jay, Apr. 8, 1776: Bancroft Coll., Rev. Papers, I., p. 37. Boast: Conn. Gazette, May 3, 1776. Letter, Apr. 6, 1776: 4 Force, V., 805.

his bitterness about losing rank promised abundantly that in effect all the former distance between them would be enforced. Arnold, for his part, had been able to mount his horse during the week before; and now, chafing from three months of inaction and burning to carry out the plans already begun upon, he hoped to make himself master at last of the ' proud city ' that he had so bravely and patiently beset. The day before Wooster appeared, his mind was boiling over with schemes; and then—another Hinman descended upon him like a candle-snuffer. In short, said Arnold, the senior officer ' did not think proper ' to consult with him.[10]

To remain as a mere spectator of events or the mere lieutenant of a jealous periwig would have driven him wild; and the only course was to get decently away.

CASTLE ST. LOUIS VIEWED FROM THE ST. LAWRENCE

Fortunately, his horse had fallen upon him the day after Wooster did, and ' violently b r u i s e d ' his wounded leg; and, after reflecting for about a week, he asked for a leave of absence. It was ' readily granted,' as he observed; and, under the color of going up to hurry the reinforcements along, he set off to take command at Montreal. This left Wooster, unembarrassed, at the apex of the pyramid to display his talents. ' I rather imagine we shall be obliged to try once more by assault,' he had airily observed to Washington. Arnold also had felt it might

10 § Sparks, Arnold, p. 56. I. N. Arnold, Arnold, p. 36. Arnold to——,
Mar. 26, 1776: 4 Force, V., 512. Id. to Deane, Mar. 30 (midnight), 1776: ib., 549.
Id. to Sch., Apr. 20, 1776: ib., 1098.

come to that, and had made preparations accordingly. But Wooster concluded to be satisfied with something more—humane; and, in substance, Arnold's other plans went on as best they could without his leadership.[11]

In fact, the day after Wooster appeared on the Heights, a battery of three 12-pounders and an 8-inch howitzer opened fire on the town from Point Levi. 'I perceive it is open overhead,' said an officer in speaking of 'that almost impregnable fortress'; and the army saw with delight that, even if they could not scale the ramparts, their iron messengers could. It was brave enough to keep on 'fagging it out' before the walls, as a soldier phrased it; but that eternal 'All 's well!' of the British sentries grew tiresome. To make the prospect now the more keenly agreeable, a certain yellowish building on the brink of the precipice—the staring bull's-eye of the town—was where the stubborn Governor lived. 'When we shall be able to plump the balls into Carleton's jaws,' cried a soldier, 'I guess they won't cry all 's well.' In short, it was hoped once more to 'catch the fox in his den.' Very 'sweetly' indeed, then, played the music of those cannon in the Americans' ears. Something would be accomplished now. Grants of houses in the city were made, it was reported.[12]

But Carleton had a reply ready on his lips. Signs of what was going on across the river had been observed: forty-nine men marching on snow-shoes in Indian file; canoes and boats passing and repassing the St. Lawrence

---

[11] § Arnold to Sch., Apr. 20, 1776 : 4 Force, V., 1098. Verreau (Sanguinet), Invasion, p. 106. Wooster to Hancock, Apr. 10, 1776: 4 Force, V., 845. Hazen to Sch., Apr. 1, 1776: ib., 751. Arnold to Sch., Apr. 3 , 1776: ib., 1155. Id. to Wash., Feb. 27, 1776 : 4 Force, IV., 1513. Ainslie, Journal, Apr. 9. Wooster to Wash., Feb. 25, 1776: 4 Force, IV., 1493. Hazen, whom Wooster had left in command at Montreal, was sent to look after Chambly and St. Johns.

[12] § Letters, Apr. 6, 1776: 4 Force, V., 804, 805. Arnold to Deane, Mar. 30, 1776 : ib., 549. Id. to Sch., Apr. 20, 1776 : ib., 1098. Finlay, Journal, Apr. 3. Haskell, Diary, Apr. 3. Letter, Jan. 27, 1776 : 4 Force, IV., 868. Letter, Mar. 10, 1776: Conn. Gazette, Apr. 19, 1776. Hodgkinson to Parents, Apr. 27, 1776: Penna. Mag., X., p. 158. Ainslie, Journal, Apr. 6. REMARK LXXII.

above; twelve horses dragging something heavy down the south shore; and men busily at work there in the snow. For ten days or more, 32- and 42-pounders and 13-inch mortars had been getting ready to answer the choir at Point Levi, and for some time, indeed, had been tuning their pipes quite vigorously. It was a splendid chance for cannon practice: bluff against bluff, not quite a mile apart; and, when the concert began, the garrison felt as well pleased as the besiegers felt hopeful. 'Infinitely superiour,' the fire of their weighty metal was pronounced; and, after about three weeks of it, they cried exultingly, 'Why do they keep on? So far they have kill'd a boy, wounded a Sailor, & broke the leg of a turkey!'[13]

This, however, was largely by way of whistling, for in reality no little damage was done. Even above the cliffs the fashion of cellar drawing-rooms became extremely popular. The first two shots hit the Convent of the Ursulines, a long distance behind the bluff; and ten or eleven balls fell in the Seminary yard or struck the building the first day. Ainslie admitted the reality of the cannonade by crying 'Diabolical!' if the Americans fired at the hour of mass. The pavement had to be torn up, to prevent shells from bursting and balls from ricocheting. The Castle was supposed to be proof, and a facetious as well as thirsty gentleman, establishing himself in the basement with good company and good wine, tossed off a bumper at every burst of a cannon; but one evening, while a party sat at cards, an iron visitor complimented them gruffly from the next room. Balls popped into the stern of the *Lizard* and splintered the foremast, opened a window in the *Hunter*, and perambulated the cabin of the *Fell*. Indeed, Barnfair the Boaster admitted that

;

---

[13] § The British Journals, *passim*; e. g., Ainslie, Journal, Dec. 13; Feb. 25 Mar. 15, 20, 21, 22; Apr. 21. 'Chalmers' Journal, Mar. 22, 25, 29; Apr. 1–3.

'great damage' was done the vessels. Red-hot shot,
hissing their way through the shingled roofs of the Lower
Town, set house after house on fire and nearly destroyed
that quarter ; and the same kind of missiles branded the
shipping. 'Let the shot be well heated,' bade Arnold on
his last day of command ; and so they were.[14]

Three other batteries were planned : a gun and a mortar battery on the Heights and a gun battery on the
farther side of the St. Charles River ; but every kind of
difficulty stood in the way. Arnold had cal'ed for more
artillery as soon as he knew the fate of his detachment,
but it came slowly. The cannon at Montreal had been
rammed full of balls, when the British retired ; and,
though Holt luckily found a man in New York who
could undo the mischief, nearly half of March had passed
before the ordnance could set out for Quebec (March 11).
St. Johns had two pieces of 24 pounds, besides a number
of smaller calibres, and several of these were tediously
worried across to Montreal, and then on to Quebec, at
about the same time. Schuyler could supply no mortars
and nothing more suitable for battering than one 18-
pounder and some 12's. At the request of Congress, the
authorities at New York ordered twelve or fourteen pieces
northward ; but, when the battle of the bluffs opened,
the most active of them had only reached Lake George.
As the British had now evacuated Boston, Washington
despatched two companies of Knox's artillery and a pair
of 13-inch mortars to Canada about the first of April ;
but a long journey lay before them. Shot and shell were

---

14 § Hodgkinson to Parents, Apr. 27, 1776: Penna. Mag., X., p. 158. An-
burey, Travels, I., pp. 50–53. Ursul. de Québec, III., p. 132. Dearborn, Journal,
Apr. 4. Ainslie, Journal, Apr. 8, 13, 14, 21, etc. Finlay, Journal, Apr. 15, etc.
Damage to Ship *Gen. Thomas :* Can. Arch., B, 42, p. 74. Barnfair to owners,
May 15, 1776 : Middlesex Journal, June 22, 1776. Rogers, Hadden's Journal, p.
10. Finlay, Journal, *passim.* Carleton to Germain, May 14, 1776 : 4 Force, VI.,
456. Pell, Diary: Mag. Am. Hist., 1878, p. 43. Caldwell, Letter, Maclean to
Barrington, May 21, 1776: Can. Arch., M, 317, p. 330. Arnold to Clinton, Apr.
1, 1776: Bloodgood, Sexagenary, p. 44.

scraped together from all sources, yet the total was absurd. About the middle of March, Wooster estimated the whole

quantity of gunpowder in the province as sixty rounds apiece for six thousand men, allowing none for the artillery. Arnold had been eager for carcasses to fire the town with; but there was no person qualified to make

PALACE GATE (OUTSIDE)

any such articles, no trained engineer to lay out the batteries, and only one artillery officer to direct the operations.

No worse time of year could have been selected. The roads overflowed with water and mud, and the streams with water and ice. In various places, nothing could possibly be moved for days and perhaps for weeks. At the end of March, nearly five feet of snow still covered the ground about Quebec, and all this had to melt and find a place for itself during the next few weeks,—in fact more, for three inches fell on the twenty-third of April, and as much more on May Day. In addition to the snow

¹⁵ § Arnold to Deane, Mar. 30, 1776:, 4 Force V., 549. Id. to Wooster, Jan 2, 1776: 4 Force, IV., 670. Holt to S. Adams, Jan. 29, 1776: S. Adams Papers. Cannon to Quebec: Verreau (Sanguinet), Invasion, p. 101. Wooster to Sch., Jan. 14, 1776: 4 Force, IV., 852. Id. to Id., Feb. 19, 1776: ib., 1483. Id. to Id., Mar. 5, 1776: 4 Force, V., 416. Sch. to Wash., Feb. 14, 1776: 4 Force, IV., 1146. Id. to Lee, Feb. 29, 1776: 4 Force, V., 356. Hancock to Lee, Feb. 19, 1776: 4 Force, IV., 1197. N. Y. Cong., Feb. 22, 1776: 4 Force, V., 299. At Ft. George : Sch. to Hancock, Apr. 2, 1776 (ib., 767). Wash. to Sch., Apr., 3, 1776: ib., 779. Id. to Arnold, Apr. 3, 1776: Writings (Ford), IV., p. 7. Wooster to Hancock, Apr. 10, 1776: 4 Force, V., 845. [Antill] to [Hazen], Mar. 28, 1776: Can. Arch., B, 27, p. 380. Wooster to Sch., Mar. 16, 1776 : Sparks MSS., No. 60, p. 77. Arnold to Cong., Jan. 11, 1776: ib., No. 52, II., p. 34. Id. to Deane, Mar. 30, 1776: 4 For V., 549. REMARK LXXIII.

there was 'Excessive heavy rain,' as even the natives called it ; and, after that, more 'very cold weather.' 'Rain Hail sleet ; ' 'soft drizzling weather,' 'heavy rain,' 'snow,' 'hard freezing,'—thus it went. 'If one steps out of the beaten path, he sinks to the knee,' wrote Ainslie ; and that was in town. April thirteenth, bare spots could be seen on some of the hilltops, which meant that all their snows were now in a liquid form down below. 'It is bad travelling,' noted Haskell that day, 'by reason of the water being in many places in the road three feet deep.' Yet water froze nearly half an inch on the second of May.[16]

However, the work went on. Pelissier advised cannonading the Palace Gate side of Quebec, because in that quarter the city had only two guns ; and fortunately a very heavy French breastwork of 1759 stood on the farther bank of the St. Charles near the ferry house. Objects were seen moving behind the alders that lined the shore there ; and at length, between nine and ten o'clock on April the twenty-second, one day after the swallows brought a promise of summer over the hills, the guns began their work. Five days later the finest piece of all—the one brass 24-pounder—was put in play ; and, though its 'axletree' broke at the first shot, the men succeeded in making it serve. Here, too, the balls were well heated ; and, as they had but a short distance to travel, they landed the redder. 'Chimneys & roofs' felt the cannonade, was Ainslie's cheerful way of putting it ; but a chimney struck by a cannon ball became a shower of missiles, and a red-hot shot landing on shingles did not simply roll down like a hailstone. Shells began dropping into town from the Heights on the evening of

16 § Sch. to Hancock, Mar. 19, 1776 : 4 Force, V., 415. Wash. to Arnold, Apr. 3, 1776 : Writings (Ford), IV., p. 7. Wooster to Sch., Mar. 5, 1776: 4 Force, V., 416. Arnold to ——, Mar. 26, 1776: ib., 512. Ainslie, Journal, Apr. 3, 4, 5, 7, 9, 10, 23 ; May 1, 2 ; etc. Haskell, Diary, Apr. 13.

the twenty-third, and more guns in the same quarter made ready.[17]

Yet, even if this bombardment rendered Quebec 'a miserable city inside,' as Lieutenant Hadden thought it, nothing vital was accomplished. It amounted essentially to the tale of Montgomery's cannon over again : few against many, small against great. 'Ten balls for one, & some shells,' recorded Ainslie one day, and that represented no doubt the usual ratio. New metal—including four 32-pounders—was brought to bear on the ferry battery ; and the guard-house near it, though built of stone and almost three feet thick, flew to pieces very soon. At Point Levi, all the American gunners could do was to wait for a lull in the terrible fire from Quebec, steal into the works, load, shoot, and run. 'We made some fine shots to-day', exulted the men in the city repeatedly ; and why not, indeed? for Captain Mackenzie of the

PALACE GATE (INSIDE)

Hunter aimed their cannon. The second day after the Point Levi battery opened, a Quebecker said it looked like a honeycomb. The mortars on the Heights were only seven inches in diameter, and the shells measured still less. The guns at the ferry lost effectiveness because they had to be elevated too

---

17 § Pelissier to Hancock, Jan. 8, 1776: 4 Force, IV., 596. Ainslie, Journal, Apr. 5, 21, 22, 23. Marr, Remarks : Can. Arch., M, 384, p. 111. Haskell, Diary, Apr. 5, 22, 23, 24, 27, 29. Carleton to Germain, May 14, 1776: 4 Force, VI., 456. Arnold to ——, Mar. 26, 1776: 4 Force, V., 512. Id. to Sch., Apr. 20, 1776: ib., 1098. [Antill] to [Hazen], Mar. 28, 1776: Can. Arch., B, 27, p. 380. REMARK LXXIV.

much. In spite of all the scraping, there was 'little ball, and less powder' still, as Arnold had said to his friend and patron, Silas Deane, so that—in Dr. Senter's phraseology—the batteries had to be 'allowanced.' By the twenty-seventh of April, substantially all of the cannon-powder had been expended. Americans picked up what British shells failed to explode, it was reported, and sold the contents for a dollar a pound ; and the British balls had to be counted upon for missiles. Still, the cannonade proved that the Americans had not given up. It might remind the garrison that Montgomery's bombardment had been followed by an assault. It was far from agreeable ; and, after so many other annoyances, it might help induce the town to yield.[18]

Even more could be expected from another style of attack, suggested by Pelissier and adopted by Arnold. With many a boom and shiver, the St. Lawrence had now broken up, and while it would take some time yet for the floating ice to leave the river below, the frigate began to bend her sails. Evidently the vessels laid up in the Cul-de-sac would soon return to their element ; and not only would they be lost, should Quebec surrender, but they might cause a great deal of trouble. To prevent that, a pair of floating batteries mounting a 12-pounder each had been fitted up, besides a number of smaller armed boats ; and Hector McNeill, formerly in the British navy, took charge of them. But Pelissier said, Burn the ships before they get afloat. Could they be set on fire, the flames might catch the palisade and open a breach ; and certainly, thought Arnold, should that be done, 'it would

[18] § Hadden, Journal, p. 10. Carleton to Tryon, May 17, 1776: Pub. Rec. Off., Am. and W. I., Vol, 186, p. 739. Ainslie, Journal, Apr. 1, 5, 8, 10, 20, 27 ; May 7 ; etc. 'Chalmers' Journal, Apr. 22, 24. 'Shortt' Journal, Apr. 4. 'Remark. Occurr.' Journal, May 1. Haskell, Diary, Apr. 21. Arnold to Deane, Mar. 30, 1776: 4 Force, V., 549. Id. to Sch., Apr. 20, 1776: ib., 1098. Senter, Journal (undated). Wooster to Cong., Apr. 27, 1776: Cont. Cong. Papers, No. 161, II., p. 309. Howell to ———, May 4, 1776: W. T. Read, G. Read, p. 154.

be impossible for the town to hold out until they could be relieved.' It was not easy to fit out a fire-ship, for the proper materials either did not exist in the province or could not be found in sufficient quantities ; there were few seamen among the troops, and no one—except Arnold himself— was exactly qualified to take the command ; but as hope- fully as possible the scheme was put in execution.[19]

Wooster, smoking his pipe upon the matter—as Jay heard—made up his mind to carry out the plan, and gave his orders. Above all things, he sagely observed, the enemy must get no inkling of it. But, a little while after, as the time of the New York men had nearly ex- pired, he made them parade and then addressed them. ' My lads,' he said with grandfatherly unction, ' I find your time is almost out, and maybe some of you think on going. But surely you won't leave me now ; you must try and stay a little longer. Don't think that I am lying here doing nothing. No, no ; you shall see a fine sight soon. I am busy building a fire-ship ; and, as soon as she is ready, will burn all their vessels up.' The precious secret was now out in earnest, and in a very little time everybody in Quebec talked of the new menace. It was feared that a conflagration would mean an assault and the Day of Judgment in general. Necks were twisted and eyes were strained, to see the dreaded monster float down past Cape Diamond.[20]

April the twenty-seventh, Sergeant Hodgkinson of Pennsylvania sat down to write his ' Honoured Parents'

---

[19] § Pelissier to Hancock, Jan. 8, 1776: 4 Force, IV., 596. Gaspé, Canadians, p. 52. Ainslie, Journal, Apr. 9. Arnold to ——, Mar. 26, 1776 : 4 Force, V., 512. Id. to Deane, Mar. 30, 1776 : ib., 549. Memor. of McNeill, Feb. 15, 1779 : Cont. Cong. Papers, No. 41, VI., p. 113. Wooster to McNeill, Apr. 23, 1776: Am. Antiq. Soc. [Antill] to [Hazen], Mar. 28, 1776: Can. Arch., B, 27, p. 380. Arnold to Sch., Apr. 20, 1776 : 4 Force, V., 1098.

[20] § Jay to Rutledge, July 6, 1776 : Corres. (Johnston), I., p. 68. (Jay's ac- count contains inaccuracies, but its substantial correctness is supported by Haskell, Diary, Apr. 18.) British Journals: e. g., Ainslie's, Apr. 9, 10, 20. Carle- ton to Germain, May 14, 1776: 4 Force, IV., 456.

in a very cheerful frame.   Necessaries in the camp were
extremely dear : ' Rum four shillings a quart, and that the
worst of Yankee. . . . Brown sugar two and sixpence,
and everything else in proportion.'   But the main interest appeared to be in good shape : ' there is no fear of
any troops to assist them till we have the honour to gain
the town, and then it will be too late.'   About ten o'clock
that evening, the sentry at the farther angle of Cape
Diamond called out, ' A fire-ship ! A fire-ship ! ' In a
moment, the alarm ran through the town.   The call to
arms was sounded.   The garrison hurried to their posts.
But the terrible fire-ship proved to be only a burning house
or pile of rubbish, with all the waters of the St. Lawrence
between it and Quebec.   ' On this discovery every man
was order'd back from whence he came '; and no doubt
the Day of Judgment seemed considerably more remote.
Once laughed at, the danger ceased to be so terrible, and
people were even able to forget it.   Still, the prospect of
a bonfire could hardly have inspired all Hodgkinson's
confidence.[21]

More and more, now, the citizens ' cast longing eyes '
in the other direction.   ' Ships from England ' began to
be the dream by day as well as night.   All understood
that it was very early for them to get up the river ; but
still there was a possibility, and it grew with every sun.
Twelve or fourteen cannon-shots had been heard from
below on the twenty-fifth of April, it was believed.[22]
Hour by hour the hope grew, and by the third of May it
had waxed rather confident.

That evening a brigantine rounded the Island of Orleans,—so like the coast of old Devonshire that a British
vessel seemed to belong there,—and sailed steadily on
toward the city.   It was now about nine or ten o'clock ;

---

[21] § Hodgkinson : Penna. Mag. X., p. 158. Ainslie, Journal, Apr. 27.
[22] Ainslie, Journal, Apr. 25.

but the welcome visitor could be made out very fairly in the brilliant moonlight. A glad cry swept through the town : ' A vessel from Europe ! A vessel from Europe ! ' All hurried to the bluff and feasted their eyes. Anxiety ended, for this must be, of course, the van of a British fleet. Congratulations, cheers, caps in the air,—the town was jubilant. Some one ran to Carleton with the happy news. ' The gunners to their places ! ' he sternly replied.[23]

Still on she came. The flagstaff on Cape Diamond ran up a blue pennant with a union below it, and five guns were touched off at the battery. That was the appointed signal communicated through Lieutenant Pringle to the government, and all awaited the response. But no response came. The stranger was hailed, and made no reply. Again they hailed, and still she was mute. The deck seemed empty. One more challenge was trumpeted : ' Who are you? Answer or we'll sink you ! ' But she only moved on in silence, and then the battery spoke. Immediately a cloud of black smoke puffed from the brigantine ; huge piles of flame burst out ; flashes of murky light ran swiftly up her rigging. Every rope changed instantly into a line of fire, her sails became sheets of blaze, and a boat could be seen putting away from her with desperate speed. At once the people took alarm : this was the fire-ship in reality. One hundred yards more,[24] and the streaming bonfire would reach the shipping ; the tarred cordage would catch like tinder ; the vessels would all burn ; the buildings would blaze ;

---

[23] § Ainslie, Journal, Apr. 27 ; May 3. 'Chalmers' Journal, May 3. Finlay, Journal, May 3. Arnold to Sch., Apr. 20, 1776 : 4 Force, V., 1098. Haskell, Diary, May 3. Senter, Journal. Howell to ———, May 4, 1776 : W. T. Read, G. Read, p. 154. Dearborn, Journal. Caldwell, Letter. Carleton to Germain, May 14, 1776 : 4 Force, VI., 456. Id. to Tryon, May 17, 1776 : Pub. Rec. Off., Am. and W. I., Vol. 186, p. 739. Verreau (Sanguinet), Invasion, p. 126. Signal : Cramahé (Hamilton) to Dartmouth, Nov. 19, 1775 (Can. Arch., Q, 11, pp. 324, 337). REMARK LXXV.

[24] Caldwell, Letter.

the palisade would probably take fire ; and, in the midst
of it, the enemy—three thousand strong[24]—would certainly fall upon them. The great bell of the cathedral
pealed furiously once more ; all the other bells hammered
and clanged ; the drums beat ; and hither and thither
men hurried to their posts. But the ship was no longer
under control ; she veered ; her burning sails lost the
wind ; tide and current bore her back ; and, in all the pomp
of gorgeous ruin, she drifted slowly down past the city,
roaring and crackling, waving her towering flames to and
fro athwart the sky, and spurting many a fresh burst of
fire, with as many loud reports, from exploding shells,
grenades, and *pots à feu*, till the flames quenched themselves at the water's edge. Once more a fatality—the
premature outbreak of the fire—had upset well-laid plans.
Once more Quebec rejoiced and trembled.[25]

Yet in spite of disappointment after disappointment,
the Americans would not give up. Famine might do what
the fire-ship and the red-hot shot had failed to do. They
did not know how Cramahé and Hamilton had written to
the government : ' To get here early in May is absolutely
necessary '; ' Provisions in the Garrison with the greatest
frugality will not last longer than the Middle of May ';
but they believed as much and even more. Indeed, one
of Lamb's men, who had escaped from Quebec some
weeks before, reported that only three ounces of pork a
day were allowed the garrison. They did not hear the
Duke of Manchester inform the House of Lords that,
according to the testimony of seamen, the ice in the St.
Lawrence did not often give way before the end of that
month ; but they knew that vessels never came up until
some time after the first, and felt sure that the winter had
been severer than usual.[26]

---

[25] See Note 23.
[26] § Cramahé to [Germain], Nov. 19, 1775: Bancroft Coll., Eng. and Amer.,

Affairs, We certainly shall have in a very few days a large reinforcement of Men Artillery Stores &c I hope every thing necessary for our future operations —

FROM WOOSTER'S LETTER TO McNEIL, APRIL 23, 1776

The heavy cannon from New York were not far distant now, and the gun battery on the Heights, within five hundred yards of the wall, would open soon. Artillerymen, infantry, and no doubt ammunition must arrive shortly. In fact, more than a week before, Wooster had written : ' We certainly shall have in a very few days a large reinforcement of Men Artillery Stores & I hope every thing necessary for our future opperations.' The enemy, on the other hand, seemed to be approaching despair. A Canadian arrested for carrying the Governor's letters, offered to take oath that both garrison and people had risen in a body and forced him to promise that, should no aid arrive within fourteen days, he would surrender ; and this had been some time ago. To be sure, he had not surrendered ; but the incident appeared very suggestive. A report went about Boston that Carleton actually offered to give up the town, though not on acceptable terms ; and, if the same story circulated in camp, as apparently it did, the soldiers must have felt the end was very nigh. Some even declared they would rather not capture the city until the British reinforcements had come. At all events the time to despair did not seem to have arrived.[27]

Aug., 1775–Dec., 1776, p. 169. Hamilton to Dartmouth, Nov. 20, 1775: Can. Arch., Q, 11, p. 339. Montreal letter, Apr. 6, 1776 : 4 Force, V., 804. Manchester : 4 Force, VI., 363. Arrival of Ships: N. Y. Calendar, I., p. 285.

[27] § Arnold to Deane, Mar. 30, 1776: 4 Force, V., 549. Wooster to McNeill, Apr. 23, 1776 : Am. Antiq. Soc. Montreal letter, Apr. 6, 1776: 4 Force, V., 804. Essex Journal, May 3, 1776. Spy: ' Shortt' Journal, Feb. 28. REMARK LXXVI.

XXIX

DARING SCHEMES

OUR analysis of the situation at Quebec, however, omitted one factor entirely. The mistake was natural. Dead men tell no tales; and prisoners of war, immured in stone walls three feet thick, have never been expected to bear a hand in the campaign. But the Kennebec detachment were no ordinary prisoners.

After laying down their arms that ill-fated morning, the Americans made their way, under very attentive escorts, to the main guard of the garrison; and, as group after group arrived, they were able to reckon up the extent of their misfortune, and find that over-praised consolation which misery has been said to love. Major Meigs broke bread very comfortably with Captain Laws, who owed him so much; the other officers had a mouthful at the guard-house; and then all of them filed off to an upper floor in a wing of the Seminary, where the Bishop resided —though not in precisely the same style—all his life. Here they passed a 'Solentary' New Year's. Few could help reflecting with Humphrey: 'Fortune was kind enough to save me from Either Starving or Drowning to bring me to this place to be maid A prisner which I think to be no great favour.' But, as Governor Ward said, they had 'acquired immortal honor,' and that counted for much; they had life, and with life hope; and the straw-beds, mattresses, and blankets made the lodging seem 'Very Cumfortable.' Meantime the privates, after soothing their fatigue and chagrin with a biscuit and a swallow

270

of rum, found their prison close at hand in the Récollet monastery, and were glad enough to rest awhile with ' a straw bed between two, and a blanket each man.' [1]

Though promised ' good quarters & Tender usage,' these unlucky patriots were hardly ' looked upon by their Captors as prisoners of war.' Caldwell, whose property on both sides the river had suffered not a little, felt decidedly unamiable toward them, and let the fact glimmer somewhat plainly through his bluff integument. Maclean, a ramrod of loyalty, with some whose old royalism had become a second—if not a first— conscience, and some whose new royalism felt the zeal of conversion, could not miss an opportunity so excellent for exalting orthodoxy. A few ' examples ' would no doubt have pleased them greatly. But Carleton viewed the situation otherwise. He looked upon the ' rebellion '

A GLIMPSE OF THE SEMINARY

of the Colonies as kindled by a few leaders, who were ' resolved to seek their own Safety and gratify their Ambition, in the Continuance of the Public Confusion and public Calamities,' and who drove on the mass of the people by representing that, after what had occurred, no hope of pardon could be entertained by any one. His desire was to isolate the chiefs by convincing their deluded followers ' that the way to mercy was not yet shut against them '; and he laid down as the true policy : ' Valor and good Conduct in time of Action, with Humanity and friendly Treatment to those, who are subdued.' [2]

[1] § See the Journals of Meigs, Dearborn, Humphrey, Melvin. Têtu, Evêques, Chap. I., p. 259. Morison, Account: Penna. Mag., 1890, p. 435. Ward to S. Ward, Jr., Jan. 21, 1776: J. Ward, S. Ward, p. 11.

[2] § Dearborn, Journal. Not pris. of war : Meigs, Petition (Cont. Cong.

Certainly Arnold's redoubtable followers needed to be safely kept, and the state of Quebec forbade any pampering of their appetites ; but, so far as possible, the Governor wished them kindly treated. Some of his officers called at the prison without delay, and he made several visits there himself. We are ' used very well,' Meigs informed his comrades outside. We were ' treated with the Greatest Humanity,' recorded Nichols. In spite of Carleton's iron resolve to have no communications with men in arms against their sovereign, they had permission to send for their belongings. Merchants of Quebec were allowed to make the rank and file a New Year's present of a large butt of porter with bread and cheese proportionate. After fuel became very scarce, parties from the garrison sallied into St. Roch more than once, their lives in their hands, ' to bring in firewood for the prisoners.' As for diet, certainly two or three bran biscuits, three ounces of pork and half a pint of thin soup each day could hardly be called luxurious; but the Americans understood that the garrison lived no better. Unfortunately a man named Dewey, appointed to look after such matters within the prison, sold a part of their supplies for his own profit; ' but,' rejoiced Morison, ' the Lord of Hosts soon delivered us out of his hands ; for he was taken with the small-pox, which swept him from off the face of the earth.' [3]

Many of the prisoners—particularly the eastern men—had never suffered from this disease ; and, as the danger from taking it in the natural way was regarded as immensely more than that from artificial infection, they petitioned to be inoculated, and the Governor granted

---

Papers, No. 42, V., p. 15). Caldwell: Porterfield, Diary (Va. Mag., Oct., 1901, p. 145). Carleton to Germain, Aug. 10, 1776: Pub. Rec. Off., Colon. Corres., Quebec, 12, p. 247. Id. to Howe, Aug. 8, 1776: Can. Arch., B, 39, p. 93.

[3] § Humphrey, Journal, Jan. 2. Henry, Journal, pp. 128, 139. Haskell, Diary, Jan. 2. Nichols, Assault. ' Chalmers' Journal, Jan. 31 ; Feb. 2, 3. Stocking, Journal, Dec. 31. Melvin, Journal, Jan. 9. Fobes, Narrative Morison, Account: Penna. Mag., 1890, p. 435.

their request. Above a hundred had to be carried to the
hospital ; and, while their hopes of an easy sickness were
not fully realized, the attentions they received proved no
slight compensation. In fact, some men pretended to
be ill in order to be taken there, or concealed recovery as
long as they could in order to remain. Lieutenant Nichols was one of these. Suffering from scarlet fever and removed to the Hôtel Dieu, he found the care of the Mother
Abbess, as he called her, and of the nuns, who sat up with
him several nights ' four at a time in turn two hours each
turn,' rather different from the rough companionship of
the prison. So he feigned to be sick for nearly a month
after he knew that he had never been sounder,—in fact,
until he chose to acknowledge his cure. It was then intimated to him that, as houses were being pulled down for
fuel, the General would like to have him go back to his
comrades. ' Never was a person treated with more Hospitality,' wrote the Lieutenant in reference to the nuns,
' than I was treated by them.' [4]

Other prisoners found a different path from confinement. When their names, ages, and places of birth were
taken, it appeared that more than a hundred of the rank
and file hailed from Great Britain. These were called
out by themselves, and addressed by the Provost-Marshal. ' My men,' said he, ' you deserve nothing but
death, for you have taken up arms against your own
country ; but, if you will take the oath of allegiance and
serve the King until the first of June next, you shall find
mercy.' Indeed, remarkable inducements were offered :
full pay, even for the time they had campaigned with
the Americans, and a free voyage ' to Britain or where
they please[d] by the first vessel in the spring.' No

---

[4] § Henry, Journal, p. 144, note. Nichols, Diary, particularly Mar. 10.
Ainslie, Journal, Jan. 3 ; Feb. 13. Councilman : Univ. Cyclop., VI., p. 261.
Henry, Journal, p. 152. REMARK LXXVII.

ordinary writhings of conscience and heart followed ; but in the end all accepted the offer.[5]

Many Quebeckers doubted whether a pledge given with a noose round the neck would prove binding, and not a few wagers were laid on that point ; but at first the plan worked well. For a fortnight, the old-country men shouldered arms and paced the ramparts fully to Maclean's taste ; but then three of the 'penitent rebels, again repenting,' disappeared. Two weeks more passed, and another trio piped the song of liberty. Ten days more went by, and a sextet vanished over the wall. Some dropped quietly off behind the artillery barracks and shot down the steep incline of thirty or forty feet, covered with snow, into a street at St. Roch ; but others chose a bolder fashion. While Cavanaugh, a 'converted rebel,' was doing sentry duty near Palace Gate in company with a British soldier, his friend Connor sauntered along in that direction, produced a bottle, and, after taking a pull as an evidence of good faith, passed the 'craythur' to the Briton. The soporific influence of the treat was deepened by a stunning blow from the butt of Cavanaugh's musket, and then the two comrades jumped for dear life into twenty-five feet of drifted snow. A ball or two followed them, but they got safely away. Finally, Carleton disarmed and disuniformed the others, and shut them up in the artillery barracks out of the reach of temptation.[6]

RETURN J. MEIGS

---

[5] § Brit. Return: Can. Arch., Q, 12, p. 159 (Recapit.). Melvin, Journal, Jan. 3. Fobes, Narrative. Ainslie, Journal, Jan. 7, 8. 'Chalmers' Journal, Jan. 7 ; Feb. 16. Caldwell, Letter. 'Shortt' Journal, Jan. 8.

[6] § Ainslie, Journal, Jan. 21 ; Feb. 6, 16. Caldwell, Letter. Finlay, Journal, Feb. 5, 16. Henry, Journal, p. 137.

The rest of the rank and file—more than two hundred and fifty—formed a cozy if not gorgeous club, and whiled away the time as best they could. Numberless tales were furbished up, length counting as a greater merit than accuracy. Cards occupied many an hour, and swearing at luck and the King disposed of occasional minutes. Some, too fastidious for these consolations, employed themselves in making wooden spoons and little boxes ; and the more artistic decorated such articles with clever figures : a beaver, an Indian sitting on a rock, or even a deer at full stretch, pursued by a hound. Far less agreeable but not less absorbing an occupation was the inevitable speculating about the future. Some of the sentries expressed the cheerful opinion that all would be shipped off to England, and ' sold as slaves to some island ' ; others said they would be sent to Boston and exchanged ; and still others maintained that a halter would certainly be the end of every mother's son in the prison. As for their own opinion, they hoped their comrades would capture the city and release them.[7]

Some ebullitions of spirit could not be avoided. Parrot found himself in irons for calling one of the Emigrants a Tory : which made it appear that even royalists considered that name opprobrious ; and Brown fared the same for answering back an uncivil keeper. When the alarm bells announced that an assault was expected, the men longed to have a share in it ; but a large guard was thrown round their prison, and a field-piece rolled up before the door. Fifteen agreed to fight their way out ; but Dewey reported them, and two were ironed. In spite of pluck, discouragement and listlessness gained a little ground each day. ' The time seems very long,' groaned

[7] § Brit. Return.: Can. Arch., Q, 12, p. 159. Melvin, Journal, Jan. 31 ; Feb. 24. Henry, Journal, p. 140.

For £105.6.9¼ Halifax Currency — Elizabeth Town 25th Sep.t 1776

Sir

Please to pay to General William
Thompson or Order, one hundred Five Pounds Six Shillings and
Ninepence halfpenny Halifax Currency, which is equal to Five
Shillings for each Pound milly Dollars, it being for the Sums
furnished myself & the Officers under my Command while in
Confinement as Prisoners in Quebec, and place the Same to
account of

Sir
Your most obe.t humble serv.t

Dan. Morgan

To

Paymaster General to the

276

Melvin ; and so did every one else even before January
ended. They felt out of the world,—mere flotsam tossed
about by the winds and waves of the contest. And then,
in a moment, the sky opened.[8]

It opened precisely when it seemed to be closing hard
upon them. About the middle of March they were transferred to the Dauphin Jail ; and, as they filed into that
dingy, gloomy sepulchre, they almost felt condemned to
a living death. Fully three feet of solid stone surrounded
them ; heavy iron bars darkened the small windows ; and
a wall twenty feet high, bristling with spikes along the
top, shut in the small yard behind. There were two
floors, with four non-communicating rooms on each, and
at night every room was carefully locked ; while the door
into the street—a very solid affair—had fastenings on the
outside. But, just as the men were bewailing their fate,
the window-bars were given a closer look, and it appeared
that many of them, deeply gnawed by rust, could easily
be removed from their sockets.[9]

A sort of council, mainly composed of sergeants, grew
together very soon, and an attempt at escape was eagerly
discussed. Evidently it would be a desperate affair.
Getting through the windows would not help the men
very much, after all. Two sentries, relieved every fifteen
minutes, waited constantly at each corner of the enclo-
sure. A guard-house, always well manned, stood nearly
opposite. St. John's Gate, occupied by thirty or forty of
the best soldiers, stood about a hundred and fifty yards
away, and no building intervened to conceal operations.
Only a few minutes would be needed to turn plenty of
cannon on the jail. Sentries patrolled the ramparts inces-

[8] § Melvin, Journal, Jan. 20 ; Feb. 15 ; Mar. 1. Tolman (Ware), Journal,
Mar. 10-13.

[9] § Melvin, Journal, Mar. 10, 13. Tolman, Journal, Mar. 10-13. LeMoine,
Pict. Quebec, p. 120. Henry, Journal, p. 145. Fobes, Narrative. Finlay,
Journal, Mar. 13.

santly with muskets ready ; and reserves lay on their arms within easy call. It was decided, then, first of all, to ask the men whether they had stomachs for such a venture. All answered, Yes; and the council then took the matter up in earnest, meeting often but always in private, lest some treachery or indiscretion should betray the plot.[10]

One thing helped the prisoners ; indeed, two things. The belief that only a few leaders really caused the opposition to England found many supporters in Quebec besides the Governor[11] ; and these fine, genial unfortunates in confinement, admired as much as feared, had now come to be looked upon ' as deluded by the fascinating sound of liberty and freedom, and induced to take up arms when . . . not at heart inimical to his Britannic Majesty.'[12] This begot a feeling that no great stringency need be used upon them ; while Maclean's eagerness to employ in active service every able-bodied man led him to place no guards within the jail and only greybeards and boys on the outside.

But arms were needed. A battle against fearful odds, Yes; mere slaughter, No.

A number of tomahawks, or small hatchets, had been secreted when the men surrendered, and brought into the prison. These were ready for action. A good many long hunting-knives, which had the same history, were now fixed at the ends of 'splits' of fir, cut from the bottoms of the lower tier of berths; and here were good spears, ten feet in length. Peeping through the keyhole of a small, locked room, an inquisitive eye discovered a pile of iron hoops two or three inches broad. The lock was carefully

---

10 § For the plot of the privates see particularly Henry's Journal, pp. 145–159 (Henry belonged to the ' council '), and Fobes, Narrative ; also the Journals of Melvin, Stocking, and Morison; and the British Journals, particularly Ainslie's. Carleton to Germain, May 14, 1776 : 4 Force, VI., 456. Caldwell, Letter.

11 E. g., Ainslie, Journal, Mar. 5.

12 Stocking, Journal, Jan. 10.

plied; it yielded; and the hoops, doubled and furnished
with wooden handles, made tolerable cutlasses, or, rather,
terrific bludgeons. Various odds and ends of iron proved
available for more spear-points; and a few old scythes were
metamorphosed into swords. An axe had to be given the
prisoners to split their fire-wood with. Somehow it was
lost; after a while a second axe also disappeared; and so,
in the course of no long time, working their way cautiously
and plausibly, the men obtained quite a number of axes.

The bottoms of some of the lower tier of berths, about a
foot higher than the floor, were taken up, and the weapons
laid away. Then the bottoms returned to their places, and
the nails, broken in the middle so they would not hold,
apparently did the same. Blankets and bundles, piled
above in seeming
confusion, hid the
work still more.
One of the men
stood guard in-
cessantly at each
end of the corri-
dor. Whenever a
British officer ap-
proached, he gave
a signal; and com-
rades appointed
to that duty fell
instantly into a heavy doze in the berths. The prison
had become an arsenal; yet every sign of danger lay as
covert as the claws of a purring kitten. Even the lock
of the small room was made to close again.

ST. JOHN'S GATE (INSIDE)

Next in order stood a plan of campaign, and reconnoitring the field threatened to be difficult. But all obstacles
vanished before such men. Ferrets as well as lions, they
contrived ways to open every door inside the prison at

will; and their day really began when the officers had locked them up for the night. Climbing into the attic and raising a trap-door in the roof, they studied the walls and the posts of St. John's Gate minutely and at leisure under the brilliant light of the moon. The cannon, the ammunition, the guard-house, the placing of sentries, the movements of the patrols were all patiently conned, until, in spite of the distance, everything of importance became perfectly clear. With equal keenness, putting out their own lights in order to see the better, they perused the guard-house across the street, only some forty yards distant. It had no shutters, and the lamps burned all night. The front door, never closed, led to a flight of stairs. In the passage there was always a light. At the top of the stairs on the right hand, going up, the muskets, with bayonets fixed, could always be found in a certain corner. About thirty men belonged there; but by morning they counted as none, for all of them lay dead-asleep on the floor. The treads in the flight of stairs were numbered, and it was reckoned that a quick man could clear them in three bounds.

The prisoners were then organized. Sergeant Aston of Lamb's company was appointed the general. McCoy and others became colonels. Majors, captains, and lieutenants also were chosen. Boyd, Cunningham, and Henry had orders to carry the guard-house opposite the jail, and were permitted to pick twenty-two men from the whole number. Aston with a hundred and fifty followers, undertook to attack the guard at St. John's Gate. A reserve under McCoy was to support him, and a smaller body had orders to fire the jail and near-by houses and then assist Boyd. So far as concerned arms, Malaysia was to fight Europe. A stiff 'bustle,' as the soldiers termed it, had to be expected; but desperation and numbers—to make no claim on the score of quality—were counted upon to win.

These men, however, had not come so far from home
simply to escape from a prison: they had come to conquer;
and, after risking life to get into Quebec, there they
were. Why not make the most of this? If the cannon
could be turned upon them, they could turn the cannon
upon the British; and, if they could take St. John's Gate,
they could certainly open it. In short, the plan of escape
turned out a plan of conquest.

As this was pondered, a great difficulty presented itself.
The cannon were loaded and primed, and boxes of ammunition stood near; but it would take the British artillerymen
only a second to throw the fuses into the ditch. Without
fuses the cannon were dead; and without gunpowder the
prisoners could manufacture no fuses of their own. Something had to be done about it; and this produced an
elaborate plot within a plot.

The boys guarding the jail were forward and inclined
to be insolent; but this lightness of head made them
easy victims to flattery. The prisoners humored them;
joked with them; pretended to learn French of them;
showed them all manner of deference. At the same time
they devised toy cannon, made of tough paper many folds
thick and very tightly rolled, and mounted them on wooden
carriages. Embrasures were cut in the opposing fronts of
the berths, and the cannon placed behind them. With an
air of infinite good-humor, the sentries were induced to
look at these forts, and their curiosity to see a battle was
cleverly worked up. Finally, they supplied some powder
for that purpose. The prisoners took sides; and, amid
roars of what sounded like simple-minded laughter, the
cannon popped and popped again, as loud as pistols. A
little of the powder, however, was reserved and secreted.

Finally the Americans, growing very fond of the mimic
warfare and requiring a good deal of this article, cajoled
the boys into purchasing small quantities of it for them;

and then, as little money could be found in their pockets, ways to obtain it had to be devised. Some were droll enough. So many of the prisoners fell sick, or feigned to fall sick in order to reach the hospital, that people outside began to think the jail unhealthy, and took pity more than ever on the unfortunate Americans. Many 'pious matrons' visited them, and never empty-handed. Elderly nuns came often; and, these—not being housewives— usually brought little gifts of money. Generosity so spontaneous would evidently bear a little stimulation; and with fine art that stimulation was applied.

Sergeant Gibson of Hendricks's company, naturally of a 'beautiful countenance,' had studied physic, knew how to care for himself, and now, amid the sallow faces of his comrades, bloomed like a rose. McCoy arranged a little room for him near the front door, so that charitable visitors might drop in there before wasting their sympathy on less public-spirited or less knowing prisoners; and then Gibson and Henry watched prudently at a window near.

'Zounds, Gibson, there's a nun!' cried Henry.

Instantly Gibson rushed into the little room; and, without stopping to disrobe, got into bed and covered himself to the chin.

The nun was admitted. Henry and others in the secret received her at the door with all politeness, and begged her to visit a sick friend. Full of pious good-will she entered, and—aided by the remarks of her escort—beheld a poor fellow in a raging fever, almost unconscious and at times even delirious. Crossing herself and murmuring a paternoster, she drew forth her little purse and emptied its contents into Gibson's hand, pushed cautiously from under the blanket. Twenty-four 'coppers,' worth two shillings, were the fruit of that haul, and they all went for powder. In devising and playing such games, the prisoners could forget their misery for a time; and, behind the veil of hoar-frost brocaded deep on the windows, a merry and even a happy company might often have been discovered. So young lions play.

Yet, unless the American army were close to the gate, the prisoners would be overpowered before it could enter. It must know of the plan, and there must be a signal to announce the outbreak. Very good. With those fellows, to state a problem was to solve it.

Two small dark cells—dungeons, perhaps—ran back from the lower floor into the yard; and, being covered with dirt, they had an elevation of some ten feet. This in effect reduced the height of the wall just there about one-half; and, as the mortar had fallen from the cracks in places, a nimble fellow might possibly, after an argument with the spikes, get over. What would happen then could only be guessed; but anyhow Martin, a small, quick man belonging to Lamb's company, volunteered to take his chances.

J. J. HENRY

A cap, an overcoat, and loose trousers, all of something white, were made for him; and, when a dark, blowy evening came, the whole body of prisoners remained, under orders from their chiefs, at play in the yard, as if trying to keep warm. Consequently, when the clanging of the front door announced that the Provost-Marshal and his file of soldiers had come to lock them up, all began to crowd through the door at once; and, as the chiefs in the rear managed things well, they got ahead but slowl This gave Martin time to slip on his disguise and mount one of the cells, where—since the doorway projected a little—he could be discovered only by going several paces into the yard. As the conspirators hoped, the impatient officer, already delayed by the tardy entrance of the men, barely looked round the inclosure from the door ; and, as he received the usual number of answers at roll-call, promptly went his way. Martin remained in the yard, though half-frozen, until night had fully descended and the cold had forced the guards round the jail into their sentry-boxes ; then over the wall he went. Presently a shot rang out, and those in the plot could hardly sleep for anxiety ; but the next day, peeping from the trap-door, they saw a knot had been tied in the American flag. Martin, almost invisible against the snow, had got safely over the ramparts, though dimly seen and vaguely fired at ; and the scheme to capture the city had the approval of headquarters.[13]

One trivial thing, however, threatened to block it after all. The men could not leave by the windows fast enough, and nothing could be done with the great door, since it was fastened on the outside. Happily, as the ground sloped rather sharply toward the street, the basement also had a front door. This was five feet wide, made of nothing worse than new pine plank, and both hinges and padlock were in plain sight. As the British officer examined the door every day, no one touched it ; but the leaders understood very well that, when the moment for action arrived, the hinges could be disposed of with little difficulty, and the padlock was not strong enough to resist for 'a moment of time.' Unfortunately, however, the basement contained a spring ; and the overflow, running down to the door, had frozen a foot deep against it. How could that fastening be undone ?

Pour boiling water on it, replied some. But the steam

---

[13] Haskell, Diary, Mar. 24 ; N. Y. Calendar, I., p. 285 ; letter, Apr. 6, 1776: 4 Force, V., 804.

QUEBEC VIEWED FROM THE RAMPARTS, 1759. THE LARGE BUILDING WAS THE URSULINE CONVENT

285

would have escaped through cracks and warned the sentry outside; and, even should that not happen, the water would cool and then freeze, adding to the mass of ice instead of reducing it.

Chop it away with hatchets, proposed others; but the noise—especially were the door accidentally struck—would almost certainly be heard.

Cut the door across above the ice, advised still others; but the ice had risen over the edge of the cross-piece. The work of cutting through two thicknesses of the plank would have taken time and most likely have been discovered before it could be completed.

Finally, the chiefs picked out sixteen or eighteen of the most active and prudent, and gave them orders to go down, two by two, on the appointed night, immediately after the curtain-raiser entitled 'Locking-up,' and softly pare the ice away from the door with knives. It was calculated that by three o'clock in the morning this could be accomplished. The hinges and lock would then receive attention; the door would suddenly be dragged down; Boyd's company would rush over it like the winds of Æolus; his first rank would dispose of the nearest sentry with the spear, while others, chosen for that office, would silence the rest of the soldiers round the jail with spears and tomahawks; and his main body would bound up the stairs of the guard-house, seize the muskets, and pin the sleeping soldiers to the floor with the bayonets,—all without a word. Aston's men, a part of them following Boyd's through the door, and a part swarming from the windows, would race to St. John's Gate and overpower the guard; and Lamb's artillerymen—a sort of third division—would instantly turn the cannon upon the town. At the same time, the prison and the adjacent houses would be fired.

In fifteen minutes, it was reckoned, all this could be

accomplished, and the smaller parties would then rejoin the main body under Aston. The flames, the uproar, and the firing would bring Arnold and the army to the gate. For the little time it would take them to arrive, the stupefied garrison could easily be held at bay. And then—'Quebec is ours!' At the very worst, should the scheme of conquest fail, the men were to scatter, and leap from the ramparts. Here and there a red spot in the snow, no doubt; but most of them would get off. To fail, however, seemed impossible. Every point had been studied and provided for. To be sure, a certain proverb about the cup and the lip crept into a brain or two; but it seemed only the creaking of the wheel. How often did a clock, wound up so carefully, fail to strike twelve at noon? Quebec was as good as captured,—captured by its prisoners; and, in spite of all their caution, the leaders went about with a gleam of exultation in their eyes that almost burned the lids.

But a couple of enterprising New Englanders, not in the counsels of the chiefs yet intensely interested, fancied that something of great importance had been overlooked, went down to the basement one night, chopped the ice away with their hatchets, wrenched off the lock, and removed two of the three hinges. The sentry heard them.

'Stop that or I'll fire,' he shouted.

An alarm was given. In a moment the guards were doubled; and, about sunrise, a number of officers came with a dozen soldiers to investigate. With aching hearts, the leaders in the plot saw a wave hurrying to demolish their costly pile of sand; but they put on a bold face and declared with perfect sincerity that they knew nothing of the affair. Satisfied at last that it was only a random venture of one or two, the visitors withdrew,—Major Murray, the highest officer, bringing up the rear. Essentially the scheme had not been touched, after all.

Fearing treachery, the chiefs had made the desperate resolve, after the alarm had been given, to kill any one attempting to betray their plans, and now, with concealed but ready knives, they gathered round the half-opened door in which Murray stood speaking to them. One of the prisoners, named John Hall, managed, however, to edge himself up to the very jamb of the door without being noticed. He had deserted from the British army at Boston the year before; and, while he had saved his neck for the moment by giving his birthplace as New England, he understood right well that any one of a dozen possible or even probable mischances might throw a hempen cord around it in a twinkling. This was his opportunity to earn a pardon. Springing through the door so suddenly that he knocked against Murray, he touched that officer on the shoulder in passing, with the words, 'I have something

HENRY DEARBORN

to disclose'; and was instantly in the midst of the soldiers, hurrying to the Castle.

Heart-broken, the leaders realized now that the clock had stopped. What arms could be thoroughly hidden were put out of the way, and the rest, so far as possible, were destroyed. In an hour or two, a squad of soldiers arrived and carried away several of the prisoners. They were forced to take an oath; and, aided by Hall, the officers put questions too precise to be evaded. The plot was avowed and justified. Nothing better could have been done, perhaps; but the logical result—in the shape of bilboes and shackles—quickly followed. These did not matter very much, to be sure. With incredible skill, false rivets or false heads were speedily contrived; and the unfortunates grew almost merry again, despite their scurvy and rags, in finding ways to escape from punishment, since they could not escape from prison. The officers always found them safely ironed, but the shackles dropped when the front door clanged. Something else, however, could not be got rid of: the bitter anguish of disappointment over the miscarriage of their plans.

Happily, the worst side of the affair lay beyond their ken. Had they been able to look forward a little when the stroke fell, they would have suffered a double anguish, for they had unwittingly imperilled the whole American army.

It was a poor plot, if it would not work both ways. The next night at the proper hour,—for Carleton did not think it safe to wait,—the whole garrison was carefully placed. Three bonfires blazed near the Dauphin Jail. Musketry rattled hotly; a great uproar burst out; men shouted, 'Liberty forever! Liberty forever!' and a couple of brass field-pieces, brought up to St. John's Gate, fired blank cartridges vigorously at the town. In short, the whole programme of the prisoners was imitated by the British. The American army turned out, paraded, and marched. But it also stopped. Such an enterprise was fit for darkness only, and the moon shone that night like a sun. Perhaps, too, Arnold observed something that confirmed his natural suspicions. Both sides awaited developments, but in vain; and when, at daylight, both broke ranks not a little bewildered, many in each army recalled that it was April the First.[14]

Evidently the officers, imprisoned in the Seminary, had no hand in the doings of their troops, but they cherished

---

14 REMARK LXXVIII.

designs of their own. Lacking the force of numbers, they could attempt nothing so heroic; but they proposed, in the case of another assault, to break out, release their men in the confusion, seize arms and ammunition from the magazine, and join in the bat-
tle. Getting wind of some such scheme, the authorities redoubled their care. A lamp burned all night in their room. A square of glass was set into the door, and eyes blinked through it almost constantly. No visitors could obtain per-mission to enter; and the sen-tries on the ground below had orders to shoot, if one should even open a window. Nobody regarded these men as mere deluded simpletons, or at any rate nobody held this opinion long; for, when Morgan was offered a commission in the British army, he answered sternly: 'I hope you will never again insult me in my distressed and unfortunate situation by making me offers which plainly imply that you think me a rascal.' [15]

A WING OF THE SEMINARY

The American officers were con-fined in the fourth story from the ground (Dearborn)

Still, the officers could not give up the idea of striking a blow; and after a long time, Thayer and Lockwood, deputed to act for all, induced a sentry, whom they called Joe, to help them. By cutting off the planking spiked to

[15] § Ainslie, Journal, Mar. 31; Apr. 20. Nichols, Diary. 'Chalmers' Journal, Feb. 21. Dearborn, Journal, Mar. 10. South. Lit. Messenger, Sept., 1854.

a door, they could scramble into the garret, and thence by a ladder and a drop of fourteen feet gain the yard. At that point, their ally was to meet them with his musket and a full supply of clubs. The four guards, it was hoped, could be satisfied with Joe's countersign; if not, then with his cudgels. Next, if nothing could be done to release the privates, they would rush to the sally-port not far away, and leap some thirty feet into the deep snow. Even should they accomplish nothing but their own escape, they would bring the army a priceless reinforcement.[16]

But, 'when thinking ourselves at liberty we were the farther from it,' Thayer presently had occasion to reflect. On April the twenty-sixth, 'all things being ready for the Event,' he went up to the garret for 'some necessary observations,' and stopped on the way to trim the door a little, while Lockwood acted as sentry. But alas! one of the priests happened to espy him at work there, and instantly sent word to the Governor. An officer, hurrying down to investigate, found him just completing the job, actually knife in hand; and, although the culprit answered very 'candidly that he wished to see where the red flag of the Americans had been moved to,' the officer evidently went away with something on his mind. Maclean himself, well attended, was presently seen approaching; and Thayer's friends, crowding round him, begged 'to undergo the same fate' as he. But the Captain, urging that it was 'better for one to suffer than such a number,' bade them good-bye, and soon found himself in the hold of an armed schooner, the only place that seemed secure enough. A lonesome abode it proved: yet not for long. Joe and a friend of his appeared too rich for their

---

station in life, and, when questioned, gave inconsistent explanations of their new wealth. A threat of prison, however, simplified their thinking. Lockwood and Hanchet went down to join Thayer, and the whole scheme collapsed : one more fatality.

Thus both privates and officers made their throw for liberty and for the cause. Certainly their schemes were boldly and well contrived. They deserved a better fate; but for the time every chance was turning against the Americans. Patient endurance now seemed to be the prisoners' only resource ; yet in a very short while something unlooked-for was to occur, and their bonds were suddenly to be eased.

XXX

THE CATASTROPHE AT QUEBEC

WHEREAS Lord George Germaine, one of His Majesty's principal Secretaries of State, has acquainted Us, by his Letter of the 4ᵗʰ of last Month, that it is the King's intention that every effort be made to send relief to Quebec; And whereas we intend that the Ship you command shall take on board one Captain, one Lieutenant, one Ensign & ninety four private Men part of the 29th Regiment doing duty at Chatham & proceed on this Service, you are therefore . . . hereby required & directed to put to Sea without loss of time; And in pursuance of His Majesty's farther pleasure signified by another Letter from Lord George Germaine (dated the 22ᵈ of last Month) make the best of your way to the Isle aux Coudres' in the River St. Lawrence, at about one half of the distance from Quebec to the mouth of the Saguenay.[1]

These were the orders of the British Admiralty to Captain Charles Douglas, the active and able commander of the 50-gun ship *Isis*, then lying at the mouth of the Thames; and on the same day, February sixteenth, 1776, equivalent orders went down to Linzee of the frigate *Surprise* and Hervey of the sloop-of-war *Martin*; while Lutridge, commanding the *Triton* frigate anchored at Portsmouth, received instructions a few days later to convoy two large transports, carrying the rest of the 29th

---

[1] Pub. Rec. Off., Admty. Secy., Out Letters, Vol. 100, p. 417. As the reader is doubtless aware, Germain's name was often spelled Germaine.

regiment, and three victuallers, laden with provisions enough to support three thousand men for a quarter, to the same point.[2]

The impossibility of despatching relief sooner had caused the Noble Lord 'great & constant Anxiety.' Authority had not been lacking, nor money, nor men, nor experience, nor stores to draw upon, nor a settled policy, all of which had come short on the other side of the Atlantic; but the 'Severity of the Weather, almost beyond what had ever been known' in the land before, had paralleled, though by no means equalled, the winter of Quebec, and greatly hindered the work of preparation. 'Every effort had been exerted,' however; and, about the twentieth of February, the nine royal vessels, weighing anchor to a cheery 'Heave-ho,' began their long voyage toward the setting sun. Two months later, but in good season, General Howe determined to send Carleton aid; and on April the twentieth, without waiting for orders from London, the 47th regiment of Foot, convoyed by the *Niger* frigate, sailed out of Halifax harbor. Yet none of these measures relieved Quebec. It was not setting out but arriving which could achieve that. Tempestuous waves, contrary gales, calms, fogs, blinding snow-storms, thick ice-floes whitening the Gulf of St. Lawrence for scores of leagues, lay before these vessels. Delays and possible shipwrecks had to be feared; and each of the expeditions might be compelled to change its course, and to enter some less northerly port.[3]

At the same time, a far larger armament also had been set on foot in England; and, even though Germain

---

[2] § See Note 1; also ib., pp., 429, etc. Germain to Carleton, Feb. 17, 1776: Can. Arch., Q, 12, p. 1. Précis of Oper.

[3] § Germain to Carleton, June 21, 1776: Can. Arch., Q, 12, p. 44. Id. to Howe, Feb. 1, 1776: Pub. Rec. Off., Am. and W. I., Vol. 431, p. 113. Précis of Oper. Howe to Secy. State, Apr. 25, 1776: Pub. Rec. Off., Am. and W. I., Vol. 305, p. 265. Weather, etc.: Admiralty Digest (4 Force, VI., 457).

deemed the 'Defeat and repulse of the Rebels at Quebec on the 31st December . . . a great and happy Event,' no pains were spared for that reason.   'Not less than 12,000

LORD GEORGE GERMAIN

fighting men,' General Howe had recommended for the recovery of Canada.   The Empress of Russia decided not to sell the lives of her people ; but a large force of Bruns-wickers was purchased, and enough British and Irish regiments were selected to complete the tax of blood.   A train of cannon was soon preparing ; a mine of gold sift-ing through the mint ; an ocean of rum gurgling into casks ; and handsome John Burgoyne—soldier, poet, play-wright, and gallant—was pluming himself to lead the

army. In short, without stay or stint, the government
intended to support the early relief-expedition with 'a
Body of Troops sufficient to retake the Town in Case it
should have fallen into the hands of the Rebels and to
effect the recovery of the Whole of the Province to His
Majesty's Possession.' Such preparations as these required time, however.[4]

While of course the orders of the British government
did not reach the American leaders, they felt sure that
something of importance would be done as early in the
spring as possible. Montgomery had scarcely entered
Montreal, when he suggested this. A month later, he
pointed out that 'if vigorous measures be adopted their
force must be levelled at the recovery of this Province ';
and everything tended to show that vigorous measures
were to be adopted. 'There will certainly be a strong
army to retake Canada in the spring,' wrote an officer
from Montreal at about the same time ; 'The General has
sent home a number of pilots to bring the fleet here
early.' The Administration, said Washington in January, 'will certainly send a large reinforcement there in
the spring.' Another month, and Wooster also took
fire : 'The Ministry will send a great force into this Province in the Spring, and our everything depends upon
our having a force upon the spot superior to them,' he
assured Congress. Even before the friendliness of the
Canadians began to be doubtful, Montgomery had given
warning that they could not 'be depended upon, especially for defensive operations' ; and from that time their
support had grown less and less reliable. Congress,
however, while sharing all these fears, believed early in
March that King George's officers intended 'to direct

[4] § Germain to Carleton, Mar. 28, 1776: Can. Arch., Q, 12, p. 4. Howe to
Secy. State, Dec. 3, 1775 : Pub. Rec. Off., Am. and W. I., Vol. 305. p. 198. Ger-
main to Carleton, Feb. 17, 1776: Can. Arch., Q, 12, p. 1. See Chap. XXXIII.,
Note 23.

their [principal] operations in the ensuing campaign against the Middle and Southern Colonies.' It felt, therefore, that a full share of troops and cannon had been sent north, and proceeded to complete its work for the present by looking for a general worthy to command there.[5]

This proved, according to Duane, 'a subject of some perplexity as well as of very great importance.' Only one thing was clear : whom not to appoint. Schuyler's health unfitted him for so arduous a task ; his activity, zeal, and knowledge of the region where he was, made him highly valuable there ; and, as New York seemed in danger of attack, his patriotic influence against the machinations of the Tories appeared likely to be no less important, perhaps. Wooster had drifted into the first position in Canada, but something better than driftwood was evidently required at the head of affairs. Arnold had shown no ambition to dominate, and had expressly declared that a general of greater experience than himself ought to be appointed. To send a new man, totally unfamiliar with the situation, seemed a misfortune but unavoidable ; and very likely his being a stranger to the jealousies and quarrels of the department would help make the wheels turn smoothly, and prove in the end an advantage.[6]

Among Washington's lieutenants at Boston, one in particular had been distinguished in the chaos of army-building for knowledge and efficiency. 'By the way,' wrote James Warren, 'I must do justice to Thomas. . . . We have no trouble with his camp ; it is always

------

[5] § Montg. to R. R. Liv., Nov. 13, 1775: Liv. Papers, 1775-1777, p. 63. Id. to Id., Dec. 17, 1775: ib., p. 89. Letter, Dec. 4, 1775: 4 Force, IV., 175. Wash. to Arnold, Jan. 27, 1776: Writings (Ford), III., p. 379. Wooster to Hancock, Feb. 13, 1776: 4 Force, IV., 1132. Montg. to Sch., Dec. 5, 1775: ib., 188. Hancock to Sch., Mar. 7, 1776: 4 Force, V., 99. Duane to Stirling, Mar. 1, 1776: ib., 37.

[6] § Duane and Hancock: Note 5. Stirling to Sch., Apr. 2, 1776: Sparks MSS., No. 60, p. 79. Hancock to Sch., Feb. 20, 1776: 4 Force, IV., 1213. Arnold to Cong., Jan. 11, 1776: Sparks MSS., No. 52, II. p. 34.

in good order, and things are conducted with dignity and spirit in the military style.' Though bred to fight that arch-enemy of mankind, disease, John Thomas had learned to combat such lesser foes as Frenchmen and Tories. Under Amherst, he made the campaign of 1759 as far as Montreal, and his merits won him the second place in the Massachusetts forces when hostilities began in 1775. During the siege of Boston he occupied the most exposed position—that at Roxbury. 'Esteemed a brave and good officer,' testified the Commander-in-chief; while the field officers of his corps united in praising his 'knowledge and experience in military movements,' his 'vigilance, prudence, and skillful management.' It was to him that Washington entrusted the occupation of Dorchester Heights with a picked force, which was followed at once by General Howe's decision to evacuate Boston.[7]

Six feet in height, erect and well proportioned, he looked the soldier that he was. His plain, honest, kindly face did not belie the sincerity and heartiness of his intentions. As a physician, he could win the confidence of the weak, as a general, that of the strong; and in Canada plenty of both classes were to be found. Strict without severity, genial without softness, energetic without imperiousness or impetuosity, brave without rashness, and prudent without vacillation, he seemed to Congress an officer 'whose military skill, courage,

JOHN THOMAS

---

[7] § Warren to S. Adams, June 21, 1775: Colburn, Am. Indep., p. 7. Coffin, Thomas, pp. 5, 6, 8, 15, 17, 18, 19, etc. Wash. to Hancock, Mar. 7, 1776: Writings (Ford), III., p. 448.

and capacity would probably ensure success'; and, on the sixth of March, advancing him to the grade of major-general, it ordered him to Canada.[8]

After allowing himself only three or four days to settle his personal affairs, Thomas hurried west through the drifts of a New England March; and, achieving the long journey in five days, arrived at Albany on the twenty-eighth. There he received his baptism, not of fire, but of cold water. The northern part of Lake Champlain—already clear of ice for a week or so—was impassable. As no road existed on either side of the water, two companies which had pushed on about forty-five miles beyond Crown Point had been compelled to encamp there as best they could, and no more dared advance on the ice. Even between Ticonderoga and Albany nothing could be done except by Herculean efforts. 'The roads are so much gullied that it will be impossible to move a step, without sledding,' the energetic Knox had confessed after the ground had frozen, though he knew that Washington stood waiting for the Ticonderoga ordnance and counting the minutes. 'The roads are so bad that it is impossible for them [the horse-sleds] to come till the lake is frozen over, that they can come on the ice,' wrote Holmes after the snow had arrived. And now these same unspeakable 'roads' were deep in the fermentation of a spring breaking-up. As late as April twelfth 'a severe snow-storm' spoiled them afresh.[9]

Day followed day, week followed week; everything

---

[8] § Coffin, Thomas, p. 30, etc. Portrait belonging to the family. Hancock to Thomas, Mar. 6, 1776 : 4 Force, V., 84. Journ. Cong., Mar. 6.

[9] § Wash to Hancock, Mar. 19, 1776: Writings (Ford), III., p. 475. Thomas to Wash., Apr. 7, 1776: 4 Force, V., 813. Id. to Hancock, Apr. 8, 1776: ib., 822. Champlain (allowing for the time required to inform Sch.) : Sch. to Wash., Mar. 27, 1776 (ib., 520). Road: Trumbull, Autobiog., p. 27. Sch. to Wash., Apr. 12, 1776: 4 Force, V., 871. Knox to Wash., Dec. 5, 1775 : 4 Force, IV., 188 ('Without sledding' was placed by Knox at the beginning of his sentence). Holmes to Bedel, Dec. 20, 1775: Saffell, Records, p. 29. Sch. to Hancock, Apr. 12, 1776: 4 Force, V., 868.

needed to be done, and nothing could be done. Crowded
where necessity penned them, some twelve hundred or
possibly fifteen hundred soldiers, the last of the reinforcements ordered by Congress in January, waited in comfort-
less repose. Little by little, the cannon from New York
—including some ponderous 32-pounders—crawled up to
Fort George and there halted. Eight tons of the precious
powder so necessary at Quebec slumbered on. A bag of
$3200 in gold and silver coins, which Congress had been
able to pick up in Philadelphia and Canada needed still
more than powder, was compelled to stop. In March,
Wooster had implored Schuyler ' For God's sake ' to forward provisions ; but even the 'very 'trifling ' supplies now
in store could not be moved. Toward the south and east,
however, the roads were open. Letters came from these
quarters, and one of them gave notice that Washington
himself despaired of obtaining more specie for Thomas.
From the north, also, came a courier, writhing through in
some desperate fashion, and with him arrived the startling
and disheartening news of the insurrection below Quebec.
Nothing whatever could be done save to worry, and in
this condition of anxiety and helplessness Thomas had to
languish nearly three mortal weeks.[10]

With almost fire enough to melt it, his eyes watched
the slowly granulating shell of Lake George ; and at
length, on the seventeenth of April, he determined to
break his way through. As men could only cleave a
passage ' by inches,' and that ' with amazing fatigue,'
forty-eight hours afterward, he probably did not advance

[10] § Thomas to Wash., Apr. 7, 1776: 4 Force, V., 813. Wooster to Sch., Mar.
26, 1776 : Sparks MSS., No. 60, p. 79. Letter from Ft. George, Apr. 20, 1776: 4
Force, V., 1001. Sch. to Wash., Mar. 27, 1776: ib., 520. Robbins, Journal, Apr.
16. Sch. to Hancock, Apr. 12, 1776: ib., 868. Id. to Wash., Apr. 12, 1776: ib.,
871. Cash : Cf. Journ. Cong., Mar. 8, 23, 1776, with letter from Philadelphia,
Mar. 18, 1776 : Pub. Rec. Off., Admirals' Despatches, N. Am., Vol. V., and
Wooster to McNeill, Apr. 26, 1776: Am. Antiq. Soc. Wash. to Sch., Apr. 3, 1776:
4 Force, V., 779.

Merits=Tavern, April 18th 1776. —

Your favor, of this day received, (Have desired
the Laker are not yet open, and you advise Capt Schair
(and me to run and find, on account of the accommodations
we are extremely much obliged to you for the advice, and
shall wait your further order. —

I am Sir with much respect humble Sir

Baron de Woedtke

rapidly, but he advanced. Four days later he had passed Ticonderoga ; and on Friday, the twenty-sixth, after candle-lighting, he entered the heavy triple door of the Château de Ramezay at Montreal, the American head-quarters. Hasty conferences with Arnold and ' other gentlemen ' followed, and then, as quickly as possible, the General set out for the front. More than a week before, ice recognized as coming from some distance above Three Rivers had passed Quebec, and so, while the King's roads had not yet ' settled,' the more royal highway of the St. Lawrence was fortunately open.[11]

After sweeping down past white farm-houses, clumsy but cozy villages, and sightly steeples on both shores of the noble river, smiling at the remains of Major Brown's hypnotic battery, calculating the strategic value of Sorel, studying the maze of islands opposite and below that point, gazing in surprise at the sudden transformation of the river into a miniature sea—twenty-five miles long and some ten or twelve wide—at Lake St. Peter, and pausing, no doubt, at the bold front of Three Rivers, Thomas must have looked about him with still deeper interest at the noisy, grey falls called the Rapids of Richelieu, some forty miles above Quebec.[12] Here, on the northern shore, a great bank of clay, bedded on rocks, lay solidly across the road, thrusting a massive shoulder into the stream, as if to defend the upper country against all comers from below. About a hundred and twenty feet high at the river and

---

[11] § Letter from Ft. George, Apr. 18, 1776 : 4 Force, V., 981. Those at Skenesborough were able to advance a little earlier. Porter reached Ti. on the 10th (Diary: Mag. Am. Hist., Sept., 1893, p. 187). Robbins, Journal, Apr. 19. Sch. to Wash., Apr. 27, 1776: 4 Force, V., 1097. Pelton: N. Y. Calendar, I., p. 285. Thomas to Wash., Apr. 27, 1776: 4 Force, V., 1104. Ice: Ainslie, Journal, Apr. 18. Roads : Hazen to Antill, April 3, 1776 (Can. Arch., B, 27, p. 395). Hazen, whose place Arnold took at Montreal, made the Château his head-quarters (H. to Antill, Mar. 26, 1776: Can. Arch., B, 27, p. 392); and it is inferred that (as tradition affirms) Arnold did the same.

[12] § Based on the author's observations and Bouchette, Descr. Topog., pp. 556, etc.

extremely steep, because continually gnawed away at the bottom, this wall extended back on a level half a mile or so, affording room for the village of Deschambault, and then sank down to the northward. In addition to its natural strength, it could easily be fortified, for the soil made little resistance to pick and spade. Where bluff ended, river began, and the billows, ledges, boulders, narrow channel, and swift current forbade vessels to ascend except by the favor of a stiff northeast wind. When Franquet went up, it required the whole attention of one sailor to look out for rocks, and he noted that the tide was full enough to permit a passage for only four hours. Even at the best, vessels could move in single file only, passing in full view—and slowly at that—before whatever cannon stood on guard at the bluff. Little in the nature of the bottom encouraged them to anchor there in the play of current and tide to return the fire; and nothing deeper than a frigate could hope to pass in any way. Lévis had seen the value of the spot, and a French battery had occupied it during the late war with England. 'A very convenient situation for a Post or a Fortification,' Engineer Marr had reported to the British government. With a proper equipment and support, it 'may be defended against all the navy and all the military force of Great Britain,' Montgomery declared as soon as he reached Holland House.[13]

Before the middle of October, President Hancock had assured Schuyler that—should Montreal be captured—the Congress would 'exert their utmost Endeavours to secure the River St. Lawrence,' and, 'by Vessels, Batteries and every Other Obstruction,' make it impossible for the

[13] § Laterrière, Mém., p. 61. Bouchette, Descr. Topog., pp. 394, 556. Marr, Remarks: Can. Arch., M, 384, p. 136. Arnold to Sch., Apr. 20, 1776: 4 Force, V., 1098. Franquet, Voyages, p. 11. Goforth to Jay, Apr. 8, 1776: Bancroft Coll., Rev. Papers, I., p. 37. Lévis, Journal, pp. 284, etc. Montg., Dec. 5, 1775: 4 Force, IV., 188.

THE CHÂTEAU DE RAMEZAY, MONTREAL

British to ascend the stream in force. Early in January, Schuyler had been instructed to have the St. Lawrence explored and proper plans determined upon ' for opposing by armed boats or otherwise any attempts of the enemy to penetrate that country by the river ' ; and in due course this order passed on to Montreal. Armed gondolas recommended themselves to Wooster, very likely because the army had no engineer qualified to lay out fortifications. Timber, nails, and spikes could be found in Canada; and he asked that ' the articles of pitch, tar, turpentine, and oakum,' besides some master-carpenters, be forwarded. Congress laid upon Schuyler the duty of procuring skilful persons to construct the armed boats, as well as to assist Wooster in reconnoitring the St. Lawrence. But Schuyler explained that his Albany ship-carpenters, though ' very good,' knew nothing about the sort of craft required, and that no pitch, tar, or oakum could be sent on before the Hudson opened.[14]

Lee, in his one Canadian mandate, informed Wooster that cannon were to go north from Crown Point, and suggested forwarding them, before it was 'too late in the season,' to Deschambault, where, he added, 'it appears to me you ought to establish a Post.' But the cannon, if Lee had time to order them sent, were no doubt stopped, like everything else, by the crumbling of the ice. Winter passed on into spring. Wooster, though he must have noticed the grand bluff, crowned with a noble grove of pines and a slender church steeple, on his wall-scaling splurge to Quebec, paid little attention to it, if he paid any ; and on the first of April Hazen exclaimed in despair, 'No preparation has, is, or can be made to guard the river, for a

---

[14] § Hancock to Sch., Oct. 12, 1775: Am. Antiq. Soc. Journ. Cong., Jan. 8 ; Feb. 5, 1776. Sch. to Hancock, Jan. 22, 1776: 4 Force, IV., 802. Id. to Wooster, Jan. 26, 1776: ib., 1003. Wooster to Sch., Feb. 13, 1776 : ib., 1218. Hazen to Sch., Apr. 1, 1776: 4 Force, V., 751. Sch. to Hancock, Feb. 20: 4 Force, IV., 1214.

very good reason—no money or men of skill to do it,' though certainly something might have been accomplished.[15]

Arnold, on his way to Montreal, halted and examined the spot carefully. With the eye of a seaman, he perceived that 'few ships could go up without anchoring near the shore, at the foot of the Rapids,' where a battery of ten or twelve cannon, supported by three or four gondolas above, would, in his judgment, 'effectually secure the pass.' Accordingly, he despatched an artillery officer at once to Crown Point for guns and shot, and also for a gondola said to be lying there. The row-galley at St. Johns had gone over the Chambly Rapids to perdition, and a floating-battery had been 'cut to pieces'; so that only one shattered gondola, mounting a single 12-pounder, was then available. Plank and timber lay ready at Chambly; but other materials were still lacking, hard money for workmen could not be had, the entrenching tools were 'very few'; and therefore Thomas found the Rapids and the bluff, after all these months of good intentions, little, if anything, save a splendid opportunity. Heaven grant, he must have prayed, that it may not be needed![16]

Just above Aspen Point another feature of the north shore doubtless arrested his eye. This was the River Jacques Cartier, a small affluent of the St. Lawrence. Bouchette called it the 'bulwark of Quebec'; but it could serve equally well, if one pleased, as a bulwark against Quebec. No bridge spanned it; and the swift, eddying current was dangerous to ford. High banks, impracticable save at intervals, permitted but few to cross at a time, and those

[15] § Lee to Wooster, Feb. 28, 1776: Am. Antiq. Soc. Bouchette, Descr. Topog., p. 556. Hazen to Sch., Apr. 1, 1776: 4 Force, V., 751. Apr. 8, Goforth wrote Jay (Bancroft Coll., Revol. Papers, I., p. 37) that not a single battery had been planted on the St. Lawrence.

[16] § Arnold to Sch., Apr. 20, 1776: 4 Force, V., 1098. Commrs. to Hancock, May 1, 1775: ib., 1166. Thomas to Wash., Apr. 27, 1776: ib., 1104. See Chap. XXXV., Note 6. REMARK LXXIX.

not without embarrassment ; and many promising points for a stubborn fight could be seen at a glance. Deschambault was a castle, and here lay its moat. But at the Jacques Cartier, as at Deschambault, there was only nature, unadorned with trenches or redoubts ; and Thomas, full of anxious reflections, hurried on past the Red Cape (*Cap Rouge*), gazed intently at the massive cliff of Cape Diamond, crowned with cannon and the high sentry-box, and at last, as the first day of May came to its close, entered the American lines in the hope of better things. Very shortly 'there fell from his eyes as it had been scales.'[17]

' To bring men [to be] well acquainted with the duties of a soldier, requires time,' Washington advised Congress. 'To bring them under proper discipline and subordination, not only requires time, but is a work of great difficulty, and, in this army, where there is so little distinction between the officers and soldiers, requires an uncommon degree of attention. To expect, then, the same service from raw and undisciplined recruits, as from veteran soldiers, is to expect what never did and perhaps what never will happen. . . . Again, men of a day's standing will not look forward, and from experience we find, that as the time approaches for their discharge, they grow careless of their arms, ammunition, camp utensils, &c. . . . To this may be added the seasoning, which new recruits must have to a camp. . . . Men engaged for a short, limited time only, have the officers too much in their power; for, to obtain a degree of popularity in order to induce a second enlistment, a kind of familiarity takes place, which brings on a relaxation of discipline.' ' Before the soldiers can be in any wise disciplined,' Ritzema informed the authorities of New York, ' their time of service is expired, and as that

---

[17] § Bouchette, Descr. Topog., pp. 188, 219, 403. Shallus, Journal, May 7. Thomas to Wash., Apr. 27, 1776: 4 Force, V., 1104. Id. to Commrs., May 7, 1776: Sparks MSS., No. 60, p. 83. REMARK LXXX.

approaches, they become mutinous and disobedient. . . . Without discipline, no obedience ; without obedience, no duty.' But these palpable truths had not yet been recognized, and the service at Quebec, like that at Cambridge, paid the penalty. ' Neither order nor subordination prevails, and of course shortly no soldiers,' wrote Hazen the first of April.[18]

On the thirtieth of March, the besieging army had numbered twenty-five hundred, nearly a third of whom were unfit for duty, while fifteen hundred were to be free the middle of April. Arnold reckoned at six hundred, or at most seven hundred and fifty, the soldiers who would insist upon going home, and Walker believed that 'it would have been an easy matter for their Gen[l] to have reingaged most of the Men, if they had begun in time ; but, deferring it until their time of service was expired, it became impracticable, for the men, perceiving that the reenforcements Artillery provisions & stores came in so slowly, peremptorily insisted upon their Discharge.' The term of Livingston's men was to expire the same day : ' very few, if any of them, will re-engage,' predicted Hazen.[19]

The consequence was an upheaval when the middle of April arrived. The Quebeckers noticed several squads of Clinton's men at Point Levi marching up the river with knapsacks on their backs, and a few days later two deserters reported in town that ' the New York troops [who had re-enlisted at Montreal] had laid down their Arms, & that those from Pensylvania & the Jerseys with some Canadians had surrounded them & made pris-

---

18 § Wash. to Hancock, Feb. 9, 1776: Writings (Ford), III., p. 406. Ritzema, Jan. 3, 1776: 4 Force, IV., 1113. Caldwell, Letter. Hazen to Sch., Apr. 1, 1776: 4 Force, V., 751.

19 § Return : 4 Force, V., 550 (present, 2505 ; sick, 786). Arnold to Deane, Mar. 30, 1776 : ib., 549. Id. to Sch., May 6, 1776; Sparks MSS., No. 60, p. 83. Walker to S. Adams, May 30, 1776 (punctuated by J. H. S.): S. Adams Papers. Hazen to Sch., Apr. 1, 1776: 4 Force, V., 751. REMARK LXXXI.

oners of them ; on which some lifted their Arms again, called out *God save King George* & fired upon the magazine,'—a performance which 'put the whole into great confusion' and ended with the imprisonment of the

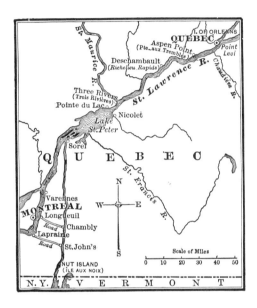

mutineers. Desperation, and not Toryism, was the cause of this outbreak, if it really took place. 'We have borne patiently the hardships of a winter campaign, in hopes of a seasonable and powerful reinforcement; but we have been kept short of money and provisions, and all the necessaries of life, and are not even thanked for our pains ': such was the language that Walker represented the troops as using. 'Our Army seemed totally neglected,' explained Lieutenant Cleghorn afterward, quite unaware

—like his comrades—of the poverty and helplessness yawning behind the bold front of Congress.[20]

'Neither art, craft, nor money will prevail on any of them to reinlist to serve in Canada,' Hazen had predicted. Some of them did it, however. Others, under pressure, remained a while in camp : though how valuable they were likely to prove, Washington's opinion suggested ; and what influence they would have on their comrades, required no explanation. But most of the men whose terms had expired were already on their way home, deaf to every call, when Thomas arrived at Montreal.[21]

Only some fifteen hundred American recruits had gone on to Quebec since March thirtieth. Hazen's meagre 'handful' of Canadians received orders to move down, and some went ; but the Colonel declared it 'impossible' to go before his men were paid, and mentioned that nearly one-half of a company that made the attempt deserted on their way. All the while, too, by day and by night, an enemy that was not remote like England, fearsome like Beaujeu's peasants, nor cautious like the Governor, marched hither and yon through the camps, and struck down victims in their very midst,—that dreadful but now familiar enemy, the small-pox. No precautions had been able to repel it ; no efforts could root it out ; and no orders availed to prevent secret inoculation from crippling the force. Deeper and deeper this unclean vulture bit its way into the vitals of the army. Medicines gave out, and hospitals overflowed. As a rule, the deaths were comparatively few, though Caldwell, some time

---

20 § 'Chalmers' Journal, Apr. 16, 18. Ainslie, Journal, Apr. 18. Those New Yorkers who re-enlisted were formed into a 'regiment' with Nicholson (recently major of the 3d regt.) as colonel (Mag. Am. Hist., Dec., 1881). Cleghorn to ———, May 12, 1776 : 4 Force, VI., 430. 'Chalmers' Journal, Apr. 18. Walker to S. Adams, May 30, 1776 (paraphrased): S. Adams Papers.

21 § Hazen to Sch., Apr. 1, 1776 : 4 Force, V., 751. Mag. Am. Hist., Dec., 1881, p. 404. Thomas to Wash., Apr. 27, 1776 ; 4 Force, V., 1104.

later, estimated 'by all accounts' that not less than five
hundred of the besiegers died of disease during the winter ; but sickness was, for the time being, worse than
death, since the invalids required care.[22]

So it was that when Thomas took account of the situation, he found its colors, which had steadily deepened as he
approached, more sombre than he could have imagined.
It was not a matter of spots on the sun but of spots on
midnight. Reduced by discharges, deaths, and desertions, the army numbered only nineteen hundred men.
Barely one thousand, officers included, were fit for duty ;
three hundred of these, no longer bound to serve, were
'very importunate' for a discharge, and in many cases
refused to do duty ; and two hundred others had been
inoculated. Five hundred reliable troops, plus two hundred with the small-pox in their veins, had to guard
the circuit of twenty-six miles, take care—with what
Canadian assistants could be got without hard money
—of nine hundred sick, and overawe three hundred countrymen indignant at what seemed neglect and oppression. Those able to work had so much to do that it took
Sergeant Hodgkinson four or five days to write a letter
home. Owing to distances and rivers only three hundred
men could be drawn together promptly in the case of
an attack. The provisions would last but six days at the
most. All the magazines together contained only a hundred and fifty pounds of gunpowder. No intrenchments
had been thrown up. Tools enough to construct them
with, although Schuyler had realized the necessity for
them in January, were not at hand. Credit had taken
flight. Only 'with great difficulty' could supplies of

---

[22] § Return: 4 Force, V., 550, note. Arnold to Sch., May 6, 1776: Sparks
MSS., No. 60, p. 83. Hazen to Antill, Apr. 20, 1776: Can. Arch., B, 27, p. 398.
Small-pox, medicine: Arnold to Deane, Mar. 30, 1776 (4 Force, V., 549); Arnold's
Ord. Book, Feb. 11 ; [Antill] to [Hazen], Mar. 28, 1776 (Can. Arch., B, 27, p. 380).
Wooster to Hancock, Apr. 10, 1776: 4 Force, V., 845. Caldwell, Letter.

any kind be worried from the 'much disaffected' people. Wooster, angry at the appointment of Thomas, dignified —no, countenanced—insubordination by vowing he would stay in Canada no longer. And yet this mockery of an army pretended, and pretended with a bold face, to besiege a walled town containing some five thousand people, with a hundred and forty-eight loaded cannon scowling on the ramparts, over sixteen hundred well men on duty, and a frigate, a sloop-of-war, and several small armed vessels available for service. On May the third, when a couple of guns opened from the Heights, the garrison replied with a musket by way of ridicule. But they staid behind the walls; and that very evening, when the fire-ship threatened to burn a hole in their defences, they looked for an assault. It was not only a caricature but a paradox of war; and, like other paradoxes, it was a Humpty Dumpty balanced on a wall.[23]

Most of the sick, however, were likely to recover, and reinforcements, cannon, powder, and a little money were certainly at hand. April the twenty-fifth had found Ticonderoga once more a busy place, for all the troops not yet gone forward had orders to embark at once. In the greatest hurry and bustle, amid shouts, cheers, laughter, and adieux, the men tumbled into sailing-craft and set out for St. Johns. Spirits rose like the wind and sparkled like the waves. 'A very respectable figure' they felt sure of cutting before Quebec; and they would

---

23 § Thomas to Commrs., May 7, 1776: Sparks MSS., No. 60, p. 83. Id. to Wash., May 8, 1776: 4 Force, VI., 453. Walker to S. Adams, May 30, 1776: S. Adams Papers. Hodgkinson, Apr. 27, 1776: Penna. Mag., X., p. 158. Sch. to Hancock, Jan. 29, 1776: 4 Force, IV., 880. Intrenchment, tools: Thomas to Wash., *supra*; 4 Force, VI., 452, note; Almon, Remembrancer, 1776, Part II., p. 195. Wooster: Senter, Journal; Arnold (i. e. Thomas) to Sch., May 6, 1776 (Sparks MSS., No. 60, p. 83). Carleton, Return, May 1, 1776: Can. Arch., Q, 12, p. 35. Précis of Oper. 'Chalmers' Journal, Apr. 13, 23, 29. May 3: Howell, May 4, 1776 (W. T. Read, G. Read, p. 153). Assault: Carleton to Germain, May 14, 1776 (Can. Arch., Q, 12, p. 7). It is rather difficult, with our incomplete data, to understand the shrinkage between Mar. 30 and May 2; and the author can only give the figures as he finds them.

soon endeavor to see what the inside of it was made of, remarked one of them suggestively. All got off that day, as well as the cannon; and, dashing past Four Brothers with a keen breeze on the twenty-sixth, they saw the white house at Iron Point at noon on the morrow, and went ashore early in the evening at St. Johns. Hopes fell a little here, for the news had but a dull ring. 'The prospects at Quebec look very dark,' sighed Chaplain Robbins; but, with more grimness if less exaltation, they hurried on down the river in their boats.[24]

On the twenty-ninth, the last of Maxwell's New Jersey regiment set out for Chambly with a fine wind; and spirits rose again as they swept on, with a bank six or eight feet high on either hand, through the rich, level wheat-lands, already touched here and there with a blush of green; studded, a few rods back with white cottages; adorned every mile or so with a tall cross; and broken at inter-

DESCHAMBAULT

vals with a sunny village, where all the people—even to the nuns—gathered to see them pass. At Lake St. Peter, whose shallow waters needed but a light wind to throw them into billows, many a young fellow had his first bitter taste of sea-sickness. But that passed; and, only two days after Thomas reached Quebec, some of the garrison observed three companies of sixty or seventy men each, as they thought, march up from Wolfe's Cove to the

[24] § Robbins, Journal. Sch. to Hancock, Apr. 28, 1776 : 4 Force, V., 1114. Letter, Apr. 20, 1776 : ib., 1001. Sch. to Hancock, Apr. 2, 1776 : ib., 767.

Heights under three standards: one red, one blue, and one white. Others had arrived the day before, perhaps; still others followed close after, no doubt; and, by sundown on the fifth of May, the first six companies of St. Clair's crack regiment, the Second Pennsylvania, were approaching the camp.[25]

Men were coming from another quarter also. Pushing up into the St. Lawrence, to the astonishment of many a big 'white' porpoise, Captain Douglas 'observed successive smokes from cape to cape, towards Quebeck,' and, on the second of May, a rumor stole through the American lines that a British fleet had entered the river. Impossible! was the reply. But, even were it so, eight hundred and forty-six miles of ice, ebbing and flowing with the tides, lay between Quebec and the ocean. After so hard a winter vessels could not arrive, people said, before the twentieth: time enough for several things to happen. The fire-ship did happen, and on the next day the soldiers detected some hints, they thought, of another assault.[26]

On the fifth, Thomas faced the cold, raw morning with a calm face, and wrote hopefully to his wife. Still, he was observing and reflecting; and, in the course of the day, he summoned Wooster and the field-officers to a council of war. At that he fully canvassed the situation. Men and artillery had not come down as fast as he had expected; vessels from England might arrive, pass up the river, and cut the line of retreat; many other 'disagreeable circumstances' had to be considered; and the council,

---

[25] § Robbins, Journal. Ainslie, Journal, May 3. Haskell, Diary, May 2. St. Clair, Narrative, p. 234. Smith, St. Clair, I., p. 15. REMARK LXXXII.

[26] (This paragraph and the next.) Dearborn, Journal, May 18. Admiralty digest: 4 Force, VI., 457. Haskell, Diary, May 2, 4. Senter, Journal. Dawson, N. Am., p. 291. May 20: Pelton, N. Y. Calendar, I., p. 285. Ainslie, Journal, May 5. Thomas to Mrs. T., May 5, 1776: Thomas Papers. Id. to Commrs., May 7, 1776: Sparks MSS., No. 60, p. 83. Council: 4 Force, VI., 454. News: ib., 452. Walker to S. Adams May 30, 1776: S. Adams Papers. The smokes would seem to have been signals made by friends of the Americans.

after voting against an assault, decided unanimously to remove the sick immediately to Three Rivers, to let the whole army follow, with its artillery and stores, 'as soon [as] it could conveniently,' and to occupy 'some important posts, where there would be a prospect of resisting with success.' Such a deliberate and formidable retreat seemed to be the only wise course, and Wooster emphasized his concurrence by setting off at once with all his baggage.

That evening, Thomas received 'certain intelligence of fifteen ships being 40 leagues below Quebec, making up the river'; but, happily, the floating ice forbade the vessels to crowd sail except at the risk of being sawn asunder, and the northwest wind almost prohibited them from advancing at all. There was still time; and immediately—or at all events very early in the morning of the sixth—men and teams began to load invalids and cannon into the waiting bateaux. Firmly planted at a strategic point, the Americans might still grip the St. Lawrence hard, even if they could not at present win Quebec.[27]

But, alas, another fatality! During the night the wind had swung round to the northeast, and Douglas had ordered Linzee to 'make the best of his way' through the ice, even at the peril of his frigate. From four o'clock on, guns were heard firing down the river, and at daybreak a tangle of masts, ropes, and spars could be seen moving up behind the nose of Orleans Island. Instantly the Canadians vanished with their teams. The American army found itself, like Pharaoh's chariots, without wheels; and the work, though it went on in a fever of haste, drave heavily. Were the Provincials to make good their retreat,

---

[27] (This paragraph and the next.) Thomas to Commrs., May 7, 1776: Note 26. Ainslie, Journal, May 5, 6. 'Remark. Occur.' Journal, May 5, 6. Admiralty digest: 4 Force, VI., 457. REMARK LXXXIII.

or would British reinforcements fall upon them in the helpless confusion of breaking camp? Long had the drama of the siege been intense; now it became agonizing.

Slowly but surely a vessel flying the cross of St. George rounded the island. Is that another fire-ship? queried the city guards. The alarm-bells rang, the drums beat to arms; the ramparts quickly turned black with men; the reserves formed on the grand parade; the gunners manned their batteries; the matches were held ready; the officers prepared to cry 'Fire!' Once more the blue pennant with a union jack below it climbed the signal mast, and five guns of the Grand Battery sent their shot across the visitor's bow. But this time the stranger answered. A blue flag, a red flag, and a union flew to the three mast-heads, and, boom after boom, one, two, three—seven flashes and roars burst from her portholes. She was a friend: in short, the frigate *Surprise*; and, bearing away from the American redoubt at Point Levi, she tacked and circled like a bird, came round by the north shore, and cast anchor as near the mouth of the St. Charles River as she could.[28]

By this time the news had flown to 'every pillow in town.' It was early still—about six o'clock—and a chill-

---

[28] § (and the rest of the chapter.) Thomas to Commrs., May 7, 1776: Sparks MSS., No. 60, p. 83. Id. to Wash., May 8, 1776: 4 Force, VI., 453. Commrs. to Sch., May 10, 1776: Sparks Corres., I., p. 512. Id. to Hancock, May 10: 4 Force, VI., 450. Arnold to Sch., May 10, 1776: Sch. Papers. Walker to S. Adams, May 30, 1776: S. Adams Papers. Porter, Diary: Mag. Am. Hist., Jan., 1893, p. 187. Journals of Senter, Haskell, Tolman, Shallus. News: 4 Force, VI., 452, note. J. Caldwell to Boudinot, May 15, 1776: Emmet Coll. Putnam (Goforth) to Wash., May 21, 1776, 4 Force, VI., 535. Wooster to McNeill, Apr. 26, 1776: Am. Antiq. Soc. Carleton to Germain, May 14, 1776: Can. Arch., Q, 12, p. 7. Id. to Barrington, May 14, 1776: War Off., N. Am., Orig. Corres., Vol. 12. Id. to Tryon, May 17, 1776: Pub. Rec. Off., Am. and W. I., Vol. 186, p. 739. Maclean to Barrington, May 10, 1776: Can. Arch., M, 317, p. 336. Id. to Id., May 21, 1776: ib., M, 317, p. 330. Id. to ——, May 25, 1776: ib., Q, 12, p. 69. The British Journals (REMARK XLV.). Pringle to Lord Howe, May 14, 1776: Can. Arch., Q, 12, p. 41. Caldwell, Letter. Admiralty digest: 4 Force, VI., 457. Almon, Remembrancer, 1776, Part II., p. 195. Return of articles captured: Can. Arch., Q, 12, p. 75. Précis of Oper. Gordon to Barrington, May 15, 1776: War Off., Orig. Corres., N. Am., Vol. 12. Mgr. de St. Vallier, Part II., Chap. IV. Barnfair, letter: Middlesex Journal, June 22, 1776. Berthelot, MS. in Can. Arch. Naval and Mil. Gazette, Feb. 1, 1851 (Mil. Antiq.). Verreau (Sanguinet), Invasion, p. 127.

ing wind swept keenly up the icy stream ; but every soul hurried to the bluff. Some of the throng were only half-dressed, but no such trifle mattered. ' God be praised! '— in that cry went up the glad heart of the city. ' At last we can breathe the fresh air of the fields! ' came next. Once more Quebec was saved.

Not far behind the *Surprise* came the *Isis* and the *Martin*, and as soon as possible their boats began landing what troops were aboard. Twenty-one trips took about eighty marines and a hundred grenadiers ashore to rein-force the garrison, and Carleton had work ready for them. Very early in the morning a woman had come to Palace Gate and reported that the Americans were ex-tremely busy loading carts with baggage, arms, and the like. Apparently they were either decamping or setting an ambush[29] ; and the Governor decided to go out and see what it meant. More than that he did not care to venture, for the Americans were now supposed to number three thousand and nine hundred, though he rather counted upon taking the new battery on the Heights and prevent-ing further damage to the town from that quarter. Nairne, with four brass field-pieces and a covering party, went first as an advance guard; and about noon, while the joy-ous bells of the city still rang and rang again, as if they could not stop, some nine hundred men, issuing from St. Louis and St. John's Gates, marched at a quick step to the Heights and formed there in columns six deep.

Though a small army, it was an impressive one, stretch-ing—as it did—quite across that historic ground from bluff to bluff, and glistening with steel. On the right, gallant Lord Petersham, heir to an earldom,[30] led the brilliant grenadiers in their scarlet coats and bearskin caps, and grizzled Maclean, eager and restless, headed the Royal

---

[29] See REMARK LXXXIV.
[30] Earldom of Harrington: Naval and Mil. Gaz., Feb. 1, 1851.

Fusiliers and the Emigrants. Stanch Caldwell occupied the left, with his British militia in green and buff; and

ST. LOUIS GATE (INSIDE)

the French militia, the marines in their dark blue, and the corps of 'artificers' in green and scarlet held the centre. Carleton himself, with a countenance rather easier than before but an eye no less cool and wary, commanded the force, and soon he directed Nairne to feel of the American outposts and guard-houses with his 6-pounders.

At once the shell of siege collapsed, like a paper balloon in a thunder-shower. Half a dozen American sentries discharged their muskets aimlessly and fled. A field-piece fired three times with as little effect. Thomas—probably warned by the flash of bayonets issuing from Quebec, which Noah Cook and no doubt many others observed—had ordered the troops under arms; but the principal camp extended about four miles by two,[31] and not over two hundred and fifty effectives were able to gather promptly at the centre. Every effort was made to rally the men under inoculation, but they threw away their muskets and fled. The soldiers already in line had to fall back; and, while they moved in good order at first, Nairne's artillery soon sharpened their pace. The troops on the low ground near St. Roch hurried up the bluff to headquarters without stopping for their baggage; but the retreat had begun when they arrived, and they could only retire with the rest.

Some of the troops formed under cover of the woods and showed fight; but a stand was impossible, and the General ordered them all to retreat. This quickened the flight.

---

[31] Hodgkinson to parents, Apr. 27, 1776: Penna. Mag., X., p. 158.

The scattered working parties and the isolated posts ran for their lives. Panic set in. Gunners abandoned loaded cannon without waiting to fire them. Clothing, provisions, ammunition, and bayonets flew this way and that. Orderly books, public documents, and private papers were forgotten. Haunted by the doom of rebels, men felt crazy to escape. Even the sick sprang frantically from their beds and staggered to the woods, falling at every step. Out of forty patients at the General Hospital, thirty-five clutched their packs with trembling fingers and tottered away.[32]

Carleton, when he saw the Americans hurrying to headquarters, concluded there would be a fight and halted in battle order; but, after waiting an hour and finding that the enemy were in retreat, he sent forward scouting parties, who put the torch to the American barracks, and opened fire on every sign of a 'rebel.' This appeared to mean pursuit. At the same time he ordered the *Surprise*, the *Martin*, and another armed vessel up the river ; and this looked as if he intended to cut off escape. At the quarters of the Second New Jersey regiment, some distance to the rear, Colonel Maxwell formed nine hundred men and placed them in 'ambush'; but Thomas, on coming up, directed all to retreat ; for a stand even there, as matters were, could only result, apparently, in vain bloodshed, and perhaps might give Carleton time to land a force above. Some of the men in the bateaux, by this time half-laden with sick and stores, pushed up the St. Lawrence close under the bank with the force of despair ; and while a part of them got ashore and fled, others lightened the boats by unloading—none too gently—their cargoes of invalids. The *Gaspé*, partially equipped for a fire-ship and now clumsily scuttled, and the schooner *Maria*, with her ten small can-

---

[32] The circumstances made any cool and complete account of the proceedings impossible, and it is difficult to piece the scraps together satisfactorily ; but there seems to be no doubt about the main features of the picture.

non and a brace of heroes too proud to retreat, were captured by the British. Two tons or so of priceless gunpowder, just going down in a bateau, about a hundred barrels of flour, and all the hospital stores met the same fate. Seven brass cannon, as many brass howitzers, more than a dozen iron cannon, and a quantity of shot—not very large, to be sure, but very precious to the Americans—were taken. General Thomas's dinner, left smoking on the table, was devoured by some of Maclean's gaunt Highlanders.

A small American force at Charlesbourg, when they saw the army retreating, plunged into the woods and found it impossible to strike the road until far above Quebec. Still worse luck befell the regiment at Point Levi. Receiving a hint rather than a notice that withdrawal had been decided upon, they moved up the river a few miles and waited eight hours for bateaux to ferry them across; but none came, and in desperation they set off by themselves, as best they could. They soon ate up their scanty stock of food, and spent their scanty stock of hard money for bread. Next, a force from one of the British vessels landed with artillery, blocking the road, such as it was; and finally the wretched fugitives had to bury themselves in the woods. As that side of the St. Lawrence, beyond a short distance, was almost a wilderness nearly to Sorel, their prospects were not brilliant.[33]

The main body, however, was little more to be envied. The scarcity of food compelled it to divide. Indeed, Thomas did not think it safe to keep more than five hundred men with him. Some stopped for the night only a dozen miles

---

[33] Robbins, Journal, May 6.

from Quebec, but more fled on with the speed of panic, and cursing Campbell made straight for Montreal. Thomas himself halted at Jacques Cartier ; but the position could easily be taken in the rear, should he make a stand there, and, posting a guard, he pressed on. The road, still deep with spring mire, was frequently almost impassable, and in some places was overflowed so badly that a circuit of several miles over the soft ground had to be made. At others, the route lay near the St. Lawrence, and shells from the British vessels, particularly where streams had to be crossed, augmented the terrors, if not the losses, of the flight. As provisions could be obtained from the people only by stark force, when they could be obtained at all, companies found it necessary to break up more and more in quest of food ; and thus on they hurried in wild confusion, spreading fear and the small-pox wherever they went ; while the poor Canadians who had sided with them, overwhelmed with even a greater misfortune than the army, tortured the fleeing host with tears, entreaties, and lamentations, and sometimes with curses or threats.[34]

At two o'clock in the morning of May seventh, news of the flight arrived at Deschambault ; and then, hour after hour, fugitives came streaming along in every conceivable shape of exhaustion, hunger, sickness, and despair : limping and reeling ; plastered with mud ; panting with fright ; hollow-eyed from lack of sleep ; equipped with little save tales of disaster. On all sides lay men dying of the small-pox ; and faster than ever sank new victims

---

[34] § For the retreat (in addition to Note 28) : Thomas to Commrs., May 15, 1776 (Cont. Cong. Papers, No. 58, p. 253); Robbins, Journal ; Journ. Cong., July 31, 1776 (the misfortunes of the Pt. Levi party were not chargeable to Thomas); Chase and Carroll to Sch., May 17, 1776 (4 Force, VI., 586); Officer (4 Force, VI., 398); Memor. of D. Campbell (Cont. Cong. Papers, No. 41, II., p. 388) ; Memoirs of J. Halsted (ib., No. 42, III., pp. 461, 463); St. Clair, Narrative, p. 234 ; Roberts, Anc. and Hon. Art. Co., II., p. 216 ; Sch. to Hancock, Apr. 2, 1776 (4 Force, V., 757); Jefferson to Page, May 19, 1776 (Emmet Coll.); Elmer, Journal (N. J. Hist. Soc. Proc., II., p. 97). Roads: Hazen to Antill, Mar. 26, 1776 (Can. Arch., B, 27, p. 392); Sch. to Hancock, Apr. 2, 1776 (4 Force, V., 757). Cleghorn to——, May 12, 1776: 4 Force, VI., 430. Germain to Howe, June 11, 1776: Pub. Rec. Off., Am. and W. I., Vol. 431, p. 145.

under the scourge.   The British vessels came up, 'firing as they came.'   At any moment their shells might drop and burst in the mob of fugitives.   Marines actually landed.

Every known terror seemed to have had notice; and, like the vultures of the desert—swooping and swooping again in ever narrower circles upon the fever-smitten Arab that has fallen but is not quite dead — fright, famine, shame, helplessness, the foe, the plague, the gloom of isolation and friendlessness, the dire prospect of total ruin, the grim visage of bloody death,—a ghastly brood,—all shook their black, foul, creaking wings over this wretched débris of huddling, fainting humanity,—each moment nearer and more near.   On every face was written panic, and on many despair cut deep its lines of agony.   'God of Armies, help us, help us!' prayed Chaplain Robbins.

An hour before noon, Thomas arrived.   Some order came with him.   A little hope glimmered; or rather despair seemed a shade less dark.   Carleton did not appear.   The marines were beaten off.   It looked as if the worst might be over,—at least for a breathing-space.

But the best possible was bad enough.   The Americans had been routed ignominiously, had fled when no man thought of pursuing, and had sacrificed stores they could hardly exist without; two regiments of regulars had now been thrown into the balance against them; and—worst of all—Carleton had at length been able to measure, and let the Canadians measure, the actual strength of the Liberators.   It was a grave, perhaps decisive, blow; and so felt both sides, as the news of it spread.   'A glorious Prospect!' rejoiced Maclean; a 'melancholy reverse,' groaned Thomas Jefferson.   It gives promise 'of putting an end to the Rebellion in one Campaign,' exulted Lord George Germain.   'Nothing but the power of an Omnipotent God, stretched forth for our relief,' cried Lieutenant Elmer, 'can preserve us from utter destruction.'

XXXI

THE APOSTLES OF LIBERTY

' I F the mountain will not come to Mahomet, Mahomet
will go to the mountain,' that astute person is said
to have remarked, when a certain eminence declined to
obey his voice ; and it has been thought very generally
that he could have done no better.

Over and over again, it had been proposed to Congress
that a committee of its members visit Canada and exert
their influence, authority, and wisdom on the scene of
action. Only a week after finding himself planted before
St. Johns, Montgomery informed Schuyler that he 'could
wish to have three members of the Congress as a council
immediately,' lest he should make some blunder. Two
months later, he still coveted 'exceedingly' such a reinforcement. On learning of the delegation sent north in
November to confer with Schuyler, he felt 'exceedingly
happy,' for he expected this body to visit Canada ; and
he informed Robert R. Livingston that he was 'no less
mortified' on hearing of its return from the lakes to Philadelphia. About the middle of October, Schuyler 'humbly' recommended to Congress that a committee with full
powers be sent north ; and, on learning of Montgomery's
tragic end, he rather impatiently repeated the suggestion.
Arnold had the same desire and made the same request.
Hazen wrote Samuel Adams in a similar strain ; and, in
specifying to Schuyler the needs of Canada, along with
' able generals, a respectable Army, a suitable supply of

325

hard cash, a printer, etc.,' he mentioned 'a Committee of Congress.' At Philadelphia itself the measure was urged persistently. ' I will be at them 'till 't is done,' promised Lynch.[1]

Congress, however, proposed with equal perseverance that Canada should send a delegation south. One could see that such a course would not only square better with the dignity of the United Colonies, but would be a long stride toward the incorporation of Canada in the Union ; and it was, perhaps, to avoid giving the mountain a good excuse for passivity, that no attention was paid to these urgent and reiterated petitions. But events at the north —particularly Montgomery's failure at the end of the year—made a closer contact with the Canadians appear more necessary, and a delegation from them less probable, than before. The wisdom of Mahomet, if not the urgency of Schuyler and Lynch, seemed to carry the day ; and, on the fifteenth of February, not only was it resolved : 'That a committee of three . . . (two of whom to be members of Congress) be appointed to proceed to Canada, there to pursue such instructions as shall be given them by Congress,' but the men were actually chosen.[2]

Then, unhappily, the Opposition seems to have made itself heard once more, and Congress could not determine what powers to give its Commissioners. At length, however, after a delay of more than three weeks, a draft of instructions was laid on the President's table. On the eleventh and twelfth of March these were 'considered' ; on the nineteenth further sections came in ; and finally, the

---

1 § Montg. to Sch., Sept. 24, 1775: 4 Force, III., 840. Id. to Id., Nov. 24, 1775: ib., 1694. Id. to R. R. Liv., Dec. 17, 1775 : Liv. Papers, 1775-1777, p. 89. Sch. to Hancock, Oct. 18, 1775 : 4 Force, III., 1093. Id. to Id., Jan. 13, 1776 : 4 Force, IV., 666. Arnold: Sch. to Hancock, Feb. 23, 1776 (ib., 1481). Hazen to S. Adams, Feb. 18, 1776: S. Adams Papers. Id. to Sch., Apr. 1, 1776 : 4 Force, V., 751. Lynch to Sch., Jan. 20, 1776: Sparks MSS., No. 60, p. 61.

2 § Wish of Cong.: Vol. I., *passim.* Journ. Cong., Feb. 15.

next day, an agreement was achieved. Represent to the
people of Canada, said Congress, 'that the arms of the
United Colonies, having been carried into that province
for the purpose of frustrating the designs of the British
court against our common liberties, we expect not only
to defeat the hostile machinations of Governor Carlton
against us, but that we shall put it into the power of our
Canadian brethren, to pursue such measures for securing
their own freedom and happiness, as a generous love of
liberty and sound policy shall dictate to them.' [3]

This meant, as the next paragraph explained, that their
interests and those of their
neighbors on the south were
'inseparably united'; and —as
the Commissioners were to represent ' in the strongest terms '
—that it was the 'earnest desire'
of Congress to adopt them as a
sister Colony. The necessity of
taking some decisive step to
place themselves under the protection of the Union was to

CHARLES CARROLL

be urged, and they were to be stimulated 'by motives
of glory, as well as interest, to assume a part in a contest, by which they must be deeply affected.' On the
other side, the rights of conscience would be held sacred,
and the whole people were to be guaranteed solemnly,
in the name of Congress, 'the free and undisturbed
exercise of their religion.' The clergy should have 'the
full, perfect, and peaceable possession and enjoyment of
all their estates,' and the entire ecclesiastical administration, beyond an assurance of full religious liberty and civil

3 § Journ. Cong., Mar. 9, 11, 12, 19, 20.

privileges to every sect of Christians, should be left 'in the hands of the good people of that province, and such legislature' as they should constitute.[4]

'With all possible expedition,' a complete Convention should be called, 'to deliberate concerning the establishment of a form of government, and a union with the United Colonies.' Jay and others objected that advising the Canadians to create a government for themselves 'without limitation' meant 'an Independency.' Richard Smith noted in his Journal that 'there was much Arg[umen]t on this Ground'; and John Adams, describing this part of the Instructions as 'one step more towards our great object—a general recommendation to the States to institute governments,' recorded that 'great zeal' was shown by the other party in opposing them; but the struggle ended with one more victory for complete self-rule.[5]

'I expect the Deputies will, in a short time, be ready to proceed to Canada,' said John Hancock four days after they were appointed; and that would have been none too soon. But it was not until the second day of April that a Hudson River sloop took them aboard at New York, and, in its leisurely fashion, set out for Albany. The fifth morning found them shaking hands with General Schuyler; and then, as the lakes could not be crossed, they settled down at what Colonel Vose called his 'very Grand farm' near Saratoga, where no doubt 'good Mrs. Schuyler,' as Franklin once described her, made them very comfortable with housewifely attentions, and her consort, steering them nervously up and down the wide, two-story veranda, made them very unhappy with Canadian facts.[6]

---

[4] Journ. Cong., Mar. 20.

[5] § Journ. Cong., Mar. 20. Smith, Private Journal. J. Adams, Works, III., p. 36.

[6] § Hancock to Lee, Feb. 19, 1776: 4 Force, IV., 1197. Rowland, Carroll, p. 147. Carroll, Journal. Sch. to Wash., Apr. 7, 1776: 4 Force, V., 812. Id. to Hancock, Apr. 12, 1776: ib., 868. Vose, Journal, p. 7. Franklin to Sch., May 27, 1776: Sparks MSS., No. 60, p. 88. Ostrander, Old Saratoga, p. 8.

Leaving this haven when the lakes opened, about the middle of April, they passed ten hard days in reaching Ticonderoga, and there took ship for the north. It was the custom for such travellers to go ashore at evening, and sleep under the trees with huge fires blazing at their feet; and some of the party spent one night under a bush hut in hunter fashion. At another time, a farmer's cabin offered its rude hospitality. Once and again, they landed to have breakfast or dine in more comfort, even if only on 'cold provisions.' But, as a rule, they got on as best they could in the crowded quarters on board. An awning was spread for them, and the beds brought from New York were made up under it each night; and in this arduous manner they tacked and tossed for three days to St. Johns. The jolting of a calash (*calèche*) to Laprairie gave them at any rate a change of sensations; and finally, threshing down the rapids, the Apostles of Liberty set foot on the sandy beach of Montreal at the close of their twenty-seventh day from New York (April 29).[7]

At the landing, General Arnold met them 'in the most polite and friendly manner'; and, entering Vaudreuil Gate amid a crash of cannons from the citadel, they passed on, escorted by all the Friends of Liberty in Montreal, through many strange sights—keen fur-traders, reckless *coureurs de bois*, strolling Indians decked out in savage finery, shy nuns, and half-scowling priests—to the dark and massive Château. 'The Committee, if any is sent, should be enabled to live in that splendour which, with Frenchmen, creates respect,' Schuyler had advised; and Arnold held the same opinion. First, the distinguished visitors were offered a glass of wine, while people of quality and importance crowded round them to pay

[7] § Carroll. Journal. J. Carroll, letter: Rowland, Carroll, p. 152. Franklin to Hancock, Apr. 13, 1776: 4 Force, V., 927. Sch. to Wash., Apr. 27, 1776: ib., 1097. Id. to Id., May 3, 1776: ib., 1182. Commrs. to Hancock, May 1: ib., 1166.

-compliments. Next, they were ushered into another apart-
ment and found themselves among ladies, most of them
French. There tea was served; and finally, after they
had chatted a becoming time, 'an elegant supper'
followed.[8]

At the head of the board sat Arnold, now famous the
world over for the wilderness march, the plucky assault,
and the wonderful perseverance of the blockade, and
quite capable of winning by his manners and conversation the 'highest esteem' of the foremost among his
guests. The chairman of the commission, placed at his

right, listening, pondering, sometimes propping his chin
with the thumb of his right hand, and occasionally sum-
ming up many words in a remark so witty and so just
as to brighten the eyes as well as the minds of all present,
bore a name honored in two hemispheres. Already past
three-score years and ten, he had felt at Saratoga that
perhaps this rough trip would 'prove too much' for him,
and had written last farewells to some of his friends ; but
he had pushed on, and now here he sat, with all the
statecraft of Benjamin Franklin and all the winning common-sense of Bonhomme Richard hard at work behind
his fatherly spectacles. Canada was no new topic with
him. Wolfe's expedition had sprung, perhaps, from his
influence. When it was proposed to give up the fruits
of the victory on the Plains, he had gone about London
'every day and hour' combatting the idea ; and he was

---

[8] § Carroll, Journal. Montreal letter in Conn. Gazette, May 24, 1776. Sch.
to Hancock, Feb. 10, 1776 : 4 Force, IV., 990. Letter from J. Carroll: Rowland,
Carroll, p. 153. Château de Ramezay : Chap. XXX., Note 11.

the author of at least one pamphlet on the future of that region.[9]

Across the table, Samuel Chase of Maryland, with a solid, well-filled body, a genial, calm, determined face, clear, steady brown eyes, and massive locks waving down toward his strong shoulders, personified good nature, judgment, and resolution.

Next him sat a man with gentle but fearless eyes and handsome, sculpturesque features toned with an air of the highest honor and courtesy. Lord Brougham extolled his learning, eloquence, character, and grace; yet his arms — two lions rampant holding a naked sword, point up, between them—were equally true to his nature.

'And do you think that writing will settle the question between us?' he had asked Chase a number of years before, when the controversy with England began to warm.

'Surely,' answered Chase; 'What else can we resort to?'

'The bayonet,' he replied.

John Adams outlined his qualifications well: 'a gentleman of independent fortune, perhaps the largest in America, a hundred and fifty or two hundred thousand pounds sterling; educated in some university in France, though a native of America; of great abilities and learning, complete master of the French language, and a professor of the Roman Catholic religion, yet a warm, a firm, a zealous supporter of the rights of America, in whose cause he has hazarded his all.' It was of him that an awestruck bystander whispered, as he unflinchingly set his hand to the Declaration of Independence, 'There goes half a million

9 § J. Carroll to Chase and C. Carroll, May 28, 1776: Emmet Coll. Familiar portrait of Franklin. Franklin to Quincy, Apr. 15, 1776: Works (Bigelow), VI., p. 10. Wolfe's exped.: Carroll, Journal, p. 23. Franklin to Hughes, Jan. 7, 1760, and Pamphlet: Works (Bigelow), III., pp. 43, 69. The seating is inferential.

at the dash of a pen!' for the name it wrote was Charles Carroll of Carrollton.[10]

Nor was he to challenge the Canadian clergy unaided. John Carroll, destined to become the first archbishop of Baltimore, had been invited by Congress to accompany the Delegates. As Abigail Adams wrote John, her spouse, the idea of taking him along was regarded by everybody, even in Puritan Quincy, as 'a master stroke,' and his learning and ability, his patriotism and zeal, his noble presence, his Catholic orthodoxy, his Jesuit diplomacy, and his persuasive eloquence, acquired and practised on the continent of Europe, seemed enough to bring even the priesthood around, were that possible.[11]

Perhaps the Carrolls had already been at work on the northern problem from a distance. ''T is said the Canadians were not a little influenced in the part they have taken by the Catholics from Maryland,' Admiral Graves had written while Montgomery was marching to Quebec.[12] At all events, they could now address both Church and people eye to eye and heart to heart; while the board of Commissioners, clothed with supreme authority over the troops and facing every difficulty with the delegated power of Congress, would surely be able to accomplish wonders. In a word, that heavy-browed old dining-room in the Château was now a rich arsenal of prestige, wisdom, tact, and authority. No doubt things had been going badly of late ; but mistakes could be corrected and misfortunes repaired.

New military forces also were at hand. Baron de Woedtke, recently a high officer of the great Frederick but now an American brigadier-general, a man looked

10 § Chase: Port. by C. W. Peale (Independence Hall, Phila.); Carroll : Port. by Lati after Stuart (Md. Hist. Soc.); Arms, etc.: Rowland, Carroll, *passim*. Chase and Carroll: Hilliard, Speeches, pp. 388, 390, 393 ; Brougham, Hist. Sketches, Sec. Ser., p. 196 ; J. Adams, Famil. Letters, p. 134.

11 § Journ. Cong., Feb. 15. Boyle, Sketches, *passim*. Carroll, Journal, Introd.

12 Graves to Stevens, Dec. 4, 1775: Pub. Rec. Off., Admirals' Disp., N. Am., Vol. 6.

upon as a hero till he proved himself a sot, had come north with the Commissioners. March twenty-fifth, Congress had requested Washington to ' detach four batallions into Canada ' as soon as the secu-

JOHN CARROLL

rity of New York and New England would permit ; and the regiments of Poor, Paterson, Greaton, and Bond, 'four of the strongest,' were selected as promptly as possible after the army reached the mouth of Hudson River. Brigadier-General Thompson, an honored graduate of the French and Indian War and recently Colonel of the First Rifles, was appointed to command this corps. 'This minute I have received orders to march to Canada,' he wrote George Read on the fifteenth of April; and in four days about two thousand hearty young fellows and their officers began clambering into sloops at New York, with a company of riflemen, a company of artisans, and two engineers besides. Two days later their sails filled plumply ; and at this very moment, while Arnold was feasting the Commissioners at the Château, they were camping cheerily in the rain at Fort Edward, only troubled lest Quebec should be taken before they could get there. Once more the omens looked auspicious; and when the weary but gratified Congressmen retired to their beds in Thomas Walker's house, fifteen or twenty rods distant— ' the best built and perhaps the best furnished in the town' —they felt they could afford to rub their hands a little.[13]

13 § Journ. Cong., Mar. 1, 16, 25. Conn. Gazette, Apr. 5, 1776. Sot: p. 440. Wash. to Sch., Apr. 15, 1776: 4 Force, V., 945. Vose, Journal, p. 4, note. Read, Read, pp. 110, 152. Wash. to Sch., Apr. 19, 1776. Writings (Ford), IV., p. 28. Id. to Hancock, Apr. 15, 22, 19: ib., pp. 17, 34 ; 4 Force, V., 985. Thompson to

One of the objects entrusted to the Commissioners was the establishment of a 'free press' in Canada. Only a single printing-office existed in the province, and that did its feeble work in the city of Quebec. Those able to read—few comparatively, but many in the sum and widely scattered—could be taught the principles of liberty only by the slow and expensive aid of the pen. To secure the approved means for awakening the intelligence of Canada, Congress had induced Fleury Mesplet, a French printer of Philadelphia, to remove with his family and appliances to Montreal; and his rude but darling press, his type, and the other accoutrements of the art preservative and destructive, bumping from sloop to wharf and wagon to bateau, breaking their master's heart at every tumble and occasionally breaking something of their own, had finally reached the island city, and now resumed their former state, under the supervision of the Commissioners, in the basement of the Château.[14]

John Carroll, with a promptness worthy of his aim, put himself in touch with the clergy at once; but here the omens proved false, for he met a wall of adamant. When he explained that no mere factiousness had caused the uprising of the Colonies, but invasions of charters and violations of well known and long recognized principles of the British Constitution, it was replied that in Canada the people had no aggressions to complain of, and that, in fact, the Quebec Bill had favored their national usages more than could have been expected. If he dwelt upon the liberal views of Congress, and pointed out that British toleration might be exchanged for American guarantees,

---

Wash., Apr. 27, 1776: 4 Force, V., 1096. Vose, Journal, Apr. 29; May 4, etc. Walker, Memorial: Cont. Cong. Papers, 41, X., p. 665. Carroll, Journal, p. 93.

[14] § Journ. Cong., Feb. 23; Mar. 20. Press: Christie, Lower Can., I., p. 25. Secret Journ. Cong., Feb. 26. Memorials of Mesplet: Cont. Cong. Papers, No. 41, VI., pp. 305, 309, 337, 341, 409. Mr. Thomas O'Leary, custodian of the museum at the Château, informed the author as to the location of the press.

the priests answered, in substance, that good treatment
actually experienced counted far more than simple promises
from an enemy in straits, pointing out that in Canada their
property had been safeguarded, their churches honored,
and their missions respected, while in some of the Colonies
their priests were not even allowed to live, and their mis-
sionaries among the Indians—Râle, for example—had been
cruelly treated.[15]

These harsh measures, explained Carroll, resulted in a
great part from the laws of the royal government.

But, they rejoined, the Colonials, though prompt and
valiant in the defence of their own rights of conscience,
have never shown themselves interested in behalf of ours.

The treatment of the Acadians, the address in which
Congress denounced the Roman Catholic faith,[16] the in-
tolerance of Wooster and other Americans in Canada
were all brought in. The injunctions of the Bishop could
not be forgotten ; and, by the well-established maxim
that allegiance was a due return for protection, the British government could claim not only neutrality but support from the Roman Church in Canada. Even John
Carroll found himself helpless against this array of objections, and he soon discovered that his appearing for the
Americans actually seemed offensive to his northern
brethren.[17]

Equally prompt and equally unfortunate, the Commissioners attacked their political problem.

A month before, Hazen had described the Canadians
as 'no longer . . . friends, but, on the contrary, waiting
an opportunity to join our enemies ' ; and their hearts
had not warmed in the interval. No more men would

---

[15] § REMARK LXXXV.

[16] See this vol., p. 215.   The dialogue form of the discussion just above is
due to the present author.

[17] Carroll, Journal, p. 30, note.

FROM FRANKLIN'S LETTER TO CHASE AND CARROLL, MAY 27, 1776

FROM CHASE AND CARROLL'S LETTER TO THOMAS, MAY 12, 1776

engage in his regiment, and he expected those already enlisted would 'go to the right about,' should the people in general turn against the Americans. Arnold endorsed Hazen's gloomy picture as in the main 'too true,' and could add several strokes of black from his own palette. His order, however unavoidable, that Continental paper must be accepted, had covered the faces of the *habitants* with 'Chagrin and discontent.' 'About fifteen thousand Dollars have been paid away,' reported Antill at the close of March, 'and with it is gone the affections of the people in general.' Beating Beaujeu at the cost of shedding Canadian blood, though it put out the flame of insurrection, had perhaps only scattered the embers of discontent. At Three Rivers, in the very ears of an American garrison, the Grand Vicar had the *Domine salvum fac regem* chanted publicly on three successive days in April. Disgusted officers and men were swarming up from Quebec; the Montreal troops could not be induced to re-enlist; and the friendly Canadians, when told that men left the army because their term had ended and that others would take their places, pronounced the American campaign a mere promenade, a mere 'go-and-come'; while the Tories had now arrived at a high pitch in Montreal, and Hazen, after exerting himself to obtain trustworthy information, declared that by and by a 'stroke' would have to be dealt there. Indeed, what else could be expected? It had already come to be generally understood among the people that whenever a royal army should arrive, it would brush the invaders from Canadian soil at once.[18]

Not many hours passed before the Commissioners real-

<hr />

[18] § Hazen to Sch., Apr. 1, 1776: 4 Force, V., 751. Arnold to Sch., Apr. 20, 1776: ib., 1098. [Antill] to [Hazen], Mar. 28, 1776: Can. Arch., B, 27, p. 380. Ursul. de T. Riv., I., p. 369. Walker to S. Adams, May 30, 1776: S. Adams Papers. Hazen to Antill, April 3, 1776: Can. Arch., B, 27, p. 395. Id. to Id., Apr. 20, 1776: ib., p. 398. Commrs. to Cong., May 1, 1776: 4 Force, V., 1166.

ized that the lack of money was the first limb of the octopus to attack. Without a military chest in camp, the American troops could not be expected to behave well nor to remain longer than they must. Even faithful Ayot sent word, that pay for the Canadians must be supplied. Unsupported by a metal base and shocked by many 'breaches of promise,' confidence had in fact collapsed. 'Our credit extends no farther than our arms,' Arnold had written a month before; and the Commissioners themselves discovered that now it fell far short of that. Within forty-eight hours after reaching Montreal, they informed Congress that it was 'impossible' to give a just idea of the lowness of Continental credit in Canada or of the harm that resulted.[19]

'Not the most trifling service can be procured without an assurance of instant pay in silver or gold,' they admitted. The express whom they sent from St. Johns to inform Arnold of their arrival and ask for conveyances to Laprairie had to wait at the ferry until a Friend of Liberty, chancing to pass, turned a dollar bill into silver for him; and, had not that same good angel promised to settle for the calashes, they would not have gone. The Commissioners had been counted upon to bring a large sum in specie, and low indeed fell the faces of all, when this expectation was disappointed. They tried to borrow, but soon found they could raise no funds on either the public credit or their own. Nobody would buy their 'sterling bills of exchange,' not even Charles Carroll's; and that would have amounted, at a later day, to refusing their cheques. Some of their friends had been drained, others pretended to be. People not already committed shrank from compromising themselves, and the

---

[19] § Ayot to Arnold, Mar. 28, 1776: Can. Arch., B, 27, p. 389. E. Antill, Certif., Dec. 1, 1784: Emmet Coll. Arnold to Deane, Mar. 30, 1776: 4 Force, V., 549. Commrs. to Cong., May 1, 1776: 4 Force, V., 1166.

Tories, naturally enough, would not part with a farthing on any terms.[20]

Some way to 'give credit to the Continental currency,' as Thomas phrased it, continued to be the problem ; and the Commissioners finally decided that, with £14,000 to pay debts—leaving Price's account aside—and £6,000 to open a bank for the exchange of Continental bills, these might perhaps be crowded into circulation. An urgent entreaty to forward the £20,000 with the ' utmost despatch ' hurried south to Philadelphia. ' With this supply, and a little success,' they added, ' it may be possible to regain the affections of the people, to attach them firmly to our cause, and induce them to accept a free Government, perhaps to enter into the Union.' In response, Congress resolved to send Canada all the specie it possessed ; but it found in its treasury less than one-twelfth of the minimum required.[21]

As regarded the Canadians, however, this fact mattered little. They felt no need of waiting to learn what Philadelphia could do. For them, the Congress itself had come to Canada ; and now, looking with their own eyes into its pockets, they found them empty. Day after day, instead of welding empires, Franklin and his colleagues could only sit like discredited idols and compare the stale odors of countless bills, ' great and small,' thrust under their noses in fists quivering with impatience. No doubts, no hopes, no pretences were possible any longer. The Grand Continental Congress is really bankrupt, said the people ; and the Commissioners concluded very promptly that, until financial credit could be restored, it would be ' improper to propose ' the adhesion of Canada to the federal Union. In short, as Arnold

---

[20] § Commrs. to Cong., May 1, 8, 1776: 4 Force, V., 1166, 1237.

[21] § Thomas to Wash., Apr. 27, 1776: 4 Force, V., 1104. Commrs. to Cong., May 1, 8, 1776: ib., 1166, 1237. Hancock to Sch., May 24, 1776: 4 Force, VI., 558.

very gently expressed it, the chief object of their mission was clearly 'at a distance.' [22]

Minor but important objects remained, however, and one of these was the general management of public affairs. If the people would not meet in convention and set up an administration of their own, something in the way of a government had to be contrived for them. What should be the guiding principle?

On this point, at least, no doubt seemed possible. The Canadians must have 'a full taste of liberty,' to show them how sweet it was. Such had been the recommendation of Joseph Hawley to Samuel Adams, and no committee of the Continental Congress could afford to adopt any other programme. This meant a radical change at Montreal. Tories were no longer sent over the lakes on suspicion. Militia captains, lodged in the dungeons at Chambly for declining to resign their commissions, had leave to go home. All the exiles languishing in Colonial Siberias were recalled. The spirit of fraternity, long preached by Congress, became a fact. [23]

But even the shining drifts of Parnassus would have seemed out of place, if dumped upon the olive grove of Academus. The principle of freedom was now inappropriate at Montreal. The time for applying gentle persuasions had passed. The imprisoned and the exiled had chewed the cud of bitter reflections until they felt that nothing could sweeten their mouths except revenge, and, on returning home, they found a host of impatient royalists asking nothing better than to follow their lead; while, by the same stroke, the Canadian allies of the Americans, the only force that could help defeat the Tory plots, were estranged.

---

[22] § Commrs. to Cong.: Note 21. Arnold to Chase, May 15, 1776: 4 Force, VI., 580.

[23] § Hawley to S. Adams, Nov. 12, 1775: S. Adams Papers. Walker to S. Adams, May 30, 1776: ib. REMARK LXXXVI.

It is impossible to give you a just idea of the lowness of the [conti]nental credit here from the want of hard money, and the [pre]judice it is to our affairs Not the most trifling service can [be pro]cured without an assurance of instant pay in silver or —
[So] The express we sent from St Johns to inform the General of [our] arrival there, and to request carriages for La Prairie, was [stopt] at the ferry, till a friend passing changed a Dollar for [him] into silver, and we are obliged to that friend (Mr. M'Carthey) [for] his engagement to pay the Calleches, or they would not have

' The Bostonians,' cried these men, ' make war only on their friends. Us they abandon to gibbets and confiscations ; but toward our enemies—enemies only because we have aided the Americans—they are merciful, humane, generous, and complaisant, giving them free license to come back to their homes again. Our foes may now roam about—well supplied with money—like gentlemen on their travels, but we are not paid for the hard cash we have loaned and the supplies we have furnished. *They* may plan to burn our houses and cut our throats ; but *we* may not lift a finger against them to disarm their malice.'

To such protests and expostulations the Delegates replied : ' A cause that cannot support itself upon the principles of liberty is not worth pursuing. We will not do evil that good may ensue. It is a most substantial wrong to exile a man five hundred miles from his own home only because he is disaffected. If the Canadians will join heartily to vindicate their liberties and rights, the few whom we have permitted to return will signify nothing ; if they will not, it will only be just to withdraw the Continental forces, for the war in Canada would be a millstone around the necks of the Colonies.'

' The means must be suited to the end,' rejoined Walker and his friends. ' Why did you seize the forts and vessels and enter our province in hostile array, except for the very purpose of overthrowing the usurpation and despotism of these few whom you now pronounce harmless ? ' But neither protests nor arguments had effect.

Some of the officers [24] at Montreal then pulled out their commissions and trampled them under their feet. ' Never again,' they vowed, ' will we take office under men who destroy by a stroke of the pen what we risked our lives to obtain '; and one even ' damn'd Mr. Chace and to his

---

[24] Walker does not state that they were Canadians, but the French words in their remarks and some of the phraseology imply as much.

face,' reported Walker, 'swearing when he prayed him to accept an important Command that he would not fire another Gun for the Congress till their Officers and Soldiers were put upon an equal footing with their Enemies.' But the Apostles of Liberty could not yield to threats.

Another task, also, fell to the Commissioners,—the superintendence of the army. Their first move was to hold a council of war the morning after they reached Montreal; and the council, besides resolving to fortify Jacques Cartier and Deschambault, voted to build four 'row-galleys or gondolas' at Chambly without delay. Some carpenters from New York had at last appeared; and the Commissioners, in order to stimulate the work, turned over for the pay of Canadian artisans a part of the specie given them for their own expenses, while Arnold sent up to Schuyler for hawsers, anchors, and seamen. But at this juncture, in the morning grey of May tenth, cursing Campbell, all mud outside as well as inside now, brought news of the flight from Quebec. Every military plan and hope staggered under the shock. Montreal became a stormy sea. Dreading that one of the British frigates would run up and cut them off, the Commissioners added to the panic by hastily quitting the city, and Franklin, attended by John Carroll, set out at once for home, both to save the ruins of his health and to make a personal report of the situation.[25]

Everything hinged now on the troops. Could they stop the enemy? Could they even escape? And on these questions, the Commissioners, like every one else, focused their attention.

---

[25] §Commrs. to Cong., May 1, 1776: 4 Force, V., 1166.   Arnold to Sch., Apr. 30, 1776: ib., 1155.   Hazen to Sch., May 1, 1776: Sch. Papers.   Commrs. to Sch., May 10, 1776: Sparks Corres., I., p. 512.   J. Carroll to C. Carroll, Sr.: Carroll, Journal, p. 109.   Winsor, Narr. and Crit. Hist., VI., p. 166.   Chase and Carroll to Cong., May 17, 1776 : 4 Force, VI., 587.   Spy's report: Can. Arch., Q, 12, p. 22. Franklin's return trip: Sparks MSS., No. 60, p. 88.

FROM THOMAS WALKER'S LETTER TO SAMUEL ADAMS, MAY 30, 1776

About noon on the seventh—that is to say, as promptly as possible after the arrival of Thomas—a council of war sat at Deschambault. 'Is it prudent for the army in its present situation to attempt to make a stand at this place?' was the first question laid before it by the president. Three lieutenant-colonels, headed by Antill, voted, Yes, but twelve officers, headed by General Wooster, voted, No; and the Noes had it. Next came the proposition to take post near the mouth of the Sorel; and to this all agreed. Wooster set off promptly; the troops began their preparations to retreat; and the sick, laid as gently as possible in the leaky boats, were rowed away in a pouring rain, some of them half buried in water. It was a dismal, a wretched, even a dreadful scene; and one feature gave it a finishing touch of poignancy. 'Row the boat, row!' sang the bateaumen over and over, incessantly, to a quaint old air. At any other time, the song would have sounded piquantly sweet, but now it seemed weird, almost ghastly, weaving its haunting melody, as it did, through the fear and horror like a sparkling lizard playing in the ribs of a murdered traveller; and the mind struggled in vain to throw off its clinging coils of gloomy fascination.[26]

Thomas understood well the danger of meeting the enemy at Deschambault. To Washington he wrote: We have 'no cannon to prevent their passing the falls of Richelieu, (the only advantageous post to fortify for this purpose); our provisions would not more than subsist the Army for two or three days; we should, therefore labor under the same disadvantages at Deschambault as before Quebeck; the men-of-war would run up the river, intercept all our resources, and soon oblige us to decamp.' He longed, however, to hold this natural fortress. Intrench-

---

[26] § Council: 4 Force, VI., 454. Robbins, Journal.

ments had been laid out and begun ; more of the troops that had followed him from Fort George—raw recruits, to be sure, but healthy and spirited—were coming in ; the wind shifted to the opposite quarter ; the British vessels went down the river ; and the next day, in spite of the council of war, hearing from Arnold that provisions and reinforcements were on the way and floating batteries were to be constructed, he answered that if he could be assured of receiving such aid in a few days, he would make a stand at the falls, putting the men on half-allowance meanwhile. Holding Maxwell at Jacques Cartier, then, as a rear-guard, he still kept about five hundred of his best soldiers with him at Deschambault, and ordered the others to fall back.[27]

Chase and Carroll, who—like the delegates of the French Convention — really commanded the generals, had very little hope of making a good fight at this point ; and when Arnold, on hearing what the council had decided, urged the opposite view, they made objections in writing. They permitted him, however, after hearing that Thomas was holding on there, to load two small vessels with flour, military stores, and what little pork—a mouthful of ten barrels —he could get ; and as soon as possible, the afternoon of the eleventh, he set out for Sorel in advance of his freight, proposing, should there be time, to take the old gondola and proceed to Deschambault with some heavy cannon. ' I tremble,' he said to Schuyler, ' for the fate of our scattered, sick, starved, and distressed Army, as well as for our friends in this country, many of whom will lose their all if we are obliged to evacuate it.' But the time was short, the distance long, the road bad, and the wind fickle.

---

[27] § Thomas to Commrs., May 7, 1776: Sparks MSS., No. 60, p. 83. Id. to Wash., May 8, 1776: 4 Force, VI., 453. Id. to Arnold, May 8, 1776 : ib., 482. Robbins, Journal, May 6, 8. 'Chalmers' Journal, May 8. Letter, May 9, 1776: 4 Force, VI., 452, note. Officer: ib., 398. Shallus, Journal, May 7. REMARK LXXXVII.

LOOKING ACROSS THE RICHELIEU TOWARD SOREL POINT

About a hundred and forty miles lay between the Falls of Richelieu and Montreal, and Arnold's vessels did not reach Sorel until the fifteenth. In the interim, news arrived that Carleton had left Quebec on the tenth to attack the Americans. On the twelfth Thomas called in his rear-guard; and, the next day, with only three pounds of meal per man and not an ounce of meat, he left Deschambault 'with great reluctance' for Three Rivers, two good days' march distant. The Gibraltar of American occupation was lost.[28]

Yet he would not give up even now all hope of fighting there ; and, leaving Maxwell in charge at Three Rivers, he set out as promptly as he could for Sorel to study the possibilities. On the seventeenth or eighteenth he arrived there, 'Steady & Calm,' and looked about him. Greaton's Massachusetts men, whom the officers found it hard to keep from rowing beyond their strength, had made all speed, staring but not stopping at many a new and curious thing, and had arrived at Sorel 'about Sun Down' on the ninth, getting 'a great Shock Indeed' when they learned of 'our People's Defeat at Quebec' and received orders to advance no farther toward the city they had come to take. Paterson's regiment had gone to Montreal ; but the other two sent north by Washington had followed Greaton. Stevens's artillery company, despatched from Cambridge, had reached Three Rivers with their two 13-inch mortars and returned thence to Sorel. The Point Levi party had escaped capture by striking into the interior, and then, re-gaining the St. Lawrence above and sending a canoe across, had obtained enough food to bring them to the same point.

---

[28] § Arnold to Sch., May 10, 11, 1776 : 4 Force, VI., 452, 480. Carroll and Chase to Franklin, May 10 ,1776: Sparks, Corres., I., p. 513. Id. to Sch., May 10, 1776: ib., p. 512. Id. to Id., May 11, 1776: 4 Force, VI., 481. Porter, Diary, May 12. Robbins, Journal, May 13. Vose, Journal, May 15. Spy's report, May 12, 1776: Can. Arch., Q, 12, p. 63. Arnold to Commrs., May 15, 1776 : 4 Force, VI., 580. Thomas to Commrs., May 15, 1776 : ib., 588. Commrs. to Sch., May 17, 1776 : ib., 586. Letter, May 17, 1776: ib., 493. REMARK LXXXVIII.

Five days before Thomas's arrival, there had been about fifteen hundred 'good troops' on the ground, and at that date Poor's had not arrived. Something had been done toward forming a navy. A schooner carrying ten small guns and a gondola equipped with three 24-pounders were now on the river, and behind them floated one row-galley mounting a 12-pounder and several armed bateaux. But, without the four new gondolas building at Chambly, these vessels could not meet the British squadron. Most of the carriages of the heavy cannon, going down to Quebec ahead of the guns, had been captured. Many of the bateaux had no doubt been lost. And above all there was the hard problem of getting the men something to eat.[29]

On hearing of Thomas's retreat from Quebec, the Commissioners had written to Schuyler, 'An immediate supply of provisions from over the Lakes is absolutely necessary.' 'Salted provisions are not in this country,' explained Arnold ; 'very little fresh, and that miserably poor.' What beef Canada could furnish had been nearly exhausted by the middle of April, and no pork at all was now to be obtained there. A small quantity of peas could be found, but no other vegetable. Lee, when appointed to command in Canada, gave notice that he would immediately buy four thousand barrels of pork, and a vote of Congress endorsing his action or supposed action made it look trustworthy; but not a barrel of this meat appeared, and so great a shortage upset calculations. As for the new regiments, they came with only enough provisions to last them ten days.[30]

---

29 § Thomas to Commrs., May 15, 1776: 4 Force, VI., 588. Arnold, May 15: Note 28. Vose, Journal, May 7, 9, 19 (dates unreliable). Sherburne to ———, June 18, 1776: 4 Force, VI., 598. Id. to Paterson, May 18, 1776: Coll. of Mr. F. A. Arnold. Walker to S. Adams, May 30, 1776: S. Adams Papers. Letter, May 14, 1776 : 4 Force, VI., 455. Arnold to Commrs., May 15, 1776: Sparks, Corres., I., p. 514, and (another letter) 4 Force, VI., 580. Thompson to Wash., May 14, 1776: ib., 448. Arnold to Sch., May 3, 1776: Sch. Papers. Id. to Wash., May 8, 1776: 4 Force, VI., 389. Id. to Commrs., May 17, 1776: ib., 592. Commrs. to Sch., May 10, 1776: Sparks, Corres., I., p. 512.

30 § Commrs. to Sch., May 10, 1776: Sparks Corres., I., p. 512. Arnold to Sch. May 11, 1776: 4 Force, VI., 480. Id. to Id., Apr. 20, 1776 : 4 Force, V., 1098.

Sick and well, the Americans at all the posts numbered now, it was estimated, about five thousand. The troops at several points had to be cut down to half-rations. Meat gave out entirely. 'If farther reinforcements are sent without pork to victual the whole Army, our soldiers must perish or feed on each other,' exclaimed the Delegates. Happily, Price — now Deputy Commissary-General of Stores and Provisions—discovered a prospect that bills of exchange for £3,000 lodged with him by Congress could be made available, and the firm of Bondfield managed to loan a sum of specie. Arnold, scouring the country about Sorel with his usual activity, ' purchased ' twenty-seven hundred bushels of wheat; but in that flat region no waterfalls, and therefore no mills, existed. Sending the wheat a long distance to grind and getting it back would take many days; and the owner of it, a ' Prerogative man,' though he had not dared refuse to ' sell,' would certainly help no more than he could be forced to do. Two hundred bags of flour came in from below; three tons bought at Montreal arrived; and twenty of the small Canadian cattle—always thin and poor at the end of the winter—were discovered; but what were all these, put together, among so many? Thomas agreed perfectly with Arnold and Thompson in longing to recover ' that grand pass ' at the Richelieu Rapids; but finally, on the twentieth, he informed the Commissioners that want of provisions made it ' absolutely necessary ' to recall Maxwell's command : and the next day the American garrison, abandoning Three Rivers, filed sadly westward.[31]

Commrs. to Sch., May 11, 1776: 4 Force, VI., 481. Lee's pork: Lee to Hancock. Feb. 27, 1776 (4 Force, IV., 1509); Journ. Cong., Mar. 8 ; W. Liv. to N. Y. Cong., Apr. 7, 1776 (4 Force, V., 813).

[31] § Commrs. to Sch., May 11, 1776: 4 Force, VI., 481. Id. to Cong., May 17, 1776: ib., 587. Arnold to Commrs., May 15, 1776: Sparks Corres., I., p. 514. Id. to Chase, May 15. 1776: 4 Force, VI., 580. Cattle: Stone (ed.), Letters, p. 13. Thompson to Wash., May 14, 1776: 4 Force, VI., 448. Arnold to Commrs., May 17, 1776: ib., 592. Thomas to Commrs., May 15, 20, 1776: ib., 588, 592. Verreau (Badeaux), Invasion, p. 215. Ursul. de. T. Riv., I., p. 369. (See E. Hutchinson to Wheelock, June 18, 1776: Wheelock Papers.)

It was now the intention to remain at Sorel, and, if possible, hold the fertile wedge between the Richelieu River and the St. Lawrence. But the breastwork already standing here was described by Colonel Porter as 'a shiftless thing indeed,' and Thomas found it a Herculean task to accomplish anything. Hardly a trace of military system now existed in his army. Necessary papers had been lost in the retreat or had gone to Montreal with Campbell, though not, like him, of their own accord. Nobody could tell what artillery and ammunition had been saved. Troops were coming, troops were going ; nobody knew how many there were, nor how many there ought to be. 'A number of us, collected without order or regularity, eating up the provisions as fast as they are brought in,' was Thompson's description of the army. Trusted officers were proving unfit. At St. Johns, the base of operations, the troublesome practice of posting sentries was given up. The generals had to be contractors and commissaries ; and the Commissioners, as they reported, had to ' become Generals, Commissaries, Justices of the Peace ; in short, to act in twenty different capacities.' ' We want words,' they groaned, ' We want words to describe the confusion which prevails through every department.'

Most of the men from Quebec had lost their baggage and were now 'naked.' Half-crazed by their trials, some of the troops plundered the house of a prominent Canadian. 'Suicides !' exclaimed Arnold, with just alarm ; but suicide looked no more dreadful to the soldiers than death by starvation. Many of the people flew about like men distracted ; some turned insolent, and

---

3 2 § Mem. of Campbell, Oct. 3, 1785: Cont. Cong. Papers, No. 41, II., p. 388. Papers captured: Maclean to ——, May 25, 1776 (Can. Arch., Q, 12, p. 69). Porter, Diary, Apr. 23: Mag. Am. Hist., Sept., 1893, p. 187. Thompson to Sch., May 19, 1776: Sparks MSS., No. 60, p. 86. Thomas to Commrs., May 15, 1776: 4 Force, VI., 588. Arnold to Commrs., May 17, 1776: ib., 592. Commrs. to Cong., May 17, 1776: ib., 587. Id. to Sch., May 17, 1776: ib., 586. Chase and Carroll to Franklin, May 10, 1776: Sparks, Corres., I., p. 513.

I concurrence with us. The Dr. has given you but a faint idea of the impertinences of our fellow traveller. The Lady had the appearance that is that the commissioners had advised with & were governed by towards enquiring who those loris were, she mentioned Dr. Robinson. Suppose the woman had so dreamed; for I believe none of you remember having seen such a man, tho' I recollect his name amongst the list of persons.

Gentlemen, I am with earnest wishes for your happiness,

Dr Gentlemen

Yr most sincere friend & humble Servt

J. Carroll

New York May 23- 1786

JOHN CARROLL'S REPORT ON MRS. WALKER'S CONDUCT

others gave the Americans false information. The small-pox, mysterious and horrible, struck such terror into the well that they almost ran from their own shadows. The enemy were coming; but nobody undertook to tell when, where, nor how many. ' No provisions, nor supplies, only men; nor half enough of them,' said one of the sufferers. Thomas, Arnold, and Thompson, to judge by their letters, remained cool, cheerful, and active; but they assumed the right of appointing officers, and probably felt driven to various other irregularities. Doubtless many below them imitated their virtues; but a lack of confidence, 'a strange discouragement' that was perhaps not so strange, after all, and even a spirit of selfish jealousy, spread from tent to tent. 'Our days are days of darkness,' mourned Chaplain Robbins.[33]

To make head against all this, Thomas needed the most absolute authority that ever a general possessed; but the pillar he should have been able to lean upon became a millstone about his neck. The mere presence of the Commissioners made him subordinate to men who, as they readily confessed, had ' neither abilities nor inclination' to command, and gave to his officers a court of appeal. Thompson, instead of reporting to him, went over to confer with Chase and Carroll, now back at Montreal, and they embodied his views in a letter of instructions to his superior. Indeed, they did not hesitate to invite letters from a subordinate officer. What was even more serious, they ignored all grades among the generals. Their idea of managing things was to have 'a meeting' of these men, ' to consult about and agree upon' a course of operations. They recommended a friendly correspondence and a free exchange of opinions among them. In a word, the town-meeting system of discipline, which had caused

[33] § Arnold to Chase, May 15, 1776: 4 Force VI., 580. Robbins, Journal, May 10, 12, 13, 16. Commrs. to Cong., May 17, 1776: 4 Force, VI., 587.

Montgomery so much trouble, was now introduced by authority. 'Sentiments,' instead of orders, became the word. To discuss, not to obey, was the rule. The methods of agitation replaced the methods of command ; and, on the complaint of a subordinate, they censured Thomas for taking what he considered a needful step ' without the least consultation with the General Officers'.[34]

This line of policy completed the achievements of the unlucky board, and, added to the other effects of their administration, marked them as Apostles of Confusion. The ' small-pox ' and the ' Commissioners of Congress ' were bracketed together as the chief scourges of the ill-starred Americans in Canada,—only the Delegates were commonly placed first. ' I have not seen a man of any party in the Army or out of it,' wrote a gentleman at Albany to Boudinot, ' who does not agree that the Commissioners have been the principal cause of all the confusion that hath reigned there.' Mrs. Walker's bitter tongue accused them to their faces of being governed by the Tories, and her husband charged them roundly with betraying their trust. Disqualified by talents and by training to command ; disqualified by their official position to obey ; convinced they had failed ; well able to see that many looked upon them as a curse ; without a function, without even a ' fixed abode ' ; appointed to win an empire but condemned to watch a sick-bed ; flitting anxiously from pillar to post and from post back to pillar in the vain hope of accomplishing something, they longed intensely to get away, yet had not even the power to leave. ' The possession of this country,' they admitted to Hancock, ' must finally be decided by the sword. We think our stay here no longer of service to the publick . . . and

---

[34] § Commrs. to Cong., May 17, 27, 1776 : 4 Force, VI., 587, 589. Thompson to Sch., May 19, 1776 : Sparks MSS., No. 60, p. 86. Commrs. to Thomas, May 26, 1776 : Sparks, Corres., I., p. 518. Arnold to Chase, May 15, 1776 : 4 Force, VI., 580.

we wait with impatience the further orders of Congress.' [35]

'Chase seems pleased with his trip to Canady,' wrote Gunning Bedford; but that was before he went. [36]

---

[35] § Caldwell, June 11, 1776: Emmet Coll. J. Carroll to Chase and C. Carroll, May 28, 1776: ib. Walker to S. Adams, May 30, 1776: S. Adams Papers. Commrs. to Sch., May 17, 1776: 4 Force, IV., 586. Id. to Cong., May 17: ib., 587.

[36] Bedford to ———, Mar. 20, 1776: Dreer Coll.

XXXII

THE CEDARS.

'A PROSPEROUS turn in our affairs,' the Commissioners felt, even when praying to be recalled, might still set the finances on a working basis.[1] That would mean a return of confidence, and out of confidence might soon grow better order and a better spirit.

The retreat from Quebec had been 'the principal source of all the disorders' in the army, they assured Congress; and certainly it was a great one. It meant almost the overthrow of organization; and an army without organization is a mob. It meant a loss of material that could not easily be replaced. It meant a fearful drop in morale. Moreover, bad as it was, the disaster had looked even worse. Few understood how logically it came to pass. Affairs at Quebec had been regarded by most people as fairly promising; Thomas himself did not realize the state of things before he reached the ground. The news of a rout came when tidings of a victory were expected; and it seemed irrational, incredible, monstrous. A 'disgraceful flight,' exclaimed the Commissioners. A 'shameful retreat,' echoed Thompson. Besides, report exaggerated the facts as usual. Maclean heard that the Americans 'made no Stop till they came to the Sorell River, 140 miles from Quebec and 40 from Montreal.'[2]

---

[1] Chase and Carroll to Hancock, May 17, 1776: 4 Force, VI., 587.

[2] § Chase and C. : Note 1. Thomas: see his letters already cited, and Vose, Journal, May 19. J. Caldwell to Boudinot, May 15, 7776: Emmet Coll. Thompson to Sch., May 19, 1776: Sparks MSS., No. 60, p. 86. Maclean to ——, May 25, 1776 : Can Arch., Q, 12, p. 69.

Little by little, however, the truth could not fail to be realized. It had already been decided in a council to retire, and the movement had begun in proper order. Only a sudden turn in the wind had brought the English fleet at that critical hour. The defection of the Canadian teamsters made it impossible to save the stores. No muskets fit for use or even worth repairing were thrown away.[3] The actual panic had extended but little—possibly not at all—beyond the men with small-pox in their veins and the soldiers forced to serve after they were legally free.[4] A stand might have been made on the Plains of Abraham, had not a cool and fearless general seen that retreat was the only logical course. For nearly a week Maxwell's Jersey volunteers, looking very trim and soldierly in their blue and white,[5] remained on guard within about thirty miles of Quebec. Their withdrawal was due, not to a lack of spirit, but to a lack of food, and, as the French representative in England noted with pleasure, the British had not come near enough the Provincial troops during the retreat to kill, wound, or capture a single man of them.[6] One victory now, even a modest one, to jog the wheels of confidence, might soon put the campaign on its feet again ; and, for some time, a good chance for such a turn had already been preparing.

An evident advantage of holding Montreal was that British supplies and presents could not reach the interior that way, and the savages found themselves at the mercy of the Colonies for their clothing, guns, ammunition, and trinkets. But this rose, like all roses, had its thorn. The Americans, cut off in turn from their own source of supply—Great Britain—could not furnish what the sav-

---

[3] British Return, Can. Arch., Q, 12, p. 75.
[4] REMARK LXXXIX.
[5] Uniform: Cf. Ainslie, Journal, Mar. 30, with Hodgkinson's expression ' Jersey Blues ' in his letter of Apr. 27, 1776 (Penna. Mag., X., p. 158).
[6] Garnier to Vergennes, June 11, 1776: Stevens Facsim., No. 873.

ages desired. Schuyler described himself as 'daily tormented by parties of Indians from all quarters' in search of goods, and it was very easy to suspect, as he did, that some of the neighborly Tories, realizing the embarrassment of the patriots, egged on the willing savages to

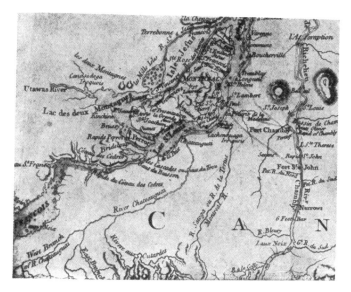

FROM FADEN'S AMERICAN ATLAS, 1777

demand what could not be supplied. The natural result came in high prices; and of that, as well as an actual scarcity, very loud complaints rolled in from the forest. Schuyler did what he could; Congress promised to exert 'strenuous endeavors'; but the problem remained unsolved; and Colonel John Butler of Niagara—acting as the Indian Superintendent in the absence of Guy Johnson—found it easy enough, when the Iroquois chiefs gathered at the grand council-house of Onondaga, the first of April, to have a demand publicly voiced for obtaining supplies by the way of Quebec once more.[7]

Nor was Butler's the only British hand masked with Indian bronze. Colonel Caldwell of the 8th Regiment, planted at Detroit, worked upon the wild tribes of that still savage region ; the post at Michilimackinack aided him ; and a rotten old fort—recently strengthened—overlooking the rich meadows at the mouth of the Oswegatchie,[8] marked another ganglion in the cord of British influence.[9]

The American leaders were not so short-sighted that posts like these could escape their notice. In 1775, Commissioners of Congress had visited Fort Pitt in order to secure the neutrality of the savages in that quarter, and they heartily endorsed a scheme of their secretary, Arthur St. Clair, to surprise Detroit. Four or five hundred young men enlisted for the expedition ; but, after many weeks of delay, the Congress disapproved of it on the ground that Arnold would capture Quebec and make the trouble unnecessary, but really, as St. Clair believed, because enough gunpowder could not be spared. A little later came other hints. ' The Forts of Niagara and Detroit, are an object which I make no doubt the Hon[ble] Congress have in View,' wrote Arnold to Philadelphia soon after the ball was taken from his leg ; and Schuyler longed to cut the British nerve at Niagara, provided the Indians thereabouts would give their consent. But the

---

[7] § Sch. to Wash., Feb. 14, 1776: 4 Force, IV., 1146. Id. to Hancock, Feb. 10, 1776 : ib., 990. Dean, Journal: 4 Force, V., 1100. R. Butler to Wilson, Apr. 8, 1776 : ib., 815. Journ. Cong., Nov. 23, 1775. Sch. to Hancock, Jan. 31, 1776 : 4 Force, IV., 898.

[8] Now Ogdensburg, N. Y.

[9] § Caldwell : Précis of Oper. Twiss, Report on Osweg., Aug. 8, 1778 : Can. Arch., B, 154, p. 29. Narrative : 4 Force, II., 1504. Carleton to Dartmouth, June 7, 1775 : Pub. Rec. Off., Colon. Corres., Quebec, 11, p. 283.

Congress had enough on its hands already, and the British agents were permitted to keep at work.[10]

Cutting deeper than a mere temporary question of supplies, they now warned the Indians over and over against the 'insincerity' of the Colonials. No doubt they pointed often at the continual encroachments of the white waves; and certainly they prophesied that, if successful against the King, the practiced arms of a greedy people would soon be turned against their too confiding neighbors. It was an old song, this, a favorite air of Colonel Johnson's, and rather hackneyed; but some one, reported Kirkland, 'had lately trumped it up so high, that it sounded very briskly in a savage ear.' Unluckily, too, an island in the Ohio River a little below Fort Pitt was surveyed about this time by a party of whites in violation of the Fort Stanwix treaty, and that fact gave a strong color to the prediction. While the Oneidas remained firm for neutrality, the 'face of things' toward the setting sun began to change, as Kirkland saw; British presents, reaching the north and east by way of the Mississippi, stimulated the hostile sentiment; the Mohawks went and came incessantly between Johnson Hall and Niagara; the tribes nearer Detroit declared they were ready to move; James Dean, journeying to attend the council at Onondaga, learned that a plot had been laid to kill him there; and Colonel Butler, announcing a grand meeting of the Indians to be held at Niagara the first of May, summoned McKee to attend it in language that suggested something important: 'It is Colonel Caldwell's orders, and mine.'[11]

Schuyler, though well aware that many of the Indians

[10] § St. Clair, Narrative, pp. 232, 233. Arnold to Cong., Jan. 12, 1776: Sparks MSS., No. 52, II., p. 34. Sch. to Hancock, Feb. 15, 1776 : 4 Force, IV., 1156.

[11] § Dean, Journal: 4 Force, V., 1100. Id. to Sch., Mar. 10, 1776 : ib., 768. Kirkland to Sch., Mar. 12, 1776: ib., 772. R. Butler to Wilson, Apr. 8, 1776: ib., 815. Presents: Extract in Tryon's of Apr. 28, 1776 (Pub. Rec. Off., Am. and W. I., Vol. 186, p. 646). Tryon to Dartmouth, Feb. 8, 1776: Pub. Rec. Off., Am. and W. I., Vol. 186, p. 305. J. Butler to McKee, Feb. 29, 1776: 4 Force, V., 818.

were unfriendly, did not think there was reason to fear them ' in general'; and he believed that the fact of Howe's evacuating Boston, which he carefully published among them, would cool their spirits not a little. In Canada, however, as winter melted away, less optimism ruled. Wooster, who could banish the Canadians from his esteem by rating them only a little higher than the Indians, could excuse himself still more effectually from prizing the Indians by placing them a little lower than the Canadians. ' The Savages hereabouts are cool,' reported Colonel Hazen from Montreal, the first of April; ' they keep aloof from us; we are to expect little or no friendship from them, and, indeed, little or no precaution has been taken for that purpose.' An unlucky embarrassment arose about the Caughnawagas, for they wished to enter the American service, but it was thought unadvisable, on account of the expense, to accept them. On their way to Canada, the Commissioners of Congress fell in with the northern deputies returning from Onondaga, and were given a promise to surrender the war-hatchet presented to their tribes by Guy Johnson the year before; but, on a suspicious pretext, the ceremony of handing it over was put off.[12]

Early in March, Lorimier, who had been the most active white leader of the Indians about St. Johns during the summer of 1775, ' stole away into the upper country ' with two comrades, and about the same time warnings began to come down. Walker, who doubtless had business connections above, notified two members of Congress on the seventh of the month that a hostile expedition might be expected from that quarter. About the same time, Wooster had ' great reason to believe,' he said, that

---

[12] § Sch. to Hancock, Apr. 2, 1776: 4 Force, V., 767. Hazen to Sch., Apr. 1, 1776: ib., 751. Caughnawagas: Wash. to Sch., Jan. 27, 1776 (4 Force, IV., 872); Sch. to Wash., Feb. 14, 1776 (ib., 1146). Commrs. to Hancock, May 6, 1776: 4 Force, V., 1214.

people at Montreal were keeping up a correspondence with Oswegatchie and Niagara, and, from a 'number of circumstances' discovered among the Caughnawagas, he feared that a plan had been laid to bring down the British troops, with what Canadians could be gathered near those points, a number of Indian traders and their workmen, and a body of savages, for a dash against Montreal. Some said the purpose was to open a way for Guy Johnson to return. The Quebeckers understood that it was intended to relieve their city. At Three Rivers, wrote Captain Goforth, reports were 'various': according to some, Montreal was to be cut off, while others believed the Indians would avoid that place, hurry down to rescue their father, Carleton, and so recover their trade.[13]

Wooster despatched a polyglot Indian, contributed by President Wheelock of Dartmouth College, to 'find out the truth,' but the essential point was evident enough already. Such widespread rumors betokened a serious attack; and when Lorimier, coming down within some thirty miles of Montreal, about the middle of April, with a fleet of bateaux and a party of soldiers from Oswegatchie, enlisted what men he could, preached massacre to the Indians, boasted that eight hundred savages with the British garrisons above and all the French inhabitants of that region would be down in twenty days, and carried back a fleet-load of supplies, the 'great convulsions' produced in that part of the country were a tocsin sufficiently wild.[14]

Congress, however, was not idle. Besides again promising the Indians, early in April, to obtain goods for them

---

[13] § Hazen to Antill, Mar. 10, 1776: Can. Arch., B, 27, p. 387. Walker to S. Adams, May 30, 1776: S. Adams Papers. Wooster to Sch., Mar. 5, 1776 : 4 Force, V., 416. Kirkland to Sch., Mar. 12, 1776: ib., 772. Ainslie, Journal, Mar. 13. Goforth (evidently some time before Apr. 1): 4 Force, V., 871. (See Badeaux in Verreau, Invasion, p. 193.)

[14] §Wooster to Sch., Mar. 5, 1776: 4 Force, V., 416. Wheelock to Wooster, Feb. 6, 1776: Wheelock Papers. Hazen to Antill, Apr. 20, 1776: Can. Arch., B, 27, p. 398. Spy: Can. Arch., Q, 12, p. 22.

and appropriating ten thousand dollars, a month later, for presents and the expenses of treaty-making, it settled in their favor the question of reopening the Indian traffic in Canada. That was a very grave and very difficult problem. In February, a committee of Montreal merchants went all the way to Philadelphia with a petition for the restoration of their trade, while Walker and Price attended Congress to show what risks it involved. Walker

THE LACHINE RAPIDS

believed that such a measure would supply the hostile posts above with ' Men, provisions & Goods for presents to the Savages '; and Schuyler, probably enlightened by Walker and Price on their way south, pointed out the weakness of the petitioners ' case as well as the danger of obliging them.[15]

But Congress doubtless thought it no more than honor-

15 § Journ. Cong., Mar. 20 ; Apr. 6 ; May 6, 1776. Wooster to Cong., Feb. 11, 1776: 4 Force, IV., 1001. Walker to S. Adams, May 30, 1776: S. Adams Papers. Sch. to Hancock, Feb. 20, 1776: 4 Force, IV., 1214.

able to keep its promises to the Indians in the only fashion
that could be discovered ; and the Commissioners, immediately on arriving in Canada, offered passports to all
traders who would ' enter into certain engagements to do
nothing in the upper country prejudicial to the Continental interests.' A busy squadron of flat-boats, thirty or
forty feet long and pointed at both ends, were soon jostling
and scraping at Lachine. Bales and boxes tumbled into
them fast. A towing line was coiled in each of the bows.
As quickly as possible, the loose, flapping sail was unfurled. The oars dipped ; a long pole wriggled in the
place of a rudder; and the traders were off,—some of
them, like Bindon, friendly to the Americans, but others
distinctly not. Had Congress and the Commissioners
acted wisely in granting this favor ? A whale has been
supposed to content himself—temporarily, at least—with
a tub: was it a whale that had floundered up the Mississippi and round into Lake Ontario, or had a shark stolen
in there to roil its blue waters ? [16]

About thirty miles above Montreal, the St. Lawrence
makes a sharp twist both horizontal and vertical. The
consequences are a bend as tense as a yew long-bow and
rapids that sweep round it, through rocks and verdure-clad
islets, with the rushing whirr of a cloth-yard shaft ; while
the highlands come down close just there, and even dip
their feet in the clear, rushing current. This place is the
Cedars ; and Colonel Hazen, temporarily in command at
Montreal, besides trying to establish a line of friendly
Indians against the danger from above, directed that stalwart scytheman and bold fighter, Timothy Bedel, to occupy this point, entrench, and be ready to defend the pass.
Shortly after, Arnold arrived from Quebec and confirmed

---

[16] § Commrs. to Hancock, May 1, 1776: 4 Force, V., 1166.   Spy: Can. Arch.,
Q, 12, p. 22.   Bouchette, Descr. Topog., p. 138.   Bindon, Memorial : Cont.
Cong. Papers, No. 41, II., p. 134.

the order. Bedel himself, however, did not move that way for some time ; but Major Butterfield, with something like half a regiment and two pieces of cannon, reached the spot about the twenty-sixth of April, and proceeded to build a stockade and a breastwork at the water's edge, placing his artillery so as to command both river and shore. The one gateway from the upper country seemed now quite solidly barred.[17]

Bedel took the small-pox not later than April the twenty-second, and, as he knew the precise day, he apparently took it by inoculation,—contrary to orders. It was the sixth of May when he arrived at the Cedars, and, as he

Timo Bedel Coll

entered the stockade, his brow hung dark with clouds. He had set out for Canada supposing that Quebec had fallen, but found that Montgomery, who got on well with him and everybody else, had met that fate instead, and that Arnold now ruled at Montreal. To command an almost independent post of the highest importance was what every brave and enterprising officer coveted, and the resources given Bedel, considering what the Americans possessed in Canada, seemed fairly ample ; yet he appeared to feel that Arnold had shown a hostile spirit in ordering him to the Cedars. Beckoning Frye Bayley to the breastwork, he demanded:

' How do you like it ? '

---

[17] § Inoculation was the introduction of unmodified small-pox virus. Lovell, Gazet., p. 279. Hazen to Antill, Apr. 20, 1776: Can. Arch., B, 27, p. 398. Arnold to Sch., Apr. 20, 1776: 4 Force, V., 1098. Id. to Wash., May 8, 1776: 4 Force, VI., 389. Verreau (Sanguinet), Invasion, p. 106. Bayley, Narrative. Aldrich: N. H. Hist. Soc. Proc., III., p. 208. REMARK XC.

' I 'm no judge,' replied Bayley, ' but it seems to me very nice and strong.'

' It is,' assented the Colonel, ' but too large.' In his judgment, the men there were not more than a quarter enough, and no reinforcements could be expected.

' I 'm unfortunate,' he added, gloomily ; ' I know not what my fate is to be.'

Very different every way seemed this man from the radiant and self-sacrificing Bedel who had written to the New Hampshire Committee of Safety a few months before : ' I have done all in my power for the good of the cause, and have brought cannon down the river, by the Fort of St. John's, and sent them to Chambly, and taken that post without the loss of a man '; and also, in a postscript : ' This moment I have got possession of St. John's . . . . and to-morrow shall march for Montreal,'—exploits that somehow got entangled with the names of Brown, Livingston, Dugan, and Montgomery. But it was a fact that, when he reached the Cedars, he had begun to suffer from the small-pox, and the next day he could not keep an appointment with Bayley.[18]

Nine days later, early in the morning, he stepped from a boat at the landing-place, Montreal, walked up to headquarters, and announced that some Indians and British troops from the upper country had come down to attack the Cedars. It was true. May twelfth, Captain Forster, under orders from Colonel Caldwell to deliver Montreal, had set out from Oswegatchie with thirty or forty regulars, a few British volunteers, some Canadians, and about a hundred and sixty Indians. Two days later, he arrived at St. Regis and called a council. The chiefs declined to stir, but gave the young men permission to go, if they would ; and forty or fifty of these joined the expedition.

18 § Bayley, Narrative. Bedel, Oct. 27, 1775: 4 Force, III., 1207.

AN EXTRACT FROM FRYE BAYLEY'S NARRATIVE

FROM A MEMORANDUM BY SAMUEL ADAMS, AUGUST 1, 1776

On the sixteenth he advanced again. A report of Bedel's fortifications and strength discouraged the Indians greatly, but news of the American retreat from Quebec arrived in the nick of time. The night of the seventeenth found the party camping at Devil's Point, about seven miles above the Cedars; and the next morning, while the canoes and boats dropped stealthily down in the shadows of the forested shore, a large band of the redskins, gotten up like so many individual nightmares, moved on by land, and crept, crawled, glided, slid and wriggled through the dense woods, in every horrid style of imp and serpent locomotion, into the neighborhood of the fort.[19]

The soil at the Cedars was peculiarly rich, and the sheltered situation especially favorable for agriculture. Before

---

[19] The chief British authority for Forster's expedition is a detailed narrative signed by Andrew Parke, Captain in the 8th regiment of Foot, J. Maurer, of the L. R. Yorkers, and Hugh Mackay, A. D. V., and also endorsed by Forster himself, entitled 'The Authentic Narrative of Facts relating to the Exchange of Prisoners taken at the Cedars.' (The author has not found a copy of this in America.) This was avowedly prepared as a defence against the American charges, but, in addition to the presumption in favor of four officers, bears numerous marks of care and good faith. A French version has been published by Marcel Ethier. Other British sources: Forster to Butterfield, May 19, 1776 (Lib. Cong., U. S. Revol., I., p. 1320); Carleton to Germain, May 25, 1776 (4 Force, VI., 575); Id. to Id., June 2, 1776 (Can. Arch., Q, 12, p. 57); Maclean to ———, May 25, 1776 (ib., p. 69); Cramahé to Germain, May 25, 1776 (ib., p. 50); Précis of Oper.; Cannon, 8th Foot, p. 67; Verreau, Invasion (Sanguinet), p. 131; (Berthelot), p. 236. American sources (the writers and dates of letters—1776 if not dated—indicate in a way to what part of the operations they chiefly relate): Commrs. to Sch., May 16 (4 Force, VI., 578); Id. to Hancock, May 17 (ib., 587); Id. to Id., May 27 (ib., 589); Id. to Thomas, May 26 (Sparks, Corres., I., p. 518); Sullivan to Sch., May 27 (4 Force, VI., 609); Sherburne to Paterson, May 18 (Coll. of F. A. Arnold); Id. to ———, June 18 (4 Force, VI., 598); Petition (N. H. State Papers, XIV., p. 476); Chase to Sch., May 31 (Sparks MSS., No. 60, p. 90); Arnold to Commrs., May 25 (ib., No. 52, II., p. 41); Id. to Id. (with Cartel), May 27 (ib., p. 42); Id. to Id., June 2 (5 Force, I., 165); Id. to ———, May 28 (Conn. Gazette, June 21, 1776); Letter, May 17 (4 Force, VI., 493); Letter (Sherburne's expedition), undated (ib., 598, note); Walker to S. Adams, May 30 (S. Adams Papers); Affidavits of Butterfield, Estabrook, and Wilkins (5 Force, I., 165, 166); Hazen, Statement (Lib. Cong., U. S. Revol., IV., Sept. 3, 1778); Bayley, Narrative; Journals of Vose, Shallus, Wells, Senter, Porterfield (Va. Mag., 1901, p. 146); Account (4 Force, VI., 599, note); Bliss to Emerson, Aug. 14 (Cont. Cong. Papers, Letters, B, 78, II., p. 79); E. to J. Sullivan, Aug. 14 (Can. Arch., B, 181, p. 32); E. Sullivan, Petition (Cont. Cong. Papers, No. 42, VII., p. 51); Wilkinson, Memoirs, I., p. 41 (W.'s letter of May 24 is also in 4 Force, VI., 566); Journ. Cong., June 15, 20, 24; July 10, 23; S. Adams, Mem., Aug., 1, 1776 (S. Adams Papers): Trumbull to Williams, July 26, 1776 (Hinman, Conn., p. 560). The newspapers contained accounts, but these add very little except errors. The cartel may be found also in 4 Force, VI., 597; Can. Arch., Q, 12, p. 59; Carleton Papers, I., p. 30. Some points of 'local color' from Bouchette, Descr. Topog. See also Dawson, Canad. Monthly, V., p, 305, who prints two letters.

May-day, the spring wheat had stood three inches high. The finest horses in Canada were raised there. Cows must have been kept, and stocks of grain must have been on hand. Butterfield, left in charge by Bedel, had the small-pox, to say the least of it ; but he was well enough to do business, and, with his three days' notice of the coming attack, might probably have filled the stockade to the eyes with provisions. Only a feeble effort, if any at all, was made ; and yet, on May eighteenth, when the attack began, there were supplies enough—counting five or six horses—to last the garrison at a pinch for, say, a week.[20] As for ammunition, while this, like every other post, lacked a full store, the bullets in the soldiers' pouches, if only one in twelve or fifteen should bite, could put every man of Forster's out of action ; one of the cannon could fire thirty rounds, and the other, if it would accept a pound of musket-balls as a charge of grape, twenty ; and there was powder enough besides, were every shot in vain, to blow the breastwork and the enemy with it into a cloud of dust. Forster, on the other side, had now rolled up his force of Indians to three or four hundred and his Canadians to at least one hundred ; but he had no cannon, and—as any one could have predicted and the sequel showed—a stout resistance would soon have discouraged and scattered his motley force. It was a splendid opportunity to prove American valor, send these painted imps yelping home up the pass, and perhaps turn the tide of fortune below.

Forster began by summoning the fort, intimating that in case of a refusal to surrender, the savages would allow no quarter ; and Butterfield consented to give up the position, if he might retire with his men and their arms. These terms were not accepted, however, and the guns

---

[20] REMARK XCI.

opened. After a time, Captain Wilkins got permission to go out and drive the enemy from a barn that stood too near. On calling for volunteers, nearly all the men stepped forward; and, sallying sharply, they taught the Canadians and Indians a lesson. But Butterfield, when he realized that scarcely a guard for his own valuable person had been left in the works, ordered the troops in, and back Wilkins had to come, literally weeping with disgust and wrath.

Sunday morning, the nineteenth, found a breastwork or intrenchment raised against the fort not very far away, and the grand onslaught seemed likely to come that night. Forster, however, had already been shown a tip of the white feather, and preferred to summon the Americans again. 'By entreaty,' he informed Butterfield, he had 'overcome the resolution formed by the savages, of allowing no quarter'; and, in order 'to take the advantage of their present favourable turn,' he proposed that the garrison should 'surrender at discretion in half an hour' In this way, and in this way only, they could save their 'lives and the cloathes' they had on. Such a proposition was an insult; but, in spite of the entreaties and indignation of his men, Butterfield agreed to it. Nearly four hundred plucky fellows—hardly scratched as yet, if scratched at all—were thrown neck and crop to the savages merely to save their commander's skin from the risk of a needed ventilation. It was a clear case of poltroonery, tempered only by the small-pox.

On hearing that a hostile party threatened the Cedars, Colonel Paterson, then at Montreal, detached a hundred and forty men of his regiment with orders to carry up supplies for the garrison as well as to reinforce it, and Major Sherburne — 'a bold stout courageous-looking man '—took command of them. Bedel accompanied the party; but at Lachine his illness, which had obligingly permitted him to leave the fort, declined positively to allow his return, and the relief-party moved on without him.[21] Pursuing the main road to upper Canada, they came to St. Anne, on the edge of Montreal Island. A

delay occurred there about boats, and they could not proceed to the mainland on the seventeenth; but, early the next morning, the provisions and a guard crossed, with orders to obtain carts and hurry the supplies forward.

RUINS OF THE FORT AT ST. ANNE

' Capt Bliss went upon that Business but before he had got 2 Miles from the Landing Place, he was met by a Scouting Party of Savages and made prisoner,' reported Sherburne. Consequently no carts appeared; but in their stead came swarms of Canadians 'with The most horrid Accts. Imaginable of their being Vast numbers of Indians in and about The Woods,' and with news of an attack upon the fort, 'Confirmed . . . by the Repeated Discharge of Cannon.' Sherburne, after remaining in a posture of defence at the landing all day, received a note from Bliss containing messages from the priest who acted as his jailer, and Lorimier, who served as head terrorizer. The upshot of it all was that four or five hundred Canadians and Indians were near at hand, and, unless the relief-party would surrender, it could expect no quarter. Bliss vouched for nothing of this himself; but the Major, thinking it 'most proper to Retreat as Soon as possible, . . . Immediately Ordered as many men into the Boats as Could possibly Stow [themselves] in them which was not more than One half' of the detachment, but among whom he thought-

---

[21] REMARK XCII.

fully included himself.   Happily, however, as no enemies or very few were near, the rest also were eventually ferried over.[22]

Sherburne expected an immediate attack and sent back to Montreal for aid, but the enemy failed to appear ; and the next morning things wore another face.   Daylight itself was cheering.   The woods, gently swaying in the wind, suggested only peace.   Very possibly he weighed the note from Bliss more carefully now.   The cannon fire had ceased.   Perhaps the story came to his ear which Walker heard : that Forster's party had been routed.   At all events he tried to embark ; but a ' very violent ' wind prevented him from doing more that day than rescue his imprisoned captain.   Bliss very likely scoffed at the fearful tales of Canadians and Indians ; and finally, on the twentieth, Sherburne crossed, set out for the Cedars, and went bravely on about half the distance, as he thought.

Forster, on hearing the evening before that a reinforcement was coming, hardly knew what to do, for so many stout prisoners required a large guard ; but he ordered Lorimier to look after it with a party of Indians, aided by some Canadians.   Accordingly, some eighty of the redskins and eighteen of their allies, posting themselves at a good place in the woods, opened fire on Sherburne about noon, with yells enough, undoubtedly, to people the whole forest with devils.   Sherburne—even after they sallied into the open—saw five hundred of them besides ' a large party ' more.   According to his feelings, the skirmish became a gory affair, and lasted an hour and forty minutes ; though by the testimony of three British officers his surrender was ' so sudden ' that another party of Canadians, despatched on the same business, could not get up in time, and only five or six of the Americans were killed.

---

[22] The quotations are from Sherburne's report to Paterson (Note 19). REMARK XCIII.

About forty of the relief expedition had been left on the way from Montreal for one reason or another ; but almost a hundred men laid down their arms unconditionally, and, like so many eels from a mud-hole, had the clothes ripped from their backs by the grinning and prancing savages.

St. Anne boasted a fort. It was a small affair, built only for defense against Indian muskets ; but Bedel's artillery could not be brought down from the Cedars in a moment, and, though garrisoned by only twenty-five men with no more than ten rounds of ammunition, the post had strength enough to halt the enemy for a time by putting on a bold front. Captain Young, however, the commander there, was a man who ' fought great battles at a distance,' according to Frye Bayley's description. Besides, he possessed altogether too much generosity to outshine his superiors, and, on a report that some Indians had landed near, he took himself out of their way without even delaying to carry off the provisions and stores. The road to Montreal was now clear ; and Forster—sending the American officers to prison, with two priests for turnkeys, at the Indian village of Conosadaga, which had taken his side, and consigning the privates to the charge of some Canadians—pushed on for his goal. Reinforcements from the neighborhood came in, though not nearly what he expected ; and, after posting the necessary guards, he still had some five hundred men.

Montreal was listening eagerly for his drums. Hazen a month before had declared, ' There is nothing but plotting & preparations making against us throughout the whole District.' When it was proposed to abandon the town after the news of the flight from Quebec arrived, Arnold feared that the people would attack his departing troops. On all sides the Tories, whom Ripley had found ' very plenty ' in March but mostly living ' like Wood-

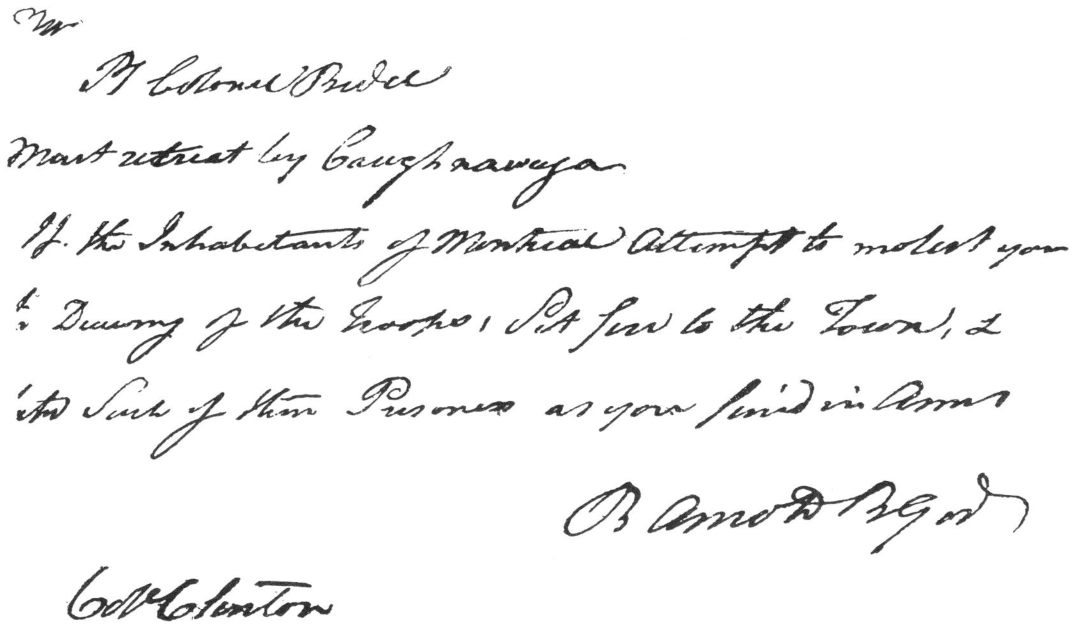
Sir

By Colonel Bedel

Must retreat by Caughnawaga

If the Inhabitants of Montreal Attempt to molest you

in Decamping of the Troops, Set fire to the Town, &

take Such of them Prisoners as you find in Arms

B Arnold B Genl

Col Clinton

POSTSCRIPT OF ARNOLD'S LETTER TO CLINTON, MAY 12, 1776

chucks underground ,' were now showing noses and even teeth. The Commissioners, getting ' daily intimations of plots hatching and insurrections intended ,' had abandoned perforce the rôle of dispensing pure liberty, filled the jails with malcontents, and sent others into the exile they had lately protested against ; but these measures did not reach the seat of the trouble. Night after night, as a sequel to Butterfield's collapse, a rising was talked of and expected ; and Lieutenant-Colonel Vose would go round the barracks, waken the men coming down with small-pox, and make them dress themselves and load their guns. ' If they do take us it shall not be for nothing ,' he quietly said ; but he could promise nothing more.[23]

At length, however, though none too soon, Forster met something hard. Arnold, hurrying up from Sorel, threw himself with a hundred men across the road at Lachine, and began to dig intrenchments like mad round a heavy stone barn or storehouse that he found there,—built perhaps by the famous La Salle, to whom the seigneury had belonged.[24] Some other troops—partly of Greaton's regiment—marched up, and Arnold at once began studying how to reach the enemy. But it soon looked as if there would be no difficulty about that. Friday evening, May the twenty-fourth, British drums could be heard in his lines. Forster's exultant horde was only a league distant. An American soldier was shot in the thigh within half a mile of the camp, and another man was taken prisoner. ' We shall be attacked within six hours ,' wrote James Wilkinson at midnight in a gloomy valedictory to General Greene ; ' The morning dawns—that morning big with the fate of a few, a handful of brave fellows.'

---

[23] § Hazen to Antill, Apr. 20, 1776 : Can. Arch., B, 27, p. 398. Arnold to Clinton, May 12, 1776 : Emmet Coll. Ripley to J. Wheelock, Mar. 7, 1776: Wheelock Papers. Commrs. to Hancock, May 8, 1776 : 4 Force, V., 1237. Walker to S. Adams, May 30, 1776: S. Adams Papers. Vose, Journal, May 25, 28.

[24] Parkman, Old Régime, p. 240.

But Forster's allies in Montreal had notified him of Arnold's operations and the gathering of reinforcements. Indeed, they drew so effectually on rumor or fancy that he supposed there were fifteen hundred men and eight cannon in the camp at Lachine that evening, and believed that a thousand more troops would arrive the next day. During the night, therefore, he beat a very quick retreat, and soon brought up at the Cedars with only eighty out of some six hundred standing by him, ' caused by most of the Canadians having returned home through fear, and the fickle disposition of the savages, who wandered as their fancy led them ,' and, seeing no further hopes of plunder, preferred to make off with their booty.[25] Nearly two hundred came back, when the truth about Arnold's force became known ; but evidently Montreal could not be taken. Retreat was in order, and what to do with almost five hundred prisoners became a serious problem.

No doubt the Indian rule in similar cases was to kill them, but Forster knew that such a deed would be an eternal shame to his uniform and his flag. He could repeat once more, however, the ruse of threatening massacre; and, under that stimulus, the captives eagerly agreed to his proposition for an exchange of prisoners, offered, he said, merely ' at the dictates of humanity,' after ' the maturest deliberation on the customs and manners of the savages in war . . . so opposite and contrary to the humane disposition of the British government.' The terms were in general fair enough ; but the second article forbade the Americans ever to bear arms against the British government again, while the men exchanged for them would be free to re-enter their companies the next day.

By this time Arnold, reinforced with Colonel De Haas's

---

[25] Authentic Narrative (Note 19).

First Pennsylvanians, hardy fellows in business-like brown
and buff,[26] and with about four hundred more from Sorel,
had begun the pursuit, first sending a number of Caughnawagas to the hostile savages with a demand for their
prisoners. 'If any are murdered,' added the General,
'I will sacrifice every Indian that falls into my hands,
& I will follow you to your Towns, & destroy them by
Fire and Sword.' The force now at his back made the
threat look substantial; but, on arriving at St. Anne
late in the afternoon, instead of surrendered comrades, he
received this reply : That all the captives had been collected together, and, should he offer to attack, every one
of them would be sacrificed and no quarter given to any
American made prisoner in the future. In fact, boats
could be seen carrying the last of the unfortunates from
an island to the British post. Arnold was furious,' torn
by the conflicting passions of revenge & humanity '; but
he could not endure to see the painted miscreants escape un-
harmed, and, sending express after express to hurry on his
bateaux, he embarked as soon as they arrived, rescued
five naked and half-starved wretches left on the island,
and pushed for Quinze Chiens, four miles distant on
the opposite shore, where Forster had now pitched his
camp.

The day was just ending as he approached the British
post. The dark waters of the Ottawa River, smooth as
glass, wore the rich blue of the sky, melting, toward the
west, into the gorgeous tints of sunset. Little by little,
as the boats advanced, shadows fell across the mirror.
The steeple of Quinze Chiens marked it with a slender, ta-
pering line of black, and the fine elms and ashes along the
flat shore threw masses of shade upon its gold and crimson.
Under the trees, the whitewashed cottages of the peasants,

---

[26] Hist. Mag., Dec., 1860, p. 353.

touched corner-wise by the slowly fading light, added a glow of homely cheer to the tranquil view. The scene invited to repose; but, near the shore and well entrenched, waited Forster's redcoats with what allies he could retain;

and presently two flashes and two puffs of smoke announced the cannon-balls that flew, an instant later, past the American flotilla. The Indians broke loose, yelled and fired, and the few regulars stood fast. Arnold had fifteen bateaux, loaded to the gunwale, and three birch canoes,—men enough to do the business; but, in the face of a resolute foe with two pieces, he could not get ashore. In vain he darted about, paddled by four Indians: he could see no chance whatever to land. The men at the oars were finally ordered to stop rowing; the

AT LACHINE

boats drifted out of range uninjured; and, as it was now too dark to attempt anything on strange ground, the baffled expedition returned to St. Anne.

What should be done? A council of war was soon discussing that question. Arnold proposed to go up the St. Lawrence, dash for the rear of the enemy, and cut him off; but Hazen maintained that the Indians could not be taken by surprise, and held that an attack would mean the butchery of their captives. As the opinion of an old ranger, this view had great weight in the meeting, and De

Haas backed it up. Arnold and Hazen grew heated; sharp words passed; but in the end it was decided—by Arnold, at least—to fight early in the morning.[27] Soon after midnight, however, Lieutenant Parke of Forster's company arrived under a flag, and brought news of the cartel already signed by the prisoners.

This put a new look on affairs. Obviously, an agreement made under such pressure could not bind the American leader, but it was both an appeal and a way of escape. It cried, Save us! and then added, We have found the means. To refuse; to condemn five hundred comrades to be shot, stabbed, hacked, and scalped in cold blood by shrieking demons was impossible. Yet Arnold could bluster and threaten, when there was an end to gain, as well as any man alive.

'I will have nothing to do with it,' he exclaimed on reading the second article; 'go back and acquaint Captain Forster that I will enter into articles for the exchange of prisoners on equal terms. If he refuses that, I am determined to attack him immediately; and, if our prisoners are murdered, I will sacrifice every soul that falls into our hands.'

The smallness of the British force gave Forster a better reason than Arnold imagined for not refusing. After some negotiations a truce for the delivery of the prisoners was agreed upon; they were landed on the south shore of the St. Lawrence; and Forster, slipping away before the truce expired, vanished into the forest while the Americans were preparing to strike. In the direct object of his mission he had failed; but it had been demonstrated to the satisfaction of many in Canada that the British lion, opening his mouth even a very little, could eat up five hundred American soldiers and retire unsinged.[28]

---

[27] REMARK XCIV.
[28] REMARK XCV.

I have this moment received
an account from Captain Forster, that he
with a detachment of the 8.th reg: some
Canadians & a number of Indians, had
taken the 19.th ins.t a fort at the Cedars,
two pieces of cannon, & 390 rebels, pri=
soners at discretion. The day following
a party of 120 rebels coming from the
island of Montreal, to their relief, these
were attacked by Mr. Lorimier &
Monsrtiny, defeated and taken.

FROM CARLETON'S LETTER TO GERMAIN, MAY 25, 1776

Little enough resemblance had this to the 'prosperous turn' craved by Chase and Carroll; and, to deepen the affliction, affairs appeared to be going to wreck and ruin almost everywhere just then. Sir John Johnson and the Highlanders of Tryon County were again making trouble, and one of the scarce American regiments had to be employed on the Mohawk. New York city, no longer a gay and busy town, was gloomily preparing to endure a siege and perhaps an assault. Stimulated by this prospect as much as the patriots were depressed, the Tories of the region were concocting schemes, and Matthew Adgate, shivering with fright, gave Washington some 'glimmering of such a plot as has seldom appeared in the world since the fall of Adam, . . . dark as hell.' At the same time Schuyler's enemies came to the front, and, making a handle of his extreme politeness to British prisoners—particularly to a nephew of Lord Barrington, the Minister of War—denounced him bitterly as a royalist at heart, sending all the provisions in the land to Canada, so that they might fall into the hands of the enemy, and even preparing to 'fall upon the country' at the head of Tory battalions from New York.[29]

Darker still was the near outlook. Hard money, the indispensable sum of it, the very least that would answer, had not arrived. On the day Sherburne surrendered, the army at Sorel had been 'entirely destitute' of meat for two days. Even bread was hard to get. De Haas's regiment, arriving hungry at Montreal, on their way to fight Captain Forster's crew, found nothing to eat; and the Commissioners were compelled to buy thirty loaves of

29 § Tryon Co.: 4 Force, VI., 493, 537, 641–648. Carroll, Journal. Plots, etc.: N. Y. Calendar, I., pp. 328–334, 338–372; Clap, Diary (Hist. Mag., Mar., 1874), p. 135. Adgate: 4 Force, VI., 438. Sch. to Hulburt, Nov. 1, 1775: 4 Force, IV., 816. Coffin, Thomas, p. 23 (letter of J. Adams). Sch. to Trumbull, Nov. 10, 1775: 4 Force, III., 1426. Id. to Hancock, Jan. 22, 1776: 4 Force, IV., 802. Wash. to Sch., May 21, 1776: Writings (Ford), IV., p. 90. Sch. to Sullivan, May 28, 1776: Sullivan Papers, N. H. Hist. Soc. Id. to Wash., May 21, 1776: 4 Force, VI., 537. (See ib., 608, 610.)

their own baker to keep the men alive. Ovens had to be laid, storehouses built ; yet many of the artisans brought from the Colonies promptly disabled themselves by inoculation. Flour threatened to fail. None could be expected from the south for some time yet, and no large quantity could be bought even in the city and island of Montreal. Dugan's bolting cloth was kept going day and night ; but it never had expected four or five thousand visitors, and no more had the mills. An army could perish while the wheat was being slowly carted from point to point and from process to process ; and, as regarded the supplies from above, all the disbanded soldiers, journeying home by leisurely stages, had to be fed, and could get the first chance at whatever was coming.[30]

' Altogether reduced to live from hand to mouth,' was the summary of Chase and Carroll, ' depending on the scanty and precarious supplies of a few half-starved cattle and trifling quantities of flour, which have hitherto been picked up in various parts of the country.' Tents were scarce. Blankets and coarse linens were ' exceedingly wanting.' Finding themselves ' all out of provisions,' the men were ' struck with terror and apprehension,' noted Robbins, when unexpectedly five boats brought them a few mouthfuls of pork. ' In the mount, God appears! ' exclaimed the Chaplain, as if it had been a miracle. There were no medicines or surgical instruments for the sick and wounded ; no bullets for the well ; and no shoes, stockings, shirts, or pay for either class. Cartridge-paper and even thread to tie it with gave out.[31]

' Our soldiers,' wrote the Commissioners, ' will be soon

[30] § Thomas to Commrs., May 20, 1776: 4 Force, VI., 592. Id. to Hancock, May 27, 1776: ib. 589. Thompson to Commrs., May 25, 1776: ib., 593. Commrs. to Thomas, May 26, 1776: Sparks, Corres.. I., p. 518. Walker to S. Adams, May 30, 1776: S. Adams Papers.

[31] § Commrs. to Hancock, May 27, 1776 : 4 Force, VI., 589. Arnold to Chase, May 15, 1776: ib., 580. Robbins, Journal, May 18. Stringer to Wash., May 10, 1776 : 4 Force, VI., 417. Thompson to Commrs., May 25, 1776: ib., 593. Chase to Sch., May 28, 31, 1776: Sch. Papers.

reduced to the dreadful alternative of starving or of plundering the inhabitants ' ; and pillage would at last drive the people to rise and cut their throats. To massacre it would soon come, then, were nothing done. A famishing man is a wolf; and a wolf—especially one with teeth of steel—will bite before he will starve. By this hard road the Delegates now found themselves goaded on to the final act of arbitrary power, and recommended—that is to say, ordered—the seizure, in exchange for promises to pay, of the goods and supplies absolutely required for the immediate wants of the men.[32]

This ensured existence for a while, but nothing more. ' You will be pleased to figure to yourselves,' Thomas had written, ' a retreating Army, disheartened by unavoidable misfortunes, destitute of almost every necessary to render their lives comfortable or even tolerable, sick, and (as they think) wholly neglected, and [with] no probable prospect of a speedy relief '; and upon this army had now fallen the shock of the whole Cedars disaster. Josiah Bartlett simply could not believe the report of that shameful affair ; and, if it seemed at Philadelphia too dreadful to be true, what colors did it wear at Sorel ? ' We must expect to meet some hard rubs,' philosophized William Whipple ; but philosophy was easier at his distance. Heart-breaking, faith-crushing examples of poltroonery had been given ; and the truce, curiously misunderstood, was taken to mean something very much like throwing up the sponge. Certain of the officers, breaking down under the strain, began to look out for themselves alone, quarrelled selfishly, and set the men a pattern of neglected duty that some of them scandalously improved upon. Unpaid, unfed, unclothed, undisciplined,

<hr>

[32] § Commrs. to Thomas, May 26, 1776: Sparks, Corres., I., 518. Id. to Hancock, May 27, 1776: 4 Force, VI., 589. Id. to Wooster, May 25, 1776: Am. Antiq. Soc. Spy: Can. Arch., Q, 12, p. 22. Letter, May 17, 1776: 4 Force, VI., 493. REMARK XCVI.

Montreal 25th May 1776.

Sir,

We think it would be proper for you to give an order to the town Major to wait on the Merchants or others having provisions or merchandize for sale and request a delivery of what our troops are in immediate want of (offering to give a receipt expressing the quantity delivered and engaging in behalf of the united Colonies to pay them for) and on refusal we think our receipt if required that force should be used to compel a delivery.

Yr most Obham. Servt

Saml Chase

Ch. Carroll of Carrollton

Gen. Wooster

the discharged soldiers felt entitled in too many cases to whatever they could lay hands on, and robbed both the government and their comrades without compunction.[33]

Early in April, Hazen had described the people as convinced that a heavy British force would soon arrive, and as anxious to secure the favor of those who were to be their masters. Now, the Canadians below Deschambault were reported as actually taking up arms against the Americans; and most of those in the vicinity, even though many still professed a vague and barren good-will, could be reckoned upon to do the same whenever the British flag should approach. Nobody could tell which of them was already planning to earn a pardon by some striking betrayal. 'Here we are in a great country,' said Chaplain Robbins, 'and know not who are friends and who are enemies.' Briand, encouraged by the American disaster at Quebec, was now preaching 'rage and fury' against this 'handful of unwarlike fellows, ignorant of the military art.' Even the Caughnawaga Indians threatened to go over. In spite of every prohibition, soldiers insisted so constantly upon inoculating themselves, that finally it was decided to authorize the process; and the troops, three-fourths of whom had never had the small-pox at home, plunged by wholesale into the business of going through that horrible disease. It was doubted at headquarters whether the men could even be held in company. 'Want of discipline and everything else necessary to constitute an army or to keep troops together,' was President Hancock's epitome of the Commissioners' reports. Yet he did not know the worst.

---

[33] § Thomas to Commrs., May 20, 1776: 4 Force. VI., 592. Bartlett to Folsom, June 6, 1776: Emmet Coll. Whipple to Langdon, June 2, 1776 : 4 Force, VI., 1024. Thompson to Wash., June 2, 1776 : ib., 684. Id. to Commrs., May 25, 1776 : ib., 593. McCarthy to Sch., May 23, 1776: Sch. Papers. Commrs. to Thomas, May 26, 1776: Sparks, Corres., I., p. 518. Bartlett to Langdon, June 17, 1776: Sparks MSS., No. 52, II., p. 139. Robbins, Journal.

'We cannot find words strong enough to describe our miserable situation,' wrote Chase and Carroll.[34]

In the midst of it all, Thomas fell sick of the pestilence, and Wooster drifted once more into the first place. That roused the Commissioners. At last they could see a plain, unmistakable duty, and they did it. 'General Wooster is, in our opinion,' they notified Congress, 'unfit, totally unfit, to command your Army and conduct the war. . . . His stay in this Colony is unnecessary and even prejudicial to our affairs; we would therefore humbly advise his recall.'

In a little while, Thomas was desperately sick, and the malady, striking at his eyes, put them out. 'Our affairs here grow every hour more gloomy,' said Chase, and both he and his colleague felt utterly helpless. At noon, the last day of May, they turned their faces homeward; and, on the second of June, with a month of agony frozen in his heart, General Thomas lay dead. Out of the meagre army, thirty-three hundred men were that day unfit for duty. The effectives at Sorel numbered exactly one-third as many, and Carleton's forces were advancing.[35]

---

[34] § Hazen to Sch., Apr. 8, 1776: Sch. Papers. Thompson to Commrs., May 25, 1776: 4 Force, VI., 593. Letter, May 17, 1776: ib., 493. Robbins, Journal, May 16. Commrs. to Hancock, May 17, 1776: 4 Force, VI., 587. Sullivan to Sch., May 27, 1776: ib., 609. Têtu et Gagnon, Mandements, II., p. 269. Têtu, Evêques, II., p. 334. Inoc.: Arnold to Commrs., May 15, 17, 1776 (4 Force, VI., 579, 592); Senter, Journal. (One of Brown's unfounded charges against Arnold was that he ordered inoculation without authority.) Thomas to Commrs., May 20, 1776: 4 Force, VI., 592. Hancock, to Wash., June 7, 1776: ib., 740. Commrs. to Hancock, May 27, 1776: ib., 589.

[35] § Commrs. to Cong., May 27, 1776 : 4 Force, VI., 589. Coffin, Thomas, p. 29. Chase to Sch., May 31, 1776 : Sparks MSS., No. 60, p. 90. Senter, Journal. Morgan to S. Adams, June 25, 1776: 4 Force, VI., 1069. REMARK XCVII.

XXXIII

THREE RIVERS

' *THE same yeare, by earthquake or some other forcible
violence, the common-place called the Forum, clave and
opened wide, welneere in the mids, and sunke downe to an ex-
ceeding depth : neither could that chincke or pit be filled up
. . . before they began to enquire, according as they were
admonished by the divine Oracles, what it might be, wherein
the most puissance and greatnes of the people of Rome consisted. (For the wisards prophesied, That if they would
have the state of Rome to remain sure for ever, they should
dedicat and offer it, whatsoever it was, unto that place.)
And when they were in doubt what this should be, it is reported, that M. Curtius, a right hardie knight and martiall
young gentleman, rebuked them therefore, because they
doubted whether the Romans had any earthly thing better
than armour and valor? Herewith, after silence made, he
lift up his eies, and beheld the temples of the immortal gods,
scituate neere to the Forum, and the Capitoll likewise ; and
stretching forth his hands, one while toward heaven, another
while to the gaping chinckes and gulfe in the earth, toward
the infernall spirits beneath, hee offered and devoted himself
to assured death. And mounting upon a brave courser, as
richly trapped and set out as possiblie he could devise, armed
as he was at all peeces, he leapt horse and man and all into
the hole.'* [1]

---

[1] Holland's Livy (Book VII.), p. 252.

The Canada enterprise, looked upon at first as promising an easy and almost sure success, now yawned wide and deep, and threatened to engulf the young state. Into this chasm, not one but many of America's worthiest sons—less famous but not less noble than Marcus Curtius, and devoted to a grander ideal—had thrown themselves with all his ardor, yet the abyss refused to close. Would a still greater sacrifice be enough? No soothsayer stood near to tell, but at all events the sacrifice was now to be made.

'The Congress, being of opinion that the reduction of Quebec, and the general security of the province of Canada,' were 'objects of great concern,' did not permit itself to forget that quarter. Not only the Adamses, Hancock, Lynch, Wythe, and Livingston, but men like Thomas Jefferson, Robert Morris, and Richard Henry Lee put their shoulders to the wheel. 'We have been very much engaged for some days in attending to the affairs of Canada,' said Thomas Stone; adding, 'I presume the Canada Department . . . will ingross our Attention for a few days [more].' Provisions, clothing, pay, transportation, cannon, ammunition, specie,—these were a few of the matters handled with great energy if but scanty power. 'That we have been a little tardy in providing for Canada, is true—owing to innumerable difficulties. However, we have been roused at last, and I hope have done pretty well,' was John Adams's complacent remark. 'The Congress . . . have left nothing undone,' attested Hancock.[2]

In due course of time, it was discovered how far short of their nominal value the reinforcements ordered north in January had proved to be; and, only two days after a cheering crowd had said good-bye to General Thompson

<hr />

[2] § Journ. Cong., Mar. 16, 25 ; Apr. 23 ; May 18, etc. Stone to Jenifer, Apr. 24, 1776: Md. Hist. Soc., Red Book, I., No. 27. J. Adams to Gates, Apr. 27, 1776: Sparks MSS., XXII., p. 92. Hancock to Wash., Apr. 23, 1776: 4 Force, V., 1036.

at Manhattan, Congress voted to despatch six more regiments. 'Weak indeed' the Commander-in-chief realized that such a draft would leave him, but he felt the importance of the northern campaign too deeply to hesitate. It was far from easy to complete the equipment of these men. Nearly two thousand muskets were lacking at New York, 'and none to be purchased at any Rate,' as an energetic officer discovered. In fact, a part of one regiment, detained for that reason, never saw Canada ; but, in one way or another, arms were obtained for the rest. In all, nearly thirty-three hundred stout volunteers, besides the officers, were present fit for duty, and the General could describe them as 'somewhat instructed in discipline.' Three hundred thousand dollars in Continental paper, snugly packed in three strong boxes, came over from Philadelphia marked 'Schuyler.' Four thousand barrels of pork and ten thousand pairs of shoes and stockings had been ordered by Congress for the northern army ; and eight hundred barrels of the meat, sixty barrels of powder, about five hundred tents, a parcel of entrenching tools, and a weighty chain to bar the St. Lawrence were in readiness.[3]

The John Stark of Bennington led one of the regiments, the Anthony Wayne of Stony Point another ; and the

----

[3] § Thomas to Wash., Apr. 7, 1776 : 4 Force, V., 813.   Journ. Cong., Apr. 23. Wash. to Trumbull, Apr. 26, 1776 : 4 Force, V., 1087.   Wayne to Johnston, May 6, 1776 : Wayne Papers.   Johnston to Wayne, June 14, 1776 : ib.   Return (3091, besides 133 present but sick, 182 sergeants, and 90 drummers and fifers), Apr. 28 : 4 Force, V., 1154. (As only three cos. of Wayne's reached Canada, the actual number going was 485 less ; see Return, 4 Force, VI., 411.)   Wash. to Sch., May 16, 1776 : Writings (Ford), IV., p. 82, note. Hancock to Wash., Apr. 25, 1776 : 4 Force, V., 1067.   Id. to Sch., Apr. 26, 1776 : ib., 1086.   Wash. to Sch., May 3, 1776 : 4 Force, V., 1179.

John Sullivan of Princeton, Trenton, and Germantown commanded the brigade. An early arrival of these troops 'may be of infinite advantage to us,' urged Washington, and all felt eager to be off. 'The tide and wind are fair—and the Vessel waiting—farewel my Dear Girl—kiss my little Girl and Boy for me—tell them their daddy sent each of them two—farewel once more—God bless and protect you adieu my Dear Polly,' scribbled Wayne to his wife. On the twenty-ninth of April, the troops began to embark; and, by the third of May, all but a few companies were afloat.[4]

At Albany new difficulties arose. As Congress had ordered too few bateaux constructed, and forwarding Thompson's brigade had exhausted Schuyler's transportation facilities, Sullivan's troops could only sit down and watch the carpenters build them boats, at the rate of six or eight a day. Dayton's regiment was needed in Tryon County to hold the Tories in check, so that the brigade lost more than one-sixth of its finest men. But all tried to make the best of the situation. Sullivan rode up and down the line of communication, and braced the workmen with Yankee snap and Irish tact. A brilliant review was held in Schuyler's meadow; and Wayne's men in their deep-blue coats faced with white, white vests, and white trousers edged with blue, Irvine's in blue turned up with red, and the other battalions in their own fresh regimentals, all equipped with martial accoutrements and bearing themselves like soldiers, had a moral effect of no slight value. The troops felt emboldened and the patriots encouraged. About two hundred and sixty Indians opened their eyes wide; and the Tories, who had

---

[4] § Wash. to Sch., May 3, 1776: 4 Force, V., 1179. Return: ib., 1154. Wayne to his wife: Wayne Papers. (He was detained at New York a few days; see Wayne to Wash., May 14, 1776: Lib. of Cong., Letters to Wash., IX., p. 155.) Wash. to Sch., Apr. 29, 1776: 4 Force, V., 1124. For Sullivan: Penna. Mag., II., p. 196. Elmer, Journal, p. 97.

been reporting all about that only three companies had arrived and that Schuyler kept them walking the streets to give an impression of numbers, hung their heads.[5]

Still another influence had time to make itself felt. Speeches and pamphlets, votes and orders, bullets and bayonets were not the only forces in the great Revolutionary contest. Ladies might not care to discuss taxation very deeply, but they had their arguments. In the midst of alarms, eyes were still gay and bright, and even the fashions continued to bloom. ' The Dress is more ridiculous and pretty than anything I ever saw—great quan-

tity of different coloured feathers on the head at a time besides a thousand other things,' gushed a Philadelphia belle from New York a little later, though times had then grown worse. Silk wraps, dainty gloves, trim shoes, hair puffed in front, gathered into a chignon behind, and always newly frizzed : these were among the points a Hessian officer noted in the region of Albany ; and he added, ' They also put on some well made and stylish little sunbonnet, from beneath which their roguish eyes have a most fascinating way of meeting yours.' [6]

Whatever power Whig beauty possessed, it now cast its mightiest spells to aid the commander of the Northern Department. Peggy Schuyler and her sister Betsy—who was destined, alas ! to weep for an illustrious husband

---

5 § Sch. to Alb. Com., May 4, 1776: 4 Force, V., 1192. Id. to Hancock, May 3, 1776: ib., 1181. Id. to Wash., May 10, 28, 1776: 4 Force, VI., 411, 608. Elmer, Journal, May 29. Sch. to Wash., May 21: 4 Force, VI., 527. Caldwell to Boudinot, June 11, 1776: Emmet Coll. Sullivan to Wash., May 16, 1776 ; 4 Force, VI., 479. Sch. to Wash., May 10, 1776: ib., 416. Uniforms: Lacey, Memoirs, p. 192 ; Hist. Mag., Dec., 1860, p. 353.

6 § Earl, Costume, p. 31.

slain by Aaron Burr—got into the serious Journal of Charles Carroll of Carrollton as a pair of ' lively, agreeable, black eyed girls.' ' Accomplished fine Sweet Girls and very handsome ', noted Wayne. How they fired Sullivan's bold, warm heart and stirred the man who talked of Molly Stark on the battlefield could be guessed. ' Had I been single—,' sighed even the devoted Wayne, on taking leave. No doubt there were other patriot belles in the retinue of Peggy and Betsy ; and all the gallant officers of the waiting brigade had their courage replenished by these priestesses of heroism. Not one could bear to think of seeing their lovely eyes beam less warmly on his return.[7]

At last the brigade got under way, but a peremptory ' Halt ! ' soon froze every man where he stood. Surrounded by an army on the brink of starvation, Chase and Carroll sent word that food was needed in Canada more than mouths ; and the reinforcements had to stop and look on, helping as they could, while provisions to keep their comrades alive passed on ahead. It was an awkward and painful check ; but, early on the twenty-fourth of May, Sullivan bade adieu to Albany. The last morning of the month found his brigade camping on the shore of Lake Champlain over eighty miles from St. Johns. ' But a fine & fair wind ' had sprung up in the night. At the roll of a drum, early in the morning, the village of canvas fell. The troops hurried into their bateaux. The tents rose again as sails. One after another, some two hundred boats took flight ; and, with Wayne's blue and white in the van and the glint of steel everywhere, the whole making ' a most formidable and beautiful appearance—I presume, something like the Gretion Fleet going to the Seage of Troy ,' as Captain

---

[7] § Carroll, Journal, p. 54. Wayne to Robinson, May 26, 1776: **Wayne Papers.** The ' Molly Stark ' story rests of course on tradition.

Lacey imagined, they swept on very briskly and reached St. Johns that evening.[8]

The next day was not a happy one for Sullivan. It rained heavily ; 'the Musketoes continually buzing' and the 'flies & knats constantly stinging' made it almost impossible to think ; the wind blew raw and cold. But these were not the troubles that he minded. 'The confused state of this country is past description,' General Thompson had found on arriving two weeks before ; and now Sullivan, after listening and looking about him that long, woeful day, summed it all up in a word : 'No one thing is right.'[9]

But he had come to set things right, and he believed it could be done. There were now troops, provisions, ammunition, muskets, and cannon. In spite of everything there was courage, there was hope. 'I am persuaded Sullivan dies or conquers. Thompson will not be behind him,' James Caldwell felt; and it was a prophecy of success to inspire such a belief. 'I hope in three weeks from this time to date my next in *Quebeck*,' Wayne had written from New York ; 'my brave fellows are Anxious to have a share in the Glory of its Reduction.' 'Matters will be soon settled,' predicted Thompson in the midst of the chaos. 'I hope we shall be able to drive them faster than they drove us,' cried a soldier at Sorel when the reinforcements approached. Arnold, though misfortune had followed misfortune before his eyes for half a year, cheerily wrote Gates : 'as Miss, like most other Misses, is fickle, and often changes, I still hope for her favours again.'[10]

---

[8] § Chase and Carroll to Franklin, May 10, 1776: Sparks Corres., I., p. 513. Sch. to Sullivan, May 13, 1776: 4 Force, VI., 449. Sullivan to Wash., May 14, 1776: ib., 449. Sch. to Wash., May 24, 1776: ib., 564. Lacey, Memoirs, p. 194. (A part of Wayne's regiment had not been able to leave New York: Sull. to Hancock, June 1 ; Lacey Memoirs.)

[9] § Lacey, Memoirs, p. 194. Scammell to Bishop, June 2, 1776: Hist. Mag., Sept., 1870, p. 136. Thompson to Wash., May 14, 1776: 4 Force, VI., 448. Sullivan to Hancock, June 1, 1776: ib., 679.

[10] § Caldwell to Boudinot, June 11, 1776: Emmet Coll. Wayne to Johnston,

The despondent Canadians along the Richelieu, deeply compromised by their friendship for the Americans, took heart afresh. ' I find the lower, and some of the higher class of French people in our favour,' reported the hopeful Sullivan at once. A militia captain waited upon him at St. Johns and brought an offer from three parishes, as he said, to contribute six hundred men, all furnished with arms and provisions. When the troops journeyed on down the river, it almost brought the tears to their eyes to see the banks ' lined with men, women, and children, leaping and clapping their hands for joy.' In a few days, the General re-ported the *habitants* as ' flocking by hundreds ' to his aid, offering wheat and flour in exchange for mere certificates, bringing their teams, when these were called for, ' with the greatest cheerfulness,' and beg-ging to have their priests arrested. Dugan, driven from the service by some accusation of Hazen's, took hold again, and brought in over two hundred armed men. ' The face of our affairs seems to be changed,' the new leader joyfully exclaimed.[11]

JOHN SULLIVAN

Thomas, after he fell ill, had suggested retreat. Indeed, most of the artillery and heavy stores were moved back from Sorel, and the troops began to retire. But now came an end of all that. ' Retreat before an enemy which no

May 6, 1776: Wayne Papers. Thompson to Wash., May 14, 1776: 4 Force, VI. 448.   Letter, May 14, 1776: ib., 455.   Arnold to Gates, May 31, 1776: ib., 649.
11 § Sullivan to Hancock, June 1, 1776: 4 Force, VI., 679.   Id. to Wash., June 5, 6, 1776: ib., 921.   Dugan to Sullivan, June 5, 1776: ib., 924.

person has seen ?' Never! Right about face! commanded Sullivan. 'All the well men, follow me !' he cried. 'Push for Sorell as Quick as Possible ,' was the order Vose received, and every one else in that quarter likewise, no doubt. Only three cannon had been set up at the mouth of the Richelieu in all the time that post had been occupied ; but now the troops took hold with a will, and the next evening not only saw the encampment nearly enclosed, but found a new three-gun battery completed on the opposite shore of the St. Lawrence.[12]

Better still, a brilliant and perhaps vital stroke at the enemy seemed to offer itself within easy reach.

Whence came the force that relieved Quebec and how strong was it? This had been almost a Sphinx's question ; but gradually the answer appeared to be found. Samuel Adams, Washington, and no doubt many others, believed that British troops driven from Boston to Halifax would find their way up the St. Lawrence. About the middle of April, the Tories in Canada began to be jubilant, and Hazen reported that General Howe was expected. This natural explanation of Carleton's reinforcements appeared to be fully confirmed by an American officer, for he recognized his own brother on one of the vessels, and knew that he did not come from abroad. In short, it was commonly, if not universally, accepted that General Thomas had been driven off by troops hailing from Nova Scotia.[13]

This meant that no grand expedition from England, and therefore that probably no very large force, had arrived,

[12] § Thomas (by Sedgwick) to Wooster, May 27, 1776 : 4 Force, VI., 580. Porter, Diary, May, 22, 23 ; June 3. Chase and Carroll to Hancock, May 27: 4 Force, VI., 589. Sullivan to Wash., June 5, 1776: ib., 921. Id.to Hancock, June 1, 1776: ib., 679. Vose, Journal, May 30 (misdated). The battery on the opposite shore (i. e. across the main channel) stood on an island.

[13] § S. Adams to Hawley, Apr. 15, 1776 : S. Adams Papers. Wash. to Sch., Apr. 24, 1776 : 4 Force, V., 1053. Hazen to Sch., Apr. 15, 1776 : Sch. Papers. Walker to S. Adams, May 30, 1776: S. Adams Papers. Elmer, Journal, May 15. Caldwell to Boudinot, May 15, 1776: Emmet Coll. REMARK XCVIII.

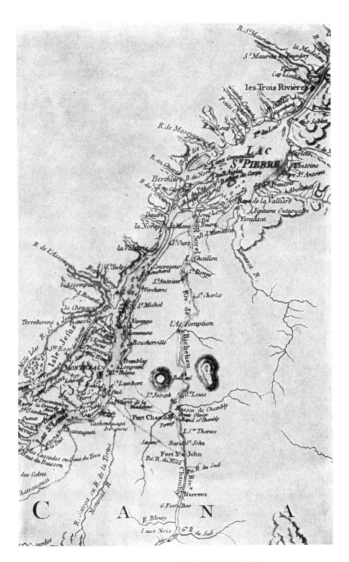

FROM FADEN'S AMERICAN ATLAS, 1777

397

for the weight of Howe's army was expected in the middle or southern Colonies. To be sure, Thomas heard that fifteen sail had entered the river, and the Commissioners that fourteen had reached the capital ; but these reports, even if correct, said nothing as to the size or character of the vessels. Some of them were very likely merchantmen, and others must almost certainly have been victualers. ' We are told an East India Ship arrived a day or two after [the sixth of May] with three or four hundred Soldiers but this wants Confirmation,' said Walker at the very end of the month. Thomas had employed ' trusty men, disguised as Canadians, to find out the number and the situation of the enemy ' ; and, on the fifteenth, he did not consider them 'very formidable.' John McCord was told by French people who came out of Quebec six days after the Americans had retreated, that only two companies of the 29th Regiment, one frigate and one transport from Halifax had caused the unhappy flight, and that no more were reported below. People said that the frigate came to ascertain whether the town had been captured, and that, as it had not been, Howe would come there ; but, even should this prove true, weeks must pass before he could arrive. Another account had it that two regiments landed; but, as Carleton was reported to be still fortifying Quebec, it did not look as if he would soon take the offensive.[14]

With so little to fear, the Americans longed more and more to regain Deschambault. Thompson was actually ordered to go there with sixteen hundred men, and expected to set out from Sorel on the twentieth of May. So confident of securing that point felt the officers, that Baron

---

[14] § Hancock to Sch., Mar. 7, 1776: 4 Force, V., 99. Thomas to Wash., May 8, 1776: 4 Force, VI., 453. Commrs. to Sch., May 31, 1776 : Sparks MSS., No. 60, p. 90. Walker to S. Adams, May 30, 1776: S. Adams Papers. Thomas to Commrs., May 15, 1776 : 4 Force, VI., 588. Commrs. to Sch., May 17, 1776: ib., 586. Thompson to Commrs., May 25, 1776: ib., 593.

De Woedtke made a formal application to command the advanced post there. Probably the necessity of sending men to check Forster put a veto on this plan; and, although Thompson proposed to re-occupy Three Rivers with a thousand men on the return of Colonel De Haas from Montreal, that idea also had to be laid aside. 'The havock made amongst the New England troops by the small-pox, and our want of ammunition, especially lead, have prevented anything being done below Sorel,' he explained to Washington later.[15]

Presently, however, the situation at Three Rivers became too attractive as well as threatening to neglect, even should Sorel itself have to be stripped. News came that Maclean, with some eight hundred regulars and Canadians, had ventured to occupy that point. Since very likely half of these troops were natives, they could not be considered very formidable; and Thompson reflected that a successful blow against them might prevent the *habitants* and Indians from taking up arms and increasing the British strength to something irresistible. Besides, as Bondfield pointed out, a league or something more below Three Rivers the deep water of the St. Lawrence ran close to the northern shore, so that a battery planted on the high bank might be able to stop, or at least delay, the enemy's fleet. Since the death of Thomas and Wooster's retirement, Arnold had stood first in rank; but, as he was above Montreal trying to catch Forster, he could not give orders at Sorel. Thompson, however, was an officer, wrote Samuel Chase, 'with sense to conceive and spirit to execute'; and he directed Colonel St. Clair, who had served at Three Rivers in the French and Indian War, to surprise Maclean's camp, if that could be done. At the

15 § Thompson to Sch., May 19, 1776: Sch. Papers. Sch. to Wash., May 31, 1776: 4 Force, VI., 639. Woedtke to Thomas, May 18, 1776: Thomas Papers. Thompson to Commrs., May 25, 1776 : 4 Force, VI., 593   Id. to Wash., May 30, 1776: ib., 628.

same time, steps were taken to support the move should it be fortunate, or to retreat nimbly should it fail. Just then, Sullivan arrived ; and, on learning from two scouts who had been despatched to reconnoitre the enemy that the British troops numbered only three hundred, he determined, after taking the sense of a council of war, to make a victory certain, and ordered Thompson himself to lead the movement, giving him enough of his best men to make up, with St. Clair's, nearly two thousand, besides a large number of Canadians.[16]

'I would by no means advise to an attack, if the prospect of success is not much in your favor,' ran his prudent instructions ; but he considered a triumph almost as good as won. Next, he would take post at Deschambault, and fortify that spot so as to 'make it inaccessible.' What ships had passed it, he would 'soon remove' below the falls ; and then—On to Quebec 'as fast as possible.' Strong, resolute, and confident, he felt it safe to be liberal with promises and good news. 'I may venture to assure you and the Congress,' he wrote to Washington, 'that I can, in a few days, reduce the Army to order ; and, with the assistance of a kind Providence, put a new face to our affairs here.' A sense of cheer soon diffused itself in all directions. 'Since Gen! Sullivan's arrival our affairs wear another faice,' Caldwell informed Boudinot. Schuyler rejoiced profoundly to find that the chaos and confusion were now 'on the point' of ending ; and the Commander-in-chief was made 'exceedingly happy' by the brilliant

---

[16] § Thompson to Wash., June 2, 1776: 4 Force, VI., 684. Id. to Commrs.. May 25, 1776: ib., 593. Goforth to Jay, Apr. 8, 1776: Bancroft Coll., Rev. Papers, I., p. 37. June 1, Wooster was at St. Johns on his way home (Sullivan to Hancock, June 1 : 4 Force, VI., 679). Arnold: Chase to Sch., May 31, 1776 (Sparks MSS., No. 60, p. 90). Chase to Gates, June 13, 1776: ib., p. 95. Thompson to Wash., June 2, 1776: 4 Force, VI., 684. Orders to St. Clair, June 2: Smith, St. Clair, I., p. 367. St. Clair, Narrative, p. 235. Letter, June 12, 1776: 4 Force, VI., p. 826. Sullivan to Wash., June 6, 1776: 4 Force, VI., p. 921. Wayne to Delaney, June 13, 1776: Wayne Papers. Orders to Thompson : Lib. Cong., Letters to Wash., IX., p. 293.

Instructions for Genl Thompson.

Dr Sir

You are to March as soon as possible with Coll. Ferris
& Coll. Warner Regiments together with those of Coll. Olf. Bairs now Arriving at this place, & Doc. Coll. & Stinson & Nicholetts & take Command of the whole party, & unlefs you find the Number of the Enemy at—

These Ophins to be such as would order an ~~regiment~~ attack upon them
Hazardous you are to bring this Other at the most convenient place,
you can & attack them. you will pay Particular attention to the Preserva=
tion of your Batteaux, keeping them at a Convenient Distance above)

prospect. Of late, he had 'almost dreaded to hear from Canada.'[17]

Thursday afternoon, June the sixth, Thompson's eager troops hurried into the bateaux, dropped down the river about thirty miles, reached Nicolet, some ten miles above Three Rivers on the opposite side of the St. Lawrence, an hour after midnight, and there united with St. Clair's detachment. A daybreak attack was intended ; and, as it could not be made that night—for the hour was already late, the men were tired, and their arms were damp—the next day was passed at this place. The people of the vicinity had shown themselves very friendly to the cause ; yet, in order to conceal the plans, a pretence was made of throwing up works. Various reports about the force at Three Rivers came in. Apparently, it might be anywhere from five hundred to fifteen hundred ; but, even at the highest, it could hardly be enough to defeat a heavy and unexpected attack in the dark, for the town had no fortifications except what Haldimand called a 'Stone House' and such intrenchments as had recently been thrown up. There seemed, then, to be no reason for abandoning the enterprise ; and the troops, filing out of camp in the paling afterglow of sunset (June 7), marched down in a long column, elbow to elbow and as quietly as possible, to the strand. The boats, rocking a little on the swell of Lake St. Peter and scraping softly one against another as if the flotilla were rubbing its hands with satisfaction, swung quickly to the landing, and the Americans—under the watchful eyes of Thompson, Maxwell, Wayne, St. Clair, and Irvine, all notable men—embarked in rapid but mathematical order. Besides officers, bateaumen, and Canadians, the force in the boats counted about fifteen hundred.[18]

---

[17] § Sullivan to Thompson, June 6, 1776 (orders): Note 16. Id. to Wash., June 6: Note 16. Caldwell, June 11, 1776: Emmet Coll. Sch. to Sullivan, June 13, 1776: Sparks MSS., No. 20, p. 260. Wash. to Sullivan, June 16, 1776: ib., p. 264.
[18] § Sullivan to Wash., June 6, 1776: Note 16. A small part of Thompson's

.It was known that a number of British vessels lay several miles west of Three Rivers, and Thompson intended to land about a league above them ; but the pilot, guiding his flotilla of fifty bateaux directly across where the last pulse of the Atlantic tides dissolved into the wide sweep of Lake St. Peter, placed him—about two o'clock in the morning—on the red soil and wild strawberry blossoms of Pointe du Lac. Possibly the man had too strong a fear of the great guns, possibly too strong a fear of the lion's paw ; but it was true that good landings could not be found everywhere on that low, soft shore. Anyhow, a little way more to tramp mattered but little. There was plenty of time, and there was a good road. Three Rivers lay deep in untroubled slumber ; and the hearts, if not the eyes, of the brave lads on the shore could make out, as if just beyond it, the spire of Deschambault and the steeples of Quebec, shining like silver in the starlight.[19]

Leaving two hundred and fifty men to guard the boats, Thompson pushed on with the rest. It was planned that St. Clair, Maxwell, Irvine, and Wayne should attack at four distinct points, all aiming at the centre and so tend-

---

men perhaps went down later in the night. Thompson to Sullivan, June 7, 1776: 4 Force VI., 1038. Ursul. de T. Riv., I., p. 363. St. Clair, Narrative, p. 235. Irvine, Journal: Hist. Mag., Apr. 1862, p. 115. Letter, June 12, 1776: 4 Force, VI., 826. Vose, Journal. For an opinion of the officers, see Chase to Gates, June 13, 1776 : Sparks MSS., No. 60, p. 95. Lacey, Memoirs. Three Rivers : Marr, Remarks (Can. Arch., M, 384); Haldimand to Jones, Feb. 25, 1774 (Can. Arch., B, 33, p. 224); Bouchette, Descr. Topog., pp. 226, 309, 556 ; Burton, Report, May 31, 1763 (Can. Arch., B, 7, p. 61); Riedesel, Letters, p. 33 ; Stone (ed.), Letters, p. 45 ; Jefferys, Nat. and Civil Hist., p. 10 ; Hadden, Journ., p. 10 ; Dawson, N. Am., p. 307. It is assumed, as seems probable, that the Americans camped near the Lake.

19 § American accounts of the expedition : Sullivan to Wash., June 6, 1776 (4 Force, VI., 921) ; Id. to Id., June, 8, 9, 12, 1776 (Sullivan Papers, N. H. Hist. Soc.); Id. to Sch., June, 19, 1776 (Sparks Corres., I., p. 531); Thompson to Sullivan, June 7, 1776 (4 Force, VI., 1038); Wayne to Delaney, June 13, 1776 (Wayne Papers); St. Clair, Narrative, p. 235 ; Irvine, Journal (Note 18); Letter, June 12, 1776 (4 Force, VI., 826) ; Arnold to Sch., June 13, 1776 (Sparks, Corres., I., p. 531) ; Lacey, Memoirs, p. 200 ; Vose, Journal ; Senter, Journal ; Porterfield, Diary, p. 150 ; Nichols, Diary ; Porter, Diary ; Alexander, Diary (Temple and Sheldon, Northfield, p. 326). British accounts: Carleton to Germain, June 20, 1776 (Can. Arch., Q, 12, p. 64). Id. to Riedesel, June 9, 1776 : Can. Arch., B, 39, p. 3 ; Id. to ——, June 9, 1776 (ib., p. 2); Almon, Remembrancer, 1776, Part II., pp. 182, 193 ; Digby, Journal, p. 106 ; Précis of Oper.; Pell, Diary (Mag. Am. Hist., 1878, p. 43 ; Verreau (Sanguinet, Badeaux, Berthelot), Invasion, pp. 133, 219, 238 ; Ursul. de T. Riv., I., p. 371.

ing to unite, while Lieutenant-Colonel Hartley, in command of the reserves, should give support wherever needed, and Thompson should oversee everything. For some reason, perhaps to avoid passing near the British vessels, it seemed best to follow a branch road, which diverged a little from the highway toward the left about a mile below the landing; and, as the two guides, Frenchmen but not Canadians and residents of parishes a little way above, did not feel perfectly sure of the ground, Antoine Gautier, a Pointe du Lac farmer, was pressed into the service.

Somebody—Gautier, perhaps—adroitly spread the story that a British post lay at a certain white house on the highway about a couple of miles beyond the fork. It seemed advisable to capture it, and for that purpose Thompson kept straight on instead of taking the branch road ; but no British were found. Should he go back then to the fork, or continue to advance by the highway? Each plan had its disadvantages ; and, when Gautier proposed cutting across country to the road first chosen, the troops were ordered to follow him.

That soon brought them into a horrible swamp, and for hours they ploughed and wallowed in miry ground and muddy bogs, amid rushes, thickets, greasy roots, decaying logs, and all the other slimy obstacles of a deep morass. This way and that way they groped in the darkness. Many lost their shoes, and even boots were sucked off by the gluey mud. Feet were bruised or actually pierced through by sharp snags ; and both strength and spirits felt the drain. St. Clair and others trusted the guide still, and believed in pushing on for the branch road ; but Thompson, a veteran surveyor and used to the wilds, knew better. In a fearful rage, he demanded to be taken back to the highway, for, once more there, he felt that he could be sure of his bearings ; and finally, after wasting as much time as he could, the treacherous guide obeyed. Then

the advance began again ; but day showed signs of breaking before the vessels could be passed, and the sloop-of-
war *Martin*, aided more or less by the lighter craft, opened
a brisk fire.

As the highway ran within fifty yards or so of the river
this was extremely annoying.   The retort of muskets and
rifles had no effect ; and, after suffering for three-quarters
of a mile, the column took a slant into the woods, intending to make a circuit
and regain the high-
way.   But that was
never done.   Before
long, the men found
themselves engulfed
once more in the
far-reaching morass,
and, with the ves-
sels threatening them
from behind, could
see nothing wiser to
do than to force their
way across it, for
evidently the town
could not be very far
distant.   Too late,
however, they sadly
repented of their
choice.   Far better
the chances of grape

ARTHUR ST. CLAIR

and shells than a struggle with 'the most Horrid swamp
that ever man set foot in,' as Wayne described it : a
trackless jungle planted in a mammoth slough 'about
mid deep in general,' as another officer said.   To surprise
Three Rivers was out of the question now.   The best possible outcome would be a stand-up fight : on the one side,

twelve hundred and fifty hungry, tired men, who had lost their sleep for two nights, besides working on fortifications the intervening day ; and on the other an uncertain, per- haps larger, number of the enemy, fresh from their beds and more or less protected. The strong probability of success that Sullivan had insisted upon could not easily be figured out.

But, as an officer phrased it, ' Canada was lost, without some notable exertion.' A resolution of Congress, pro- nouncing it ' of the highest importance that post be taken at Dechambeau,' had arrived at Sorel just before Thomp- son set out, and this appeared to be the last chance of obeying that behest. Washington had said to Thomas, ' The lower down you can maintain a stand, the more advan- tageous will it be ' ; and the wisdom of the principle stood out in bold relief. ' This misfortune must be repaired, if pos- sible,' had been his comment on the flight from Quebec ; and it could not be repaired by a flight from Three Rivers. A victory there—to quote him once more—would be ' of the most essential service.' Even those who did not know what Washington thought on these points, could hardly fail to think as he did. Sullivan himself, in his orders for the expedition, had sounded a high note of ' bravery ' as well as advised prudence ; and, after ridiculing other troops for retreating before an enemy whom no person had seen, he could hardly be expected to commend his own for so doing. Moreover, these officers and these men had spirit of their own. ' It might have been, perhaps, pru- dent to have retreated—but no one would propose it,' said one of them afterward. Should withdrawal prove neces- sary, it could be ordered later, they felt. The boats were waiting and guarded. Forward, then, in Heaven's name, and at least have a sniff of gunpowder !²⁰

---

²⁰ § Letter from Sorel, June 12, 1776 : 4 Force, VI., 826. Secret Journ. Cong., May 25. Sullivan to Wash., June 6, 1776 : 4 Force, VI., 921. Wash. to Thomas,

For two or three hours the Americans fought the morass, the slimy brooks, the forest, and the bushes. Every moment they expected to find solid ground and space to form, and every moment brought a fresh disappointment. Toward eight o'clock, however, word passed along of a clearing and horses discovered about a quarter of a mile ahead, and this gave fresh hope. All pressed on, badly divided by this time—indeed, badly scattered—but all bound for the goal; and finally Wayne, with his small division of two hundred, reached ' a more Open piece of bad Ground.' At the same instant, he found a body of regulars bearing straight down upon him.

Here and now Mad Anthony had the baptism of fire. His fine person seemed to expand; his high and handsome forehead shone, as he swung his hat; his dark hazel eyes darted and flashed; his voice rang in bugle tones; and at the same time, as little disarranged by enthusiasm as by danger, his mind worked like a clock.[21] Throwing forward a company of light infantry and a company of riflemen to check the enemy, he formed the rest of his men as well as he could. The two advanced corps then wheeled to right and to left, threatening the British flanks; and his main body, pushing up between them opened a smart fire. Plastered with mud and here and there streaked with crimson, the lines of blue and white moved onward steadily, and, though regulars and more than twice as many, the enemy blenched. At first they retreated in good order,

May 24, 1776: Writings (Ford), IV., p. 102.   Id. to Sullivan, June 16, 1776: Sparks MSS., No. 20, p. 264.   Orders: Note 16.   Letter, June 12, 1776: 4 Force, VI., 826.
[21] Contemp. Description of Wayne: Hazard, Penna. Register, June 13, 1829.

but soon they broke and ran; and the Indians on their flanks, forgetting to shoot and yell, took to their villainous heels.

While this was going on, Thompson and the other divisions gained the edge of the woods, and pressed forward without a sign of fear. Bursting impetuously through a fringe of thickets, they could at last see where they were. Far yonder ran the blue St. Lawrence, bitten short off by a bluff that rose sharply from the meadows which bounded the river for many miles. Back from it straggled two or three hundred low wooden houses, culminating in the spire of a church. The wooden convent of the Ursulines and the stone monastery of the Récollets stood up rather grandly above the black roofs; and the old Governor's House of solid masonry, dominating the town and the environs, dignified a scene full of quiet and simple charm. They had not missed their aim: Three Rivers lay before them. But between them and their goal ran a line of new intrenchments, the fresh earth crumbling to sand in the June heat; and behind these, pausing and gazing with astonishment, they discovered—what they had not dreamed of seeing.

With the exception of a few men detained by contrary winds a short distance below, the entire 29th Regiment had reached Quebec by May fifteenth, and with it the 47th Regiment sent from Halifax. 'I hope we shall follow the Rebels closs at their heels,' cried Maclean; and it was rumored that he himself—'Beloved, Dreaded & indefatigable,' as Pringle described him—was to lead the advance immediately. Carleton, however, now that his tedious office of Shield had been resolutely fulfilled, sprang eagerly to that of Sword, placed himself at the head of the two regiments, and, amid the booming of cannon from ships and town, set off up the St. Lawrence. But, as the usual northeasters would not blow, he found himself compelled to halt a little below Three Rivers. There he posted a Canadian guard, to report whatever the Americans undertook to do, and returned to direct operations at Quebec. The ' rebels ' in the province were believed to number not less than five thousand, and both a spy and a New York newspaper had given notice of Sullivan's march; so that he understood the need of caution.[22]

Before he reached the capital, ten more vessels had entered the harbor (May 27). Others were continually arriving; and. the first of June, as the sun was going down, a fleet of sixteen dropped anchor there amid the crash of salutes. In these transports and ships of war, came the main expedition organized for the recovery of Canada, and this represented the best that His Britannic Majesty and the English pound sterling could accomplish. General Burgoyne, seven regiments from Ireland, one from

ANTHONY WAYNE

England, and some two thousand Germans hired out by the Most Serene Prince of Brunswick were aboard. Over £185,000 of real money on the *Juno* and *Blonde*, ships of war, supplemented the £20,000 just received by the

22 § Gordon to Barrington, May 15, 1776: War Off., Orig. Corres., N. Am., Vol. 12.   Carleton to Germain, May 14, 1776: Can. Arch., Q, 12, p. 14.   Maclean to Germain, May 10, 1776 : ib., p. 39.   Pringle to Howe, May 14, 1776: ib., p. 41. Humphrey, Journal, May 22.   Verreau (Sanguinet), Invasion, p. 130.   Maclean to ——, May 25, 1776: Can. Arch., Q. 12. p. 69.   Carleton to Germain, June 2, 1776: ib., p. 57.   Cramahé to Germain, May 25, 1776: ib., p. 50.   Spy: ib., p. 53.

Triton. Absolute completeness had been aimed at. Not only had one hundred and twenty-five thousand gallons of rum been provided, but new instruments also, to see whether it was ' of due Proof' withal.[23]

In spite of every effort, some delays had occurred in Great Britain, and the winds had not been favorable; but now the utmost pains were taken to save every minute. Pilots were sent down the St. Lawrence to guide the transports to Quebec, and other pilots were engaged for the river above. Frigates and armed vessels took post at proper points to assist and escort the fleet. ' The Transports Victuallers and Store Ships, to proceed with the utmost expedition,' ran Carleton's orders, ' as high as the wind & other circumstances will permit, [and] on being stoped the Troops are to land and proceed by the North [Side] with the same diligence.' Provisions for the shore parties were carried to suitable points. To render cantoning easy, the men had orders to march in squads of three hundred; and, for the sake of speed, they were to carry only thirty rounds of ammunition.[24]

Maclean, the indefatigable, remained at Quebec to hurry them along. Many of the transports were not allowed even to cast anchor there. Red tape was dispensed with. Carleton did not stop to make reports. To reach Three Rivers, the appointed rendezvous, was the one duty. By the second of June, General Fraser, with a part of the troops from Ireland and some transports, appeared there. By the seventh, enough more had arrived

---

23 § LeMoine, Port, p. 41. Germans : Can. Arch., B, 153, p. 6. Sailing: Germain to Howe, May 3, 1776 (Pub. Rec. Off., Am. and W. I., Vol. 431, p. 141); Précis of Oper. Germain to Burgoyne, Mar. 28, 1776: Pub. Rec. Off., Am. and W. I., Vol. 131, p. 743. Id. to Fraser, Mar. 19, 1776: Pub. Rec. Off., Am. and W. I., Vol. 431, p. 121. Robinson to Burgoyne, Mar. 29, 1776: Can. Arch., B, 38, p. 41. Substantially, if not literally, the whole of the expedition had reached Quebec by June 2 (Carleton to Germain, June 2, 1776: Can. Arch., Q, 12, p. 57).

24 § Germain to Carleton, June 21, 1776: Can. Arch., Q, 12, p. 44. Précis of Oper. Advices: 4 Force, VI., 1089. Carleton's orders, May 28, 30, 1776: Can. Arch., B, 83, p. 1.

by land to make upwards of a thousand, including some artillery with their field-pieces; and, on the evening of that day, while Thompson was leaving Nicolet, twenty-five vessels came up, some dropping anchor off the town, others advancing three or four miles beyond it.[25]

About four o'clock the next morning, an officer on a transport at Three Rivers opened his eyes laboriously and fought his way back to consciousness with a vague sense of noise. Could somebody be calling? Aye, somebody was calling. It was Fraser; and he was crying:

'For God's sake, wake up, and send ashore every gun you possibly can. The rebels are coming, two or three thousand of them. They're within a mile of the town.'

While Gautier was teaching the Americans to chase the *Will-o'-the-Wisp*, Landron, Captain of the militia at Pointe du Lac, had slipped round and given the news to a British out-picket. Like a flash in tinder the alarm spread. The troops, braced by their long voyage and weary of confinement, sprang eagerly to their work. The batteries already ashore were reinforced. The armed vessels prepared their broadsides. And so, when the Americans advanced far enough to survey Three Rivers and examine the new intrenchments, they found themselves face to face with some thousands of redcoats, many of them well posted behind breastworks.

Yet the sight did not unnerve them. Maxwell's division leading, they pressed boldly on and opened a sharp fire of musketry, while the riflemen farther back hurried up to support it. Small-arms and field-pieces replied from the intrenchments, and shot and shell from the fleet

---

[25] § Maclean to ——, May 25, 1776: Can. Arch., Q, 12, p. 69. Carleton to Germain, June 2 (and P. S., June 6), 1776: ib., p. 57. Germain to Carleton, June 21, 1776: ib., p. 44. Almon, Remembrancer, 1776, Part II., p. 192. Porterfield, Diary (May 27), p. 146. Carleton to Barrington, June 21, 1776: War Off., Orig. Corres., N. Am., Vol. 12. Digby, Journal. Sullivan to Wash., June 12, 1776: Sull. Papers, N. H. Hist. Soc. Carleton to Germain, June 20, 1776 : Can. Arch., Q, 12, p. 64. REMARK XCIX.

volleyed across the meadows.   Thompson ran to the front. Irvine, his fine head thrown high and his genial countenance aflame, led on his men.   St. Clair drew his long lips tight, pointed his mighty chin at the enemy, and pressed

THE WATER-FRONT, THREE RIVERS

forward.   H a r t l e y brought up the reserves.   The Americans heard B r i t i s h soldiers encouraging one another with the cry, ' We are three to one!' yet they quailed not ; and in massive columns they charged the breastworks.

But a tremendous fire converged upon them, while they now found themselves outflanked on one side by the ships and on the other by the overwhelming numbers of the British infantry. ' Indeed it was Impossible for them to support it longer,' said Mad Anthony himself; and they gave way. Thompson ordered them to retire fifty paces into the woods, and there he and his officers did everything possible to organize another attack ; but the ranks crumbled as fast as they were formed. Then partial rallies were made. One company planted itself within eighty yards of the enemy under the full fire of the ships. Riflemen posted behind trees taught the victors caution. A sharp musket fire from thickets reinforced the lesson. But, under that storm and on that ground, to form again and advance in full force was out of the question. 'Our men would fight,' said an officer a few days later, 'but we had no ground for it. We had no covering, no artillery, and no prospect of succeeding, as the number of the enemy was so much superior to ours.' Retreat was the only choice.

But there came the rub. General Nesbitt, a cool veteran who had seen service in almost every clime where British legions campaigned,[26] had landed a strong force from the vessels above the town, and hurried to cut the Americans off from their boats. Fraser, with a heavy column, struck for their rear. Grant set out for the bridge over the River Du Loup, some distance above. To regain the road and concentrate was impossible, for the instant a squad emerged from the woods, a gust of cannon-fire swept it back. The fleeing army, already divided, became badly scattered. In the midst of 'small timber,' where nothing could be seen twelve yards away, officers lost their men and men their officers.

At one time, Wayne collected about seven hundred and tried to reach the British flank, but in vain; yet, with only twenty-five who stood fast, he checked the enemy for an hour, making them believe the whole body was in the thicket still. Then he retreated in tolerable order, finding a good path and rolling up another ball of seven hundred as he retired, though all were exhausted, famished, perishing of thirst, and completely lost.

St. Clair, who knew the region somewhat, made his way with a strong party to the landing; but there, instead of the bateaux, he found Nesbitt's troops. Forming

---

[26] Nesbitt to Barrington, June 6, 1776: War Off., Orig. Corres., N. Am., Vol. 12.

as if to charge, he forestalled and delayed their attack, and then, moving suddenly to the right, threw a point of woods between himself and the enemy. By this bold stratagem he escaped, but it was only to plunge again into the woods and mire. ' Nature,' said Irvine, ' perhaps never formed a place better calculated for the destruction of an army.' Indians tirelessly stalked the fugitives, and Canadians ambushed them at every turn. As night fell, they could only drop where they were; and the next morning their heart-breaking flight began again.

Thompson and Irvine, like the rest, wandered all day. The swamp—which, according to a British account, was thirteen miles long—seemed endless ; and, whenever signs of open ground cheered them on either hand, the usual fire of musketry or field-pieces drove them back. All night they plodded on at random and in vain. When light broke, they found themselves not only worn out but completely surrounded; and, rather than be shot down from the bushes by the lurking Canadians, delivered themselves up as ' prisoners at discretion ' to a British guard.

Such promised to be the hard fate of all, Wayne and his party not excepted, for Major Grant now held the one door of escape. But fortunately Carleton himself arrived at Three Rivers that evening. Believing in the possibility of winning the honest masses away from their rebellious leaders, he longed to prove that the door of mercy stood ajar. After the Americans retreated from Quebec, he issued a proclamation inviting the sick, who had fled to the woods in fear of the rebel's halter, to surrender, promising them ' free Liberty ' to return home as soon as restored to health, and commanding the militia officers to ' make diligent search for all such distressed Persons and afford them all necessary Relief' at the King's charge. As soon as the flight of their comrades from

I have the honor to be with
profound respect & most faithful esteem

Your Lordship's
most obliged
and faithful humble servant J. Grignon

Quebec permitted, he visited the daring prisoners and ordered their irons removed ; and ere long they had a supply of fresh provisions. Great pains were taken to make them understand the kindness of his intentions ; unpleasant speeches to them were rebuked ; and later they were dismissed on parole with substantial presents. So now, in this temper of mingled policy and humanity, he said to Captain England of the 47th :

'What would you do with them ? Have you spare provisions for them ? Or would you send them to Quebec to starve ? No, let the poor creatures go home and carry with them a tale which will serve his Majesty more effectually than their capture'; and, recalling Major Grant, he threw open the door of escape.[27]

By hard rowing, all of the bateaux save one, though closely pursued by the troops and armed vessels, got away. A scouting-party of riflemen went across the St. Lawrence from Sorel to meet and direct the fugitives. And, by evening of the third day (June 11)—their veins almost sucked dry by the 'Musketoes of a Monsterous seize and innumerable numbers'—the wretched troops found themselves again at the mouth of the Richelieu. Of Wayne's own regiment, a quarter part was left behind ; and the total losses amounted to some two hundred and thirty-six captured, besides an unknown number dead. The hurt inflicted on the British signified little.[28]

'A very bold enterprise indeed,' was Carleton's description of this affair. 'The most audacious rascals existing,' exclaimed Joshua Pell, Jr., of the British army. 'The King of Prussia when on the brink of ruin never

27 § Verreau (Badeaux), Invasion, p. 219. Carleton, Proc , May 10: Can. Arch., Q, 12, p. 27. Melvin, Journal, May 7; June 5 ; Aug. 5. Henry, Journal, p. 165. Nichols, Diary (July 26), p. 509. Porterfield, Diary, May, 7, 9. Humphrey, Journal, May 7. Carleton to Howe, Aug. 8, 1776 : Can. Arch., B, 39, p. 93. Id. to Douglas, June 13, 1776: ib., p. 7. Id. to Pownall, June 28, 1776: ib., p. 37. Wilkinson, Memoirs, I., p. 55, note (W. had Carleton's words from England). REMARK C.

28 REMARK CI.

planned better,' admitted another officer. But, in spite of enterprise, deep strategy, and brave fighting, the British had won another decided triumph. To be sure, the real victor was neither Fraser nor Nesbitt, neither redcoat noi cannon. 'Had they not lost their road, they would have been an hour sooner and must have carried their point,' said a candid enemy. ' If Gen. Thompson had been one hour sooner,' it was understood in Quebec, ' he would have carried the post.' The real victor was the stubby, wriggling, dirt-brown clodhopper, An-toine Gautier. It was his grimy, horny fist that had held the distaff of fate. 'To the left,' from his tobacco-stained lips, at the fork of the road, would have given a great nation the first of its many victories in the field ; ' to the right,' meant an exultant Ministry and a jubilant King. 'So much for chance,' commented Lieutenant Nichols grimly.[29]

No matter who won, however, America lost. After listening for hours to the fire of cannon and musketry, which could not only be heard but distinguished at Sorel, Sullivan wrote to the Commander-in-chief, ' I am almost Certain that victory has Declared in our favor'; and the disappointment of their confident hope struck him and his army to the heart. But this terrible failure signified a great deal more. The six fresh and spirited regiments were already buried like the others in the bottomless gulf of disaster, want, plague, and chaos, and it was very plain that powerful British forces were near at hand. If the Americans had not been able even to hold their own before, what was to become of them now ? More than ever the pestilence walked abroad. ' Out of eight thousand men, that we have in this country, not five thousand effectives can be mustered,' said Arnold ; and very likely he did not

---

[29] See Note 19. The description of Gautier is inferential.

know the worst. 'Colo Graton is with me without a Single man all under innoculation' wrote Sullivan; 'Colo Bond with all his Reg^t in the same Situation Colo Patterson has Six only Colo Stark about forty Colo Reed, & Colo Poor Nearly in the Same Situation. . . . This Colony it seems has been of Late Considered as the General Hospital of America.' But, if a hospital, it was a very poor one. Dr. Lind, who had seen it, described the medical department in Canada as 'one scene of confu-

John Greaton

sion and anarchy.' 'It is a very dying time,' noted Frye Bayley with all seriousness in his diary. The fact was, Congress had given no person authority to establish a general hospital beyond the frontier,—still less provided the means to do so.[30]

So much was owing, and the expenses of the army—suddenly increased by ten regiments—mounted so fast, that Schuyler's $300,000 in paper money seemed little more than a heavy dew. 'Extremely deficient still,' said his Deputy Paymaster-General; adding very truly, 'A paymaster without money, is but a ridiculous animal.' Once more Congress poured all its cash into Schuyler's hands. It amounted to £1,662 sh.1 d.3. 'Every method to collect hard money for the army in Canada' had been tried, admitted the President; and here was the result.[31]

---

[30] § Sullivan to Wash., June 8, 1776: Sull. Papers, N. H. Hist. Soc. Porter, Diary, June 8. Arnold to Sch., June 6, 1776: Sparks MSS., No. 60, p. 93. Morgan to S. Adams, June 25, 1776: 4 Force, VI., 1069. Bayley, Narrative, June 15.

[31] § J. Trumble, Jr., to Hancock, May 21, 1776: 4 Force, VI., 537. Hancock to Sch., May 24, 1776 (two letters): ib., 558.

The prospect of starving seemed excellent, however. While Sullivan's brigade was approaching Sorel, Walter Livingston, the Commissary-General at Albany, wrote: ' This minute an Express arrives from Genl Schuyler who informs me that our Army will again be in danger of wanting provisions unless Pork is speedily sent up. I have not a barrel more to spare. If possible send more up. I have sent all round the Country, and cannot procure any more.' Were the meat obtained and landed at Albany, it would then have to go ten miles by boat, twelve by wagon, twelve by boat, two by wagon, three and a half by boat, half a mile by wagon, eight miles by boat, fifteen by wagon, thirty-six by boat, a mile and a half by wagon, and an equal distance by boat. At the end of this journey it would be off Ticonderoga. For the hundred and twenty miles to St. Johns, the reliance would have to be on sailing craft, liable to be 'detained by contrary winds, or by getting aground,' and on bateaux, liable also to founder by the wholesale in a sudden storm. Finally, it would have to go down the Richelieu about fifty miles, taking its chances in two series of rapids.[32]

Upon these difficulties, all sorts of minor embarrassments were piled. Even in the principal street of Albany wagons got mired. Lazy and tricky teamsters betrayed the best of schedules, and those the most upright did not care to work for nothing. Vexed by the demands of the soldiers, they all threatened to quit work and many did so. Provender for the draught animals was hard to get. An Indian scare could be relied upon to send the laborers flying home, and Schuyler discovered that the savages were moving. A single British vessel in the Hudson might cut the line of

[32] § Liv. to Josh. Trumbull, June 2, 1776: Trumbull Papers, Conn. Hist. Soc. Transportation: 4 Force, VI., 565. Sch. to Wash., May 21, 1776: ib., 537. The author infers there were rapids at St. Ours from the fact that at present a fall of five feet exists there, and vessels pass through a lock: Dawson, N. Am., p. 302 ; E. Townships Map.

supplies from New York, and many British vessels were looked for at the mouth of that river. In short, the Canada army was in the position of a Japanese juggler's umbrella balanced on a column of clay pipes; only it had no parachute quality, and all kinds of circumstances were being thrown all the time at the pipes.[33]

Making the necessary allowance for losses, General Schuyler estimated the daily requirement of the army at the north, after Sullivan's arrival, as twelve thousand pounds of pork and as much of flour. During May, by the utmost exertions, he kept the average shipment of pork from Lake George nearly up to that figure, but the flour was less than two thousand pounds a day. A certain amount of Canadian wheat helped out somewhat; but, on the other hand, all the laborers, guards, and crews beyond Fort George had to be fed, and the supply of Canadian wheat was precarious. The loss of Deschambault had cut off 'in a great measure' what might have been obtained, and Schuyler heard, at the end of May, that the army was 'in great straits' for it. In a word, only about one-half of the required weight of provisions was really forwarded. How, then, was the army to be fed in June? And what would follow should a serious accident occur? Schuyler could not escape 'the most poignant anxiety.'[34]

Looking for the enemy in force at New York, Washington could spare no more troops, and Schuyler felt that no help could be expected from the militia in case of an emergency. Powder, bullets, cannon-balls, and intrenching tools were still needed. The New York Congress could suggest no place to get lead save 'in and on the dwelling-

---

[33] § Munsell, Coll., III., p. 404. Sullivan to Wash., May 16, 18, 1776: 4 Force, VI., 479, 502. Sch. to Wash., May 10, 1776: ib., 411. Id. to Putnam, June 3, 1776: ib., 692.

[34] § Sch. to Price, May 7, 1776 : 4 Force, VI., 414. Report, Ft. George, May 31: ib., 639. Arnold to Sch., May 10, 1776: ib., 452. Sch. to Hancock, May 31, 1776: ib., 639. Id. to Wash., May 16, 1776: ib., 479. Walter Liv.'s letters to Sch. (Sch. Papers) tell much about the difficulty of supplying the army, etc.

houses.' Pennsylvania had found it necessary a month before to take up the lead clock-weights in Philadelphia in exchange for iron ones. Connecticut was just about to authorize the purchase of all the lead in the Colony, except that in sheets on the buildings, or—if the owner would not sell—the confiscation of it. No tents had yet been furnished for the reinforcements that preceded Thompson. 'Notwithstanding the most diligent pains,' Washington himself could gather 'but a small part of the Nails' required by Schuyler, and Congress was not able to obtain the shoes and stockings ordered for the Canada army. A competent engineer was at length found and appointed, but the man declined to serve. Schuyler, liable every day to

THE SWAMP, POINTE DU LAC

an attack of illness, harassed by the 'infamous manœuvres' of officers who tampered with his transportation arrangements, and 'infamously scandalized and ill-treated' by the 'assassins and incendiaries' who circulated 'diabolical tales' about him, had little chance to grow in patience and tact. Even his buoyancy failed, and almost his duty. 'I enclose you two Resolutions of Congress,' he wrote dishearteningly to the over-taxed Sullivan; 'I have not much hopes that either of them will have the happy effects which Congress expects.' [35]

35 § Wash. to Putnam, June 3, 1776: Writings (Ford), IV., p. 108. Sch. to Hancock, Apr. 2, 1776: 4 Force, V., 767. Id. to Sullivan, June 13, 1776: Sparks MSS., No. 20, p. 260. Id. to Wash., June 11, 1776: Lib. Cong., Letters to Wash., IX., p. 323. Wash. to Putnam, May 22, 1776: 4 Force, VI., 543. Lead: Invoice, note (4 Force, VI., 563); Penna. Com. Safety, May 9, 1776 (ib., 652); Conn. Assembly (ib., 878). Sch. to Hancock, June 1, 8, 1776: ib., 677, 762. Wash. to Sch.,

Gloom and confusion among the troops, despite the new blood, were inevitable. 'A starving army is actually worse than none,' wrote the Iron Duke soon after glorious Talavera ; 'The soldiers lose their discipline and spirit. . . . The officers are discontented and are almost as bad as the men'; but at Sorel the danger of starving was only one of a dozen afflictions. 'Almost lifeless' the troops had appeared when Sullivan came ; and now, when his new regiments—the sheet-anchor of what little hope remained—went down vainly into the gulf of disaster, disease, and despair, what chance of salvation was there ? No fewer than forty officers begged leave to resign, and the privates were 'filled with horror at the thought of seeing their enemy.' The atmosphere seemed a-tremble with panic. And, while Carleton's army gathered like a phalanx, the country itself closed in upon the doomed Americans like the walls of a contracting dungeon. ' Our enemies are daily increasing, and our friends deserting us,' testified Arnold.[36]

May 17, 1776: Writings (Ford), IV., p. 84. Journ. Cong., May 7. Wrixon to Hancock, Apr. 28, 1776: 4 Force, V., 1110. Sch. to Wash., May 26, 28, 31, 1776: 4 Force, VI., 578, 608, 639. Id. to Sullivan, June 13, 1776: Sparks MSS., No. 20, p. 260.
    36 § Hamley, Operations, p. 18. Sullivan to Sch., June 19, 1776 : Sparks, Corres., I., p. 531. Arnold to Sch., June 6, 1776, Sparks MSS., No. 60, p. 93.

XXXIV

HOPE WITHERS BUT SHOOTS AGAIN

'A FATALITY seems to attend every one of our
enterprises,' reflected Arnold gloomily.[1] But the
mischances of the wilderness march, the assault of Quebec,
the fire-ship, the attempt of the American prisoners to
escape and conquer, the sudden arrival of the British
fleet, Forster's legerdemain at the Cedars and Gautier's
handling of the distaff at Three Rivers were trivial indeed
compared with the fatality that seemed to be preparing
now.

' If we are not immediately supported with eight or ten
thousand men, a good train of artillery, well served, and
a military chest well furnished, the Ministerial troops, if
they attempt it, will regain this country ': such words,
written to Schuyler by Arnold about the middle of April,
had no lack of precision. ' In short,' advised the Commissioners of Congress eighteen days later, ' if [hard]
money cannot be had to support your army here with
honour, . . . we report it as our firm and unanimous
opinion, that it is better immediately to withdraw it '; and
this warning also rang as clear and sharp as Roland's
horn.[2]

Yet such letters, however precise, did not paint the
situation. What it required was to be drawn like Michel-

---

[1] Arnold to Commrs., June 2, 1776 : 5 Force, I., 165. (Arnold omitted 'one.')
[2] § Arnold to Sch., Apr. 20, 1776 : 4 Force, V., 1098. Commrs. to Cong.,
May 8, 1776 : ib., 1237.

angelo's *Last Judgment* and colored like an impressionist
Gehenna. The fagged and preoccupied brains at Philadelphia needed to be blistered with details. Washington,
although he had read many despatches, assured Hancock
after talking with Chase and Carroll, 'Their account
. . . cannot possibly surprise you more than it has done
me.' Even a verbal statement needed much amplifica-
tion to be understood. 'Let us know the truth, which
has too long been hidden from us!' John Adams exclaimed after the Commissioners had reported in person.
The broad facts looked incredible. 'Matter of wonder
and astonishment,' some of them appeared to Jonathan
Trumbull. Consequently, distant from the field and
lacking complete knowledge, Congress acted largely in
the dark still.[3]

On the other hand, the importance of holding Canada
seemed to grow more and more plain. Two great objects
were pointed out by Congress itself : ' the protection and
assistance of our Canadian friends, and the securing so
much of that Country as might prevent any communication between our enemies and the Indians.' In this way
the frontiers could be safeguarded, an armed invasion
would be averted, and the driving of a wedge from the
north into the midst of the Union would be made impossible. '*Resolved*, That the commanding officer in Canada,
be informed, that the Congress are fully convinced of the
absolute necessity of keeping possession of that country,'
recorded the Journal near the end of May ; and the President solemnly declared at the same time that, should
the province be abandoned, it was not ' in human wisdom
to foretell the consequences.'[4]

---

[3] § Wash. to Hancock, June 10, 1776: Writings (Ford), IV., p. 129. Adams
to Sullivan, June 23, 1776 : Works, IX., p. 407. Adams appears from the con-
text to include facts as well as causes. Trumbull to Williams, July 26, 1776:
Hinman, Conn., p. 560.
[4] § Journ. Cong., May 22, 24. Secret Journ., May 25. Hancock to Thomas
May 24, 1776: 4 Force, VI., 558, 559.

Of course it was known that a hard task had been set for the northern army, but at Philadelphia it did not look impossible. Charles Carroll of Carrollton, for one, doubted whether the force of the enemy exceeded 4,000. ' It is a woody country,' he suggested, ' and by intrenching, making abbaties, breaking up the roads, harassing the enemy on their march, and reducing the campaign to a war of posts, in forcing of which they will lose many men, we may probably keep a footing in Canada this summer.' On the approach of winter he believed that Carleton would have to withdraw his fleet from the upper St. Lawrence to save it from the ice. The American troops, heavily reinforced, could then drive the hostile army to Quebec; the passes of the river could be fortified ; and it would thus be made impossible for the British to go up again the following spring. As Washington, Gates, and Mifflin

had by this time been called upon to advise Congress, and Carroll would not have presumed to offer military ideas of his own at variance with theirs, this opinion probably represented what the legislators had learned from the generals. At any rate, Congress decided to ' expect ' the forces in Canada to ' contest every foot of the ground,' and pronounced it ' highly necessary ' to make a stand below the mouth of the Richelieu. This language did not favor a retreat from Sorel ; and thus, in effect, a rotten pest-house of a sloop was bidden to challenge a royal fifty-gun man-of-war fresh from the painters. Paul Jones in the *Bon Homme Richard* dared far less.[5]

---

[5] § Carroll to Gates. June 14, 1776 : Sparks MSS., No. 60, p. 101. Journ. Cong., May 23, 24.

Sullivan made a fit primer for this rashness. His intelligence and military knowledge were no doubt ample to point out the weakness of his position. Sorel was a flat, unhealthful beach, rising little and very gradually above the water. Lying at the junction of the St. Lawrence and the Richelieu, the spot looked extremely important, and the French had there erected forts and minor works, though little or nothing valuable of them now remained. A few days after the Americans had retreated from Quebec, a breastwork of sand facing the St. Lawrence was begun, and the troops worked at it for ten days or more. They accomplished little, however; but Sullivan promptly ordered five hundred men to the spades, and implored them in general orders to ' Exert themselves,' ' the preservation of the Country as well as their own honour and Safety ' appearing to depend upon their efforts. A battery for ten guns on the right bank of the Richelieu, a battery for eight guns on the left bank, a three-gun battery on St. Ignatius Island over against Sorel, many smaller fortifications, proper lines of intrenchments, an abatis, and a stockade were rapidly completed. ' Pretty good works,' an officer observed cheerfully as he looked about; and, behind the defences, at least the fourteen pieces of cannon—several of them 32-pounders—that a British spy had touched and counted in May, were now in position.

But, at a little distance in the rear, could the enemy reach it, there was high ground commanding all these fortifications. The abatis had been made of tall sapling pines, the only wood at hand, planted upright in the sand;

6 § Senter, Journal, near end (undated). Bouchette, Descr. Topog., p. 226. Canad. Antiq., Jan., 1875. Lévis, Journal, p. 293. Shallus, Journal, May 12, 13. Vose, Journal, June, 8–10. Woedtke's and Sullivan's Ord. Book, June 10: Lib. Cong. Sullivan to Wash., June, 5, 1776 : 4 Force, VI., 921. Almon, Remembrancer, 1776, Part II., p. 194. Lacey, Memoirs, p. 201. Letter, June 12 (13), 1776: 4 Force, VI., 826. Spy, May 12, 1776: Can. Arch., Q, 12, p. 54. Thompson to Sullivan, June 7, 1776: 4 Force, VI., 1038.

and these, drying quickly under the hot sun, made an admirable combination of tinder and match-wood, while they would actually have aided the enemy by masking his approach. What St. Clair considered ' a good boat-able stream ' ran behind Sorel and emptied into Lake St. Peter. The high water had prevented Arnold from sink-ing a *chevaux-de-frise*, as he called it, at a narrow place in the St. Lawrence five miles below; and evidently, as the flood still continued, the chain brought from New York proved useless. A correct return of the army could not possibly be made, but Sullivan found only twenty-five hundred men round him, the best of them little more than spectres ; and these had to do a three-fold duty,—as troops, as laborers, and as nurses. Canadians were com-ing in ; but, warned Hazen, ' they will leave us in the hour of difficulty.' Sufficient pork had been arriving of late ; but, during the first eight days of June, only flour enough for three days had left Fort George. The chance of holding the enemy in check at Sorel under these con-ditions appeared rather dark.[7]

That, however, was only the first syllable of the dan-ger. To fight with a river at one's back has always been considered perilous ; and a river lay at Sullivan's back lengthwise, with a big lake, also lengthwise, behind that. Chambly boasted a large garrison—of small-pox invalids. St. Johns, the very pivot of the campaign, had only a sergeant and twelve men for a guard, swamped by another host of the sick. ' Not one stroke done to fortify the Camp, the engineer a perfect Sot , ' Arnold found when there on a tour of inspection. Crown Point, Ticonderoga, and Fort George lay defenceless. Butler at Niagara had

[7] § Senter, Journal : Note 6. St. Clair, Narrative, p. 240. Arnold to Commrs., May 17, 1776 : 4 Force, VI., 592. Thompson to Sullivan, June 7, 1776: ib., 1038. Return : ib., 915, note. Sullivan to Sch., June 19, 1776 : Sparks, Corres., I., p. 531. Hazen to Sullivan, June 13, 1776: Sparks MSS., No. 60, p. 108. Sch. to Hancock, June 8, 1776: 4 Force, VI., 762. Lamb, Return : ib., 763.

induced the greater part of the Senecas, Cayugas, and Onondagas to enlist for the King. Hostile bands were known to be gathering at Oswego. Sir John Johnson had stolen away northward some time before with a body of his angry Highlanders and all the savages he could muster ; and nobody knew what point he would strike. Some regulars, with five hundred Scotch, Canadians, and Indians were hovering round Montreal, watching for a chance to deal a blow ; and numberless Canadians, like Antoine Gautier, felt eager to make their peace with England by betraying America. Some of these many hostiles might almost be expected to cut Sullivan's line of support, and Schuyler, frequently shaking with the ague so that his signature could hardly be recognized, had little strength or spirit for new and fearful emergencies.[8]

And yet even this was by no means the worst of it. The St. Lawrence ran almost parallel to the Richelieu ; the road along the north shore was open to the British ; and Arnold with only two guns, no matrosses to serve them, and but four hundred and fifty infantry, outnumbered already by his prowling foes and well aware that many of his men had been inoculated, could not undertake to prevent the enemy from crossing to the south side. Let the British but reach Longueuil with a strong column by this route, ignoring or amusing the forts at Sorel, and they could march to Chambly, only four leagues distant, for a morning promenade. Sullivan, almost fifty miles below, would then be absolutely ruined. A dozen miles

---

[8] § St. Johns : St. Clair, Narrative, p. 241. Arnold to Sullivan, June 13, 1776 : Sparks MSS., No. 20, p. 258. Returns : 4 Force, VI., 915, 917. Lansing to Sch., June 14, 1776 : ib., 942. Sch. to Wash., June 17, 1776: ib., 939. Wynkoop to Sch., June 20, 1776: ib., 1058. Kirkland to Sch., June 8, 1776 : ib., 764. Sch. to Sullivan, June 13, 1776: Sparks MSS., No. 20, p. 260. Johnson: Carleton to Germain, July 8, 1776 (Pub. Record Off., Colon. Corres., Quebec, 12, p. 191) ; (see Id. to Barrington, War Off., Orig. Corres., N. Am., Vol. 12, wrongly dated June 8) ; Blackburn to Claus, July 30, 1776 (Can. Arch., M, 104, p. 224). Verreau (Sanguinet), Invasion, p. 133. Arnold to Sullivan, June 5, 1776 : Sparks, Corres., I., p. 524. Id. to Sch., June 10, 1776: ib., p. 527. Sch. to Sullivan, June 20, 1776: Sullivan Papers, N. H. Hist. Soc.

more to St. Johns, and Arnold also would be cut off. Every American in the province would surrender. Then, leaving the Canadians to guard his prisoners, Carleton would embark his troops in the bateaux, sail to Ticonderoga, march to Albany, rush down the Hudson, co-operate with Howe's powerful army, stamp out Washington, and scatter the Conscript Fathers. No Declaration of Independence could then appear ; and the only real question would be, How many insurgents to hang? Tryon was looking for such a descent from the north ; General Howe was planning for it; and the British Government expected it. Precisely this was the ' one campaign ' which Lord George counted upon for 'putting an end to the Rebellion.'[9]

Yet Sullivan, though he must have seen this danger, refused to be impressed by it.

In the first place, he would not credit the Governor's reported numbers ; and, in the next, he assumed that his enemy would attack him at Sorel. Perhaps he argued that ships were so very convenient for the transportation of men and provisions that Carleton would not abandon his fleet ; and possibly, being a fighter himself, he could not believe that a good soldier would ignore a saucy ' rebel ' waiting for him with so big a chip on his shoulder. Should the vessels dare attack him,—Prescott's fleet had yielded to one sham battery, and Carleton's might well surrender to three real ones ; and this looked the more probable because, according to Price, nothing so deep as a frigate could pass Lake St. Peter with her burthen. Besides, the gallant Sullivan had 'his little tincture of vanity' and ' an over desire of being popular, ' as Washington

---

[9] § Arnold to Sullivan, June 5, 1776 : Sparks, Corres., I., p. 524.   Id. to Id., June 11, 1776: Sullivan Papers. Carleton to Germain, June 20, 1776: Can. Arch., Q, 12, p. 64.   Tryon to Germain, July 8, 1776: Pub. Rec. Off., Am. and W. I., Vol. 186, p. 735.   Howe to Germain, June 7, 1776: ib., Vol. 131, p. 423.   Précis of Oper. Germain: p. 324.

had observed ; and, after his glowing reports and sanguine predictions, he little cared to retreat. Ambition also
had a place in his thoughts. Like Samuel Chase, he
doubtless believed that ' laurels were still to be reaped in
Canada ' ; and, under the veil of asking that Washington
or Lee take the command there—neither of whom, as he
well knew, could do so—he announced his intention to
resign should any one else be set over him. This was a
bid for the supremacy in that quarter, and he could not
easily relinquish the prospect.[10]

A variety of other influences aided in stiffening him.
The orders of Congress and the prayers of his countrymen
awoke a loyal response in his heart. The idea of letting
Carleton off without a fight he could not bear. The
danger itself nerved him ; and his courage rose as the
incoming tide of the Kenmore swelled past the home of
his fathers. ' At all hazards,' he would stay at Sorel till
a reinforcement could arrive. ' I am determined to hold
it as long as a person will stick by me,' he promised the
Commander-in-chief. Even when satisfied of Carleton's
preponderance, he did not flinch. ' I now think only of
a glorious death or a victory obtained against superior
numbers,' he assured Schuyler.[11]

Meanwhile, the British army gathered rapidly at Three
Rivers and was organized in six brigades. Almost exactly
ten thousand effectives answered at roll-call, and around
them buzzed a cloud of Canadians and Indians. Some
holds of the transports were opened with all speed, and a
good number of field-pieces got ready for their work.
Fraser set off with a strong column by land along the

[10] § Sullivan to Sch., June 25, 1776: Bancroft Coll., Sch. MSS. Commrs. to
Thomas, May 12, 1776: Emmet Coll. Wash. to Hancock, June 17, 1776: Wash.,
Writings (Ford), IV., p. 156. Chase to Gates, June 13, 1776 : Sparks MSS., No.
60, p. 95. Sullivan to Wash., June 7, 1776: Bancroft Coll., Rev. Papers., I., p. 93.
[11] § Sullivan to Sch., June 19, 1776: Sparks, Corres., I., p. 531. Id. to Id., June
25, 1776: Bancroft Coll., Sch. MSS. Id. to Wash., June 12, 1776 : 4 Force, VI.,
1037. Sch. (quoting Sull.) to Wash., June 20, 1776: ib., 976.

north shore. The rest of the grenadiers and light infantry embarked in the leading ships, the light artillery in the next, and then the remaining troops in their order. Arrangements were made to have forces march by the south shore, in case that should be necessary. But a favorable wind sprang up; from vessel to vessel the heave-ho of the capstan sang out; the anchors came slowly up loaded with the clean sand of the St. Lawrence; the sails filled; and, Thursday afternoon, June thirteenth, the fleet passed up into Lake St. Peter, coming to off Nicolet as the breeze died away. 'We hear the enemy now firing; this will be a hot week,' wrote an American officer at Sorel, as he listened to the signal guns; 'we are determined to fight inch by inch.' But the British general had a shrewder idea than that.[12]

JAMES WILKINSON

At one o'clock in the morning, the wind rose again; the *Rousseau* transport came up, with Carleton aboard; and the fleet got under way immediately. Not long afterward, shots were heard on the shore; an express arrived; and the Governor ordered the anchors dropped. But the alarm proved nothing serious, and, in less than

---

1 2 § Orders, June 12: Can. Arch., B, 83, p. 7. Numbers: Pub. Rec. Off., Am. and W. I., Vol. 290, p. 127; Précis of Oper. (Very likely there were in fact over 10,000, for an estimated deduction of 30 non-effectives per regiment was made, and at this stage the estimate was probably too large.) Almon, Remembrancer, 1776, Part II., pp. 182, 193. Carleton to Germain, June 20, 1776: Can. Arch., Q, 12, p. 64. Orders, June 14: Can. Arch., B, 83, p. 9. Digby, Journal. Letter, June 12, 13, 1776: 4 Force, VI., 826.

an hour, the ships moved on again. Little by little, the sky flushed with grey and then with gold and crimson; and at length full daylight revealed a splendid scene. Sixty vessels filled the eye with a cloud of white, warmed into loveliness by the tinge of sunrise. Their decks, clean-scoured and orderly, were populous with trained soldiers rosy with eagerness for combat. The black band of the 29th with red feathers in their hats, who looked so ' extrornery neat,' merely fitted their surroundings. The German officers, in blue regimentals with red facings, broad lace and silver frogs, actually seemed to ' shine'; the English scarlet, gold-laced and gold-epauletted, positively did shine; and the polished muskets and cannon, sword hilts and bayonets more than shone, for they flashed. The British government, after centuries of splendid fleets and armies, called it a ' great Armament'; and King George himself would have been proud to look upon it.[13]

The soft murmur and light sparkling foam of ripples at the prow of every vessel seemed like a welcome to the expedition. The grave stillness of the dark forests that rimmed the lake; the white cottages, here dotted and there clustered at the shore; the orchards and gardens decked in their holiday June attire of pink and white; the puffs of invisible incense breathing eddies of perfume into the soft wind; and the faint song and chirp of countless birds, blending in a sylvan allegro, kindled the feelings and roused the spirit. Winding in and out among the wooded islands at the upper end of the lake, the vessels appeared to multiply. Nothing seemed wanting to illustrate the grandeur and power of the armament save a total contrast,—a glimpse of the low, grovelling, earth

13 § Orders: Can. Arch., B, 83, p. 9. Digby, Journal. Almon, Remembrancer, 1776, Part II., pp. 182, 194. Humphrey, Journal, May 19. Porterfield, Diary, p. 148. Précis of Oper.

ramparts at Sorel; and finally these could be seen. The issue now stood clearly forth. It was health against sickness, confidence against defeat, plenty against want, gold against paper, four against one; and Sullivan's bravery, even should the enemy condescend to fight him, could only dash itself and the army to pieces. ' The destruction of a large part, if not the whole' of the American army in Canada was the prospect that Washington saw on learning the facts.'[4]

But Sullivan's bravery had suddenly acquired wisdom. Thompson had early pronounced Sorel untenable. St. Clair had expressed the same opinion from ' the first Moment' he saw it. Arnold, satisfied ' by the best accounts,' that Carleton had ten thousand men, pointed out that he would strike for the American rear, and urged an instant retreat from Sorel. The plan to incorporate Canada in the Union of Colonies, he told Sullivan, had failed. To hold a mere scrap of the country would be of ' little or no service '; and a battle against such a superiority would risk everything. ' I am content to be the last man who quits this Country, and fall so that my Country rise—but let us not fall all together,' he implored. Hazen and Antill gave equivalent advice. The general opinion at 'Sorel ran the same way; and desertion began to show the feeling of the troops. Yet Sullivan would not stir. But at length Fraser's column was actually seen, on that Thursday, stealing along the north shore toward the rear. At night a council of war met, and nearly all the field-officers in camp begged the General to retire.

' If you persist in occupying your present ground and any ill consequences follow,' they said firmly, ' you alone must answer for it.'

----

[14] § Digby, Journal. See Knox: Parkman, Montcalm, II., p. 364. Wash. to Sch., June 24, 1776: 4 Force, VI., 1053.

Sullivan made no reply. But he reflected; and, after meditating for some time, he answered,

' I believe you are right; and I will immediately order the boats to be got above the rapids.' [15]

So, when the grand British fleet drew near the sandy beach of Sorel, all was bustle and activity behind the rusty foliage of the pine abatis. With feverish haste, wan, ragged, hungry-looking figures were loading cannon, stores, invalids, and arms into the bateaux. Spades were levelling the intrenchments, and, that done, they also went into the boats. Tents, camp-kettles, and every last object followed. The troops embarked and pulled away with all their might. And, one hour later—when a blue ensign, floating to the peak of a British frigate, gave the signal—a force of grenadiers and light infantry, supported by a part of Nesbitt's brigade, rowed through the gloaming, landed, and crunched across the shingly beach to the dismantled works. [16]

Very early the next morning more troops went ashore, and that day Burgoyne, eager to exert ' every faculty ' he possessed for the King's pleasure, began the pursuit with about four thousand men and six field-pieces. The Americans, worn in heart and in body, fatigued by a desperate day's work, little refreshed by a night's repose wherever they happened to drop, and burdened with every impediment, well knew how little chance they had in a race with

---

15 § Thompson to Wash., May 30, 1776: 4 Force, VI., 628. St. Clair to Sch., June 19, 1776: Coll. of Mr. F. A. Arnold. Arnold to Sch., June 13, 1776: Sparks, Corres., I., p. 531. Id. to Sullivan, June 13, 1776 : Sparks MSS., No. 20, p. 258. Hazen to Sullivan, June 13, 1776: ib., No. 60, p. 108. Antill to Sullivan, June 13, 1776: Cont. Cong. Papers, Letters to the Pres., A, 78, 1, p. 5. Sullivan to Sch., June 19, 1776: Sparks, Corres., I., p. 531. Desertion : Hazen to Sullivan, June 13, 1776 (Sparks MSS., No. 60, p. 108). St. Clair, Narrative, p. 240.

16 § References for Sullivan's retreat : Sullivan to Sch., June 19, 1776 (Sparks, Corres., I., p. 531); St. Clair, Narrative, p. 240 ; Shallus, Journal ; Vose, Journal ; Lacey, Memoirs, p. 202 ; Arnold to Wash., June 25, 1776 (4 Force, VI., 1107); Maxwell to Sch., June 25, 1776 (Sch. Papers) ; Wilkinson, Memoirs, I., p. 51 ; Alexander, Diary (Temple and Sheldon, Northfield, p. 326) ; Digby, Journal; Almon, Remembrancer, 1776, Part II., pp. 182, 193 ; Pell, Diary, p. 43 ; Carleton to Germain, June 20, 1776 (Can. Arch., Q, 12, p. 64). Orders: Can. Arch., B, 83, pp. 9, 10.

fresh, lightly weighted troops ; but they resolved to do their best. While the bateaux vexed the Richelieu with all possible speed, the shore contingent marched at an equal rate about three miles in the rear. Many tributaries of the river crossed the highway ; and as the troops, after plunging down the little pitch leading to each of the rough bridges, hurried up the other side, they looked inquiringly back for a line of scarlet and steel.[17]

But Burgoyne did not appear. It was no part of his duty to hurry the Americans back to St. Johns. To alarm, annoy, and delay them, if he could, would be useful ; but his orders were to hazard nothing until the rest of the army had secured its position, and the Governor sailed on as quickly as possible for Longueuil. With the breeze holding as it now blew, he would reach that point by Saturday evening (June 15)[18] ; and the next morning, striking the American van at Chambly, he could also reach out for the boats waiting at St. Johns. Only one question remained : Would the breeze hold ? The weathercock was the distaff now. A puff of air more or less might decide the whole future of America.

For a time the fleet sailed gaily on. The narrow St. Lawrence above Sorel was gorged with vessels. Brown's imitation battery had no effect. The crews and the troops were jubilant. But after a time the ripples at the prows died out; the pennants drooped; the sails fluttered and then flapped. The wind—truly a wind of destiny—had failed. Helms were abandoned and anchors dropped.

This gave Sullivan a respite. But he needed more than a respite. Ahead of him stood Chambly Rapids, a tumbling wall of strong water, seventy-five feet in vertical

---

[17] Burgoyne: see facsimile on page 437. Stone (ed.), Letters, p. 49.

[18] Cf. Carleton to Germain, June 20 (Note 16) with Arnold to Wash., June 25 (Note 16).

height. Even to go down that reeling staircase of grey-white billows was difficult and perilous. ''T is truly astonishing that a bateau can live in such places,' Chaplain Robbins had exclaimed. What chance, then, of ascending the falls? 'I much question,' Charles Carroll had remarked; 'I much question whether the batteaux could be brought up.' [19]

Fortunately, however, Sullivan understood this kind of navigation, and he was in earnest. His well-rounded, handsome, beaming face hot and dripping, his lips tightly set when they were not speeding commands, his great brown eyes lightening incessantly amid the storm of his countenance, his athletic figure hurrying from point to point, straining at a rope or bending to the wheel of a cannon, he toiled like a demigod and taught the rest how to labor like heroes. Some of the boats went round in Canadian carts; and the others, hugging the shore, were drawn through the rapids with long ropes by men often ' up to their armpits in Water,' while soldiers on board kept them off the rocks and banks with poles. In the midst of terrible heat, without a moment's rest day or night, this Herculean labor went on. At last, by the General's personal attention and exertions, as St. Clair testified, the miracle was wrought; and on Monday (June 17), about an hour after noon, murky flames, darting into the sky from the fort and storehouses of Chambly, announced that Sullivan had completed his work. Then, with his artillery and baggage at the front and a guard to prevent any person, whether officer or man, from passing them and in that way suggesting flight, he moved on in some kind of order, and reached St. Johns that evening. The troops in pursuit, softened by their long confinement on shipboard and almost melted by the sun, had not as yet been able to

---

[19] § Dawson, N. Am., p. 302. Robbins, Journal, Apr. 28. Carroll, Journal, p. 94.

BURGOYNE'S PLEDGE ON SAILING FOR AMERICA

annoy their enemy ; but, at 9 o'clock the next morning, Burgoyne was inspecting the smoking ruins at the foot of the rapids.[20]

Arnold, for his part, had made a tour of observation some days before, ordered Antill to fortify St. Johns, directed Hazen to remove the valuable stores and the sick from Chambly, and then returned to Montreal. 'I shall remain,' he grimly notified Schuyler, 'until I have orders to quit it, or am attacked, when it will be too late.'[21]

Saturday forenoon (June 15), he sent off Captain James Wilkinson in a 12-oared bateau with despatches for Sullivan at Sorel; and the Captain, about three o'clock, as he approached Varennes, fourteen miles below, heard a cannon boom not far away, and then another. Wondering what this could mean and landing to investigate, he found a tide of redcoats inundating the village streets and a skyful of poles growing out of the river beyond the point. Carleton was there and the breeze had just failed him.

Leaping a fence and stealing away under cover of a thicket, Wilkinson came to the big stone windmill and found a horse at the door. Without asking the owner for a saddle, he sprang instantly upon the animal's back, left his men to care for themselves, and galloped the dozen miles to Longueuil at full speed. There, he forced a Canadian at the point of his sword to help launch a canoe, got a paddle by the same argument, and about five o'clock burst upon Arnold at the Château with the news that his retreat was being cut off. Word having just arrived that Sullivan had left Sorel, Arnold felt free to evacuate Mon-

---

20 § Amory, Sullivan, p. 9. Portraits of Sullivan, particularly one in oils in the State Library, Concord, N. H. Note particularly St. Clair, Narrative, p. 241, and Lacey, Memoirs, p. 202. REMARK CII.

21 § For evacuation and occupation of Montreal: Arnold to Sch., June 13, 1776 (Sparks, Corres., I., p. 531); Id. to Sullivan, June 13, 1776 (Sparks MSS., No. 20, p. 258); Id. to Id., June 16, 1776 (Sullivan papers, N. H. Hist. Soc.); Id. to Wash., June 25, 1776 (4 Force, VI., 1107); Wilkinson, Memoirs, I., pp. 38, 49 ; Lacey, Memoirs, p. 199 ; Bayley, Narrative ; Orders, June 16 (Can. Arch., B, 83, p. 10) ; Verreau (Sanguinet), Invasion, pp. 132–134. REMARK CIII.

treal. In two hours, the sick, the baggage, and the garrison—reduced by this time to three hundred men—embarked in eleven bateaux; and, in two hours more, a procession of carts, escorted by the troops, set out from Longueuil for Laprairie and St. Johns.

While this was going on, Arnold reflected : his retreat would be slow, the enemy must soon learn of it, the next day they would be upon him ; and, calling Wilkinson, he ordered him to find Sullivan and obtain a reinforcement. It was a dark and stormy night ; but Wilkinson discovered a horse at the priest's door in Longueuil, mounted without asking troublesome questions, and at nine o'clock entered Chambly.

Here 'the front of our retreating army ,' he wrote in his Memoirs, 'overwhelmed with fatigue, lay scattered in disorder over the plain and buried in sleep, without a single sentinel to watch for its safety.' Not halted, not even hailed, he rode through the encampment, crossed the drawbridge of the fort, and presented himself at headquarters. No slumber there, however. Depressed but determined, Sullivan, St. Clair, Maxwell, and Hazen sat planning for the morrow.

The news from Varennes burst upon them like a shell. 'Be the Lord ,' cried Maxwell with his brave Scottish burr, 'it cannot be possible !'

But very possible indeed it was ; and, after some discussion, Wilkinson was directed to find Woedtke, who commanded the rear, and give him the order to detach five hundred men for Arnold. It was then raining torrents, but the Captain set out. Every house, every cabin, every barn and hut along the road were filled with soldiers, 'men without officers and officers without men,' all plunged in deep gloom ; but nobody could direct him to the Baron. Demoralization seemed complete ; the army was no more. At length, discovering a vacant spot on a filthy floor, Wilkinson threw himself down and fell asleep.

At daybreak, he began his quest again ; and, meeting Lieutenant-Colonel Allen of the Second Pennsylvanians, a brave, active officer,[22] he inquired for Woedtke.

' No doubt the beast is drunk and in front of the army,' was the reply ; ' but Col. Wayne is in the rear, and if any one can do it, he is the man.'

In half an hour the hero of Three Rivers appeared, ' as much at his ease as if he were marching to a parade of exercise,' thought Wilkinson ; and—quite of Allen's opinion about the Baron—he promptly accepted the commission. A guard was posted at the next bridge. It halted men without reference to their regiments ; and, in less than an hour, the needed corps was cheerfully marching off, ready to fight old Carleton and all his bloody-backs, or for that matter the devil himself, should he be in company. There might no longer be an army, but there were still men. Fortunately, two miles on they met an express, and learned that Arnold now felt himself out of danger. Breaking down the bridges and felling trees across the road, he passed safely to St. Johns on Sunday (June 16), and none of these gallant fellows that marched out with Mad Anthony had to spill a drop of their heroic blood.

Just before leaving Canada, Chase, foreseeing the evacuation of the country, had urged Schuyler to send all the vessels and boats he possibly could to St. Johns ; but Arnold, on reaching that point, received notice this had not been done. Congress, determined to hold on, had ordered six thousand militia sent north, and the boats were detained above for their transportation. The instructions to fortify St. Johns had not been carried out,—doubtless because they could not be. By Monday evening, Sullivan's army was there, exhausted, defenceless, and, in spite

---

[22] **Chase to Gates, June 13, 1776: Sparks MSS., No. 60, p. 95.**

of all that its leaders could do, confused 'beyond description'; and the next day found Carleton, Fraser, and Burgoyne focusing upon it and not far away. Burgoyne had the lead, with men enough at his back to ruin the Americans. All the bridges above Chambly had been destroyed, but he rebuilt them rapidly. For a while, Sullivan's rearguard was supposed to be an attacking column, and preparations to receive it caused a delay ; but, something like two miles from St. Johns, the mistake was discovered, and three companies of light infantry were ordered on at the double quick.[23]

A little distance ahead, two men sat calmly on their horses and reconnoitred the British advance. These were Arnold and Wilkinson. Presently they turned and galloped back to St. Johns. Warned by Colonel Poor of the real situation, Schuyler had concluded to send the boats. A council of war had resolved unanimously to give up the place. The sick and the well had embarked. Artillery, stores, baggage, and every individual scrap of American property there—even to the last dull axe—had been loaded in. Colonel Hazen had crossed the river and set fire to his own mansion. The fort also was in flames. Arnold looked about him : not a thing remained to do. He and Wilkinson then shot their horses and tossed the saddles and bridles into the waiting boat. Bidding an affectionate farewell to Chief Louis of Caughnawaga, the one inhabitant of Canada waiting to say good-bye, Arnold ordered all hands on board, and, pushing the boat off himself, sprang into the stern. Before it was fairly out of musket range, the British van charged swiftly into St. Johns.[24]

---

[23] § Chase to Sch., May 31, 1776: Sparks MSS., No. 60, p. 90 ; Arnold to Sullivan, June 16, 1776 : Sullivan Papers, N. H. Hist. Soc. Militia: Journ. Cong., June 1 ; Sullivan to Sch., June 19, 1776 (Sparks, Corres., I., p. 531). Cushing, Journal. Carleton to Germain, June 20, 1776: Can. Arch., Q, 12, p. 64. Id. to Fraser, June 17, 1776: ib., B, 39, pp. 11, 12. (Letters, ib., pp. 13-18, throw further light on the British movements.) Digby, Journal.

[24] § Sch. to Wash., June 20, 1776: 4 Force, VI., 975. Sullivan to Sch., June

At that moment, Lorimier with a gang of the redskins was hurrying toward a narrow place in the river above. But he arrived too late ; and, as the night fell (June 18), the last of the Americans in Canada rowed silently and sadly for Nut Island. The wall of pines and firs on the right threw upon the river a pavement of shadows, wider and deeper every moment, broken into where the Americans had camped the year before, and touched at intervals by a glance from the sunset sky darted almost straight across it. Here and there a bat, hunting the swarms of hovering insects, winged his restless, distracted flight like the soul of a lost hope, and now and then an owl, deep in the forest, cried a sepulchral ' Who ? Who ? ' like the challenge of a Stygian sentry; but of the British nothing was seen and nothing heard. As Napoleon meanly said of Moreau's escape through the Valley of Hell, it was only a retreat ; but a retreat like Moreau's or Sullivan's is a triumph.[25]

' The Troops halt tomorrow,' read Carleton's general order the next day, for without boats he could not pursue; but the Americans had foes that would not stop. The plight of the sick, thrown hastily on the island so that the boats could go back for more, made Dr. Meyrick weep till he could weep no longer ; and the well seemed hardly less to be pitied. After the frightful exertions of the past few days, they were ' almost weried to Death.' Meyrick thought the men who rowed him from St. Johns ' would fall from their seats.' The malarial air of the island found them just ready for its germs. The camp-

19, 1776: Note 23. Id. to Wash., July 2, 1776 : 4 Force, VI., 1219. Bayley, Narrative. Wilkinson, Memoirs, I., p. 54. Vose, Journal. St. Clair, Narrative, p. 242. Lacey, Memoirs, p. 202. Arnold to Wash., June 25, 1776: 4 Force, VI., 1107. Cushing, Journal. Meyrick to Trumbull, June 1, 1836: Trumbull, Autobiog., p. 299. Alexander, Diary : Temple and Sheldon, Northfield, p. 326. Letter, July 3, 1776: 4 Force, VI., 1252. Carleton to Germain, June 20, 1776: Can. Arch., Q, 12, p. 64.

25 § Verreau (Lorimier), Invasion, p. 284. Cushing, Journal. Scammell to Bishop, June 2, 1776: Hist. Mag., Sept., 1870. The bat and owl are inferential. REMARK CIV.

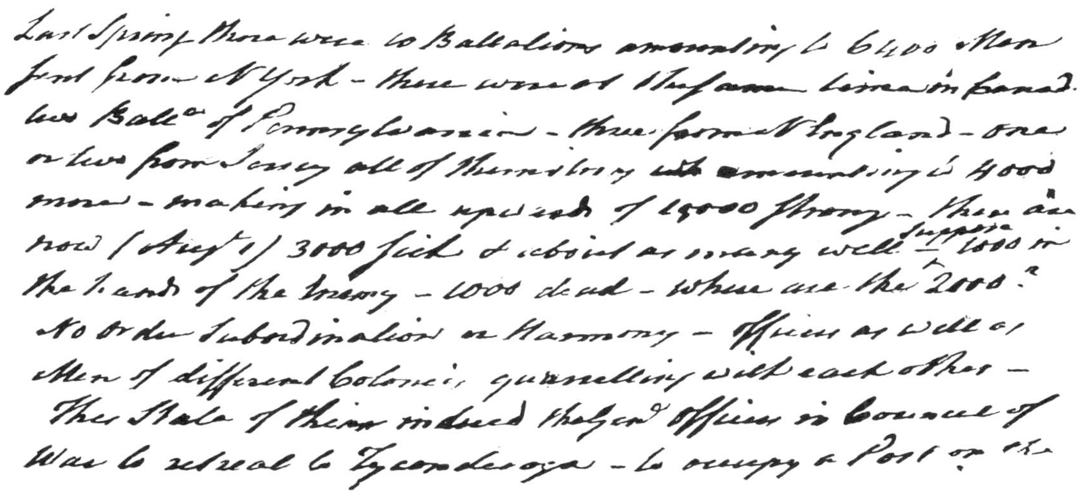
Last Spring there were 10 Battalions amounting to 6400 Men
sent from N York - there were at the same time in Canada
two Batt^s of Pennsylvania - three from N England - one
or two from Jersey all of them being ... amounting to 4000
more - making in all upwards of 12000 strong - there are
now (Augt 1) 3000 sick & about as many well - suppose 1000 in
the hands of the Enemy - 1000 dead - where are the 2000?
No Order Subordination or Harmony - Officers as well as
Men of different Colonies quarrelling with each other -
This State of things induced the Genl Officers in Council of
War to retreat to Tyconderoga - to occupy a Post on the

FROM A MEMORANDUM BY SAMUEL ADAMS, AUG. 1, 1776

disorder struck down one quarter of the army within
forty-eight hours ; and the small-pox, ' in its most viru-
lent and deadly form,' laid low ' whole regiments in
the course of a few days,' as Sullivan himself reported.
There were not enough tents for the sick, and no boards
to make shelters. Salt pork and flour—a part of the
time salt pork alone, and some of that rancid—made up
the list of delicacies. Medicines gave out, and doctors
also. ' Oh the Groans of the Sick ! ' cried Bayze Wells ;
and in many and many a case the groans had one and the
same end. All day long the dead-pits were open ; and this
poor body after that, lying mute and still in its rags on a
dirty blanket, passed down to an unknown grave ' without
a sie from a Friend or relative, or a single morner to follow
it.' Unable to bear such ' scenes of horror ' longer without a respite, several excellent officers deliberately sat
down together 'in good Earnest,' and calmly drank
themselves insensible. ' This wretched Army, now perhaps the most pitiful one that ever was formed,' its
commander described it.[26]

The council of war had advised a complete withdrawal
to Crown Point, and that was the only sensible course.
Not only had Nut Island little to recommend it as a place
of residence, but the British could plant small field-pieces
on the shores above it in a little while, and cut off the
army's communications. Yet Sullivan, still haunted by
the point of honor, declared that he ' could not ' retreat
farther on his own responsibility with men able to do
duty ; and, sending Arnold to Schuyler for orders, he
busied himself in reconnoitring Iron Point, transporting
the sick to the upper end of the lake, and assisting the
people near him to move beyond reach of the enemy. As

---

[26] § Order: Can. Arch., B, 83, p. 10. Lacey, Memoirs, pp. 202–206. Meyrick.
etc.: Trumbull, Autobiog., pp. 27, 28, 299. Sullivan to Wash., June 24, 1776:
4 Force, VI., 1220. Arnold to Sch., June 13, 1776: Sparks, Corres., I., p. 529,
Wells, Journal, etc., p. 267. Sullivan to Wash., June 24, 1776: 4 Force, VI., 1220.

promptly as possible, the orders to withdraw came ; and, during the first days of July, the wreck of the army gathered itself painfully and pitifully at Crown Point, humiliated, woe-begone, and utterly demoralized. 'A truly melancholy scene,' lamented Governor Trumbull. Three thousand able to crawl and as many sick were all that remained. For the rest of the brave fellows who had sailed into the north so hopefully, no living man would undertake to account.[27]

Up to this point, then, our endeavor to win Canada has run through several distinct phases, each with its own chance of success.

What Samuel Adams despatched Brown to inaugurate, was a campaign of political agitation and enlightenment.

That could not possibly have brought Canada into the Union. The British element there counted too small a number, was too divided in sentiment, and had interests too much threatened by the commercial policy of the Colonies ; while the Canadians, besides lacking political tastes, experience, and knowledge, had too little education to profit much from pamphlets or even speeches.

After the capture of Ticonderoga, the campaign became both political and military ; and in this form it ought not to have failed. More decision and force on the part of either Congress or General Schuyler might clearly have ensured the capture of Quebec during the summer or the autumn. The elimination of any one of a series of mischances would probably have enabled Arnold to accomplish his mission. Only a succession of accidents prevented

[27] § Sullivan to Wash., June 19, 1776 : Sparks, Corres., I., p. 531. Sch. to Sullivan, June 20, 25, 1776: Sullivan Papers, N. H. Hist. Soc. Arnold to Wash., June 25, 1776: 4 Force, VI., 1107. Sullivan to Sch., June 24, 1776 : ib., 1201. Cushing, Journal. Porter, Diary. Lacey: Note 26. Shallus, Journal. Meyrick, etc.: Trumbull, Autobiog., pp. 28, 299. S. Adams, Mem., Aug. 1, 1776: S. Adams Papers. Trumbull to Williams, July 26, 1776 : Hinman, Conn., p. 560. Sullivan to Cont. Cong., July 2, 1776: Cont. Cong. Pap., 160, p. 15. J. Adams, July 7, 1776: Smith, Pittsfield, I., p. 261. Spy: July 11, 1776: Can. Arch., B. 181, p. 10. Robbins, Journal. Bayley, Narrative. Wilkinson, Memoirs, I., p. 61. REMARK CV.

the assault from carrying the Lower Town, and very possibly—not to assert more—that would have won the whole. Had Quebec fallen during 1775, in all likelihood Canada would have sent delegates to the Continental Congress ; and, had it fallen before the end of November, she would almost infallibly have done so.

It has been said that the Canadians and Americans could not have fraternized ; but the scenes at Chambly and St. Johns, in the Chaudière valley, before Quebec, and at Aspen Point disproved this theory by substantial facts. There were peculiar and powerful influences just then and there to weld the two peoples. The Canadians had learned to be guided in political affairs by Saxon Protestants rather than by French priests. The mass of Colonials feared ' papists' not from hatred to any mystical theory of transubstantiation or devotion to any particular exegesis of a text about keys, but from a vivid recollection of thumb-screws and iron boots, confiscations and auto-da-fés. It was, in short, the political aspects of the Roman Church they abhorred ; and the Canadians, abjuring clerical guidance in temporal affairs to espouse the principles of English liberty, not only ceased to excite alarm, but became peculiarly interesting and appealing. Sooner or later, the priests were doubtless to recover their ascendancy ; but, if the Americans had prospered, this would not have come to pass until after the political attitude of Canada had been determined.

Had the capture of Quebec and the complete expulsion of the British troops occurred in time to swell the rising tide of Canadian confidence, giving it no chance to ebb, the people would almost certainly have reached the stage anticipated by Mr. Bondfield, and become ' so deeply engaged in the present contest as to render their vigorous exertion acts of necessity and self defence.' [28] And Great

28 Bondfield to R. Morris, Feb. 4, 1776: N. Y. Hist. Soc. Coll., 1878, p. 399.

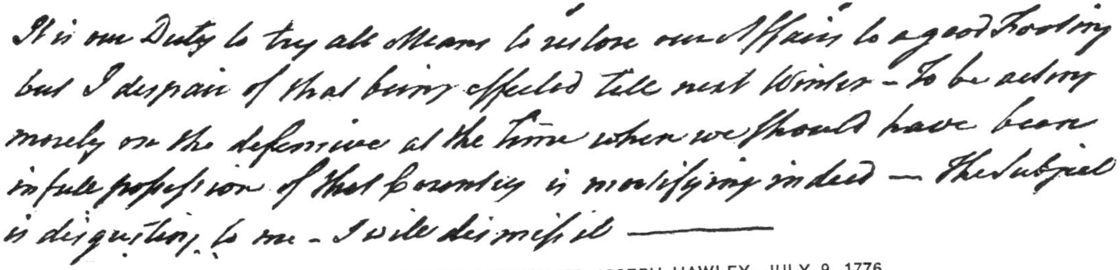

It is our Duty to try all Means to restore our Affairs to a good Footing but I despair of that being effected till next Winter — To be acting merely on the defensive at the Time when we should have been in full possession of that Country is mortifying indeed — The Subject is disgusting to me — I will dismiss it ——

FROM SAMUEL ADAMS'S LETTER TO JOSEPH HAWLEY, JULY 9, 1776

Britain, seeing this, might have chosen to abandon an alien, costly,[29] and undervalued province, which she had probably thought of letting France reoccupy.

Had she chosen the opposite course, the adhesion of the Canadians might not have enabled the Americans to hold that province during the war. Even if, as has been represented on the other side of this proposition, Canada possessed fifteen thousand fighting men, it is certain that no *levée en masse* would actually have taken place. In 1779, the United States had 435,000 men of the military age; yet in 1781, when the country needed every ounce of its power, only 29,340 soldiers—militia included—took the field.[30] Besides, the great majority of the Canadian volunteers would have been young and inexperienced; and they would have evinced no greater constancy than the men of 1759. There would not have been time to organize an army capable of meeting the British strength which arrived in May. Once driven from the province, the Americans would not have been likely to force its doors against the guards Britain would have established; and—even had they done so—they could not have made it impossible for her naval power to go up the St. Lawrence.

Yet, had the Canadians once taken the American side emphatically, a considerable number of men would have enlisted, and these would have been forced, like Hazen's regiment,[31] to find a refuge in the States. The British government would have been compelled to treat the people as traitors instead of truants, with steel instead of birch; and the fear of this or its consequences would have sent many more across the border. All these refu-

---

[29] Coffin, Quebec Act, pp. 362, 363.

[30] Fiske, Critical Period, p. 102.

[31] Hazen, Memorial, Apr. 8, 1783; Cont. Cong. Papers, 42, III., p. 451; N. H. State Papers, XVIII., p. 911. In the later Chapters will be found much to confirm this paragraph.

gees would have proved cords of union, and they would have kept open and rankling every wound inflicted in Canada by British severity. The expense and annoyance of holding the country—great even as matters turned—would have been, under such conditions, immense. They would have taxed and wearied the government; the chance of making the province loyal and peaceable would have seemed remote; and, when the war ended, even if British troops held Quebec, England might perhaps have surrendered Canada quite as cheerfully as New York.

After Montgomery fell, the Canadians in general were regarded as doubtful, indifferent, even hostile. The campaign became then almost purely military; and this, however it should turn, was doomed to failure. In other words, to capture Quebec in April would have been profitless, for the confidence and friendship of the people had then been chilled, and they could not possibly have been warmed again in time to co-operate. Here one does not have to theorize about what might have been. Carleton's despatches at the end of November fixed the policy of Great Britain for the ensuing year, so far as Canada was concerned. A powerful expedition for its recovery was ordered and was sent; and its arrival, while the Canadians were still outside the American Union, was sure to determine their attitude.

In fact, the capture of Quebec in April would have proved a misfortune, for it must have tended to commit the Colonies to a struggle where their money would not circulate and the people were not in their interest. The battering train[32] in Burgoyne's transports would almost certainly have driven the Americans from any works they were then able to raise at Deschambault; or,

---

[32] A. Lee to Franklin, Feb. 13, 1776: 4 Force, IV., 1125 ; Germain to Carleton, Feb. 17, 1776: Can. Arch., Q, 12, p. 1.

had it not, the mere cost of carrying on a war at arm's length would have exhausted the poor, feebly organized, and inexperienced military administration of the young States. Their only chance of success lay in a tedious defensive contest, with distances, difficulties of the ground, popular feeling, the instinct and necessity of self-defence, the granaries and the looms all working in their favor. In a sense, then, one phase of the campaigns for Canada —the third—succeeded; for the only possible success at that stage was to fail.

The collapse of so glorious an expectation and the failure of so costly an effort stirred the Colonial leaders profoundly. Many, to be sure, found comfort in Sullivan's brilliant retreat. Under the circumstances, this was ' a most fortunate event,' maintained Washington with his invincible constancy. 'We have got out of Canada pretty well considering the situation we was in,' reflected Colonel Greaton cheerfully. Some braced themselves without looking for compensations. 'We ought to be prepared in our minds for greater changes and more melancholy scenes still,' proclaimed John Adams grandly; while the pious Trumbull urged that the disappointment should be received 'with that steadiness and fortitude which becomes the soldier and the Christian, who believes that Heaven will never forsake the cause that is just.' But others felt a chagrin too deep to bear. 'The subject is disgusting to me—I will dismiss it,' cried Samuel Adams, though dismiss it he could not.[33]

All joined, however, in John Adams's outburst, ' For

33 § Wash. to Hancock, June 30, 1776: Wash., Writings (Ford), IV., p. 196. Greaton to Heath, July 31, 1776: Heath Papers, I. J. Adams, July 26, 1776: 4 Force, VI., 1083. Trumbull to Sch., June 28, 1776: ib., 1126. S. Adams to Hawley, July 9, 1776: S. Adams Papers.

God's sake explain to me the causes!' And many tried, with honest hearts, to find them. A committee of Congress, appointed for that purpose, named short enlistments, the lack of hard money, and the small-pox. Samuel Adams, though he dared not state what he took to be the real difficulty, suggested that 'Our secret Enemies had found Means to sow the Seeds of Discord and Faction there.' To Jefferson, the want of gold and silver, the pestilence, and an unlucky choice of officers, explained the sad outcome. 'Pray did not opening the trade to the upper country and letting loose the tories bring upon us so many disasters?' demanded John Adams; while at another time he traced the misfortune partly 'to the indecision of Philadelphia and partly to the mistakes or misconduct of our officers in that department.' Whoever has followed the events carefully has observed every one of these causes and some others; and at the bottom of nearly all, except the small-pox and personal errors, he has found what the President of Congress laid bare: 'We were compelled, unprepared, hastily to take up the weapons of self-preservation, and have, consequently, had numberless difficulties to struggle with; of which the expedition into Canada has been a continued scene.'[34]

Yet America had reason to congratulate itself upon the northern campaigns. Only the invasion of Canada prevented Carleton from regaining the command of Lake Champlain, rolling up a substantial force and coming south in 1775; and the effect of such a movement upon the situation in that year and the next would have been serious, perhaps decisive. The invasion did still more. It caused a division of the British strength, which other-

---

[34] § J. Adams to Sullivan, June 23, 1776: Works, IX., p. 407. Journ. Cong., July 30, 1776. S. Adams to J. Hawley, July 9, 1776: S. Adams Papers. Jefferson to Fleming, July 1, 1776: Jeff., Writings (Ford), II., p. 39. J. Adams to Bullock, July 1, 1776: Works, IX., p. 414. Hancock to Sch., Apr. 26, 1776: 4 Force, V., 1086.

FROM JOSEPH HAWLEY'S LETTER TO SAMUEL ADAMS

wise would very likely have been concentrated against
us, as a wedge of steel, at New York.   This, to be sure,
might have proved a doubtful advantage, had the northern British army succeeded in coming down by the
Hudson.   But that, as will presently appear, the war in
Canada prevented.[35]

Other advantages, also, ripened on the same thorny
tree.   The early successes at the north inspirited the
patriots and attracted volunteers to the ranks.   The bright
instances of heroism set an example for the Americans,
and ennobled them in the eyes of the world.   The martyrs'
blood was seed for the cause.   Even the common people,
who seldom perceive a principle until it strikes them, came
to realize the value of discipline and the evil of short
enlistments.   The idea that officers ought to manage
affairs after the manner of a caucus gave way in Congress
to a saving belief in authority.[36]   The meaning of war
and some knowledge of its methods got abroad, as they
could not from a mere fight like Bunker Hill or a mere
investment like that round Boston.   Many volunteers
had time to graduate as veterans.   Many clever, preten-
tious rogues, who had got into uniforms for the sake of
the buttons, the sword, and the epaulettes, were sternly
sifted out ; and sterling officers had a chance to show
themselves and qualify before the real tussle began.   The
manufacture of munitions and equipments gained a start.
In short, the Canada struggle was a dress rehearsal for
the war.   It revealed weak points ; it made plain some
things that could be done and some that could not ; and
perhaps its failure was a schooling that made the Revolution succeed.

Politically, it created a compulsive common interest and

[35] REMARK CVI.   See also the next Chapter.
[36] Chase to Gates, June 13, 1776: Sparks MSS., No. 60, p. 95.

helped evolve the nation in several other ways : particularly two.

The first was internal. At the beginning of the northern campaigns, Colonies addressed one another almost as foreign states. Repeatedly during their stress, trouble, and disappointments, provincial jealousies, jibes, and accusations did great and evident mischief; but at its close, before the real war began, the Congress instructed Schuyler 'to recommend, in the strongest terms, harmony between the officers and troops of the different states ; to discountenance and suppress all provincial reflections and ungenerous jealousies of every kind, and to promote, by every possible means, discipline, order, and zeal in the public service.' This was a lesson not too dearly learned.[37]

Externally, the war in Canada helped lead a confused agitation to its logical goal. One after another, step by step, a series of exigencies not met with at Cambridge drew Congress and the country toward a plain issue : independence or subjection. Events in Canada taught that the army must have a flag and the Colonies must have constitutions. 'Our Declaration of Independence has given Vigor to the Spirits of the People,' wrote Samuel Adams ; 'Had this decisive Measure been taken Nine Months ago it is my Opinion that Canada would now have been in our hands.' 'Had a declaration of Independency been made seven months ago,' declared his cousin, John, 'we should have mastered Quebec, and been in possession of Canada.' What these men felt so strongly in July, 1776, they and others must have foreseen long before. Joseph Hawley, for one, on hearing of the flight from Quebec, exclaimed : 'Will your Congress now delay for a Moment the most explicit declaration of *independence ?* ' And the fact that such leaders understood

---

[37] Journ. Cong., July 19, 1776.

RICHARD, VISCOUNT HOWE

455

what aid this measure would give, tended to bring it about.[38]

While Sullivan's routed army lay gasping at Nut Island in the last extremity of wretchedness, while defeat and gloom seemed to overwhelm the patriot cause, Richard, Viscount Howe, parading grandly in ' His Majesty's Ship, the Eagle, off the coast of the Province of Massachusetts Bay, ' flung broadly to the wind ' free and general pardons to all those who in the tumult and disorder of the times might have deviated from their just allegiance, and who were willing, by a speedy return to their duty, to reap the benefits of the Royal favour.'[39] Could sane men, with two such pictures before their eyes —the wretched failure and the easy escape—could sane men dream of rejecting the King's offer and defying the power of Great Britain ?

Dr. Senter, who had watched the long series of ' most peculiar and unparalleled rebuffs and sufferings' from the Kennebec to Montreal and from Montreal to Nut Island, concluded his Journal in these words : ' Thus ended an expedition of nine months continuance, the ill success of which in any other cause would have induced us to have renounced the principles.' It was not a shrewd calculation of self-interest but devotion to a cause that controlled the hearts of the patriots, and therefore no thought of surrender could be entertained. This gave immense dignity to the attitude of America. But the circumstances of the hour added vastly to its dignity. To challenge Great Britain, even under a sunny sky, for the sake of an ideal, would have been grand ; to do that under the cloud of July 4, 1776, was sublime. Were there nothing else to say for those campaigns in Canada, as a background for the

---

[38] See pp. 64, 328. S. Adams to R. H. Lee, July 15, 1776: S. Adams Papers. J. Adams to Mrs. Adams, July 3, 1776: Works, IX., p. 419. Hawley to S. Adams, May 22, 1776: S. Adams Papers.

[39] Howe, June 20, 1776: 4 Force, VI., 1001.

Declaration of Independence they were fully worth what they cost.

And their significance reached farther. In spite of many human frailties displayed in the struggle, the lofty patriotism, the keen intelligence, the bold initiative, the dauntless courage, and the splendid fortitude exhibited there made it a fit prologue of our whole national career ; while, as if in return, the bell of the first glorious Fourth rang in a new era, not only for the cause of self-government, but for the hopes of those—and they were not few—who still dreamed of securing Canada.

XXXV

FROM THE SUBLIME TO GENERAL GATES

'UNTIL that,' cried the venerable Joseph Hawley when praying for a declaration of independence; 'Until that the Continent will never act compactly and with vigor—but will entertain thoughts of returning back into Egypt—until that the Tories will look with hopes and some assurance—until that the Conclusions and resolves of your Congress will be languid and like a lamp burning in a cold damp Vault.' And now the glorious Declaration had been flung to the free winds.[1]

What the campaign in the north had suffered from the impediments that Hawley pointed out, measured how greatly the cause was to profit by this change ; and other gains also could be expected. The army would have a flag now,— the flag of a great and popular hope. The Canadians could be offered something precious and inspiring,—self-government and partnership in a nation. The Colonies, no longer kneeling at the foot of a contemptuous throne but appealing as a free, brave people to the admiration and sympathy of generous humanity,[2] were sure to win aid for the emancipation of the fourteenth as well as the thirteen. Indeed, they themselves had now more reason than ever to labor for it, since—if they became independent—the northern province must be either a support

---

[1] § Hawley to S. Adams, May 22, 1776: S. Adams Papers.
[2] E. g., Doniol, La F., p. 15 ; Id., Particip., I., p. 632.

or a menace, either a partner or a possible foe, not merely during the settlement of a quarrel with England but for many years, perhaps forever. 'Canada, Canada is the Object,' exclaimed Hawley himself when begging for the Declaration.

First, however, the retort expected from the very hour Ticonderoga was seized, had to come and be met. Carleton's pursuit of the Americans halted perforce on the shore at St. Johns, but he began at once his preparations 'to return the visit of the rebels,' as he pleasantly phrased it.[3]

When Lieutenant Pringle went over to England, the November before, the Governor had enjoined very urgently upon him to call for 'a number of flat bottomed Boats, and materials prepared and ready to be joyned together, with all their apparatus for rigging, arming &c'; and that officer obeyed his orders with great zeal and thoroughness. 'Representations' were made to the Admiralty for 'a number of armed ships drawing little water'; and, as that Board had no such vessels to send, steps were taken to find them. By the first of April, they were reported as 'nearly fitted out.'[4]

The Governor, however, not venturing to take anything for granted, bent all his power toward the building of a fleet. The next day after his army halted, he requested Commodore Douglas to have 'every means' employed in forwarding materials for 'armed vessels' to sail

---

[3] Carleton to Hamilton, July 19, 1776: Can. Arch., B, 39, p. 76. The paragraphs that follow, dealing with the invasion of the Colonies by Carleton and Burgoyne, do not properly belong in this work, for the people of Canada had only the most incidental connection with the operations; but it has seemed desirable to insert them as 'connective tissue.' The author has used many original documents, but has not undertaken to investigate matters thoroughly, and gives references in special cases only.

[4] § Carleton to Germain, Sept. 28, 1776: Can. Arch., Q, 12, p. 188. Id. to Phillips, Nov. 18, 1776: Can. Arch., B, 39, p. 258. Robinson to Burgoyne, Mar. 29, 1776: Can. Arch., B, 38, p. 41. Sept. 26, 1776, Carleton reported that ten boats and materials for building fourteen one-gun boats had arrived. These were evidently very little toward gaining control of Lake Champlain. Besides a fighting navy, it was necessary to construct boats for the transportation of troops.

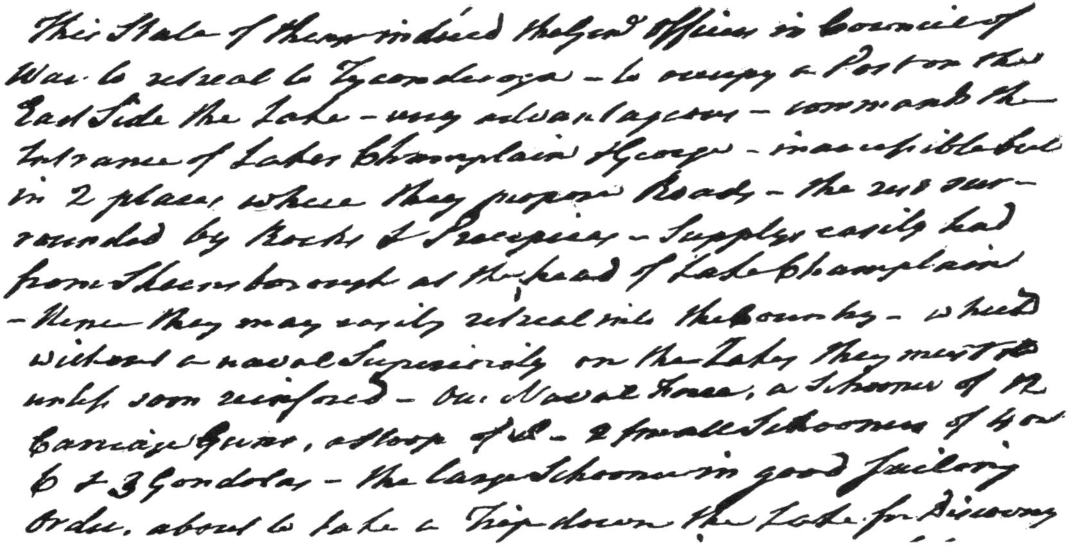

FROM A MEMORANDUM BY SAMUEL ADAMS, AUG. 1, 1776.

the lake and in sending men to work them up. Cool though he was, he confessed his 'impatience in this, so essential, point.' Artisans were drafted from all departments of the service, wherever found; a squad arrived by water at Quebec; and General Phillips, Commodore Douglas, and the rest did their all to advance the work. There was 'a prodigious deal to execute,' as the Governor found; materials could not easily be obtained; many of the workmen fell sick; but at length, on the twenty-eighth of September, Carleton found himself able to announce, ' I expect our fleet will soon sail.' [5]

On the other side, equal efforts were made. Before the fleeing Americans reached Crown Point, Arnold pronounced it 'of the utmost importance that the Lakes be immediately secured by a large number (at least twenty or thirty) of gondolas, row-galleys, and floating-batteries.' [6] His advice was followed as well as it could be; Arnold himself took command of the fleet; and, early in September, a line of American vessels, moored across the outlet of Lake Champlain, permitted not so much as a bateau, hailing from the north, to ruffle its liquid glass. Apparently the Americans meant fight. Carleton saw he must reckon upon that; and priceless days were spent by the British in preparing to meet them. At last, not only was the fleet ready to sail, but in the weight and also in the number of available guns, it had the superiority. [7]

Arnold, for his part, studied the situation with masterly insight. What were his vessels good for? To beat the British, if possible, but at all events to delay them; for

[5] § Carleton to Douglas, June 21, 1776: Can. Arch., B, 39, p. 29. Id. to Id. July 3, 1776: ib., p. 55. Id. to Germain, Aug. 15; Sept. 28, 1776: Can. Arch., Q, 12, pp. 170, 188. Id. to Cramahé, Aug. 27, 1776: Can. Arch., B, 39, p. 116.

[6] The exact distinctions between these three kinds of vessels are not fully understood. The galleys appear to have been larger and quicker than the gondolas: see Mahan, Scribner's Mag., Feb., 1898, p. 150.

[7] § Arnold to Wash., June 25, 1776: 4 Force, VI., 1107. Gates to Cont. Cong., July 29, 1776: 5 Force, I., 649. Arnold to Gates, Sept. 7, 1776: 5 Force, II., 223. Carleton to Germain, Sept. 28, 1776: Note 5.

a check signified a victory.   Already the season was late, and soon the campaign must end.   Horatius-at-the-Bridge represented the correct policy, then.   Vessels and men should be hurled at the enemy and all sacrificed without hesitation, if need be, to gain time.   Yet not a point was

to be thrown away ; and the admiral, after exploring and reflecting, decided to station his fleet
in the strait between Valcour
Island and the New York shore,
near the lower end of the lake.
Should the enemy attack him
there from the north, a knob in
the middle of the passage might
catch a vessel or two ; while,
should they sail past the long,
high screen of the island, nòt

aware the Americans lay behind it, and attack from the south, they would have the wind more or less against them.

It was the second chance that befell ; and, on the eleventh of October, Carleton's fleet, discovering its enemy after passing the island, sailed back as well as it could and brought as much as possible of its force to bear.   A single one of his vessels—the square-rigged *Inflexible*, carried to St. Johns in sections from the St. Lawrence—was probably more than a match, in a good wind, for everything Arnold had ; but she could not work effectively until late in the day.   A schooner, however, and a flotilla of gunboats got soon within half-musket range, and, like dwarfs battling for the prize of titans, the two little fleets hammered one another for hours.   Arnold's principal vessel—the *Royal Savage*, captured at St. Johns—ran aground at the beginning of the action, and was taken by the enemy. His men were mostly a 'very indifferent lot,' in need of shoes and stockings, breeches and blankets, hats and caps, and there had not been powder enough to practise often with the heavy guns; whereas the British had been able to draw from a large fleet, from an army of regulars, and from overflowing magazines. On his own galley, Arnold found it necessary to point most of the guns himself. Yet the Americans bravely stood to their work, and played a noble prelude to Macdonough's glorious fight at Cumberland Head (1814). 'The cannonade was tremendous,' testified Riedesel. Arnold's galley was hulled a dozen times, and seven shot struck her between wind and water. A second vessel lost every officer but the captain. A third sank.[8]

Toward evening, the British drew back for a better spring the next morning, anchoring in a line from the island to the mainland. But, when darkness had arrived, bringing with it a mist, the American fleet silently got under way, passed the British line without detection, and sailed south until its hurts compelled it to halt for repairs. On the thirteenth, Carleton and his mortified comrades, favored by the wind, overtook the fugitives. A hopeless running fight ensued; and after some hours, finding himself at the end of his cable, Arnold ran five of his vessels into a creek, set them afire, watched them burn with their colors flying, and then retreated by land; while the remaining five of his original fifteen, less closely pursued, managed to reach Crown Point.

Some of the Americans thought it a shame to break so beautiful an egg merely for the sake of an omelet. It was an excellent fleet, groaned Maxwell, till Arnold,

---

[8] § For the naval campaign, see paticularly Mahan: Scribner's Mag., Feb. 1898, p. 150. Arnold's account of the battle at Valcour Id.: 5 Force, II., 1038. Carleton's reports of the two battles: Can. Arch., B, 39, pp. 218, 219; Q, 12, p. 224. Indifferent: Arnold to Gates, Sept. 7, 1776: Sparks MSS., No. 52, II., p. 45. Id. to Id., Oct. 10; Sept. 21, 1776: 5 Force, III., 932, 440. Carleton to Douglas, June 28, 1776: Can. Arch., B, 39, p. 35.

MOUNT DEFIANCE AND UPPER LAKE CHAMPLAIN SEEN FROM TICONDEROGA.

465

'our evil genius to the north . . . got us clear' of it.
But Carleton understood the case better.   About a week
after the struggle ended—if not before—he realized that
his army could accomplish nothing in the Colonies that
season.   He pushed on, indeed, occupied Crown Point,
and sent for tools to build quarters there; but all that he
counted upon was to draw the attention of the Americans,
'and keep back part of their force from General Howe.'
This done, so far as possible, he returned to Canada early
in November ; and Lord George Germain's great hope of
seeing him strike hands with the New York army fell to
the ground.[9]

But the fleet and the troops were still there ; and the
first day of July, 1777, saw a commander setting out from
Crown Point for the south, whom every lady driving in
St. James Street would have pronounced the ideal soldier:
a man that believed in gallantry instead of humdrum
study, relied on spirit rather than prosy knowledge, and
seemed so much a general that he had little strength
left to be one.   It was General Burgoyne, of course ;
or, as he described himself, 'John Burgoyne, Esquire,
Lieutenant-General of His Majesty's forces in America,
Colonel of the Queen's regiment of Light Dragoons,
Governour of Fort William in North Britain, one of the
Commons of Great Britain in Parliament, and commanding an army and fleet employed on an expedition from
Canada' ; and, as one column of scarlet moved against the
'rebels' at Ticonderoga, while another moved against the
new Fort Independence on the opposite side of the lake,
and a line of floating batteries swept the water, he flung
a decisive watchword to the breeze : ' This army must not
retreat.'   Victory was now assured.[10]

---

[9] § Maxwell to Gov. Liv., Oct. 20, 1776: 5 Force, II., 1143.   Carleton to Ger-
main, Nov. 17, 1776 : Can. Arch., Q, 12, p. 236.   Id. to Burgoyne, Oct. 14, 1776;
Can. Arch., B, 39, p. 216.   Id. to Howe, Oct. 20, 1776: ib., p. 224.   Id. to Germain,
Sept. 28, 1776: Can. Arch., Q, 12, p. 188.

[10] § For Burgoyne's campaign, see Burgoyne, State of the Expedition, etc.,

General Gates, who had commanded at the lake in the previous autumn, had considered Mt. Defiance—which overlooked both forts—inaccessible, and therefore had left it unfortified. Naturally the British now dragged cannon to the summit; the poor little force of Americans had to flee as best they could; and Burgoyne went south to Skenesborough in pursuit. Here came a pause. General Schuyler at Fort Edward, after gathering the fugitives, could muster less than 4,500 men fit for duty, while Burgoyne had nearly 8,000.

But he appealed to nature. Houses were abandoned, provisions carried away, cattle driven off, pastures and fields turned into ponds or morasses, bridges torn down, roads destroyed, trees felled. Burgoyne's wise policy was to go back and take the water-route by Lake George. But no! 'This army must not retreat,'—must not even seem to retreat, for to Burgoyne *seeming* meant a great deal; and in twenty-four days his soldiers, exhausted with toil, melted by the heat, and drunk up by the insects, made twenty-six miles. Nature, then as ever, was on the side of liberty.

On the British left, Baum soon found himself in a closing circle of fire at Bennington, and the people learned how easy it really was to beat the regulars. On the right, Gansevoort at Fort Schuyler—threatened, like Butter-

particularly p. 17; Burgoyne, Orderly Book; Hadden, Journal; Riedesel, Letters; Letters of Brunswick and Hessian Officers; I. N. Arnold. B. Arnold; the standard histories; Can. Arch., Q, 13 and 14; etc. The literature is very extensive. His titles: Thacher, Mil. Journal, p. 97.

field at the Cedars, with Indian vengeance—indignantly refused to yield, and, aided by a Herkimer instead of a Sherburne and by the same Arnold that had stopped Foster at Lachine, proved, by routing St. Leger, what Bedel might have done.   More fatal, perhaps, than either of these misfortunes, Burgoyne's Indian allies atrociously murdered poor Jane McCrea, and in a moment the name of an obscure girl became a battle-cry that roused the very mountains.   Burgoyne himself, at the centre, found his provisions failing, the enemy gathering fast, his Canadians wilting, and his Indians taking French leave.   No doubt he might still have saved his main body ; but the army could not retreat.

As the old New England feeling against Schuyler had now gathered great force, he was removed, and that ' old midwife,' Gates —as the British general described him— took command of the department.   But Arnold (though Congress had promoted juniors over his head), the chivalric Lincoln, and the lion-hearted Morgan were there to prop him ; and when Burgoyne, at the first battle of Saratoga, laid a plan to outflank Gates's left while amusing him in front, Arnold struck so furiously at the British centre that the scheme failed.   Burgoyne could now advance as little as he could retreat.

Then came the second battle of Saratoga.   Arnold, not even mentioned in Gates's report of the previous affair and in effect relieved of his command, heard the noise of the fight and exclaimed : ' No man shall keep me in my tent today.   If I am without command, I will fight in the ranks; but the soldiers, God bless them, will follow my lead.   Come on !   Victory or death ! ' and soon a coal-black thoroughbred was seen dashing into the fight, while an aide of Gates's, far in the rear, pursued the horseman with an order to leave the field.

On the side toward the Hudson, Poor had shattered the

British left; on the other, Morgan and Dearborn were driving the right; but the tough German centre stood firm. Placing himself at the head of his old division, Arnold blew the men to a mad heat and poured them like molten iron upon the foe. In the former battle, if backed with some of Gates's 11,000 idle troops, he might have won a complete victory: so now he determined to find his own support. Wherever he saw an available corps, he swept it into his fight as a tornado carries off a hayrick. Now here, now there he dashed. To make a short cut, he would run the gauntlet of both fires. First, he drove the Germans into their defences, and then he stormed the fortifications. Musketry, cannon, abatis, breastworks—nothing could stop him. When the day ended, the central British position lay open; and it was only then, as his charger sank and he himself fell inside the enemy's works, with his Quebec leg fractured by a ball, that Gates's aide overtook him.

Burgoyne found now that he could retreat, but he had learned the lesson too late; and about a week after, riding jauntily to the American headquarters in all his scarlet and gold, he gracefully doffed his cocked hat and pleasantly remarked, 'The fortune of war, General Gates, has made me your prisoner.'

A new chapter could now be added to the history of the war in Canada. The stubborn perseverance of the northern army in 1776, which prevented Carleton from building water-craft early enough in the season to accomplish his mission toward the south, probably saved the cause of America. Only four weeks more, exclaimed General Riedesel at the close of the campaign, and 'everything would have been ended this year.' Even more brilliant was the other side of this result. Carleton's merely negative success in 1776, misunderstood by the government, cost him the King's favor for a time. As a consequence, it was Burgoyne that directed the invasion, and under him the British troops marched to the Caudine Forks instead of the Capitol. Bennington and Saratoga gave us the French alliance; and the aid of France ensured our independence. [11]

Almost immediately on Burgoyne's capitulation, the American commander at the north began to think of returning the attack. Before the month was out, Colonel Bedel appeared suddenly at Dartmouth College, and, without a word of explanation to the President, ordered all the St. Francis Indians to go home. Poor Dr. Wheelock felt not a little troubled; but, had he been calmer, he might have suspected that his pupils were needed for some service in Canada. Ten days later, the Colonel—who had been court-martialled from the army after the Cedars episode but was a power still in his neighborhood —received a new commission from President Laurens of the Continental Congress. Under orders from Gates, he sent scouting parties into the north, and gathered Indians at Coös. In short, a movement against Canada was on the tapis. Jacob Bayley, of Newbury, pronounced it 'highly necessary' to visit St. Johns without delay; and at the Albany headquarters, in a certain pigeon-hole, lay 'A plan of an expedition An order by the Honble. Maj Genl. Gates Commander in Chief of the Northern Department.' [12]

On the fifteenth of November, the contents of the pigeon-hole took final shape in the form of definite instructions to Colonel Bedel. Without delay but with the ' greatest

---

[11] REMARK CVI.

[12] § Wheelock, Diary, Oct. 27, 1777: Wheelock Papers. N. H. Hist. Soc. Proc., III., pp. 204, 217. Bedel to Gates, Nov. 29, 30, 1777 : N. H. State Papers, XVII., p. 152. Id. to Sch., Nov. 30, 1777: ib. Plan: Force Transcripts of Gates Corres., Lib. of Cong. The Plan bears no date; but the heading shows that it was drawn up before Gates became Prest. of the Bd. of War. 'Coös' was the western side of Coös Co., N. H., but the term covered also Newbury, Vt., and its vicinity.

FROM SAMUEL ADAMS'S LETTER TO TRUMBULL ILLUSTRATING THE NEW ENGLAND FEELING AGAINST SCHUYLER.

secrecy,' said the order, enroll five hundred men ; and, about noon on the first day of February, giving out that you intend to join the army, take the direct road for Albany. The next morning at daybreak, however, 'turn short about to St. Johns,' and go on that way, pretending that your mission is to cut off a strong scouting-party of the British. In case you can surprise the fort, seize it and 'instantly' put the torch to that, the shipping, and 'every article that can be Burnt.' If your scouts describe the post as beyond your strength, attempt only to burn the vessels ; but, whatever you do, return at once to Coös and send me word immediately. Enlist only reliable Indians and 'Staunch Whiggs'; appoint John Wheelock, son of the President, your Lieutenant-Colonel, and Whitcomb, the dreaded scout, your Major ; and let not a soul, except these two, know the truth about your plan. ' I have in contemplation a stroke of importance ,' Gates informed the President of Congress.[13]

Five days later, James Duane, then at Livingston Manor, wrote to Gates : 'Congress have been pleased to appoint Brigr Gen Stark to the Command of an Enterprise which they have much at Heart'; and so extremely private is the affair that I have been sent on to explain matters to him 'in a personal Conference at Albany.' Congress, also, it appeared, had a secret stroke in view, and—stranger yet—it was the same as Gates's.[14]

In brief, that body had voted, on the third of December, to burn the British vessels at St. Johns. The idea was that 'the adventurous spirit of the Inhabitants in those parts, the Dangers to which they must be exposed while

---

[13] § Gates to Bedel, Nov. 15, 1777: Bedel Papers, p. 52 ; N. H. State Papers, XVII., p. 150. Gates to Prest. Cong. (from Albany), Dec. 11, 1777: Force Transcripts of Gates Corres., Lib of Cong. Wash. to Cong., Nov. 20, 1778: Chase, Hanover, I., p. 396.

[14] § Duane to Gates, Dec. 16, 1777: Force Transcripts of Gates Corres., Lib. of Cong.

the British Vessels commanded the Lakes, and the prospect of a great Reward if they should succeed in the Attempt,' would be inducements enough to call out three or four hundred volunteers ; though a choice between the reward and double pay was offered. To clinch matters, the command was given to General Stark, now so famous and so popular in that region, 'and in every other respect qualified for the undertaking.'[15]

Duane, not knowing where he could place his finger upon Stark, sent a letter for him to Gates ; and the General, little suspecting to what it referred, forwarded it ' by special express.' ' Not a moment is to be lost,' urged the delegate from Congress ; and Stark, with Bennington fire already kindled in his piercing light-blue eyes, hurried to Albany.[16]

At first he seized upon the plan hopefully ; but on considering it longer, he concluded ' that a Reward which depended only on a prosperous Issue, was too slender a Motive for the undertaking.' As evidently Duane agreed with him, it was decided to ask Congress for ' pay at all events, & the bounty [also] in case of Success ' ; and, counting upon this favor, Stark began work immediately. For one thing, he went across to Bennington, and roused the Council of Safety ; for another, he applied to the Committee of Vermont for aid, and was promised ' all the Assistance in their power ' ; and for a third he wrote to Bedel. Evidently something was to be done. If Molly Stark's John could not bury the British fleet with firebrands, in Heaven's name who could ?[17]

15 § Secret Journ. Cong., Dec. 3, 1777. Duane to Wash., Mar. 13, 1777: Coll. of C. H. Swan, Esq. The quotations are from this letter. REMARK CVII.

16 § Duane to Gates, Dec. 16, 1777: Force Transcripts of Gates Corres., Lib. of Cong. Gates to Stark, Dec. 17, 1777: ib. Duane to Stark, Dec. 16, 1777: C. Stark, Gen. Stark, pp. 79, 93.

17 § Duane to Wash. : Note 15. Stark to Council of Safety, Bennington, Feb. 3, 1778 ; Proceedings of Council ; Wilkinson to Wash., Feb. 22, 1778: all in Cont. Cong. Papers, Letters, No. 78, W, XXIII., pp. 451–456. Bedel to Gates, Mar. 14, 1778: N. H. State Papers, XVII., p. 218.

At this precise juncture, however, a grand shifting of scenes took place.

A certain opposition to the Commander-in-chief had now grown up in the country. It was impossible for the generality to understand his character; therefore not a few questioned it. He stood apart from the common and rather aloof; and some, governed by the sort of wolfish instinct that often rules us, noting that he did not run with the pack, looked upon him as an alien and enemy. Others, observing that he did not seem to be dominated by their own very ordinary motive for doing right—the fear of opinion—concluded that he had no principle. Still others, finding their eminent wits could not see through him, decided that he must be wrapping up some villainy within. When a man is different from those about him, many cannot bear to imagine that he may be superior. To misconstrue and denounce answer all questions and soothe all misgivings.

There were also more tangible objections to him. Some wearied of hearing Aristides called the Just. Others —Clark, of New Jersey, for example—believed that he was overriding the people's rights. Not a few, judging by the plausible standard of immediate results, felt that he had proved no great success as a general, and pointed, by way of contrast, at Gates's great achievements against Burgoyne. Many, forgetting that the pen is mightier than the sword and that a march is easier on paper than on land, wondered why the combinations they could suggest far surpassed those actually carried out. Still others, or their friends, had been disappointed in personal hopes, exposed in some crookedness, compelled to do their duty, or thwarted in unrighteous designs. Self-seeking was common enough in the Revolutionary epoch, and even reasonable wishes could not always be gratified. To make matters worse, Tories in disguise observed this rift and labored to widen it, thinking in that way to damage the cause of independence.[18]

John Adams asserted stoutly in his autobiography that he was a firm supporter of Washington in 1777, as at all other times, and that his reputation for a contrary stand was chargeable to Tom Paine, 'that insolent blasphemer of things sacred, and transcendent libeller of all that is good.' But Adams was undoubtedly piqued by the praise accorded Washington ; he had a just grievance, as he believed, against the Virginia group, because the jealousy felt toward Massachusetts made it wise to yield them posts of distinction that belonged, perhaps, to him ; he affiliated with men found acting later against Washington ; and he condemned sharply the 'timorous, defensive' military policy of the Commander-in-chief as the cause of 'so many disasters.' Naturally enough, then, many besides Tom Paine have classed him with the Opposition. Lafayette did so ; and, though Adams took leave of Congress on the eleventh of November, 1777, to represent the nation abroad, his influence had been exerted, and it remained behind.[19]

Samuel Adams had scarcely any points of contact with George Washington. A democrat, a Puritan, a civilian, a town-meeting man, a puller of strings, an apostle of talk, how could he understand an aristocrat, an Episcopalian, a sportsman, a believer in strong rule, a fighter, upreared by a grand force of character—but silently and imperceptibly—into the sublime, divinely patient Atlas of the national cause, self-communing and unknown ? Though equally opposed to oppression, they stood otherwise at the antipodes from each other ; and the greater part of the word antipodes reappears in 'antipathy.'

18 Sparks MSS., No. 32, I.: MS. on the Cabal found at Lafayette's residence.
19 § J. Adams, Works, II. p. 439 ; III., p. 93 ; Lodge, Wash., I., p. 215. Morse, J. Adams, pp. 133, 134. Laf., Mém., I., p. 38. On the sectional feeling, see also Gérard de Rayneval: Durand, New Materials, p. 173.

We the underwritten, being the Committee of Congress for secret Correspondence, do hereby certify whom it may concern, that the Bearer, the Honourable Silas Deane Esquire, one of the Delegates from the Colony of Connecticut, is appointed by us to go into France, there to transact such Business, commercial and political, as we have committed to his care, in Behalf & by Authority of the Congress of the thirteen united Colonies. In Testimony whereof we have hereunto set our Hands and Seals at Philadelphia, the second Day of March. 1776—

[SIGNED BY FRANKLIN, HARRISON, DICKINSON, JAY, AND MORRIS.]

By principle also, as well as by prejudice, the agitator drew away from the soldier. Adams well knew how many times in the past freedom had been shamelessly betrayed by its trusted guardian. He believed that vigilance was the price of liberty, and that another name for vigilance was distrust. He felt that Washington might prove not only a weak champion of liberty but even its worst foe. And, though he charged John Hancock, now his bitter enemy, with giving him a false color of antagonism to the General, he too has been fixed so fast in this group that he never can escape. Richard Henry Lee of Virginia—who possibly had some local or personal pique —was a confidant of Samuel Adams and stood, like him, in the Opposition; and of course the Adamses had the other New England Congressmen at their back.[20]

What these men might have done, had the circumstances developed and organized their sentiment, no one can say. Probably they themselves did not know, and so far their disclaimers were justified. They were not ready to call for Washington's removal. They were not even plotting against him. A gentleman who had important dealings with them at the time wrote to the Commander-in-chief, 'every honest man in Congress is your friend.' Yet, lacking that appreciation of his character and policy which time alone could give and profoundly discouraged by his military non-success, even the most sincere patriots among them could reasonably doubt whether the cause ought to be bound up wholly in this one man. Apparently, it was felt that there should be a second in reserve, to take the place of Washington should he fall, fail, or prove untrue; and it was largely for this reason, or to serve as a curtain-raiser for

---

[20] § Distrust: Luzerne (Durand, New Materials, pp. 234, 235). Hosmer, S. Adams, pp. 338-341. Laf., Mém., I., p. 38. Lodge, Wash., I., p. 214. R. H. Lee to S. Adams, July 29, 1776: S. Adams Papers.

Charles Lee, that Gates had been brought forward in the Burgoyne campaign.[21]

There his fortune, if not his merits, had filled his supporters with joy; and now, at precisely this point, a still more distinguished place was found for him. Realizing the imperative need of a military executive, Congress had maintained for some time a Board of War; and, at the very close of November, Gates was elected the President, or rather—one may say— the Dictator of this body. In requesting him to come to York and assume his new responsibilities, it was voted that he be informed of 'the high sense' Congress entertained of his abilities and his peculiar fitness for this office; 'upon the right execution of which,' added the Resolution, 'the success of the American cause does eminently depend.' In effect, then, he was now the Secretary of War.[22]

Parallel with the Opposition in Congress, which had secured this action, ran a short line of officers in the army, the foremost of whom was Gates himself.

Viewed in the abstract and at a distance, the idea of a competition between George Washington and Horatio Gates appears ridiculous; but, in the actual world, things are not done at a distance nor in the abstract. Gates belonged to the same class as beau Burgoyne and cursing Campbell, standing about midway between the extremes. Like them, he made an impressive appearance, as Lafayette said; and why not?—this was perhaps the one matter that he studied. Four times out of five, it is the principal thing demanded by the public, and the superficially smart

---

[21] § Laf. to Wash., Feb. 23, 1778 : Sparks MSS., No. 87 (unpaged). Morse, J. Adams, p. 134. J. Adams, Works, I., pp. 265, 282 (C. F. A.). S. Adams appears to have originated the plan of having a chief in reserve. Hosmer, S. Adams, p. 339. Lee : Laf., Mém., I., p. 38 ; MS. on the Cabal found at Laf.'s residence (Note 18). It should be noted that on Dec. 30, 1777, Congress extended until April 10 certain extraordinary powers previously vested in Washington,—perhaps a sign that it was not bent upon unhorsing him.

[22] § Journ. Cong., Oct. 17 ; Nov. 7, 17, 27, 1777.

discover that fact early in life. When the squealing mountebank won the popular verdict against the farmer with a real pig in his blouse, it was doubtless because his attitudes, his gestures, and his grins convinced people that he was a clever fellow and must be able to squeal better than a simple, honest countryman like themselves. A general cry for roast pork would have turned the tables, but famines are rare.

Gates was vulgar[23]; but millions have enjoyed Sairy Gamp and called her a good soul. He was an inferior person ; but he had been trained in the regular army, knew military routine better than his chief, and at Cambridge, as the adjutant-general, had been given opportunities enough to ascertain that fact. Just because he was an inferior person, he could not realize the comparative unimportance of this technical proficiency.

He was doubtless a very clubbable fellow : always ready to inform a hunched-up circle how matters could be finished ; well able to reel off yards of messroom strategy; and abundantly qualified, like every one-eyed man that cares for such subjects, to be king among the blind. After the manner of his class, he possessed a streak of cunning. Some diffident little fellow, back in the circle, would venture a suggestion and be promptly sat upon by all present ; whereupon Gates would quietly pocket the idea, carry it home, turn it round, cock the brim, dent the crown, and flourish it as his best head-gear for the next week or ten days. In this way, he could seem to be quite a thinker.

With liquor for the convivial—well mellowed himself every afternoon, according to report[24]—with abundant military small-talk, with more or less veracious chapters from his experience in the British army, with large

---

[23] A case: Arnold, B. Arnold, p. 202.
[24] F. Bayley, Narrative.

schemes and liberal promises, with an impressive appearance, and with Burgoyne's defeat as a foundation for every
assumption : with all this and a pretty talent for intrigue,
he made a formidable showing against the reserved, preoccupied Washington ; and, by common opinion, he as-
pired at this time to the Commander-in-chief's epaulettes.[25]

HORATIO GATES.

The brilliant Mifflin asserted most emphatically, in a
confidential letter at this very period, that he loved his
country too much to desire a change at the head of the
army ; but he certainly thought Washington had erred,
and, like other brilliant men, he probably said quite as
much as he thought.   As a Pennsylvanian, he bitterly

[25] § Sparks, Wash., I., pp. 247–250. Lodge, Wash., I., pp. 214–222, 224
Marshall, Wash. (London, 1805), III., p. 282. Thacher, Mil. Journal, p. 202.

mourned the loss of Philadelphia. He knew that he was
not a favorite at headquarters. No independent command,
save in the trifling affair at Lechmere's Point, had been
entrusted to him. It went upon the records of the Board
of War, of which he was a member, that he expressed ' A
Warm Sollicitude' to have Gates for its President ; and
Lafayette cannot have erred greatly in saying that Mifflin
aided the Opposition.[26]

One other officer—perhaps only one—belonged to the
group. This was Thomas Conway, a man of Irish descent
employed in the French service, who had thought the
shortest road to promotion in France ran through Philadelphia. Washington had stood squarely in his way.
With but little to lose, Conway could afford to be outspoken in his disparagement of the General and persever-
ing in his intrigues against him ; and since a mishap to him
would injure no American, others felt particularly free to
make him say what they wanted expressed, and possibly
even to charge him with what they wished he had said. In
this manner, he came to represent in a way the sentiment of
opposition, and perhaps really thought himself the leader
of a party. Indeed, people speak now, for convenience,
of the Conway Cabal ; but in reality he led the vague,
unorganized spirit of antagonism to Washington, not as
a head, but as a great toe. Strong or weak, however,
Conway's influence was hostile.[27]

It was under these circumstances that Gates's project
and the Stark project came together on his arrival at York,
where Congress was then sitting. The two schemes com-

---

[26] § Mifflin: Mem. Penna. Hist. Soc., II., Part II., pp. 124, 125. Bd. of War
Papers, I., Nov. 21, 1777. Laf., Mém., I., p. 38.

[27] § Statement of Troup: Sparks MSS., No. 49, I., p. 20. Sparks, Wash.,
pp. 248, 250. Aim : Conway to Sullivan, Jan. 3, 1778 : U. S. Revol. MSS.,
III., Lib. of Cong. Disparage: Conway to Hancock, Oct. 19, 1777 (Sparks MSS.,
No. 52, III., p. 133). Tool: Laf., Mem., I., p. 38 ; Durand, New Materials, p. 191 ;
Doniol, Particip., III., p. 264 ; Sullivan to Wash., Dec. 1, 1779 (Wash., Writings
(Ford), VIII., p. 140, note).

bined, of course. Very naturally, too, as Duane put it later, 'the Plan was enlarged.' It was decided, Stark soon heard, 'to penetrate into Canada instead of St. Johns,' and this involved—since the American army would march among the Canadians, instead of merely battering the door of their province—a recasting of the whole affair. It offered Gates another opportunity to distinguish himself, and it gave the whole sentiment of opposition another occasion to develop a policy.[28]

Prominent among the lively young officers at Metz, France, while Schuyler was preparing to attack St. Johns in 1775, was a certain precocious young fellow, married at sixteen, a captain of dragoons a month later, and now in his eighteenth year. One evening he dined, as he often did, at the table of his commander and friend, the Comte de Broglie ; and there he heard a chance guest—an Englishman, the brother of George III.—give some news of a revolt in America. America?—where was America? Never mind ; people determined to be free lived there; and, while others listened indifferently to pass a few idle minutes, he drank in the spirit of our Revolution. Instantly the blood of his mountain ancestry took fire. ' The Moment I heard of America, I lov'd her,' he wrote later ; ' the Moment I knew she was fighting for freedom, I burnt with the desire of bleeding for her.' Thus the spirit of American independence, appealing to generous humanity, bore fruit.[29]

Silas Deane, sent across the water as an informal representative of the Colonies in France, encouraged these aspirations. He and the Frenchman made a sort of contract ; and already this precocious young enthusiast, the

[28] § Duane to Wash.: Note 15. Stark to Council: Note 17.
[29] § Doniol, La F., pp. 17, 18. The Nation, LXXVI., p. 513. Doniol, Particip., I., p. 651. Charavay, La F., p. 6. Laf. to Cong., Sept., 23, 1778: Cont. Cong. Papers, 156, p. 27.

Marquis de Lafayette, after fighting bravely in the American army, was a Continental major-general. His blood, his title, his ardor, his abilities—how could they fail to stir the Canadians, were he to go among them?[30]

All in authority saw this, and many saw farther. Intimately connected, as the Marquis was, with the French court and with many leaders in the public affairs of that country, it might be worth an immense deal to pay him a substantial compliment; and an independent command, especially one so conspicuous, would certainly delight him, his friends, and his nation. The assistance of the French government was eagerly hoped for; such a factor might be decisive; and, in consequence, the prestige of securing a grand alliance might accrue to the promoters of this plan.

Others could see still more. Conway was eager to have Lafayette speak a good word for him at home; and, particularly since the Board of War proposed to make him the second in

LAFAYETTE'S AGREEMENT TO COME TO AMERICA

---

[30] Wharton, Revol. Dipl. Corres., I., p. 560. Doniol, La F., p. 20. Marshall,

command, he favored the programme with all his energy. Gates had been carrying on an affectionate correspondence with the Marquis, and, only a little while before, had received this from him : ' The knowledge I got of your character adds infinitely to the pleasure my heart feels in receiving the assurance of your future affection towards a young soldier who desires it very heartily ' ; so that Gates doubtless felt that by advancing Lafayette's fortunes he could improve his own. Besides, the creation of this independent command would damage the prestige of Washington, tend to isolate him, lessen the importance of his army, and possibly provoke him into resigning. Finally, the whole Opposition deemed it wise, very probably, to detach Lafayette and all that he represented from too close an affiliation with the distrusted Commander-in-chief.[31]

So it came to pass that Major-General the Honorable Horatio Gates, Esquire, became the head of the department of war, and that under his direction Major-General the Marquis of Lafayette received orders to lead an 'irruption' into Canada. One of the consequences was that Brigadier-General Stark suddenly found himself deposed, ' for wise and prudential Reasons,' from the leadership of a raid against St. Johns, and learned that he was expected to assist young Lafayette in ' promoting the Interest, and political Views of the United States in Canada.'[32]

This, however, was not the only nor the greatest surprise that followed.

Wash. (London, 1805), III., p. 329.   Gates to Laf., Jan. 14, :778: Bancroft Coll., Revol. Papers, III., p. 267.   Journ. Cong., July 31, 1777.

[31] § Conway : Laf., Mém., I., p. 135 ; Gates to Laf., Jan. 24, 1778 (Bancroft Coll., Revol. Papers, III., p. 267).   Gates to Laf., Nov. 12, 1777, and Laf. to Gates, Dec. 14, 1777 : Force Transcripts of Gates Corres., Lib. of Cong.   Detach: Doniol, Particip., III., p. 264 ; Laf., Mém., p. 72.   REMARK CVIII.

[32] § Journ. Cong., Jan. 22, 23, 1778.   Gates to Laf., Jan. 24, 1778: Note 31.   Id. to Wash., Jan. 24, 1778: Bancroft Coll., Revol. Papers, III., p. 263.   Id. to Stark, Jan. 24, 1778 : Mag. of Am. Hist., 1885, p. 90.

XXXVI

A BRIEF CAMPAIGN

LAFAYETTE abounded in sentiment, and it was only fair to allow General Gates a taste ; but for Washington he felt a regard far above that plane. Consequently, when he received the notification of his Canadian appointment, not from—but merely through—the Commander-in-chief, with a few words revealing at the same time the General's personal attachment and his aloofness from this matter, he felt surprised and troubled. A committee of Congress on military affairs, of which Gouverneur Morris was a member, chanced to be in the camp, and to them Lafayette applied for counsel. He found that they did not approve of the plan and probably he learned something of the spirit behind it. It was his impulse then to decline the commission ; but Washington pointed out that in any event he would conduct himself so as to win distinction, while the blame, should misfortune be the outcome, would fall upon the projectors of the campaign ; and he decided to accept the place.[1]

He varied from his orders, however. Gates had requested that he should ' immediately repair to Albany, ' adding that his instructions would be forwarded by Con-

---

[1] § Gates to Wash., Jan. 24, 1778: Bancroft Coll., Revol. Papers, III., p. 263. Laf., Mém., p. 73. Laf. to Cong., Jan. 31, 1778: Cont. Cong. Papers, 156, p. 5. Journ. Cong., Jan. 10, 20, 1778. Diary of the Com.: U. S. Revol. Papers, III., Lib. of Cong. G. Morris to B. Arnold, Feb. 21, 1778: Freeman's Journal, July 18, 1781. Sparks, Wash., p. 250. Morris appears to have arrived at the camp on Jan. 26 (Laf. to Laurens, P. S., rec'd Jan. 27, 1778: So. Car. Hist. and Gen Mag., vii., p. 126).

way ; but the Marquis thought—and so did the committee of Congress—that he should first go to York for a look at the bottom of the scheme ; and, with a firm determination to show his Washington colors at the first opportunity, he rode away toward the west.[2]

The opportunity soon came. On arriving at Gates's house, he found a merry company at table ; and, with all his liveliness and good-fellowship, he joined them. Toasts followed the dinner, and in those, too, he bore a convivial part. But finally, as the company began to rise, he remarked, with an edge of seriousness on his gayety :

' One toast, gentlemen, has been omitted, and I will give it.'

All filled their glasses.

' The Commander-in-chief of the American armies.'

Down went the wine, perforce ; but it went so hard that a little of it—the color, at least—got into the faces of some in the party.[3]

The committee of Congress had been surprised at the young fellow's mature judgment, and probably he did not spend many hours at the old court-house in the middle of York square, where the Delegates met, before that body felt the same. ' My first step toward albany will be decisive for my fate,' he believed ; and he proposed to take it carefully. First of all, he was determined not to be cut adrift from Washington. I think it a higher honor, he chivalrously declared, to be considered ' only as an officer of his under his immediate orders, than if I was in any other light.' A 'detachment of his excellency's army ' he was determined his command should be, and on no other basis would he move. Congress found it necessary to yield that point.[4]

---

[2] § Gates to Laf., Jan. 24, 1778: Bancroft Coll., Revol. Papers, III., p. 267. Laf. to Cong., Jan. 31, 1778: Note 1.

[3] § Laf., Mém., I., p. 39. Ami du Gal. Lafayette (MS.): Lib. Cong. Sparks, Wash., p. 251, note.

[4] § Maturity: G. Morris to Cont. Cong., Jan. 26, 1777, i. e., 1778 (Cont. Cong.

Next, he proceeded to oust Conway from the second place. At the camp, he had called attention to the danger of exciting jealousies, were the two best positions occupied by foreigners, and the imprudence of trusting 'a Person whose object it was to push his Fortunes in France' with an opportunity to 'imbue the Minds of the Canadians with a Love of the Grand Monarque'; and no doubt similar ideas came forward at York. However this may have been, he certainly pronounced Conway 'most disagreeable' on account of his attacking and abusing Washington, and, when he found the authorities inclined to insist upon carrying out the plan agreed upon, threatened that he would 'go to france with most all the french officers in the army.' 'No canadians will join under that

G. MORRIS

irish man,' he added, 'principally when they will see us going of and publishing the reasons'; and, in short, he required Congress to accept the terms he proposed,—also, to accept them 'immediately.' By way of lever, perhaps, General McDougall was proposed by the Marquis for the second place; and then, as McDougall was very ill at the time, Lafayette remarked, 'there is the Baron De Kalb'; he has 'seen more wars' than any other officer in the army; he desires to go, and I recommend him strongly; and at last, as there was no escape, Conway accepted the third position. Whatever the expedition was now, it could no longer be called anti-Washington.[5]

Papers, Letters, 78, M, XV., p. 295). Court House: Lossing, Revol. Field-Book, II., p. 133. Laf. to Cong., Jan. 31, 1778 : Cont. Cong. Papers, 156, p. 5. Laf., Mém., p. 39. Ami du Gal. Laf.: Note 3.

[5] § G. Morris: Note 4. Laf. to Laurens: So. Car. Hist. and Gen. Mag., VII.,

Finally, the Marquis inquired into the means for carrying out the plan, and again everything seemed to favor him. '*At a low estimate*,' 2,500 effectives would be found ready, he was assured ; and informally ' a much larger body was foretold.' There needed to be no concern on his part about provisions, forage, and transportation. The trifle of clothing would, also, take care of itself, for the clothier-general had been ordered to furnish everything the stores afforded. The ships could be burned with the straw collected by the British. Stark would be on hand, and very likely would touch off this bonfire before his chief could arrive. Consternation would throw down the rest of the barriers, and Lafayette would be in Montreal. What gave all this an air of certainty was the fact that Gates, the famous Gates, had been in command at Albany until a few weeks before. How could Lafayette imagine that perhaps he had fallen into that pit which always yawns for men who win their glory by others' toil,— the blunder of taking things for granted? The General himself suspected nothing of the sort. Let there be a victory and there was a victory, summed up fairly well what he knew about the defeat of Burgoyne ; and now he said, Let there be an expedition to Canada. Such confidence is always impressive, and Lafayette set out.[6]

On the ninth of February, as the chilly day came to a chillier close, a young man drew rein at the unpretending inn of Flemington, in the State of New Jersey, eagerly entrusted his tired horse to a servant, made his way to the fireplace, and rapidly threw off his outer garments. A tall, erect, strongly built figure was his, with large

pp. 126, 179, 182, 183. Unsigned letter from Fishkill to Gates, Nov. 27, 1777: Force Transcripts of Gates Corres., Lib. of Cong. Laf to Cong.: Note 4. Bd. War Papers, I., p. 469. The Nation, LX., p. 222.

[6] § Laf. to Bd. War, Feb. 20, 1778: Cont. Cong. Papers, Canad. Affairs, 166, p. 97. His statements are borne out by his Instructions: U. S. Revol. Papers, III., Lib. of Cong. Duane to Wash., Mar. 13, 1778: Coll. of C. H. Swan, Esq. Gates had been at Albany as late as Dec. 28, 1777: see his letter of that date to Greaton in Force's Transcripts of Gates Correspondence., Lib. of Cong.

limbs and broad shoulders,—though he looked as if consumptive tendencies might have asserted themselves, but for the active out-of door life he evidently enjoyed. A high and ample forehead, a large, long nose, reddish hair, bushy eyebrows projecting over fine, animated, hazel eyes, mobile, interesting, though not symmetrical features, gestures that would have been graceful if less hurried, and an air that blended real dignity with a sort of lightness completed his person.[7]

The loungers about the fire concluded very promptly that a rare bird had flown into their humble cote, and they were right. No ordinary traveller was this, indeed, but a beautiful, romantic, pathetic figure; Keats's poetic youth, 'forever panting and [alas!] forever young,' forever loved yet in vain forever pursuing; now a stripling of twenty in a rude hostelry, but fated to be known in a few years the world over; a leader who, gifted with more wisdom or less honor, might sit in the very front rank of historical figures; a favored son of fortune, destined to hold France in his hand but not know what to do with it; a noble, true patriot, whose chiefest honor was to be the epithet Noodle[8] from that arch-traitor, arch-brigand, and arch-cutthroat, Napoleon: in a word, Washington's bright French moon—Lafayette—in his first and loveliest quarter.

'Very slow' the Marquis had found his journey. Great cakes of ice in the Susquehanna had threatened to sink him; and, after escaping that peril, he had toiled painfully on, 'angry against' the roads, against his horse, against every obstacle that delayed him, 'sometimes drenched by rain, sometimes covered by snow,' with only a country inn

---

[7] § Laf., Mém., p. 40. Pers. appear.: Thacher, Mil. Journal, p. 186; Charavay, La F., p. 6; Atlantic Monthly, VIII., p. 660; Niles' Register, XIII., p. 141, etc. It seems fair to infer, since Laf. stopped at F. long enough to write to Wash., that he ended his day's journey there. The scene is constructive.

[8] Bigelow in Encyc. Brit., 'Lafayette.'

THE MARQUIS DE LAFAYETTE

to solace the close of his day. Very different had been the gay fellowship round the table of the Count at Metz. Very different a leading place at Marie Antoinette's balls. Very different the jolly and intimate *camaraderie* at the restaurant of The Wooden Sword (*A l'Epée de Bois*) at Paris.[9]

Yet it was none of these things that printed the look of anxiety on his lively features. Many desires—most ardent ones—thronged his bosom, and each presented itself now with a face like a challenge. He desired to merit the confidence of Washington and of Congress: would it be possible to do so on this mission? He longed to strike a blow for America and for liberty; to humble the pride of ' that insolent nation,' Great Britain, which had brought his country low a few years before; to prove his fitness for a high command in France; to gratify his friends; to slake his intense and ever-raging thirst for distinction and praise: and was all this likely to be accomplished on the Canada expedition?[10]

The military problem—could it be as simple as the Board of War supposed? And if it were, would not the officers who had gone on ahead of him reap the honors? Alas, yes; even that was possible. ' I expect to meet them at the Governors house in Quebec,' wrote the Marquis half-seriously.[11]

And those ' political Views ' of which Gates had written to Stark and no doubt said much to Lafayette! ' If upon your entering Canada,' said his Instructions, ' you find a general disinclination of the Natives, to join the American

[9] § Laf., Mém., p. 40. Laf. to Wash., Feb. 9, 1778 : Sparks MSS., No. 87 (unpaged). Id. to Laurens (undated) : So. Car. Hist. and Gen. Mag., VII., p. 187. Charavay, La F., p. 6. Doniol, Particip., I., p. 663.

[10] § Laf. to Bd. War., Feb. 20, 1778: Cont. Cong. Papers, Canad. Affairs, 166, p. 97. Doniol, Particip., I., p. 4 ; III., pp. 443, 447. Doniol, La F., p. 45 and *passim*. Jefferson's remark in Bigelow, ' Lafayette,' Encyc. Brit. Laf. to Wash., Feb. 23, 1778: Sparks MSS., No. 87 (unpaged).

[11] Laf. to Wash., Feb. 9, 1778: Sparks MSS., No. 87 (unpaged).

Standard,' you will destroy the British works as far as Chambly and return at once; but 'If, on the contrary the Canadians are ardently desirous of assisting to establish the Freedom and Independence of America, you will inform them, that when they embark in the common cause, they must determine to receive the Resolves of Congress and the Currency of America, with that Reverence and Alacrity, which have ever been manifested in the Acts and Dealings, of the Subjects of the United States'; must send delegates to the American Congress; and must 'conform in all Political Respects to the Union and Confederation.' Ah, how difficult it might be to decide, without a vote, what the sentiment of Canada really was! How many shades of feeling there might lie between a general disinclination and an ardent desire! How much skill it might need to bring even an ardent desire to the acceptance of paper money and the rest of the American policy![12]

And this was not all of the difficulty. Evidently some members of Congress had become rather frightened after commissioning Lafayette, Kalb, Conway, and a small army of minor French officers to lead troops into Canada. Such trustfulness did not reign in every American breast. France was eyed askance by not a few. Hugh Hughes had written Samuel Adams in February, 1776, that he feared the French would try to recover Canada. According to Thomas Walker, the Commissioners of Congress had stated in May that, rather than call in the assistance of France, 'they would come to a reconciliation wth G[reat] B[ritain] upon *any Terms*'; and Joseph Hawley had cautioned Samuel Adams at about the same time,

---

[12] U. S. Revol. Papers, III., Lib. of Cong.

'Dont put too much trust in Strangers.' Gouverneur
Morris promptly called attention to the danger of sending
these French officers north, and Wayne was alarmed at
the bare idea that Lafayette was to lead the expedition.
' Is it not worth some reflection,' he asked Gates at once;
' does it not deserve a serious thought before you determine
to commit the command to a *Stranger?* ' [13]

Much in this tone doubtless rained upon the Board of
War, and so a cautionary section was hastily tacked on
to Lafayette's orders. The ' grand Object,' it explained,
was the destruction or capture of the enemy's property
on the lake and at Montreal; and 'the holding the Country or prevailing upon the Inhabitants to confederate with
the States' was ' not to be undertaken but with the greatest Prudence, and with a Prospect of durable Success.'
The contrast in spirit between this and what had gone
before was evidently wide; and it suggested that perhaps
the Board of War, in their own minds, had really quite
abandoned the political views, only—for the sake of con-
sistency—they did not wish to state that fact.[14]

Turning it all over, Lafayette could find but few 'handsome thoughts about the projected incurtion into Canada.' 'Lake Champlain is too cold for producing the
least bit of laurels,' he wrote to Washington. But he fell
back once more upon the evident fact that Gates could
not afford to blunder. 'This project is yours, Sir,' the
Marquis had reminded him two days before, 'therefore you
must make it succeed. If I had not depended so much
on you, I would not have undertaken the operation.'
And, with this comfort, he said a hasty good-bye to

[13] § Secret Journ. Cong., Feb. 2, 7, 11, 1778. Laf. to Wash., Feb. 23, 1778 :
Sparks MSS., No. 87 (unpaged). Hughes, [Feb. 4, 1776] : S. Adams Papers.
Walker to S. Adams, May 30, 1776: ib. Hawley, May 22, 1776: ib. G. Morris to
Prest. Cong., Jan. 26, 1778 : Note 4. Wayne to Gates, Jan. 26, 1778 : Bancroft
Coll., Revol. Papers, III., p. 271. REMARK CIX.

[14] § Laf.'s Instr.: U. S. Revol. Papers, III., Lib. of Cong. Gates to [Cong.]:
Cont. Cong. Papers, 156, p. 63. REMARK CX.

Flemington, struggled on through bleak New Jersey, and crossed the Hudson above New York.[15]

Then he turned to the north and soon found himself in the Highlands, among scenes that fitted his thoughts. Stern Donderberg, pushing into the stream, looked down upon him with a defiance gloomy as night; and, though its old Dutch goblin in trunk-hose and sugar-loaf hat

AT ANTHONY'S NOSE

that roused the summer storms lay asleep under the drifts, every dark ledge topped with snow seemed an eyebrow raised at his undertaking. Just beyond, Anthony's Nose—descending to the stream like a black cliff hurled from the battlements of heaven—seemed to bar his progress as it had seemed to bar brave Henry Hudson's long before. At the upper gateway, Storm King and Cro' Nest scowled a parting menace; and the lovely bay of Newburg, bound fast now in chains of ice, reminded him how scarce the laurel must be at Lake Champlain. But at Poughkeepsie, George Clinton's manly, genial face and hearty voice bade him welcome and God-speed; and, when he reached Manor Livingston, the roaring hearth of the great patroon roared louder than ever in honor of such a guest.[16]

On the fifteenth of February, he took leave of this hos-

15 § Laf. to Wash., Feb. 9, 1778: Sparks MSS., No. 87 (unpaged). Id. to Gates, Feb. 7, 1778: Sparks MSS., No. 22, p. 129.

16 § Hudson: Pictur. Amer., II., p. 17. Clinton: see portraits, particularly frontis. of Clinton, Public Papers, I. Met Clinton: ib., II., 865. Duane to Wash., Mar. 13, 1778: Coll. of C. H. Swan, Esq.

pitable mansion and set out, with the ghostly Catskills at his left, on the final stretch of his four hundred frigid miles.   Beside him rode now the long-nosed New York attorney, James Duane,—lately the messenger of Congress to John Stark.   In Duane's mind, too, boiled many ideas.   For one thing, he doubtless pictured to himself the thin, set lips and vise-like jaw of that rough-and-ready war-horse, when he found that not only a boy-aristocrat, but the peaceful McDougall, an Irish adventurer, and a German hireling had all been preferred to him. But he deemed it wise to keep his opinions to himself, and the Marquis reached Albany (February 17) with no counsel but his own tumultuous thoughts and the suggestions of the Highland scenery.[17]

One man, he soon found, was deeply in earnest about the expedition and had been working energetically for nearly a fortnight.   Colonel Moses Hazen, who was to be the Quartermaster-General, had arranged with General Heath at Boston to send a small party down the Chaudière and scatter word that an army was to invade Canada by that route; had obtained authority from the Massachusetts Legislature to impress all the needed ' carriages' in Berkshire and Hampshire Counties; had secured a similar power from the New York authorities; had collected provisions enough, as he believed, besides fat cattle, snow-shoes, felling-axes, and what not; had made sure of the necessary forage; had set Easton at work enlisting men : had stimulated Bayley and Bedel; and had written pressingly to the Council of Safety at Bennington.   He felt prepared to transport the hospital and military stores; and his Canadian soldiers were ' so

---

[17] § Duane: Note 16.   Engraved portrait of Duane.   Stark : C. Stark, J. Stark, frontis. and p. 93.   Kalb: Laf., Mém., p. 73 ; Wharton, Dipl. Corres., I., p. 416.   K., by birth a German, was in the French service.   17th: Laf. to Bd. War, Feb. 20, 1778: Note 10.

warm for the expedition that they would consent to go almost naked into Canada.'[18]

But sleds and provisions did not make an army ; and, when Lafayette looked for his 2,500 men, he did not find them.[19] Gates, in his comfortable way of taking things for granted, had accepted the muster-rolls as Gospel ; and the rolls had not been correct. Soldiers had figured there, for example, who had been dropped in hospitals hundreds of miles distant and had sent no report of themselves since. ' By this Means,' explained Richard Varick later, 'Congress is amuzed by the abstracts of the D[eputy] M[uster] M[aster] Gen¹. with Returns of a Large Army of Men, who are most probably not in Existence, or at least, not now in their Service.' Others were ill at Albany, no doubt ; desertions and furloughs had thinned the rest ; and, in all, only 960 effectives of the rank and file could be discovered, a number of whom, boys of twelve or patriarchs of sixty, were quite unfit for the proposed march.[20]

As for the clothing required by a winter campaign in Canada, these poor fellows might about as well have been in breech-clouts and nose-rings. Three hundred and

---

[18] § Gates to Wash., Jan. 24, 1778: Bancroft Coll., Revoi. Papers, III., p. 263. Id. to Laf., Jan. 24, 1778 : ib., p. 267. Hazen to Bedel, Jan. 29, 1778 : N. H. State Papers, XVII., p. 212. Id. to Laf., Feb. 18, 1778 : Cont. Cong. Papers, 166, p. 67. Id. to Conway, Feb. 17, 1778 : ib., p. 103. Id. to Gates, Feb. 20, 1778 : ib., p. 117. Laf. to Wash., Feb. 19, 1778 : Sparks MSS., No. 87 (unpaged).

[19] § For the state of things at Albany : Note 18 ; Conway to Hazen, Feb. 18, 1778 (Cont. Cong. Papers, 166, p. 65); Return, Feb. 20 (ib., p. 77); Clinton to Conway, Feb. 17, 1778 (ib., p. 87); Sch. to Conway, Feb. 17, 1778 (ib., p. 93); Return of provisions, Feb. 18, 1778 (ib., p. 101) ; Arnold to Conway, Feb. 16, 1778 (ib., p. 71); Lincoln to Conway, Feb. 16, 1778 (ib., p. 81); J. Pierce, Jr., to Bd. War, Feb. 20, 1778 (ib., p. 115); Laf. to Conway, Feb. 19, 1778 (Bancroft Coll., Revol. Papers, III., p. 287); Troup to Gates, Feb. 19, 1778 (ib., p. 283); Id. to Id., [Feb. 6, 1778] (ib., p. 279); Laf. to Bd. War, Feb. 20, 1778 (Cont. Cong. Papers, Canad. Affairs, No. 166, p. 97); Id. to Hazen, Feb. 18, 1778 (ib., p. 59); Conway to Gates, Feb. 19, 1778 (ib., p. 111); Laf., Mém., p. 41 ; Ami du Gal. Laf. (Lib. of Cong.).

[20] § Varick to Gates, Nov. 28, 1777 : Cont. Cong. Papers, Letters, 78, V, Vol. XXIII., p. 69. Id. to Id., Mar. 23, 1778 : ib., p. 77. V. was Dep. M.-M.-Gen'l, No. Dept. Conway and Troup to Gates, Feb. 19, 1778 : Note 19. Clinton to Conway, Feb. 17, 1778 : Cont. Cong. Papers, 166, p. 87. Remarks on the Return of Feb. 20 : Note 19.

sixty-nine coats, seven hundred 'vest-coats,' three hundred and twenty-one pairs of breeches, one thousand and thirty-five shirts, seven hundred and eighteen ' hoses,' seven hundred and twenty-one pairs of shoes, two hundred and ninety-two caps, four hundred and twenty-nine pairs of leggings, nine hundred and eighty-eight pairs of socks, and six hundred and fifty-seven blankets were needed. Instead of obtaining every necessary from the clothier-general, the Marquis had to report: ' there is nothing, or almost nothing at all' in his boasted stores. The energetic Hazen had procured some clothing in Boston, but only about enough for his own men. Clinton wished he could help, but the New York authorities could barely furnish a small number of shirts.[21]

THE HIGHLANDS OF THE HUDSON VIEWED FROM WEST POINT

Funds could have eased things a great deal, no doubt ; but money was literally a minus quantity. Four hundred thousand dollars in Continental paper had seemed ample to the Board of War; but, when the first half of the amount landed at Albany, this report went back to York : ' Words

[21] § Remarks on Return of Feb. 20 ; Laf. to Bd. War, Feb. 20; and Clinton, Feb. 17: Note 19. Hazen to Gates, Feb. 20, 1778: Cont. Cong Papers, 166, p. 117.

cannot express the distress we are in for want of Money—
and this is but a small sum in comparison of what is
absolutely wanted in the Department.' Back pay and the
like amounted to nearly $500,000. Half as much more was
owing for the militia, the staff, and the rations ; and there
were many other debts. Needless to say, with pay already
due them for more than five months and a half and only
shivers to keep their blood in circulation, the soldiers
received the announcement of an expedition to the north
with no great enthusiasm. ' I found here a general Aver-
sion to the expedition,' reported Conway ; and Troup
added, The men are ' almost ready to mutiny for want
of pay.'[22]

Bedel—annoyed, perhaps, by the shifting ground of
the campaign—had lost faith in it, and, though he kept
men scouting, felt little inclination to move. Provisions
were costly in his region ; and naturally, as Gates forwarded no money, Lieutenant-Colonel Wheelock found
them very hard to purchase. Hazen's urgent orders and
$5,000, received about the seventh of February, had finally
set the wheels in motion ; but only two hundred and
fifty men could be raised, and those would not march,
Bedel reported, without such equipments as blankets,
moccasins, and Indian stockings,—that is to say, according to Conway's gloss, 'every Necessary article of Cloath-
ing.' Nothing, then, could be counted upon in that
quarter.[23]

---

[22] Pierce, Conway (Feb. 19), Troup (Feb. 19): Note 19.

[23] § Bedel to Hazen, Feb. 7, 1778 : Cont. Cong. Papers, 166, p. 63. Id. to
Gates, Mar. 14, 1778: N. H. State Papers, XVII., p. 218. Wheelock to Gates,
Dec. 30, 1777 : Force Transcripts of Gates Corres. Bd. War Papers, I., p. 465.
Wheelock, receipt, Feb. 7, 1778 : N. H. State Papers, XVII., p. 218. Troup to
Gates, Feb. 19: Note 19. Hazen to Bedel, Jan. 29, 1778: N. H. State Papers,
XVII., p. 212. Hazen to Laf., Feb. 18, 1778 : Note 19. Conway to Gates, Feb.
19, 1778: Note 19. Bedel stated to Gates (Mar. 14 : N. H. State Papers, XVII., p. 218)
that he received word on the day he would have marched that the expedition
had been given up (see Conway to Bedel, Feb. 15, 16, 1778 : N. H. State Papers,
XVII., pp. 213, 217); but how many men he really had is somewhat cloudy : see
Chase, Hanover, I., pp. 390–393.

GENERAL JOHN STARK

Stark had decided that, as Congress had pretty well forgotten his enterprise, he would do the same, and blandly wrote to Lafayette (February 3) : 'Being Informed by the Hon'ble General Gates that you are appointed to Command an expedition against the British troops in Canada, & that I am to go on the same expedition, should be glad to know as soon as possible what Number of troops you expect I shall Bring with me what States I shall Raise them in, the place of rendevouz & when to Be rendevouzed.' To the Bennington Council he said: the plan has been changed,—' I hope,' for the best ; and, as for the officers who wish a bounty for recruiting, I have no doubt that Congress will reward them according to their merit. In short, the fiery Stark was neutral and passive, which—from a man like him—seemed antagonistic. According to Troup, Congress had expected fifteen hundred volunteers from this direction ; but Schuyler declared, the day Lafayette reached Albany, that Stark had not yet 'raised a single man,' and Conway repeated the same words two days later. To expect ' the least assistance ' from him would be ' folly,' said Colonel Troup.[24]

The Council at Bennington had resolved to furnish three hundred old rangers and their officers, but had added that it would be necessary to provide them with shoes, stockings, and blankets, and highly desirable to settle back pay, before asking them to re-enlist. In other words, these men could not be expected. Of Easton's four hundred, nothing was heard ; but news did come, in a roundabout way, that Colonel Fellows had called the Berkshire officers together, and it had been decided, ' after mature deliberation,' that unless ' a proper encouragement was

---

[24] § Stark to Laf., Feb. 3, 1778 : Cont. Cong. Papers, 166, p. 57. Id. to Benn. Council : Cont. Cong. Papers, Letters, 78, W, XXIII., pp. 451–456. Sch., Conway, and Troup (Feb. 19) to Gates : Note 19. Stark's letter to Prest. Cong., May 24, 1778 (C. Stark, Gen. Stark, p. 150) seems to imply that, on hearing of Laf.'s appointment, he dismissed men already enrolled.

given . . . it was unnecessary to attempt raising any men.' That accounted for western Massachusetts.[25]

To leave no stone unturned, Lafayette heaved also at the Albany Committee. But it would not budge. We can do little, for we are cut off from our seaport, was the reply. Enlisting troops is not our affair. The question of forage belongs to the commissary. There is little to be had—we can tell you so much—for the enemy took what they could in the late campaign, the American troops used up a deal, and, as many farmers were called from their hay-fields to serve in the army, much of the grass was not cut. As for transportation, Hazen has authority to im-

R. R. LIVINGSTON

press 'carriages,' and certainly they can be got in that way; but, 'owing to the Averseness' of the people to so tedious and hazardous a journey, it will take time. Besides, if this is done, the transportation of supplies to the other garrisons will probably be delayed. But of course we will do everything we can,—certainly.[26]

Before Lafayette's arrival, Conway, who had preceded him three days, had asked the advice of the general officers on the ground, and his ' first word' to the Marquis was: 'quite impossible.' The advice fully supported him. Lincoln said that all ideas of prosecuting the plan should be abandoned, and the sooner the better. Schuyler added that Congress itself would consider the force

[25] Cont. Cong. Papers, Letters, No. 78, W, XXIII., pp. 451-456.

[26] § Laf. to Alb. Com. and reply, Feb. 19, 1778: Cont. Cong. Papers, 166, pp. 105, 107. Peter Kalm, who visited Albany, said that if a Jew were to settle there, he would be ruined: Munsell, Coll., II., p. 13.

inadequate, else it would not have promised one so much greater. Arnold was 'fully of Opinion' that nothing could be done, and even that an attempt to carry out the scheme as matters actually stood would be to 'deviate' from the instructions given the Marquis. Duane and the minor officers consulted held similar views. Nobody believed that Hazen would be able to accomplish what he promised. Out of a hundred and fifty sleds that he expected, only thirteen arrived. Lafayette distrusted his motives; and that officer himself, though 'greatly hurt' by the thought of giving up, conceded that such a lack of men and clothes was fatal. To crown the whole, so moderate had been the weather, that it seemed a question whether the ice on Lake Champlain would bear.[27]

Such a crown merited a rare gem to top it, and this Arnold offered to supply. In his judgment, the expedition was essentially imprudent and ought not to have been undertaken. Should it fail, how could the troops return? The ice would not hold so late in the season. Should it succeed, how were they to be subsisted? They could not carry provisions enough to last them; none could be purchased without hard money; and what could be obtained by force—aside from the folly of using such means—had already been taken by the British. As for getting military aid from the Canadians, they had neither arms nor ammunition. To send away the Continental troops at Albany would leave only militia to defend the Hudson and back Fort Schuyler. There were no signs that Burgoyne's expedition was to be repeated; therefore

---

[27] § Conway arrived on the 14th (Laf. to Wash., Feb. 19, 1778 : Sparks MSS., No. 87). In Sparks MSS., No. 12, p. 327, the letter to Lincoln is dated Feb. 6 ; but the letters of Lincoln and Clinton to Conway prove that the date should be Feb. 16. Laf., Feb. 20, 1778 (Conway, Hazen, Duane, etc.), Lincoln, Sch., Arnold, Troup (Feb. 19) : Note 19. Sleds: Conway to Gates, Feb. 19, 1778 (Cont. Cong. Papers, Canad. Affairs, 166, p. 59). Suspected : Laf. to Wash., Feb. 19, 1778 (Sparks MSS., No. 87). Hazen to Gates, Feb. 20, 1778: Note 18. Duane to Wash., Mar. 13, 1778: Coll. of C. H. Swan, Esq. Ice: Arnold to G. Morris, Feb. 2, 1778 (Freeman's Journal, July 18, 1781).

the vessels on Lake Champlain could do no great harm. And the best way, after all, to secure Canada was to enable Washington, by sending him all the troops that could be had, to 'drive Mr. Howe and his banditti from the country.'[28]

Then, to polish the jewel, it appeared that perhaps the situation in Canada was not so promising as Gates had supposed. John Nevill, an American soldier captured on the retreat from Quebec, after serving a long while in Maclean's Highland Emigrants, had taken French leave; and he now reported under oath upon the present state of things at the north. According to his testimony, the British kept a party at Iron Point, which could no doubt, even if surprised, send notice of the expedition; about four hundred men and thirteen cannon were on guard, under the brave Nairne, at Nut Island; as many or more lay at St. Johns, with at least a hundred pieces of artillery; some five hundred Hessians were scattered between Montreal and the Richelieu; Sir John Johnson's regiment of Tories occupied Laprairie; two or three hundred regulars were in garrison at Montreal; there were now three redoubts and a blockhouse at St. Johns; nearly all the shipping lay under their guns, and no straw to burn the vessels with had been stowed away in their holds.[29]

Heavy artillery could not be transported by Lafayette; and 'if they do their duty [at St. Johns] ten thousand men cannot take it with small arms,' remarked Arnold. To imagine that such a bristling series of posts would suddenly be overwhelmed with ' consternation ' was absurd ; yet that was the very nub of Lafayette's instructions.

---

[28] Arnold to Morris, Feb. 2, 1778: Freeman's Journal, July 18, 1781. The point about money was urged by Franklin also: Wharton, Dipl. Corres., III., p. 215.

[29] § Nevill, Statement: Cont. Cong. Papers, 166, p. 75. Laf. to Bd. War, Feb. 20, 1778: Note 19. Id. to Wash., Feb. 19, 1778: Note 27.

Deerfield 15 Feby 1775

Sir

Being Informed by the Honble
General Gates that you are appointed
to command an expedition against
the British troops in canada, & that
I am to go on the same expedition.
Should be glad to know as soon as
possible what Number of troops you expect
I shall bring with me what states I shall
raise them in, the place of rendivouz & when
to be rendevouzed, & I shall leave no method
untried to answer your expectations

I am
dear general
your most obedt.
Humble servt.
John Stark

The Honble Genel de lafayette

507

'They suppose the Enemy are to be pannic Struck & fly,' said the impartial Clinton, after a careful look at the document. Besides, if men could come south with interesting information, men could go north with as good, making a surprise impossible; and prudence had to reckon more or less on what actually occurred: loyalists carrying news to the British. To sum up: scarcely one pale ray of encouragement filtered upon the enterprise from any quarter.[30]

Dazed, at first, rather than enlightened by the terrible truth, Lafayette determined to push on with what he had. But soon he realized that it would be mad, even wicked, to squander the men's lives; and finally he determined to ask the advice of Congress, keeping at work meanwhile and listening eagerly to every scheme suggested.[31]

It was not a happy family, that group of officers in Albany. By this time, more than twenty Frenchmen had come up,—every one a Hannibal, in his own opinion, except the Scipios; and all they could do was to climb the hill for a look at the ruined fort, watch the steaming breath of a Dutch housewife poking skeptically at frozen deer-meat in the little market, or sit on one of the front stoops, in summer so carefully scoured but now swept by the zero gales, and listen to the resinous creak of horses' hoofs on the snow. On Sunday, as a special treat, they could hear the English bell on St. Peter's chapel in the middle of State Street; or they could file into the old Dutch church and see a black figure slowly rise in the octagonal oak pulpit, invert the hour-glass on the bracket in front of it, and then lay out a series of

---

[30] § Arnold to Morris: Note 28. Clinton to [Alex. Hamilton]: Clinton, Pub. Papers, II., p. 865. Powell to Carleton, Mar. 2, 1778: Can. Arch., B, 129, p. 1. See also Can. Arch., B, 100, p. 17.

[31] § Conway to Hazen, Feb. 18, 1778: Cont. Cong. Papers, 166, p. 65. Laf. to Bd. War, Feb. 20: Note 19. Id. to Wash., Mar. 25, 1778: Sparks, Corres., II., p. 93. Id. to Gates, Feb. 23, 1778: Sparks MSS., No. 22, p. 130.

'heads' as if sands could not run; but even this did little toward satisfying their dreams of glory and riches. Colonel Troup, Gates's aide-de-camp and confidant, who had pronounced Lafayette—after his famous toast at the banquet—'strongly tinctured with the Fabian principles of Head Quarters,' was still sniffing discontentedly at his heels like an ill-bred black-and-tan. Conway was thoroughly vexed with Congress for making General De Kalb, whom he described as his junior in France, outrank him in America, and especially for sending this rival to lord it over him at Albany. Hazen felt deeply disappointed and bitterly angry with Arnold. Lincoln was painfully curing a severe wound. Schuyler—although, like the gentleman and patriot that he was, he had buttoned a civilian coat about him and gone over to congratulate Gates on Burgoyne's defeat—could not feel reconciled to the disgrace of removal. And Arnold, still in his bed, was raging like a furnace over his enemies and his leg.[32]

THE DUTCH MEETING-HOUSE, ALBANY

But all of this misery, piled together, would not have equalled Lafayette's. The 'most solemn promises' had been made him that he should 'find here a large field of glory.' An 'immensity of laurels' had been predicted. He had been induced to inform his friends and 'let know

32 § Laf. to Wash., Feb. 23, 1778: Sparks MSS., No. 87. Troup, Statement: Sparks MSS., No. 49, I., pp. 20, 21. Fleury to Laurens, Feb. 14, 1778: Emmet Coll., F. Munsell, Coll., II., pp. 12, 13, 24, 26, 27, 374. Porter, Diary Apr. 1, 1776. Troup to Gates, Feb. [6], 19, 23, 1778: Bancroft Coll., Revol. Papers, III., pp. 279, 291, 299. Conway to Gates, Feb. 24, 1778: ib., p. 303. Hazen to Gates, Feb. 20, 1778: Cont. Cong. Papers, 166, p. 117. Sch.: Stone, Memoir, p. 81. I. N. Arnold, B. Arnold, pp. 213, 214. G. Morris to Arnold, Feb. 21, 1778: Freeman's Journal, July 18, 1781.

to the whole europe,' that he stood at the head of an American force 'directed to do great things.' As a letter to his wife showed, he had felt convinced in his sanguine moments that it would be impossible to keep his movement within any small bounds. All Canada would be freed from the British yoke, and his army would swell to an 'immense' host. There had been, indeed, a 'charming prospect,' as he said; but now—'the people [in Europe] will be in great expectations, & what shall I answer?' 'I shall be laughed at,' he groaned; 'I will become very ridiculous.' What his 'perhaps too quick and too warm heart' felt, could not be measured. Said an eye-witness, James Duane, Esq., it was 'unexpressible chagreen.'[33]

His one consolation was that he felt sure where to place the blame, and he made considerable use of it. 'What business had the board of war to hurry me thro' the ice & snow without knowing what I should do neither what they were doing themselves?' he exclaimed. In his judgment, it was tardiness at York that had ruined the plan. 'If proper orders, proper monnies had been sent sometime ago we should have been able to carry the expedition,' he informed the Board itself; 'if as soon as the intended expedition began to [be talked about] in the streets of york General Washington had been desired of giving me the order to repair to Congress, we should have had some time before hand.' A 'hell of blunders, madness, and deception,' was his picture of the case. 'Your deceived friend,' he described himself to his General.[34]

---

[33] § Laf. to Bd. War., Feb. 20, 1778: Note 19. Id. to Wash., Feb. 19, 1778: Sparks MSS., No. 87. Id. to his wife, Feb. 3, 1778: Laf., Mém., p. 151. Id. to Laurens, rec'd Jan. 28, 1778: So. Car. Hist. and Gen. Mag., VII., p. 179. Id. to Gates, Feb. 23, 1778: Sparks MSS., No. 22, p. 130. Duane to Wash., Mar. 13, 1778: Coll. of C. H. Swan, Esq.

[34] § Laf. to Wash., Feb. 19, 1778: Note 33. Id. to Bd. War, Feb. 20, 1778: Note 19. Id. to Wash., Mar. 25, 1778: Sparks, Corres., II., p. 93. Id. to Laurens, Feb. 19, 1778: So. Car. Hist. and Gen. Mag., VII., p. 189.

Nor was Congress happy at this time. For one thing, Washington's attitude did not seem precisely reassuring. When Gates invited him, after the orders to Lafayette had been issued, to give his opinion and advice on the matter, the Commander-in-chief had replied to what was a perfunctory, if not a patronizing, letter: 'as I neither know the extent of the objects in view, nor the means to be employed to effect them, it is not in my power to pass any judgment upon the subject.' Evidently Washington felt no desire to be connected in any way with the expedition ; and while no doubt his sense of propriety and his regard for Lafayette combined to prevent any public criticism upon it, an equal sense of duty may have led him to make some remarks to the committee of Congress.[35]

At any rate, the committee worked hard against the scheme. 'We have taken every measure in our power to ruin the Canada expedition,' wrote Gouverneur Morris ; 'it is necessary that we should destroy it, or it will destroy us.' One letter of theirs in particular disturbed Congress so much that, on the sixteenth of February, the Board of War were directed ' to report specially thereon, and to lay before Congress a copy of the orders given to the officers commanding the irruption.' Whatever was thought of the extravagant orders, it cannot have been reassuring to find that one part of them—and that the final, cautionary part—had been lost, and could only be given from memory.[36]

Arnold had very promptly, very cheerfully, and very emphatically written to Gouverneur Morris against the expedition ; and, as this was a prime opportunity to settle scores with both Gates and Hazen, he doubtless ex-

---

[35] § Gates to Wash., Jan. 24, 1778 : Bancroft Coll., Revol. Papers, III., p 263. Reply, Jan. 27, 1778: Wash., Writings (Ford), VI., p. 296.

[36] § Morris to Arnold, Feb. 21, 1778: Freeman's Journal, July 18, 1781. (This was in reply to Arnold's of Feb. 2; but, as that did not arrive until Feb. 20, the action of the Com. was not due to Arnold's advice.) Secret Journ. Cong., Feb. 16, 1778. Memory: Gates's memorandum (Cont. Cong. Papers, 156, p. 63).

if I have ever been intitled to ask any favor from Congress of the united states, I beg in this
occasion your and their particular attention for what I am to tell them by this letter— the love
of this country, the desire of complying with the ardent wishes and dangerous hopes of myself (So
I think) the matter represented to me, and the most solemn promises which have been made to me

that I should find her a large field of glory, have engaged me in the present entreprise —

I hope you will leave my instructions represented to you, and I trust you will not find my
confidence in what they contain greater than this while I consider an honest man— let not
Mention the promises which have been told, but only that which have been wrote to me—

I was to find at a low estimate two thousand five hundred combattans only with the troops
mentioned in the instruction—but a much larger body was foretold.

Gal Stark would have been ready with his men, and indeed the board of war thought the [?]
could be burnt before my arrival—

pressed his opinion to other friends of his in Congress. Lincoln and Schuyler, understanding the difficulties, very likely did the same. Evidently some persons addressed remarks to the Board of War itself ; and, on the twenty-third, sundry papers from that body, communicated to Congress, were referred to a special committee with orders to consider them, 'collect the best information' it could upon the subject, 'and lay the same before Congress as soon as possible.' This led, the next day, to a vote that Lafayette should be 'particularly attentive' to the matters of clothing and provisions, and that, if he could not obtain sufficient men and supplies, he should 'regulate his conduct according to the probability of success.' [37]

By the second of March, Lafayette's full report of the situation, with the returns and the opinions of the officers, evidently arrived. ' I hope it will open their eyes,' the Marquis had said ; and that it did. Congress voted that, ' Whereas, it appears from authentick accounts, that difficulties attend the prosecution of the irruption . . . which render the attempt not only hazardous in a high degree, but extremely imprudent,' it should be suspended for the present, and the officers—in particular, the Marquis—be treated to the most appreciative and complimentary phrases. A few days later, Washington was authorized to recall Lafayette and Kalb to the 'grand army.' On the morrow, a snub was administered to the Board of War by voting down its recommendation in favor of Conway's aide-de-camp. Still later, Conway was ordered to join McDougall ; Schuyler offered Louis, the faithful Caughnawaga chief, a thousand dollars in specie if he would burn the vessels at St. Johns, thus fitly winding up Gates's great military and political operation as an attempt at arson ; Lafayette's passionate mortification

---

[37] Secret Journ. Cong , Feb. 23, 24, 1778.

grew calm enough to laugh—rather grimly, no doubt—at the whole affair; and finally all traces of the many anxious, hurrying feet melted away with the snows of Albany into Albany mud.[38]

One thing, however, did not melt : the idea of using, as a lever on Canada, the affection of its people for France.

---

38 § Secret Journ. Cong., Mar. 2, 13, 14, 1778. Laf. to Wash., Feb. 19, 1778: Note 33. Bd. War. Papers, I., p. 551. Conway to Gates, Apr. 2, 1778: Bancroft Coll., Revol. Papers, III., p. 323. Sch. to Prest. Cong., Mar. 15, 1778 ; Cont. Cong. Papers, 170, p. 261. Laf. to Wash., Mar. 25, 1778: Note 34. Mar. 10, 1778, Wash. wrote consolingly to Laf. (Writings, Ford's ed., VI., p. 410). RE-MARK CXI.

XXXVII

REASONS OF STATE

PERSONAL sympathy and aid such as Lafayette's—
however cheering, however valuable—were not the
principal reinforcement which the Declaration of Independence ensured. That act opened the way to foreign
alliances ; and when France, precisely as the Marquis was
about leaving Valley Forge for Albany, concluded a treaty
with the United States, we found ourselves on intimate
terms with the beloved fatherland of the Canadians. A
great change then occurred in the northern problem. It
ceased to be an affair of quick dashes, of personal enthusiasm and address ; and it became a question of high
diplomacy and far-reaching strategy, with all the advantages and all the disadvantages which that new fact
implied.

Another change, also—a military one—took place now
in the schemes for invading Canada. The fleet at St.
Johns had not been burned. The British still held full
control of Lake Champlain, and seemed very likely to retain it. Schuyler suggested that perhaps vessels enough
to beat them could be secretly constructed somewhere on
those waters; but, as Washington pointed out, this was
extremely improbable. In a winter campaign, the fleet
would have been helpless, no doubt ; but military operations at that season were exceedingly exhausting and
required the costliest preparation. Consequently, some

Resolved ~~that it is expedient~~

That these United Colonies are, and of right ought to be, free and independent States, that they are absolved from all allegiance to the British Crown, and that all political connection between them and the state of Great Britain is and ought to be, totally dissolved.

That it is expedient forthwith to take the most effectual measures for forming foreign Alliances

RESOLUTION MOVED IN CONGRESS, JUNE 7, 1776

other convenient route into the north seemed quite essential.[1]

Fortunately, that problem appeared to have been solved in advance. As early as December, 1775, Jacob Bayley of Coös—more precisely Newbury, Vermont—proposed to Washington the building of a road to Canada from the Connecticut River at that point, and Washington laid the matter promptly before Congress. In February, 1776, Frye Bayley and two comrades went from Coös to Montreal and described the region they crossed in Vermont as 'the best country for a road' that any of them had ever seen, 'through any woods of the same length.' The distance from Boston to St. Johns along that line was found to be eighty-two miles less than by Crown Point, no slight advantage ; and the settlements of Coös appeared to give the route a solid fulcrum. Private interests would be served, no doubt, by carrying out the project, but that was true in every such affair. Samuel Adams, as well as Washington, recommended the plan ; and in May Congress ordered the road built.[2]

Under Washington's orders it was promptly begun ; and by the first of July, according to a loyalist informer, the route had been marked all the way to St. Johns. At the southern end, to the infinite astonishment of many a catbird and lynx, the trees and bushes were cleared away for a breadth of twenty-two yards, a carriage road levelled half as wide, and strips of trees killed along the way by girdling, so that the sun might dry the ground. In this fashion, the work proceeded thoroughly to Peacham

---

[1] Wash. to Sch., Nov. 20, 1778: Wash., Writings (Ford), VII., p. 265.

[2] § Wash. to Cong., Dec. 25, 1775: Wash., Writings (Ford), III., p. 297. Bayley *et al.*, Report: 4 Force, IV., 1500. Bayley to Wash., Apr. 15, 1776: 4 Force, V., 947. Wash. to Cong., May 5, 1776: Wash., Writings (Ford), IV., p. 59. Johnson, Journal: 4 Force, V., 948. Wells, S. Adams, II., p. 402. Wash. to S. Adams, Mar. 22, 1776: S. Adams Papers. Id. to Bayley, Apr. 29, 1776: 4 Force, V., 1113. Private: Bayley, Narrative. S. Adams to Wash., May 15, 1776: S. Adams Papers. Journ. Cong., May 10, 1776.

and several miles beyond. Then, as a consequence of the American retreat from Canada, the British seemed likely to attack the laborers at any moment. In fact,

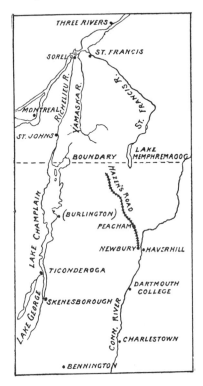

news came that a party was close upon them, and the work hastily ended. But the line had now been laid out and the road could manifestly be completed with no great difficulty. That done, an American force could strike St. Johns by land, or—passing down one of the rivers just east of the Richelieu—arrive at the St. Lawrence without encountering any of the British forts.[3]

Gates, not wholly pleased with the results of his Lafayette 'irruption,' felt very ambitious to carry through some scheme for the invasion of Canada; and, in the month of July, 1778, Traversie, one of the principal Canadian scouts, presented himself to Colonel Bedel with this mysterious

---

[3] § Wash. to Bayley, Apr. 29, 1776: Note 2. Work was ordered to be begun before Congress acted. Bayley to Wash., May 28, 1776: 4 Force, VI., 611. Informer to Carleton, July 11, 1776: Can. Arch., B, 181, p. 10. Wells, Newbury, p. 76. Bittinger, Haverhill, p. 170. Bedel to Gates, Aug. 25, 1778: N. H. State Papers, XVII., p. 265.

letter: ' Traversie has my directions to acquaint you with a message I have sent by him,'—*Horatio Gates.*[4]

Louis Vincent was called in to interpret, and with his aid the message was written down: ' General Gates Ordered me to tell Col° Bedel to Chuse a proper Person for a Pilot to find out a Road to Saint Francois. I was to Consult with them about the same, [and] when the Road is looked out to send Lieu^t Col° Wheelock to him and no other Persons, with the Proceedings, to be done with the utmost despatch. . . . Genl Gates also told me not to Inform Generals Schuyler or Starks of the same on pain of Punishment. Genl Gates in Person wo^d March this way with the troops. Genl Gates upon his arrival at Saint Francois wo^d divide the Army into two Divisions and wo^d be in Canada in September, where there is plenty of Provisions, and that the French would come up the River.' To this Traversie put his mark in the presence of two safe witnesses, and before long Colonel Hazen arrived to confirm it ; while Gates, to protect the secret still further, assured Stark: ' You need be under no manner of concern of another Canada expedition being needlessly undertaken,'—saving himself by the adverb.[5]

Bedel replied that ' No kind of difficulty ' was to be feared about a route. There were three practicable ways to go north from Coös, all of them indicated on Hazen's plan, and they should be examined and marked at once. Further, he would send three parties of spies to as many different sections of Canada for intelligence ' with orders to return with all possible expedition,' and would hold himself in readiness with his men. Within five days,

[4] § Ambitious: Gates to Wash., Mar. 4, 1779 (Sparks, Corres., II., p. 256). Id. to Bedel, June 26, 1778, etc.: Chase, Hanover, I., p. 392.

[5] § Message: Wheelock Papers (Chase, Hanover, I., p. 392). Gates to Stark, July 14, 1778: C. Stark, Stark, p. 181. What warrant Gates had for saying the French would aid, the author does not know. Perhaps he made the statement merely to rouse the Canadians. François is, of course, the French form of Francis.

the surveyors and spies were out. Fifteen hundred or two thousand volunteers, Bedel assured Wheelock, could be found for the expedition in those parts. Don't delay about recruiting, he added.[6]

But now came one of those whirls that kept the Canadian operations perpetually waltzing. Within a week Hazen wrote : ' Our proposed expedition to Canada, must be Post poned,' for Congress and the generals are busy shutting up Howe's fleet, ' in hopes of Burgoyning Clintons Army.'[7]

Soon, however, and under better auspices, another plan for invading the north by this route began to take shape. It was a general belief that Great Britain would soon evacuate the States ; and, were that done, the men and resources for an expedition could be spared. Still firm in his opinion that Canada ought to make a part of the Union, Washington lost no time. Gates, Bayley and Hazen were appointed as a Board of Officers, to con-

FROM TRAVERSIE'S MESSAGE

---

[6] § Bedel to Gates, July, 14, 1778 : Chase, Hanover, I., p. 393. Bedel to Wheelock, July 19, 1778: N. H. State Papers, XVII., p. 243 ; Wheelock Papers.
[7] Hazen to Bedel, July 25, 1778 : N. H. State Papers, XVII., p. 248.

sider ' what would be the most eligible plan ' ; and, about
the middle of September, the Commander-in-chief sent
their findings to Congress with his own cautious and
conditional endorsement. ' Essential advantages ' might
be derived, he thought, from such a movement, should
Congress regard it as warranted by the circumstances. In
the interim, he had ordered stores of provisions and
forage gathered at Coös, and the best possible answers
obtained in Canada to a series of important questions.
As Colonel Hazen was deputed to carry and supplement
the letter, Congress was evidently to hear all that could
be said for the project. To send him was itself an
argument.[8]

Then the kaleidoscope turned again. Lafayette also
found the glamour of the north too strong to resist. In
August, he sent an engineer to examine the route from
Coös, and in October he proposed the co-operation of
France and the United States in a vigorous invasion.
Congress took the project up at once, and, on the twenty-
second of the month, in the form of Instructions to Doctor Franklin, the American representative at Paris, an
elaborate scheme was adopted.[9]

By this plan, sixteen hundred chosen men of the rank
and file were to be gathered at Fort Pitt from Virginia and
Pennsylvania, and march by the first day of June against
Detroit. A nearly equal force, drawn from Pennsylvania
and New Jersey would rendezvous in the Wyoming valley on the upper Susquehanna, and move not later than
June the first against Niagara ; and a third party of the

[8] § Wash. to Jay, Apr. 14, 1779: Wash., Writings (Ford), VII., p. 393. Id. to Carter, May 30, 1778: ib., p. 37. Id. to Cong., Sept. 12, 1778: ib., p. 191 and note. Bayley to Bedel, Oct. 13, 1778: N. H. State Papers, XVII., p. 276.

[9] § Engineer to Lafayette, Aug. 25, 1778: N. H. State Papers, XVII., p. 264. Wash. to Jay : Note 8. Journ. Cong., Oct. 21, 22, 1778. Secret Journ. Cong., Oct. 22. Instructions: Cont. Cong. Papers, Reports of Committees, 25, I., p. 35: The Committee were G. Morris, Chase, Drayton, S. Adams, R. H. Lee, and Witherspoon.

same strength, assembled on the Mohawk, would march west at about the same time, destroy the hostile Indian towns on its route, and join the Susquehanna men on the way to Niagara.

Twenty-five hundred more, drawn in part from the regular army and in part from the militia of New York, Massachusetts, and Connecticut, would advance from the Mohawk as early as possible to Oswego, and proceed—suitable preparations having been made in the winter—to build vessels of force, gain control of the lake, and assist the work at Niagara by alarming the Indian country.

Further, a body of five thousand Continentals, rank and file, gathered in the course of the winter on the upper Connecticut, would advance as early as they could to St. Francis, and gain possession of Montreal, St. Johns, and Lake Champlain. A detachment would then join the forces at Oswego, and as many as possible of the troops assembled there would finally go to Niagara, where the Detroit party, also, whether successful or not, was to end its campaign.

Meanwhile, ' a Body [of] from 2,000 to 5,000 French Troops,' convoyed by four ships of the line and as many frigates, would pass up the St. Lawrence, and about the first of July reach Quebec, which 'they would in all Probability find quite defenceless' on account of the demand for troops in the west. After occupying that capital, gathering and arming the Canadians, and planting a small garrison of marines and regulars, they would go on with the frigates and transports to St. Francis, and combine with the Americans for the operations against Montreal and St. Johns. Should the Americans not have arrived, a part of the French troops would await them, and the rest advance in the lightest vessels. ' By the latter End of July or about the Middle of August the Reduction of *Canada* might be so far compleated that the Ships might

proceed to the Investiture of Halifax' aided by a ' considerable Body of American Troops . . . with the Militia
of the States of Massachusetts and New Hampshire '; and,
by the beginning or middle of October, the victorious
forces might occupy Newfoundland.

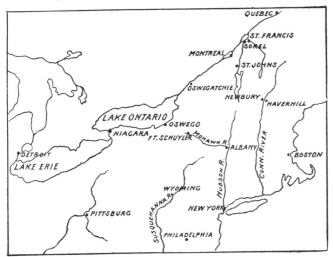

Shrewd plans were laid for deceiving the British.
Whereas the other parts of the scheme were to be kept
profoundly secret, the movements against Detroit and
Niagara might be judiciously mentioned. While the
real destination of the French troops was to be given out,
their clothing and stores were apparently to ' designate
them for the West Indies '; but each soldier was to have
' a good Blanket of a large Size to be made into a Coat '
when the weather grew cool; regular winter clothes were
to be despatched separately; and arms for the Canadians
were to be marked ' as for the Militia of one of the French
Islands ' in the Antilles.¹⁰

10 § Instructions : Note 9.   Secret Journ. Cong., Oct. 22, 1778 ; Jan. 1, 1779.

The state of things in Canada at this time invited an attack. Carleton had turned over the government to General Haldimand in July; and the new head, though capable, had found it an immense labor to gather up the reins of Greater Quebec, a line of champing steeds that reached from Labrador to the Mississippi. The mere distances were enough to make his work difficult. The task of transporting provisions to the upper posts was by no means a light one, and at present a dearth of supplies could be seen in the near future. The walls of Quebec were still pronounced ' rotten,' and repairs or new works were needed at other points also. A ' swarm of Privateers ' infested the Gulf of St. Lawrence, as the Governor himself admitted,—greatly injuring trade, almost ruining the fisheries in that quarter, and undermining confidence in the power of Britain; and, for almost six months of the year, the intense cold paralyzed work so completely, that anxious Haldimand was driven to dancing and fierce Maclean to getting up theatricals.[11]

The Governor's most serious difficulty, however, was the temper of the people.

Canada had not found the expulsion of the Americans an unqualified boon. The day Carleton's army halted in its pursuit of them, he directed the *habitants* to ' hold themselves in readiness to March ' as soon as the chase could be resumed. Four days later General Phillips, in charge of the naval preparations, ' sent an order for the assembling the Country people with their Tools.' Only during the harvest were they exempt from forced labor (*corvées*). Troops were billeted upon them; and, as many petitions revealed, they squirmed lustily under the burdens of unpaid work and uninvited guests. Burgoyne tried to coax

11 §Hald. to Germain, July 25, 1778: Can. Arch., B, 42, p. 6.   Id. to Id., Sept. 14, 1779: ib., 54, p. 178.   Id. to Id., June 7, 1779: ib., 54, p. 85.   Id. to Id., Oct. 24, 1778: ib., 54, p. 47.   Id. to Buda, Mar. 1, 1779: ib., 66, p. 105.   Maclean to Mathews, Dec. 11, 1780: ib., 129, p. 191.

BAYLEY'S MEADOW AND THE CONNECTICUT SEEN FROM NEWBURY

them; but, when coaxing failed, he put six hundred of the young men under guard, and forced them to march south on his ill-fated excursion. 'Cuff and kick them well about!' appeared to be the general prescription of the regular officers for making Canadians work; and very possibly the poor *habitants* remembered now the occasional exactions of the American troops as almost acts of kindness.[12]

Besides these afflictions, which fell like the rain on the just and the unjust alike, that large percentage of the people which had sided with the Americans found a heavy hand upon them. 'The rewarding those who had preserved their Loyalty and the punishing those who had forsaken their Allegiance,' was recommended by Germain; and Carleton himself, however excusable he considered the people, realized the sound policy of this rule. At the first anniversary of Montgomery's assault, a service of thanksgiving was held in the cathedral with Bishop Briand upon his throne; and eight Canadians who had taken part with the invaders had to present themselves with ropes about their necks, do penance before the congregation, and humbly 'crave pardon of their God, Church and King.'[13]

More substantial punishments also were meted out. Not Rusoe d'Eres and his family alone, but many others of the people, found themselves persecuted. Carleton 'has rendered himself very odious to the Canadians by levying contributions on them in general,' said Thomas Jefferson, '& confiscating the estates of all those who followed our army or who abscond'; and of course he did

---

12 § Carleton to Burgoyne, June 20, 1776: Can. Arch., B, 39, p. 25. Foy to Fraser, June 24, 1776: ib., 39, p. 31. Harvest: Carleton to Powell, Aug. 24, 1776 (ib., 39, p. 110 (inference)). Foy to Marr, Aug. 18, 1777: ib., p. 678. Billeting; petitions: Can. Arch., B, 218, pp. 12, 90, 101, 106, 221, 266; 219, pp. 39, 100, etc. Bayley, Narrative. Burgoyne: Rey to S. Adams, 1780 [?] (S. Adams Papers). 'Cuff': Liv., Journal, Oct. 19.

13 § Germain to Carleton, Aug. 22, 1776: Can. Arch., Q, 12, p. 88. Carleton to Germain, May 23, 1777: ib., 13, p. 160. Stone (ed.), Letters, p. 66.

not make the statement without grounds. Jean Menard, and nobody knows how many others, were cast into prison and there vegetated until the war came to an end. A German staff-officer saw the houses of many disloyal *habitants* pulled down. Moreover, the Tories doubtless went far beyond, when they could, the Governor's official sternness. Haldimand suggested their temper by lamenting later that too little severity was shown at this time. Goulet's American commission was burned to ashes in his hand at the church door by royalist neighbors, and continual insults finally drove him from the country. No wonder the German officer could write : ' I have indeed passed through Parishes in which the faces of all the habitans seemed to betray their rebellious tendencies ' (November, 1776). [14]

St. Leger's failure and still more Burgoyne's disaster had naturally a great effect in Canada. At first deserters, and then fugitives, made ' very unfavourable impressions' upon the minds of the people, reported the Governor. The brilliant prowess displayed by the Americans cancelled the bad effects of their repulses in Canada, and it was necessary to make special efforts ' to raise the spirits of the [loyal] People from that Dejected state into which they had been plunged.' Once more the Tories felt abandoned, as in 1775 ; and sympathy with the Americans gathered force. Carleton's departure deepened the gloom. ' No people ever loved their ruler more than the Canadians do theirs,' testified a German ; and his resignation, growing out of just resentment against Lord George Germain, could but stimulate the reaction. [15]

---

[14] § C. D. R. d'Eres, Memoirs, *passim*. Jeff. to Page, Aug. 20, 1776: Jeff., Writings (Ford), II., p. 85. Menard, Petition: Cont. Cong. Papers, No. 35, p. 157. Stone (ed.), Letters, pp. 24, 29. Hald. to Germain, June 7, 1779: Can. Arch., B, 54, p. 85. Goulet to Wash., Jan., 1781 : Wash. Papers, VI., p. 250, Lib. of Cong.

[15] § Carleton to Germain, June 10, 1778: Can. Arch., B, 37, p. 187. Stone (ed.), Letters, p. 20.

Influences from beyond the border had a powerful effect in the same direction.

Every effort had been made by the British to build a voice-proof wall on the frontier, with gates of bronze and no latch-string. Parliament prohibited all intercourse ; King George, to give the law a special sanctity, put his royal hand to the parchment ; and Germain ordered Carleton to pay this command 'the most punctual and exact obedience.' All strangers were jealously watched. The pass of the Chaudière was guarded. Scouts were glued upon all the avenues leading into Canada from Oswego and Fort Schuyler. At St. Johns and Nut Island the sharpest precautions were taken. When any person arrived at a British post or vessel, whatever papers he carried were seized, ' packed up, sealed & directed to the Commander in Chief or Officer Commanding at Montreal to be forwarded to him,' and the bearer was then passed along under guard from post to post, in a silence as deep as possible, to the same destination. Caughnawagas assured an officer of Stark's that, on a mere suspicion of dealings between them and the States, 'our friends in that Country would be instantly secured and obliged to suffer at least a Close Confinement.' In fact, a party from the south under a flag of truce, conducting an exchanged British officer back to Canada, were arrested and held as prisoners.[16]

Every effort possible was made to catch the American spies. In the Chaudière district, both sides of the river were patrolled, and scouts went long distances back and forth across the country at right angles to the stream. If Carleton heard that three St. Regis Indians or two from

---

[16] § Germain to Carleton, Feb. 26, 1776: Can. Arch., B, 37, p. 126. Carleton to Cramahé, Aug. 27, 1776: Can. Arch., B, 39, p. 116. Id. to Officer, Jan. 21, 1777: ib., 39, p. 339. Precautions, e. g.: Carleton to Germain, June 10, 1778 (Can. Arch., B, 37, p. 187). Circular to officers, Aug. 19, 1778 : ib., 62, p. 88. Cochran to Stark, Oct. 20, 1778 : Emmet Coll. Arrested : Bayley, Narrative.

Caughnawaga had been talking with 'rebels,' he ordered the matter investigated. 'I employ all methods,' reported Haldimand, 'to become acquainted with the intricate & secret Paths,' by which American scouts reach the parishes.'[17]

But 'all methods' were not methods enough. Many a bold and wary eye, trained to read the moss on the tree-trunks, familiar with every dell and crag, acquainted with each peasant's inmost feelings, threaded safely those intricate paths. Colonel Hazen was known to visit Canada, but he could not be found. Major Whitcomb, a mild, benevolent-looking justice of the peace at home, but a hard, cunning, restless dare-devil when on British soil, was a frequent invader, and his tall, thin figure, broad shoulders, rough-hewn face, light-brown hair tied behind, blue vest, flask-pockets, leather breeches, grey woollen stockings, and flapped hat with a gold cord round it, were made known to every British officer; yet he went and came as he pleased. Traversie, a 'famous Canadian Rebel,' as Haldimand described him to Germain, did the same. Goulet, Boileau, Cadieux, and Gosselin were some of the other Canadian spies. Bayley and Bedel kept men out almost constantly. Stark and Schuyler busied themselves in the same work. Messengers came and went by Oswegatchie; and, now and then, volunteers in the cause ventured south, even to Philadelphia, with information.[18]

The field was too large and the arts of secrecy were

---

[17] § Foy to officer, Dec. 8, 1776 : Can. Arch., B, 39, p. 295. Carleton to Maclean, Aug. 21, 1777: ib., 39, p. 680. Hald. to Germain, Oct. 15, 1778: ib., 54, p. 30.

[18] § Powell to Hald., July 30, 1778 : Can. Arch., B, 129, p. 16. Whitcomb: Morris, Address, pp. 19, 21, etc.; F. Bayley, Narrative ; Burgoyne, Gen. Ord., July 23, 1776 (Can. Arch., B, 83, p. 27). Traversie: Hald. to Germain, Oct. 15, 1778 (Can. Arch., B, 54, p. 30) ; Gates to S. Adams, Aug. 23, 1779 (S. Adams Papers); Verreau (Badeaux), Invasion, p. 187; etc. Wash. Papers, VI. and VII., passim; particularly VII., pp. 244-247, 249, 250-253, 361. N. H. State Papers, XVII., pp. 133, 152, 218, 241, 243, 265, 276. etc. Herrick to Stark, May 19, 1779: C. Stark, Stark, p. 195. Sch., Colon. N. Y., II., p. 275. Cochran to Stark, Oct. 20, 1778: Emmet Coll. Cramahé to Foy, Sept. 17, 1778: Can. Arch., B, 95, p. 44.

ADMIRAL D' ESTAING

too many for the Governor's patrols to accomplish much. Chambly Mountain was a roomy hiding-place. Any big hollow log served Whitcomb for a nest. A tipsy Indian might be Traversie. Women, stealing to the woods at night with little packets, could bear priceless documents. Invisible messages were easily written with milk and brought out before a fire, or the signature of a letter could be torn off and forwarded separately. While the British scouts were peering at stumps in Sertigan, illicit papers could be laid on door-sills or fastened to doors at Three Rivers. While the bearer of an American flag of truce was being clapped into the guard-house at St. Johns, a man with a scar on his cheek, dressed in a blue coat with a crimson velvet collar, could slip into a cottage near Quebec, utter a few words, and vanish. I cannot discover the channels of communication, admitted Haldimand, precisely while Congress was meditating on Lafayette's plans. The province was full of secret American agents, he discovered at about the same time. 'People receive Earlier Intelligence of the state of Affairs in all quarters than I can possibly obtain,' he lamented helplessly.[19]

These operations of the American scouts were sure evidence that many people in Canada sympathised with their cause, and they were also sure evidence that what the scouts carried north would increase this kind feeling. Countless exhortations from the Canadian refugees naturally made up a large part of the papers and messages that entered the province. News of the military operations and the military outlook, inevitably colored, were no

---

[19] § Genevay to Schmid, May 18, 1780: Can. Arch., B, 117, p. 184. Morris, Address, p. 17. Deserters, June 20, 1779 : Can. Arch., B, 181, p. 197. Hald. to St. Leger, June 28, 1779: ib., 139, p. 17. St. Leger to Mathews, Jan. 17, 1781: ib., 134, p. 5. Maj. Carleton to Hald., July 30, 1780: ib., 205, p. 64. Secret letters: ib., 205, *passim*. Affidavit, June 14, 1779 : ib., 175, p. 60. Affidavit, Mar. 23, 1779: ib., 184, 1, p. 50. Hald. to Gugy, Nov. 1, 1778: ib., 62, p. 294. Id. to Buda, Oct. 24, 1778: ib., 66, p. 92. Ib. to Germain, June 18, 1779: ib., 54, p. 109. The later letters doubtless illustrate what existed earlier.

doubt another part; and information as to the political doings and prospects of the young nation went in company. Under this last head, the Articles of Confederation were transmitted with an Address; and the Canadians found that, in laying the foundations of the new Republic, the Congress had left one place vacant. Their province and no other, whenever her people should choose, might occupy it; and such an opportunity was itself an inducement.[20]

All the while, in the same clandestine manner, the campaign of political education went on. Ideas and arguments crept unseen from mind to mind, from parish to parish. We have at length satisfied the Canadians 'of the natural rights of man in the social state,' asserted a leader in this business while Lafayette's plan was under consideration; they are not willing to have their civil and religious institutions depend upon the will of a foreign state; they desire the power to legislate on such matters for themselves: in brief, they wish the liberty and self-government of the American States. Many were the 'conversions' to this agreeable doctrine, it was reported. Even the noblesse and the clergy were said to realize at last that all their privileges depended, as Congress had pointed out, upon the nod of a Minister.[21]

As the result of everything, Haldimand felt satisfied that the Canadians—except the nobles, the clergy, and some of the people in the towns—could not be relied upon; and a spy declared that the suspects, who filled the jails and overflowed into the churches, rejoiced in their sufferings and received constant encouragement 'from multitudes of the inhabitants.' Even the King's chief

---

[20] § Powell to Hald., July 2, 1779: Can. Arch., B, 133, p. 122. Colored, e. g.: Gosselin to wife, Oct. 19, 1778 (Can. Arch., 184, 2, p. 595); Indians (ib., 133, p. 57). Art. Confed., XI. Van Tyne, Am. Revol., p. 202.

[21] —— to Estaing, Dec. 31, 1778: Sparks MSS., No. 22, p. 74.

interpreter was accounted a friend by the American agents.[22]

But the grand, the essential, the deeply exciting message that crossed the border was the news of an alliance between the United States and France. The supreme military fact and prospect for the Canadians were that the flag of the lilies was to march now with the flag of the stars. Nothing could have interested them more. As Haldimand admitted, a cordial feeling toward the Americans was 'undoubtedly raised in numbers of them, who in regard of the Rebellion were unquestionably attached to Government'; and the symptoms of the change were 'everywhere manifest.' In all quarters, the *habitants* became 'adherents to the united Cause of France & the Americans.' Even the gentry cooled. 'What!' exclaimed Lafayette, on meeting some of them detained as prisoners at Boston, 'What! you fought in order to remain colonials instead of becoming independent! Remain slaves, then!' and the logic of the sarcasm could be felt, even where the remark was not heard. Few of them, said the Governor, had sagacity enough to see the bearings of the French alliance; and some, on hearing that an ambassador from the Court of Versailles had arrived at Philadelphia, resigned their places in the British service at once. The clergy, too, fell off. Already the French priests in Canada had been restive for years, and now their Canadian brethren yielded to the contagion. American spies were aided by clergymen, and men of the cloth even stole across the border.[23]

[22] § Hald. to Germain, July 25, 1778: Can. Arch., B, 42, p. 19. (At this date the effect of the French alliance had not had time to declare itself.) Bedel to Gates, July 15, 1778: N. H. State Papers, XVII., p. 241. Interpreter: J.Wheelock to Gates, Dec. 30, 1777 (Force Transcripts of Gates corres., Lib. of Cong.).

[23] § Hald. to Germain, Oct. 15, 1778: Can. Arch., B, 54, p. 30. Id. to Id., June 7, 1779 (concerning an earlier time): ib., 54, p. 85. Id. to Id., Sept. 19, 1779: ib., 54, p. 178. —— to Estaing: Note 21. Laf. (traditional, perhaps): Institut Canadien, Centenaire, p. 58. Cramahé to Hillsborough, July 25, 1772: Can. Arch., Q, 8, p. 160. Bayley to Gates, Jan. 1, 1779: Letters of Gates, No. 171, Lib.

About the time Lafayette's plan was under discussion, messengers from Canada went down to Philadelphia and called upon the French ambassador, to see with their own eyes that no lie had been told about the alliance; and from him they journeyed over to Boston for a long look at the banner of Estaing's fleet. Already the Admiral had in mind an address to the Canadians. This appeared to him the very time for launching it; and, on the twenty-eighth of October, the press of his flag-ship issued a striking yet subtle appeal.[24]

'I will not say, as a Gentleman of France,' he exclaimed, 'I will not say, as a Gentleman of France, to those of you born Gentlemen like myself, that only one august house exists in the universe, under which the Frenchman can be happy & serve with delight, since its head & those nearest him in blood have been pleased, through a long succession of Monarchs, during all epochs, & are more pleased today than ever, to bear this very title, which Henri IV. regarded as the noblest he possessed. I will not evoke regret for those dignities, those badges, those decorations,—precious treasures to all who think as we do, but at present, by our common misfortune, beyond the reach of the French Americans who knew so well how to merit them. Their zeal, I venture to hope & to promise, will soon win them in plenty: they will deserve such rewards when they dare to become the friends of our allies.

'I will not ask the comrades of Monsieur the Marquis de Lévy, those who shared his glory, who admired his talents [and] his military skill, who cherish the memory of his cordiality and frankness—the essential characteristic

---

of Cong. F. Bayley, Narrative. Bedel to [Sch.], Jan. 11, 1779 : N. H. State Papers, XVII., p. 311. Spy's report, Oct. 16, 1778 : ib., p. 276.

[24] Doniol, Particip., III., pp. 180, 423.

of our noblesse—whether, among other peoples, they can find names beside which they would rather place their own. The Canadians who saw the brave Monsieur de Montcalm fall in their defense, could they be the enemies of his nephews, fight against their former leaders & take up arms against their own relatives? At the mere name, these arms would fall from their hands!

' I will not point out to the Ministry of the altars that their apostolic labors will need the special protection of providence, if [heretical] examples are not to undermine faith, if temporal interests are not to gain the upper hand, if the kindness of the Sovereigns—due to necessity—is not to diminish as the Sovereigns have less and less to fear. [I will not point out] how needful it is for the cause of Religion that its ministers form a Body in the State, & that no Body would be more esteemed nor more able to do good than that of the Priests of Canada, taking part in the Government; for their worthy conduct has won the confidence of the public.

' I will not remind this people, all my Fellow-countrymen in general, that a vast Kingdom having the same Religion, the same customs, the same Language, where relatives, old friends, & brethren are to be found, is an inexhaustible [source] of Commerce, & of Wealth, more easily to be gained & better secured by union with powerful neighbors than with Strangers in another hemisphere among whom everything is foreign, [and] that soon or late jealous & tyrannical Sovereigns will treat them as vanquished,—indeed, even worse, no doubt, than did their Fellow-countrymen of a former day, the actual conquerors. I will not suggest to a whole people when it is gaining the right to think and act, [and] understands its interests, that to link itself with the United States is to ensure its happiness: but I will declare, as formally I do in the name of His Majesty, who authorized & commanded me so to act, that all his former subjects in North America who shall cease to recognize the supremacy of England may count upon his protection & upon his aid.' [25]

Most seductive to the Canadian heart, Governor Haldimand rightly pronounced this bit of minstrelsy. Hopes, ambitions, pride, vanity, race instincts and darling memories, were all deftly thrilled. Followed, as it was, by 'a multiplicity of Papers of the same Tendency,' the document set a still more dangerous edge upon the defection of the people, and Haldimand could observe 'a very visible alteration amongst all Ranks of Men.' [26]

In a word, then, by the time the expedition against Canada was to be in motion, the province had become a honeycomb. American prisoners could always find ways to escape. Captain Lawe described the whole parish where he was as hoping for rebellion. The spirit of revolt seemed almost ready to burst into flames. The Jesuits were found intriguing against the government; the priests in general showed an 'extraordinary' aloofness; and the Governor believed that a glimpse of white uniforms and a French vessel or two in the St. Lawrence would 'most probably' turn all the *habitants* into rebels. To such a sentiment, the news of Hamilton's disaster at Vincennes (February, 1779) made an admirable primer. [27]

All this while, the Indians of the north had been studying the faces of their Canadian brethren and the signs of the time. Whatever influenced the peasants affected them. The Caughnawagas kept up a correspondence with the Americans. Some at St. Francis did the like.

---

[25] Cont. Cong. Papers, 35, p. 105 (the second half). In order to make the translation clear, the punctuation of the original has been slightly changed.

[26] § Hald. to Budé [?], June 17, 1779: Can. Arch., B, 66, p. 137. Id. to Clinton, May 26, 1779: ib., 147, p. 51.

[27] § Hald. to Rouville, Apr. 19, 1779: Can. Arch., B, 66, p. 117. Lawe to ———, Feb. 7, 1779: ib., 181, p. 157. Hald. to St. Leger, June 5, 1779: ib., 139, p. 12. Id. to Montgolfier, Feb. 15, 1779: ib., 66, p. 102. Id. to Germain, Sept. 19, 1779: ib., 54, p. 178. Intelligence, Sept. 18, 1779: ib., 181, p. 242. Hamilton: Hald. to Clinton, May 26, 1779 (ib., 147, p. 49); to Germain, June 7, 1779 (ib., 54, p. 85).

DÉCLARATION
ADRESSÉE
AU NOM DU ROI
A TOUS LES ANCIENS FRANCOIS
DE L'AMÉRIQUE SEPTENTRIONALE.

LE fouffigné autorifé par Sa Majefte, & reveru par là, du plus beau des Titres; de celui qui efface tous les autres : chargé au nom du Pere de la Patrie & du Protecteur bienfaifant de fes fujets, d'offrir un appui à ceux qui étoient nés pour goûter les douceurs de fon Gouvernement ; à tous fes Compatriotes de l'Amérique Septentrionale.

Vous êtes nés François, vous n'avez pû ceffer de l'être : une Guerre qui ne nous avoit été annoncée que par l'enlévement de prefque tous nos Matelots , & dont nos ennemis communs n'ont dû les principaux fuccès qu'aux courage, au talent, & au nombre des Braves Américains qui les combattent aujourdhui, vous a arraché , ce qui eft le plus cher à tous les hommes , jufqu'au nom de votre patrie; vous forcer à porter malgré vous des mains parricides contre elle , feroit le comble des malheurs, vous en êtes ménacés : une nouvelle Guerre doit vous faire redouter qu'on ne vous oblige à fubir cette loi la plus révoltante de l'efclavage : cette Guerre à commence comme la précédente, par les dépradations de la partie la plus intéreffante de notre commerce. Les prifons de l'Amérique contiennent depuis trop longtems un grand nombre de François infortunés ; vous entendez leurs gemiffemens. Cette Guerre à été déclarée par le meffage du mois de Mars dernier , par l'Acte le plus authentique de la Souveraineté

By October, 1778, the latter tribe become 'very ungovernable.' Not only did many of the savages, reaching the conclusion that King George had the weaker arm, grow lukewarm toward the British, but some even showed signs of joining the other side. And now, at this critical juncture, a trumpet note—sweet and magical yet darkened with an undertone of menace—addressed itself to their ears.[28]

'My Children,'—it was the voice of Lafayette that spoke; 'My Children . . . You remember that when your Fathers [the French] left you, they said that some day they would Return; . . . nor have you forgotten your promise to join Them as soon as they should begin War upon the English. Well, my children, they are going to keep their word, and it is for you to keep yours.' Already France and the States are bound together as brothers. Our struggle with Great Britain has begun, and both French and Americans have brought the English banner low. 'You will soon see us arrive in Canada with General Washington, the Great War Chief of the Americans, and we shall know our friends from our Enemies.' Hard would it be for you to strike your Fathers, and for them to strike you,—they who fought with you in the late war and loaded you with benefits. 'I hope soon to hear that my Words have passed through your ears and rested in your Hearts, and to be able to Report to the King, your Father, that you all wish to be his friends, and that you renounce his Enemies for all time to come.'[29]

Some of the Indian chiefs wore still on their necks the medals of Vaudreuil. Many had guns and knives from the

---

[28] § Cochran to Stark, Oct. 20, 1778: Emmet Coll. Hald. to Germain, Oct. 15, 1778: Can. Arch., B, 54, p. 30. Id. to Id., June 7, 1779: ib., 54, p. 85.

[29] Boston, Dec. 18, 1778 (in French): Sparks MSS., No. 13, p. 36 ; Can. Arch., B, 181, p. 260. The effects of this letter could not be learned before the decision regarding Lafayette's plan was made, but they could be foreseen. The punctuation of the extracts has been slightly altered to make the sense of the translation clear.

arsenals of Louis XV. In reality or in fancy, all had
listened to Montcalm's inspiring voice and eaten at his
generous table. The hearts of those who saw Estaing's
white flag waving in Boston harbor had danced within
them. Every bosom was ready for the message ; and
soon ' the faithful Traversie ' was hurrying with it from
Coös to St. Francis. Ere long the trumpet note penetrated all the forest villages and set every tall pine above
the cabins murmuring ; and Haldimand realized that
another had been added to his catalogue of perils.[30]

And what forces had the Governor, to hold all these
dangers under safe control ?

He himself answered the question. Below Lake
Ontario there were only about sixteen hundred
British regulars fit for duty, and these were so divided
that, even on the ' greatest emergency,' he could not
reckon upon assembling more than a thousand, while
he felt that he ought to have eight times that number,
besides adequate garrisons for all the posts. The
small body of Highland Emigrants, made up of
several nationalities, lacked solidity. Sir John Johnson's
regiment of Tories, though ornamental in their blue-and-
white and handy with the axe, could not be depended
upon with the firelock. And the German troops, numer-
ically the largest corps, were for the most part ' only the
refuse of those who accompanied Genl Burgoyne,' and
all of them 'both by nature and Education totally unfit
for an American War.' Moreover, they had 'imbibed the
Principles of the Inhabitants,' and frequently deserted in
numbers ' even from the most secure Cantonments in the
Province.' As for a naval force, the only vessel to be
near Quebec at the end of May, 1779, was a small old
sloop of little value. In short, reported Haldimand for-

[30] § Doniol, Particip., III., p. 423. Gates to Bedel, Dec. 22, 1778: N. H. State
Papers, XVII., p. 290. Hald. to Maclean, May 26, 1779 : Can. Arch., B, 150, p. 6.

mally, about the time Lafayette submitted his plans to Congress, 'this Province cannot be preserved should the Rebels exert the efforts against it, which it is evidently not less their inclination to attempt, than it is their interest to prosecute.'[31]

Naturally, the Governor did not favor Congress with copies of his reports, but others did what they could to atone for this neglect. It was as easy to bring information out of Canada as to carry it in. Some of the refugees—particularly Hazen's men—did so much in this way that Haldimand proposed to pardon the whole corps, in order to get them home. Indians helped ; and the American scouts were active in all parts of the border. Very important also was the aid of a deserter. According to his account, the total force in Canada, as far west as Niagara, was less than four thousand men ; the garrison of Quebec numbered only four hundred ; that of St. Johns was but three hundred ; and, while two thousand soldiers lay at Sorel, they had no defences. General Bayley believed that two thousand Americans, with the aid of the Canadians, could have 'Burgoyned the Tote of them without much Risque.' From another source, it was learned that no works had been erected at Point Levi or the Island of Orleans. The approaches to Quebec, then, were open ; and, even should notice of an expedition be received in that city, little or nothing could be done to fortify it before the opening of navigation in the spring would allow a French squadron to arrive. The Canadians were described as ' very desirous to see us come in Earnest.' Frye Bayley, held as a prisoner in Canada for months, was told by a British officer that all the people east of the St. Lawrence were hostile to the government ;

<hr />

[31] § Hald. to Clinton, May 26, 1779: Can. Arch., B, 147, p. 51. Id. to Germain, Oct. 15, 1778: ib., 54, p. 30. Uniform: Loyalists to Hald., Dec. 2, 1778: ib., 161, p. 6. Hald. to Hughes, May 29, 1779: ib., 150, p. 10.

and he reached home with his news in October.   At least three-fourths of them were said by one of the spies to be prepared for action.   The horses were kept fat so they could be in readiness for a campaign.   And all this information from the north, with much more, doubtless went regularly on to Congress.[32]

At the same time, that body was eagerly stimulated by Lafayette.   'How happy I would be,' he wrote with contagious enthusiasm ; 'How happy I would be to serve with these cooperating [French] troops, I hope I need not to say.'   In one sentence he appealed to their fears : 'if the bad luck of America makes a peace without joining these Provinces to the United States, I shall ever be fearful for their safety and liberty' ; and in another he excited their hopes: 'Anything Congress will ask [of France] in the name of mutual friendship, & in the view of removing the English, I dare say they will obtain if possible provided the French Court sees that America makes exertions on her side.'   Congress, as it put on record a little later, had the emancipation of Canada and her union with the States 'greatly at heart' still, and the enthusiasm over these broad, large plans rose high. 'Nothing is spoken of but the conquest of Canada,' wrote Kalb ; and, to borrow Lafayette's phraseology, 'all imaginations put on snow-shoes and went skimming across Lake Champlain.'[33]

But some in Congress had a very cooling recollection

<hr />

[32] § Hald. to Germain, Sept. 13, 1779: Can. Arch., B, 54, p. 149.   All parts: J. Wheelock to Wash., Nov. 20, 1778 (Chase, Hanover, I., p. 397).   Bayley to Gates, Jan. 1, 2, 1779 : Cont. Cong. Papers, Letters of Gates, 171, Lib. Cong. Bedel to [Sch.], Jan. 11, 1779 : N. H. State Papers, XVII., p. 311. ——— to Estaing, Dec. 31, 1778: Sparks MSS., No. 22, p. 74.   Bedel to Gates, July 15, 1778: N. H. State Papers, XVII., p. 241.   F. Bayley reported personally to Wash.: see his Narrative ; Bedel to Wash., Nov. 5, 1778 (N. H. State Papers, XVII., p. 281). Id. to Hazen, Nov. 5, 1778 ib., p. 282.   To Congress : Gates to Bedel, Dec. 22, 1778 (ib., p. 290).   REMARK CXII.

[33] § Laf. to Cong., Nov. 29, 1778: Sparks MSS., No. 52, III , p. 172.   Secret Journ Cong., Jan. 1, 1779.   Kalb to Comte [de Broglie], Nov. 7, 1778: Stevens Facsimiles, No. 1987.   Laf. to Estaing, Oct. 1, 1778 (in French): Doniol, Particip., III., p. 417.

Head Qrs Novr 11: 1778 —

Sir

An uneasy afternoon herewith

letter from the Hon ble Mr be wherewith, of

the Committee for foreign affairs enclosing

have and sundry Resolutions of Congress for

attaching Canada/Personal Campaign in

conjunction with the forces of his most

Christian Majesty; and request tonight my order.

FROM WASHINGTON'S LETTER TO CONGRESS (HARRISON'S WRITING)

of a certain Canada expedition planned about a year before, and this time it was decided to consult Washington.[34]

After careful reflection, the Commander-in-chief submitted the 'observations' requested.   It would be impolitic, he pointed out, 'to enter into engagements with
the Court of France for carrying on a combined operation
without a moral certainty of being able to fulfill our
part,' and this, he went on to show, did not exist.   Unless the British army should evacuate the States—which
could not safely be predicted—it would be necessary first
of all to attack it, or at least to protect the neighboring
country against its incursions.   Indeed, no other policy
would satisfy the people.   To provide men at the same
time for such extensive northern operations, would require about double the force which the utmost efforts had
been able, so far, to place in the field ; and this, too,
when both army and nation seemed to be losing interest
in the war, and the pay of the soldiers was constantly
diminishing in value.

The difficulties of transporting and subsisting what
troops could be raised, had proved 'extreme'; how
then, with Continental money sinking in credit every
day, could a greater load be supported?   The cost of
provisions was already 'enormous,' and much had to be
feared from the spirit which had even created an 'artificial scarcity' in order to raise prices.   Besides, the northern expeditions would have to cross wide stretches of
wilderness, 'incapable of affording any aid, and great
part of it hostile,' so that regular magazines, in place of
the local and occasional supplies relied upon in the
States themselves, would need to be provided, and the
expense of gathering and transporting the stores—in case
it should be possible to obtain them—could be 'more easily
conceived than described.'

[34] Secret Journ. Cong., Oct. 22, 1778.

546 Our Struggle for the Fourteenth Colony

To send five thousand men, with an immense train of wagons, to St. Francis, a hundred and fifty miles beyond Coös, through a country in great part uninhabited and trackless, would prove extremely difficult. Probably not more than four thousand effectives would reach their destination,—fewer still, were posts established to guard the road and protect the convoys of supplies ; and, at the St. Lawrence, fresh obstacles would be encountered, for the British, if they could not make head against the attack, would lay waste the country, remove all the boats, and destroy everything required for building water-craft. As for Niagara, it was a very strong fortress indeed ; and the reduction of it would probably, at the very best, prove slow and tedious.

Our allies, for their part, might have no less trouble. The secret of the expedition could not be kept, and the English, ' now greatly superior ' to the French on the sea, could surely intercept the squadron proposed as a convoy, or destroy it in the St. Lawrence. Nor was it certain that Quebec would surrender at once. The authorities in Canada might decide to sacrifice the western posts, ' and collect their strength at the heart.' Nothing more would be essential than to defend Quebec and Montreal ; and this, with the troops already in the province and the reinforcements that might, and probably would, arrive in the spring, could well be done.

But, over and above the lack of a moral certainty on our part and the many objections to the plan in detail, it was a scheme of co-operation, and this co-operation was 'as delicate and precarious an enterprise as could be imagined.' The impediments and delays of a march like that proposed to St. Francis 'almost exceed conception,' and the American troops might be very late in reaching this point ; while a tempest or a British fleet might prevent the French from ever arriving. The plan, in short, was 'not only

too extensive and beyond our abilities, but too complex ';
and to succeed required ' such a fortunate coincidence of
circumstances ' as could not be counted upon.[35]

HENRY LAURENS

All this was true, too true ; and it fell like a Niagara of
ice upon the enthusiasm of Congress. Yet was there not
something singular about it ? Why did the Commander-
in-chief limit himself to destructive criticism ? Why did
he not prune, amend, adjust, reinforce the plan ? Was it
pique ?

No, it was not. Washington felt that the scheme must

[35] Wash. to Cong., Nov. 11, 1778: Wash., Writings (Ford), VII., p. 239.

positively be discarded, and this letter was designed to give sufficient public reasons for shelving it; but he wrote something still more serious to President Laurens.[36]

France had been the mistress of Canada, and could not have forgotten that fact. Only force had shaken off her grip. Her subjects had been loyal; and the very encouragements brought by the spies indicated how eager the people were, as might have been foretold, to see the white banner waving over them again. The policy of the French regarding that province did not stand forth clear and explicit; their minister had thrown cold water upon the plan of Congress; and, above all, Estaing's proclamation said ten words for France while saying one for the States. 'You were born Frenchmen, and such you have not ceased to be,' it ran; you were 'born to enjoy the favors' of His Majesty, 'the beneficent Protector of his subjects.' They were French memories that he evoked, and French honors that he promised; and what he bade the Canadians rely upon, was the support and aid of the French king.[37]

All this Washington had observed, and now he felt it his duty to speak. There exists another objection to the Canadian plan, he informed Laurens, 'which is, in my estimation, insurmountable, and alarms all my feelings for the true and permanent interests of my country. This is the introduction of a large body of French troops into Canada, and putting them in possession of the Capital of that Province, attached to them by all the ties of blood, habits, manners, religion, and former connexion of government.'

To France, Canada would mean a great territory, full

---

[36] Wash. to Laurens, Nov. 14, 1778: Wash., Writings (Ford), VII., p. 260. Note the reply of Laurens: ib., p. 264, note.

[37] § Sparks, G. Morris, I., p. 189. Cont. Cong. Papers, 35, p. 105.

of the supplies needed in her West India islands.   It
would mean a rich trade with the savages ; control of ' the
finest nursery for seamen in the world,' and strategic security for her insular possessions in the Atlantic.   Already the strongest military power in Europe, and, if aided
by her ally, Spain, superior to England on the sea, with
Canada on the north enthusiastically loyal, with the Indians on the west—' a people so generally friendly to her,
and whom she knows so well to conciliate '—active in her
interest, and with New Orleans, by some arrangement
with Spain, co-operating in the south, France might have
the power 'of awing and controlling these States, the natural and most formidable rival of every maritime power
in Europe.'   Such advantages could not be ignored by
that nation ; and moreover, even were she actuated at
present by the purest of motives, events or the wishes of
the people might render it impracticable for her, once in
Canada, to withdraw.

Both letters from Washington were carefully studied
by Congress, and he was invited to confer personally
with a committee.   His military objections halted the
plan of campaign ; and his political objections, though
nothing could be said publicly about them, had no doubt
still greater weight.   Far better, evidently, that Canada
remain a discontented, mutinous British province, than
become a firm strand in a coil round the neck of the
United States, with France pulling at the end of it.
Hard indeed it was to draw the curtain upon the brilliant
hopes that had been entertained.   For weeks, Congress
labored over the situation.   But finally, on the first of
January, 1779, it was voted that the invasion of the north
' should be deferred till circumstances should render the
co-operation of these states more certain, practicable, and
effectual,' with other phrases pointing in the same direction ; and so Lafayette's grand scheme for sweeping the

British from the continent found itself laid, for good and for all, upon the table.[38]

Great was the disappointment. Congress was disappointed, though convinced. The Marquis was disappointed. Hazen, Bayley, Bedel, the refugees, and the scouts were disappointed. But greatest of all, perhaps, was the disappointment in Canada. In October, Gosselin had sent word : The French fleets will go up the St. Lawrence in the spring ; the French generals also are going with their troops ; the great General Washington will drive all the beggars out ; there is nothing to worry over, now. And the glad news, coming no doubt from more than one source, had quickly spread through the province in circles that grew no fainter as they widened. 'There is scarcely a Rebel, or Canadian, or Indian, in, or near the Province but believe' the fleet is coming, said the Governor ; '& I fear most even expect it with Pleasure.' Great quantities of provisions—secreted by peasants, as Whitcomb reported, for the use of the allies—were ready. Notice of a sail in the river set the people all agog. Not much would be required, Haldimand admitted, to 'raise the whole Country in Arms' against England. He even suspected members of the Legislative Council. But spring passed on into summer, summer into autumn ; and no Bourbon pennants fluttered into the Basin at Quebec, no white lines chalked the green Plains of Abraham, no loud ' *Vive le Roi!* ' burst from charging columns.[39]

Yet this did not settle the Canada question, after all. The war did not end then ; and so wide, so deep a feel-

[38] § Journ. Cong., Nov. 19 ; Dec. 17, 24, 1778. Secret Journ. Cong., Dec. 5, 1778 ; Jan. 1, 1779. See Wash. to Cong., Dec. 13, 1778 : Wash. Writings (Ford), VII., p. 285 ; Laurens to Wash., Nov. 20, 1778 : Note 36. REMARK CXIII.

[39] § Gosselin to his wife, Oct. 19,1778 : Can. Arch., B, 184, 2, p. 595. Hald. to Germain, June 18, 1779 : ib., 54, p. 109. Whitcomb : report of loyalists, July 13, 1779 (ib., 181, p. 215). Hald. to Germain, Oct. 24, 1779 : ib., 54, p. 199.

ing, as that in the north, based on substantial causes, could not soon die out. Indeed, the Governor himself was obliged to feed it by repressive acts. And Washington, instead of dismissing all thoughts of Canada, ordered the preparations to move that way continued.[40]

---

[40] § Hald. to Germain, Sept. 13, 1779 : Can. Arch., B, 54, p. 135.   Wash. to Sch., Nov. 20, 1778 : Wash., Writings (Ford), VII., p. 265.   Bayley to Bedel, Nov. 30, 1778: N. H. State Papers, XVII., p. 283.

XXXVIII

THE LINE IS DRAWN

HOW little the men who shape the destinies of the world can shape their own destinies! The leader leads, because, when the people are halted by a door, the little key that he finds in his pocket slides the bolt, while other men's keys do not fit. He passes on, therefore, and the people follow. At the next door, simple-minded fellow that he is, he steps up to offer his key again; but now, perhaps greatly to his astonishment, the bolt refuses to yield. Another man has the right implement this time, and the recent hero—for a moment the supreme, the essential being, worthy a whole pedestal of epithets—becomes as absurd, possibly, as the pathetic starling would be, if it still cried, ' I want to get out, I want to get out ! ' after the gate of its cage had been thrown open. Fortunate indeed is the great man who dies before he becomes an anachronism.

Samuel Adams began to drift into this condition before the Revolutionary War ended. He believed thoroughly in freedom; but liberty found itself sternly limited by the necessity of discipline in the army. He favored a system of conducting public business that should make oppression impossible; but the need of efficiency required some concentration of power. He understood and relied upon the methods of the agitator; but the best means of dissolving old bonds were not the best means of solidifying new ones. He saw the importance of jealously watching

552

those in authority ; but the common-sense of the nation
realized that it must believe in its leaders and trust
them amply. For all these reasons, the influence of
Adams waned ; and his distrust of Washington tended
the same way.[1]

Nor were these his only misfortunes. Very naturally,
he looked upon France with no excess of confidence.
Not only was fear of that power widespread among the
leading Americans, but there was a substantial reason
for it aside from her suspicious glances toward Canada. At the beginning of the American revolt, it had
been seriously proposed in France to have the Comte de
Broglie command the republican armies, become the
Dictator or at least the Stadtholder of the new nation, and
tow it hither and yon in the wake of his own country ;
and the fact that Silas Deane had considered the plan
worth laying before Congress was a further proof that
patriots needed to be awake. Early in 1777, it was whispered in Paris that King Louis might be willing to help
England reduce her Colonies, if England would give up
Canada in return ; and possibly some inkling of this
reached Adams. At all events, he doubtless understood
that policy, not affection, was actuating the cabinet of
Louis XVI., and distrusted it accordingly. Such motives, added to his principle of watchfulness, his dislike
of all foreign influences, and his innate gift of leadership,
made him prominently, though not offensively, anti-
French. But, as matters stood, the alliance with France
and her armed assistance were looked upon with favor
by the American army and people, and therefore Adams's
jealousy of her threw him still farther to one side.[2]

---

[1] § Most of these points have already been brought out. Public business:
Durand, New Materials, p. 240 (Luzerne); Hosmer, S. Adams, pp. 316–337, 343,
346.

[2] § Widespread: See note by Laf. on a copy of a letter of his which he sent
to Sparks (Sparks MSS., No. 85, p. 20). The Broglie affair may be traced at
length in Doniol, Particip., II., Chap, II.; Wharton, Revol. Dipl. Corres., I.,
pp., 392–396; Doniol, La F., p. 15 ; etc. Durand, New Materials, pp. 200, 201, 215,

When peace began to be seriously talked of in the spring of 1779, he found himself again with the minority. He dreaded negotiations in which a foreign state was to have a voice, and though he pretended—said the envoy of France, Gérard—on account of the popular clamor, to favor a settlement with Great Britain, he was regarded as an obstacle. Vergennes, the French minister of foreign affairs, even hinted that he was really ' sold to England.' Finally, he stood squarely for Arthur Lee, the enemy of Franklin and the friend of no wise man. He even did all in his power to have Lee placed in charge of our foreign office; and he brought upon himself, in consequence, a crushing blow, for the French envoy refused flatly to do business with that gentleman.[3]

All this weakened the influence of the eastern States in Congress, and other causes aided. Hancock had become the bitter and unreasonable enemy of Samuel Adams. John Adams had gone abroad. And as New England—in 1775 the national martyr, for whom all hearts bled, whom all hearts burned to aid—hardly felt the weight of a British hand after March, 1776, she naturally fell in the general interest and regard.

The possession of Canada was coveted there in 1779 as keenly, perhaps, as in 1775. The position of the province made it no less dangerous as an enemy, and its ocean treasures made it no less desirable as a partner. ' Is not the Fishery as valuable to America and more so to old [?] Massachusetts,' cried Samuel Adams, ' than the Tobacco Fields of the middle States & the Rice Swamps of the South?' All the representatives from that quarter continued to demand a northern expedition. If our resources

---

241, 249. Stormont to Weymouth, Feb. 5, 1777: Stevens Facsimiles, No. 1428. Policy: Doniol, Particip., I., pp. 2, 4, 8, 568, etc. Favor : e. g., Rochambeau, Mém., I., p. 314.

3 § Wharton, Revol. Dipl. Corres., III., p. 194, etc. Durand, New Materials, pp. 202, 203, 209, 215, 234, 235, 241.

We talked of a Proclamation to the Canadians — If it is not already done, I think it ought not to be delayed — If framed be in your own or a more ——) and have as much as possible an air of probability. Perhaps it will be more politic not to tell them to have too different kinds, & much ——

One is to march into them that the arrival of a french fleet and army to cooperate with them soon is to be expected, and next dwelling on the happy of fraternity ——)

were small, so had they been in 1775. But now, said Gérard, the other States declined to sacrifice their own interests or opinions for the sake of New England; the military plans were arranged without special reference to her wishes; and when—early in 1779—it seemed best, on the score of economy, to make the next campaign purely defensive, Washington called a halt in the preparations for an advance into Canada. This closed the record of one year more.[4]

In 1780, however, the sky brightened. Hazen's regiment had been sent up to Coös the preceding summer, and the road toward the north had been pushed on to a notch in the soapstone ledges quite near the boundary. The main object of this movement was doubtless to alarm Haldimand, and warn him to keep his troops at home; but, whatever the reason for making it, the road existed, and barracks, ovens, and storehouses waited.[5]

In May, 1780, the New Hampshire Committee of Safety urged all residents on the Connecticut River to hold their wheat and flour till these could be purchased for the United States. At the end of that month, Hazen went to Boston; and, a week after, he reported that every one in authority there was disposed to 'under Take' what he and his friends desired. Nine days later, he wrote from New Jersey, 'Northern opperations are now on the Carpit,' 'The Marques is warm & the commander in Cheif is steady to the point'; and, on the fourth of July, he added,

---

[4] § Durand, New Materials, p. 195. S. Adams, Apr. 27, 1779 : S. Adams Papers. Wells, S. Adams, III., p. 66. Marbois to Vergennes, Mar. 13, 1782: Hale, Franklin in France, II., p. 163. Cooper to S. Adams, Mar. 14, 1779 : S. Adams Papers. Wash. to Jay, Apr. 14, 1779: Wash., Writings (Ford), VII., p. 393. Id. to Cong., Jan. 15, 1779: Wash., Writings (Sparks), VI., p. 158. Id. to Sch., Mar. 25, 1779: ib., p. 375. An expedition against the Indians was the only exception.

[5] § Road: Hazen to Charlestown, Apr. 22, 1779 (N. H. State Papers, XVII., p. 331); Id. to Bedel, Aug. 24, 1779 (ib., p. 345); N. H. Hist. Soc. Proc., III., p. 217; Avery to McClure, June 26, 1779 (Wheelock Papers); Collins, Vt., p. 44. Object: Wash. to Sch., Mar. 25, 1779 (Wash., Writings (Ford), VII., p. 379). Bedel to Clinton, Jan. 6, 1779: N. H. State Papers, XVII., p. 310. REMARK CXIV.

everything is Perfectly right in this Quarter to the
utmost of our wishes.' Scouts were to be sent into
Canada at once.[6]

What Washington really designed was, at first, only to
remind Haldimand again of his own vitreous tenement;
and, with that in view, he urged Lafayette in May to get
up a proclamation or two announcing a northern campaign. ' The more mystery in this business the better,'
he suggested; ' It will get out, and it ought to seem to be
against our intention.' But, after a little, he began to
look more hopefully on the idea, and discussed it seriously
with the Marquis; for, by this time, he had probably
observed France long enough to feel safer about her policy.
In June, his principal officers were asked their judgment
as to a plan of campaign, and a strong sentiment in favor
of attempting Canada came out. Wayne opposed the
scheme; Stark thought the season already too late; but
Greene, St. Clair, and Hand recommended it. Lafayette's
hope began to spring again, and the French minister took
the matter in earnest.[7]

' I am fully sensible,' General Bayley argued to Samuel
Adams in August, 'that the present expence of defending
our Frontiers is greater than to take possession, and Keep
the District of Montreal. I am fully of the opinion that
the Enemy have done as much damage to our Frontiers,
as would pay the cost of one Campaign into Canada, with
a force sufficient to take possession of said District.' Almost that same day, ' the principal inhabitants on Connecticut river on both sides,' north of Charlestown, met
in the shadow of Dartmouth College with an officer of the
College for their clerk, and petitioned Congress to secure

---

[6] § N. H. Hist. Soc. Coll., VII., p. 217. Hazen to Bedel, June 6, 1780: N. H.
State Papers, XVII., p 363. Id. to Bedel and to Chase, June 15, 1780: ib., pp.
365, 367. Id. to Bedel, July 4, 1780: ib., p. 368.

[7] § Wash. to Laf., May 19, 1780 : Wash., Writings (Ford), VIII., p. 280.
Officers, June, 1780: Sparks MSS., No. 57, II. Doniol, Particip., IV., p. 370.

the long-coveted Quebec, presenting, in addition to many other arguments, this very point of expense. ' We had almost said,' they urged, ' the enemy destroy and take yearly from the frontiers bordering on Canada as much in value as the cost of reducing and holding that country—we are sure the defence of our frontiers costs more.' Here was an argument that economy itself could feel.[8]

In September, Washington met the Comte de Rochambeau and Admiral de Ternay at Hartford to concert operations, and among his papers—doubtless on the top —lay a plan in Hamilton's clear hand, that gave special attention, among the three projects offered for consideration, to the idea of a northern campaign. But the French leaders declared positively for an attack upon New York, the 'Centre and Focus of all y^e British Forces,' as they termed it; and at once the Canada scheme—although, said Hazen, ' the wish of every one '—vanished from sight once more.[9]

ROCHAMBEAU

In 1781, the French troops and fleet were blockaded for months at Newport, while the Americans had enough to do in the south ; but finally the allies combined their forces happily in Virginia, and the surrender of Cornwallis at Yorktown ended the campaign with glory. In winning this victory, Washington had another opportunity

[8] § Bayley, Aug. 31, 1780: S. Adams Papers. Petition, Aug. 30, 1780: Cont. Cong. Papers, 40, I., p. 559.

[9] § Plan: Sparks MSS., No. 52, III., p. 340. Opinion of Roch. and Ternay, and substance of their agreement with Wash., Sept. 22, 1780: ib., No. 57, II., pp. 168, 171. Rochambeau, Mém., I., p. 250. Hazen to Bedel, Oct. 12, 1780: N. H State Papers, XVII., p. 379.

for studying his allies ; and evidently he became still less suspicious of their designs. Accordingly, about the first of November, he himself proposed to Luzerne, the French minister, a joint invasion of Canada.[10]

The situation there still invited it; and, as the Governor still bore witness that nothing could be kept from the Americans, no doubt they understood the case.[11]

The Bishop stood firm, and did his all to carry out Haldimand's blunt injunction that, in view of the benefits received from the King, the clergy should teach their people fidelity, zeal, and respect for His Majesty. But the Governor still believed that, since France had taken part in the contest, 'many of the Priests' had changed their opinions, and he strongly suspected that clergymen were the principals in a serious combination against the government. American papers were found to have been secreted in a church and circulated by the curé. A priest arrived at Fort Edward with five Indians and as many Tory prisoners, and stated that he was on his way to Congress with despatches. A Récollet was reported as leaving for the south with 'a great Number of Letters,' and a Jesuit who knew of his intention did nothing to thwart it. Father Floquet, another Jesuit, was described as a rebel emissary ; and Haldimand referred to the Order in general as attached to the Americans. As for the nobles, ' I have for many months,' wrote the Governor about the time Washington proposed his plan to Luzerne, ' I have for many months observed in the Canadian Gentry Expectations of a Revolution.' ' I say ready to join us, if they think we can hold the Country ,' was General Bayley's digest of the information, touching both clergy and nobles, that he received from his agents.[12]

---

[10] Doniol, Particip., IV., p. 565.

[11] Hald. to Shelburne, Aug. 17, 1782 : Can. Arch., B, 55, p. 204.

[12] § Hald. to Germain, July 6, 1781 : Can. Arch., B, 55, p. 54. Id. to Briand, Oct. 14, 1779 : ib., 66, p. 161. Briand, circular, Jan. 17, 1781 : ib., 171, p. 48. Hald.

The peasants ' are all in our favour,' added Bayley. Three-fourths, was the estimate that Pillon sent Washington of the number now prepared to act. Calvet, another leader of the seditious, had more than two hundred at his call, ready to join an American advance-guard. Arbitrary, though unavoidable, acts of severity had continued to alarm and anger the people. To ease their consciences, a theory went about that, as twenty-one years had passed since the capitulation, the oath of allegiance was no longer binding ; and the surrender of Cornwallis, added to the success of the French fleet off Chesapeake Bay, could not fail to have a profound influence. As regarded the Indians, finally, Haldimand believed they were ' from Habit as well as the assiduous Persuasion of the Canadians strongly attached to the French,' and that they ' would undoubtedly declare for them upon the appearance of a french Army.' [13]

LUZERNE

The fortifications were now in a tolerable state, though it had been found impossible to build the regular citadel

to Germain, Oct. 25, 1780: ib., 54, p. 339. Combination : Id. to Clinton, Jan. 3, 1781 (ib., 147, p. 287). Flood's depos., Mar. 10, 1780 : ib., 184, 2, p. 523. Sherwood to Powell, Dec. 12. 1779: ib., 182, p. 131. Récollet: Maclean to Hald., Dec. 13, 1779 (ib., 129, p. 80). Jolibois, affidavit, Oct. 26, 1784 : ib., 205, p. 301. Hald. to North, June 19, 1783: ib., 57, 2, p. 535. See also Hald. to Germain, Nov. 23, 1781: ib., 55, p. 130. Nobles: Hald. to Germain, Nov. 23, 1781: Can. Arch., B, 55, p. 130. Bayley to S. Adams, Aug. 31, 1780: S. Adams Papers.

13 § Bayley: Note 12. Pillon, Sept. 7, 1780: Can. Arch., B, 205, p. 70. Du Calvet to his son, Sept. 9, 1780: ib., p. 77. Arbitrary: Hald. to Germain, June, 7, 1779 (ib., 54, p. 85); Id. to Id., July 6, 1781 (ib., 55, p. 54); Mathews to Maclean, Mar. 30, 1780 (ib., 131, p. 44); etc. The Cont. Cong. Papers contain interesting documents relating to Du Calvet, Cazeau, and others of that class. Theory : Maj. Carleton to Hald., July 9, 1780 (Can. Arch., B, 133, p. 204). Hald. to Germain. Nov. 18, 1781: ib., 55, p. 122.

planned for Quebec. Troops, however, the real defence, were lacking. The best in Canada had been stationed at the western posts, and those within Haldimand's reach were still mostly Germans,—in the main, invalids rejected by General Burgoyne or 'Recruits Totally Ignorant of Military Discipline.' To meet an invader, not more than 2,500 men 'Capable of Keeping the Field two Months' could be assembled,—'many of them' ready to join the Americans at their first opportunity. On the other hand, six thousand excellent French troops had actually landed on American soil, so that co-operation was no longer a precarious undertaking, and, as Spain had allied her red and yellow to the red, white, and blue, Britannia no longer ruled the waves.[14]

The time for sweeping England from the Continent seemed to have arrived, then; the besom was ready; and Washington himself proposed the enterprise. What could possibly occur now to prevent the long-hoped-for consummation? Would Congress object? By no means; but— the French minister said, No. The King had taken up arms to help America win her independence, not make conquests, he explained; and there was enough work still to do in the southern States.[15]

What did this mean? Two years before, the minister had informed Washington that His Christian Majesty felt a sincere and disinterested wish to see Canada form a part of the confederacy, but would make no move in that direction until the plan had been approved by the leader of his allies.[16] Now, that leader himself proposed the plan, and his proposition was rejected. Was this a

---

14 § Rey to S. Adams, 1780 [?]: S. Adams Papers. Hald. to Germain, Oct. 15, 1778 : Can. Arch., B, 54, p. 30. Id. to Townshend, Oct. 22, 1781: ib., 55, p. 73. Id. to Id., Oct. 25, 1780: ib., 55, p. 9. Troops : Hald. to Germain, Nov. 23, 1781 (ib., 55, p. 130).

15 § Doniol, Particip., IV., p. 565. Durand, New Materials, p. 195.

16 Conference, Sept. 16, 1779: Wharton, Revol. Dipl. Corres., III., p. 319.

temporary whim of the minister? Was it the settled policy of his government? What could it signify?

It signified, for one thing, that probably Washington had given himself unnecessary trouble in vetoing the great scheme of October, 1778 ; for, had he not intervened, France would almost certainly have done as much.

The Duc de Choiseul, recently the prime minister of Louis, had been so eager to strike England through the revolt of her North American subjects, that he had thought it worth while to sacrifice the national hope of regaining Canada, and Bonvouloir was instructed to assure the Americans unofficially, in 1775, that France had no design of re-establishing herself on the continent ; yet the hope still existed beside or below the pledge. At the same time it was felt that, should England retain Canada, the United States would have a lasting need of French support. Lafayette urged France to liberate her oppressed sons in America by helping them join the Union, and win as her reward the fur business, the Indian trade, and the gratitude of the people ; but Spain, on the other hand, suggested that she recover the province, and insisted, as a condition—more or less explicit—of taking part in the war, that it should not be given to the United States. Moreover, the obvious difficulty and expense of driving England from the St. Lawrence counted with the French cabinet.[17]

A subtle, obscure policy was the natural consequence. The upshot of it was that France determined to make no direct move towards regaining Canada, to let the Americans win it if they could, to give them pleasant words but no real help to that end, and meanwhile—in view of the possibilities—to keep a firm hold upon the affection

---

[17] § Doniol, Particip., I., pp. 129, 241 ; IV., p. 43 ; III., pp. 156, 292. Laf. to Vergennes, July 18, 1779: Sparks MSS., No. 85, p. 20, and a note written in the margin by Laf.

and confidence of the Canadians. Hence the orders to
Estaing to aid the Americans against Canada by nothing
more than a cruise or an attack upon the outposts, and,
should anything seem likely to be accomplished there, to
assure Canadians and Indians of the King's protection.
Hence the instructions to Gérard, the first French envoy,
to express in general terms, provided it should be neces-
ray to say something, the King's desire to do whatever

H S. CONWAY

would benefit America, but avoid—if possible—commit-
ting himself in regard to Canada. Hence Luzerne's cordial
but guarded assurances to Washington in 1779; and
hence, finally, his refusal to co-operate in 1781.[18]

Yet even now the American leader did not give up the

[18] § Doniol, Particip., III., pp. 191, 192 ; V., p. 164, note ; III., pp. 156, 157; IV.,
p. 43. Note Garnier's advice (to Vergennes, Aug. 16, 1776: Stevens Facsimiles,
No. 891; Gérard's reflections, 1775 (ib., No. 1310); and Kalb's remarks to
Broglie (ib., No. 1987).

idea. May the first, 1782, he drew up a survey of the field, and dwelt upon the advantages of securing Canada. Lafayette, also, had the north still in mind. But peace was at last in sight. On Washington's birthday, General H. S. Conway, a good friend of America, had moved in Parliament that war cease between Great Britain and her former Colonies. One vote, one only, had defeated the motion ; and, on the fourth of March, the day we inaugurate our Presidents, it was voted that all were to be considered enemies to His Majesty and the country, who should undertake to continue the hostilities. The news of this action was very welcome in America. The nation desired rest ; and it was clearly impolitic to cloud the prospect by an annoying activity. As the months passed, this view of the situation grew stronger and stronger, and the last chance of reaching Quebec now was evidently by the winding road of diplomacy.[19]

Here, if nowhere else, all the recent efforts in the north bore fruit ; for they had kept the British government in constant anxiety about Canada, hampered its operations in other quarters, and aided in preparing it for concessions. In December, 1777, Lord Shelburne informed the House of Lords that Carleton was in the greatest distress, fearing every moment to lose the province. In October, 1778, Haldimand assured the government that Congress declared no peace could be made until Canada had been secured, and that, unless heavy reinforcements were sent, they would carry out their design. In 1779, in 1780, in '81, and in '82, it continued to be essentially the same story : sedition, conspiracy, the ' rebels ' coming, troops needed, works needed, provisions needed, ships needed, money needed.[20]

---

[19] § Wash., Writings (Ford), IX., p. 490. Laf., Mémoire : Stevens Facsimiles, No. 1642. See Journ. Cong., Feb. 20. 1783. Winsor, Narr. and Crit. Hist., VII., p. 95.

[20] § Noailles to Vergennes, Dec. 12, 1777 : Stevens Facsimiles, No. 1772.

Clinton felt a constant anxiety about the province, and inevitably transmitted a share of his worry to London. In November, 1779, he wrote : 'you must look to Canada next year ' ; in May, 1780 : ' I think that [French] armament is intended against Canada ' ; in the following August : ' I shall tremble for Canada next year ' ; and in February, 1782, he felt satisfied that now the crisis was at last impending. He was put under orders, early in 1778, to send whatever troops Haldimand should require of him, and this compelled him to plan operations without knowing how long his arm was to be. A year and a half later, a call from the north found him distressed for men, yet he despatched four regiments. A storm scattered the transports ; about four hundred Hessians fell into American hands; and there were probably other losses.[21]

From the very first, in the negotiations for peace, Franklin proposed the cession of Canada. Great Britain, he charmingly suggested, ought to offer the province willingly, in order to obliterate a frontier that might be troublesome and make easier an adjustment of sundry other matters. Personally, he was good enough to give it as his advice that England yield the point, in order to cement the two countries more firmly together ; and he went so far as to say that no pleasant or peaceable relations could be expected unless this were done. What he had not succeeded in accomplishing at Montreal, he in-

---

Hald. to Germain, Oct. 15, 1778: Can. Arch., B, 54, p. 30. It seems unnecessary to set down references to the many documents which are before the author, after what has been already stated in the text.

[21] § Clinton to [Eden], Nov. 10, 1779 : Stevens Facsimiles, No. 1032. Id. to Id., May 12, 1780 : ib., No. 726. Id. to [Id.], Aug. 14, 1780 : ib., No. 1043. Id. to Hald., Feb. 22, 1782 : Can. Arch., B, 148, p. 8. Eden, minute, July 29, 1778 : Stevens Facsimiles, No. 508 ; Germain to Clinton, Mar. 8, 1778: ib., No. 1062. Clinton to Hald., Sept. 9, 1779: Can. Arch., B, 147, p. 85 ; Wash. to Laf., Oct. 20, 1779: Wash., Writings (Sparks), VI., p. 382 ; Maclean to Hald., Dec. 3, 1779: Can. Arch., B, 149, p. 108. In March, 1780, Haldimand still had authority to call on Clinton for aid: Germain to Hald., Mar. 17 (Can. Arch., B, 43, p. 20).

tended to bring about at Paris ; and John Adams, another of our Commissioners, took a similar stand.[22]

But Great Britain, though probably willing—while she held the other Colonies—to let France have Canada, did not wish now to part with it. In the scheme of October, 1778, Congress itself had mentioned two reasons : first, by holding Quebec and Nova Scotia, she could easily attack the United States and the French possessions ; and, secondly, she needed these provinces to supply her West India islands with bread and lumber, and to furnish her army and navy with hospitals and dockyards. The Canadian trade was precious, and the seamen of the fisheries were almost invaluable. For Great Britain, said Washington, the loss of Canada ' would be a deadly blow to her trade and empire.'[23]

At Whitehall, this was understood quite as well. In April, 1778, when there was talk of a peace, Lord North exclaimed, ' If we have recovered & preserved that province by arms, we must take care not to lose it by Treaty.' When Hartley, his agent, was asked in Paris the same month whether he had powers to treat, he replied that he would certainly have them very soon, ' if it were possible to open negotiations on conditions admissible by England'; and he intimated that Great Britain would recognize the independence of the United States, provided Canada and Nova Scotia were solemnly conceded to her. To Germain, the holding of Canada seemed essential. Though he sometimes found it impossible, or judged it unnecessary, to supply Haldimand with everything desired, he was willing that, should the case prove critical, Clinton should strip himself of troops to reinforce the Governor.

---

[22] § Doniol, Particip., V., pp. 99, 134, 163, note. Wharton, Revol. Dipl. Corres., V., pp. 476, 540, 541, 542, 544, 545. Hale, Franklin in France, II., p. 115, etc.

[23] § Instructions to Franklin, Cont. Cong. Papers, Reports of Committees, 25, I., p. 35. Wash. to Cong., Nov. 11, 1778: Wash., Writings (Ford), VII., p. 239.

GEORGE WASHINGTON

And Shelburne, on coming into power, said the preservation of Canada was so important that His Majesty himself had ordered the new British Commander-in-chief—
General Sir Guy Carleton—to leave New York and go
there personally, should he deem it necessary, taking
with him as many of the troops as he should think
required.[24]

For the United States, on the other hand—fighting for
its very existence as a nation, and struggling not only
against enemies but against allies—Canada was highly
desirable yet not essential, and it seemed by no means
wise to risk the vital for the valuable. In 1779, Congress had declared that while it was ' of the utmost importance to the peace and commerce of the United States
that Canada and Nova Scotia be ceded ', yet ' a desire
of terminating the war' prevented it from making the
cession of them a *sine qua non* of peace ; and the same
reasoning held good in 1782.[25]

For a time, indeed, it looked as if the hope of the American diplomats to obtain the northern province would
be realized. Oswald, the British agent, spoke that way.
Yet he spoke with a singular reserve ; and, when the formal project of a treaty was submitted by the Americans
in October, 1782, no allusion to the matter was made.
Apparently, the subject had simply evaporated, as if
struck by some thirsty breeze from the desert. In fact,
nobody seemed even to note its disappearance, and neither
Franklin, Jay, nor Adams ever cared to explain the mys-

---

[24] § North to Eden, Apr. 23, 1778: Stevens Facsimiles, No. 447. Francés to
[Vergennes], Apr. 26, 1778: ib., No. 1919. Doniol, Particip., III., p. 281. Reasons
for not sending reinf.: Germain to Hald., Aug. 3, 1779 (Can. Arch., B, 43, p. 169);
Mar. 2, 1780 (ib., 44, p. 3); Apr. 12, 1781 (ib., 50, p. 83); May 4, 1781 (ib., 44, p. 86);
Admiralty to Hald., Aug. 7, 1779 (ib., 49, p. 86) ; etc.   Germain to Clinton,
Nov. 4, 1779: Sparks MSS., No. 58, p. 18.   Shelburne to Hald., Apr. 22, 1782 : Can.
Arch., B, 50, p. 164.

[25] § Wharton, Revol. Dipl. Corres., III., p. 295.   R. R. Liv. to Franklin
(giving the views of Congress), Jan. 7, 1782: Sparks, Dipl. Corres., III., p. 268.
See ib., IV., p. 339 ; X., p. 75.

tery. Very likely, indeed, they felt that any one who desired could solve the apparent riddle for himself. The plain truth doubtless was that it seemed impossible to carry the project through or unwise to make the attempt. Though Oswald had permitted Franklin to convince him that England might well cede the province, and Lord Shelburne had probably thought it unnecessary to throw cold water upon the incipient negotiations by fully stating his views to Oswald, the British government had at the proper time emphatically rejected the idea ; and our Commissioners understood now that France also opposed it. They felt, therefore, as Congress had anticipated, that it would be sounder policy to battle for other points ; and so it came to pass that, when the treaty of peace was agreed upon, it drew an invisible yet adamantine line between the United States and Canada. The long struggle for that rich and beautiful province, the fourteenth Colony, the fourteenth State that might have been, was at last over.[26]

Eight Years of Failure the whole series of plans and measures to win it might be called. Yet they were by no means altogether a failure. In the first place, their indirect benefits, already pointed out,[27] were neither few nor slight. In the second, two great facts of enduring significance were graven deep upon the Laurentian cliffs : that our fathers, the builders of this republic, believed that Canada should form a part of it ; and that only force, aided by remarkable circumstances, prevented this consummation. In the third, while the centre of the American advance was checked, each wing secured a victory : on the east, the use, if not the ownership, of the fisheries

[26] § Doniol, Particip., V., pp. 162, 163, and note. Wharton, Revol. Dipl. Corres., V., pp. 548, 549. Hale, Frankin in France, II., p. 115. Winsor, Narr. and Crit. Hist., VII., pp. 101, 104, 109. Lewis, Admin., pp. 47, 48. J. Adams, Works, I., p. 360.

[27] See pp. 451–458 of this volume.

was gained ; and, on the west, the portion of Canada—
as defined by the Quebec Act—that fell into our possession
has to-day three times the population of all that England
retained.

Even where the failure was greatest, we are not utterly
without comfort. The fathers did not succeed in ensuring
peace on the northern frontier by bringing our neighbor
within the Union, yet their hopes and plans do not hover
like unshriven ghosts about the rocky pinnacle of Quebec;
for the days of Frontenac, those dreaded days, have never
returned. Upon the grave of the American martyr by
the St. Lawrence the flag of his country sheds no con-
soling benediction, yet he sleeps in peace ; for above his
resting-place floats in amity—so may it ever float !—the
starry banner of the deep Canadian sky.

REMARKS

XLII. (see page 10)

According to Lindsay (Can. Rev., No. 5, Sept., 1826, p. 89) Indians brought word 'on the 1st of November' that Arnold was rapidly approaching. But, as this account (though from a man present in Quebec at the time of the siege, and based, to a greater or less extent, on documents) was apparently written long after the events, the author has concluded that the date was a mistake or was intended in a general sense for 'very early in November.' Ainslie gives Nov. 3 as the date, and this seems more probable.

XLIII. (see page 21)

Ainslie says that Maclean brought 'a party' of Emigrants and a few Fusiliers; Finlay that he brought 200 Emigrants and Fusiliers; Ogden (Nov. 14) that the Americans heard he came with 200 Emigrants and 'about 80 of the Eighth' [doubtless a slip for Seventh]. The official report for Nov. 16 included no Fusiliers and only 200 Emigrants, so that—since a part of the men from Newfoundland and St. John's Island had no doubt enlisted as Emigrants—Maclean must have brought less than 200. He seems in fact to have come with about 120. (See Vol. I., p. 451.) Hamilton (Can. Arch., Q, 11, p. 339) said 'about 100 of his men.' Caldwell (Letter) wrote the same.

Some other small difficulties present themselves: e.g., a Quebec Letter of Nov. 7 (4 Force, III., 1396) says that no regulars were there, Lindsay (Can. Rev., No. 5, Sept., 1826, p. 89) concurs, and Caldwell (Letter) says the same in effect ('not a soldier'); but the official return of Nov. 6 mentioned 6 artillerymen. Whence came they? However, these difficulties are of slight importance.

XLIV. (see page 26)

Thayer states in his Journal that shortly before the river was crossed a council decided, against a strong minority, not to assault the town immediately after landing. Ogden, however, says this matter was left to the Colonel's pleasure, and that, as he believed it ought to be done, the scaling ladders and pikes were taken to the place of embarking, with a view to carrying them across that night. Whatever the fact about the council, the question seems to have come up after the crossing. For Arnold's attitude after the crossing, see Marshall (i.e. Heath), Life of Washington, II., p. 294; for Morgan's, see Graham, Morgan, p. 85. Marshall (*loc. cit.*) says Arnold did not urge an assault strongly.

Who ordered the firing on the barge? Thayer wrote (Journal) that the barge ' was hail'd by col arnold myself and 4 more But on her not coming too we fir'd at her.' As Arnold was in the party he must almost certainly have given the order. In his letter of Nov. 14 to Montgomery he wrote ' we fired into her.' Arnold's letter to Montgomery, Nov. 14, represents the affair of the barge as what prevented him from surprising the town. Fobes, writing long after, said that ' if Arnold and the soldiers had kept still the boat and crew might have been taken without alarming the city ' ; but that is more than he could prove. That the report of the affair did not reach the Lt.-Gov. till the next day is stated in Account, 4 Force, III., 1723; see also Marshall, Washington, II., p. 295.

What is the proof that a gate was open? It was so stated to the Americans shortly afterward by Quebec people (Henry Journal, p. 83 ; Marshall, Washington, II., p. 295). Fobes said : ' St. John's gate was open. We stopped a man that had just come out of it and could have entered, with nothing to hinder.' (Apparently this must have been after the Americans had marched to Caldwell's, for when he marched up the bluff Arnold supposed that Maclean had been aroused.) And it was reported in Quebec that on the next day the keys of St. John's gate could not be found, ' and the fastening in such a situation that they were obliged to procure handspikes and ropes ' (4 Force, III., 1723). This last account states that it was necessary to send to the *Lizard* for matches for the cannon, Nov. 14; also, that the gate was in the keeping of the French militia. Jan. 8, 1776, an American soldier wrote from Montreal that two French gentlemen, just arrived there, said that ' Arnold might have march'd into Quebec, when he first arrived ' (in Tryon's No. 30, Feb. 8, 1776: Pub. Rec. Off., Am. and W. I., Vol. 186, p. 309).

From the return of Nov. 16 one can see that the garrison consisted at this time of 243 men besides the militia, for the sailors had not yet been organized ; but Arnold wrote Washington, Nov. 20, that by the night of the 13th, the garrison had been ' augmented to near seven hundred men, besides the inhabitants ' (Me. Hist. Soc. Coll., I., p. 379). To enter an open gate (where there might be an ambush) and attack an alert enemy (such as Arnold then supposed Maclean to be) who had (as Arnold believed) superior numbers as well as all the advantages of position, besides more or less help from the militia, could not seem prudent. Now that (as Arnold concluded) a surprise was impossible, the only chances lay in producing a revolt within the town, or drawing the garrison out.

Could Arnold have pursued a different course and succeeded ? The author holds that—as the text intimates—he might have done so. But this inquiry has often been confounded with a distinct one : Ought Arnold, in view of the evidence, to have adopted a different course, and was he to be blamed for not succeeding? To these questions the author would reply in the negative.

Gordon, on the other hand (Hist. U. S., I., p. 430), says that Arnold should have taken the scaling ladders across, concealed himself, and tried a coup-de-main the next night ; and this is perhaps as reasonable a criticism as could be suggested. But (1) it was important first to get men across, since a small party left on the north shore might have been discovered and destroyed ; it was therefore wise to leave the ladders for the last trip ; and circumstances prevented that trip. (2) The chance that 500 men could remain close to Quebec undiscovered for twenty-four hours, especially when a considerable number of people were on the lookout for them, seems very small. (3) As a matter of fact, Arnold's presence was discovered by the guard boat. As for the wisdom of hailing and firing upon that boat, it depended on delicate circumstances which no one can be sure about now, and we cannot decide that Arnold acted wrongly.

XLV. (see page 27)

Several of the American Journals become wholly or partially silent after Nov. 14 ; but Meigs, Dearborn, Humphrey, Thayer, Topham, Senter, Haskell, Henry, and Melvin continue about as before. Of the Canadian Journals the fullest and perhaps the best is that of Thomas Ainslie, Collector of Customs, which may be found in the Sparks MSS., No. 1. (For convenient evidence that he was the Collector : letter, Dec. 16, 1775, 4 Force, IV., 290.) The 'Chalmers' Journal (Sparks MSS., No. 142) was kept by an important officer of the garrison. This name (in default of any other) is given it because George Chalmers found and bought it. Finlay's Journal (Quebec Lit. and Hist. Soc., 4th ser.), there is good reason to believe (as Malcolm Fraser endorsed upon the MS.), was kept by a prominent official named Hugh Finlay. The 'Shortt' Journal (edited by W. T. P. Shortt, London, 1824) is represented as 'collected from some old MSS. originally written by an officer,' and is, of course, less authoritative. A 'Journal of the Most Remarkable Occurrences in Quebec' was published in the N. Y. Hist. Soc. Coll., 1880 ; it presents itself as ' By an Officer of the Garrison.' The same Journal is quoted by Smith, Canada, II., beginning with p. 81. In 1905, a very similar Journal bearing substantially the same title was published at Quebec (Würtele, ed.). Both of these were perhaps based upon Ainslie's. It is not considered necessary to give references to the Journals for minor details.

XLVI. (see page 31)

Was it Arnold's purpose, when he retired from Quebec, to join Montgomery ? Such was the plan announced in his letter to Montgomery of Nov. 8, 1775 (4 Force, III., 1634). The letter in Henry's Journal (p. 185) says that Arnold found it absolutely necessary to halt until he could provide the men with footgear ; and that implies an intention to go farther. But Arnold's letters of Nov. 20 to

Montgomery and to Washington, and that of Nov. 27 all say it was judged prudent to 'retire to this place.' One cannot be sure therefore, as to his purpose. Perhaps he himself did not feel certain what he should do, but did not care to admit either indecision or disappointment.

XLVII. (see page 35)

The author searched Pointe aux Trembles and the district around it for traces of the Americans, and found, besides vague traditions of their friendly behavior there, this song:

> ' Yankee doddle [*sic*]
> Tiens toi bien!
> J'entends la musique!
> Ce sont les Americains
> Qui viennent prendre le fort Pique.' *

XLVIII. (see page 41)

The habits of Lake Champlain signify so much in this campaign that the author took pains to inform himself by careful inquiry of people concerned in navigating it. He was informed that the northern part is not usually covered with solid ice before about the middle of February. The Committee of Congress wrote that the lake might 'take' about the beginning of that month (4 Force, IV., 442), which marks that as the earliest possible time. Much depends, of course, upon the severity of the winter. The southern end of the lake as far down as Crown Point closes during the first half of December, as a rule. See [Bedel] to Schuyler, Dec. 19, 1775: Sparks MSS., No. 60, p. 39; Schuyler to Hancock, Nov. 22, 1775: 4 Force, III., 1633.

XLIX. (see page 53)

In this and the following paragraphs, the author has made no attempt to be exhaustive, for in this work the subject is of course only incidental; but it is hoped that enough illustrative cases are cited to justify his position. See REMARK CXV.

L. (see page 73)

Three weeks and more appear to have been wasted by Congress at this juncture, for the orders to raise or assign troops might and should have been issued at Philadelphia not later than Nov. 1. Even in the summer, although (as stated above) Congress kept 'abreast' of the events, it was unfortunate that more was not done and in particular that Schuyler was not aided and urged to carry out the order of June 27 promptly.

---

* The grounds by the site of the present Parliament building at Quebec.

LI. (see page 86)

Attention has been called to the story that Arnold sent Burr in disguise from Lake Megantic to Montgomery. According to Parton (Burr, I., p. 71) this was done when Arnold neared Quebec. But the reply is as before: Arnold's letter introducing Burr to Montgomery was dated Nov. 30, more than two weeks after he reached Quebec. Montgomery was at that time nearly down to Arnold, on his way to attack Quebec, so that Parton's tale of Burr's lying concealed at Three Rivers on his way to find Montgomery at Montreal is incredible. Besides, under date of Nov. 19 (4 Force, III., 1682) Montgomery wrote to Schuyler that his expresses passed freely between the two cities, so that there was no occasion for either disguise or concealment.

LII. (see page 87)

Strangely enough, it is not certain on what day Montgomery landed. Humphrey's careful Journal has been followed in the text, and most of the accounts which apparently disagree with that can in a measure be reconciled with it. As Montgomery was known to be close at hand on the 1st, he could be said to have arrived on that date; and, as he could not begin work until the 3d, that day could be given. Wooster wrote Schuyler on December 4 that he had a letter of the second instant from Montgomery who was then at Pointe aux Trembles (Schuyler Papers). Fortunately, nothing depends upon certainty about this point. See the various Journals and Arnold's Orderly Book, Dec. 2, which seems to confirm the date in the text.

J. Livingston (Jan. 25, 1819: Bancroft Coll.) said that the cannon had to be landed because the boats conveying them were frozen in at Lake St. Peter; but this, written long after, seems doubtful.

LIII. (see page 98)

LeMoine (Quebec Past and Present, p. 201) names the Commander of the Canadians Col. Lecompte Dupré; but Caldwell wrote, 'old Voyer, their Colonel'; and this is confirmed by Sanguinet (Verreau, Invasion, p. 37).

It needs to be remembered, in reading accounts of these events, that British officers were often given a higher title in Canada than their rank in the regular service. E.g., Carleton speaks of Captain Hamilton as 'Colonel.'

LIV. (see page 99)

According to Ritzema (Journal), Montgomery took from Montreal, Nov. 28, a part of Lamb's Co., Cheeseman's and Weisenfel's Cos. of Ritzema's Regt., one Co. of the 2d regt., two Cos. of the 3d regt.; and, on Dec. 1, Zedtwitz set out for Quebec with the

Cos. of Mott, Varick, and Quackenbos. A letter of Dec. 17 from Montreal (Conn. Gazette, Jan. 26, 1776) states that Weisenfels, Cheeseman, Mott, Varick, and Quackenbos were before Quebec, Willet at St. Johns, Goforth and Lyon at Montreal.

The name St. Roch seems to have been written quite commonly St. Roques or St. Roc in 1775.

LV. (see page 104)

Force (4, IV., 289) prints, as the letter of Dec. 16, what the author has described as that of Dec. 6. There seems no lack of evidence (Note 26) that the letter was written on the latter date, and it fits that case. Was the same letter sent on the 16th? (1) It does not contain an offer of a safe-conduct, which Montgomery said he made (see also letter, Dec. 16, 4 Force, IV., 290). (2) The object on the 16th (as Montgomery wrote R. R. Livingston: Note 31) was 'to prevail on Mr. Carleton' to give him peaceable possession, and the menacing tone of the former letter was not well adapted to that end.

LVI. (see page 117)

Parton (Burr, I., p. 72) says that, after two weeks of work, Burr completed on Dec. 20 the drilling of a forlorn hope, which was to storm Quebec under his command. The preparations began, then, Dec. 6. But this seems inconsistent with Montgomery's cautious way of approaching the matter with the soldiers and masking his design from Carleton. Besides (even though the plan of attack was changed) it is hard to understand why, if Burr picked and prepared a forlorn hope, his corps did not figure at all and he himself did not appear prominently in the assault. A reliable forlorn hope was precisely what Montgomery needed and did not have. Parton's account contains so many errors that it cannot be considered authoritative in the least.

LVII. (see page 124)

The opinion has often been expressed that Montgomery intended to force the passage to the Upper Town (e. g., Smyth, Précis, p. 115; Cullum, Sketch, p. 14), and censure has been meted out accordingly; but there seems to be no evidence for this view, while plenty of evidence for the view of the text is given in the footnotes. Further: Ainslie (Journal, Jan. 1) says, 'It was reported before daylight that the Lower town was in Mr. Montgomeries possession; this acceptable piece of news, brought all the blackguards of the adjacent Parishes to St. Roc to wait the surrender of the upper town.' I. e. it was commonly understood on the American side that the Upper Town would yield were the Lower Town captured.

That Montgomery had carefully studied Wolfe's campaign is

proved, e. g., by his letter to R. R. Livingston : 4 Force, III., 1638.

One is surprised to hear nothing of Major Brown in the accounts of the assault (REMARK LX). One is also surprised by Ritzema's statement that Montgomery had 466 men (Journal, Jan. 2, 1776), whereas the accounts represent him as followed by the New Yorkers only. Smith (Pittsfield, I., p. 258) says that Montgomery had, besides the New Yorkers, a part of Easton's regiment (with which Major Brown would have gone, since he was the commander of it), and that the force led by Jacob Brown (Remark LX.) was a newly formed corps, composed of men just about to be disbanded. This would seem to solve the riddle ; but (1) the accounts give it no support, (2) it is hard to understand why a new corps should be formed of men not yet free, and (3), if the men of Easton's regiment followed Montgomery, as Smith states, it is not easy to see whence such a new corps could have come. To be sure, it might be surmised that some of Arnold's troops went into it ; but the disaffection in his detachment seems to have been confined to the captains, and, as Senter (Journal, Dec. 30) intimates, the soldiers would naturally wish to fight in company with their tried comrades of the wilderness march. The author has, therefore, followed the accounts and left the riddle unexplained.

LVIII. (see page 127)

This is based upon the letter, of which the owner, Hon. John D. Crimmins of New York, kindly gave the author a copy. The letter was written after midnight, for the date is Dec. 31. As the attack, ordered the evening before (see, e. g., Macpherson's letter, dated Dec. 30, Note 20) was conditional only upon the weather, it must be inferred that the storm gave signs of ceasing. Evidently the letter was not sent, for a white flag could not have been seen in the darkness and storm. It must have been written to be sent after daybreak. It seems to have been intended as a *ruse de guerre.*

LIX. (see page 128)

The author's study of the assault would make a volume, and would be published as such did there seem likely to be a general call for so extended a treatment of the subject. Selecting about fifty of the most valuable sources, he gave each a number and then resolved each into separate statements. These were grouped, and after each was placed the number or numbers of the source or sources in which it occurred. The following extract from this compilation will show what is meant (the reference is to Arnold's attack).

The front got lost in the storm: 9
The main body missed their way: 1.
The path made by Arnold, Morgan, and Lamb was almost imperceptible because of the falling snow : 3.
The main body were led astray: 4, 6.

Thayer undertook to guide them : 9.
The piece of artillery had to be abandoned : 6, 14, 27.
On account of the snow the field-piece had to be abandoned : 1, 4, 19.
Another reason was the difficulty of the way : 1, 4, 15, 19, 25.
The streets were narrow and crooked : 6.

By carefully studying this digest, bearing in mind the relative value of each source, and adding the valuable points of the other sources, the author felt that a fairly complete and trustworthy narrative could be produced, though in not a few cases the evidence is conflicting. Necessarily, many details come from single witnesses, and the fight was observed under circumstances not favorable to precision ; but nothing hangs upon the strict accuracy of these details (except in certain cases specially studied below), and the picture is really truer to the reality with some fairly supported yet not scientifically proven details in it than it would be without them.

LX. (see page 130)

For the Canadians, see Montgomery to Wooster, Dec. 16, 1775 ; Sparks MSS., No. 52, II., p. 60 ; Schuyler to Hancock, Jan. 13, 1776 ; 4 Force, IV., 666 ; Henry, Journal, p. 104 ; Senter, Journal, Dec. 31. J. Livingston (Jan. 25, 1819 : Bancroft Coll., separate) said that a shifting of the wind, favorable to the city, prevented his attempt to burn St. John's Gate from being completely successful. Brown's men are said to have numbered 94 (Ritzema, Journal, Jan. 2), and were led by Captain Jacob Brown, Major John's brother, possibly in consequence of the latter's having become compromised in the cabal against Arnold. See Campbell, Mar. 28, 1776 : Livingston Papers, 1775-1777, p. 145 ; Smith, Pittsfield, I., p. 258.

LXI. (see page 130)

Ritzema (Journal, Jan. 2, 1776) says that Arnold had 560 men, to whom, we may add, as an estimate, 40 Canadians and Indians. Carleton's official report gave 431 as the number of the prisoners, including the wounded (Can. Arch., Q, 12, p. 37). The killed (including those who died in the snow of wounds) may perhaps be estimated at 100, and those who skulked or escaped at 50. We thus have 581 as his force at the beginning, plus the Canadians and Indians. We may get at the figures in another way. Arnold stated (to Washington, Jan. 14, 1776 : 4 Force, IV., 674) that all of his detachment except about 200 'sick and on command' were captured, i. e. (as he says nothing of the wounded) this number went into the fight. If we add 60 men of Lamb's and 40 Canadians and Indians we get 575. If 'about 200' meant 175, we then have 600 as the total. Arnold had all but 7 or 8 of Lamb's Co. (Campbell to ——, Mar. 28, 1775 : Livingston Papers, 1775-1777, p. 145).

LXII. (see page 141)

Caldwell (Letter) complained that ' had the officer of the Canadian

Militia, who commanded there [at the Cape Diamond blockhouse], done his duty, great havoc might have been made among the enemy'; but Engineer Marr (Report, July 1, 1778 : Can. Arch., B, 154, p. 6) said that the blockhouse was 'too high to fire upon people passing below unless when the snow falls so deep as to make an inclined plane to the water's edge,' and perhaps this state of things had not been reached when the Americans passed.

LXIII. (see page 144)

The Americans advanced through what is now called Dog Lane or the Canoterie ; the second barrier was probably at St. James St., protecting the ends of St. Peter and Sault au Matelot Streets; and the house entered by Nairne and Dambourgès is believed to have been where the No. 5 fire-engine station is at present. Lymburner's house, from the windows of which cannon fired on the Americans, stood where the Quebec Bank has been erected. See LeMoine, Quebec P. and P., pp. 316, 318.

The text states that Morgan went over the barrier first and Porterfield immediately after him. Some good authorities reverse this order. It is hard for the author to believe that Morgan would have been second at such a time ; but, so far as glory is concerned, an instant's difference either way would signify nothing.

LXIV. (see page 146)

It is impossible to be sure with reference to the losses on either side. According to the account published by Congress, about 60 Americans were killed or wounded and 300 captured. Arnold called the 'prisoners and missing' about 400 (to Cong., Jan. 11, 1776 : Sparks MSS., No. 52, II., p. 34). Dearborn estimated the number of sergeants, corporals and privates killed and wounded in Arnold's detachment as about 100, and those captured unhurt as about 300. No American could really know. At Près de Ville the killed were 'about 15,' said one who was present (4 Force, IV., 582), and Ainslie (Journal) recorded that 13 bodies were brought in. Two wounded men crawled to the guard-house ('Chalmers' Journal). Carleton's official report of the American loss (Can. Arch., Q, 12, p. 37) was : 30 killed, 42 wounded prisoners and 389 unwounded prisoners, besides whom he believed that 'many perished in the River' (to Germain : Can. Arch., Q, 12, p. 14). As the slightly wounded and some of those badly hurt went or were carried to the Hospital until the sally into St. Roch occurred (Senter, Journal), as some escaped in the confusion at the end (e.g., Dearborn, Journal), as some (including some or most of the Canadians and nearly all of the Indians : Henry, Journal) took their chances on the ice, and as many of the dead were hidden in the snow, this report seems to tally fairly well with what we know or believe regarding Montgomery's forces. The total American loss might, then, be called about 500. Maclean, however, wrote, May

25, 1776 (Can. Arch., Q, 12, p. 69), 'we buried 220 and since the snow went away we found 20 more'; and Carleton wrote Howe (Can. Arch., Q, 12, p. 11) that the American loss was 600-700 men and 40-50 officers killed, wounded and captured. But these statements can hardly be reconciled with Carleton's official return or with the numbers that Arnold had after the assault.

Of the British accounts, Ainslie gives 5 killed and 14 wounded as the loss on that side, while Carleton wrote Howe (Can. Arch., Q, 12, p. 11) of 'only' three dead and two wounded; but Henry (Journal, p. 114) says the sentries who guarded the prisoners 'frequently admitted of 40 or 50 killed and many more wounded.' As the space between the two barriers was held first by the British and then by the Americans and to a large extent the costumes of the two sides were similar, one is tempted to suppose that some of the American killed referred to by Maclean were really British; but this seems hardly credible.

For an official list of the Americans captured, see Can. Arch., Q, 12, p. 159. For the principal American list of the losses, see 'Ware's' Journal (N. Eng. Hist. and Geneal. Register, April, 1852). For partial lists, see, e. g., Dearborn, Journal; Hinman, Conn., p. 554; 4 Force, IV., 708.

LXV. (see page 146)

It is extremely difficult (indeed impossible) to satisfy oneself perfectly as to the details of the assault at Sault au Matelot, because the reports are incomplete, and, on account of the darkness and excitement, necessarily inaccurate; but the difficulties concern details. On the other hand, the essential features of the affair at Près de Ville are in question. To feel sure about them is impossible; but it seems a duty to inquire closely.

I. What were the defences? The text follows Henry's account. This, to be sure, was written about thirty-five years later; but (1) Henry's honesty and intention to be careful cannot be questioned; (2) while a prisoner at Quebec he felt extremely desirous of examining the spot, and, when permitted to do so, went there expressly for the purpose of observing; (3) he undoubtedly did his utmost to fix the facts in his memory; and (4), as no doubt he told scores, if not hundreds, of times what he saw, his recollection became confirmed. Campbell represented the house as 'in the line of the pickets'; but so it would have appeared—especially in the feeble light—if viewed from a little distance, and Campbell's remark seems to signify only that he did not pass or come very near the second palisade. Caldwell states (this part of his letter has not been correctly printed) that there were 'four cannon, 3- and 4-pounders'; and he was quite likely to know about this.

II. What men were there? Thompson, who had been appointed Supt. of Mil. Defences at Quebec and had charge of the palisading, etc., said in 1828 (LeMoine, Quebec Past and Present, p. 206) that Sergt. Hugh McQuarters had charge of the barrier guard, and

LeMoine (p. 204) accepts this on the ground of the 'immemorial usage of the British army to have a trusty N[on] C[ommissioned] O[fficer] of artillery at every guard where there was a gun'; but, as Quebec had only one officer of artillery, this rule could not be carried out, and Thompson's recollection, fifty-three years after the event, as to a detail that he had no special reason for keeping fresh in his mind, is of very little value. Sanguinet (in Verreau, Invasion, p. 121) says that Chabotte (Chabot) and Picard ordered the cannon fired, and the Canadian writers credit these two with a joint command of the guard; but (1) Sanguinet's account of this affair came from hearsay and contains many errors, and (2) a joint command would not have been appointed by Carleton : the two officers might have paralyzed the operations by disagreement. Caldwell says what is given in the text. That Barnfair (the correct spelling) had charge of the gunners seems very probable : (1) we know that many of the seamen could work guns (Verreau, Invasion, p. 112), but can hardly suppose the Canadian militia were able to do so, (2) Barnfair's letter is evidence, and (3) it is improbable that, when Carleton relied upon the sailors and distrusted the Canadians, he would place these guns in the keeping of the latter.

III. Did Montgomery's approach cause a panic? (A) There was a panic at some stage, as is proved by ample testimony. (B) Caldwell says that the panic occurred (after Montgomery had been repulsed) in consequence of a report by 'some old women' that Arnold had got into the Lower Town, and that a Mr. Coffin, aided by Barnfair, stopped it in a very heroic manner ; but (1) Caldwell was not there ; (2) Caldwell himself makes the story improbable by saying that, during the panic caused by news of S. au Matelot being surprised, Arnold's division might have taken the Lower Town and 'let their friends in at the other side,' for this implies (since news no doubt travelled there as rapidly as the Americans could have felt their way across) that the post at Près de Ville heard of the entry of the Americans at S. au M. (since the Americans at P. de V. were but a few moments in a position to be let in) before Montgomery made his attack ; (3) men capable of one panic were capable of two panics ; (4) if only one panic occurred, it was more likely to come when the guard suddenly found that the enemy had passed two lines of defence and were upon them, than after the guard had won a victory, had only old women's tales of a distant enemy, and knew that the whole force of the garrison could either interpose between them and this enemy or assail this enemy in the rear ; (5) the story about Coffin was a mistake, for he presented to the government later an application for assistance, and made no mention of what (had it occurred) would have been a far stronger basis for his claim than what he offered (Can. Arch., B, 42, p. 21 ; see also B, 54, p. 244); (6) Henry (Journal, p. 131) said that the guard was intoxicated and fled ; that a half-drunk sailor returned, etc.; and that some of those very sailors, a part of the guard over the Americans that same morning, said so ; (7) the report that the guard fled was current among the Americans (e. g., Journals of Meigs and Dearborn) and was believed by Sanguinet,

(Verreau, Invasion, p. 121); (8) the writers of the British Journals were not likely to hear the truth, especially as Barnfair (see his letter) was evidently a bold braggart, nor, if they heard, to record it ; and (9), in spite of the natural interest in smothering accounts of such a panic, reports 'in print, representing the guard at Près de Ville as paralyzed by fear' became so current in Canada before 1834 that Hawkins (Picture) felt obliged to contradict them, which he did (in spite of ample evidence to the contrary) by denying that *any panic at all* occurred. From the 'Chalmers' Journal and Campbell's account it would seem that, as the Americans did not advance, the guard returned to their post and did some more firing, both with cannon and with muskets. Possibly this may explain some stories of vigorous action earlier.

IV. What firing was done? Along with the author's conclusion about the panic goes naturally the opinion that, as Henry heard, a half-drunken sailor went back and fired a gun. Barnfair's letter is of some value as confirming this. As he asserts, he himself was probably the man. The letter sounds like it. Perhaps, as he says, he fired two guns. If he did, he was in such haste that probably they went off almost at the same instant, and so it was said that only one gun was fired. Perhaps some of his comrades followed him back and made the hasty fire of small arms reported by some of the authorities ; or perhaps there were (as Thompson states) bullets in the cannon, and this fact gave rise to the report that muskets were fired.

V. Did Montgomery pass the second palisade? (1) Henry (p. 130) so states ; (2) Montgomery seems to have fallen in the act of charging, sword in hand, and he would not have charged upon an intact palisade ; (3) had there been a strong palisade between the Americans and the enemy, the British fire would not have been so deadly ; (4) Campbell mentions ordering the carpenters on to the second palisade some time before Montgomery fell.

VI. What did Burr do? It has been denied that Burr went with Montgomery (e. g., by Cullum), and certainly Arnold's letter of Dec. 31 sounds at first as if Burr had been with him. But the testimony of Campbell and Lieut. Platt (Parton, Burr, I., p. 75) proves that he did ; and, as he was Montgomery's aide, he could hardly have fought elsewhere. But he does not seem to have played an important part. If, as Parton intimates (Burr, I., pp. 73, 75) Burr had actually led the storming party, it is inconceivable that no one of the eye-witnesses should have mentioned the fact, and that the accounts should represent Montgomery himself as leading the attack and Cheeseman as heading the first company.

This brings us to the famous tale of Burr's attempting to carry off Montgomery's body (Parton, Burr, I., p. 76). The stories of Burr's doings already discredited (REMARKS XXXIX., LI.) show how this one should be approached, and the evidence confirms our presumption. The testimony of Thompson, who found the American dead (Anderson, Siege and Blockade, p. 65), seems to prove that Montgomery's body was not moved from the spot where it fell. An officer who saw his body on the ground made a statement to Henry

(Journal, p. 131) which confirms this. Further : Parton says (Mag. Am. Hist., Apr., 1884, p. 454) that Burr carried it 'down the hill,' whereas he would have carried it along the river bank, and that he was forced to leave it by the pursuing foe, whereas we find no sign of any pursuit. Parton (Mag. Am. Hist., Apr., 1884, p. 454) relied especially on the testimony of Spring, who, Parton says, 'saw' the body carried 'some distance,' whereas Spring belonged to Arnold's detachment and according to Henry (p. 109) helped Arnold to the Hospital. Spring's testimony was not given until about forty-five years after the events, and was not reported until 1838, nineteen years after he died (Parton, Burr, I., p. 374).

Dearborn's company had been stationed on the farther side of the St. Charles River, and the sergeant-major, carrying the order to march, was delayed by the tide. Dearborn set out, however, when he had evidence that an attack had begun, and met with the same difficulties as the others. His company became divided, and both parts fell a prey to the party that sallied from Palace Gate.

Smith had been stationed at the Island of Orleans, and had no personal share in the battle.

LXVI. (see page 152)

For Montgomery's burial, etc., see : Lindsay (Can. Rev., No. 5, Sept., 1826, p. 89); Henry, Journal, p. 170 ; Dearborn, Journal, Jan. 4 ; Mass. Hist. Soc. Coll., First Series, I., p. 111 ; Warren, Am. Rev., I., p. 268 ; LeMoine, Quebec Past and Present, pp. 205-208 (Thompson); Ainslie, Journal, Jan. 1, 4. He seems to have been buried at once and without ceremony, but a lady who afterward married Cramahé begged him to show the dead hero more respect. J. Livingston (to ——, Jan. 25, 1819: Bancroft Coll.) said that Campbell knew Cramahé and wrote him, asking that Montgomery might be decently interred ; but Meigs appears to have been the only channel of communication, and, as he did not return to Quebec until after Montgomery had finally been buried, Campbell's letter—if actually written—had nothing to do with the matter (cf. Haskell, Diary, Jan. 5, with Ainslie, Journal, Jan. 4). The consent of the Governor was doubtless obtained ; and on Jan. 4 the body, enclosed in a suitable coffin, was privately but respectfully interred with the services of a Protestant clergyman. For the spaniel, see Gaspé, Mémoires, p. 40. Gaspé's uncle, Charles de Lanaudière, hearing that a dog had been lying for three days on Montgomery's grave, went to the place and found him howling, moaning, and scratching the ground. The word 'Montgomery' caught its attention, and after 'a week of efforts' the dog was induced to leave the spot. Montgomery's body was laid before burial in the house which is now No. 72, St. Louis St. Ainslie traces the identification of Montgomery's body to a report of his disappearance brought by two deserters. The bodies were then shown to prisoners.

For the transferring of Montgomery's remains to New York in 1818, see Harper's Mag., LXX., p. 358 : Niles's Register, July, 1818 ; LeMoine (*supra*) : Lossing, Am. Rev., I., p. 201, note.

If the visitor at Quebec turns from St. Louis St. toward the Citadel near St. Louis Gate, he soon passes a tablet in the end of a building, recording that thirteen of the American killed were buried below. A few rods from this tablet, in a yard surrounded by buildings, four cannon balls may be seen on the ground. At the centre of the square of which they suggest the corners, is a flat stone. Under this, as a responsible military officer informed the author, Montgomery lay and Cheeseman and Macpherson rest still.

LXVII. (see pages 116, 154)

Campbell (to ——, Mar. 28, 1776: Livingston Papers, 1775–1777, p. 145) asserted that Arnold wished the powder removed from the magazine, and Campbell represented himself as the one determined to keep it there. It is not difficult, however, to decide which of the two was likely to favor a backward move. To the author it seems necessary to regard this very interesting letter of Campbell's with much reserve, (1) because of the writer's conduct and character, (2) because it was a private letter which he did not expect to be challenged, and (3) because —though he knew (see the letter) that very serious charges against him were current—he does not seem to have desired an official investigation.

It is impossible to tell just how many effectives there were, Jan. 1. Arnold's figures vary. Writing Wooster on Jan. 5, he said that by an 'exact return,' made on the 2d, there were not quite 800, including Livingston's corps. This is the basis of the text, Campbell (*supra*) said 450 [Americans]. The men appear to have been quartered in buildings, perhaps hired, perhaps 'borrowed' from British partisans.

LXVIII. (see page 175)

Hancock informed the N. H. Com. Safety (4 Force, IV., 654) that a battalion should include eight companies, each company to have seventy-six privates, a drummer, a fifer, four corporals, four sergeants, two lieutenants, one ensign, a surgeon, a quartermaster, an adjutant, and the captain.

LXIX. (see page 190)

According to Schuyler's ledger, Wooster was sent £10,691, sh. 7, d. 1¼ in specie during Jan. and Feb., 1776. This was probably reckoned in 'York' currency, and was therefore equivalent to about $28,000. This is inferred from Schuyler's referring to 'something above £2,100' as about $5,300 (to Hancock, March 6: 4 Force, V., 91; to Trumbull, Mar. 9: ib., 147).

LXX. (see page 234)

It is necessary to form an idea of Wooster's rule at Montreal mainly from hints and inferences, as we have very few documents relating to that period. If it be thought that the author is severe with him, one should reflect that, at a period when the Continental Congress was almost or quite timid in its desire to avoid giving offense, he was summarily ordered home. Lotbinière (to Sullivan, undated, Cont. Cong. Papers, Letters, 78, Vol. XIV., p. 423) represents Wooster as the one insurmountable obstacle that prevented the Americans from winning Canada.

LXXI. (see page 235)

A thoughtful writer on this subject has expressed the opinions: (1) that the Americans were trusted up to about May 1, 1776, and (2) that even paper money failed early ; but the references for this and the succeeding paragraphs appear to disprove both points, though no doubt there was a delay in sending the paper. See also Wooster to Schuyler, Feb. 19, 21, 1776: 4 Force, IV., 1483, 1499; and Arnold to Deane, Mar. 30, 1776 : 4 Force, V., 549.

LXXII. (see page 257)

Accounts differ as to the precise location of this battery. Finlay (Journal, Mar. 20) said it was 200 yards to the 'east of where Wolfe's was ' ; but a letter written by a soldier who had visited the ground (Conn. Gazette, Apr. 19, 1776) stated (Mar. 10) that 'the King's old battery' was to be refitted. See map of the Siege of Quebec (Jefferys). The old works appear to have been reinforced with fascines (Haskell, Diary, Mar. 16) and perhaps earth also, for Arnold reported that the frost was out of the ground before the snow disappeared (Arnold to ——, Mar. 26, 1776 : 4 Force, V., 512).

LXXIII. (see page 260)

In some cases we find three batteries mentioned and in other cases four. The explanation seems to be that the gun battery and the mortar battery on the Heights could be spoken of either as one or as two. Maclean, for example, said 'two' (May 25, 1776: Can. Arch., Q, 12, p. 69).

Did the Americans obtain shot and shells from the Forges St. Maurice? According to Ursul. de T. Rivières (I., p. 369), Yes. An article in Proc. and Trans., Roy. Soc. of Can., 1886, Sect. II., p. 77, states the same. Badeaux (Verreau, Invasion, p. 207), says Pelissier was to begin making shells May 1; which would mean, No, so far as shells were concerned. Apparently he contributed but few, if any.

LXXIV. (see page 262)

The battery at the ferry was not included in Arnold's scheme (see his letters of Mar. 26 and 30 : 4 Force, V., 512, 549). Work upon it began on Apr. 5 (Haskell), and the 24-pounder, intended by Arnold for use on the Heights, was transferred to it. This very likely offended Arnold. The battery is said to have had two guns ; but Haskell's account proves there were more. According to Carleton (May 14) there were two guns and a howitzer. Caldwell (Letter) said 'three guns.'

LXXV. (see page 266)

As Arnold stated, another fire-ship (the *Gaspé*) was preparing above the city, but the work did not reach completion (Ainslie, Journal, May 7). Possibly the fire-ship of May 3 was a vessel of Arnold's. That opinion prevailed in Quebec (Ainslie, Journal, May 3). Ainslie stated that a brigantine of his wintered below, and the Journ. of Remark. Occurr. (Jan. 25) that a vessel laden with rum was driven ashore on Orleans Island 'November last.' Arnold's vessel (I., p. 502) would have been likely to have a cargo of that sort.

Adjt. Anderson, who had charge of the fire-ship was very badly burned by the premature ignition of the combustibles (caused perhaps by the fire of the garrison), but threw himself from a porthole and got safely ashore. Very possibly had the vessel been a little earlier, it would have reached its destination, for the wind was N. E. but the tide had begun to ebb.

The Cul-de-sac occupied the space between Queen's wharf and the jetty on the west (LeMoine, Pict. Queb., p. 197). Ships were bedded there on the clay bottom for the winter. Dearborn (Journal, May 4) 'heard' that an assault would have been made had the fire-ship succeeded; and Porter says that the ladders were carried near the walls, under cover of darkness and a fog (Diary, Apr. 30 : Mag. Am. Hist., Jan., 1893, p. 187).

LXXVI. (see page 269)

One is surprised that heavy cannon were not sent to Quebec earlier, since Arnold called for them on Jan. 11 (Sparks MSS., No. 52, II., p. 34); but it appears from a letter of T. Walker to S. Adams, May 30, 1776 (S. Adams Papers), that it was not believed such ordnance could be transported over the ice. Walker, however, declared that the ice would have borne them.

LXXVII. (see page 273)

Félix de Bercy, head of the Récollets of Quebec, defending his Order against Du Calvet's charges in 1784, said that upwards of 400 American prisoners had the small-pox in their convent, and that only one died (Can. Arch., Report, 1888, p. 55); but this was a mistake. It is completely disproved by the Journals and Carleton's report.

LXXVIII. (see page 290)

It was very natural for the prisoners to decide to wait for a dark and stormy night for their outbreak. Ainslie, whose report doubtless came from Hall, states that they did so. Stocking concurs. This may explain why Arnold was suspicious.

According to Fobes, a number of pistols were obtained by the prisoners; but Henry, who was in a better position to know the facts, states the contrary.

LXXIX. (see page 308)

Wooster wrote to Congress on April 27 (Cont. Cong. Papers, 161, II., p. 309) that he had sent a company to take post and fortify at Deschambault and proposed also to fortify at Jacques Cartier; but evidently very little if anything had been done when Thomas passed, for on April 30 Antill ordered Desdevens (often called Dudevan by the Americans) to take measurements of the old fort at the mouth of the Jacques Cartier river with a view to drawing a plan, and Desdevens was employed also on May 1 and 2 in drawing this plan and studying the course of the river at Deschambault so that batteries might be planted there (Cont. Cong. Papers, 35, pp. 222, 227). Wooster's action seems to have been caused by something written him by Arnold, for had he moved on his own initiative he would not have waited so long after seeing these two points, and we know that Arnold took hold at once after going up the river.

LXXX. (see page 309)

It is inferred that Thomas arrived late in the day from the fact that while he states that he arrived on May 1, Haskell (Diary) and Alexander (Journal: Temple and Sheldon, Northfield, p. 326) recorded that he came on May 2. Porter says that he arrived on the morning of the second (Diary: Mag. Am. Hist., Jan., 1893, p. 187).

LXXXI. (see page 310)

Besides the New Yorkers who re-enlisted to April 15 at Montreal (Chap. XXII.) and Livingston's men, Warner's regiment agreed to serve only to about that date (Morey to Weare, Mar. 7, 1776: 4 Force, V., 117; Arnold to Deane, Note 19); but these were spoken of as still in the service the latter part of May (Schuyler to Washington, May 24, 1776: 4 Force, VI., 564), though the report seems questionable. The same was true of Col. Fellows's Berkshire men (Schuyler to Hancock, Jan. 22, 1776: 4 Force, IV., 802). Arnold reported (Mar. 30) the following corps: Warner, 373; Maj. Cady, 132; De Haas, 225; Brown, 170 (as 132 of these were under inoculation, it would appear that most of them were recruits); Wooster, 90; McDougall, 191; Van Schaick, 158; Clinton, 227; Holmes, 114; Livingston, 206; Arnold, 167; Wool (artillery), 31; Dugan, 123; Maxwell, 216; Fellows, 82 (4 Force, V., 550). Perfect accuracy regarding the figures was not attained at the time and cannot be now.

LXXXII. (see page 316)

It is impossible to be exact about the arrival of troops. Haskell says that Thomas came on the 2d with 500 men, and makes no mention of others. This seems to mean in a general way that Thomas was supposed to be followed by that number of troops, for it is not probable, in view of what Robbins tells of their movements above, that so many arrived together on May 2. St. Clair says that on May 11 he arrived somewhere near Quebec; but his date must be wrong, for he adds that he was just in time to cover the movement which took place on May 6.

LXXXIII. (see page 317)

It has often been said that the Americans ought to have retreated before, and so Thomas himself suggested forcibly, somewhat influenced, no doubt, by chagrin at finding himself forced to give up the siege so unfortunately. Perhaps that is true ; but the importance of taking Quebec, the belief that Carleton could not hold out, the expectation that the fire-ship would accomplish something, the news of reinforcements at hand, the uncertainty about the arrival of the British, and the danger of destroying the confidence of the friendly Canadians, were powerful arguments for holding on until the last possible moment. Several times at Quebec, caution had defeated the Americans when victory lay within their grasp. It is a suggestive fact that one of the transports had not reached Quebec on May 15, being 'detained by contrary winds' (Gordon to Barrington, May 15, 1776 : War Off., Orig. Corres., N. Am., Vol. 12). Doubtless it was true, as Marshall suggested, that the American leaders feared they would be blamed, should they retire from Quebec, and also that they were extremely reluctant to abandon or alarm the Canadians. It seems, however, as if a plausible pretext could have been found for placing the hospitals a considerable distance up the river, and certainly Wooster could not be excused for neglecting to entrench. What tools the army had (and they had some : Ainslie, Journal, May 6), with what could have been obtained from the people, would have enabled them to throw up something respectable in a month's time. Some fortifications with troops and cannon behind them would probably have justified Thomas in making a stand, prevented the panic, and changed a rout into a retreat. Further, it was Wooster's plain duty to push forward with more energy the plans for the fire-ships and batteries, so that—should all the offensive measures fail—there might be ample time for retreat before the British vessels could possibly arrive. He seems to have had almost no power of initiative, perhaps none whatever.

LXXXIV. (see page 319)

Walker, in his letter to S. Adams, May 30, 1776 (S. Adams Papers) charged Thomas with indiscretion for attempting to retreat in daylight. But (1) Ainslie's Journal shows that the work began before the arrival of the *Surprise;* (2) the fact that the Canadians helped *until* the arrival of the vessels became known proves the same; (3) since an effectual stand could not be made, the quicker the flight the better, in case Carleton should decide to sally immediately; (4) should Carleton delay, a quick flight might soon harden into an orderly retreat; (5) a delay on Thomas's part might have enabled Carleton to cut the line of retreat; (6) from Shallus's Journal it appears probable that Thomas had *intended* to complete (or perhaps begin) the retreat in the night of May 6–7. Walker thought the retreat caused the sally; but, even if this was true, it would have done as much harm or more had it been made later, for whenever made, it was sure to be known by Carleton through some disaffected Canadian.

LXXXV. (see page 335)

For the discussions between Carroll and the Canadian clergy, see Têtu, Evêques, p. 332, and particularly Campbell on Carroll, U. S. Cath. Mag., III., p. 244. Campbell obtained his information from Bishop Fenwick of Boston, who was given the points on a visit to Canada by a priest who had met Carroll (Carroll, Journal, p. 30, note). Aside from this evidence, the position attributed to the Canadian priests could be inferred from their known views. The references to the bishop and the Americans in Canada have been added.

Ainslie (Journal, May 7) praises 'the steady & distinguish'd loyalty of the Canadian Clergy.' The Abbé Casgrain, a well-known writer on Canadian history, expressed to the present author his emphatic opinion that it was the religious question which held Canada on the British side at the time of the American Revolution. Our study of the situation has perhaps shown that so concise an explanation can hardly be complete; but these and many other evidences which might be adduced, in addition to those cited in the Notes, are enough to prove that the influence of the Church, as an organization, was thrown against the Colonies. See also Verreau, Invasion, p. 95.

LXXXVI. (see page 340)

This and several following paragraphs are based mainly, in default of any other adequate source of information, upon Walker's letter of May 30 to S. Adams (Walker suggests, though he does not express, the dialogue form; his diction has been slightly emended). He was hostile to the Commissioners and therefore liable to give a prejudiced account of their doings; but (1) his hostility is an evidence that they adopted the policy he denounced, (2) he was too shrewd a man to state things to Adams about Adams's colleagues which they could refute, (3) the principles to which the Commissioners were committed made it impossible for them to pursue any other policy. and (4) the consequences alleged by Walker, given the state of feeling that certainly existed, were sure to follow.

LXXXVII. (see page 346)

Just what new troops reached Thomas at this time it is impossible to say. At the Deschambault Council were Col. Burrell, of the Conn. regt., who probably left Chambly with a considerable part of his men on May 3 (Robbins, Journ.); Lt. Col. Buel, who left Chambly on that day (Robbins, Journal); Lt. Col. Irvine of the First Penn. Regt. (DeHaas); Lt. Col. Shreve, Lt. Col. Allen of the Second Penn. Regt. (St. Clair); and Lt. Col. Williams.

But regiments were often divided ; and the fact that the colonels of these were not present would of itself suggest that some of the men were not.

LXXXVIII. (see page 349)

The author has not been able to discover all the letters that passed at this time, and some points are not perfectly clear. For example, Arnold wrote on May 15 from Sorel that Thomas proposed to make a stand at Deschambault ; why, then, since his vessels arrived that day (Vose, Journal) at Sorel, did he not go on ? It was perhaps because, after writing this letter, he received word (before he had a chance to sail) that Thomas had retreated. Possibly Vose was wrong about his date, as he certainly was in several cases; but, if so, the date should probably be the 13th, and the query remains.

LXXXIX. (see page 358)

'Jacob Shallus, Esq., of Philadelphia,' who went to Quebec as a volunteer and whose Journal proves that he was intelligent and self-possessed, states that about 900 men were formed by Maxwell at the time of the British sally, 'ready to receive the Enemy.' Thomas (to Washington, May 8 : 4 Force, VI., 453) reported that he had (probably on May 2) only 500 men besides the classes excluded in the text. It seems doubtful whether many more than 400 new troops had come down by the forenoon of the 6th. James Caldwell wrote to Elias Boudinot, May 15, 1776, that only one battalion of Thompson's had arrived (Emmet Coll.).

XC. (see page 366)

Bayley's 'Narrative,' which will be referred to a number of times, was written in 1826 to give his son Enoch an account of their family and of his life. Frye Bayley, the author, belonged to the same family as Jacob Bayley of Newbury. His home was at Peacham, Vt. His narrative, which is quite long and very minute, is not a diary but evidently must have been based (so far as his own life was concerned) upon something of that sort. In fact, a portion of his Journal for 1776 is given by Wells in his Hist. of Newbury, p. 383. The writer was plainly a very careful, conscientious man, and he evidently took great pains with his narrative. To the present author it seems highly trustworthy.

Bayley went to Canada, not as a soldier, but to guide a part of Bedel's regiment. He declined an ensign's commission, which Bedel offered him, but consented to remain three weeks in order to carry word back how Bedel fared with the small-pox. Then he drifted into the service because capable and willing to help at a time when such men were scarce. The Journal shows that he was on very good terms with Bedel.

XCI. (see page 370)

Arnold (then at Sorel) counted upon Price, the Commissary, to keep the Cedars supplied with provisions, and put the Commissioners in mind to make sure that he did so (Arnold to Commrs., May 15, 1776 : 4 Force, VI., 579). Bedel reported, May 16, that the garrison had been 'four days without any other provisions than bread' (Commrs. to Hancock, May 17, 1776: 4 Force, VI., 587); but Capts. Estabrook and Wilkins made oath that when attacked they had 3 bbls. pork, 1½ do. beef, 20 bu. meal, and 5 or 6 horses. The barrelled provisions could not have been obtained from the neighbors after Bedel left the fort, and did not go from Montreal, for Bedel brought the first notice that supplies were needed. The same officers testified as to the quantity of ammunition (5 Force, I., 166).

XCII. (see page 372)

As the text suggests, the author found himself driven to the conclusion that Bedel did not do his duty. A somewhat extended study of the affair was prepared for insertion at this point ; but as the book is quite large and the question of Bedel's responsibility is no way essential, it has been omitted. Bedel said that he left the Cedars to attend an important Indian council; but this representation did not save him at the court-martial and does not bear examination now.

XCIII. (see page 373)

Arnold (5 Force, I., 166) wrote that on strict inquiry he found that Sherburne had acted with 'great prudence, spirit and resolution'; but the British account and Bayley's narrative do not exactly bear that out. Indeed, scepticism as to Sherburne's conduct seems to have arrived soon. Col. Greaton wrote from Ticonderoga to Gen. Heath, July 31, 1776 (Heath Papers): 'You rote me about Maj. Sherburne's great honours to himself amongst you, it is not so here.'

According to Dawson, the village in which the American officers were confined is that now called Oka, and Quinze Chiens was the present Vaudreuil.

XCIV. (see page 380)

Wilkinson tells of the trouble at the council (of which he acted as the secretary). Arnold reported the decision to attack as unanimous ; but, mindful perhaps of the unpleasant reputation he had gained at the lakes, he seems to have avoided in his letters every suggestion of quarrelling.

XCV. (see page 380)

The truce was to last six days (the British account says four), Forster declaring that he could not agree to deliver all of the prisoners within a shorter time. Apparently he told the truth about this, for some of them had to be purchased of Indians who did not wish to give them up. Besides other inducements, it was urged that the prisoners, if permitted to live, could be used in the process of exchange to free British soldiers from captivity (Lorimier in Verreau, Invasion). Forster agreed to deliver the prisoners as soon as possible, and professed great eagerness to begin hostilities (on due notice being given) when that had been done. Arnold wrote the Commissioners that the truce did not cover the Indians, but apparently he found that it did.

The cartel was rejected by Congress and great bitterness arose on both sides. Congress asserted that the prisoners were plundered and stripped, contrary to the agreement, and forced to live for about a week in cold weather in the open ; that they were nearly starved ; that some were murdered ; and that when the last of the prisoners were leaving the north shore they were fired upon. The evidence presented to Congress appeared to support all these complaints. The British, on the other hand, charged Congress with falsehood, slander, and a breach of faith.

The version of Congress was no doubt honestly intended; but (1) it was designed to be as favorable as possible to the American side, (2) it was prepared under the stress of extreme chagrin and irritation, (3) Congress was far from the scene and the witnesses, (4) both feeling and self-interest inclined the actors in the affair to color their reports, and (5) the British account had not yet been issued. To expect good history from such conditions would be unreasonable.

The account prepared by the British officers admitted but explained the plundering. By the terms of capitulation, Butterfield's men were entitled only to the clothes they wore. They made up packs, however ; and, in spite of a warning from Forster, took them out of the fort, because two chiefs, without consulting the rest, gave them permission to do so. The consequence was dissatisfaction among the Indians and some pillage. Sherburne's men, surrendering unconditionally to the Indians, could not be saved from plundering. Finally, when the two parties of prisoners were lodged together in the barracks at the Cedars, some Indians, going in to take things from Sherburne's men, took things also from Butterfield's. (The death of a distinguished Seneca chief in the fight with Sherburne's party had made the Indians peculiarly rabid.) Of course, the British could not provide new clothing. Ample provisions, it was asserted, and the same quantity given the British, were allowed the prisoners. (Perhaps their Canadian guards appropriated a part.) The charge of butchery was roundly denied ; but the British officers were not present when Sherburne surrendered, and some of the wounded at least appear to have been murdered at that time. Perhaps one or two more were killed later ; on this point the evidence is contradictory. The prisoners, it was maintained, were treated as well by the British as the necessities of the case permitted ; and there seems no reason to doubt in general the truth of this or to deny that Forster and his officers tried hard to protect them.

The British admitted that some of the Indians fired their guns when the last prisoners were leaving, but denied that they injured or intended to injure any one. How it could be known what the savages intended is hard to see ; and certainly it was more difficult still for the prisoners—now a long time under the threat of massacre—to have any faith in their tenderness or decency. This firing was naturally construed as an act of war by the Congress, and as justifying a refusal to confirm the cartel. Of course, Forster did not wish the Indians to fire ; but, as he had had the advantage of employing irresponsible savages, he could not reasonably complain of now suffering the disadvantage.

Four American captains (Stevens, Green, Sullivan, and Bliss) were left in the hands of the British, but were finally permitted to go quietly home. Eben Sullivan, one of them, wrote his brother, General John Sullivan, vigorously against the course of Congress (Can. Arch., B, 181, p. 32). The Americans had had enough of war and most of them promptly deserted, so that it was not practicable to send them back to the British (Schuyler to Sullivan, June 17, 1776 : Sullivan Papers, N. H. Hist. Soc.).

Forster certainly used sharp practice and it galled the Americans keenly that he could control the savages well enough for the interest of his own side but not for the protection of the other.

The British account of the prisoners was : 'The cartel had indorsed on the back, 2 majors, 9 captains, 21 subalterns [in the American copies of Sparks and Force, 20] 443 privates; Total 475 ; to whom let us now add, hostages remaining at Montreal, 4 ; Canadians released, 8; prisoners who remained with, and were afterwards bought from the savages, and are now at Montreal, 8; yet remaining with the savages, 2; thus do we account for 497 prisoners, being the full number who fell into the hands of the savages ' (Authentic Narrative). A factor of uncertainty is introduced, however, by Hazen's statement, nearly two and a half years later (Note 19), that a subaltern and sixteen men from his company were not included in the exchange. Half a dozen unanswerable queries are at once suggested ; but, if these men were regarded all the way through as outsiders, the above reckoning is not affected. The British government, though not ready to make a formal exchange of prisoners with the 'rebels,' approved of this cartel as necessary under the circumstances (Germain to Carleton, Aug. 22, 1776 : Can. Arch., Q, 12, p. 84).

The losses were not positively known, but were small. A prisoner who escaped reported to Arnold on May 25 that only ten American privates had been killed and that Forster had lost twice as many ; but that was not authoritative.

Arnold, after returning to Montreal, gave De Haas positive orders to destroy Conosadaga and all the people within it. This harsh measure appears to have been as justifiable as the punitive expeditions of Sullivan and Wayne, which have been so much praised. De Haas, however, not wishing to do the job, laid the order before a council of war, and the council voted against it. De Haas pretended that seven hundred Indians threatened him (Arnold to Commrs., June 2, 1776 : 5 Force, I., 165 ; Shallus, Journal ; Wilkinson, Memoirs, I., p. 47). Arnold also ordered the burning of the fort at St. Anne, which belonged to the leader of Forster's Canadians ; and this was done. The course of De Haas was obviously rank insubordination. Arnold's order was the basis of one of John Brown's charges against him (Smith, Pittsfield, I., p. 272). It has often been said that Brant led the Indians in this affair ; but he had gone to England with Guy Johnson in November, 1775, and did not return until he landed at New York on July 29, 1776 (Trans. Can. Inst., V., p. 246).

XCVI. (see page 384)

The seizure of goods was justified on two grounds : (1) That it prevented the troops from getting food by miscellaneous plundering with the consequence of bloodshed ; (2) and that the owners had forfeited all claim to protection by acting or conspiring against the Americans. May 12, Carleton issued a proclamation forbidding all persons who left Quebec in November, 1775, (to avoid bearing arms in the militia) to re-enter Quebec without permission in writing (Can. Arch., Q, 12, p. 31). This amounted to a partial confiscation of the property of all not actively zealous for the King (Walker to S. Adams, May 30, 1776 : S. Adams Papers). Admitting that Montgomery's capture of Montreal gave the Americans a right to govern there, their act of seizure would seem quite as justifiable as Carleton's. Besides, they at least promised to pay. It was alleged that the seizures were contrary to the terms on which Montreal had capitulated. But Montgomery expressly refused to give any terms of capitulation ; and the protection which he promised was undoubtedly based upon the understanding that the people of Montreal would not be hostile.

XCVII. (see page 387)

One is surprised at first to find no signs of Thomas's activity at

Sorel. But he did not arrive there until May 17 (or early on the 18th), and on May 21 he wrote Wooster that he had been taken with the small-pox and desired to be removed from the camp (Thomas Papers). See Trumbull, Autobiog., p. 27.

XCVIII. (see page 396)

The fact that men of the 29th Regiment had arrived at Quebec was evidence that reinforcements had been sent direct from England ; but the Americans could not be expected to understand that.

XCIX. (see page 411)

Nothing more will be heard in this campaign of the Royal Fusiliers (7th Foot), for the officers went home to enlist new men, and the privates were drafted into the 47th (Carleton to Barrington, May 21, 1776). Fraser was a lieutenant-colonel (24th Regt.); but in this campaign he had local rank as a brigadier-general. The same was true of Nesbitt (47th), Powell (53d), and Gordon (29th) : Carleton to Barrington, June 22, 1776 (Can. Arch., Q, 12, p. 68).

In Am. and W. I. (Pub. Rec. Off.), Vol. 290. p. 127, is the following :

'State of the Army in Canada at the beginning . . . of the campaign, 1776. BRITISH : 11 Batt^{ns} of Foot viz.: the 8th, 9th, 20th, 21st, 24th, 29th, 31st, 34th, 47th, 53^d and 62nd, at 677 each . 7,447
Supernumeraries to the British Regulars 150
1 Battn. Maclean's Emigrants, incomplete . . . 150
British Artillery, about 400

8,147

FOREIGN : 1st Div^n of Brunswickers. . 2,280
1 Batt^n. Hanau 684   2,964

Total strength at the beginning of the Campgn.   11,111

. . . N. B. It is to be observed that the 8th Reg! did duty in the Back Forts, and was not with the Army. If this Reg! and 30 Non-effective Men p! Batt^n from the British and Foreigners, making about 1,127 Men, are deducted from 11,111, the remainder 9,984 will show nearly what was the effective strength at the opening of the Campaign.'

C. (see page 416)

One is surprised that a general alarm was not given the British by the vessels that fired upon the Americans above; but the Americans may have been seen very indistinctly, may have been believed to be a small party, and may have been thought to have taken flight.

For Carleton's treatment of the American prisoners and his policy regarding them, see also: Diaries and Journals of the prisoners (e. g., Dearborn, May 16; 'Ware' (Tolman), June 5; Morison, at end; Porterfield, June 14; Nichols, Diary, Aug. 10); Carleton to Douglas, June 13, 1776 (Can. Arch., B, 39, p. 7); Id. to Pownall, June 28, 1776 (ib., p. 37); Id. to Howe, Aug. 8, 1776 (ib., p. 93); Id. to Germain, Aug. 10, 1776 (Can. Arch., Q, 12, p. 135).

CI. (see page 416)

Sullivan wrote to Schuyler, June 19, 1776, that his loss amounted to 'about 150'; but, in the chaotic state of the army, it was doubtless impossible to ascertain it. The British list of prisoners (Can. Arch., Q, 12, p. 149) gives 236 names. 'Upwards of fifty' dead were found in the woods (Digby). As many must have fallen in the attack, and as the pursuit continued for many miles, it would appear safe to reckon the total loss as not under 400. Carleton (June 20) reported his killed and wounded as 12 or 13; other accounts made the number a little larger (e. g., Digby, 19). Instead of a bridge, St. Clair speaks of a ford across the Du Loup; but he evidently refers to the same spot, for he mentions it as the only way to escape.

CII. (see page 438)

Sullivan had to leave three poor iron cannon at Chambly and burn his gondolas there. The British found two bateaux and took two prisoners at that point (Digby). Digby says no bridges were destroyed between Sorel and Chambly. The American guard at Berthier, not joining the army when ordered to do so, were met by the British, forced to abandon their nine bateaux and make for Chambly by land.

CIII. (see page 438)

Did Arnold at his own instance evacuate Montreal and then return to the place by order of Sullivan? Senter states (Journal, near the end) that the troops evacuated Montreal on June 9, and implies that he himself left at that time, so that he ought to know; but Senter's Journal contains many inaccuracies. Sullivan mentions with much regret a report that Arnold was about leaving Montreal. On the other hand, we find no evidence of such a movement in Arnold's letters or Sanguinet's Journal, nor an order sending him back. June 6, Arnold wrote Schuyler that he should remain at Montreal 'until I receive orders to leave it, or am obliged to quit it, by a superior force' (Sparks MSS., No. 60, p. 93); and neither of these conditions was fulfilled before June 15. What seems even more convincing is the fact that, had he evacuated Montreal, the place would no doubt have been occupied at once by the Scotch, Cana-

dians and Indians who were hovering near. It is clear that about
this time he reduced his force from 450 to 300 men (very likely by
sending off those under inoculation), and this might easily explain
what Senter and Sullivan wrote.

As the author does not consider it a part of his duty to discuss
Arnold's character, it seems unnecessary to examine the charge
that he seized goods at Montreal on his own account and had them
sold at Albany, as Wilkinson charged in his Memoirs ; but a word
may be said. The seizures in general were made by authority, e. g.,
Schuyler gave Thomas orders for ' bringing away from Montreal
all the goods you possibly can ' (4 Force, VI., 711). Arnold wrote
about them repeatedly and as openly as about any other military
operations. Very likely he would not have scrupled to take a case
of wine for his own use or a bundle of silks for some friend. But
how he could have managed to get any large quantity of goods
conveyed surreptitiously to Albany under the circumstances, it is
impossible for the author to imagine. Sept. 7, 1776, Arnold wrote
Gates (Sparks MSS., No. 52, II., p. 45) : ' He [Samuel Chase] ob-
serves my character is much injured by a report prevailing in Philadelphia of my having sequestered the goods seized in Montreal.
As you have had an opportunity of hearing that matter canvassed
on the trial of Col. Hazen [charged by Arnold with failing to take
proper care of the seized goods], I beg you will be kind enough
to write your sentiments to him on the matter.' In other words
Arnold was willing to rest his case on the judgment of a superior
officer so placed as to hear all that could be said about the matter.
Conscious innocence could not have taken a fairer or more dignified attitude. As the seized goods were neglected (contrary to
Arnold's orders), broken into and plundered (Arnold to Sullivan,
June 13, 1776 : Sparks MSS., No. 20, p. 258), some of them may have
been taken by the thieves to Albany and sold there. Wilkinson's
statement was evidently based upon hearsay, and his testimony is
always to be cautiously used. Arnold seems during this campaign
to have been under the spell of Washington's influence and eager
to prove himself worthy of his confidence.

The account of Wilkinson's doings rests upon his own testimony;
but in this case there was little motive for misrepresentation, and
all that he tells appears probable.

CIV. (see page 442)

Did Carleton favor the escape of the Americans here as he did at
Three Rivers ? So Wilkinson thought. The presumption is, however, very strongly against that idea, for the question this time was
not the capture of a few wretched prisoners, but the possession of
a strategic point and of priceless boats, and the complete elimination of the only army that stood between the British and New York.
An examination of Carleton's letters and orders shows no sign of a
desire to forego these immense advantages, and he was not the man
to conceal his views. His plan to reach Sullivan's rear, the caution
enjoined by the affair at Three Rivers, the softness of his troops

(see particularly Digby) the difficulties of transportation, the failure of the wind, and the extraordinary activity of the Americans appear to explain the case.

CV. (see page 445)

Jonathan Trumbull (Hinman, Conn., p. 560) estimated that at least 10,400 men went into Canada in 1776. (Substantially all who were there prior to Jan. 1 came away (Schuyler : 4 Force, VI., 939), some time before the province was evacuated.) Of these, he charged 'perhaps' 1,000 dead to the enemy and 1,000 to disease. This left 2,400 to be accounted for. Of course many deserted ; but, lacking accurate returns of any sort and none at all of desertions and deaths by disease, it is useless to figure on the losses.

CVI. (see pages 453, 471)

June 2, Carleton wrote Germain that he had returned to Quebec to see about refitting and building bateaux. June 28, he directed Cramahé to 'employ every possible means to procure 200 flatt bottom boats for the use of the army, and then to send them up without loss of time to Chambly' (Can. Arch., B, 39, p. 34). Other letters of about the same date had the same burden (ib., pp. 35, 39, 40, 51). It may be said on the other hand that Carleton had asked Germain to send boats for the lake service and therefore would not have begun to build until he knew that enough had not been supplied. But (1) when Carleton asked to have such boats sent, he did not expect to be able to build them in the spring; (2) his ship-building operations in August, 1775, are evidence that he would have begun the same in 1776 as promptly as possible, for so experienced a man would not have risked the chances that enough suitable boats would be sent, would escape the American cruisers, and would have favoring gales to bring them in time (see his letter to Germain, Sept. 28, 1776 : Can. Arch., Q, 12, p. 188); and (3) there is no evidence (but much probability the other way) that, when he began taking steps to collect boats as stated above, the transports had been overhauled thoroughly enough to show what materials and sections of boats they contained (see his letter of Sept. 28, *supra*, and that of Aug. 10, 1776 : Can. Arch., Q, 12, p. 119).

For Carleton's loss of favor see, e. g., Précis of Operations; Carleton to Germain, Sept. 28, 1776 : Can. Arch., Q, 12, p. 188 ; Germain to Carleton, Mar. 26, 1777 (Separate) : Can. Arch., Q, 13, p. 73; Carleton to Germain, May 20, 1777, printed in Can. Arch., Report 1885, p. CXXXII. ; and Germain to Carleton, July 25, 1777, ib., p. CXXXVI. Burgoyne (State of the Expedition, p. 2), in order to clear himself from the charge of having intrigued to obtain a command belonging of right to Carleton, says that it was decided before the result of the campaign of 1776 was known in England that Carleton should remain in Canada, (1) because the civil government of the province required his presence there, and (2) because his Commission did not permit him to pass the frontier; and it is true that, in his letter of Aug. 22, 1776 (Can. Arch., Q, 12, p. 88), Germain ordered Carleton to return to Quebec and put the civil administration in order, detaching some officer to advance with the troops. But, as for (1), this task once accomplished, the order ceased to operate. As for (2), Carleton's authority extended over his frontiers (Dartmouth to Carleton, Aug. 2, 1775: Can. Arch., Q, 11, p. 198; Carleton to Germain, May 20, 1777), and this was an elastic term, as

I am with all due respect

My Lord

your Lordships

Most Obedient

most humble servant

Guy Carleton

TO LORD GERMAIN, MAY 25, 1776 (Note the word ' due ')

Germain's letter of Aug. 22, 1776, illustrated. As a matter of fact, Carleton did pass the frontier in 1776. The main point, however, is not whether Carleton was personally to lead troops south, but whether he was to direct such an expedition, as he could have done without leaving the province; and Germain's letter of Mar. 26, 1777 (confirmed by Carleton's of May 20, 1777) indicates clearly that it was the result of the campaign of 1776 which led to taking the command of the invasion from Carleton and giving it to Burgoyne. Carleton showed that he felt great bitterness because this was done.

One who goes over the correspondence between Carleton and Germain may discern signs of contempt on the one hand and enmity on the other before the open breach occurred; and personal feeling may have influenced Germain.

It is of course possible that an army would have been sent to Canada in the spring of 1776 even if the Americans had not invaded that province, and that the British army would not have been able to reach Albany even under Carleton's direction.

CVII. (see page 474)

Lossing (Life of Schuyler, II., p. 391) states that on Nov. 4, 1777, Schuyler wrote to Congress at length, recommending a winter campaign against Canada. The author has searched for the letter carefully but without success. This by no means proves, however, that Lossing was in error.

CVIII. (see page 485)

Conway's correspondence seems to prove conclusively that he was not on the terms of a fellow conspirator with either Gates or Congress. See his letters to Charles Carroll (Nov. 14, 1777: Cont. Cong. Papers, No. 159, p. 461); to Gates (Nov. 9 and 11, 1777: Force Transcripts of Gates's corres.); Gates to Conway (Dec. 3, 1777: ib.); Conway to Gates (Feb. 24; April 2, 1778: Bancroft Coll., Revol. Papers, III., pp. 303, 323); etc. Lafayette observed at Albany that Conway was on excellent terms with Gates's enemies (Lafayette to Laurens, Feb. 19, 1778: S. Car. Hist. and Gen. Mag., VII., p. 189). Even Conway's famous letter to Gates in criticism of Washington (reported by Wilkinson and Stirling) points in the same direction, for by the time two men are deep in a cabal together, they have ceased to speak in that way to each other. He was, to be sure, elected as an Inspector General at this time ; but such an officer was needed and his long military experience appeared to have qualified him particularly well to drill American recruits. Even Lafayette, writing to Laurens, spoke very strongly of his qualifications (S. Car. Hist. and Gen. Mag., VII., p. 63). In his letter of Apr. 2 to Gates, he stated that he had not sought employment in America 'but was frequently solicited by your agent,' and, so far as this was true, Congress was under an obligation to employ him. At the same time, his election is suggestive of the feeling against Washington, even though not an evidence that Conway governed Congress. Conway's complaints and his vain protests against Kalb's promotion are proof enough under the latter head ; and no less significant is the fact that Lovell, the most outspoken New England critic of Washington (Lodge, Washington, I., p. 214), took strong ground in Congress against Conway (Conway to Ch. Carroll, Nov. 14, 1777: Sparks MSS., No. 52, III., p. 137).

CIX. (see page 495)

The letters of Morris and Wayne are later than Lafayette's

Instructions ; but (1) they show what was in people's minds and doubtless made itself felt in Congress as soon as the matter was made known ; (2) this paragraph was not in the original Instructions and probably was considerably later than they, for Gates spoke, in writing Congress, of something 'superadded' (evidently this paragraph) the draft of which could not be found. The copy of the Instructions in Revol. Papers, III., Lib. of Cong., has no date except on the back.

CX. (see page 495)

There are two copies of Lafayette's Instructions in the Library of Congress. That in Cont. Cong. Papers, No. 156, p. 55 (printed by Tower, *Lafayette in the Am. Revol.*, I., p. 274) appears to be the one sent to Congress by the Board of War. It does not contain the cautionary appendix ; but is followed by a note in the hand of Peters, signed by Gates, giving the substance of that appendix from memory. The other copy is in U. S. Revol. MSS., III. This is in the handwriting of President Laurens, and was probably made for Washington after Lafayette received the original. Omitting a concluding paragraph which advised Lafayette to call upon the New York authorities at Poughkeepsie, this copy adds three paragraphs, the first of which refers to Hazen's regiment while the other two embody the cautionary remarks. This copy seems therefore to be the real and entire Instructions received by Lafayette, and it is the one used by the present author.

CXI. (see page 514)

One of the most competent of the American writers on this expedition has taken the ground that it was 'nothing but a plot,' solely intended to draw Lafayette over from Washington to the Opposition party. But (1) the facts laid before the reader (not all of them known to this writer, probably) seem quite enough to prove that the expedition was seriously intended and seriously believed in by Congress ; (2) this is confirmed by the history of its genesis through the Bedel and Stark schemes ; and (3) Gates and the Opposition would have been imbeciles to think of winning Lafayette by deliberately getting him to take the leading place in a ridiculous fiasco. In fact, it looks as if Gates had expected the expedition to go through without Lafayette if not with him, for Troup wrote him on [Feb. 6]: ' My opinion is, that he [Lafayette] will be too tardy to reap the benefits Congress promise themselves from the Expedition. I shall therefore endeavour to forward it not only by delivering my packet by Gen. Conway, but by every other means in my power.' Troup had been ordered to reach Albany in the quickest possible time (Lafayette to Laurens, rec'd Feb. 4: So. Car. Hist. and Gen. Mag., VII., p. 185).

CXII. (see page 543)

It will be noted that, here and elsewhere, letters bearing upon the state of things in Canada are applied to a period some months distant from their date. In some instances the writer refers expressly to an earlier time ; and, in general, since the temper of the Canadians changed but slowly and evidently remained about the same from 1777 to 1782, such a use of the letters seems right. It should be remembered, too, that, since reports from Canada were constantly coming to the Americans, it is safe to assume that the state of things at any given time was fairly well understood. Most of the reports quoted in this paragraph were too late to affect the decision upon Lafayette's plan, but they indicate what was doubtless reported earlier.

It is natural to suppose (particularly as information of this kind was secret) that the documents in our possession are merely specimens of what actually existed. On the other hand, it is obvious that the reports of spies needed to be discounted somewhat.

CXIII. (see page 550)

Wells (S. Adams, III., p. 40) attributes the paternity of this plan to a letter from Arnold to Congress. The author has looked for such a letter in all the accessible places where it seemed likely to be, but without success. This, however, does not prove that it was not written nor even that it does not exist ; but Washington, who suspected the plan was suggested by France (letter to Laurens), and Laurens (Sparks, Corres., II., p. 233) believed ' on good ground ' that it originated with Lafayette, probably encouraged by Estaing. Besides, Arnold had argued strongly in February against making an attempt upon Canada.

CXIV. (see page 556)

The road toward Canada is commonly called Hazen's Road, because the greater part of it was built under his direction. It ends at ' Hazen's Notch ' in Westfield, near the line between that town and Montgomery. So far as possible, it ran through the hardwood timber on the high ground. A letter of Hazen's (N. H. State Papers, XVII., p. 276) shows that he completed his work in the latter part of August, 1779. See *The Vermonter*, Nov., 1906, and a map in the office of the Sec. of State, Montpelier, Vt.

CXV. (see pages 57, 58)

Why, if peaceful measures were expected to bring England to terms, was it deemed necessary to convince her that we would fight? A prudent man, in a case of shipwreck, takes a life-preserver if he can, even though confident of his ability to swim without it. Besides, some had not full faith in the peaceful measures. (This REMARK is out of place because at first the author thought—probably he was right—that it was unnecessary.)

INDEX OF PERSONS, PLACES, AND SUBJECTS

ABBREVIATIONS.—*Adjt.*, Adjutant; *Amer.*, American or Americans; *Brig.-Gen.*, Brigadier-General; *Brit.*, British; *Can.*, Canada; *Canad.*, Canadian, Canadians; *Com.*, Committee; *Cong.*, Congress; *Conn.*, Connecticut; *Crown Pt.*, Crown Point; *Dept.*, Department; *Eng.*, England; *Exped.*, Expedition; *Gen.*, General; *Gov.* Governor; *Gt. Britain*, Great Britain; *Ind.*, Indian, Indians; *Maj.*, Major; *Mass.*, Massachusetts; *Montg.*, Montgomery; *N. H.*, New Hampshire; *N. J.*, New Jersey; *N. Y.*, New York; *Penn.*, Pennsylvania.

Index of Persons, Places, and Subjects 609

Brown, John—*Continued.*
with Hanchet against Arnold, 121;
not mentioned in the accounts of
the Quebec assault, REMARK LVII.;
trouble with Arnold renewed, 222
and *note* 17; an unfounded charge of,
against Arnold, 387, *note* 34; his mission to Can., why doomed to fail, 445.
Brunswick (Me.), i., 21.
Bunker Hill, i., 3, 105.
Burgoyne, John, i., 36; to lead the
main Brit. army for the relief of
Quebec, ii., 296; reaches Quebec,
409; signature, 415; in pursuit of
Sullivan, 434; his object, 435; his
pledge, 437; reaches Chambly, 438;
St. Johns, 441; his expedition
south, 467–71; sketched, 467; occupies Ticonderoga, 468; baffled
by Schuyler, 468; defeated at Sara-
toga, 469–70; surrenders to Gates,
470–71; political consequences, 471.
Burke, Edmund, i., 88, 227; protests
against the Quebec Act, i., 72.
Burke, William, on the Quebec Act,
i., 73.
Burr, Aaron, i., 124; enthusiasm for
Kennebec exped., i., 506–07; at the
Great Carrying-Place, 548; not sent
disguised to Montg., REMARKS
XXXIX. and LI.; Montg.'s second
aide, ii., 116 and REMARKS LVI.,
LXV. (p. 584)
Burrell, Colonel, ii., 195.
Bute, Lord, i., 80.
Butler, John, supports the Iroquois
on the supply question, ii., 359–60;
induces the Ind. to enlist for the
king, 427–28.
Butterfield, Major, fortifies the
Cedars, ii., 366; attacked by Forster,
370–71; his poltroonery, 370–71;
surrenders, 371.

C

Caldwell, Colonel, in command at Detroit excites the Ind. against the
Amer., ii., 360; orders Forster to
deliver Montreal, 367.
Caldwell, Major, i, 201, 219, 337, 401;
ii., 18, 93, 312; picture of his mill
ii., 19; Arnold's men quartered in his
mansion, 26; commands the Brit.
militia at Quebec, 79; on Morgan's
lost opportunity, 134; complains of
those at Cape Diamond blockhouse,
REMARK LXII.; helps check the
Amer., 144; attitude of, toward
Amer. prisoners, 271; in Carleton's
move against the Heights, 320.
Callender, Amos, captures Ft.
George, i., 145
Calvet, P. du, leader of seditious
Canad., ii., 560.
Cambridge (Mass.), i, 109, 164, 165;
Arnold at, i., 119; Arnold to bring
Ticonderoga cannon to, 171; Wash-
ington's headquarters at, 493; the

riflemen at, 509; Arnold's troops
leave, 516,
Camden, Lord, i., 199, 200.
Campbell, Donald, i., 420; sketch of,
ii., 115–16 and *note* 7; retreats with
Montg.'s detachment, 143; his
assertion as to the powder magazine,
Heights of Abraham, REMARK
LXVII.; brings news to Montreal of
the retreat from Quebec, 343.
Campbell, Major, i., 177, 277, ii., 233.
Canada, i., 4, 8, 29, 31, 46, 47, 48, 58,
60, 66, 70, 71, 74, 85, 90, 92, 94,
111, 140; first voyage into (Cartier),
i., 13–14; second voyage into
(Champlain), 14–17; Jesuit mis-
sionaries in, 17; growth under set-
tlers, 17; entrusted to a trading Co.,
17; 1663, a royal province., 17;
under Frontenac, 18; Ind. troubles
in, 18; wars with the Brit. colonies,
21–27; falls into Eng. hands, 24;
becomes an Eng. colony, 27; the
social elements in, 27–40; indebt-
ed to Brit. Canad. traders, 38;
struggle for self-government in,
46–49; effect of Quebec Act on, 60–
68; J. Brown in, 92–106; feared by
Americans 173–76; receives news of
Lake affairs, 211–13; letters from
the Colonies, 213–15; course of the
Brit. Canad. in, 218–19; of the French
Canad., 218–19; martial law in, 220–
28; speedy invasion of it necessary,
248; map of N. Y.-Canad. boundary
line, 306; threatened, 341–42; loses
St. Johns, 460; and Montreal, 481–
83; efforts of Cong. to secure
delegates from, ii., 37–38, 326;
the mission of the Delegates from
Congress to, 327–28; Americans
withdraw from, 441–42; review of
the endeavor to win, 445–50; Gates's
proposed movement against, 471–
513; Arnold suggests the best way to
secure it, 506; well protected against
invasion, 506–08; the changed policy as to its invasion, 515; the new
road to, 517–18; under Haldimand
524–28; the reaction in, 528–35;
through the failures of St. Leger
and Burgoyne, 528; through American spies, 529–35; vain efforts to
keep out the spies, 529–35; reported
weak, 541–42 and REMARK CXII.;
and ripe for revolt, 550; the possession of, still coveted in 1779, 554;
Washington plans to invade in
1780, 556–58; and in 1781, 559–61;
the attitude of its classes toward
the Americans, 559–60; the state of
defence in 560–61; anxiety
of the British concerning, 564–65;
Franklin proposes its cession, 565;
why valuable to Great Britain, 566–
69; desired by the United States,
569; no allusion to, in the treaty of
peace, 569; and the probable reason,